A HISTORY OF THE WORLD

IN THE

TWENTIETH CENTURY

Volume I

Western Dominance, 1900–1947

A HISTORY OF THE WORLD

IN THE TWENTIETH CENTURY

Volume I
Western Dominance, 1900–1947

J. A. S. GRENVILLE

The Belknap Press of
Harvard University Press
Cambridge, Massachusetts

1997

Printed in the United States of America

First Harvard University Press paperback edition, 1997

Library of Congress Cataloging-in-Publication Data

Grenville, J. A. S. (John Ashley Soames), 1928–
A history of the world in the twentieth century / J. A. S. Grenville.
p. cm.
Originally published: HarperCollins, 1980.
Includes bibliographical references and index.
Contents: v. 1. Western dominance, 1900–1947 – v. 2. Conflict and liberation, 1945–1996.
ISBN 0-674-39961-7 (v. 1). – ISBN 0-674-39962-5 (v. 2)
1. History, Modern – 20th century. I. Title.
D421.G647 1997
909.82 – dc21 97-20993

CONTENTS

PART IV: *The Continuing World Crisis, 1929–1939*

PART V *The Second World War*

PART VI *Post-War Europe, 1945–1947*

MAPS

ILLUSTRATIONS

PREFACE

Interest in world history has grown enormously in recent years. Jet travel has shrunk the globe. People are now less confined to their own part of the world than ever before. Migrations have resulted in multicultural societies on every continent; different ethnic groups have a desire to learn more about each other. Another major reason for the growth of interest is that events and developments in any part of the world – wars, revolutions, the movement of trade, changes in economic conditions – impact on the rest of the world.

To write a world history is a formidable task. I began sixteen years ago, adding to the islands of knowledge I had researched in the previous twenty-five years of academic study. In 1980 the first part of the *Collins History of the World in the Twentieth Century,* covering mainly Europe, Asia and the United States from 1900 to 1945, was published by Fontana Press and has since been widely used. Twelve years later I reached the 1990s and widened the scope of the history to Africa, Latin America and Australasia. I am grateful to Stuart Proffitt for his encouragement and for suggesting that the first volume should be revised and that the work should now cover the whole of the twentieth century. His support has made the realisation of my original concept possible.

One way of writing world history is to concentrate on general movements affecting the world as a whole, to describe the underlying forces of history – population growth, increasing literacy, the technological revolution, for instance – to reveal how the twentieth century became the 'age of the masses'. A number of excellent books have appeared based on this approach. But if we ignore the fact that our world in the twentieth century is a world of nations we leave out of account one of the mainsprings of historical change in this century.

Clearly we have to deal with the enormous impact made by social and economic changes in the twentieth century across national frontiers, the consequences of industrialisation, the clashes of cultures as the West came to dominate Africa and Asia, reactions and counter-reactions making themselves felt to the present day. The varied responses to conflict, change and maladjustments were not confined in the twentieth century to national borders: the appeals of socialism and communism, of totalitarian state organisations, of Western parliamentary government, of fascism and Nazism, all crossed land frontiers and the oceans and continents of the world.

What a writer of world history cannot do without seriously distorting its understanding is simply to ignore and discard national frontiers and national influences beyond a country's frontiers. International co-operation was and still is too weak to reduce national frontiers to no more than historical and cultural boundaries. On the other hand, though world trade has made nations more dependent on each other for their prosperity and perhaps even survival, this interdependence is not a relationship of free equals, great and small! The moment we analyse more closely the actual nature of that interdependence we come back to questions of national power. That is why a world history cannot make 'interdependence' the central theme.

In this century technological and scientific advances have resulted in startling transformations: journeys have been made to the moon by lone astronauts; more usefully the masses can be carried by air from one continent to another in a few hours; communication by the single political leader with millions by means of radio, and later television too, has profoundly affected the conduct of politics; from artillery projectiles capable of killing a hundred people at once we have moved to the capability of obliterating several millions with a barrage of nuclear missiles. And yet, accepting the twentieth century in its way as a revolutionary stage of historical change, it was not the first nor is it likely to be the last such stage. Historical change has not in the past come about by gradual steps; the pace quickens and slackens.

The first half of the twentieth century was a period during which intercontinental rivalries frequently played a role in world history, but we have to be precise in showing the interrelationships. Industrial power ceased to be a virtual European monopoly. Two devastating wars occurred in Europe and the first furthered the partial triumph of the new revolutionary ideology of communism. The problems of eastern Asia were both a consequence of Western impact and the result of Asian conflicts. They are too frequently viewed through Western eyes alone. After 1945, the part played by Western Europe, important though it remains, shrinks when viewed within a global perspective. The significance in world affairs of Africa, the Middle East and Latin America increased. The nations of these continents asserted their national rights and imposed on the most powerful nations of the world a sense of the limits of their own power.

I have put forward no startling new theories or hypotheses about world history. Space limits what can be written on any one topic: some have had to be omitted altogether, since only by means of a degree of selectivity can anything be written in depth and I have preferred to do this rather than to provide an encyclopaedic account of many more subjects. On the subjects I have written about I have endeavoured to keep abreast of present research so far as this is humanly possible.

A technical note. First, some basic statistics are provided of population, trade and industry in various countries for purposes of comparison. They are often taken for granted. Authorities frequently disagree on these in detail; they should therefore be regarded as indicative rather than absolutely precise. A comparison of standards of living between countries is not an exact science. I have given per capita figures of the gross national product (GNP) as a very rough guide; but these represent only averages in societies where differentials of income may be great; furthermore they are expressed in U.S. dollars and so are dependent on exchange rates; actual costs of living also vary widely between countries; the per capita GNP can not therefore be simply translated into comparative standards of living and provide but a rough guide. Secondly, the transliteration from Chinese to Roman lettering presents special problems. The Pinyin system of romanisation was officially adopted by China on 1 January 1979 for international use, replacing the Wade-Giles system. Thus where Wade-Giles had Mao Tse-tung and Teng Hsaio-ping, Pinyin gives Mao Zedong and Deng Xiaoping. For clarity's sake, the usage in this book is not entirely consistent: the chosen form is Pinyin, but Wade-Giles is kept for certain older names where it is more easily recognisable, for example Shanghai, Chiang Kai-shek and the Kuomintang. Peking changes to the Pinyin form Beijing after the communist takeover.

The reception of this book has far exceeded the author's expectations, and I would like to thank the many colleagues who have written to me from all over the world. The onerous task of typing was undertaken by Miss G. Briggs, Mrs. S. Atkins and for this edition by Mrs. P. Roberts.

At HarperCollins, I was fortunate to have an excellent editor, Peter James; overall editorial control was in the capable hands of Philip Gwynne Jones, and Caroline Wood was the indefatigable picture researcher. They brought this large project to successful fruition. To Harvard University Press, I am grateful for urging me to work on this new edition; in particular, I am grateful to Aïda D. Donald, Editor-in-Chief, for her infectious enthusiasm, to Elizabeth Suttell, Senior Editor, for important suggestions, to Christine Thorsteinsson, Paperback Editor, for her care and attention, and to the rest of the staff at the Press, a team effort. The work is dedicated to my wife, who makes it possible for me to be happy writing.

The Institute of Advanced Studies, The University of Birmingham.

PART I

Social Change and National Rivalry in the West, 1900–1914

CHAPTER 1

The World in the Twentieth Century

Historical epochs do not coincide strictly with centuries. The French Revolution in 1789, not the year 1800, marked the beginning of a new historical era. The beginning of the twentieth century too is better dated to 1871, when Germany became unified, or the 1890s, when international instability became manifest in Europe and Asia and a new era of imperial rivalry which the Germans called *Weltpolitik* began. On the European continent Germany had become by far the most powerful military nation and was rapidly advancing industrially. In eastern Asia during the 1890s a modernised Japan waged her first successful war of aggression against China. In the Americas the foundations were laid for the emergence of the United States as a superpower later in the century. The United States no longer felt secure in isolation. Africa was finally partitioned between the European powers. These were some of the portents indicating the great changes to come in the new century. There were many more.

Modernisation was creating new industrial and political conflict and dividing society. The state was becoming more centralised, its bureaucracy grew and achieved control to an increasing degree over the lives of the individual. Social tensions were weakening the tsarist Russian Empire and during the first decade of the twentieth century Russia was defeated by Japan. The British Empire was at bay and Britain was seeking support, not certain which way to turn. Fierce nationalism, the build-up of vast armies and navies, and unquestioned patriotism that regarded war as an opportunity to prove manhood rather than a catastrophe characterised the mood as the new century began. Boys played with their tin soldiers and adults dressed up in the finery of uniforms. The rat-infested mud of the trenches and machine guns mowing down tens of thousands of young men as yet lay beyond the imagination. Soldiering was still glorious, chivalrous and glamorous. But the early twentieth century also held the promise of a better and more civilised life in the future.

In the Western world civilisation was held to consist not only of cultural achievements but also of moral values. Despite all the rivalries of the Western nations, wanton massacres of ethnic minorities, such as that of the Armenians by the Turks in the 1890s, aroused widespread revulsion and prompted great-power intervention. The pogroms in Russia and Romania against the Jews were condemned by civilised peoples, including the Germans, who offered help and refuge despite the growth of anti-Semitism at home. The Dreyfus affair outraged Queen Victoria and prompted Émile Zola to mobilise a powerful protest movement in France; the Captain's accusers were regarded as representing the corrupt elements of the Third Republic. Civilisation to contemporary observers seemed to be moving forward. Before 1914 there was no good reason to doubt that history was the story of mankind's progress, especially that of the white European branch.

There was a sense of cultural affinity among the

aristocracy and bourgeoisie of Europe. Governed by monarchs who were related to each other and who tended to reign for long periods or, in France, by presidents who changed too frequently to be remembered for long, the well-to-do felt at home anywhere in Europe. The upper reaches of society were cosmopolitan, disporting themselves on the Riviera, in Paris and in Dresden; they felt that they had much in common and that they belonged to a superior civilisation. Some progress was real. Increasingly, provision was made to help the majority of the people who were poor, no doubt in part to cut the ground from under socialist agitators and in part in response to trade union and political pressures brought about by the widening franchise in the West. Pensions and insurance for workers were first instituted in Germany under Bismarck and spread to most of the rest of Western Europe. Medical care too improved in the expanding cities. Limits were set on the hours and kind of work children were allowed to perform. Universal education became the norm. The advances made in the later nineteenth century were in many ways extended after 1900.

Democracy was gaining ground in the new century. The majority of men were enfranchised in Western Europe and the United States. The more enlightened nations understood that good government required a relationship of consent between those who made the laws and the mass of the people who had to obey them. The best way to secure co-operation was through the process of popularly elected parliamentary assemblies, which allowed the people some influence – government by the will of the majority, at least in appearance. The Reichstag, the French Chambers, the Palace of Westminster, the two Houses of Congress, even the Russian Duma, all met in splendid edifices intended to reflect their importance. In the West the trend was thus clearly established early in the century against arbitrary rule. However much national constitutions differed, another accepted feature of the civilised polity was the rule of law, the provision of an independent judiciary meting out equal justice to rich and poor, the powerful and the weak. Practice might differ from theory, but justice was presented as blindfolded: justice to all, without favours to any.

Equal rights were not universal in the West. Working people were struggling to form effective unions so that, through concerted strike action, they could overcome their individual weakness when bargaining for decent wages and conditions. Only a minority, though, were members of a union. In the United States in 1900, only about 1 million out of more than 27 million workers belonged to a labour union. Unions in America were male dominated and, just as in Britain, women had to form their own unions. American unions also excluded most immigrants and black workers.

Ethnic minorities were discriminated against even in a political system such as that of the United States which prided herself as the most advanced democracy in the world. Reconstruction after the Civil War had bitterly disappointed the black Americans in their hopes of gaining equal rights. Their claims to justice remained a national issue for much of the twentieth century.

All over the world there was discrimination against a group which accounted for half the earth's population – women. It took the American suffragette movement half a century to win in 1920 the right to vote. In Britain the agitation for women's rights took the drastic form of public demonstrations after 1906, but not until 1918 did women over thirty years of age gain the vote, and those aged between twenty-one and thirty had to wait even longer. But the acceptance of votes for women in the West had already been signposted before the world war. New Zealand in 1893 was the first country to grant women the right to vote in national elections; Australia followed in 1908. But even as the century comes to an end there are countries in the Middle East where women are denied this basic right. Moreover, this struggle represents only the tip of the iceberg of discrimination against women on issues such as education, entry into the professions, property rights and equal pay for equal work. Incomplete as emancipation remains in Western societies, there are many countries in Asia, Latin America, Africa and the Middle East where women are still treated as inferior, the chattels of their fathers or husbands. In India, for example, orthodox Hindu marriage customs were not changed by law until 1955. As for birth-control education, which began in the West in the nineteenth century, freeing women from the burden of repeated pregnancies, it did not reach the women of the Third World until late this century – though it is there that the need is greatest.

The limited progress towards equal rights achieved in the West early in the twentieth century was not mirrored in the rest of the world. Imperialism in Africa and Asia saw its final flowering as the nineteenth century drew to a close. The benefits brought to the indigenous peoples of Africa and Asia by the imposition of Western rule and values was not doubted by the majority of white people. 'The imperialist feels a profound pride in the magnificent heritage of empire won by the courage and energy of his ancestry,' wrote one observer in 1899; '. . . the spread of British rule extends to every race brought within its sphere the incalculable benefits of just law, tolerant trade, and considerate government.'

In 1900 Europeans and their descendants who had settled in the Americas, Australasia and southern Africa looked likely to dominate the globe. They achieved this tremendous extension of power in the world because of the great size of their combined populations and because of the technological changes which collectively are known as the industrial revolution. One in every four human beings lived in Europe, some 400 million out of a total world population of 1600 million in 1900. If we add the millions who had left Europe and multiplied in the Americas and elsewhere, more than one in every three human beings was European or of European descent. The Europeans ruled a great world empire with a population in Africa, Asia, the Americas and the Pacific of nearly 500 million by 1914. To put it another way, before 1914 only about one in three people had actually avoided being ruled by Europeans and their descendants, most of whom were unshaken in their conviction that their domination was natural and beneficial and that the only problem it raised was to arrange it peacefully between them.

To the Asians and Africans, the European presented a common front with only local variations: some spoke German, others French or English. There are several features of this common outlook. First, there was the Westerner's feeling of superiority, crudely proven by his capacity to conquer other peoples more numerous than the invading European armies. Vast tracts of land were seized by the Europeans at very small human cost to themselves from the ill-equipped indigenous peoples of Asia and Africa. That was one of the main reasons for the extension of European power over other regions of the world. Since the mid-nineteenth century the Europeans had avoided fighting each other for empire, since the cost of war between them would have been of quite a different order.

Superiority, ultimately proven on the battlefield, was, the European in 1900 felt, but one aspect of his civilisation. All other peoples he thought of as uncivilised, though he recognised that in past ages these peoples had enjoyed a kind of civilisation of their own, and their artistic manifestations were prized. China, India, Egypt and, later, Africa were looted of great works of art. Most remain to the present day in the museums of the West.

A humanitarian European impulse sought to impose on the conquered peoples the Christian religion, including Judaeo-Christian ethics, and Western concepts of family relationships and conduct. At his best the Western coloniser was genuinely paternalistic. Happiness, he believed, would follow on the adoption of Western ways, and the advance of mankind materially and spiritually would be accomplished only by overcoming the prejudice against Western thought.

From its very beginning, profit and gain were also powerful spurs to empire. In the twentieth century industrialised Europe came to depend on the import of raw materials for its factories; Britain needed vast quantities of raw cotton to turn into cloth, as well as nickel, rubber and copper. As her people turned her into the workshop of the world in the nineteenth century, so she relied on food from overseas, including grain, meat, sugar and tea, to feed the growing population. Some of these imports came from the continent of Europe close by, the rest from far afield – the Americas, Australasia and India. As the twentieth century progressed, oil imports assumed an increasing importance. The British mercantile marine, the world's largest, carried all these goods across the oceans. Colonies were regarded by Europeans as essential to provide secure sources of raw materials; just as important, they provided markets for industrialised Europe's output.

Outside Europe only the United States matched, and indeed exceeded, the growth of European industry in the first two decades of the twentieth century. Europe and the United States accounted for virtually all the world trade in manufactured goods, which doubled between 1900 and 1913. There was a corresponding increase in demand for raw materials and food supplied by the Americas, Asia and the less industrialised countries of Europe. Part of Europe's wealth was used to develop resources in other areas of the world: railways everywhere, manufacture and mining in Asia, Africa and

North and South America; but Europe and the United States continued to dominate in actual production.

Global competition for trade increased colonial rivalry for raw materials and markets, and the United States was not immune to the fever. The division of Asia and Africa into outright European colonies entailed also their subservience to the national economic policies of the imperial power. Among these were privileged access to colonial sources of wealth, cheap labour and raw materials, domination of the colonial market and, where possible, shutting out national rivals from these benefits. Thus the United States was worried at the turn of the century about exclusion from what was believed to be the last great undeveloped market in the world – China. In an imperialist movement of great importance, Americans advanced across the Pacific, annexing Hawaii and occupying the Philippines in 1898. The United States also served notice of her opposition to the division of China into exclusive economic regions. Over the century a special relationship developed between America and China that was to contribute to the outbreak of war between the United States and Japan in 1941, with all its consequences for world history.

By 1900 most of Africa and Asia was already partitioned between the European nations. With the exception of China, what was left – the Samoan islands, Morocco and the frontiers of Togo – caused more diplomatic crises than was warranted by the importance of such territories.

Pride in an expanding empire, however, was not an attitude shared by everyone. There was also an undercurrent of dissent. Britain's Gladstonian Liberals in the 1880s had not been carried away by imperialist fever. An article in the *Pall Mall Gazette* in 1884 took up the case for indigenous peoples. 'All coloured men', it declared, 'seem to be regarded as fair game,' on the assumption that 'no one has a right to any rule or sovereignty in either hemisphere but men of European birth or origin'. During the Boer War (1899–1902) a courageous group of Liberals challenged the prevailing British jingoism. Lloyd George, a future prime minister, had to escape the fury of a Birmingham crowd by leaving the town hall disguised as a policeman. Birmingham was the political base of Joseph Chamberlain, the Colonial Secretary who did most to propagate the 'new imperialism' and to echo Cecil Rhodes's call for the brotherhood of the 'Anglo-Saxon races', supposedly the British, the Germans and white Americans of British or German descent. Americans, however, were not keen to respond to the embrace.

After the Spanish–American War of 1898 the colonisation of the Philippines by the United States led to a fierce national debate. One of the most distinguished and eloquent leaders of the Anti-Imperialist League formed after that war denounced US policies in the Philippines and Cuba in a stirring passage,

> This nation cannot endure half republic and half colony – half free and half vassal. Our form of government, our traditions, our present interests and our future welfare, all forbid our entering upon a career of conquest.

Clearly, then, there was already opposition to imperialism on moral grounds by the beginning of the twentieth century. The opponents' arguments would come to carry more weight later in the century. Morality has more appeal when it is also believed to be of practical benefit. As the nineteenth century came to an end competition for empire drove each nation on, fearful that to lose out would inevitably lead to national decline. In mutual suspicion the Western countries were determined to carve up into colonies and spheres of influence any remaining weaker regions.

The expansion of Western power in the nineteenth and early twentieth century carried with it the seeds of its own destruction. It was not any 'racial superiority' that had endowed Western man with a unique gift for organising society, for government or for increasing the productivity of man in the factory and on the land. The West took its knowledge to other parts of the world, and European descendants had increased productivity in manufacturing industries in the United States beyond that of their homelands. But high productivity was not a Western monopoly: the Japanese were the first to prove, later in the century, that they could exceed Western rates.

The Wars of American Independence demonstrated that peoples in one region of the world will not for ever consent to be ruled by peoples far distant. By 1900 self-government and separate nationhood had been won, through war or through consent, by other descendants of Europeans who had become Australians, Brazilians, Argentinians,

Canadians and, soon, South Africans. These national rebellions were led by white Europeans. It remained a widespread European illusion that such a sense of independence and nationhood could not develop among the black peoples of Africa in the foreseeable future. A people's capacity for self-rule was crudely related to 'race' and 'colour', with the white race on top of the pyramid, followed by the 'brown' Indians, who, it was conceded, would one distant day be capable of self-government. At the bottom of the pile was the 'black' race. The 'yellow' Chinese and Japanese peoples did not fit easily into the colour scheme, not least because the Japanese had already shown an amazing capacity to Westernise. Fearful of the hundreds of millions of people in China and Japan, the West thus conceived a dread of the yellow race striking back – the 'yellow peril'.

The spread of European knowledge undermined the basis of imperialist dominance. The Chinese, the Japanese, the Koreans, the Indians and the Africans would all apply this knowledge, and goods would be manufactured in Tokyo and Hong Kong as sophisticated as those produced anywhere else in the world. A new sense of nationalism would be born, resistant to Western dominance and fighting it with Western scientific knowledge and weapons. When independence came, older traditions would reassert themselves and synthesise with the new knowledge to form a unique amalgam in each region. The world remains divided and still too large and diverse for any one group of nations, or for any one people or culture, to dominate.

All this lay in the future, the near future. Western control of most of the world appeared in 1900 to be unshakeable fact. Africa was partitioned. All that was left to be shared out were two nominally independent states, Morocco and Egypt, but this involved little more than tidying up European spheres of influence. Abyssinia alone had survived the European attack.

The Ottoman Empire, stretching from Balkan Europe through Asia Minor and the Middle East to the Indian Ocean, was still an area of intense rivalry among the European powers. The independent states in this part of the world could not resist European encroachment, both economic and political, but the rulers did succeed in retaining

The public execution of a 'Boxer' after suppression of the Rising.

some independence by manoeuvring between competing European powers. The partition of the Middle East had been put off time and time again because in so sensitive a strategic area, on the route to India, Britain and Russia never trusted each other sufficiently to strike any lasting bargain, preferring to maintain the Ottoman Empire and Persia as impotent buffer states between their respective spheres of interest. Much farther to the east lay China, the largest nation in the world, with a population in 1900 of about 420 million.

When Western influence in China was threatened by the so-called Boxer rising in 1900, the West acted with a show of solidarity. An international army was landed in China and 'rescued' the Europeans. Europeans were not to be forced out by 'native' violence. The Western powers' financial and territorial hold over China tightened, though they shrank from the responsibility of directly ruling the whole of China and the hundreds of millions of Chinese living there. Instead, European influence was exerted indirectly through Chinese officials who were ostensibly responsible to a central Chinese government in Peking. The Western Europeans detached a number of trading posts from China proper, or acquired strategic bases along the coast and inland and forced the Chinese to permit the establishment of semi-colonial international settlements. The most important, in Shanghai, served the Europeans as a commercial trading centre. Britain enlarged her colony of Hong Kong by forcing China to grant her a lease of the adjacent New Territories in 1898. Russia sought to annex extensive Chinese territory in the north.

With hindsight it can be seen that by the turn of the century the European world empires had reached their zenith. Just at this point, though, a non-European Western power, the United States, had staked her first claim to power and influence in the Pacific. But Europe could not yet, in 1900, call in the United States to redress the balance which Russia threatened to upset in eastern Asia. That task was undertaken by an eastern Asian nation – Japan. Like China, Japan was never conquered by Europeans. Forced to accept Western influence by the Americans in the mid-nineteenth century, the Japanese were too formidable to be thought of as 'natives' to be subdued. Instead the largest European empire, the British, sought and won the alliance of Japan in 1902 on terms laid down by the Japanese leaders.

Europe's interests were global, and possible future conflicts over respective imperial spheres preoccupied its leaders and those sections of society with a stake in empire. United, their power in the world was overwhelming. But the states of Europe were not united. Despite their sense of common purpose in the world, European leaders saw themselves simultaneously ensnared in a struggle within their own continent, a struggle which, each nation believed, would decide whether she would continue as a world power.

The armaments race and competition for empire, with vast standing armies facing each other and the new battleship fleets of Dreadnoughts were symptoms of increasing tension rather than the cause of the great war to come. Historians have endlessly debated why the West plunged into such a cataclysmic conflict. Social tensions within each country and the fears of the ruling classes, especially in the Kaiser's Germany, indirectly contributed to a political malaise during a period of great change. But as an explanation why war broke out in 1914 the theory that a patriotic war was 'an escape forward' to evade conflict at home fails to carry conviction even in the case of Germany. It seems almost a truism to assert that wars have come about because nations simply do not believe they can go on coexisting. It is nevertheless a better explanation than the simple one that the *prime* purpose of nations at war is necessarily the conquest of more territory. Of Russia and Japan that may have been true in the period 1900–5. But another assumption, at least as important, was responsible for the Great War. Among the then 'great powers', as they were called in the early twentieth century, there existed a certain fatalism that the growth and decline of nations must inevitably entail war between them. The stronger would fall on the weaker and divide the booty between them. To quote the wise and experienced British Prime Minister, the third Marquess of Salisbury, at the turn of the century,

> You may roughly divide the nations of the world as the living and the dying. . . . the weak states are becoming weaker and the strong states are becoming stronger. . . . the living nations will gradually encroach on the territory of the dying and the seeds and causes of conflict among civilised nations will speedily appear. Of course, it is not to be supposed that any one of the living nations will be allowed to have the monopoly of

curing or cutting up these unfortunate patients and the controversy is as to who shall have the privilege of doing so, and in what measure he shall do it. These things may introduce causes of fatal difference between the great nations whose mighty armies stand opposed threatening each other. These are the dangers I think which threaten us in the period that is coming on.

In 1900 there were some obviously dying empires, and the 'stronger nations' competing for their territories were the European great powers and Japan. But during the years immediately preceding the Great War the issue had changed. Now the great powers turned on each other in the belief that some must die if the others were to live in safety. Even Germany, the strongest of them, would not be safe, so the Kaiser's generals believed, against the menace of a combination of countries opposing her. That was the fatal assumption which more than anything led to the 1914–18 war. It was reducing the complexity of international relations to a perverse application of Darwinian theory.

The First World War destroyed the social cohesion of pre-war continental Europe. The Austro-Hungarian and Ottoman Empires broke up; Germany, before 1914 first among the continental European countries, was defeated and humiliated; Italy gained little from her enormous sacrifices; the tsarist Russian Empire disintegrated, and descended into civil war and chaos. In their despair people sought new answers to the problems that threatened to overwhelm them, new ideals to replace respect for kings and princes and the established social order. In chaos a few ruthless men were able to determine the fate of nations, ushering in a European dark age in mid-century. Lenin, Trotsky and Stalin were able to create a more efficient and crueller autocracy than that of the Romanovs. The new truths were held to be found in the works of Karl Marx as interpreted by the Russian dictators, who imposed their ideas of communism on the people. In Italy disillusionment with parliamentary government led to fascism. In Germany, democracy survived by a narrow margin but was demolished when her people despaired once more in the depression of the early 1930s. Hitler's doctrine of race then found a ready response, and his successes at home and abroad confirmed him in power.

Different though their roots were, what these dictators had in common was the rejection of Judaeo-Christian ethics, a contempt for the sanctity of human life, for justice and for equality before the law. They accepted the destruction of millions of people in the belief that it served desirable ends. They were responsible for a revolution in thought and action that undid centuries of progress.

Stalin and Hitler were not the first leaders to be responsible for mass killings. During the First World War, the Turks had massacred Armenians, ethnic hatred inflamed by fears that in war the Armenians would betray them. Stalin's calculated killing of 'class enemies' and his murderous purges of those from whom he suspected opposition were the actions of a bloody tyrant, by no means the first in history. The ruthless exploitation of slave labour, the murder of the Polish officers during the Second World War and the expulsion of whole peoples from their homes revealed the depths to which an organised modern state was capable of sinking. But nothing in the history of a Western nation equals the Nazi state's application of its theories of good and bad races which ended with the carefully planned factory murder of millions of men, women and children, mostly Jews and gypsies. There were mass killings of 'inferior Slavs', Russians and Poles, and those who were left were regarded as fit only to serve as labour for the German masters.

The Nazi evil was ended in 1945. But it had been overcome only with the help of the communist power of the Soviet Union. As long as Stalin lived, in the Soviet Union and her satellite states the rights of individuals counted for little. In Asia, China and her neighbours had suffered war and destruction when the Japanese, who adopted from the West doctrines of racial superiority, forced them into their cynically named 'co-prosperity sphere'. The ordeal was not over for China when the Second World War ended. Civil war followed until the victory of the communists. Mao Zedong imposed his brand of communist theory on a largely peasant society for three decades. Many millions perished in the terror he unleashed, the class war and as a result of experiments designed to create an abundant communist society. In Asia too the regime of Pol Pot in Cambodia provided a more recent example of inhumanity in the pursuit of ideological theories amounting to genocide.

By the close of the century the tide finally turned against communist autocracy and dictatorship. The suffering and oppression all over the world in the twentieth century was much greater than it had been in the nineteenth. Only the minority whose standards of living improved, who lived in freedom in countries where representative government remained an unbroken tradition, had the promise of progress fulfilled through greater abundance of wealth. But even in these fortunate societies few families were untouched by the casualties of the wars of the twentieth century. Western societies were spared the nightmare after 1945 of a third world war, which more than once seemed possible, though they were not spared war itself. These wars, however, involved far greater suffering to the peoples living in Asia, Africa and the Middle East than to the West.

The Cold War had divided the most powerful nations in the world into opposing camps. The West saw itself as the 'free world' and the East as the society of the future, the people's alliance of the communist world. They were competing for dominance in the rest of the world, in Africa, Asia, the Middle East and Latin America, where the West's overwhelming influence was challenged by the East. That struggle dominated the second half of the century. Regional conflicts in the world came to be seen through the prism of the Cold War. Within the two blocs differences also arose, of which the most serious was the quarrel between the Soviet Union and China, which further complicated developments in Asia. That the Cold War never turned to a real war between its protagonists was largely due to MAD, the doctrine of mutual assured destruction. Both sides had piled up nuclear arsenals capable of destroying each other and much of the world, and there was no sure defence against all the incoming missiles. Mutual assured destruction kept the dangerous peace between them. The battle for supremacy was fought by other means, including proxy wars between nations not possessing the 'bomb' but armed and supported by the nuclear powers.

The abiding strength of nationalism from the nineteenth century right through the twentieth has generally been underestimated by Western historians. Hopes of peace for mankind and a lessening of national strife were aroused by the formation of the League of Nations after the Great War of 1914–18. But long before the outbreak of the Second World War the principle of 'collective security' had broken down when the undertakings to the League by its member states clashed with perceived national interests. The United Nations began with a burst of renewed hope after the Second World War but could not bridge the antagonisms of the Cold War. Both the League and the UN performed useful international functions but their effectiveness was limited whenever powerful nations refused their co-operation.

Despite growing global interdependence on many issues, including trade, the environment and health, national interests were narrowly interpreted rather than seen as secondary to the interests of the international community. Nationalism was not diminished in the twentieth century by a shrinking world of mass travel and mass communication, by the universal possession of cheap transistor radios and the widespread availability of television nor by any ideology claiming to embrace mankind. To cite one obvious example, the belief that the common acceptance of a communist society would obliterate national and ethnic conflict was exploded at the end of the century, and nationalism was and still is repressed by force all over the world. Remove coercion, and nationalism re-emerges in destructive forms.

But the world since 1945 has seen some positive changes too. Nationalism in Western Europe at least has been transformed by the experiences of the Second World War and the success of co-operation. A sign of better times is the spread of the undefended frontier. Before the Second World War the only undefended frontier between two sovereign nations was the long continental border between Canada and the United States. By the closing years of the century all the frontiers between the nations of the European Union were undefended. Today the notion of a war between France and Germany or between Germany and any of her immediate neighbours has become virtually unthinkable; a conflict over the territories they possess is inconceivable, as is a war prompted by the belief that coexistence will not be possible. To that extent the international climate has greatly changed for the better. But the possibility of such wars in the Balkans, in eastern Europe, in Asia, Africa and the Middle East remains ever present.

No year goes by without one or more wars occurring somewhere in the world, many of them savage civil wars. What is new in the 1990s is that these wars no longer bring the most powerful nations of the world into indirect conflict with each other. The decision of Russia and the United States to cease arming and supplying opposing contestants in the Afghan civil wars marked the end of an indirect conflict that had been waged between the Soviet Union and the United States since the Second World War in Asia, the Middle East, Africa and Latin America. But this understanding will not banish wars. Intervention, whether by a group of nations acting under UN sponsorship or by a major country acting as policeman, is costly. UN resources are stretched to the limits by peacekeeping efforts in Cyprus, Cambodia, Yugoslavia and other trouble-spots. No universal peacekeeping force exists. Intervention would therefore be likely only when the national interests of powerful countries were involved, as they were in the Gulf in 1991. It would be less likely, unfortunately, where the motive was purely humanitarian.

The world's history is interwoven with migrations. The poor and the persecuted have left their homeland for other countries. The great movement of peoples from eastern to western Europe and further west across the Atlantic to the United States, Canada, the Argentine, Australasia and South Africa continued throughout the nineteenth century, most of the emigrants being unskilled workers from rural areas. But this free movement of peoples, interrupted by the First World War, was halted soon after its close. In countries controlled by Europeans and their descendants quotas were imposed, for example by the United States Immigration Act of 1924, denying free access to further immigrants from Europe. These countries so arranged their immigration policies that they slowed down to a trickle or excluded altogether the entry of Asians and Africans. In the United States the exclusion of Asians from China and Japan had begun well before 1914. They had been welcome only when their labour was needed. The same attitude became clear in Britain where immigration of West Indians was at first encouraged after 1945, only to be restricted in 1962. The demand for labour, fluctuating according to the needs of a country's economy, and the strength of racial prejudice have been the main underlying reasons for immigration policies. While the West restricted intercontinental migrations after the First World War, within Asia the movement continued, with large population transfers from India, Japan and Korea to Burma, Malaya, Ceylon, Borneo and Manchuria. Overseas Chinese in Asia play a crucial role, as do Indian traders in sub-Saharan Africa.

After the Second World War there were huge migrations once more in Asia, Europe and the Middle East. Millions of Japanese returned to their homeland. The partition of the Indian subcontinent led to the largest sudden and forced migration in history of some 25 million from east to west and west to east. At the close of the war in Europe, West Germany absorbed 20 million refugees and guest-workers from the East. Two million from Europe migrated to Canada and to Australia; 3 million North Koreans fled to the South.

The United States experienced a changing pattern of immigration after the Second World War. More than 11 million people were registered as entering the country between 1941 and 1980. The great majority of immigrants had once been of European origin. After 1945 increasing numbers of Puerto Ricans and Filipinos took advantage of their rights of entry. There was a large influx of Hispanics from the Caribbean; in addition probably as many as 5 million illegal immigrants crossed the Mexican border to find low-paid work in burgeoning California. The proportion of Europeans fell to less than one-fifth of the total number of immigrants. The second-largest ethnic influx came from Asia – Taiwan, Korea and, after the Vietnam War, Vietnam. The United States has become more of a multicultural society than ever before. But, unlike most blacks and Hispanics, the Asians have succeeded in working their way out of the lower strata of American society.

Although the migration of Europeans to Africa south of the Sahara after 1945 was less spectacular in terms of numbers – probably less than a million in all – their impact as settlers and administrators on the history of African countries was crucial for the history of the continent.

One of the most significant developments in the Middle East after 1945 was the creation of a whole new nation, the State of Israel. Proportionally, migration into Israel saw the most rapid population increase of any post-war state. Under the Law of Return any Jew from any part of the world had the right to enter and enjoy immediate citizenship. Between May 1948 and June 1953 the population doubled and by the end of 1956 had tripled to 1,667,000.

There are no accurate statistics relating to the peoples of the world who, since 1945, have been driven by fear, hunger or the hope of better opportunities to migrate. They probably exceed 80 million. As the century draws to a close more than 10 million are still refugees without a country of their own; political upheavals and famines create more refugees every year. The more prosperous countries of the world continue to erect barriers against entry from the poor countries and stringently examine all those who seek asylum. In Europe, the Iron Curtain has gone but an invisible curtain has replaced it to stop the flow of migration from the East to the West, from Africa across the Mediterranean, from the poor South of the world to the North.

The only real solution is to assist the poor countries to develop so that their populations have a hope of rising standards of living. The aid given by the wealthy has proved totally inadequate to meet these needs, and loans have led to soaring debt repayments. The commodities the Third World has to sell have generally risen in price less than the manufacturing imports it buys. The natural disadvantage is compounded by corruption, economic mismanagement, the waste of resources on the purchase of weapons, wars and the gross inequalities of wealth. But underlying all these is the remorseless growth of population, which vitiates the advances that are achieved.

There has been a population explosion in the course of the twentieth century. It is estimated that 1200 million people inhabited planet earth in 1900. By 1930 the figure reached 2000 million, in 1970 it was 3600 million and by the end of the century the world's population is expected to total 6000 million. Most of that increase, some 90 per cent, has taken place in the Third World, swelling the size of cities like Calcutta, Jakarta and Cairo to many millions. The inexorable pressure of population on resources has bedevilled all efforts to improve standards of living in the poorest regions of the world, such as Bangladesh. The gap between the poor parts of the world and the rich widened rather than narrowed. Birth-control education is now backed by Third World governments, but, apart from China's draconian application of it, it has not yet made an impact on reducing the acceleration of population growth. Despite the suffering caused, wars and famines inflict no more than temporary dents on the upward curve. Only the experience with Aids may prove different, if no cure is found: in Africa the disease is widespread, and in Uganda it has infected one person in every six. The one positive measure of population control is to achieve economic and social progress in the poorest countries of the world. With more than 800 million people living in destitution the world is far from being in sight of this goal.

At the end of the twentieth century many of the problems that afflicted the world at its beginning remain unresolved. The prediction of Thomas Robert Malthus in his *Essay on the Principle of Populations* published in 1798 that, unless checked, the growth of population would outrun the growth of production still blights human hopes for progress and happiness in the Third World. According to one estimate, a third of all children under five, some 150 million, in the Third World are undernourished and prey to disease. Of the 122 million children born in 1979, one in ten were dead by the beginning of 1981. In Africa there are still countries where one child in four does not survive to its first birthday. In Western society, too rich a diet has led to dramatic increases in heart disease. In the Third World, according to the UN Secretary-General in 1989, 500 million go hungry and every year there are 10 million more. The Brandt report, *North–South: A Programme for Survival* (1980), offered an even higher estimate, and declared that there was 'no more important task before the world community than the elimination of hunger and malnutrition in all countries'. No one can calculate the figures with any accuracy. The world community has reacted only to dramatic televised pictures of suffering and famine, for example in the Horn of Africa, but there is no real sense of global agreement on the measures necessary to tackle the problem. Now that the Third World is politically independent, the former Western colonial powers are conveniently absolved from direct responsibility.

The political independence of the once Western-dominated globe represents an enormous change, one which occurred much more rapidly than was expected in the West before the Second World War. But in many countries independence did not lead to better government or the blessings of liberty. Third World societies were not adequately prepared, their wealth and education too unequally distributed to allow any sort of democracy to be established – although this was accomplished in India. But on the Indian subcontinent, as elsewhere in the former colonial states, ethnic strife and blood-

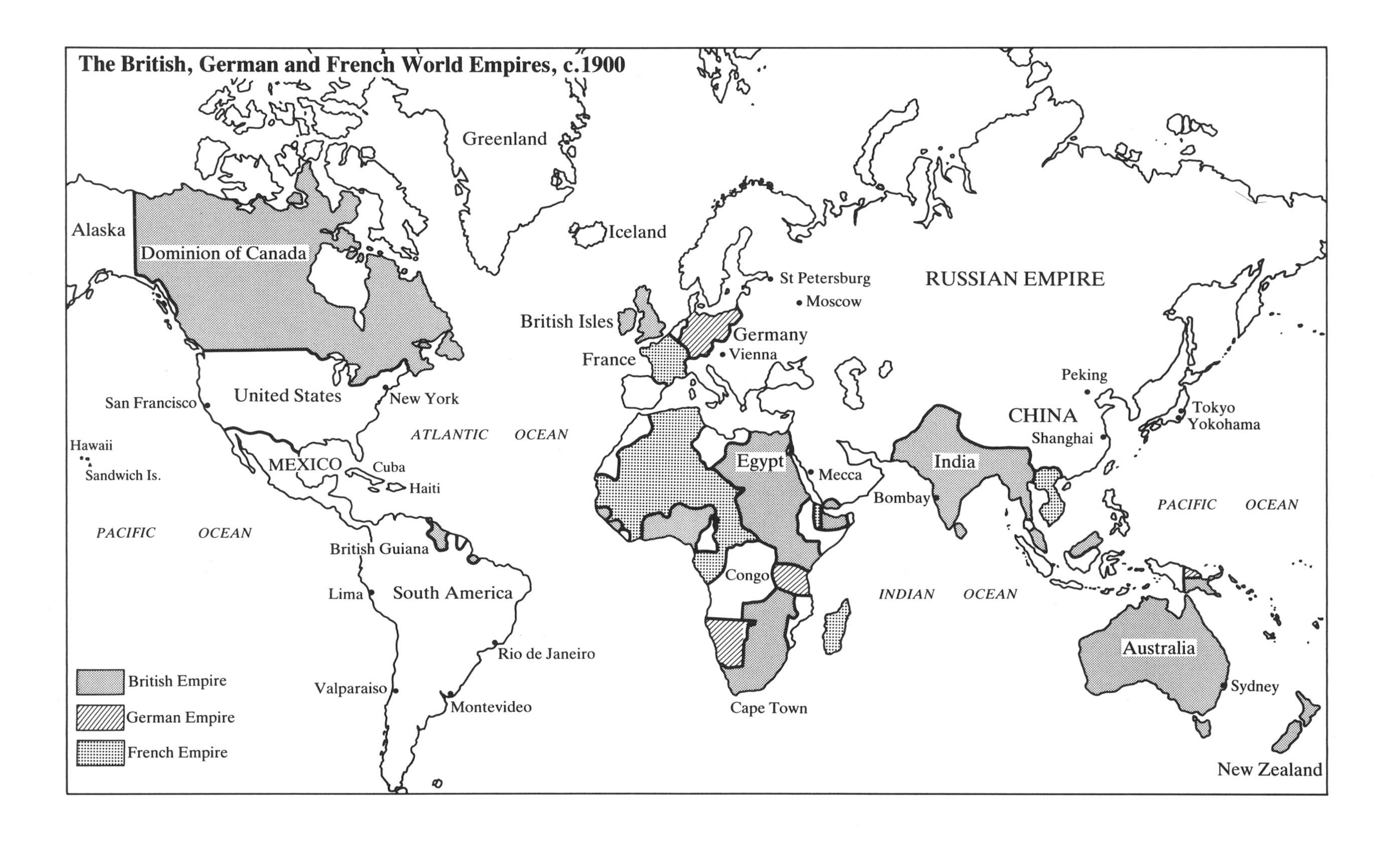

The British, German and French World Empires, c.1900
Greenland
Alaska
Dominion of Canada
Iceland
St Petersburg
Moscow
RUSSIAN EMPIRE
British Isles
Germany
Vienna
France
Peking
United States
New York
San Francisco
CHINA
Tokyo
Yokohama
Shanghai
ATLANTIC OCEAN
Hawaii
Sandwich Is.
MEXICO
Cuba
Haiti
Egypt
Mecca
India
Bombay
PACIFIC OCEAN
PACIFIC OCEAN
British Guiana
Congo
Lima
South America
INDIAN OCEAN
Australia
Rio de Janeiro
British Empire
German Empire
French Empire
Valparaiso
Montevideo
Cape Town
Sydney
New Zealand

shed persist. Corruption, autocracy and the abuse of human rights remain widespread.

In eastern Asia at the beginning of the century the partition of China seemed to be at hand, and Japan already claimed to be the predominant power. But China proved too large to be absorbed and partitioned. The military conflict between Japan and her Pacific neighbours ended only in 1945. By the close of the twentieth century she has emerged as an economic superpower decisively influencing world economic relations. China, economically still weak, but developing rapidly remains by far the largest and most populous unified nation in the world. By the end of the century the last foreign outposts taken from her before the twentieth century, Hong Kong and Macao, will become part of her national territory again. Apart from Vietnam, Cuba and North Korea, China in 1993 is the last communist state in the world.

At the beginning of the century Karl Marx had inspired socialist thinking and indeed much political action in the Western world. The largest socialist party in 1900 was in the Kaiser's Germany. But these socialist parties believed that the road to power lay through constitutional means. Revolutionaries were on the fringe, one of them the exiled Lenin in Zurich, their prospects hopeless until the First World War transformed them and created the possibility of violent revolutions in the east. By the end of the century, in an overwhelmingly peaceful revolution communism and the cult of Marxism–Leninism has been discredited in the Soviet Union. Whatever takes its place will change the course of the next century. The unexpected revolutions that swept through central and Eastern Europe from 1989 to 1991 were on the whole no less peaceful. In every corner of the globe the autocratic, bureaucratic state faced a powerful challenge. The comparative economic success and social progress achieved by the West through the century proved desirable to the rest of the world, as did its institutions, especially the 'free market' and 'democracy' with a multi-party system. But how will these concepts be transferred to societies which have never practised them?

'Freedom', 'democracy' and the 'free market' are simple concepts but their realisation is beset by ambiguity. In societies lately subjected to autocratic rule, how much freedom can be allowed without risking disintegration into anarchy and disorder? There is no Western country which permits a free market to function without restraint, without protecting the interests of workers and consumers. These institutional restraints, embodied for example in the successful 'social market economy' of Germany, have taken years to develop. How large a role should the state play? Not everything can be privatised, and certainly not instantly. How large a welfare system needs to be created? 'Communism' too has lost precise meaning. Communism in China today is very different from the communism of thirty years ago, now that private enterprises are flourishing. Labels change their meaning. Nor do simple slogans provide the answers.

At the beginning of the century one could believe that a better world was gradually emerging. History was the story of progress. For some this meant that socialist ideals would lead to a utopia before the century had come to an end. In mid-century that faith in human progress and in the inevitable march of civilisation was shattered. The power of National Socialism and its destructive master-race doctrine were broken; it was the end of an evil empire but not the end of tyranny. At the close of the century there is a little more cause for optimism. The horrors, corruption and inefficiency of autocracy, with its denial of humanity, lie exposed. But the problems that face mankind as a new era of history begins remain daunting. With the collapse of the Soviet model of communist autocracy there superficially appears to be a consensus in the world (except in China) that only 'democracy' and the 'market economy' can reconcile the people and their government and master the complex economic requirements of today's societies if progress is to be achieved and the people are to be deflected from revolution. Is it then the 'end of history', an end to the great ideological debate about the direction in which mankind is going to travel? Can we be more sure about our future? The world is far too diverse for that to be likely. New apparent certainties will no more survive immutably than did the old.

Right to the end the great events of the century did not turn out the way contemporaries expected. Having considered some of the overall changes, comparing the beginning of the century and the end, the chapters that follow will recount the tumultuous history that lies between.

CHAPTER 2

The German Empire: Achievement and Excess

Imperial Germany symbolised success. Created in three victorious wars, she had replaced France as the first military power in Europe. The Prussian spirit was seen to be matched by astonishing progress in other directions. In all branches of education and scientific discovery, the German Empire stood second to none. In manufacture, German industry grew by leaps and bounds. The secret of her success seemed to lie in the Prussian genius for organisation and in the orderliness and self-discipline of her hard-working people. There were a lot of them, too – nearly 67 million in 1913; this made the Germans the second-largest nation of Europe, well ahead of France and Britain, and behind only the vast population of Russia.

By the turn of the century Germany had become a predominantly industrial nation, with large cities. For every German working on the land, two were engaged in manufacture on the eve of the First World War. Once far behind Britain in coal production, by 1914 Germany had almost closed the gap, and after the United States and Britain was the third industrial power in the world. Coal, iron and steel, produced in ever larger quantities, provided the basis for Germany's leap forward, challenging Britain's role as Europe's leader.

Between 1871 and 1914 the value of Germany's agricultural output doubled, the value of her industrial production quadrupled and her overseas trade more than tripled. Germany's progress aroused anxieties among her neighbours, but there was also co-operation and a recognition that the progress of one European nation would, in fact, enrich the others. Germany was catching up with Britain, the pioneer of the industrial revolution, but Britain and Germany were also important trading partners.

Unlike Britain, the German Empire was transformed in a relatively short time from a well-ordered, mainly rural country to a modern industrial nation. In contrast with her industrial progress, the pace of Germany's political development was slow, deliberately retarded by its ruling men. The government of the Prussian–German Monarchy after 1871 was a mixture of traditional mid-nineteenth-century institutions, together with an imperial parliament – the Reichstag – more in harmony with the new democratic age. But the old traditional Junker society found allies after 1871 among the big industrialists in its opposition to the advance of democracy. The cleavage so created between the powerful few and the rest of society, in the name of maintaining the power of the Crown, was responsible for the continuation of social and political divisions in Wilhelmine Germany down to the outbreak of war.

The constitutional arrangements for the German Empire of 1871 did nothing to heal these divisions. On the contrary, Bismarck, their creator, intended to block any possibility that the old Prussia should be submerged by the new Germany. In Britain during the period of rapid industrialisation half a century earlier, the ruling wealthier groups of society had, in the end, acquiesced in the necessary political and social adjustments and admitted the

Coal, Iron and Steel Production in Germany and Britain
(annual averages)

	1875–9		1910–13	
	Germany	Britain	Germany	Britain
Coal and lignite *(million metric tons)*	49.9	135.7	251.5	292.0
Pig iron *(thousand metric tons)*	1,791.0	6,483.0	14,829.0	9,792.0
Steel *(million metric tons)*	0.97 (1880–4)	1.82	15.34	6.94

less wealthy to participate in government through radical electoral reform; not so in Prussia.

The German Empire consisted of a federation of twenty-five states; the largest was the kingdom of Prussia with a population in 1890 of some 30 million; it overshadowed the second largest state, Bavaria, with a population of 5.5 million. By preserving state parliaments and extensive state rights, Bismarck not only appeased the feelings of the other states, but above all preserved Prussia's own position. In Prussia, the parliament elected on a mid-nineteenth-century three-class system, not even by secret ballot, ensured the permanent predominance of the landed aristocracy, the Junkers, and also of the wealthy merchants and industrialists, and the socially conservative groups. Whereas some other states introduced democratic franchises, Prussia retained her totally undemocratic parliament until 1917.

The Reichstag for the empire as a whole was an entirely separate parliamentary body, democratically elected by universal manhood suffrage. The basis of parliamentary power lies in parliament's control of the purse-strings of government. But Bismarck had done his best to draw the teeth of parliamentary control. In the first place most of the imperial budget was spent on the military; by various means annual control over the army budget was removed from the Reichstag. The Reich's increasing expenditure in the twentieth century necessitated asking for more money from the Reichstag, which then acquired more significance for government.

The power to raise taxes was divided between the democratically elected Reichstag and the undemocratic Prussian (and other state) parliaments. The Reichstag controlled only indirect taxes, the rate of custom duties, duties on tobacco, sugar, brandy, salt, which weighed most heavily on the poor. Taxes on income and property could be voted only in the state parliaments. The Reichstag was thus virtually powerless to secure greater social justice through the introduction of more progressive taxation of the wealthy and the landed Junkers. These groups in their turn were determined to resist all attacks on their privileged position from the Reichstag, and as long as they could preserve the constitutional settlement with its divided parliaments they were able to block all serious attempts at constitutional reform. Bismarck wanted to ensure that there would never be parliamentary government on the British model.

The constitution of 1871 also gave tremendous powers to the emperor; he alone could appoint and dismiss the chancellor; he was supreme commander of the military forces and final arbiter of war and peace. The chancellor was nominally responsible to the Federal Council formed by delegates from the federal states – the Bundesrat – but this Council exercised no real power. The system so devised could operate as long as the Reichstag demanded no real control over government policies.

In fact the Reichstag was far from quiescent. By refusing to increase indirect taxation it could deny the imperial government the money it needed. 'Government', however, is rather a misnomer for the frequently chaotic executive of Wilhelmine Germany. The heads of the army, the navy and the civil branches of government and administration were often in conflict. The chancellor had to attempt to find a consensus and, if he succeeded in doing so, either to circumvent the Kaiser altogether or to win his consent. Sometimes the chancellor was too late, and the impressionable Kaiser had been led in a different direction already. After Bismarck no chancellor succeeded in dominating the state.

The Reichstag's political leaders too were in an isolated position. They debated vigorously and bargained with the chancellor, but their actions were not tempered by the responsibility of office. Divorced from government, the parties of the left, centre and right lacked the incentive of reaching workable and stable compromises. The parties of the left were insistently calling for reform and an end to the privilege so entrenched in Prussia. The conservative right, or agrarians as they were called, demanded tariffs on the import of grain to protect themselves. The left opposed tariffs because they meant dearer food for the people. So it became increasingly difficult for the chancellors of the empire to find majorities for the budget and other legislation from the shifting coalitions of parties from the centre to the right which they tried to form for their support after 1890; meanwhile the support of the Reichstag became indispensable in the new century as government expenditure on the navy, the army and the colonies rose rapidly. The scope of political manoeuvre available to the chancellor was, furthermore, narrowed by the growth of the Social Democratic Party; it had become, by 1912, the largest single party with 110 seats out of a total of 391.

Reichstag Election, 1912 (*number of seats*)

Conservatives & Free Conservatives	57
National Liberals	45
Progressives	42
Centre	91
Social Democrats	110
Nationalities	33
Anti-Semitic	13

The Social Democratic Party was denounced as revolutionary, its members as 'enemies of the state' – an extraordinary and unwarranted attack on a party operating fully within the law. The defeat of social democracy was the main purpose of the Conservatives and the men surrounding the Kaiser. They could not conceive of including the Social Democrats within the fabric of the political state. This was more understandable while the Social Democratic Party was indeed Marxist and revolutionary. But as the twentieth century advanced the great majority of the party members in 1913, led by the pragmatic Friedrich Ebert, had become democratic socialists working for gradual reform; their Marxist revolutionary doctrine was becoming more a declaration of outward faith than actual practice, or immediate expectation. In a number of the state parliaments, Social Democrats had already joined coalitions with Liberals to form a responsible base for governments, thus abandoning their revolutionary role. But in Prussia this was unthinkable.

One consequence of the narrow outlook of the Conservatives was that they would never consent to constitutional change which would have made the chancellor and his ministers responsible to the Reichstag as the government in Britain was to Parliament. The Conservatives thus had no alternative but to leave power, in theory at least, ultimately in the hands of the Kaiser. The Kaiser's pose as the 'All Highest' was ridiculous, and even the fiction could not be maintained when, after the Kaiser's tactless *Daily Telegraph* interview in 1908, when he claimed that he had helped Britain during the Boer War, his own ministers sought to restrain him.

Kaiser Wilhelm II did not have the strength to lead Germany in the right direction. He was an intelligent man of warm and generous impulse at times, but he was also highly emotional and unpredictable. He felt unsure of his fitness for his 'divine calling', and posed and play-acted. This was a pity as his judgement was often intuitively sound. He did not act unconstitutionally, leaving control of policy to his ministers and military men. But when, in an impasse or conflict between them, the decision was thrust back to him, he occasionally played a decisive role. More usually he was manipulated by others, his vanity making him an easy victim of such tactics. He wanted to go down as the people's Kaiser and as the Kaiser of peace; also as the emperor during whose reign the German Empire became an equal of the world's greatest powers. His contradictory aims mirrored a personality whose principal traits were not in harmony with each other.

The Kaiser, and the Conservative–industrial alliance, were most to blame for the divisiveness of German society and politics. There was constant

Kaiser Wilhelm II and General Helmuth von Moltke, who as Chief of the General Staff was responsible for carrying through the Schlieffen Plan. After an ignominious performance at the Marne, he was relieved of his command in November 1914 and replaced by von Falkenhayn.

talk of crisis, revolution or pre-emptive action by the Crown to demolish the democratic institutions of the Reich. Much of this was hysterical.

But the Wilhelmine age in German development was not entirely bleak. The judiciary remained substantially independent and guaranteed the civil rights of the population and a free press; there was a growing understanding among the population as a whole that Kaiser Wilhelm's pose as the God-ordained absolute ruler was just play-acting. Rising prosperity was coupled with the increasing moderation of the left and the growth of trade unions. The political education of the German people proceeded steadily, even if inhibited by the narrowly chauvinistic outlook of so many of the schoolmasters and university professors, by the patronage of the state as an employer, and by the Crown as a fount of titles, decorations and privileges. Significantly, the anti-Conservative political parties on the eve of 1914 commanded a substantial majority, even though they could not work together.

The deep political and social divisions never really threatened Germany with violence and civil war in the pre-war era. Over and above the conflict, the German people, including the Social Democrats, felt a strong sense of national pride in the progress of the 'fatherland'. Furthermore the last peacetime chancellor of imperial Germany, Theobald von Bethmann Hollweg, recognised that constitutional reform was a matter of time. But there was not sufficient time.

The Social Democrats, the Progressives and Centre, who had won a majority in the 1912 elections, demanded a constitutional monarchy responsible to the Reichstag. The Conservatives chose to regard this challenge as provoking a constitutional crisis, threatening the Wilhelmine state. But did they unleash a war deliberately to preserve their position and to avoid reform? To be sure, there were Conservatives and militarists who saw a successful war as a means of defeating democratic socialism. The Chancellor, Bethmann Hollweg, was not one of them. Nevertheless it was an element in the situation that the Kaiser and his supporters saw themselves in a hostile world surrounded by enemies at home and abroad. There developed in the increasingly militarised court a wild and overheated atmosphere, a fear and pessimism about the future. While German society as a whole had good reasons for confidence and satisfaction on the eve of the war, the increasingly isolated coterie around the Kaiser suffered more and more from hysterical nightmares inimical to cool judgement.

They were carried forward in 1914 by a tide of events they had themselves done much to create. In the summer of 1914 war was seen as a last desperate throw to stave off Germany's otherwise inevitable decline. Bethmann Hollweg laid the blame for the outbreak of war on cosmic forces, on the clash of imperialism and nationalism, and specifically on British, French and Russian envy of Germany's progress. Germany, so he claimed, could have done little to change this. But did her growth of power make the struggle in Europe inevitable or did her own policies contribute to war and her 'encirclement'?

Twenty-six years earlier, in 1888, at the time of the accession of Wilhelm II, Germany appeared not only secure but on the threshold of a new expansion of power, world power. The contrast of mood and expectations between then and 1914 could not have been greater. Bismarck had raised German power to the position where Berlin was the centre of diplomacy. European affairs revolved around the triangular-alliance relationship of Berlin, St Petersburg and Vienna. Bismarck had accomplished this by convincing Europe that Germany's power would be used only in her own defence, that Germany was a satiated nation, looking for no more territorial expansion, and that he would join with other peace-loving nations to preserve the general peace of Europe. After twenty years of peace, Germany's pacific intent could not seriously be doubted. Bismarck followed this policy to avoid what Bethmann Hollweg three decades later in August 1914 claimed to be inevitable, the formation of a hostile coalition to check the growth of German power in Europe and the world.

All this fundamentally changed in 1890 after the Kaiser's dismissal of Bismarck. The harm was not done by dropping the 'old pilot'. Bismarck was not indispensable. What proved so harmful to Germany's interests was that the basic aim of his policy in Europe was deliberately abandoned. Germany's leaders were blinded by a vision of *Weltpolitik*. They forcefully argued that the German Empire could not be content with her position on the European continent alone but must become a 'world power', otherwise her decline would be certain. Germany, so they thought, needed colonies, world markets, the certainty of securing raw materials, a merchant marine, and a navy no one would dare challenge, to protect her overseas commerce. They placed themselves at the head of, and stimulated further, the chauvinism of some sections of German society. No wonder that fear of Germany in the end bound together her neighbours in alliance against her. One of the most consistent advocates of this *Weltpolitik* from its inception was Admiral Alfred von Tirpitz.

The one overmastering purpose of Tirpitz's life was to build up a great German battleship fleet that would match on the high seas the primacy of the army on the land. He pursued this aim with tenacity and political skill. The Kaiser was obsessed with being respected and loved by the British. What better way to achieve this than to build up a rival navy, he thought, and so supported Tirpitz. The trouble was that a large navy in addition to a large army entailed heavy expenditures. Was it really necessary? Tirpitz set out to persuade the Reichstag. The first Navy Law was passed in March 1898. Tirpitz had claimed that it was a matter of survival to protect Germany's interests on the high seas; without their defence in the new age of *Weltpolitik* German decline was certain. For Foreign Minister Prince von Bülow, the navy would be a means of pressurising the European imperial powers, who had got there first, into making way for Germany, so that she too would have her 'place in the sun'. But how could the German navy hope to catch up with the large navies of France, Russia and above all Britain?

To meet the arguments that to attempt to build a large offensive fleet was a waste of German effort, Tirpitz developed facile and yet, to his contemporaries, plausible theories. He postulated that given Britain's widespread global commitments a German battleship fleet only two-thirds of the size of the British would suffice for victory, provided the German fleet was concentrated in the North Sea. Then there was his famous risk theory: Britain might strike at the incomplete German battleship fleet as Nelson had struck at the enemy in Copenhagen. Therefore until her fleet was large enough Germany would pass through a period of risk. During this period she must avoid war. Tirpitz calculated that this risk period would end in 1920, by which time, if his construction programme were adhered to, Germany would possess sixty battleships. Then what? Tirpitz publicly argued that the fleet would act as a deterrent, so ensuring Britain's neutrality in any future conflict; indeed he and others claimed that Britain would respect and only deal 'fairly' with Germany when Germany possessed enough naval force to impress on her the dangers of conflict. With Britain deterred from acting against her, Germany's plans for continental hegemony could be realised. Tirpitz professed to believe, taking a longer view, that since empires came and went in history, there would come the time for a new global share-out of territory; then Germany would be able to take her proper place only if she possessed a navy strong enough. Secretly he wrote that the fleet would need to defeat the British navy in war before Britain would cease to oppose Germany's rise to world power. Did Tirpitz believe in all his theories or just in a large navy? Were the theories really no more than propaganda to persuade the Kaiser and the Reichstag to accept the burdens of constructing the navy? Probably Tirpitz, like so many dynamic men of action, convinced himself by arguments first devised to persuade others.

Tirpitz's campaign of persuasion was certainly very successful. To the industrialists supplying the steel and to the owners of the shipyards, the battleship fleet plan could be presented as both patriotic and highly profitable. The cause of the navy was popularised among the people through a Navy League; the Pan-Germans were wooed as were all those who believed in Germany's *Weltpolitik*, from patriotically ardent professors to Reichstag deputies. One harmful consequence of all this propaganda, not actually welcome to Tirpitz while Germany passed through the risk years, was that German chauvinism was greatly increased. The difficulty of persuading the Reichstag to grant more money also added to the empire's constitutional difficulties and this, in turn, aroused the fears of Germany's rulers. Tirpitz's navy helped to stimulate a belligerent, restless spirit of dissatisfaction. The direct impact on Anglo-German relations was considerable too during the years of the 'naval race' after the launch of the first Dreadnought-class battleships in 1906, though it was not the naval challenge as such that brought Britain to the side of France and Russia. The British government knew it could maintain a margin of superiority over Germany and outbuild whatever the Germans could manage. But there was a fear that Germany might

Europe prepares for Armageddon. The Krupps 'Cannon Workshop No. 5' in Essen here turns out 15-inch guns for Germany's new 'Super-Dreadnoughts'.

soon launch herself on a general course of aggression endangering the whole European continent.

It was clear for all the world to see that the leaders of Wilhelmine Germany did not regard the German Empire any longer as satiated. The Germans saw no *moral* reason why they should be denied a 'place in the sun'. There were plenty of good practical reasons which would have made more responsible men hesitate.

While the Kaiser and the navy looked into the yonder of the wider world, the military had their eyes firmly fixed on the problem of how Germany in the centre of Europe could overcome the disadvantage of facing two enemies, Russia and France, at the same time and emerge dominant. The outcome was the Schlieffen Plan, which laid down that the bulk of the German army should be thrown against the French army, leaving the east for two months only lightly defended against the Russians.

The Schlieffen Plan was remarkable for two aspects of German official thinking: the complete disregard for international morality, in the interests of military advantage; and the excessive faith the German military mind placed on theoretical planning that disregarded the human factor and the unexpected. Despite its increasing remoteness from reality, the Schlieffen Plan acquired the authority of Holy Writ. It was the work of Count Alfred von Schlieffen, Chief of the German General Staff from 1891 to 1906. In all its versions, beginning with the first plan of 1899, Belgian neutrality would be violated – although Germany was a party to its perpetual guarantee. This would be justified by 'military necessity', claimed Schlieffen, and no one dared dispute that the General's plan overrode any treaty obligations. Schlieffen saw as his model Hannibal's victory at Cannae, achieved 2000 years earlier by turning both flanks of the Romans. Schlieffen's plan, however, concentrated on one wing, the right wing only, which would sweep around the French armies, 'crush the enemy's flanks . . . and complete the destruction by attack upon his rear'. The plan assumed that the French in the centre would not withdraw in time; that the war in the west could be won before the Russians could be ready to mount a serious offensive in the east; that France would be defeated more or less precisely in thirty-nine days and would then seek peace. The plan was based on many unsupported political and military assumptions. It was in truth a desperate gamble designed to achieve victory on one front in what was from the beginning a three-front war (Germany against France in the west, Germany against Russia in the east, Austria–Hungary against Russia in the south-east).

Imperial Germany began to give expression to her new post-Bismarckian orientation of foreign policy in 1890 by abandoning the alliance with Russia and drawing closer to England. Her intention was to regain a 'free hand' and exploit international rivalries to advance Germany's global objectives. Republican France and tsarist Russia thereupon drew together in alarm and concluded a defensive alliance directed against the possibility of German aggression (page 28). Fear of Germany was the main rationale of this otherwise incongruous alliance.

The policy of the 'free hand', of exploiting international differences, was thought out by one of Bismarck's pupils and erstwhile admirers, the publicity-shy head of the political section of the German Foreign Ministry, Baron von Holstein. To exploit Germany's freedom while the other powers confronted each other also became the guiding motive of policy during the years presided over by Bernhard von Bülow as Foreign Minister and Chancellor (1897–1909). These were fateful years for Germany. At the turn of the century a number of pro-German British ministers, led by the Colonial Secretary Joseph Chamberlain, were seeking a closer alignment with Germany as a counter to Russia's global expansion. There probably never was a possibility that Britain would have been ready to sign a formal alliance with Germany during the years 1898 to 1901, but she was ready to work in close collaboration with Germany. The chance for a far-reaching Anglo-German entente was rejected by Holstein and Bülow except on the impossible terms that Britain should share portions of her empire with Germany. The Germans expected the hard-pressed British to become more amenable later. The British found another way and managed without Germany's support. As Prime Minister Lord Salisbury had foretold in 1898 when speaking to the German Ambassador, 'You ask too much for your friendship.'

The 'other way' for Britain was to reach compromise settlements with imperial rivals. That was achieved with the French in the spring of 1904. The settlement involved allowing France predominance in Morocco. It was German policy that began turning the Anglo-French settlement of their differences into a partnership against Germany. The

Germans also had rights in Morocco and were not going to be ignored. The Kaiser made a dramatic visit to Tangier in 1905 and promised to support the Sultan of Morocco against the French. It is unlikely that the German military were looking for a pretext for war against France while France's ally, Russia, was internationally impotent, having to face the consequences of her unsuccessful war against Japan both abroad and at home. The Kaiser and Bülow in any case did not want war. Their aim was to bully France and Britain and to frighten them out of their recent entente. The result was the opposite. The Germans gained nothing from the conference which they convened at Algeciras in 1906 to deal with the Moroccan question, and British and French officers began secret discussions on military co-operation. French fears of Germany were strengthened.

But in 1905 the Kaiser's personal diplomacy did lead to one spectacular scoop. Constantly on the move, the Kaiser was cruising in his yacht just north of Stockholm in the Bay of Björkö; there he met the Tsar from close-by Russian Finland and talked him into signing a German–Russian alliance. In St Petersburg and Berlin the ministers were aghast. The Russian ministers would not abandon the French alliance against Germany. The treaty was stillborn.

Four years later in 1909, the Germans more successfully bullied Russia during the Bosnian crisis (page 59) and in 1911 attempted to coerce the French again over Morocco (page 30). The ineptitude of German policy is striking. The threats of war were bluff. Despite Germany's military superiority during these years, the Kaiser and his ministers did not wish to unleash an aggressive war. As long as the leaders of imperial Germany felt themselves to be stronger than their country's neighbours, they maintained the peace. Aggression was to stem from a growing sense of weakness, from the conviction after 1912 that Germany's superiority was slipping away.

Bülow's disastrous direction of German foreign policy came to an end with his resignation in 1909. He was succeeded as chancellor by Bethmann Hollweg. The dour philosophical new chancellor was conscious of, and opposed to, the excesses of German policy, of the naval programme and of the wilder shores of *Weltpolitik*. He hoped by patient diplomacy to allay the fears of Germany's neighbours and, above all, to improve relations with Britain. He began with the right ideas but soon found that in Wilhelmine Germany others, besides the responsible chancellor, had the ear of the Kaiser and could nullify the chancellor's efforts. British attempts, initiated by Richard Haldane and Winston Churchill in 1912, to cool down the naval competition all failed. British naval arrangements with France and Russia to share the defence of the oceans followed in 1914. In this way Germany herself tightened the coalition formed to contain her.

Bethmann Hollweg's efforts had also been undermined by the Secretary of State for Foreign Affairs, Alfred von Kiderlen-Wächter, who in 1911 turned France's attempts to increase her hold over Morocco into a second trial of strength and another international crisis. A German gunboat was sent to Agadir in Morocco to frighten the French. British reaction was unambiguous: Britain would stand by France if Germany attacked her. The Kaiser was all the more annoyed as this had not been his intention; finally the Germans withdrew from the Moroccan affair with 'compensation' – a strip of African territory which France relinquished to Germany. But there was no hiding the fact that imperial Germany had suffered a humiliating diplomatic defeat.

The Moroccan setback only reinforced Germany's desire to become stronger. It also drove her to support her one reliable ally, Austria–Hungary, and so to link Germany's fate with that of the Habsburgs. Germany's leaders were unwilling to contemplate a future based on their own calculations of a *relative* decline of power. General Ludendorff, the second most influential planner after the Chief of Staff General Moltke (the younger), urged a preventive war before it was too late. The year 1912 marks the turning point in the once confident thinking of the Kaiser and his entourage. By now they recognised that the possibility of building a German fleet sufficiently large to inflict defeat on Britain on the seas was a pipedream. Germany could not match Britain's naval construction. The naval race was lost for all to see. With it *Weltpolitik* faded.

Much more immediate and serious for Germany was the situation on the continent of Europe. The Habsburg ally appeared in dire straits, weakened by the dispute among the nationalities composing the empire. Russia had recovered from defeat by Japan and was launched on a colossal programme of military expansion and preparedness. With so little to show for so much effort in the cause of *Weltpolitik*, with the position of the Habsburg monarchy weakening, and Russia's strengthening in the Balkans where her protégés were in the ascendant after their victory in the first Balkan war, with more Social Democrats in the Reichstag after the elections of 1912 than ever before, an air of desperation can be discerned in the attitudes of the Kaiser's military advisers.

Bethmann Hollweg, from 1912 to 1914, consistently worked for better Anglo-German relations, but his efforts to detach Britain from her support of France failed. He did not rule out war as a solution to Germany's problems in Europe but it would need to be a war for what he saw as the right objectives, the survival of Germany as the strongest continental power, providing a base also for a share of imperial world power; diplomatically, he believed, this would mean loosening the Triple Entente and neutralising Britain. In its illusions Bethmann Hollweg's policy was as disastrous as his predecessor Bülow's had been.

The army command was clearly growing jittery in 1912. Bethmann Hollweg could still count on Tirpitz and his ever-unready navy to aid him in urging a delay in bringing about conflict. The desirability of launching a preventive war against France and Russia was discussed by the Kaiser and his principal military advisers, meeting in a so-called war council, in December 1912. The Kaiser had had one of his periodical belligerent brainstorms, this time brought about by a warning received from Britain that she would not leave France in the lurch if Germany attacked her. Nothing aroused the Kaiser to greater fury than to be scorned by Britain. But the secret meeting of 8 December 1912 did no more than postpone war. A consensus among all those present was achieved in the end; Admiral Tirpitz had opposed the army, which urged that war should be unleashed quickly; all in the end agreed to wait but not for much beyond 1914. They were also agreed that Germany would lose all chance of defeating Russia and France on land if the war was longer delayed. Speedier Russian mobilisation would make the Schlieffen Plan inoperable because Russia would be able to overwhelm Germany's weak screen of defence in the east before the German army in the west could gain its victory over France.

The most sinister aspect of the meeting of December 1912 was the cynical way in which the Kaiser's military planned to fool the German people and the world about the true cause of the war. It was to be disguised as a defensive war against Russia in support of the Habsburg Empire. In the coming months, they agreed, the German people should be prepared for war.

Still, a war postponed is a war avoided. Bethmann Hollweg was not yet convinced or finally committed. Wilhelm II could and, in July 1914, actually did change his mind. As the German Chief of Staff rightly observed, what he feared was not 'the French and the Russians as much as the Kaiser'.

Nevertheless, in 1913 the needs of the army did become first priority; a bill passed by the Reichstag increased the hitherto fairly static standing army by calling up an additional 136,000 conscripts. This measure was designed to bring the peacetime strength of the army to nearly 800,000 men by the autumn of 1914.

Bethmann Hollweg scored one success. The abrasive *Weltpolitik* overseas was downgraded. Instead, Germany now pushed her interests in Asia Minor and Mesopotamia and developed her new friendship with Turkey. The projected Berlin-to-Baghdad railway was to be the economic artery of this Germany's new imperial commercial sphere. The intrusion of German interests in the Middle East was not unwelcome to Britain since Germany would help to act as a buffer against Russian expansion.

In the Balkans, where a second Balkan war had broken out in 1913, Bethmann Hollweg and the British Foreign Secretary Sir Edward Grey worked together to localise the conflict and to ensure a peaceful outcome. The Kaiser's conference of December 1912 had at least made it much easier for Bethmann Hollweg to follow a pacific policy in 1913 and he could show some success for it, though not a weakening of Britain's support for France, his main objective. Nevertheless, the drift to war in Germany was unmistakable. Her leaders were accustoming themselves to the idea of a war, persuaded by the seemingly irrefutable logic of the military. In the end, in the summer of 1914, Bethmann Hollweg too would be carried forward with the Kaiser over the brink.

CHAPTER 3

Republican France during the 'Belle Epoque'

The German Empire symbolised to contemporaries in 1900 discipline, union and progress; France was generally seen as a country divided, whose politicians' antics could scarcely be taken seriously, a society sinking into corruption and impotence. The malevolence of that corruption had been demonstrated in the highest reaches of the army, the Church and politics by the Dreyfus affair, the innocent Captain having been found in 1899 yet again guilty of espionage. The slander against the Jews living in France achieved a degree of viciousness not seen anywhere in a civilised country. Only Russia could compete. Yet the better-off flocked to France. Paris was acknowledged as perhaps the most beautiful city in the world, certainly the artistic capital of Europe. The Riviera was becoming the holiday playground of European society.

Foreigners of course realised that there was more to France than the surface glitter of Paris and the Riviera. Few of them could understand a country so varied, so divided and so individualistic. Governments changed so frequently that in any other country such a state of affairs would have meant the nation was close to chaos, ungovernable. Yet in everyday life France was a stable country, with a strong currency and well ordered. Monarchial Europe looked askance at republican France with her official trappings derived from the revolution of 1789. Yet France was far more stable than she seemed and by 1914 had achieved a quite remarkable recovery as a great power.

Can we now discern more clearly how government and society functioned in France, something which so clearly mystified contemporaries?

The key to an understanding of this question is that the majority of Frenchmen wished to deny their governments and parliaments the opportunities to govern boldly, to introduce new policies and change the course of French life. France was deeply conservative. What most Frenchmen wanted was that nothing should be done that would radically alter the existing state of affairs in town and country or touch their property and savings. Thus the Republic became the symbol of order, the best guarantee of the *status quo* against those demanding great changes. The monarchist right were now the 'revolutionaries', something they had in common with the extreme left.

One explanation for this innate conservatism is that France did not experience the impact of rapid population growth and rapid industrialisation. For close on half a century from 1866 to 1906 the occupations of the majority of the working population altered only gradually. Whereas in 1866 half the working population was engaged in agriculture,

Population (*millions*)

	1880	1900	1910
France	37.4	38.4	39.2
Germany	45.2	56.4	64.9

French and German Coal, Iron and Steel Production *(annual averages)*

	1880–4		1900–4		1910–13	
	France	Germany	France	Germany	France	Germany
Coal and lignite *(million metric tons)*	20.2	65.7	33.0	157.5	39.9	247.5
Pig iron *(thousand metric tons)*	1,518.0	2,893.0	2,665.0	7,926.0	4,664.0	14,829.0
Steel *(million metric tons)*	0.46	0.97	1.7	7.7	4.09	15.34

fisheries and forestry, by 1906 it was still nearly 43 per cent. Employment in industry during the same years scarcely changed at all, from 29 per cent to 30.6 per cent. The tariff protected what was in the main a society of small producers and sellers. In industry small workshops employing less than five people predominated, as did the old-established industrial enterprises of clothing and textiles. But this is not the whole picture. Productivity on the land and in industry rose. New industries such as electricity, chemicals and motorcars developed with considerable success. France possessed large iron reserves in French Lorraine which enabled her to become not only an exporter in iron but also a steel producer. Large works were built at Longwy on the Luxembourg frontier, and the Le Creusot works rivalled Krupps as armament manufacturers. Coal mining in the Pas de Calais developed rapidly in response; but France remained heavily dependent on Britain and Germany for coal imports to cover all her needs. Production figures show that France, with a stable population, was overtaken dramatically as an industrial nation by Germany, whose population increased (see tables). For this reason France's success in maintaining her position in exports and production, judged per head of population, can easily be overlooked.

In one respect – the provision of capital finance for Europe – France won first place, and the large proportion of her total investment overseas which went to Russia between 1890 and 1914 became a major factor in international relations.

The majority of Frenchmen did not wish to face the fact that new problems were arising which required new solutions; they saw the 'defence' of the Republic in terms of combating the political aims of the Church and the army. But in the early twentieth century the growth and concentration of industry and a new militancy among groups of workers also threatened the Republic from the left. The majority groups of the parliamentary lower Chamber were determined to defeat these threats from the extreme right or the left. Political power depended on the management of the elected Chamber; governments came and went, but the legislation prepared by the Chamber provided the necessary continuity. Actual office was confined to a number of leading politicians who reappeared in ministry after ministry. In this scheme of things few Frenchmen cared how many ministries were formed. Their frequency in itself was a healthy obstacle to too much government, for Frenchmen had singularly little faith in their politicians.

There existed side by side with the elected government an administration with an ethos of its own and which had little connection with the democratic roots of government. This centralised administration had been little modified through all the constitutional change since its creation in 1800 by Napoleon. It made the head of state the chief executive, while the prefects were the state's representatives and administrators in each of the ninety geographical departments into which France was divided. They were appointed, and could be transferred or dismissed, by the Ministry of the Interior.

The prefects dealt directly with each ministry and on the whole kept aloof from politics; they were hand-picked administrators who carried out the decrees of the state. Each prefect in his department had his own administration which could be appealed against only by putting the case to the Council of

State in Paris. The prefects were not, of course, elected; they deliberately did not grow local roots but represented, in theory at least, an impersonal justice. They were powerful men who controlled enormous patronage in their department; they could make appointments to many paid posts from archivists to some grades of schoolteachers, tax collectors and small tobacco and post-office staff. They stood at the head of the social hierarchy, and were a guarantee of stability and conservatism. In this way France was at one and the same time both highly centralised but also decentralised; for the ordinary Frenchman 'government' in practice meant what the prefect and his administration did, not what was happening in far-off Paris. France has had the good fortune to attract to this type of higher administrative service, over a long period of time, many capable men.

The Republic stood for the defence of property and a well-ordered, static society. At the same time it was identified in the minds of its supporters as the bastion of the enlightenment and so, curiously, despite their frozen attitude towards the desirability of social change, republicans saw themselves as the people who believed in progress and the modern age. This was only possible because they could identify an 'enemy to progress' in the Church and its teachings. More passion was expended on the question of the proper role of the Church and the state during the first three decades of the Third Republic than on social questions. In every village the secular schoolteacher represented the Republic and led the ranks of the enlightened; the priest led the faithful; the Church demanded liberty to care for the spiritual welfare of Catholics not only in worship but also in education. Republicans decried the influence of the Church as obscurantist and resisted especially its attempts to capture the minds of the rising generation of young Frenchmen.

The Church was supported by the monarchists, most of the old aristocracy and the wealthier sections of society; but 'class' division was by no means so complete and simple as this suggests: the Church supporters were not just the rich and powerful. The peasantry was divided: in the west and Lorraine, they were conservative and supported the Church; elsewhere anti-clericalism was widespread. In the towns, the less well-off middle classes and lower officials were generally fervid in their anti-clericalism. Their demand for a 'separation' of state and Church meant in practice that the Church should lose certain rights, most importantly, its right to separate schools. The Catholic Church in France by supporting the losing monarchial cause was responsible in good part for its own difficulties. In the 1890s the Vatican wisely decided on a change and counselled French Catholics to 'rally' to the Republic and to accept it; but the *ralliement* was rejected by most of the French Catholic bishops and the Church's monarchist supporters. The Dreyfus affair polarised the conflict with the Church, the monarchists and the army on one side and the republicans on the other. Whether one individual Jewish captain was actually guilty or not of the espionage of which he stood accused seemed to matter little when the honour of the army or Republic was at stake.

Dreyfus' cause united all republicans and they triumphed. In May 1902, though the electoral vote was close, the republicans won some 370 seats and the opposition was reduced to 220. There now followed three years of sweeping legislation against the Church. Church schools were closed wholesale; a number of religious orders were banned; in 1904 members of surviving religious orders were banned from teaching. In December 1905 a Law of Separation between Church and state was passed. This law represents both the culmination of republican anti-clericalism and the beginning of a better relationship. Freedom of worship was guaranteed and, despite the opposition of the Vatican, the bitter struggle was gradually brought to a close. Anti-clericalism declined, and the monarchist right lost its last opportunity of enlisting mass support with the help of the Church. Extreme anti-clerical governments were now followed by more moderate republicans in power.

French governments before 1904 remained dependent not on one party but on the support of a number of political groupings in the Chamber; these groups represented the majority of socially conservative voters: the peasants who owned their land, shopkeepers, craftsmen, civil servants and pensioners with small savings. Governments were formed around groups of the centre, sometimes veering more to the 'left' and sometimes to the 'right'. But 'left' in the French parliamentary sense did not mean socialism. Once the predominant groupings of radical republicans had succeeded in defeating the Church, their radicalism was mild indeed. They stood for defending the interests of the peasant land proprietors, the shopkeepers, the less well-off in society; their socialism went no further than wishing to introduce a graduated income tax. The radical republicans were not in fact in the least radical but were 'firmly attached to the principle of private property' and rejected 'the idea of initiating class struggles among our citizens'. Their reforming record down to 1914 was indeed meagre. Even progressive income tax had to wait until 1917 before it became effective.

Socialism developed late but rapidly in France. Jean Jaurès and the more orthodox Marxist, Jules Guesde, led the parliamentary party, which gained 103 deputies and 1 million votes in the elections of 1914. But they never shared power with the parties of the centre for two reasons: the Socialist Party adhered to the line laid down in the International Socialist Congress of 1904 by refusing to co-operate in government with bourgeois parties, and in any case it was excluded by all the anti-socialist groups, which could unite on this one common enmity.

Besides the extreme left, the extreme right was also ranged against the Republic. From the debris of the Dreyfus case there had emerged a small group of writers led by Charles Maurras who formed the Comité de l'Action Française. Under the cloak of being a royalist movement, Maurras' ideas were really typical of some aspects of later fascism; fanatically anti-democratic and anti-parliamentarian, he hated Protestants, Jews, Freemasons and naturalised Frenchmen. An aristocratic elite would rule the country and destroy the socialism of the masses. The Action Française movement could not really appeal to the masses with its openly elitist aims. Yet it appealed to a great variety of supporters. Pius X saw in the movement an ally against the godless Republic; its hatreds attracted the support of the disgruntled, but it did not become a significant political movement before the war of 1914. The Action Française enjoyed notoriety through its daily paper of the same name, distributed by uniformed toughs, the so-called *Camelots du roi*; uninhibited by libel laws, the paper outdid the rest of the press in slander.

Far more significant than right extremists was the revolutionary workers' movement known as syndicalism, which emerged during the early years of the twentieth century. The factory worker had become a significant and growing element of society between 1880 and 1914. The trade unions, or *syndicats*, really got under way in the 1890s. Unlike the parliamentary Socialists, the syndicalists believed that the worker should have no confidence in the parliamentary Republic, which was permanently dominated by the propertied. The unions were brought together in the Confédération Générale du Travail (CGT). By 1906 the CGT firmly adhered to a programme of direct action, of creating the new state not through parliament but by action directly affecting society; its ultimate weapon, its members believed, would be the general strike. They accepted violence also as a justifiable means to bring about the 'social revolution'. The attitude of the CGT had much in common with the British phase of revolutionary trade unionism in the 1830s. Although most workers did not join the syndicalist CGT – only some 7 per cent in 1911 – nevertheless with 700,000 members their impact was considerable; they organised frequent violent strikes which were then ruthlessly put down by the army. The syndicalists declared they would not fight for the Republic and on 27 July 1914 demonstrated against war. Socialism, by being divided as a movement – for syndicalists rejected any community of interest with parliamentary Socialists – was much weakened in France. The result was a deep alienation of a large group of working men from the Third Republic. The defence of the fatherland, the almost unanimous patriotism in 1914 against the common enemy, was to mask this alienation for a time.

The assertiveness of France in the wider world stands in remarkable contrast to the conservatism of French society at home. The national humiliation and defeat at German hands in the war of 1870–1 did not turn France in on herself; the growing disparity between French and German power after 1870, whether looked at in terms of population or industrial production, did not, as might be expected, inhibit France's efforts abroad.

During the Bismarckian years from 1871 to 1890, France was isolated in Europe by the Iron Chancellor's diplomacy. Even so, a sense of security began to return. The rest of Europe was not likely again to stand by idly if Germany chose to attack France once more. To protect themselves against the danger of a German hegemony in Europe the other powers would seek to check Germany. French weakness thus gave to France paradoxically a certain international strength. But every French leader also knew that France could only count on help if she were the victim of aggression; no ally would ever be willing to risk war with Germany merely in order to help France recover the lost territories of Alsace-Lorraine. The cry for *revanche* was a stance, a sentiment, and in any case grew gradually weaker; it never became the basis of practical policies.

The choice confronting France towards the end of the nineteenth century was clear. A policy of reconciliation and trust in imperial Germany could have been followed. This would have been based on the fact that Germany had not exploited her superior strength for twenty-five years to foist another ruinous war on France. Alternatively, France could follow a deterrent policy. Unable ever to be strong enough to match Germany alone, she could with the help of an ally contain her by making the chances of success for Germany in war much more hazardous. This was the policy generally followed by the governments of the Third Republic after 1890. They first sought an alliance with tsarist Russia, and after its conclusion in 1894 made its maintenance the bedrock of French foreign policy. The alliance made it possible for France to continue to conduct policy as a great power despite her relative inferiority in population and production. Reliance on good relations with Germany would have made her dependent on her goodwill, a weaker and in the end junior partner as long as relationships were seen purely in terms of national power.

The path to the alliance with Russia was smoothed by the large loans raised on the Paris money market which Russia needed for her industrial and military development. From close on 3000 million francs in 1890 they rose to 12,400 million francs in 1914, representing between a third and a quarter of the total of France's foreign investments.

At the heart of the Franco-Russian alliance lay the military convention, concluded in 1892 and ratified in 1894. This stated that if France were attacked by Germany or by Italy supported by Germany, then Russia would attack Germany with all her forces; and that if Russia were attacked by Germany, or by Austria supported by Germany, then France would fight Germany with all her forces (Article 1). That was a clear though strictly defined and limited defensive-alliance commitment for both sides against a German attack. Of equal practical importance was the second article, on mobilisation, because mobilisation in conditions of modern warfare leads almost inevitably to war. According to this article, if any one of the Triple Alliance powers mobilised, that is Italy, Austria or Germany, then France and Russia would immediately mobilise. The practical consequences of the first and second article did not coincide. The French realised that the second article might very well undo the careful limitation (restricting the contingency to conflict with Germany) of the first. Under the first article France was not committed to go to war if Austria and Russia alone fought; but under the second article she was bound to mobilise if Austria did so, and this mobilisation would lead to German mobilisation and in this way to certain war between France and Germany. Thus in practice France could become involved in war with Germany over an Austro-Russian quarrel. Both sides had grave misgivings that the alliance would either prove worthless or drag one side into war over the national ambition of the other. Yet there was one common interest: fear of having to face Germany in isolation.

In other respects Russian and French ambitions did not coincide. Russia had her eyes on the Balkans, the Middle East and China, the French on Africa and the Mediterranean. Russia's rivals were Japan, Austria and Britain and France's rivals in different regions of the world were Britain and Italy for a time, then Germany over Morocco. Before 1912 neither Russia nor France was in the slightest interested in engaging in a great European war of life and death merely as a consequence of the other power's expansionist desires in the Balkans or Morocco. Before 1912 the French invariably advised the Russians to exercise caution and warned them against the use of the alliance to push national regional interests. The Russians for their part gave exactly the same advice. This happened when the French asked for and failed to secure Russian support against Britain in the 1890s and Germany in 1905 and 1911; the Russians similarly got no help from France in Asia in 1904 and 1905 or in the Balkans during the Bosnian crisis in 1909 (page 59).

What then kept the alliance alive despite these setbacks? It was the threat which was felt both in Russia and France of imperial Germany's growing might and the fear that Germany with her ally Austria–Hungary was seeking continental hegemony.

It is a remarkable fact that France's relative weakness on the European continent before 1914 did not throw her whole diplomacy on the defensive. On the contrary, successive French governments followed well-thought-out expansionist aims overseas and, to the bafflement of their German neighbours, refused to be intimidated. Only the threat of war led them to draw back when clashing with Britain in 1898 at Fashoda over control of the Sudan and the Upper Nile. But French colonial policy had enormously extended the French Empire from the 1880s to the turn of the century: in West Africa, in North Africa (where Tunis was added to Algeria) and in eastern Asia in Indo-China. This policy drew for support on no popular enthusiasm. Colonies excited few Frenchmen. It was the work of but a small number of politicians, explorers and soldiers. But when in consequence of colonial expansion there occurred a clash with a European neighbour, then ardent patriotism would sweep through the country. Until 1903 this animosity was directed far more against Britain, which blocked French imperial ambitions, than against Germany. During the Boer War (1899–1902) no country exceeded France in expressions of popular hatred of Britain.

Then in 1905 occurred an extraordinary and unanticipated change. Germany suddenly loomed large as the obstacle to French colonial ambitions and Britain became the friend. This was partly accidental and partly a deliberate result of French and German policies. The French were determined to gain control of Morocco, which would round off her large African empire stretching from Tunisia and Algeria through the Saharan desert hinterland to French West Africa. In April 1904 the French Foreign Minister, Théophile Delcassé, reached a comprehensive settlement with Britain over rival colonial interests all over the world. The main purpose was to gain Britain's consent to French predominance in Morocco, in return for which France would cease to make difficulties for Britain as the occupying power of Egypt.

The only two major international crises France faced after the agreement with Britain were due to French attempts to make good that bargain. The Germans, who also had treaty rights, had been left in the cold. Belatedly, in 1905, they reacted with a visit to Tangier by the Kaiser, emphasising dramatically Germany's interests in the future of the Sultan's dominions. What was really at issue for the Germans, however, was not the future of Morocco but France's new international position. France had escaped from the Bismarckian shackles of isolation, first by concluding an alliance with Russia in 1894 and now by reaching agreement with Britain and establishing the *entente cordiale*. To the Germans it seemed that their position of strength was an illusion and that the tables were being turned on Germany herself, now threatened with isolation and 'encirclement'. They used the Moroccan issue in 1905 and again in 1911 to attempt to tear asunder the alliances and alignments France had constructed.

The Germans in 1905 timed their diplomatic strike extremely well. With Russia fully engaged in an unsuccessful war in China, and her navy annihilated by the Japanese, the Russians were in no condition to provide any military support to France. The French military staff had always recognised that because of Russia's slower mobilisation, the German armies would all be hurled against France at the outset of the war. This was in fact the essence of the Schlieffen Plan, which sought to meet the dangers for Germany of a two-front war by defeating France before Russia could be ready to advance in the east. So, conversely, from the French point of view the vital importance of Russia's military role would be to strike against Germany as soon as possible after the outbreak of war and thus relieve the outnumbered French. In 1901 the Russian General Staff had promised to begin their offensive even before they were fully mobilised, on the eighteenth day after the outbreak of war.

It was clear to the French in 1905 that the Russians could no longer fulfil this commitment. A year later the Russian General Staff formally confirmed this. The new entente partner, Britain, was no substitute for Russia. The British refused a formal alliance commitment and warned the French right down to 1914 that they could not count on British military support. Even if British support did materialise it would be confined to 100,000 men. Until Russia had recovered sufficiently to resume her military commitment to France in 1912, France found herself in a position of desperate military inferiority. Yet this fact did not alter her basic policy in Morocco.

The French appeared to give way in 1905. The Germans demanded the removal of the architect of the Moroccan policy, Foreign Minister Delcassé; the French government obliged by forcing him to resign. The French also agreed to a conference to be held at Algeciras in 1906. But when the powers assembled at the conference, France's special position in Morocco was recognised by the majority of powers, whose support had been secured by Delcassé's earlier diplomacy. Similarly in 1911 during the second Moroccan crisis Germany failed in her main objective. France's alliance and alignments held. Again France showed her willingness to acknowledge German claims by ceding other colonial French territory to the Germans in compensation. But she secured Morocco. Britain, alarmed by Germany's bellicosity, also drew closer to France. But the Kaiser did not in 1905 or in 1911 press German policy to the point of war.

The following year in 1912 Raymond Poincaré, a tough nationalist, impeccable republican, orthodox anti-clerical and conservative in social questions, became premier, and subsequently president in 1913. Army appropriations were increased; even so in 1913 the French army of 540,000 would be facing a German army of 850,000 if war should break out – a catastrophic prospect. To reduce this gap a bill lengthening service in the French army from two to three years became law in 1913. The French Chamber had turned away from the left Socialists, and the army became more respectable in the eyes of the leading politicians in power, as it had proved a valuable and reliable instrument in crushing strikes and revolutionary syndicalism. Poincaré was determined that France should never find herself at the mercy of Germany. A strong alliance with Russia became the most cherished objective of his diplomacy. So he reversed earlier French policy and assured the Russians in 1912 that they could count on French support if their Balkan policy led to conflict with Austria–Hungary; if Germany then supported her ally, France would come to the aid of Russia. This was a most significant new interpretation and extension of the original Franco-Russian alliance of 1894; it ceased to be wholly defensive. Poincaré also encouraged the Russians to reach naval agreements with the British.

Against the growing power of Germany Poincaré saw that France was faced with a grim choice: either to abandon her status as a great power and to give in to German demands (the manner of their presentation had been amply demonstrated during the Moroccan crisis of 1911); or to strengthen her own forces and draw as close as she could to her Russian ally (even at the risk of being sucked into war by purely Russian Balkan interests) and to the British entente partner. In staff conversations the Russians in 1912 agreed to resume their offensive military role and to start their attack on East Prussia on the fifteenth day of mobilisation. France had come through her years of 'risk' giving up very little. The other side of the coin is that imperial Germany had not exploited her military superiority during the years from 1905 to 1911 by launching a so-called 'preventive' war.

The years from 1912 to 1914 marked a vital change. Fatalism about the inevitability of war was spreading among those who controlled policy, and ever larger armies were being trained for this eventuality on all sides of the continent. With Poincaré as France's president, Russia would not again be left in the lurch by her ally whenever Russia judged her vital interest to be at stake in the Balkans and the Ottoman Empire. But French diplomacy conflicted increasingly with public sentiment. There was strong domestic opposition to strengthening the army; foreign dangers, the left believed, were being deliberately exaggerated by the right. On the very eve of war in 1914, the French elections gave the majority to the pacifist groups of the left. But it was too late. Poincaré's support for Russia did not waver during the critical final days before the outbreak of war and was a crucial factor in the decision the Tsar and his ministers took to mobilise, which made war inevitable in 1914.

CHAPTER 4

Italy: Aspirations to Power

What happens when a parliamentary constitution is imposed on an underdeveloped society? The answer is not without relevance to conditions in the Third World in the twentieth century. Italy provides an interesting early case history. In population size Italy, Austria–Hungary France and Britain belong to the same group of larger European nations; but the differences between their development and power are striking. The greater part of Italy, especially the south, was in the late nineteenth century among the poorest and most backward regions of Europe. But her rulers in the north imposed parliamentary constitutional government on the whole of Italy, over the more developed as well as the undeveloped regions. Furthermore, a highly centralised administration was devised dividing the whole country into sixty-nine provinces, each governed by a prefect responsible to the minister of the interior.

Parliamentary institutions suited well enough the north-western region of Italy, formerly the kingdom of Piedmont, the most advanced region of Italy, where parliamentary government had taken root before unification. The problem arose when the Piedmontese parliamentary system was extended to the whole of Italy in 1861; it was now intended to cover the very different traditions and societies of the former city states, the papal domains and the Neapolitan kingdom. It was a unity imposed from above. For many decades 'unity' existed more on paper than in reality. Italy had the appearance of a Western European parliamentary state.

A closer look at the Italian parliament shows how very different it was from Britain's. To begin with, only a very small proportion, 2 per cent, of Italians were granted the vote. This was gradually extended until in 1912 manhood suffrage was introduced. But in the intervening half-century, the small electorate had led to the management of parliament by government; a few strong men dominated successive administrations. There were no great political parties held together by common principles and beliefs, just numerous groups of deputies. The dominating national leaders contrived parliamentary majorities by striking bargains with political groups, by bribes of office or by the promise of local benefits. When a government fell, the same leaders would strike new bargains and achieve power by a slight shuffling of political groupings.

In such a set-up, parliamentary deputies came to represent not so much parties as local interests; their business was to secure benefits for their electors. Politicians skilled in political deals dominated the oligarchic parliamentary system from 1860 to 1914. (In the early twentieth century Giovanni Giolitti became the leading politician.) These leaders can be condemned for their undeniable political corruption as well as for undermining the principles of constitutional parliamentary and, eventually, democratic government. The ordinary voter could scarcely be aroused in defence of parliament which seemed to assemble only for the benefit of politicians and special-interest groups.

On the other hand the particular conditions of

recently united Italy have to be taken into account. It had a strong tradition of local loyalties. Central government was regarded as an alien force. The difficulty of building bridges between the political oligarchy of those who ruled and the mass of the people was great. Outside Piedmont there was little tradition of constitutional parliamentary government of any sort. At the time of unification three-quarters of the population could neither read nor write. The poverty of southern and central Italy was in great contrast to the progress of the north. And the enmity of the papacy, which had lost its temporal dominion, meant that Catholics obedient to the pope were alienated from the state and would not participate in elections. In a country so rent by faction and regional rivalry as well as so backward, it can be argued that the firm establishment of unity and the solid progress achieved represented in themselves a notable success. The franchise was extended, and illiteracy greatly reduced so that by 1911 almost two-thirds of the population could read and write; in the south the proportion of literate to illiterate was reversed.

Politics cannot be divorced from society and poverty. Compared to France and Britain, Italy was a poor country; the greater part of Italy, especially the south, was caught in the poverty trap of a backward agrarian economy. A larger proportion of the population remained dependent on agriculture right down to the First World War than in any other Western European country, including France. Some agricultural progress was achieved as landowners and peasants turned to exporting olive oil, fruit and wine, but protection against the influx of low-cost wheat from the Americas benefited principally the great landowners of the south, while high food costs bore most heavily on the poorest landless labourers. The masses of the south were exploited in the interests of the north. Deforestation, exhaustion of the soil and soil erosion, taxation and overpopulation forced some of the peasantry to emigrate in search of a less harsh life elsewhere in Europe or across the Atlantic. During every year of the 1890s, on average 280,000 people left Italy, rather more than half this number to go overseas; this human stream rose to 600,000 a year in the first decade of the twentieth century and reached 873,000 in 1913, by which time about two-thirds went overseas, principally to the United States. No European state suffered so great an exodus of its population in the early twentieth century. By 1927, the Italian government calculated there were more than 9 million Italians living abroad, where they formed concentrated communities: among them, half a million in New York, 3.5 million in the United States as a whole, 1.5 million in the Argentine and 1.5 million in Brazil.

The alliance between northern industry and the large and frequently absentee landowners growing wheat in the south impoverished the mass of the peasantry: protected by a high tariff, these landowners were able to farm large tracts of land inefficiently and wastefully without penalty; unlike in France, no class of peasant proprietors, each with his own plot of land, would emerge. Almost half the peasants had no land at all; many more held land inadequate even for bare subsistence.

By the turn of the century, there was a growing recognition that there was a 'southern question' and that the policies of United Italy had been devised to suit the conditions of the north; special state intervention would be necessary to help the south. In December 1903 Giolitti, when prime minister, expressed the will of the government to act: 'To raise the economic conditions of the southern provinces is not only a political necessity, but a national duty,' he declared in parliament. Genuine efforts were made by legislation to stimulate industrial development in the Naples region, to improve agriculture and reform taxation, build railways and roads, improve the supply of clean water and, above all, to wage a successful campaign against the scourge of malaria. But too little was done to improve the wealth of the peasants and to increase peasant proprietorship; the middle class was small and, in the absence of industry, mainly confined to administration and the professions. Government help on the economic front was but a drop in the ocean of widespread poverty and backwardness. Despite the undoubted progress, the gap between the north and south continued to widen. Little would be achieved until after the Second World War, but even in the last quarter of the twentieth century the problem of the south persists.

Italian industrialisation was handicapped by the lack of those indigenous resources on which the industrialisation of Britain, France and Germany was based: the amount of coal in Italy was negligible and there was little iron ore. But helped by protection (since 1887), Italian industry developed in the north. The first decade of the twentieth century was (apart from the brief depression of 1907 to

1908) a period of exceptionally fast growth, overcoming the depression of the 1890s. Textile production, led by silk, rapidly expanded in Piedmont and Lombardy and dominated exports. Large quantities of coal had to be imported but as a source of energy coal was supplemented by the exploitation of hydroelectrical power, in which large sums were invested. Italy also entered into the 'steel age', building up her steel production to close on a million metric tons by the eve of the First World War, a quantity five times as large as in the 1890s. A start was made, too, in promising new twentieth-century industries in typewriters (Olivetti), cars (Fiat), bicycles and motorcycles. A chemical industry producing fertilisers rapidly developed. State aid, in the form of special legislation aiding shipbuilding or by stimulating demand through railway construction and through tariff protection, contributed to this spurt of industrialisation in the early twentieth century. The banks provided investment funds; the help of tourist income and the money sent back by Italians abroad enabled a greater investment to be made than was earned by the industrial and agricultural production of the country.

Population (*millions*)

	1900	1910
Italy	32.4	34.7
France	38.4	39.2

Italian Production (*annual averages*)

		Italy	France
Raw-cotton consumption (*thousand metric tons*)	1895–1904	125.7	174.0
	1905–13	186.0	231.0
Raw-silk output (*thousand metric tons*)	1895–1904	53.6	7.9
	1905–13	43.5	6.8
Pig-iron output (*thousand metric tons*)	1900–4	47.0	2,665.0
	1910–13	366.0	4,664.0
Steel output (*million metric tons*)	1900–4	0.15	1.7
	1910–13	0.83	4.09
Electric-energy output (*million kilowatt hours*)	1901	220.0	340.0
	1913	2,200.0	1,800.0

But a weakness of Italy's industrialisation was its concentration in three north-western regions, Piedmont (Turin), Lombardy (Milan) and Liguria (Genoa), thus widening further the gap between administrative political unification and industrial economic unification.

The growth of industry in the north led, as elsewhere in Europe, to new social tensions as factory workers sought to better their lot or simply to protest at conditions in the new industrial centres. During the depression of 1897 and 1898 riots spread throughout Italy, culminating in violence and strikes in Milan. They were met by fierce government repression. But the year 1900 saw a new start, a much more promising trend towards conciliation. The Socialist Party was prepared to collaborate with the Liberal parliamentarians and accept the monarchy and constitution in order to achieve some measure of practical reform. This was the lesson they learnt from the failure of the recent violence in Milan. Giolitti, who became prime minister for the second time in 1903, saw the involvement of the masses in politics as inevitable and so sought to work with the new forces of socialism and to tame them in political combinations. But he looked beyond this to genuine social and fiscal reforms.

The rise of socialism in the 1890s had one beneficial result for the embattled state. It alarmed the Church and led to a revision of the papal interdiction against such activities as participation in government and parliamentary elections. The temporal rights of the Church – the 'occupation' of Rome – were becoming a question of history rather than one of practical politics. Pope Leo XIII expressed the Church's concern for the poor and urged social reform as a better alternative to repressive conservativism on the one hand and atheistic socialism on the other. The Church was coming to terms with twentieth-century society. His successor, Pope Pius X, though more conservative, in 1904 permitted Catholics to vote wherever Socialists might otherwise be elected. This marked the cautious beginning of collaboration between Church and state, and a beginning too in creating a Catholic political force (Christian Democrat) to keep the Socialists out of power in collaboration with other groups.

Catholic support was welcome to Giolitti. His progressive social views did not mean he wished to allow Socialists a decisive voice in government.

From 1903 onwards the Socialists were split into violently hostile factions: a minority, the reformists, were still ready to collaborate within the constitutional framework and to work for practical reform; the majority, the syndicalists, were intent on class revolution to be achieved by direct action and violence through syndicates or trade unions. The weapon which they hoped would overthrow capitalist society was the general strike. The split into reformist socialists, revolutionary socialists and syndicalists further weakened the Socialists, faced in the new century with the overwhelmingly difficult task of changing a well-entrenched capitalist state. The great strikes of 1904, 1907 and 1908 were defeated, the Socialist Party in parliament was small, the forces of law and order strong; a Catholic labour movement, too, successfully diverted a minority of peasants and industrial workers from socialist trade unions.

The absence of strong parties and the commanding position established by a few politicians were the most noteworthy characteristics of Italian political life before the First World War. The Catholic political group was embryonic, unlike those in neighbouring France and Germany. Italian socialism could not overcome the handicap of the fierce factional struggles which characterised the emergence of socialism in Europe. Regionalism, the Church and the backwardness of much of the country also prevented the development of a broadly based conservative party. So government was dominated by the 'liberal' groupings of the centre, agreeing only on the maintenance of law, order and national unity, and bound by a common opposition to conservative extremism and revolutionary socialism. Were these characteristics of Italian political life the inevitable consequence of this stage of uneven national development, of the continuing regional particularism of a sharply differentiated society and of a limited franchise? Or should the arrested form of parliamentary government be regarded as forming the roots of the later fascist dictatorship and the corporate state? It is not helpful to look upon Giolitti as a precursor of Benito Mussolini. The two men and their policies must be examined in the context of the conditions of their own times. The shattering experience of the First World War separated two eras of modern Italian history, Giolitti's from Mussolini's.

Giolitti was a politician of consummate skill in parliamentary bargaining. He followed broad and consistent aims. The first was to master the whirlpool of factions and to reconcile the broad masses of workers and peasants with the state, to accept the upsurge of mass involvement in politics and industrial life and to channel it away from revolution to constructive co-operation. 'Let no one delude himself that he can prevent the popular classes from conquering their share of political and economic influence,' he declared in a remarkable parliamentary speech in 1901. He clearly accepted the challenge and saw it as the principal task of those who ruled to ensure that this great new force should be harnessed to contribute to national prosperity and greatness. He was not prepared to accept revolutionary violence, yet repression, he recognised, would only lead to unnecessary bloodshed, create martyrs and alienate the working man.

Giolitti utilised the revulsion against the strikes of 1904 to increase his parliamentary support by calling for a new election which he fought on a moderate platform. His tactics succeeded and he never, down to 1914, lost the majority of support he then gained. But this support was based as much on the personal loyalty and dependence on political favours of individual deputies as on agreement with any broad declaration of policy. His management of parliament (and the electoral corruption) undeniably diminished its standing and importance.

Enjoying the support of King Victor Emmanuel III, Giolitti's power was virtually unfettered for a decade. He used it to administer the country efficiently, to provide the stability which enabled Italy in the favourable world economic conditions to make progress and modernise her industry. His concern for the south was genuine, and state help pointed the way. In order to preserve the state, Giolitti appeased the left and claimed to be a conservative. His most startling move towards the politics of the masses, away from those of privilege, was to introduce a bill in 1911 to extend the electorate to all males. The bill became law in 1912. It was not so much the new extension of the franchise which undermined Giolitti's hold over his parliamentary majority: he secured the return of a large majority in the new parliament of 1913. What transformed Italian politics was the unleashing of ardent nationalism by the war with Turkey in 1911 which Giolitti had started in quite a different spirit of cool calculation.

*

It was Italy's misfortune to be diverted in the twentieth century from the path of highly necessary internal development to a policy of nationalism and aggressive imperialism. Italy lacked the resources and strength for an expansionist foreign policy. But for her own ambitions, Italy could have remained as neutral as Switzerland.

Italy was favoured by her geographical position in that she did not lie in the path of the hostile European states confronting each other. Luckily for Italy, her military forces represented to her neighbours a 'second front' which they were most anxious to avoid opening while facing their main enemy elsewhere. However little love they had for Italy, they were therefore anxious to preserve Italian neutrality and even willing to purchase her benevolence with territorial rewards. Thus the diplomatic tensions and divisions of Europe were extraordinarily favourable to Italy's security, which her own military strength could not have ensured.

One of the most virulent forms of nationalism is that known as 'irredentism', the demand to bring within the nation areas outside the national frontier inhabited by people speaking the same language. There were two such regions adjoining the northern Italian frontier: Trentino and Trieste. Both were retained by Austria–Hungary after the war with Italy in 1866. A third area, Nice and Savoy, which had been ceded to France in return for French help in the war of unification, also became the target of irredentist clamour. Besides this irredentism, Italian leaders also wished to participate in the fever of European imperialism. Surrounded on three sides by the sea, Italians looked south across the Mediterranean to the North Africa shore where lay the semi-autonomous Turkish territories of Tunis and Tripolis and perceived them as a natural area of colonial expansion. They saw to the west the island of Corsica, now French, but once a dependency of Genoa; to the east, across the Adriatic, the Ottoman Empire was the weakening ruler of heterogeneous Balkan peoples.

All these possibilities for expansion presented Italian governments with choices as to which neighbours would be friends and which enemies. Italian foreign policy from 1878 to 1915 is really the story of Rome's manoeuvres between the powers to secure the particular prize or objective of the moment. It is this national 'egoism' which gives Italian policy the appearance of faithlessness and inconsistency. But it would be facile to make the moral judgement that Italian nationalism was either better or worse than that of the other European powers. What can be said with certainty is that it served Italian interests ill, but then it would have required vision and statesmanship of the highest order to have resisted the imperialist urge which swept over all the European powers.

The French occupation of Tunis in 1881 brought Italy a year later into the Austro-German alliance group, and a Triple Alliance was concluded in 1882. Italy remained a formal member of this alliance down to the First World War, but it helped her achieve her territorial ambitions hardly at all. At the turn of the century she made further agreements with France and Britain whereby the spheres of interest along the North African coast were divided. The 'tariff war' between France and Italy ended. Meanwhile Italy had established a protectorate in east Africa and dreamt of conquering Abyssinia. These ambitions were checked in a most humiliating way when the Abyssinians, the 'natives', defeated an Italian force at the battle of Adowa in 1896. The Italians, however, did not lose their appetite for influence and empire. Austria–Hungary's annexation of Bosnia in 1908 stimulated the Italians to search for compensation in the far-flung and loosely controlled Ottoman Empire. But the terrible Messina earthquake in December 1908 riveted national attention on Sicily for a while.

The Italians did not wait very long, however. The Moroccan crisis of 1911 between France and Germany pointed to the North African coast as a region where the Europeans would complete their colonisation soon. Perhaps, some Italians feared, the Germans foiled in Morocco would descend on Tripoli instead. Giolitti's 'imperialism' was much more opportunist. He was more interested in the effect which the agitation for colonial expansion had on his domestic position than in imperialism as such. He regarded the nationalists as just another group to be appeased at home, another group to be brought into his broad parliamentary front of supporters. When he assessed the international situation in 1911 he concluded that Italy would get away with the seizure of Tripoli. His domestic hold on power would be much strengthened by a successful little war.

In October 1911 the Italians, after declaring war on Turkey, landed troops in Tripoli. A month later Giolitti announced the annexation of Libya. But the Turks refused to give in. The Italians now escalated the war, attacking in April 1912 the Dardanelles and occupying a number of Aegean islands. By October 1912 the Turks had had enough and the war ended.

The consequences of the war were, however, far from over. As peace was signed, Montenegro, Serbia, Bulgaria and Greece began a new war, the first Balkan war, attacking Turkey. Italy's policy cannot be said to have caused the Balkan wars but her success, and Turkey's proven isolation, had certainly encouraged the Balkan states. Setting the Balkans alight was the last thing Giolitti wanted, yet that is what occurred. Just as serious were the reactions at home. Giolitti desired only limited expansion, but a reversion to a cautious pacific policy had been difficult. The nationalists thirsted for more colonies, more territory. And so it came about that Giolitti had unleashed a political force more powerful than he could control.

CHAPTER 5

The British Empire: Premonitions of Decline

At the height of her imperial greatness, there is discernible in the Edwardian Britain of the early twentieth century a new mood of uncertainty, even of apprehension about the future. Why should this be so?

British society had shown itself remarkably successful in adapting to new conditions brought about by the industrial revolution. The inevitable social changes were taking place without violence. Britain had passed peacefully through some two decades of difficult economic conditions. The apprehensive mood was related more to her future role in the world. On the face of it the British Empire was the most powerful in the world: the navy 'ruled the waves'; Britain's wealth was matched by no other European state; a war in South Africa had been brought to a successful end in 1902, though it had not enhanced Britain's military reputation. Superficially the Edwardian age was elegant and opulent, the King giving a lead to fashionable society and doing little else, despite the myth about his influence on affairs of state. But it was obvious that in the years to come Britain would face great changes.

The effects of trade on British industry were widely discussed. It was argued that British industrial management was not good enough. If British industrialists did not wake up, authors of books like *Made in Germany* (1896) and the *American Invaders* (1902) warned, Britain would be overtaken and become a second-rate industrial power.

People feared another depression and rightly sensed that British industry was lagging behind that of the United States and Germany. This can indeed be seen in the comparative growth in value of manufactured exports of the world's three leading industrial nations.

Britain's economic performance during the years from 1900 to 1914 showed several weaknesses. The 'first' industrial revolution was spreading to the less developed world. A textile industry was being built up in Japan and India. But Britain continued to rely on a few traditional industries such as cotton textiles, which for a time continued to grow strongly because of worldwide demand. Then the coal industry, employing more than a million men in 1914, still dominated the world's coal export trade due to the fortunate fact that British coal mines were close to the sea, making possible cheap transportation to other parts of the world. Together with iron and steel, coal and textiles accounted for the greater

Value of Exports (*US$ millions, 1913 prices*)

	1899		1913	
	Manufactures	All exports	Manufactures	All exports
Britain	479	912	624	969
Germany	437	691	925	1285
United States	272	1366	535	1850

part of Britain's exports. After 1900 British exporters found increasing difficulty in competing with Germany and the United States in the developing industrial countries. At home, foreign manufacturers invaded the British market. The speed of the American and German growth of production is very striking. This success was partly due to the increasing disparity between Britain's, Germany's and America's populations.

Population (*millions*)

	1880	1900	1910	1920	1930
Britain*	35.6	44.3	45	46.9	45.8
Germany	45.2	56.4	64.9	59.2	64.3
United States	50.2	89.4	92.0	118.1	138.4

* Including Ireland and Northern Ireland respectively.

The story these statistics told was one people felt in their bones. Of course it would be mistaken to believe that Britain and her industry was set on an inevitable course of rapid decline. There were successful 'new' industries of the 'second' industrial revolution, such as the chemical and electrical industry. Britain was still in 1914 immensely strong and wealthy because of the continuing expansion of her traditional textile industry and large coal reserves, the world dominance of her mercantile marine, her investment income from overseas and the reputation of the insurance and banking institutions which made the City of London the financial centre of the world. But there was already in 1900 a doubt as to whether Britain would move sufficiently fast in changing conditions to maintain her leading industrial place in the world.

Then industrialists felt doubts about the continuing co-operation of labour. The trade union movement had revealed a new militancy which posed a threat to industrial peace. The movement was no longer dominated by the skilled artisans sharing the values of the Victorian middle class. The new unions of the poor working men formed in the last two decades of the nineteenth century looked to the state for decisive support, for a redistribution of wealth.

The Labour political movement also emerged during the last decade of the nineteenth century, though the ultimate break between 'Liberal' and 'Labour' politics did not take place until after the First World War. In 1900 the trade union movement became convinced that involvement in parliamentary politics was now necessary if the working man was to improve his standard of life. The Labour Representation Committee, embracing a broad alliance of socialist parties and trade unions, was formed in 1900. In the election later that year two Labour candidates succeeded in winning seats in the House of Commons. The founders of the Labour movement were practical men who realised that in the foreseeable future Labour members would be in a minority. They resolved accordingly that they would co-operate with any party ready to help labour. In Britain, the Labour Party was prepared to work within the parliamentary system, and turned its back on revolution and violence. In turn it became accepted, and enjoyed the same freedom as other political parties.

The Conservatives, who were in power until the close of 1905, followed cautious social–political policies. A state system of primary and secondary schools was introduced, partly because of the belief that it was their better educational provisions that were enabling America and Germany to overtake Britain in industrial efficiency. When the Liberals came to power in 1906 their attitude to social and economic reforms was equally half-hearted, much of the party still believing in self-help and a minimum of state paternalism. The surprise of the new Parliament of 1906 was the election of fifty-three Labour members, though that number owed much to an electoral arrangement with the Liberals. Among this Labour group were a few genuine socialists, such as Keir Hardie and Ramsay MacDonald, who had nothing in common with the Liberals; but other Labour members were less interested in socialism than in securing legislation to benefit the working men – for example the Trade Disputes Bill which protected union funds from employers' claims for compensation after strikes.

In 1908 Herbert Asquith succeeded to the premiership. In the same year, one of the few major reforms was introduced – old-age pensions, which removed fear of the workhouse from the aged. The famous budget of 1909, however, sparked off a political crisis. Introduced by the Liberal chancellor of the Exchequer, David Lloyd George, it increased indirect taxes on spirits and tobacco – which was unpopular with the poor – but also modestly increased the burdens on the better-off. The House of Lords – quite unjustly – sensed in these measures the thin edge of the wedge that would destroy their privileges. The Liberals pressed the issue of constitutional reform as a means of reviving the party's popularity in the country. The power of the Conservative-dominated House of Lords to veto bills passed by the Liberal majority in the Commons was to be curtailed so that within the life of one Parliament the House of Commons majority would prevail.

An impasse was reached in Britain's political life, not dissimilar from that in imperial Germany at about the same time. Should the conservative hereditary lords have the power to block even the mild reforming legislation of an elected Liberal majority? Unlike in Germany, the constitutional turmoil was resolved. In November 1909 the House of Lords threw out the budget with the intention of submitting the issue to the electorate. This readiness by government and Parliament to accept the wishes of the people on the one hand and the constitutional monarch's acceptance of the same verdict (though George V did insist unnecessarily on *two* elections) on the other was the essential difference between imperial Germany and Britain. The Liberal tactic of taking the constitutional issue to the country misfired. They lost their overall majority and now ran neck and neck with the Conservatives. By the close of the second election in December 1910, each party had precisely the same strength in the House of Commons. But the Liberals, supported by Labour members and the Irish Nationalists, commanded a substantial majority over the Conservatives. The House of Lords in the summer of 1911 gave their assent to the bill limiting their powers. No social upheaval threatening the influence of wealth and property followed. But common sense, and a respect for the wishes of the majority of the House of Commons on which parliamentary constitutional government was based, prevailed. Britain would continue to follow the political and social path of evolution, not revolution.

A suffragette demonstration in Britain, May 1913. As is evident here, the movement often brought sexes and social classes together in common cause.

A National Insurance Bill of 1911 covered most workers against ill health, but only those in the cyclical building and engineering trades against unemployment. What Liberal policies did not do was to satisfy the working man who resented paying (with employers) compulsorily for national insurance and whose real wage in the recent years had not risen. The years 1911 and 1912 witnessed an unprecedented number of strikes and an increase in the power of the trade unions. The Liberal Party did not win the support of organised industrial labour. Nor did it seize the chance to earn the gratitude of potential women voters by granting their enfranchisement. The Liberals, for all Lloyd George's dash and clamour as chancellor of the Exchequer, were simply not ready to embark on bold social policies.

Many prominent British politicians believed that the future safety and prosperity of Britain depended on revitalising and drawing together the strength of the empire. Only in this way, they thought, could Britain hope to face the other great powers on an equal footing. But the questions were also asked: Will the empire last? Does it rest on permanent foundations or is it only a political organism in a certain state of decomposition? Will the younger nations, as they grow to maturity, be content to remain within it, or will they go the way of the American Colonies before them . . . ?

The 400 million peoples of the British Empire had reached different stages of advancement to independence by the close of the nineteenth century. The division of the empire was largely on racial lines. The white people of the empire, where they predominated or even formed a significant minority of the country, were granted 'self-government', only a step short of total independence. In practice, 'self-government' was brought about by applying the pattern of British parliamentary government to these countries; this, together with a federal structure, created the Dominions: Canada in 1867, New Zealand in 1876, the Commonwealth of Australia in 1901 and, in 1909, seven years after the conclusion of the bitter Boer War, the Union of South Africa. The responsibility to protect the 'native' inhabitants of lands conquered and colonised by Europeans was recognised by Britain. But little that was effective was done by the imperial government in London. Indians in Canada, Maoris in New Zealand and Aborigines in Australia were largely left to struggle alone for their rights. In southern Africa, the black Africans formed the majority of the inhabitants but democratic rights were denied them and they were left to the control of the white peoples. British governments in London were not prepared to jeopardise their relations with the white ruling inhabitants. Racial discrimination was a grievous flaw in the British Empire, though a paternalistic concern for the 'natives' was perfectly genuine. Those parts of the empire not granted self-government were controlled and ruled in a bewildering variety of ways, more the result of accident than design, as Crown Colonies (in the Caribbean and West Africa, for instance) or indirectly through local rulers – as, originally, in the Indian States, and later in the Malay States and the protectorates of tropical Africa. Of these 'realms in trust' the most populous and extensive was India. Ruled by British viceroys under the Crown as a separate empire, some 300 million Indians were Britain's responsibility from 1858 until 1947.

In 1900, a British Empire which did not include India would have seemed as unlikely as London without the Tower. But already the voice of India had been heard calling for autonomy and independence. In 1885 the first Indian National Congress had met. Those who gathered represented the Western viewpoint and admired the British. But rule by the British was seen as alien rule, and independence through the stage of Dominion status as an achievable goal for the future. The British brought unity, external and internal peace to India, and with the active co-operation of those Indians who had traditionally ruled the various states, established an incomparable administration all over the subcontinent. It was made possible by the marriage of Anglo-Indian traditions. But India was exploited too. Little was done for the masses of the poor. Economically, India was a dependency of Britain. The splendour of the British Raj never stilled British doubts about their role, so strongly reinforced by the Indian mutiny of 1857; the British were conscious that they, a mere handful of aliens, were ruling over millions of people. Would the people always so consent? In 1905 a senior member of the British ruling caste of India summed up the general view held by those responsible for British policy in India: British rule, he wrote, rested on 'its character for justice, toleration and careful consideration of native feeling', but it was also based on bayonets, on the maintenance of an 'adequate' force of British soldiers in India and the absolute command of the sea. If Britain weakened, her domination of India would come to an end through an uprising, perhaps helped along by a hostile foreign power, in all probability Russia. That was regarded as the ultimate disaster.

The dynamic Colonial Secretary, Joseph Chamberlain, was the principal advocate of an imperial movement for greater unity. In his great 'tariff reform' campaign from 1903 to 1905 he sought to win British support for a protected and preferential empire market which he believed would cement imperial relationships; but, as it would also have entailed higher food prices for the British people, he failed to carry the whole country. In a different way, the attempt to create a more unified system of imperial defence also failed; the self-governing Dominions were not willing to give up their independence. The cause of imperial unity was destined to fail. But in the era from 1900 to 1945, the British Empire remained very much a reality, as the prodigious effort in two great wars was to show. Co-operation between the Dominions and the mother country, however, was voluntary, based on a variety of changing institutions devised to meet no more than immediate needs.

The most striking aspect of Britain's world position in 1900 was the contrast between the appearance of her world power and its reality. Anyone looking at a map of the world with the British Empire painted red might well think that Britain dominated the world. This was certainly not the case.

The security of the British Isles and the empire came to depend on three circumstances: in North America on peaceful good relations; in eastern Asia on the assistance of an ally; in Europe on a continued 'balance of power' between the great continental nations.

Even with the largest navy, Britain could not continue relying entirely on her own strength and on temporary allies whose own interests happened to coincide with Britain's at any particular moment of crisis. There was a widespread feeling that Britain was over-committed and that some change of course in her foreign relations would be essential. There were those who favoured an alliance with Germany. But the Germans proved coy. They saw no advantage in helping Britain against Russia, except perhaps if Britain were to pay the price of sharing her empire with Germany. An alliance was never really on the cards and discussions about such a possibility ceased in 1902.

Others thought the sensible course for Britain would be to reduce the number of potential opponents all over the world. A successful start was made by removing all possibility of conflict with the United States. On the British side, the readiness to defend British interests in the Americas by force, against the United States if necessary, was abandoned in the new century. The British government signified its willingness to trust the United States by allowing the Americans control of the future Panama Canal, by withdrawing the British fleet from the Caribbean, and by leaving the Dominion of Canada, in practice, undefended. On the United States' side the idea that the absorption of Canada was part of the United States' manifest destiny faded. Plans for war were for some time still drawn up by the military on both sides of the Atlantic; but the political realities were quite different. In the twentieth century it really became unthinkable that Britain and the United States would ever go to war against each other again.

Britain liquidated with equal success the long-drawn-out imperial rivalry with France in many parts of the world. As late as 1898 it had seemed possible that Britain and France would be at war again, as they had been in the early nineteenth century. There was very little love for Britain in France, where Britain was most bitterly condemned during the South African War. But the French government made its prime objective the control of Morocco. Eventually, in April 1904, Delcassé, the French Foreign Minister, was ready to secure British support by settling amicably all outstanding imperial differences with Britain. German threats against France, in 1905 and later, turned this settlement into one involving British promises of support against Germany, though never an alliance in peacetime; the increasingly intimate relations between France and Britain became known as the *entente cordiale*.

Britain's attempt to reach a settlement with her most formidable opponent in the world arena, Russia, was far less successful. Russia's occupation of Manchuria in China, which began in 1900, alarmed the British government. The China market was seen as vital to Britain's future prosperity. Unable to check Russia, or to trust her, Britain concluded an alliance with Japan in 1902.

This alliance marks a significant stage in the history of Western imperialism. In the division of empire the European powers had been locked in rivalry and confrontation one against the other, though this rivalry had not led to war between them since the mid-nineteenth century. It was the Africans and Chinese, the peoples whose lands were parcelled up, who had suffered the ravages of war. The Europeans, though fiercely competitive among themselves, acted in this their last phase of expanding imperialism on the common assumption that it was their destiny to impose European dominion on other peoples. Now, for the first time in the new century, a European power had allied with an Asiatic power, Japan, against another European power, Russia.

In the Middle East Britain was determined to defend against Russia those territorial interests which in 1900, before the age of oil had properly begun, were largely strategic: the road to India which ran through the Ottoman Empire, Persia and landlocked mountainous Afghanistan. India was the greatest possession and jewel of the British Empire and tsarist Russia was credited by the British with the ultimate desire of ousting Britain from India and of seeking to replace Britain as the paramount power of southern Asia. The defence of India and Britain's own supremacy in southern Asia had been the foremost objective of British policy in the nineteenth century and remained so in the new century.

But it became increasingly difficult to defend the 'buffer states' which kept Russia away from the classic land-invasion route to India. The Ottoman Empire, once dominated by British influence, had turned away from Britain. No British government could easily have come to the defence of an empire which under the Sultan Abdul Hamid, 'the Damned', had murdered defenceless Christian Armenians in Asia Minor. In Persia, Russia's influence was steadily advancing.

In 1904 occurred a dramatic change. Russia became embroiled in war with Japan over China (page 58). Her military weakness became apparent to the world. Tsarist Russia desperately needed years of peace after 1905 to recover. The British Foreign Secretary, Sir Edward Grey, therefore found the Russians more ready in 1907 to reach an agreement with Britain to partition their imperial spheres of interests in the Middle East. But Grey believed this agreement only provided a temporary respite.

British security in Europe had been based on an effective balance of power on the continent. It had been a part of Britain's traditional policy to seek to prevent any one power gaining the mastery of continental Europe. After the defeat of Napoleon there seemed to be no serious possibility that any single nation either harboured such ambitions or could carry them through. But around 1905 doubts began to arise as to whether this fundamental condition of safety might not be passing. Germany's ambitious plans of naval expansion were being seriously noted. Germany's aggressive reaction in 1905 to the Anglo-French deal over Morocco aroused graver fears that Germany might be contemplating another war against France. Britain gave unhesitating support to France. From 1905 to 1914 the golden thread of British policy was to endeavour to preserve the peace, but in any case to avoid the possibility of a German hegemony of the continent which would result from a German victory over much weaker France.

Accordingly, on the one hand British policy towards Germany was pacific and the prospect of helping her achieve some of her imperial ambitions was held out to her as long as she kept the peace. But she was warned that, should she choose to attack France in a bid for continental hegemony, she could not count on the British standing aside even if Britain were not directly attacked. The Liberal Cabinet from 1906 to 1914 was not united, however, though Grey's policy of growing intimacy with France in the end prevailed. Several Liberal ministers were more anti-Russian than anti-German; strongly pacific, they saw no cause for war with Germany or anyone. Grey went his own way of constructing a barrier against the threat of Germany, supported by the two prime ministers of the period, Campbell-Bannerman and Asquith, and a small group of ministers. In secret discussions between the French and British military staffs, military plans were drawn up after the second Moroccan crisis of 1911 to land a British army of 150,000 men in France if Germany invaded France. At the same time Grey continued to emphasise that the French should place no reliance on Britain as there could be no formal alliance between the two countries. It was a curious policy dictated partly by differences among his ministerial colleagues and partly by Grey's own desire to play a mediating role in present and future conflicts. This compromise between 'alliance' and the 'free hand' in fact worked quite well down to the outbreak of war in 1914. Grey made a notable contribution to calming Europe during the Bosnian crisis of 1909 (page 65) and in collaborating with Germany during the Balkan wars in 1912 and 1913 in order to help preserve European peace.

Alarm at Germany's intentions nevertheless grew in Britain from 1910 onwards. In the public mind this had much to do with the expansion of the German navy. Efforts to moderate the pace – the War Secretary, Richard Haldane, visited Berlin for this purpose early in 1912 and Winston Churchill, First Lord of the Admiralty, called for a 'naval holiday' in 1913 – all came to nothing. The German ministers in return had demanded that Britain should tie her hands in advance and promise to remain neutral if Germany went to war with France. The Germans continued to be warned that Britain, in her own interests, would stand by France if France found herself attacked by the numerically superior German military machine. This threat, rather than Germany's naval challenge, motivated British policy. As Grey put it in 1912, Britain was in no danger of being involved in a war 'unless there is some Power, or group of Powers in Europe which has the ambition of achieving . . . the Napoleonic policy'.

The British government knew that it possessed the resources to keep pace with any increase in Germany's naval construction. By 1914 Britain had twenty new super-battleships of the Dreadnought class, against Germany's thirteen; in older battleships Britain's superiority was even greater – twenty-six to Germany's twelve. By making arrangements with France to concentrate this fleet in home waters, leaving the Mediterranean to be defended by the French fleet, British naval superiority over Germany was assured and, also significantly, her ties with France were strengthened.

Still trying at the same time to assure Germany of Britain's general goodwill, Grey concluded two agreements with her in 1913 and 1914. The first, a rather dubious one, divided up two Portuguese colonies in Africa, Mozambique and Angola, allowing Germany a good share should Portugal choose to dispose of these possessions. The other agreement helped Germany to realise plans for the final sections of the Berlin–Baghdad railway project and so facilitated German commercial penetration of Asia Minor and Mesopotamia. It was concluded on the very eve of the outbreak of war in Europe.

Grey endeavoured to steer a difficult middle path. He had met the Russian threat by the agreements of 1907, just as his predecessor in the Foreign Office, Lord Lansdowne, had removed the imperial rivalry with France in 1904 by a general settlement. But the British never thought that agreements with Russia, unlike the French settlement, would allow more than breathing space from her inexorable pressure. Yet in every one of these agreements made to protect Britain's empire there was a price which the British Cabinet would have preferred not to pay. To protect her enormous stake in China, Britain had concluded the alliance with Japan in 1902 sanctioning Japanese aggression in Korea and making war in eastern Asia with Russia more likely. After Japan's victory in 1904–5, Japan was set on the road to dominate China. Then there was the agreement with France over Morocco and Egypt in 1904, which was bound to offend Germany. Britain would have preferred to appease Germany by allowing her a share of Morocco. The French would not allow that. So Britain once more gained her imperial objective – predominance in Egypt – at the cost of increasing tensions in Europe. The most striking example of Britain protecting her empire at the cost of international tension was the settlement reached with Russia. With the conclusion of this agreement with Russia in 1907 over spheres of influence in the Middle East, Sir Edward Grey, the British Foreign Secretary, well understood that the Germans would increasingly feel 'encircled'.

The question that has to be asked is why, if Russia continued to be considered even after 1907 to present the main threat to the heart of the British Empire in Asia, did Britain go to war with Germany in 1914? There were no direct Anglo-German territorial disputes or differences over spheres of influence that were not capable of settlement. It is not easy to answer that question but there are clues in what Grey wrote and said. Agreement with Russia rather than enmity bought time. Then looking to the future, how could Britain best maintain her position as a great power in Europe? She certainly wanted the peace of Europe to be maintained. But Grey feared that Britain might be faced with too powerful a combination of countries in Europe in coalition against her. However, he also repeatedly warned against Britain becoming dependent on Germany.

Britain's distrust of Germany was certainly growing in the Edwardian period. The Kaiser was regarded as over-emotional and unstable. German manufacturers were competing with the British in the world. Of course Germany was an excellent market for British goods, something that was taken for granted. Above all, the German naval build-up touched the public to the quick. As Sir Eyre Crowe, a senior member of the Foreign Office, put it in 1907, a hostile Germany was disregarding the 'elementary rules of straightforward and honourable dealing' and Britain would have to defend her position in the world, her naval supremacy and the European balance of power. Still, there were others who deplored the Germanophobia, among them the bankers, industrialists, politicians and many ordinary people who preferred the 'clean' Germans to their Latin neighbours with their supposedly more dubious morals and awful lavatories. Tsarist autocratic Russia, with her record of abusing human rights, was regarded as the one European country which not only threatened Britain in Asia but least shared British democratic ideals and respect for human rights.

Grey did not share the Germanophobia, but he believed it essential to preserve and strengthen the entente with France as the primary objective of British policy in Europe. He hoped to gain some influence over French policy in return for supporting France against unreasonable German behaviour. He could not hope to exercise such influence over German policy. As it turned out he could exercise little influence over the French either. But it was the bedrock of Grey's policy that friendly relations with Germany should never be established at the expense of France. In the end it meant that Britain was more influenced by French objectives than the other way around. To please the French and Russians in 1914, Grey for instance consented to Anglo-Russian naval conversations which unnecessarily but dramatically increased German fears of encirclement. On the eve of 1914 the well-informed Grey perceptively assessed German apprehensions:

> The truth is that whereas formerly the German Government had aggressive intentions . . . they are now genuinely alarmed at the military preparation in Russia, the prospective increase in her military forces and particularly at the intended construction at the instance of the French Government and with French money of strategic railways to converge on the German Frontier.

Yet for all these insights, when the crisis came in July 1914. Grey's mediating efforts, limited as they were by previous constraints, proved unavailing.

On the eve of the Great War, the most serious problem facing the British government seemed to be not abroad but at home: the question of maintaining the unity of the United Kingdom. Ireland was Britain's heel of Achilles. British governments had been too slow in attempting to satisfy Irish national feeling by devolution or limited 'home rule'. Ireland's problems had been allowed to languish until after the elections of December 1910. Now the decline of the Liberals' fortunes forced Asquith into more active collaboration with the Irish Nationalist Party in the House of Commons. Not for the first time the Irish held the parliamentary balance of power. The Liberals with the support of the Irish Nationalists had staked their future on reforming the House of Lords. Asquith in return was committed to home rule for Ireland. In April 1912 he introduced the Home Rule Bill in the Commons. Ulster Protestant militants, strong in the north of Ireland, were determined to kill the bill or at least to demand partition. Sinn Fein, the Irish republican movement, was equally determined to preserve a united Ireland. Both sides raised private armies which on the eve of the Great War in 1914 threatened to plunge a part of the United Kingdom into civil war. The outbreak of the war gave Asquith the opportunity of postponing the Irish confrontation. What with suffragettes resorting to spectacular demonstrations to gain the vote for women, industrial unrest, Ireland seemingly on the brink of civil war, Britain presented a picture of disarray. It was deceptive. A united Britain and Empire entered the Great War of 1914.

CHAPTER 6

The Emergence of the United States as a World Power

The emergence of the United States as a superpower by the mid-twentieth century is one of the most striking changes of modern history. The state of the American economy and America's decision as to where and in what manner to intervene in any part of the globe have profoundly affected every continent. The United States came to wield an influence such as no other single nation has exercised before. What is striking is that this impact on the world has been so recent, scarcely predating the turn of the century. How did it come about and where are the roots of American world power?

The growth of the population, and of the industrial and agricultural production of the United States, were phenomenal. Their sustained increase through the nineteenth and twentieth centuries, overcoming two depressions in the mid-1870s and the mid-1890s as well as the serious depression of the 1930s, is one of the 'economic wonders' of modern history. There was a contemporary awareness of America's good fortune, and 'growth' was both expected and regarded as the unique 'American way'. When we compare the population growth of the United States with that of the European great powers, we see clearly how relatively sudden the transformation of the United States into the present-day colossus has been. In 1880 the total population of the United States was about the same as Germany's ten years later and only 5 million more than Germany's at the same time. Thus in population the United States only just ranked in the same league as the largest of the European nations. But, from then on, the United States' rapid outdistancing of previously comparable countries was one fundamental reason for the emergence of the United States as a superpower.

Population (*millions*)

	1880	1900	1920	1930
United States	50.2	76.0	105.7	122.8
Germany	45.2	56.4	59.2	64.3

A crucial factor in this growth of population was another feature of the New World, the large-scale emigration from Europe. Driven largely by poverty and the hope of a better life a great mass of humanity flooded into the United States, more than 13 million between 1900 and 1914 alone. Most of them were peasants from central and southern Europe. The majority of these 'new immigrants' (to distinguish them from the 'old' immigrants from Britain, Ireland, Germany and Scandinavia) settled in the towns where they preferred to join their countrymen who had kept close together in the cities and found unskilled industrial work. Immigrants contributed significantly to the growth of major cities, reinforced economic expansion and helped to bring about the mass market which is characteristic of twentieth-century America. Of the 13 million, more than a million were Jews leaving the pogrom-ridden

Coming to America. Ellis Island was the gateway to the New World for immigrants from Europe. Between 1881 and 1910, 17,729,545 settlers were admitted to the United States and of these more than 90 per cent came from Europe. The picture (left) *shows a dining room, c.1900, for those who were detained for further questioning. Others were cleared to pass on swiftly* (top)*; they settled in tenement flats and lived in cramped conditions* (right)*, almost invariably with fellow-immigrants from their 'homeland'.*

Russian Empire; they helped to make New York into one of the great clothing manufacturing centres of America.

The rich cultural variety of the United States, the diversity of ethnic groups from west and east, as well as the sheer numbers of immigrants, are among the unique features of America's national growth. America, as one historian put it, was less a 'melting pot' – intermarriage and common allegiances did not speedily obliterate national differences of origin – than a 'salad bowl'. All the same, the fusion of peoples of every national origin and religion and, over a much longer period, the fusion of the races black and white, into a national community has proved a more powerful force than national and racial differences and conflict.

In the twentieth century the shared experiences of two world wars were powerful influences in making for more toleration and mutual acceptance – one of the most significant aspects of the development of the United States for world history.

The immigrants added immensely to the vitality of the United States. Starting from nothing, they and their descendants acquired new skills and an education. The United States was the country where the accident of a father's social status mattered least in the Western world. As far as the blacks were concerned, this generalisation did not hold true. As long ago as 1868 some of the framers of the fourteenth amendment of the constitution sought to protect the rights of blacks. The amendment declared that Americans enjoyed equal rights and equality before the law and specifically laid down that no state could 'deprive any person of life, liberty, or property, without due process of law'. However, as a protection of the civil rights of the blacks the fourteenth amendment proved worthless because it was not enforced. It was used instead by the rising industrialists and financiers to amass greater fortunes and influence through combinations and mergers.

The age distribution of the immigrants and their tendency to have larger families than the American-born kept the increase of population at a much higher level than could otherwise be sustained. America was in reality, and in self-image, a young country constantly renewing herself. At the turn of the century, the United States had just recovered from the depression of the mid-1890s, and Americans faced the twentieth century with much optimism believing, rightly as it turned out, that their country was on the threshold of industrial expansion and the accumulation of wealth. Between 1900 and 1914 manufacturing production nearly doubled and overtook agriculture as the main source of national wealth. The traditional America was a nation of farmers, artisans and small businessmen. The America of the twentieth century was predominantly industrial, with the growth of cities, and railways linking the industrial midwest and the east. Industry was increasingly dominated by the giant corporations such as John D. Rockefeller's Standard Oil Company or the Trusts of J. Pierpont Morgan, though small businesses also persisted. The absolute growth of population, the opening up of virgin lands in the west, made possible simultaneously a great expansion of agricultural output despite the population movement to the towns. This increasing output was more than enough to feed the growing American population and leave sufficient to export. Meat packing and food canning became important industries. The vast continent of the United States was singularly blessed in all its resources – fertile land, forests, coal, iron and oil. Their simultaneous successful development provided the dynamic of American economic growth which no European nation could match, and meant that Americans were less dependent on imports or exports than any other advanced Western nation.

An assembly line in a Ford car factory, 1913. Henry Ford (1863–1947) is said to have died with a stop-watch in his hand.

In the early twentieth century, American business nevertheless expanded American exports to industrialised Europe, seeing this as a necessary insurance against a glut in the market at home – yet these exports were only a small proportion of America's total production, which was protected at home by a high tariff. In the early twentieth century the application of electricity as a new energy source provided a further boost, and electrical machinery together with automobiles – Henry Ford alone producing 125,000 cars a year by 1913, half the nation's total output – were the 'new industries' maintaining America's lead as the world's first industrial power.

America's explosive growth was not achieved without severe political and social tensions. This was the other side of the optimism expressed at the turn of the century about the future. People began to ask who would control the destinies of the United States. Would it be the new breed of immensely successful and wealthy financiers and businessmen? Was not their influence already the main reason for the corruption of government, no longer a government for and by the people but for the good of business? The cleavage between the rich and poor appeared to widen as the Vanderbilts, Morgans, Rockefellers and Harrimans displayed their wealth.

The western farmers were exposed to the vagaries of the seasons and also to the increases and falls of world grain prices. A good harvest could drive the prices farther down and the farmers seeking a cause for their misfortunes focused on the high interest they had to pay on the loans they needed – the result, as they saw it, of government dominated by the industrial east. The southern United States remained relatively stagnant, unable to diversify when, after the worldwide drop in cotton prices, cotton could no longer yield the same profit as before the Civil War.

The American workers in the mines and factories also tried to organise to meet the increased power of business. Socialism as a political force had developed in the United States as well as in Europe during the nineteenth century, and for a short while after 1872 the headquarters of Marx's First International was in New York. But the Socialist Labor Party of North America could not establish itself as a serious force in politics. In the early twentieth century, under the charismatic leadership of Eugene V. Debs, the Social Democratic Party attempted to win over the worker from trade union economic bargaining to politics, but was unsuccessful on a national scale, though Debs, when he became a presidential candidate, secured almost 900,000 votes. When labour unions expanded it was under the direction of men like Samuel Gompers who rejected political socialism as utopian and saw themselves as practical men seeking to improve the wages and conditions of labour day by day without ulterior ends in view. In 1886 they organised the American Federation of Labor but in the 1890s found that union militancy could not prevail against the employers supported by the federal government. There were some successes to set against the failures, with the gradual introduction of maximum working hours and the ending of the abuse of child labour. Theodore Roosevelt, when president, showed more sympathy for the workers. Strikes of national concern, like the coal strike in Pennsylvania in 1902, were no longer settled by the federal government siding with the employers. President Roosevelt intervened and refused to back the mine owners, who had to concede higher wages. Roosevelt's action was characteristic of one aspect of a new spirit collectively known as the Progressive Movement.

But Roosevelt's outlook was not shared by all the states, which had retained extensive rights under the constitution. In 1903 and 1904 the Governor of the state of Colorado, for instance, had mobilised the militia, jailed the union leaders of the striking copper miners and beaten down the strikes with violence and bloodshed; and in all this he was eventually supported by the Supreme Court. Gompers himself was imprisoned by federal courts after another strike and denounced as a dangerous rabble-rouser subverting the law. Against this onslaught of employers, and with business dominating the courts and the state governments, Roosevelt could do little. Though the American Federation of Labor expanded from half a million to 2 million members by 1914, it could scarcely hold its own. Only the boom brought about by the Great War and the shortage of labour enabled the more moderate unions to gain acceptance and to negotiate better terms for workers. But the mass of the unskilled and the blacks remained largely outside the unions. The AFL's successes were mainly won on behalf of the skilled craft unions and the semi-skilled.

After the depressed 1880s and mid-1890s the farmers, who had been a major force behind the rising challenge to eastern business dominance, became quiescent. From 1897 until 1914 they enjoyed a short 'golden age' of prosperity, the *value* of their crops doubling during this period.

Looking at the United States as a whole, the only safe generalisation is that the problems which forced themselves on the attention of people varied enormously from one region to another, as did the responses of those in power in any particular state. Thus, in contrast to the conduct of Colorado's government, the Governor of Wisconsin, Robert M. La Follette, passed many practical reforms in his state, as did Woodrow Wilson after becoming governor of New Jersey in 1911.

'Progressive' became a loose label denoting little more than a recognition of the many varied ills besetting American society and politics during years of rapid change and a desire to remedy whichever of these ills a particular progressive felt to be the most injurious. The ills were well publicised by a new breed of journalists who proudly accepted what was meant to be an insulting description of their work – 'The Muckrakers'. Their targets were manifold – political corruption, the inequality of wealth, the domination of politics by big business; they investigated most aspects of American life; they attacked the doctrine of freedom which allowed the grasping entrepreneur to develop America at too great a price; they stressed the undermining of democracy; and argued the need for more regulatory government, not less.

In domestic politics the president's powers are limited by the rights of the two Houses of Congress, the Senate and the House of Representatives, and by the Supreme Court, the final arbiter of any dispute about constitutional rights. What President Theodore Roosevelt and his successors – the more conservative William Howard Taft, and then the Democrat Woodrow Wilson – actually achieved in legislation was less important than the fact that the presidency gave a reforming lead and so helped to change the climate of American public opinion. The Progressives were successful in the passage of child-labour laws in over forty states, and of laws governing the working conditions of women, but their attempts to clean up politics and smash the power of party machines failed. Lack of supervision to ensure enforcement also weakened much of the social legislation passed. After the Great War was over, in 1919, one reform dear to many Progressives, Prohibition (of alcoholic drinks), was enacted by Congress nationwide. Here too a large gap soon became apparent between law and actual observance.

Theodore Roosevelt was the first president of the United States to play a role as world statesman. As in his domestic policy, where he was inhibited by political constraints, so in his 'world' diplomacy he was circumscribed by America's lack of military power and the unwillingness of American people to make sacrifices to back up a 'large' American foreign policy. Superficially Roosevelt succeeded in drawing international attention to the United States and to his own role as diplomatist. In this respect his greatest achievement was to act in 1905 as mediator between the Japanese and Russians and to host the peace conference at Portsmouth, New Hampshire, ending the Russo-Japanese War. The United States next played a part in the international Moroccan conference at Algeciras in 1906. The following year, in a characteristically ostentatious gesture, Roosevelt sent the newly constructed United States Navy on a world cruise to show the flag. Roosevelt made America's presence felt. But what really lay behind these great-power posturings was apprehension that the conditions which had given the United States security for the past century were passing away.

For this feeling, which actually anticipated dangers that still lay in the future, there were two principal reasons: the likely direction of European imperialism and the consequences of America's own flirtation with imperialism at the turn of the century. Both can be seen clearly at work during the course of a war just won, the 'splendid little' Spanish–American war of 1898.

The American response to European imperialism, which had led to the partition of Africa and China, was to try to anticipate a serious challenge to the Monroe Doctrine, with its Declaration of US opposition to any further European colonial extension within the Western hemisphere. What if the Europeans next sought to extend their influence in the Caribbean and Central America and so surrounded the United States with armed bases? Captain A. T. Mahan, in his day the most influential writer and proponent of the importance of sea power, was writing at this time that such a danger did exist since crucial strategic regions of significance in world trade would inevitably become areas of great-power rivalry. One such artery of trade would be the canal (later Panama Canal) which it was

A prescient view of American imperialism from the satirical German magazine Kladderadatch, *1894.*

planned to construct across the isthmus of Central America. The backward and weak independent Caribbean island states were also easy prey for any intending European imperialist. The island of Cuba, lying close to the mainland of Florida was, then as now, a particularly sensitive spot. Before the war with Spain, Cuba was a Spanish colony, in chronic rebellion and anarchy. The war on the island was barbarous as most guerrilla wars are apt to be, and American opinion, genuinely humanitarian, was inflamed by the popular 'yellow' press. But the hidden aspect of the situation as seen by the administration was that a weak Spain as the sovereign power on the island might be replaced by an aggressive Britain or Germany.

A group of Americans, including a number of senior naval officers, Theodore Roosevelt (then an up-and-coming politician) and Senator Henry Cabot Lodge, discussed ways and means of taking precautionary action before these dangers materialised. They were later seen as 'imperialists' or 'expansionists' and indeed this was the practical outcome of their ideas, but their motivation was essentially defensive – to preserve American security in the coming conditions of the twentieth century.

Imperialism was inextricably bound up with this defensive attitude. The Americans intervened and made themselves the gendarmes of the Caribbean. After the war with Spain in 1898, Cuba, though proclaimed an independent republic, became a virtual protectorate of the United States. A US naval base was constructed on the island and the land needed for it was ceded to the United States. This American presence was intended to ensure that no European power could take over Cuba or reach the inner naval defences of the United States before meeting the US Navy in the western Atlantic. The United States also imposed conditions on Cuba which allowed the United States to intervene in case of internal discord. Another Caribbean island, Puerto Rico, was simply annexed for similar strategic reasons. In 1904 Theodore Roosevelt extended the right of the United States to act as a policeman throughout Central and Latin America, invoking the Monroe Doctrine as justification. By helping the Panamanian revolutionaries against Colombia in 1903, Roosevelt established another American protectorate in all but name in the new state of Panama. Nor did the United States hesitate to intervene in the independent republics of Dominica and Nicaragua. Although Woodrow Wilson, when he became president, attempted to revert to the earlier spirit of inter-American collaboration, he did not himself hesitate to intervene in Mexico from 1914 to 1916.

In contrast to the advanced industrialised and agriculturally developed North American continent, the habitable regions of South America supported a growing population in, for the most part, abject poverty. (For a fuller discussion of Latin America see Part XIV.) The descendants of the Spaniards and Portuguese and the immigrants from Europe who formed the minority of inhabitants enjoyed the wealth and political power of the American 'republics'. There was much variety in the politics and society of Latin America. Their revolutions, though, had been revolutions from above in the early nineteenth century. The new states remained authoritarian, despite their elaborate constitutions modelled on the French or American, and their professed ideals of democracy, with a few notable exceptions, proved a façade for governments based on force: they were governments of the generals or of dictators who commanded the military forces of the state. Violence was the language of politics. Trade with Europe, especially (in the later nineteenth century) with Britain and Germany, was considerably greater than with the United States, to which there was much hostility, on account of her claims to pre-eminence in the Americas. The possibility of 'Yankee' interference was the object of particular Latin American suspicion and animosity.

In 1900 strategic planners in the United States clearly saw the discrepancy between the pretensions of the Monroe Doctrine and the inability of the United States to exert any military and naval influence south of the Amazon in Brazil. What if the partition of Africa were followed by European domination of South and Central America? In fact the

The Americas, 1990
GREENLAND
ALASKA
Anchorage
C A N A D A
HUDSON BAY
Edmonton
Regina
Vancouver
Ottawa
Quebec
Detroit
Toronto
Chicago
New York
Washington
A T L A N T I C
O C E A N
U N I T E D
S T A T E S
San Francisco
Los Angeles
Houston
BAHAMA ISLANDS
WEST INDIES
CUBA
HAITI
DOMINICAN REPUBLIC
PUERTO RICO
Monterrey
MEXICO
Mexico
BELIZE
JAMAICA
GUATEMALA
CARIBBEAN SEA
VENEZUELA
EL SALVADOR
GUYANA
HONDURAS
SURINAM
NICARAGUA
FRENCH GUIANA
COSTA RICA
Caracas
PANAMA
Bogota
Quito
EQUADOR
COLUMBIA
PERU
BRAZIL
Lima
Salvador
P A C I F I C
O C E A N
La Paz
Brasilia
BOLIVIA
PARAGUAY
Rio de Janeiro
Asunción
São Paulo
Santiago
Buenos Aires
URUGUAY
Montevideo
CHILE
ARGENTINA
0
1000
2000 miles

conflicts in Europe, the Mediterranean and Near East, in Africa and in Asia absorbed the military resources of the European Western powers. Britain, the major European power with colonies and commercial interests in Latin America and an empire extending from colonies in the Caribbean to the Dominion of Canada in the north, furthermore made clear her intention not to challenge the United States' claim for regional supremacy. At the turn of the century Britain and the United States signed the Hay–Pauncefote Treaty which granted the United States the sole right of defence of the future Panama Canal. This was followed by Britain withdrawing her fleet from the Caribbean and settling all outstanding disputes with the United States. Britain could not afford to risk the enmity of the United States as well when her interests were more endangered at home, first by Russia then by Germany, in the Mediterranean, in Asia and in Europe. And so a war between Britain and the United States became increasingly unthinkable as the twentieth century progressed. In this way the conflicts of the European powers in the early years of the twentieth century continued to serve the security of the United States in her hemisphere.

But in the Pacific and eastern Asia the United States became more deeply involved and exposed. US interests in the trade of China date back to the foundations of the American republic herself. Not until the close of the nineteenth century, however, did the United States acquire a territorial stake in the Pacific. The annexation of Hawaii in 1898 could still just about be fitted in with the notion that the island was an essential offshore base of defence for the western seaboard of the United States. There could be no such claim for the annexation of the Philippines after the Spanish–American War of 1898. An American army crushed the Filipino struggle for independence (1899–1902). This was imperialism. The United States staked her claim for a share of the China market whose potential was overestimated. The appearance of the United States in eastern Asia as a Western colonial power aroused the alarm of Japan and marks the origins of a new conflict in eastern Asia in the twentieth century. Theodore Roosevelt had recognised that the Philippines were indefensible; they were, to use his words, America's 'heel of Achilles'.

In the military sense, America's role as a world power was potential rather than actual during the first decade and a half of the twentieth century. The American army was small – adequate to deal with Indians and Mexicans; her warships in the 1880s had been called in Congress a collection of washtubs. How soon the United States could turn military potential into reality is illustrated by the amazingly rapid construction of the modern US Navy. In the 1890s American naval power was puny, just enough to cope with Spain's antiquated warships; by 1920, the United States Navy could match the British. But to exercise world power requires not only the means – and no one could doubt in the early twentieth century America's capacity – but also the will. Before 1914, it did not seem realistic to suppose that the United States would become involved in war over the conflicts of the other Western powers. The American people saw no need for war. The large navy, which could ensure the security of the North American continent and its approaches, and the small professional army indeed point to the overwhelmingly defensive attitude of the United States. How nevertheless she was to be involved in war in 1917 will be examined in a later chapter (pages 116–19). But it was only with great reluctance that Americans came to accept that the United States' circumstances had fundamentally changed from the times when George Washington could advise that the United States should not entangle her fortunes in the rivalries of Europe.

CHAPTER 7

The Russian Empire: Absolutism and Adaptation

As the world entered the twentieth century there was a large question mark over the largest Western state, the Russian Empire. The total size of Russia's population remained ahead of the United States'. But in industrial development Russia lagged behind the Western world. She was what would be termed today a vast underdeveloped country, stretching from the European frontiers with Germany and Austria–Hungary through the Middle East and Asia to the shores of the Pacific Ocean. The only nation larger than Russia was China, which in 1900 seemed on the verge of disintegration. Would Russia also disintegrate in the new century? Would revolution sweep away the Romanov dynasty, or would Russian autocracy prevail and continue to send the largest army in the world to conquer more and more territory and continue to incorporate more and more nationalities into the Russian Empire? Russia possessed all the resources of iron and coal to turn her into a major industrial power. How would her neighbours be able to resist Russian expansion as she modernised?

Population *(millions)*

	1880	1900	1910	1920	1940
Russia	97.1	132.1	155.7	145.3	195.0
United States	50.2	84.4	102.4	118.1	150.6

Her potential threat to the interests and security of all the countries surrounding her hung over them all, and increased in proportion to the actual growth of Russian power in the nineteenth and twentieth century.

By 1914 some hundred distinct national peoples had been incorporated into Russia. This made her the largest and most varied multinational empire. Government was highly centralised and absolute loyalty to the tsar was demanded of every national group. The predominant Russian people, the largest single population group by far, believed in the superiority of their culture, their Orthodox form of Christianity and the superiority of Slavs. The tsar sought to impose Russification on the other peoples and to suppress other religions. The Orthodox Church also formed a pillar of the tsar's autocracy and justified it as ordained by God. The most persistently persecuted minority were the Jews, who were deliberately made scapegoats for the ills besetting Russia. Anti-Semitism and discrimination, and even persecution of Jews, were endemic throughout Europe, but most virulent in Russia. Liberal and progressive European opinion was shocked and offended by the tsarist regime's treatment of the Jews.

It is difficult to look objectively at the history of Russia during the period of the last Tsar's rule, 1894 to 1917, knowing what followed. Was the development of Russia in the reign of Nicholas II a kind of blind alley bound to lead to collapse and revolution and the triumph of the Bolsheviks, or was she already on the road to reform and change before the outbreak of the First World War? An affirmative answer to the question of fundamental change can most confidently be given when industrialisation is considered. Rapid acceleration in the growth of the Russian economy began some forty years later than in the United States. Growth was uneven during the period 1890 to 1914, rapid in the 1890s when it more than doubled, was checked by a serious depression during the early years of the twentieth century, then from 1910 onwards resumed rapid expansion until the war. Not before 1928 would the Soviet Union again reach that level of production and so recover from war, revolution and civil war. Industrialisation was purposefully promoted by the state and masterminded in the 1890s by Sergei Witte, the Minister of Finance. He recognised that to maintain her status as a great power, Russia must break with past traditions and catch up with her rapidly industrialising European neighbours. A protective tariff (1891), a stable currency linked to gold, and high interest rates attracted massive foreign capital, especially from France, and encouraged capital formation in Russia. The expansion of railways had a widespread and stimulating effect on industrial growth. Besides the small workshops which in 1915 still employed two-thirds of all those employed in industry, there had also developed large-scale and modern industry.

Russian Production (*annual averages*)

	1880–4	1900–4	1910–13
Railways (*kilometres*)	22,865 (1880)	53,234 (1900)	70,156 (1913)
Raw-cotton consumption (*thousand metric tons*)	127.6 (1879–84)	281.2 (1895–1904)	388.5 (1905–13)
Pig-iron output (*thousand metric tons*)	477.0	2,773.0	3,870.0
Steel output (*million metric tons*)	0.25	2.35	4.20
Oil output (*thousand metric tons*)	764.0	10,794.0	10,625.0
Coal and lignite output (*million metric tons*)	3.7	17.3	30.2

The statistics set out in the table give some indication of Russian economic growth.

It must also be remembered that population growth was very rapid during these years so that the increase calculated per head of population was much less impressive. But because Russia was so large, her total production ranked her in world terms by 1913 the fifth industrial power after the United States, Germany, Great Britain and France.

In 1913, in comparison with the United States, Russia still lagged far behind. She was also behind Germany and Britain, but Russian output became comparable to that of France and Austria–Hungary in a number of leading industries. With a population four times as large as that of France, Russia only achieved roughly the same total industrial production. All these figures on the one hand show Russia's great progress since 1890 compared with earlier decades, while on the other hand they reveal that in comparison with the United States, Germany and Britain, she remained backward and the gap was still wide.

Even in 1914 Russian society remained overwhelmingly rural. Precise classification is extremely difficult as many workers in factories retained their ties with their village and returned seasonally at harvest time. But not less than 80 per cent of the population were peasants, or muzhiki, who led a hard life, close to subsistence and dependent on weather and harvests. Religion was their solace but less a reasoned Christianity than ritual and superstition. More than half the peasantry were illiterate. Oppressed, the muzhiki symbolised the Russian masses revering the tsar as father and autocrat, yet, when driven by hunger and deprivation, resorting to violence and destruction. Those peasants recently forced by destitution into the crowded tenements or factory barracks of St Petersburg and other industrial centres to work even lived separated from their families.

At the heart of the problem of a Russia seeking to modernise and move into the twentieth century lay this vast peasantry. It was mainly on their heads too that the burden of industrialisation had to be placed, because they provided a cheap labour force and generated the necessary surplus of wealth which made investment in new and expanding industries possible. Exports of agricultural produce had to provide the greater part of capital to pay for all that the state spent on the huge army, on administration and on industry. In the early twentieth century the heavily burdened peasantry was ripe for large-scale violent protests. In town and country sporadic violence was to turn into the explosion of 1905.

The year 1905 marks a turning point in the history of Russia. The peasantry looted and burnt the countryside and appropriated the landlords' land. The immediate reason was the loss of authority suffered by the tsarist autocracy during the Russo-Japanese War (page 88). Violence also flared in St Petersburg and the towns. The defeat of the Russian armies in China and the despatch of the Russian fleet to the bottom of the ocean by the Japanese at the battle of Tsushima in May 1905 weakened the hold of the autocratic Tsar and his ministers.

The capital, St Petersburg, became the scene of violence and brutal repression. It was the enigmatic leadership of a charismatic priest, Father Georgei Gapon, who had initially worked for the tsarist regime, that led to bloodshed. As trade unions were forbidden in Russia the tsarist authorities developed an ingenious scheme to provide a safety valve for industrial grievances and a link with the government workers. Associations, carefully guided in their loyalty to the Tsar and led by reliable supporters of autocracy were promoted. One of these associations, formed with the blessings of the Ministry of the Interior, was Gapon's in St Petersburg. Gapon proved an unreliable supporter. He organised a mass strike and in January 1905 the whole of industrial St Petersburg was shut down by strikes. On what became known as Bloody Sunday, 22 January, he led to the Winter Palace a huge demonstration of workers, their wives and children, perhaps as many as 200,000 in all, dressed in their Sunday best, to seek redress of their grievances from the Tsar. At the Narva Gate the head of the procession was met by Cossacks, who charged with drawn sabres at the masses before them, maiming and killing indiscriminately; soldiers fired into the crowd. Killing continued all morning. Several hundred, possibly as many as 1000, innocent people perished. The spell of a beneficent tsar was broken. The Tsar would never entirely recover his authority or the faith and veneration of the masses who had seen him as their 'little father'.

Throughout the borderlands – Poland, Baltic, Finland and the Caucasus – there followed widespread unrest and insurrection. To the earlier victims of assassination now, in February 1905, was added another illustrious victim, the Grand Duke Sergei, the Tsar's uncle. Terrorism, strikes, student agitation and a rioting peasantry, together with the defeated and demoralised army and navy, added up to a picture of Russian autocracy in complete disarray. The prospect of disaffected armed forces on which autocracy relied was a spectre reinforced in June 1905 by the celebrated mutiny of the battleship *Potemkin* in Odessa harbour. Russian autocracy had reached a critical point: the Tsar could go on shooting and follow a policy of harsh repression or seek to master the situation by some timely concession and reform. He chose the latter, though at heart he remained a convinced, unbending autocrat.

Yet from the low point of his reign in 1905 to the outbreak of the war nine years later the Tsar managed better than many would have foretold at the outset. For a short while he placed the able Sergei Witte in charge of the immediate crisis. Witte had a true, if cynical appreciation of the problem of governing the empire. 'The world should be surprised that we have any government in Russia, not that we have an imperfect government,' he remarked in July 1905. Witte was convinced that chaos would follow if the Tsar's rule was allowed to fail; the nationalities and the conflict of classes would tear Russia apart. Autocracy was the only answer to lawlessness and dissolution. Faced with so much popular opposition, Witte saw clearly enough that the Tsar must either now resort to repression far more bloody than any that had preceded or put himself at the head of the 'reform' movement and limit its scope. Above all the Tsar must stop drifting in a sea of indecision. Witte's personal inclination was for the maintenance of undiluted autocracy but he recognised that this was not likely to succeed, and the Tsar had neither the nerve nor the stomach for total repression. The Tsar gave way to those who argued that a form of constitutionalism should be introduced. A renewed wave of strikes in October overcame his final resistance. The outcome was the October Manifesto of 1905.

In the previous February, Nicholas had declared that he would call into being a consultative assembly, to be known as the Duma. In August the complicated method of election was announced which allowed as little influence as possible to the disaffected workers. Now the October Manifesto promised to bring to life a genuinely parliamentary body with whom the Tsar would share power. No law would be promulgated without the consent of the Duma.

These promises made no impression on the workers who had formed themselves into soviets, or workers' councils, spontaneously. In St Petersburg and Moscow they openly called on the army to come to the side of the revolutionary movement. But the loyalty of the army to the Tsar was never seriously in doubt, the soviets were dispersed, their leaders arrested, and gradually during 1906 in town and country the tide of revolution passed.

With the need for compromise pressing, the Tsar soon showed his true colours. There were four meetings of the parliamentary assembly: the Duma of 1906, the second Duma of 1907, the third from 1907 to 1912, and the last from 1912 to 1917. In the first Duma, a new party emerged, the Constitutional Democratic Party, or Kadets as they were known. They were moderate and liberal and hoped on the basis of the October Manifesto to transform Russian autocracy into a genuine Western parliamentary constitutional government. Together with the moderate left, they outnumbered the revolutionary socialists, who had mostly boycotted the Duma, and the ultra-conservatives. But the Tsar would have nothing to do with a constitutional party or their leader Pavel Miliukov. After the short second Duma, which saw a strengthening of revolutionary socialists, the Tsar simply changed the electoral rules, ensuring tame conservative majorities in the third and fourth Dumas.

The opportunity of transforming Russia into a genuinely constitutional state by collaborating with moderate liberal opinion was spurned by the Tsar. As long as Nicholas II reigned, genuine constitutional change on the Western model was blocked. In 1917 the liberals as well as autocracy would be swept away by the forces of revolution. Yet before the war the actual hold of the various revolutionary socialist parties over the urban workers and the peasants was tenuous. Therein lies the extent of the lost opportunity to modernise and transform Russia while avoiding the terrible violence which after 1917 accompanied that process.

Despite the undoubted political repression and reactionary policies of the Tsar and his ministers, there was also a genuine effort made to tackle some of Russia's basic problems and so to cut the ground from under the widespread discontent. In 1906 the Tsar entrusted power to a ruthless but able man, Peter Stolypin, as chairman of the Council of Ministers, a position he held until his assassination in 1911. Stolypin lived up to his reputation as a 'strong man', and through draconian measures such as military court martials executed hundreds and smothered revolutionary agitation. There were also, of course, revolutionary attacks on government officials whose victims equally ran into many hundreds killed and wounded. Stolypin launched a war on terrorism. He suppressed the rights of the nationalists; the Jews again particularly suffered, associated as they were in the Tsar's mind with sedition and socialism.

It took no great discernment to recognise that something needed to be done to help the peasantry. In November 1905 the peasants' redemption payments for the land they farmed were cancelled (as from 1907). This made it possible for a peasant to become the legal proprietor of the land. But as most of the land was held within the organisation of a village commune (*mir*), his freedom was still heavily circumscribed. The change Stolypin aimed at was a transformation of the existing communes into a whole new class of peasant proprietors, each farming his own land, not in strips as before, but consolidated into one viable farm.

The independent well-to-do peasant proprietors were already a phenomenon, especially in western Russia. The purpose of the land reform associated with Stolypin's name was to increase their number in all parts of Russia. Legislation passed in 1906, 1910 and 1911 facilitated the redistribution of land within the commune and gave the right to the peasant to secede from the commune and claim the land he farmed. How successful did these reforms prove? The problem of Russian agriculture was gigantic, due to over-population, lack of capital, lack of knowledge and simple peasant resistance to change. It has been calculated that by 1916 about 2 million households had left the communes and set up their own farms. It was no more than a beginning, but a significant one. But since by 1916 more than 80 per cent of the land was already being farmed by peasants, redistribution of land by taking it away from the larger landlords and the Church could no longer solve the continuing problem of land hunger caused by over-population. The peasantry was being divided between the richer, the poorer and the landless peasant driven into the towns to swell discontent there. Rapid industrialisation promoted by the state, the spread of education,

Nicholas II with his family (including four nephews) in January 1916. His wife (not in the photograph) and children were murdered with him two and a half months later. To the left of the Tsar an officer is in attendance. On the extreme right of the picture is the Tsarevitch; next to him the Grand Duchess Anastasia.

political agitation, the continuing increase of the population all produced severe social tensions.

Nicholas II was quite unequal to the Herculean task of ruling Russia. He was more and more dominated by his wife, the Empress Alexandra, devoted but equally narrow-minded, and she in turn was influenced by the 'magic' of Rasputin, whose spiritual healing was alleviating the agonies of their son, the sick Tsarevich.

Yet by the eve of the 1914 war a succession of energetic ministers such as Witte and Stolypin had brought about some change. Higher agricultural prices and reforms did benefit rural Russia and pacify the peasants. But in the towns the standard of living of the workers did not improve. Workers had gained limited rights to form trade unions. Bad conditions and an increasing political awareness that change was necessary and possible led after 1910 to strikes. The only answer the government knew was repression, which reached its horrifying peak in the Lena goldfields in 1912 when the troops killed 170 miners striking for higher wages. 1913 and 1914 saw a renewal of massive strikes especially in St Petersburg and Moscow and, significantly, they became increasingly political.

Faced with these internal disorders, the Tsar and his ministers had to weigh, during that fateful July of 1914, the question of war and peace. Would war release a patriotic spirit that would drown the voice of revolution; or would it spark off the great upheaval? The Tsar's agonising over the fateful mobilisation order indicates vividly how he was fully aware that he might be signing the death warrant of his autocratic rule, perhaps his dynasty. Certainly during these last critical weeks, decisions which required the utmost coolness of judgement were being taken under the daily tensions of unrest much more immediate and severe than those facing the Kaiser in Berlin. How had the Tsar allowed Russia to be brought to so dangerous an international position in 1914 when what Russia most needed was peace?

Throughout the nineteenth century Russian foreign and imperial policy sought, generally speaking, the lines of least resistance. Hence the great expansive drive into central Asia and the extension of Russian territory and power to the Sea of Japan with the establishment of Vladivostok as a naval port rather than expansion into western Europe. In western Europe, Russia followed a policy of maintaining good relations with Prussia and Austria–Hungary. The three kingdoms shared a common conservatism and would each be endangered by the revival of nationalism in Poland, that unfortunate kingdom having been partitioned between them in the eighteenth century. In Asia, by the third quarter of the nineteenth century, Russia came in conflict with British imperial interests on a very wide front. In Europe, Russia never ceased to fear that the effect of a hostile occupation of Constantinople and the Straits would be to close the maritime routes of southern Russia and, worse, to provide a springboard for an attack on Russia herself. Yet despite this vital interest Russia always shrank from provoking a coalition of powers against her by attempting to conquer the region. So faced with powerful neighbours in Europe, Russia for a century had followed a path of caution.

The co-operation with Germany and Austria was first breached in 1887 when the Three Emperors' Alliance was not renewed and then more decisively in 1890 when the Germans refused to extend the separate Russo-German 'Insurance' treaty. This was not because the Russians wanted to change the direction of their policy fundamentally, but because the new course had been inaugurated by Wilhelm II, whose advisers persuaded him after the fall of Bismarck not to renew the Russian alliance (page 19). The Russians felt themselves menaced by their isolation, especially when simultaneously Germany drew closer to Russia's imperial rival in Asia, Britain. Fear of isolation drove the Russians reluctantly into the defensive alliance with France in 1894.

During the next five years, little reference was made to the alliance, though France became increasingly important as the provider of foreign loans. The alliance had so far proved of little use and in the new century the French seemed anxious to come to an amicable settlement with Britain just at a time when Russia was faced with the prospect of grave complications in China.

Russia was determined to leave her own way open to the exploitation of Manchuria and northern China while keeping the other European powers and Japan away from the Russian frontiers in eastern Asia. As so frequently happens, a sense of weakness and a desire to defend territory and interests led the Russians into *offensive* action. Following the German appearance on the Chinese mainland when they seized the port of Kiaochow in 1897, the Russians countered by forcing the Chinese to lease to them strategically important Port Arthur. During the years from 1898 to 1903 Russia penetrated deeply into northern China. The peaceful policy advocated by Witte of working with the Chinese and seeking economic dominance with the help of a Russian-constructed and -controlled Manchurian railway was abandoned. The Boxer rising in 1900 gave Russia the opportunity to occupy large parts of northern China under the guise of rescuing the Europeans and suppressing the Boxers. At the same time Russia also sought to dominate the neighbouring kingdom of Korea.

The military expansion of Russia in eastern Asia greatly alarmed the Japanese (page 87). With Britain's alliance in 1902, the Japanese were sure that they could not be overwhelmed by a European coalition if they chose to resist Russia. They demanded that Russia withdraw. The Tsar and his ministers knew in 1904 that they faced war unless they withdrew. But with their own sense of 'white' superiority – they referred to the Japanese as baboons – it seemed unthinkable to Nicholas II that he should give way to mere Asiatics. The Minister of the Interior even thought that 'a little victorious war' would calm the revolutionary agitation at home.

War broke out in February 1904. There were two unexpected results. The first was the Japanese surprise attacks on the Russian fleet at Port Arthur during the night of 8/9 February 1904 without the benefit of a declaration of war. The second was that the Japanese won. Russia's military, and even more her naval, performance during the Russo-Japanese war presented a sorry spectacle. Port Arthur finally fell to the Japanese troops investing it in January 1905. In February and March 1905 the Japanese inflicted heavy defeats on Russia's land forces in Manchuria at Mukden. The crowning disaster was the annihilation of Russia's European

Baltic battlefleet which had sailed halfway round the world to the straits separating Korea and Japan only to be sunk at the battle of Tsushima on 27 May 1905.

The war ended by compromise. The Japanese were equally anxious to end the war once they had gained their objective. With the help of Theodore Roosevelt's mediation, the peace of Portsmouth was concluded on 5 September 1905. Russian influence in southern Manchuria and Korea was at an end. She remained predominant in northern Manchuria and outer Mongolia. In peaceful agreement with Japan, Russia's frontier of interest in China was now drawn.

No doubt the revolutionary outbreaks at home had persuaded the Tsar to accept this humiliation. Even more compelling was the necessity of rebuilding the army and navy in the face of the ever present danger of European complications. The menace to the security of the empire in Europe was not a limited one but threatened its very existence.

Russia had no choice but to remain conciliatory and pacific in Europe. The French had to be told that Russia for the time being was militarily in no position to fulfil the military obligations of the alliance (page 29). In the Balkans, the policy of friendly co-operation with the Habsburgs was continued. The empire had to have peace. In August 1907, agreement with Britain settling their imperial rivalries in Persia, Afghanistan and Tibet removed the greatest immediate dangers of conflict. Peaceful relations with all her neighbours, agreements of compromise rather than active extension of Russia's influence – those were the guidelines for the Russian foreign ministers during the years from 1906 to 1908. For a brief period the 'Russian threat' loomed less darkly in Europe and Asia.

From 1909 to 1914 the rapid recovery, reorganisation and planned enlargement of the Russian army alarmed her neighbours. Unlike the German army, the Russian – and this may cause surprise – was never simply the bastion of class privilege. The nobility and gentry played a prominent role as officers but two out of every five officers up to the rank of colonel had risen from the peasantry or lower-middle class. The fathers of many officers had been serfs. The industrial upsurge and the recovery of agriculture rapidly increased the income of the state during these years and together with foreign loans from France enabled the government to budget for the huge additional expenditure on the army, on the navy and on new railway construction.

By 1914, it has been calculated that Russia was already spending more than Germany on her army and navy; when the armaments programme was completed in 1917 the Russian army on paper would enjoy overwhelming superiority with a peacetime strength of nearly 2 million men; what is more, by 1917 they could be mobilised in eighteen days, against Germany's fifteen days. The Schlieffen Plan, which was based on quickly defeating France before Russia was ready to attack Germany (page 21), would then be done for; France could not be defeated in three days. Germany, thrown on the defensive, would be overwhelmed. To be sure, this gloomy prognostication by the German military staff left out of account Russia's poor planning, inefficient command structure and wasteful military expenditure. It also took no account of her lack of communications or her industrial weakness. But there can be no doubt that at the time the German military leadership was thrown virtually into panic by believing that Germany's conditions of safety would soon vanish. The 'Russian danger' was greatly exaggerated in Berlin in 1914.

In 1908 the Balkan fuse was lit. The resumption of Austro–Russian tension in the Balkans began paradoxically with an agreement between the Russian Foreign Minister Alexander Izvolski and Count Aehrenthal, the Habsburg Foreign Minister. Both wished to score some external success to revive the flagging status of their respective empires. Izvolski desired to change the 'rule' of the Straits of Constantinople, which closed them to all warships when Turkey was at peace, to a new rule which would allow Russian warships to pass them. Russia had always regarded control of the Straits as one of her most vital interests. Aehrenthal, less ambitious, wished to convert the occupation of the two Turkish provinces of Bosnia and Herzegovina into an actual annexation. They promised each other mutual support. In October 1908 Aehrenthal collected his side of the bargain, but British opposition prevented the Russians from realising their objective (page 43). The 'Bosnian crisis' marks a turning point in the relations of the powers before 1914. Slav Serbia, resenting the annexation of Bosnia–Herzegovina, appealed to Russia for support; Austria relied on Germany. No one was ready to fight. But good relations between Austria and Russia were at an end. Also ended was the Austro–Russian understanding to settle their imperial rivalries in the Balkans. Now they intrigued against each other and the fuse leading to war in 1914 was lit.

Other European nations with their own ambitions added to the breakdown of stability in the Balkans. The Ottoman Empire was attempting to reform itself after the Young Turk revolution of 1908. But Turkey was weak. Italy attacked Turkey in 1911 and annexed Tripoli. The small Balkan states, equally greedy, wanted Turkish territory in Europe and were ready to fight each other over the spoils.

Turkish weakness, Balkan nationalism and the rivalry of Austria and Russia destabilised south-east Europe.

At first the Balkan states went to war against Turkey. The Balkan League of Serbia, Bulgaria, Greece and Montenegro attacked the Turks in October 1912 and defeated them. As a result of the war Serbia greatly increased her territory, to the alarm of Austria. All the great European powers stepped in to supervise the peace and Russia had to agree to Austrian demands limiting Serbia's gains.

But hardly had the question been settled in London in May 1913 when the members of the Balkan League fought each other. Bulgaria now attacked Serbia and Greece; Montenegro, Romania and Turkey joined Serbia and Greece in attacking Bulgaria. Bulgaria was forced to make peace and yield many of her gains from the first Balkan war.

The conflicts of the Balkan states would have mattered comparatively little outside their own region of the world, but for the effects on Austria–Hungary (pages 61–66) and on Russia. There was little consistency about Russian policy in the Balkans. Strong Pan-Slav feelings motivated Russia's ambassadors in the Balkans and these were backed by sections of public opinion within Russia. But the official line taken by Sergei Sazonov, Izvolsky's successor at the Foreign Ministry in St Petersburg, was caution. The result of the Balkan wars was to weaken Russia's position as well as Austria's. For Russia the future appeared full of uncertainties in the Balkans. The eventual alignment of the individual Balkan states, with Austria–Hungary and Germany on the one side and Russia and France on the other, was unpredictable. Only Serbia was still Russia's firm ally and that was not for love of Russia but due to her enmity of Austria–Hungary.

These uncertainties made the Russians much more nervous about the future of the Straits of Constantinople. They were not only vital strategically but, with the upsurge of the Russian economy, they also formed an increasingly important link in the chain of Russia's trade with the rest of the world. Three-quarters of her grain exports were shipped from the Black Sea through the Straits, and grain constituted some 40 per cent of Russia's total export trade. The Russians wished the Turks to remain the guardians as long as they did not fall under hostile influence until the Russians were strong enough to control them. Germany now had become a double threat: as Austria–Hungary's ally and, since 1909, as Turkey's 'friend'. The appointment of a German general, Liman von Sanders in November 1913 to command the army corps stationed in Constantinople greatly alarmed St Petersburg. Russian protests this time worked. General von Sanders was promoted to the rank of field marshal, which made him too grand merely to command troops in Constantinople.

On the plus side for the Russians was the attitude of the French who in 1912 strongly revived the Franco–Russian alliance (pages 29–30). But Russian policy would in the end be dictated by Russian interests. Until Russia's military reorganisation was completed, and while still faced with strikes and unrest at home, Russia wanted to avoid war. That was still the view of the Council of Ministers called to debate the question in January 1914 just a few months before the outbreak of war.

CHAPTER 8

The Closing Decades of the Habsburg Empire

The Habsburg Empire had been a formidable European power for more than four centuries. Was its disintegration in the twentieth century the inevitable consequence of the two most powerful currents of modern history: nationalism and industrialisation? These threatened respectively the common bond of loyalty which the nationalities composing the Dual Monarchy felt for the dynasty and the acceptance of an existing social order. In many ways industrialisation and nationalism were contradictory forces in Austria–Hungary. The large market of the empire and free trade within it helped industrial progress; socialism, which grew with industrial expansion, also called for an allegiance that cut across the ethnic differences of nationality. Nationalism, on the other hand, was divisive and threatened to break up the empire. But nationalism contained the seeds of conflict within itself. There could be no easy agreement in a part of Europe where the nationalities were so intermingled as to what precise national frontiers should be drawn, or who should form the majority in a state or which peoples must acquiesce in remaining a minority. There would be conflicts and tensions however matters were arranged and the majority of the emperor's subjects felt 'better the devil we know'. There was much to be said for the supranational solution which the Habsburg Monarchy represented. Multinational states break apart when the central power is weakened beyond point of recovery. This did not happen in the Habsburg Empire until 1918. In defeated Russia, Lenin and Trotsky were able to restore the authority of the central power through civil war, but no such Habsburg recovery was possible in 1918. Nevertheless it took four years of devastating war to break Habsburg power and the cohesion of the Monarchy.

Austria-Hungary's Population
(in millions)

1900	1910
46.9	52.4

It has frequently been claimed that central power had been eroded half a century earlier with the constitutional settlement of 1867. But the settlement stood the test of time when judged by central European standards. The greatest threat to the Monarchy was Hungarian independence. After 1867 there was no longer a serious possibility of this. The extensive rights which the Magyars were granted in the historic kingdom of Hungary reconciled them to the unity of the empire under the personal link of the emperor–king. For the Magyars the continuation of the empire meant that the entire power of the Monarchy was available to defend their position against external and internal enemies.

The settlement of 1867 granted to each half of the empire its own government with control of internal affairs; this included, importantly, powers to decide what rights were to be conceded to the other nationalities living within the jurisdiction of the kingdom of Hungary and Cis-Leithania, as the Austrian half of the empire was officially called. But the central power of the empire remained strong and real after 1867. Finance, foreign affairs and military matters remained the responsibility of the imperial ministries in Vienna, whose ministers were chosen by the emperor. The emperor was commander-in-chief of the imperial army. In another important way this unique imperial constitution actually strengthened central power. The democratic constitutional trend of the nineteenth and twentieth century could not be entirely halted in the empire. But franchise concessions were granted for the separate parliaments sitting in Vienna and Budapest. In Austria the year 1907 saw the introduction of manhood suffrage. The Magyars refused to accept any substantial reforms. But the Hungarian parliament exercised much more real power over the Hungarian government than the Austrian over the Austrian government. There existed no parliament for the empire as a whole which could influence or control the crucially important joint imperial ministries.

Indirect parliamentary influence was in theory provided for by the system of the 'delegations', representatives of the Austrian and Hungarian parliaments meeting separately and together (in theory) to deal with questions affecting the joint ministries. In practice, what concerned the delegations mainly was finance, customs, commercial policy and the contributions to the common budget to be paid by Austria and by Hungary. These questions were settled, after much wrangling based on obvious self-interest, for ten years at a time. The emperor's 'reserved' powers in foreign and military affairs remained virtually absolute through his choice of ministers and refusal to take notice of any parliamentary disapproval. His power would not have been so completely preserved in the twentieth century, and with it a strong central power, but for the dualism of the empire and so the absence of a single imperial parliament. Consequently imperial policies in war and foreign affairs were conducted by just a handful of men. These included the heads of the three joint ministries, with the minister of foreign affairs presiding; on important occasions the prime minister of Hungary, who had a constitutional right to be consulted on questions of foreign policy, and other ministers were invited to join in the discussion.

Among some of the Slavs, dualism was seen as a device for excluding the Slav majority from their rightful and equal place in the empire. By dividing the empire, the Magyars and Germans constituted the majority each in their own half. The majority of the 21 million Slavs (approximate 1910 figures) in the empire as a whole was thus turned into minorities.

Of course the 'Slavs' were not unified in religion, social structure or tradition. The rivalries and hostilities between them were at least as important as their supposedly common interests. The Magyar–German compromise of 1867 led to parallel small compromises within each half of the empire. In Austria, the Polish gentry were given privileges at the expense of the Ruthenes; the Czechs were from time to time allowed special rights; but Serb, Croat and Slovene cultural development was restricted. The struggle between German-speaking Habsburg subjects and the other nationalities was bitter at the local level and in parliament, but it was not, as in Hungary, systematic government policy. In Hungary, the Magyars allowed a special status to the Croats but excluded the Slovaks and Serbs and Romanians from any share of power or from exercising autonomous rights.

Nationalities of the Dual Monarchy, 1910

	Austria	Hungary
Germans	9,950,000	2,037,000
Czechs	6,436,000	–
Poles	4,968,000	–
Romanians	275,000	2,949,000
Ruthenians	3,519,000	473,000
Serbs & Croats	783,000	2,939,000
Italians	768,000	–
Slovenes	1,253,000	–
Slovaks	–	1,968,000
Magyars	–	9,945,000

The politics of 'Austria' and of Hungary also diverged in other respects in the twentieth century. In Austria one striking development was the emergence of a socialist party led by Victor Adler which gained a sizeable parliamentary following in 1907. Austrian politics were marred by the antics of the German nationalists and the anti-Semitic Christian Socialists inspired by Karl Lueger. Conflicts between nationalists in Austria frequently paralysed parliament. The industrialised and prosperous Czechs demanded autonomy. The Germans in Bohemia sought to keep the Czechs in an inferior national status. The focus of the struggle was over the official use of language. When the emperor's ministers made concessions to the Czechs, the Germans refused co-operation to the government and when concessions were made to the Germans the Czechs went into bitter opposition. In any case parliament was regarded by the emperor as no more than an 'advisory body'.

The introduction of manhood suffrage in Austria in 1907 was intended to break the nationality deadlock. For a brief time the Social Democrats sat together, irrespective of national origin, whether German or Czech. It did not last. From 1908 to 1914 the old nationality conflict reasserted itself with as much vehemence as before. The conflict of the national parties reduced the parliament in its splendid and imposing building in Vienna to impotence. With such a record, parliamentary government could win little respect among the population as a whole.

In Hungary, extensive franchise reforms were blocked by the Magyar gentry as likely to undermine Magyar predominance. Relations with the non-Magyar nationalities remained bad down to 1914. Repression was the only policy consistently adopted. Hungarian politics revolved around largely unsuccessful attempts to modify the compromise of 1867 so that the Magyars could gain greater control over the army. But this was fiercely resisted by Francis Joseph, who threatened force against any Hungarian government or parliament seeking to tamper with the royal prerogatives.

When now we marvel at the continued resilience of the Habsburg Empire, despite national and constitutional conflicts, which seemed to increase rather than diminish during the last years of peace, we tend to overlook one question. Who had anything to gain from driving the conflict to extremes and threatening the Habsburg Empire with disintegration? Not the Magyars, not the Germans, nor the Poles, who enjoyed greater liberties under Austrian than Russian and German rule; not the Jews, whose talents transformed cultural Vienna; not the Czechs who believed their own security necessitated the empire; not even the majority of Serbs and Croats in the annexed provinces of Bosnia and Herzegovina. Everywhere the mass of the peasantry was attached to the Habsburg dynasty. Agitation for independence, whether of Czech or southern Slavs, was largely the work of a minority among the more educated. The great majority of Francis Joseph's subjects wanted the empire to continue even though they differed so bitterly on the kind of empire they wanted. Meanwhile the dynasty and its central power, the imperial civil service and administration, and the imperial army all carried out their duties sustained by the common consent of the great majority of the people.

Francis Joseph had won the affection of his subjects simply by always having been there. His family misfortunes bravely borne, his simplicity and honesty, and pride in his robustness in very old age combined to make him the most respected and venerated monarch in Europe. And all this despite the fact that he had made war on his own subjects in 1849 (Hungary) and had lost all the wars in which Austria had engaged since his accession against Italy, France and Prussia. It was a remarkable achievement.

During the last years of the nineteenth and during the early twentieth century, the empire emerged as a modern state. In Hungary the administration was virtually Magyarised. This applied also to the judicial administration. But the country enjoyed a high reputation for justice, with admittedly the important exception of what were seen as 'political' offences. The kingdom of Hungary was Magyar: patriotism meant Magyar patriotism; dissent from this view was treated harshly. But, despite this fierce attempt to Magyarise the nationalities on the peripheries of the kingdom, the policy met with little success; the nationalities preserved their identities. In the Austrian half of the empire the governments sought to arrive at settlements between Germans, Czechs and Poles acceptable to all sides, but with little lasting success.

That the empire was on the whole so well governed was in no small part due to an incorruptible and, on the whole, intelligent and fair-minded bureaucracy of civil servants and jurists. It is true that in the Austrian half of the empire the Germans constituted some 80 per cent of the civil servants though by population they were entitled only to a third. The much better education of the Germans accounts for some of this predominance. In Hungary deliberate Magyarisation led to more than 90 per cent of government service being in Hungarian-speaking hands. In the central imperial administration the Germans also played the major role, with more than half the civil servants German-speaking. But one can certainly not speak of a totally German-dominated imperial administration. In the principal joint ministries of the empire, Francis Joseph ensured that the three common ministers never came from the same half of the Monarchy. The senior Foreign Ministry was held in turn by a Saxon German, a Hungarian, an Austrian German, a Pole, a Hungarian and an Austrian German.

To say when we turn to the economic development of the empire that it was disappointingly slow in the latter part of the nineteenth and early twentieth century implies a comparison with western and northern Europe. But the empire's centre was in the Balkans, the grain-producing Hungarian plain. Within the empire lay regions such as the Czech provinces, which achieved a development comparable to the most advanced areas of Europe, and such poverty-stricken provinces as Galicia.

The empire thus provides great contrasts between comparative wealth and stark poverty. Agricultural backwardness and an increasing population condemned the peasants of Galicia to continuous poverty. Large-scale emigration was one consequence. (The empire's population grew from 46.9 million in 1900 to 52.4 million in 1910.) In Bohemia, and in upper and lower Austria, agriculture, as well as industry, turned these regions into the most prosperous in the empire. In Hungary the owners of the great landed estates led the way to the introduction of better farming methods. The central Hungarian plain became one of the granaries of Europe. The imperial customs union, freeing all trade within the empire, opened up to Hungary's agriculture the market of the more industrialised Austrian half of the empire.

In the twentieth century Austria–Hungary achieved a fast rate of industrial growth in the favoured regions. Nevertheless the empire as a whole lagged far behind the more advanced western and northern European nations. Regional variations were as marked in industrial as in agricultural development. The most successful agricultural parts of the empire were also the most industrially advanced: upper and lower Austria, Bohemia, Moravia and Silesia and Hungary proper. Industrialisation had made little impact in Galicia, Dalmatia or Transylvania. In 1911, textiles and clothing, tobacco and foodstuffs together with wood, leather and paper accounted for nearly two-thirds of the Austrian half of the empire's industrial output. But imperial policies of free trade within the empire tended to maintain these regional differences of progress and backwardness. On the other hand, it needs to be remembered that without state aid in the development of the railways, without good administration and internal peace and security throughout the empire, the economic conditions of the people would have been far worse than they actually were.

Austria-Hungary's Production
(annual averages)

	1900–4	1910–13
Raw-cotton consumption *(thousand metric tons)*	135.4 (1895–1904)	191.4 (1905–13)
Coal and lignite output *(million metric tons)*	38.8	50.7
Pig-iron output *(thousand metric tons)*	1,425.0	2,204.0
Steel output *(million metric tons)*	1.2	2.46

It is remarkable that the empire, beset by so many problems internally, backward in economic development and also poor, achieved a high reputation in the arts and was still acknowledged to be one of the great powers of Europe. The Monarchy's universities were second to none, the musical, literary and theatrical life of Vienna, Budapest and Prague, and the renown of Freud and Liszt and Strauss, were celebrated throughout the Western world. The Monarchy's status as a great power had been diminished, it is true, but not extinguished by defeats in the nineteenth-century continental wars that created united Italy and Germany. In 1900 the empire was still considered one of the foremost military powers of Europe, a bulwark against the possibility of the Russian or German dominance of south-eastern Europe. The territorially large Habsburg Empire was thus a major element in the pre-1914 European balance of power whose disappearance, the other powers felt, would create grave new problems.

Actually the empire's military capacity was overrated. The perennial lack of funds was one reason for its weakness. Another unique problem was that it was largely officered by German-speaking Austrians and a smaller number of Hungarians; the troops themselves were composed of all the nationalities and spoke in many languages. Even worse was the incompetence of the General Staff. Only in the two years before the war of 1914 was the army increased to a potential wartime strength of 1.5 million men. Military and economic weakness made the Monarchy's foreign ministers cautious and conservative.

There is a shape, logic and consistency to Habsburg foreign policy in the nineteenth century with its emphasis on the importance of tradition and of dynastic rule and its opposition to nationalism. The loss of the Italian provinces was therefore seen as a particularly heavy blow. If the neighbours of the Habsburg Empire, Romania and Serbia, followed the example of Piedmont in the wars of Italian unification, justifying their efforts by an appeal to the right of national self-determination, then the Habsburg Empire must disintegrate altogether. Serbia cast in the role of Piedmont was the nightmare vision that drove the Emperor and his ministers to stake the future of the empire on the field of battle in July 1914. But they also recognised that the real threat had not been Piedmont but Piedmont in alliance with France in 1859 and with Prussia in 1866. The real threat in 1914 was felt to be not Serbia but Serbia in alliance with Russia.

Security and integrity are basic objectives of any state's foreign policy. But the great powers of pre-1914 Europe also considered it axiomatic that they should possess spheres of influence and control beyond their own state frontiers. In the nineteenth century the Habsburgs were forced to abandon their traditional role of influence first in the Italian and then in the German states. By the twentieth century the only 'frontier' left open was the Balkan. Not to suffer a third defeat on this last frontier was seen as a matter of vital importance for the future of the empire.

With the decline of the Ottoman Empire in Europe the future of the Balkan peoples, divided and intermingled in religious beliefs, in tradition, in culture and in socio-economic structure, preoccupied the European great powers. But the Balkan states pursued policies of their own and were locked in rivalry over the disposition of the still Turkish or formerly Turkish lands.

Once Russia had recovered from defeat in the Far East, the attention of St Petersburg reverted to the Balkans and a rediscovery of Russia's Slav mission. A much more active Russian policy now coincided with a new period of Ottoman weakness caused by the internal upheavals of the Young Turk movement (1908 to 1910). It also coincided with the growing ambitions and rivalries of the Balkan states, themselves casting covetous eyes on Macedonia and other territories still ruled by the Turk. The Balkans were becoming a powder barrel. Austro-Russian co-operation might have contained these tensions. Instead Russia's ambitious ministers at the various Balkan capitals were adding to the growing turmoil. The turning point came in 1908/9.

In the Monarchy, the Foreign Minister Count Aehrenthal was a well-known advocate of a policy of co-operation and agreement with Russia. He regarded Austria–Hungary as a 'satiated' state that needed no more territories and no more Slavs. But as a final step of consolidation – almost a technical consolidation – whose purpose was to regularise and remove all uncertainty, he wished to convert the Monarchy's position in Bosnia–Herzegovina from that of the permanently occupying power (since 1878) to one of sovereignty. He was prepared to pay compensation to the Turks and to give up the occupation of another Turkish territory, the strategically important land known as Novipazar. This withdrawal would also convince the Russians that Austria–Hungary had abandoned all thought of territorial expansion. Talks were arranged with the Russian Foreign Minister, Alexander Izvolski. Their famous, and unrecorded, conversation took place at the castle of Buchlau in 1908. From the available evidence it seems clear that the whole basis of these talks was the intention to strengthen Austro-Russian co-operation. Izvolski said that Russia would diplomatically support Austria–Hungary's wish to annex Bosnia–Herzegovina. In return he asked for, and obtained, Aehrenthal's promise of diplomatic support for a Russian proposal to the powers to change the rule of the Straits (page 59). Aehrenthal soon after, while Izvolski toured western Europe and had not even time to consult the Tsar about the Buchlau 'bargain', announced the annexation of Bosnia–

Herzegovina to Europe. Izvolski was furious. He had no success with his attempt to change the rule of the Straits: Britain rejected the proposal outright. To save face, Izvolski now claimed he had been tricked by Aehrenthal.

From here on the threads lead to the catastrophe of 1914. Out of the breakdown of relations between Izvolski and Aehrenthal grew the prolonged Bosnian crisis. Serbia's nationalist feelings had been wildly aroused by the Monarchy's annexation of Bosnia and Herzegovina, inhabited by many Serbs. Russia backed Serbia and was insistent on 'compensation' for Serbia; also that the Monarchy should submit the whole question of annexation to a conference of powers. With the German ally's support, Aehrenthal refused both demands. Russia and Britain and France backed away. Serbia did not. In 1909 Serbia and Austria–Hungary came close to war, with Russia acting as Serbia's protector. In reality neither Russia nor any of the powers were ready for war in 1909. One cannot help speculating how different a course history might have taken if Austria–Hungary had used her superior strength to defeat Serbia then. As it was, Izvolski drew back. On Germany fell the odium of having threatened Russia with a peremptory note that unless she recognised the annexation at once, Germany would not hold the Monarchy back from attacking Serbia. Izvolski could now claim that the German 'ultimatum' forced Russia to give way. More important, the crisis marked the end of tolerably good Austro-Russian relations. Were their Balkan differences really so irreconcilable? The collision of the two empires was due to miscalculation rather than deliberate intent. In 1909 Russia was the more aggressive of the two states.

The Russian diplomats in the years after 1909 redoubled their efforts to re-establish Russia's damaged prestige among the Balkan states. These moves coincided with the intrigues and national ambitions of the Balkan states themselves, whose policies in the end could not be controlled by the Russians.

In 1911 the Italians made war on the Ottoman Empire (page 35). This started a new period of continuous Balkan tensions. In 1912 the Habsburgs believed that the Russians had inspired a Balkan League of Greece, Serbia, Montenegro and Bulgaria to attack Turkey. These states had temporarily buried their own disputes over Macedonia and other territorial disputes to grab more lands from Turkey. Then they in turn fell out over the booty in 1913 when Bulgaria attacked Serbia and Greece and was herself defeated by a new alliance of Balkan states (page 60).

Apart from the certainty of Austro-Serb enmity, there were no other certainties in the Balkans during the last years before 1914. Neither Russia nor the Monarchy could be sure at any point of crisis which of the other Balkan states would side with whom. The unhappy consequence for the peace of Europe was that Russia and Austria–Hungary felt equally threatened by the diplomatic intrigues of the other! Russia, with promises of French support, was both fearful and active. The Dual Monarchy could never assume that the German ally would stand behind her. As for Italy, her alliance was nominal. Italy was regarded as a potential enemy. So the Habsburgs felt unsure of the future.

Austria–Hungary's bitter opponent, Serbia, had emerged greatly enlarged from the two Balkan wars. In 1913, by helping to create independent and friendly Albania, Austria–Hungary succeeded in checking Serbia's further expansion to the Adriatic. This was achieved not so much by the 'conference of European' powers as by the Dual Monarchy's own threats delivered to Serbia. Count Leopold Berchtold, Aehrenthal's successor at the Foreign Ministry since 1912, learnt from these experiences that Austria–Hungary must needs rely on her own firmness. Behind Serbia stood Russia. But Francis Joseph and his ministers believed that firm diplomacy could still break the hostile ring of states and Russia's manifest design to encircle the Monarchy, provided Germany loyally backed the Habsburg Empire. Sarajevo changed all that.

CHAPTER 9

Over the Brink: The Five-week Crisis, 28 June to 1 August 1914

The Great War disrupted and destroyed lives on a scale never known before. More than 60 million men were mobilised and 8.5 million were killed, 21 million were wounded and in every town and village in Europe the blinded and maimed victims served as daily reminders decades after the war was over. In every town and village war memorials commemorate the names of those who gave their lives for their country. The war which involved millions and for which millions suffered was launched by the decision of just a few men negotiating and conspiring in secret. They bear a heavy responsibility. What made these men act the way they did? Were they aware of what they were doing, or did they just muddle into war through confusion and error?

There was a widespread illusion about the course the war would take. The troops left for the front believing that they would be home by Christmas. With the new mass armies it was thought that the war would be decided by the devastating battles fought at the outset. But no one expected that this would be just another war, like those of the mid-nineteenth century, ending with the victors exacting some territorial and financial punishment from the vanquished and leading to a new balance of power. There was, however, no illusion about what was at stake. Grey's famous words about the lights going out all over Europe expressed a sentiment that would have been well understood in Paris, Berlin, Vienna and St Petersburg. Bethmann Hollweg gloomily predicted the toppling of thrones and the victory of socialism. In Vienna, the future existence of the Habsburg Monarchy was felt to be at stake: defeat would lead to her dissolution. Tsarist Russia was beset by serious internal disturbances and French society was deeply divided on the eve of the war. There were no illusions about the devastating consequences of this war from which a new world would emerge. There were hesitations on the brink of war. It was then too late. How had the powers allowed the crisis caused initially by a terrorist crime, the assassination of an archduke, the heir to the Habsburg throne, to escalate until there was no way out but a devastating European war? There seems to be no obvious connection between the murder committed by a young man in Bosnia and the clash of armies of millions.

The assassination of the Archduke Francis Ferdinand in Sarajevo on 28 June 1914 was the work of a handful of Bosnian youths who had romantically dedicated their lives to Serb nationalism and had been greatly influenced by the Russian terrorists in exile. They received their weapons from the secret Serbian conspiratorial Black Hand organisation headed by Colonel Dragutin Dimitrijević, who was also in charge of army secret intelligence. The Bosnian youths, who had spent some time in Belgrade, had been helped across the Serb frontier by Serbian agents. The Prime Minister of Serbia, Nikola Pašić, and King Alexander were powerless against the army officers and the Black Hand. But Pašić did send a vague warning to Vienna that

Gavrilo Princip is seized by police, moments after mortally wounding Archduke Francis Ferdinand and his wife.

the Archduke would be in danger when he visited Sarajevo.

The amateur assassins almost bungled their task. On the morning of 28 June, the first attempt failed and the bomb thrown by one of the six conspirators exploded under the car following the Archduke. Incredibly the Archduke, his wife and the Governor of Bosnia drove through the open streets again the same afternoon. When the Archduke's chauffeur hesitated which way to go, by mere chance one of the conspirators, Gavrilo Princip, found himself opposite the Archduke's stationary car. He aimed two shots at the Archduke and the Governor of Bosnia; they mortally wounded Francis Ferdinand and his wife.

The government of Serbia did not want war in 1914, for the country had not yet recovered from the exertions of the Balkan wars. But the government could not control the army nor prevent the secret societies from fomenting and aiding anti-Habsburg movements in Bosnia and Herzegovina. The assassination of the Archduke was unwelcome news to the government, for the King and his government would now be called to account for allowing anarchical political conditions which gave the terrorists their base and power.

In Vienna, the Dual Monarchy's foreign minister, Count Berchtold, before those fateful shots at Sarajevo had given no serious thought to war. He did not judge the internal state of the Habsburg Monarchy as so desperate. Serbia and Russia would surely be restrained by firm Austro-Hungarian diplomacy backed by imperial Germany. The Habsburgs could continue to rely upon the divisions and mutual antagonisms of their Slav subjects. The Slovenes were Catholics and loyal to the Crown. The Croats were Catholics too, and union with the Greek Orthodox Serbs was opposed by the majority of them. Nor were the Serbs in favour of any general union of southern Slavs, 'Yugoslavia', which would place them in the minority of such a new state. They dreamt of a 'Greater Serbia', but this would have placed the Croats in a minority! The idea of 'Yugoslavia' had won the adherence of only a minority of students and intellectuals. The majority of the southern Slavs had no thought of leaving the Habsburg Monarchy in 1914.

Every Austro-Hungarian minister since 1909

realised that the threat to the existence of the Habsburg Empire was due not to the challenge of any of the small Balkan states such as Serbia, but to Russia utilising Balkan discontents against the Dual Monarchy. That is why the misunderstanding and dispute between Russia and Austria–Hungary – the so-called Bosnian crisis – is such a significant milestone on the road to war.

Russia had been forced to back down when faced with Germany's determined support of Austria–Hungary. In this way, the changed status of two provinces in the Balkans – which made no real difference to the map of Europe – led to disastrous consequences out of all proportion to the issues involved. Henceforth, the good Austro-Russian understanding, designed to prevent the two powers from becoming so entangled in local Balkan conflicts that thereby they could be dragged into hostility with each other, was broken by crises that threatened the peace of Europe. Rivalry, suspicion and intrigue in the Balkans replaced the co-operation of former years. The final crisis was occasioned by the assassination of the Archduke.

In Vienna, news of the assassination entirely changed the attitude of Berchtold and the majority of the Monarchy's ministers. A diplomatic offensive was no longer thought enough. Habsburg prestige was now so seriously involved that, unless Serbia was 'punished', the empire's role as a great power would be at an end. Serbia could not be allowed to get away with this last and most serious provocation by sheltering behind Russia. If the Monarchy could prove that Russian protection could not save Serbia from her wrath, the lesson would not be lost on the other Balkan states and Austria–Hungary's international position of power would be reasserted. Berchtold concluded that Serbia's hostility must be broken and that only Serbian submission to the will of the Monarchy should be allowed to save her from war and conquest.

There were three obstacles. The Austro-Hungarian army was not ready for war: it would need more than a month to prepare. The Chief of Staff, Conrad von Hötzendorf, moreover, pointed out that, if Russia intervened, the Austro-Hungarian army would need German military co-operation to cope successfully with a war on two fronts, the Serbian and Russian. The Monarchy's ministers were in any case convinced that the Monarchy could not risk war with Russia unless the German ally stood side by side with Austria–Hungary in war. Would the imperial German government support the Monarchy now? The third obstacle to war was internal, the opposition of the Hungarian Prime Minister, Count Tisza.

On 4 July 1914, the Council of Ministers, meeting in Vienna, decided that the first step was to ascertain the attitude of the Kaiser and his ministers. Count Hoyos was sent to Berlin with a personal letter from the Emperor Francis Joseph to the Kaiser, and a set of questions from the Monarchy's ministers. They did not beat about the bush, but wanted to know whether Germany would come to Austria–Hungary's help if Russia chose to intervene on behalf of Serbia. They also explained what was in store for Serbia. Serbia would be eliminated 'as a power factor in the Balkans'.

From a variety of recorded conversations, some of which have only recently come to light, it is possible to gain close insights into what the Kaiser and Bethmann Hollweg and the military thought. For two years and more there had been mounting fears about the planned expansion of Russian military power. The weakness of the Habsburg Monarchy became increasingly apparent, and there were serious doubts about her future after the old Emperor's death, which could not be long delayed. There were also nagging doubts about Austria–Hungary's loyalty to the alliance with Germany. Would the alliance survive if Germany once again forced the Monarchy to desist from doing what she thought imperative for her survival – to show she was stronger than Serbia and would not tolerate Serbian hostility? Imperial Germany felt she needed the support of Austria–Hungary if the mass Russian Slav armies were to be checked. A war with Russia arising out of an Austro-Serb conflict would ensure the Monarchy's support. A war starting between Germany and Russia, or Germany and France, might not find Austria–Hungary on Germany's side. Then there was a calculation of quite a different kind. Bethmann Hollweg hoped to weaken, perhaps even to break up, the alignment of Russia, France and Britain. Bethmann Hollweg's calculations were all based on 'ifs'. If Russia should decide to back Serbia and then applied to Paris for backing, and if France then refused to risk war with Germany so that Russia might threaten Austria–Hungary with war, Russia would discover that the French alliance was, in reality, worthless. *If* all this happened then Germany would be in a position to win back Russia's friendship, perhaps even her alliance. If, on the other hand, it should come to war, then better now than later. But the Dual Monarchy must initiate the war so that at home it could be presented as being fought in defence of Germany's ally against tsarist Russia. Russia would be cast in the role of aggressor.

The critical discussions between the Kaiser, Bethmann Hollweg and the military took place immediately after the arrival of Count Hoyos in Berlin. The decision, when it was reached, was not the Kaiser's alone. That is a myth which was believed for a long time. The decision was to back Austria–Hungary to the hilt, with German military support if necessary, should Russia intervene to prevent the Dual Monarchy from dealing with Serbia. The Habsburg ministers were given a free hand to settle with Serbia in any way they thought appropriate. That was the message to Vienna on 6 July, the Kaiser's famous 'blank cheque'. The Habsburg ministers were also urged to act quickly against Serbia while the governments of Europe were still shocked by the assassinations at Sarajevo. In Germany, the Chief of Staff, General Moltke, continued his health cure at the spa of Karlsbad. Admiral Tirpitz stayed away from Berlin and the Kaiser departed on his yacht to cruise in the North Sea. Everything was done to avoid an air of crisis, to camouflage the impending Habsburg action. Why? It could only have been to allay British, Russian and French suspicions that Germany secretly stood behind Austria–Hungary. A diplomatic triumph for Austria–Hungary and Germany was still preferable to war. Europe was to be faced with a sudden *fait accompli*.

What went wrong? In Vienna the ministers were not unanimous, even after receiving the German assurances. Count Tisza, the powerful Hungarian Prime Minister, remained opposed to war at their meeting on 7 July and the following week gave way only on condition that the Dual Monarchy first agreed not to annex any Serbian territory after the expected victory. Tisza, a Magyar, wanted to see no more Slavs added to the population of the empire. Then there was further delay as the army asked for more time. Berchtold used it to compile a justificatory dossier of Serbia's recent wrongdoings for presentation to the chancelleries of Europe when the time for action eventually came. Then Berchtold decided to wait until the French President, Poincaré, and the French Prime Minister, René Viviani, had ended their visit to St Petersburg. Thereby he hoped that Austria would act at the very moment when Russia would find it more difficult to consult her French ally.

More than three weeks had now elapsed since the assassination of Francis Ferdinand at Sarajevo. The Austrians had worked in greatest secrecy, and Europe had been lulled into a false sense of calm. On 23 July the Austro-Hungarian ultimatum was presented in Belgrade, and in just six days Europe plunged headlong from peace to certain war. On 25 July, Serbia mobilised her army and, in a cleverly worded reply later that day, appeared to accept many of the Austrian demands, although not to the point of submitting Serbia to Austrian supervision. The same evening, the Austro-Hungarian Ambassador left Belgrade and Austria–Hungary mobilised against Serbia. Even though the Austro-Hungarian army would not be ready for another three weeks, Austria–Hungary declared war on 28 July, and to make war irrevocable bombarded Belgrade on 29 July.

Between the break of diplomatic relations and the actual declaration of war, Sir Edward Grey attempted mediation and sent proposals to Berlin in an attempt to preserve the peace of Europe. Bethmann Hollweg wanted no such interference and Grey's efforts came to nothing. When the Kaiser learnt how the Serbians had replied to the ultimatum, he was personally delighted. So much for the myth that he was thirsting to go to war. He immediately wrote a note on the morning of 28 July from his palace in Potsdam, expressing his evident relief that now there was no longer any need for war – 'On the whole the wishes of the Danube Monarchy have been acceded to, every cause for war has vanished' – and he added that he was ready to mediate. But by then Bethmann Hollweg and Berchtold had instigated the Austro-Hungarian declaration of war on Serbia which the Kaiser heard about later that day. Bethmann Hollweg now made every effort to localise the war. On 30 July, he urged Vienna to exchange views with St Petersburg. He resisted calls for mobilisation in Berlin and he initiated the Kaiser's personal telegrams appealing to the Tsar not to mobilise.

The weak Tsar was under pressure from his own military advisers to mobilise. The French military, too, were urging mobilisation and the French Ambassador in St Petersburg, Maurice Paléologue,

Europe in 1914
ICELAND
FINLAND
NORWAY
SWEDEN
Helsinki
GREAT BRITAIN &
IRELAND
Oslo
Stockholm
ATLANTIC
OCEAN
NORTH
SEA
RUSSIA
DENMARK
Copenhagen
Dublin
NETHER-
LANDS
London
Elbe
Berlin
Warsaw
GERMANY
BELGIUM
Cologne
Seine
Paris
Prague
Rhine
Danube
Vienna
HUNGARY
LUX.
Munich
Budapest
FRANCE
SWITZ.
AUSTRIA
Belgrade
ROMANIA
Rhône
ITALY
Bucharest
PORTUGAL
SERBIA
BULGARIA
Sofia
Madrid
CORSICA
(French)
Rome
MONTE-
NEGRO
SPAIN
SARDINIA
(Italian)
GREECE
TURKEY
GIBRALTAR
(British)
Athens
SICILY
ALBANIA
Spanish Protectorate
DODECANESE
(Italian)
Algiers
Morocco
(French
Protectorate)
ALGERIA
(French)
MEDITERRANEAN SEA
CRETE
(Greek)
Tripoli
CYRENAICA
(Italian)
TUNISIA
(French)
TRIPOLITANIA
(Italian)
EGYPT
0
1000 miles
0
1000 km

pressed their views on the Foreign Minister, Sazonov. The French General Staff was terrified that war would begin in the west and find the Russians unprepared. Russia, if she went to war, could count on French support; the Tsar had known this for certain ever since the visit of President Poincaré and Prime Minister Viviani to St Petersburg (20–23 July). But the Russians, in so vital a question for the empire, would reach their own decisions just as the Austrians had had to do.

The reaction of the Tsar, Sazonov and his ministers was to seek to 'localise' the crisis in a way neither Germany nor Austria–Hungary had in mind. When Bethmann Hollweg spoke of 'localisation', he meant that the Dual Monarchy should be allowed to dictate terms to Serbia. The Tsar and Sazonov, on the other hand, hoped that Germany and the other powers would stand aside while Russia supported Serbia to prevent Austria–Hungary from attacking Serbia. To the Russians, the Austrian ultimatum to Serbia was hurling down the gauntlet. But could Russia risk war now? There was much civil disturbance and there were large-scale strikes; the army would be in a much stronger position three years later. The news of the ultimatum reached Sazonov on the morning of 24 July. His first reaction was to advise the Serbians to surrender to Austrian demands and not to fight. But later that afternoon, the Russian Council of Ministers agreed to recommend to the Tsar a 'partial' mobilisation against Austria–Hungary only. Russian involvement in the fate of Serbia was also officially announced. The line was now to put pressure on Austria–Hungary.

The following day, 25 July, the Tsar at an imperial council confirmed the need for preparatory military measures in anticipation of partial mobilisation. By 26 July, these secret preparations were in full swing. The news of the Austrian declaration of war on Serbia and bombardment of Belgrade on 29 July threw St Petersburg into a frenzy. The Tsar agreed to a general mobilisation, but after receiving the Kaiser's telegram changed this to a 'partial mobilisation', against Austria only. In reality, though, the Tsar's motive was to avoid pushing Germany into mobilisation – partial or total made no difference, for the Austro-Hungarian–German alliance and campaign plans would necessitate German mobilisation anyway. It was too late in Berlin to continue playing the game of 'localising' the Austro-Serbian war. With the military in Berlin now also in a frenzy, Moltke insisting on the need to mobilise, Bethmann Hollweg and the Kaiser could not resist the 'military imperative' much longer. On 31 July, the Russian military persuaded the Tsar that a 'partial mobilisation' was technically impossible, and Nicholas II consented to general mobilisation. But the nature of German military planning had made war inevitable after the Russian partial mobilisation on 29 July.

The very concept of the Schlieffen Plan was responsible for the situation that mobilisation meant war. Its implications may not have been grasped fully by the Kaiser and Bethmann Hollweg in July. But in militaristic Wilhelmine Germany, the generals' views on military necessity were conclusive. Until the moment of Russian mobilisation, Moltke, the Chief of Staff, was ready to leave control to Chancellor Bethmann Hollweg. But, when on 30 July it became clear that the Chancellor's policy of frightening Russia into acquiescence had failed, there was not a moment to lose. France had to be defeated before Russia could complete her mobilisation. The German onslaught must now start without delay against Belgium and France. Ultimatums were sent to Russia and France and war was declared with unseemly haste on Russia on 1 August 1914, on France two days later. The German invasion of Belgium was followed by a British ultimatum and declaration of war on 4 August.

It was the same Schlieffen Plan which was responsible for forcing the pace in St Petersburg and Paris. That the Germans would at the outset turn the mass of their armies against France and not Russia was known. The Russian–French military plans were constructed accordingly, with the promise of an early Russian offensive to relieve pressure on the French. That is why the French military were so worried about 'partial mobilisation' against Austria–Hungary. In the event of war they wanted Russia's military effort to be directed against the main enemy, Germany. No wonder Paléologue was urging full mobilisation in St Petersburg. In this way was Bethmann Hollweg's diplomatic 'offensive' matched by the offensive strategy of the German General Staff with its aim of destroying the French will to resist by seeking total victory in the west.

Behind the 'governments' – the handful of men who made the decisions in Berlin, Vienna, Paris and St Petersburg – stood populations willing to fight for Republic, King and Emperor. Only a tiny minority dissented. For the largest Socialist Party

To Arms. Marching off to war with no conception of what lay in store for them, everybody expected that the war would be over and the troops home by Christmas. In August 1914, all the combatants looked equally optimistic – witness the French, left, *and the Germans,* right. *Even in 1917, the soldiers of the last nation to enter the First World War – the United States – still seemed gleeful, despite being poorly trained and ill-equipped* (top).

in Europe, the German, the war was accepted as being fought against tsarist Russian aggression. The different nationalities of the Dual Monarchy all fought for the Habsburgs, the French socialists fought as enthusiastically in defence of their fatherland ruthlessly invaded by the Germans.

The responsibility for starting the conflict in July and August must rest primarily on the shoulders of Germany and Austria–Hungary. Russia and France reacted and chose to fight rather than to withdraw from the confrontation, which would have left the diplomatic victory to Germany and Austria–Hungary. Whether they had wisely interpreted their national interests is another question. For Britain it was a preventive war. Not directly threatened by Germany, Britain was looking to the future and what that future would hold for her if Germany were able to gain the mastery of continental Europe. But Britain's was a 'preventive' war in quite a different sense to Germany's. The British government had done everything possible to prevent war from breaking out, but could not afford to stand aside.

Yet Britain cannot be absolved from blame. War broke out in 1914 not only as a consequence of the shots at Sarajevo. The tensions that had been building up in Europe and the wider world for two decades and more had created the frame of mind that led the European chancelleries along a fatal path. For Britain, faced with the relative decline of her power, the problem of defending her empire loomed ever larger. She negotiated a division of interests with France of territory – Morocco and Egypt – that did not exclusively belong to either. Russia also was appeased for a time. Inevitably fears and hostilities in Europe were raised. British foreign secretaries were well aware of this and would have preferred it not to be so. But Britain's immediate interests were placed before international harmony. That is the darker thread that ran through British policy. During the last decade before the war Britain too tended to follow Bismarckian *Realpolitik*. Just as she wanted to avoid imperial clashes with Russia, so too Britain feared that the entente with France might not prove strong enough to prevent Germany and France reaching a settlement of their differences. Then Britain would have been isolated in the world. British policy was too compromised to allow Grey in the summer of 1914 a strong mediating role. But, given German war plans and the small size of the British army at the outset, the hope that London might influence decisively the course of events in Europe during July 1914 was an illusion anyway.

Nowhere were domestic political considerations the decisive influence. The war was about national power, and ambitions, and also fears as to how national power would in the future be exercised. Russia was not satisfied with her already huge empire. France was conscious of her secondary status in Europe which, if she were left without an ally, would leave her at Germany's mercy. Austria–Hungary wished to annihilate Slav hostility beyond her frontiers. For imperial Germany, a future in which her military power was no longer superior to the combined military forces of her potential enemies was not to be tolerated. This had to be averted by diplomacy or so-called 'preventive' war. Germany's own diplomacy had contributed much to the French and British feelings of insecurity. It had finally placed her in the unenviable position of being on bad relations with her neighbours in the east and the west. The working out of the Schlieffen Plan saddled her with the guilt of violating a small neutral state and with the necessity to strike the first blow, for it was Germany who had to declare war in order to keep to the timetable of the famous war plan. What the coming of the war in 1914 reveals is how a loss of confidence and fears for the future can be as dangerous to peace as the naked spirit of aggression that was to be the cause of the Second World War a quarter of a century later. A handful of European leaders in 1914 conceived national relationships crudely in terms of power and conflict, and the future in terms of a struggle for survival in competition for the world. For this, millions had to suffer and die.

PART II

The Response of China and Japan to Western Dominance

CHAPTER 10

China in Disintegration, 1900–1929

About one-fifth of humanity lives in China, the most populous nation of the world. But until the nineteenth century, though in touch with the West, China followed her own path of historical development unaffected by Western contact. Some features of this historical development are remarkable.

The hugeness of China in land area and population makes it all the more extraordinary that for more than a thousand years a concept of unity was maintained. Other peoples were absorbed as China expanded. The ethnic origin of some of these peoples survives to the present day in the form of national minorities with which about one in eighteen Chinese identify – though intermarriage has obliterated the majority. In traditional China, to be considered Chinese was not a matter of race or nationality in the Western sense but depended on an acceptance of Chinese customs and culture. Those who did not accept them – even people within Chinese frontiers – were considered 'barbarian'. The living traditions of Chinese culture were so strong that they absorbed the alien peoples who conquered China and so turned them into Chinese. These included the Mongol dynasty and, in the mid-seventeenth century, the Manchus who ruled from then until the revolution of 1911 as the Ch'ing dynasty. Foreign peoples were incorporated by conquest or else absorbed by China when they conquered the empire from without. The political and cultural continuity of China persisted, overcoming periods of internal rebellion and war: integration, not disintegration, was the dominant theme of more than a millennium of Chinese history until the mid-nineteenth century. But how should historians interpret the century that followed?

If we stop the clock in 1925 it would certainly seem that the disintegration of China had proceeded so far that the long tradition of the national unity of the Chinese Empire could never be restored. It was then a country torn by internal strife, economically bound to the West and Japan, yet without significant progress, as far as the mass of Chinese were concerned, to show for Western economic penetration, politically divided, and with parts of China dominated by foreign powers. From the later Ch'ing period in the 1840s until the close of the civil war in 1949, China knew no peace and passed through a number of phases of disintegration which no single ruler who followed the Ch'ing dynasty after 1911 could halt. But from the perspective of the 1990s the picture looks quite different again. The Chinese Empire is unified once more and has reasserted her right to recover territories once Chinese or over which suzerainty was asserted. Tibet has been reabsorbed already. After the Second World War, China wanted to eliminate all foreign penetration and special privileges in her country – Japanese, Russian, British, American, French and Portuguese. But the total eradication of foreign rights and settlements secured by earlier 'unequal' treaties could not be achieved in 1945 or 1949. The British Crown Colony of Hong Kong, as it turned out, proved of inestimable economic value as a trading partner. Nevertheless, faced with the expiry in 1997 of the lease of the so-called New Lands (without which the rest of Hong Kong would become untenable), China successfully insisted on regaining sovereignty over the whole colony. China now takes her place among the world's great powers and her rulers control the whole of mainland China. The ancient traditions of China were overlaid by Western democratic ideals, coupled with national self-assertion, imperial claims and after 1917 the ideology of Marxism, influences which were in many respects antagonistic to one another. Yet there has evolved, too, some common ground: it seems as if China has absorbed some features from each to form a unique Chinese blend, in which one constant is a readiness to change and modify. But in the process China has been transformed.

The essence of the traditional culture of China, dating from the age of Confucius in the sixth century before Christ, was to emphasise the wholeness of the universe in which the ultimate goal of all people was to strive together to achieve harmony and universal peace. Harmony was to be attained by the individual's virtue and understanding, and by the right ordering of the family where the older enjoyed seniority over the younger, and men over women, and every member of the family accepted his or her obligations and responsibilities; the right ordering of the state would then follow. The theory of state was based on the family, on the affection between its members, extended to relationships between families to the community and between communities to the whole empire. The ruler of the empire ruled by the Mandate of Heaven. By his deeds he showed whether he enjoyed that mandate and when the people deemed that he did not, then it was their duty to rebel and to depose their ruler. The Confucian tradition is idealistic: it is centred not in religion and a belief in a God creator assuming an entity separate from the wholeness of the universe, but in humanity and a concern to bring about harmonious relationships between each individual and between rulers and ruled. It emphasises virtue and happiness and the values of humanism. Its focus is on the individual family unit tilling its soil; and in a vast land overwhelmingly peopled by peasants it thus strengthened local economic and social responsibility. But the millions of family units were part of a whole ruled over by an emperor and his officials. This was the utopian vision of harmony.

The emperor's role was that of a virtuous head of his family of all the Chinese people; and as a father his powers were not restricted. In practice his powers were delegated to the class of scholar–officials, China's unique contribution to government, an elite group selected by a system of examinations and drawn from each region of the empire in proportion to the population. A body of censors was responsible for investigating corruption in administration. In the localities a gentry, again selected by examinations rather than birth, acted as intermediaries between the imperial officials and the people, holding the people under their influence and raising local defence forces for their protection whenever necessary. The Confucian spirit extolled contentment rather than change and development, and it is a mistake to apply Western yardsticks of progress and technical innovation or use them to make contrasts unfavourable to Chinese history. Within traditional technology China coped with almost a tripling of her population from 150 million in 1700 to 420 million by the early nineteenth century, maintaining living standards just above subsistence level at all times, except when natural disasters struck. Does that compare so unfavourably with contemporary efforts by the less economically developed parts of the Indian continent, Africa and Latin America where population increases lead to famine, and natural disasters to death?

In the nineteenth century a double crisis threatened the cohesion and stability of China and undermined traditional China and the rule of the Ch'ing dynasty. A great blow to central authority was the defeat of the Manchu Ch'ing dynasty by the invasion of the 'barbarians' of the West. The West saw an opportunity to trade in China and made wars to force their way in. The British fought the Opium Wars (1839–42) and China ceded her territory (Hong Kong) and was forced to accept the opening of her trade to Britain. An even more fundamental cause of unrest was that population growth was no longer matched by an increase in the lands under cultivation. Amid the general distress occurred the greatest rising in world history – the Taiping Rebellion of 1850–64 – which led to huge destruction and to the loss of between 20 and 30 million lives. The rising was mastered in the end by gentry-led regional armies. China was thereby pushed along a path where regional independence and strength asserted themselves against central authority. During this period and later in the nineteenth century other Western nations followed the British example and secured concessions; and so began a process whereby the Western powers acquired territorial settlements, colonies, leases, rights to trade in 'treaty ports', and concessions in some eighty towns on the coast and inland. The foreigners not only enjoyed immunity from Chinese government but in their settlements in effect ruled over the Chinese inhabitants as well. The largest, the foreign settlements of Shanghai, in 1928 comprised a Chinese population of more than 1 million subordinated to 35,000 Westerners. China was not only defeated and forced to accept the 'unequal treaties' by the West, but during the last decade of the nineteenth century was attacked by Japan as well.

The impact of the West and Japan as well as China's internal upheavals led Chinese intellectuals to question China's future role. Yet their initial reaction was to seek to preserve Chinese traditions. China should strengthen herself through the adoption of Western industrial and military techniques. But little real headway could be made materially. It was not Confucian tradition which blocked the path but economic reality. China remained a peasant society with a surface scratch of industrial development, largely in the foreign-dominated enclaves. The movement of 'self-strengthening' was nowhere near sufficient to counter the forces of disintegration. The Ch'ing dynasty under the formidable Empress Dowager Tz'u-hsi attempted in a last spasm to adopt Western techniques in government and education, but always with the underlying conservative purpose of strengthening traditional China. The reforms were undertaken in the wake of the disastrous Boxer rising of 1900, which attempted to throw out Western influence – economic, political, territorial and religious – by force and was in its turn crushed by a Western international army joined by the Japanese. China was placed further in debt to the West and lost control over even more territory since the Russians refused to leave northern China and Manchuria. Then the Chinese had to stand aside as Russia and Japan in 1904 and 1905 fought each other for dominance over this portion of China (page 58). China was breaking apart into foreign spheres of influence; simultaneously the regions were asserting their autonomy from central government. In 1908 the Empress died and the strength of the Ch'ing dynasty was spent. If the misery of the condition of the country and its people could prove such a thing, then the Ch'ing dynasty had lost its Heavenly Mandate.

Among the small group of conservative intellectuals and administrators there were some who under the impact of the experience of their own lifetime looked at the world beyond China more realistically and knowledgeably. They contrasted Japanese success in maintaining national independence, in throwing off discriminatory treaties in their homeland and in inflicting military defeat on a great Western power with China's weakness and helplessness. China had, in theory, preserved her sovereignty over all but small portions of her empire. The reality, however, was different since foreigners controlled her commerce, built her railways and established industries under their ownership. (Here, though, it is necessary to distinguish the few Westerners who were dedicated to serving the interests of China as they saw them. These were officials like Robert Hart, head of the Maritime Customs Service, who warned in the aftermath of the Boxer rising that the Western powers should take care how they treated the Chinese: 'a China in arms will be a big power at some future day', he wrote; the Western powers should make sure that 'the China of the future might have something to thank us for and not to avenge'.) There were some Chinese reformers who sensed that China stood at the parting of the ways. China could emulate Japan or suffer the fate of India and south-east Asia, then part of the colonial empires of the Dutch, the British and the French.

Many of these reformers had received part of their education in Japan or the West. Yan Fu, one of the most important, spent time not only in Japan but also in England. In his writings he contrasted the Chinese ideals of harmony and stability with Western encouragement of the thrusting individual, competition and the goal of progress. Yan Fu translated into Chinese seminal Western works on politics and the economy, books by T. H. Huxley, John Stuart Mill and Adam Smith among them. His translations and his own advocacy stimulated demands for a break with Confucian traditions and the adoption of a Western-style form of constitutional government. Another reformer of great influence in the first decade of the twentieth century was Liang Qichao, the intellectual leader of the

China looks to the West.

young Chinese progressives, who wrote extensively about Western political leaders and thinkers in the hope of opening up a new world to the Chinese and thus transforming them into a new people. In its last years, not so much directly influenced by the reformers but reacting to the same stimuli – a desire to strengthen China against the foreigner – the Ch'ing dynasty promulgated reforms thick and fast, promising the gradual introduction of constitutional government, a process which when set in motion was to lead to its own downfall and the revolution of 1911.

Thousands of students in the first decade of the twentieth century travelled and studied abroad. Their ideas were far more radical than those of the reformers. Their goal was a revolution against the 'foreign' Ch'ing dynasty and the establishment of a republic. They identified with another Western-educated revolutionary, Dr Sun Yat-sen. A farmer's son, like many Chinese he had emigrated abroad joining, at the age of twelve, his brothers in Hawaii. He was educated in a British missionary school there and, later, in Hong Kong, where he graduated in medicine. He did not practise long as a doctor, instead seeing that his task was to awaken China to revolution. In breach of Chinese tradition, Sun Yat-sen encouraged the Chinese to view themselves as a distinctive race. The removal of the foreign Manchu Ch'ing dynasty provided a focus for the revolutionary movement. Sun Yat-sen wished to create a modern Chinese nation state, with a constitution based on that of the United States together with some Chinese traditions grafted on to it such as a control branch of government – the old censors, under a new name. In Japan he founded the revolutionary League of Common Alliance, an organised political movement which in 1912 joined with other groups to form the Kuomintang or Nationalist Party. Not until after his death in 1925, however, did the Kuomintang play a leading role in China's history.

Sun Yat-sen summed up his political programme and aims in three principles: first, the restoration of the Chinese identity, which came to mean the removal of both the 'foreign' Manchu dynasty and foreign imperialism. China, Sun Yat-sen said, lacked a national spirit; the 400 million people of China were 'just a heap of loose sand', and China the weakest and poorest nation – 'other men are the carving knife and serving dish; we are the fish and meat'. China must seek its salvation by espousing nationalism and so avert the catastrophe of 'China being lost and our people being eliminated'. The foreign oppression, he pointed out, was not just political, which was easily recognised, but economic, transforming China 'into a colony of the foreign powers'. The second principle was democracy, by which he meant the creation of a strong executive central power and the ultimate sovereignty of the people expressed in an electoral process. The third principle, socialism, was the vaguest; in theory it stood for landownership equalisation and some state control to prevent the abuse of monopoly capitalist power, but since the Kuomintang drew support from businessmen, the principle was blurred. Sun Yat-sen developed these ideas throughout his political life though in his own lifetime they found little application.

The advocates of Westernisation always faced one serious emotional and intellectual problem. The very people they wished to emulate showed their belief in Chinese inferiority. Foreign residents, whether missionaries or merchants, only too frequently looked down on the Chinese, regarding their culture as pagan. The roles of the civilised and the barbarians were reversed. In Shanghai there were parks reserved exclusively for the Westerners, characteristic of the racial prejudice of the time. The Christian missionaries saw themselves engaged in saving souls otherwise lost to heathen ways. So the Chinese reacted to Western ways with both admiration and intense hostility. The political and economic behaviour of the Western powers could only strengthen that hostility.

The course of the revolution of 1911, which soon

ended the monarchy, was not determined by Sun Yat-sen, though a Chinese republic did come into being. A strong Chinese nation dedicated to the objectives of his loose Alliance movement did not emerge when the revolution had succeeded in its first task of overthrowing the Manchus. The membership of Sun Yat-sen's party amounted to only a few thousand within China. More significant in determining the subsequent course of events were the men of influence in the provinces – the merchants and the gentry – who took advantage of constitutional reform to assert the independence of the provinces in the newly elected assemblies. The spark for starting the revolution was provided by a rising of a small group of revolutionary soldiers in Wuchang in central China in October 1911 with only the weakest links with Sun Yat-sen's Alliance. Sun Yat-sen at the time was in Denver in the United States. The rising could easily have been suppressed. But so weak had the power of the central government become that province after province in October and November 1911 declared its independence from the central court government. Hostility to the dynasty was widespread. The court turned to Yuan Shikai, recently a governor-general of a northern province, where he had built up a modern Chinese Northern Army.

Yuan Shikai was in retirement when the revolution broke out; the dynasty saw him now as the only man considered capable of commanding the loyalty of the officers of the Northern Army, whose military strength might still re-establish the dynasty's authority. Yuan Shikai, however, was determined to be his own master. He negotiated with the revolutionaries. They agreed to his assuming the presidency of the Chinese republic provided he could secure the abdication of the Ch'ing dynasty. In February 1912 the abdication decree was published and in March 1912 Yuan Shikai became the first president of China as the man most acceptable to the provincial gentry and merchants. These men were basically conservative, and Sun Yat-sen's revolutionary movement was abhorrent to them. There was to be no social revolution. The republic and its new parliament representing the unity of China were frail institutions. During the last four years of Yuan Shikai's life, from 1912 to 1916, he ruled more and more as a military dictator through the army and shortly before his death attempted to revive the monarchy with himself as emperor. Through his hold over the army, the provinces were unable to assert complete independence from Peking. But Yuan Shikai could establish no genuine national unity and with his death the disintegration of China accelerated.

The years from 1916 to 1928 mark the warlord era in modern Chinese history. To the outside world the republic of China was governed from Peking. In reality this was just one of the hundreds of governments, each headed by a warlord with a personal army which had gained control of an area sometimes small, sometimes covering a whole province. The warlords intrigued and fought each other in hundreds of wars throughout twelve years of constant strife and bloodshed. The peasants suffered from pillage, tax oppression, destruction of their property and bloodshed. But during this bleak period a continuous process of state-building also took place.

This same period, however, also saw more positive developments. The combination of China's misfortunes internal and external welded together a new national movement which tried to recapture the objectives set by Sun Yat-sen but totally disregarded after the revolution of 1911.

Foreign encroachments on Chinese integrity provoked the strongest reaction among the young students and intellectuals. Peking University became the centre of the intellectual ferment and participated in what became known as the New Culture Movement. Japan's Twenty-one Demands in January 1915 took advantage of the preoccupation of the European powers with winning the war in Europe to demand of the Chinese government its practical subordination to Japan (page 89). In China they were met with a storm of protest. An even greater outburst of indignation greeted the decisions of the Paris Peace Conference in 1919. China was an ally, yet Japan had been accorded the right to take over Germany's extensive concessions in the province of Shantung, and the warlord government in Peking, representing China, had accepted this transfer of what was after all still Chinese territory.

The fourth of May 1919 is an important date in the history of modern China. It was later seen as marking the moment when China reasserted her national identity once more in angry response to imperialism. Some 3000 students in Peking University launched a national protest movement which took its name from that date. The government had arrested some students and the protest was directed equally against the government and national humiliation. In the burst of publications that followed, the May the Fourth movement had a powerful effect on stimulating the young intellectuals to reject the social and political traditions of old China, including the Confucian ideals of duty and filial obedience and the subordination of women. A boycott of Japanese goods in turn led to the organisation of Chinese labour in the ports. But the intellectual revolution also had a divisive effect as the mass of the countryside and the peasantry was virtually untouched by the fever for change.

During the warlord period there occurred not only the intellectual ferment making a decisive break with the traditional past but also the revival of one political party, the Kuomintang, and the establishment of a new party, the Communist Party; their rivalry divided China during the 1930s and 1940s. They began by joining forces, the communists in obedience to orders from Moscow. Then in the 1930s and 1940s they fought a triangular struggle – together against the Japanese invader, and also against each other. That struggle reached its climax during the years following the defeat of Japan in 1945 and China was once more divided by civil war. In 1949 the era of war ended at last and mainland China was set on the course of national unity. So although the actual power the Kuomintang and the Communist Party exerted beyond their base in Canton was weak in the early 1920s, and they

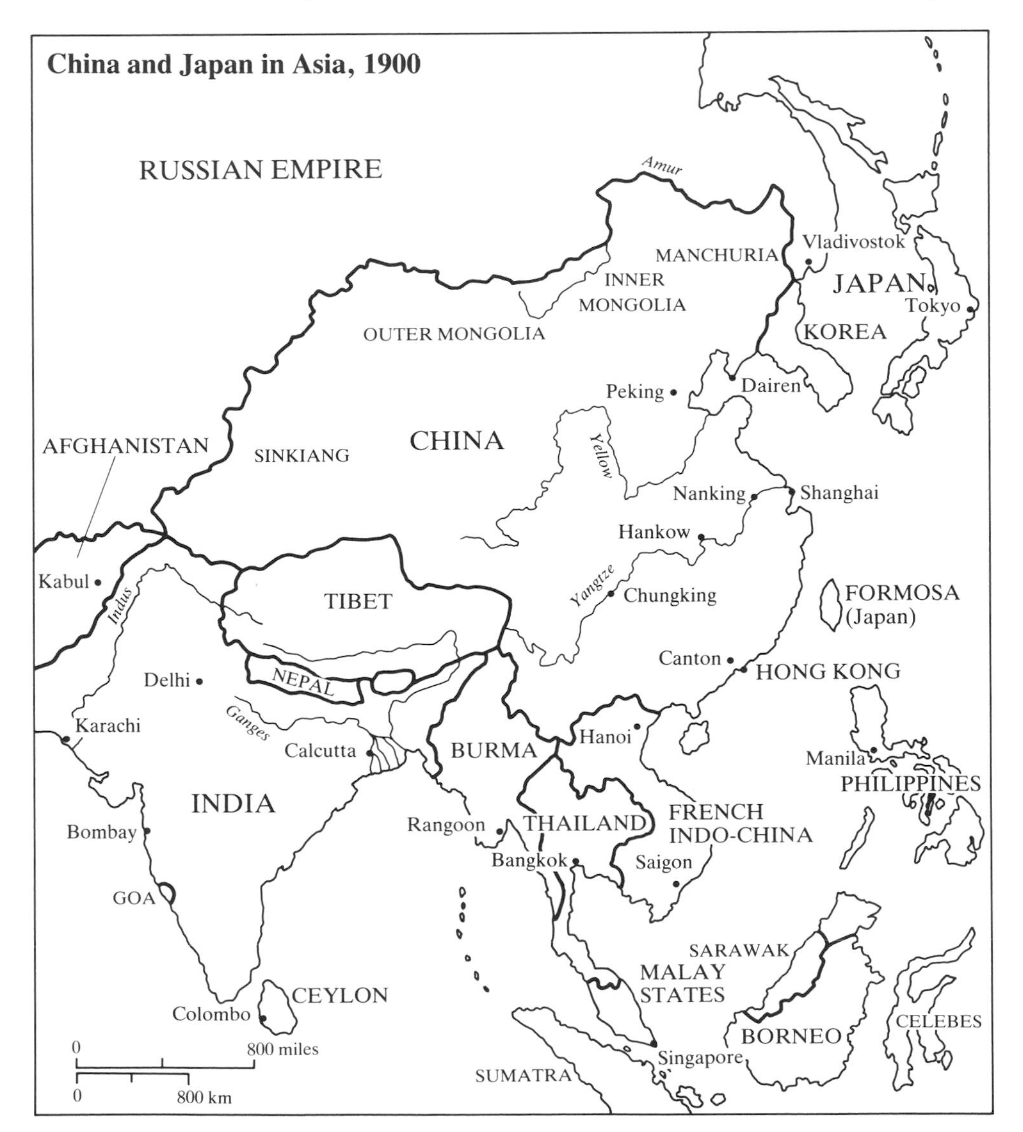

too were dependent on the protection of a warlord, they emerged to dominate contemporary Chinese history.

In 1923 Sun Yat-sen was looking for ways to strengthen his enfeebled Kuomintang Party, which was nominally ruling Canton but in reality was dependent on the local warlord. He turned for help to the tiny Communist Party, numbering less than a thousand members. The Comintern welcomed any opportunity to strike a blow against Western imperialism and agents were sent from Moscow. The co-operation of Sun Yat-sen and his Russian advisers soon bore fruit. Sun Yat-sen adapted his principles to the new situation and the Comintern ordered the Chinese communists not to form an alliance but to subordinate their interests and fuse with the Kuomintang. The communists, now forming the left wing of the Kuomintang, never lost their sense of identity. The party, with the help of Russian advice, was reorganised, and communist influence among Chinese labour working for Western interests rapidly grew; strikes were fomented and supported. In the countryside too the Kuomintang made headway among the peasants in encouraging the seizure of landlord's land.

The right wing of the Kuomintang controlled the national revolutionary army it was organising. The task was assigned to one of Sun Yat-sen's loyal young followers, Chiang Kai-shek. In 1923 Chiang Kai-shek went to Moscow to study the new Soviet Red Army. On his return he was placed in charge of training the officers of the Kuomintang's revolutionary army. In 1925 Sun Yat-sen died. There was no obvious successor. For a time the party continued under a collective leadership amid increasing strains between the left and the right. But Chiang Kai-shek soon made clear his opposition to the left of the Kuomintang. Chiang Kai-shek turned against the socialist plans of his communist allies. He also vied for the assistance of the propertied and for help from the West. Meanwhile the communists in following Moscow's orders fared disastrously. In April 1927 the Nationalists and their supporters crushed organised workers in Shanghai and shot protesters. In the countryside peasant risings were bloodily put down. By the end of that year the break between the communists and Nationalists was complete. Driven out of the towns, the communists establised base areas in remote regions. Mao Zedong, then in his thirties, created the most important in Jiangxi. Here the Red army was trained by Zhou Enlai and taught to help and not plunder the peasants. Other significant reforms ended the sale of girls into forced marriages, while the peasants' greatest need was land reform. After five years, surrounded by Chiang's forces, the base became untenable. Daringly at night on 16 October 1934, leaving behind a rearguard and the sick and wounded, the communists broke through the encirclement and fought their way north for six thousand miles on the epic 'Long March'. Yet it was not civil war that dominated the 1930s but the Japanese invasion in 1937. Once more, fervent national feelings created a sense of unity in resisting the brutal aggressor. Before his decisive breach he utilised the strength of the communists to support the northern military expedition started in 1926 to convert what was a local government into a national one. It was a tremendous feat to sweep successfully north from their base in southern China to Peking. There was some hard fighting; some warlords agreed to accept Chiang Kai-shek's authority on behalf of the Nationalist government now established in a new capital in Nanking.

Chiang Kai-shek took care at this stage not to offend the Western powers in China. He smashed the anti-Western movement of the communists in the Kuomintang. He set himself as his first task to gain military control over China. But, though his success had been astonishing, he had not broken the power of all the warlords and by the close of the 1920s controlled less than half of China. In 1930 he quelled a rising in the north in large-scale battles. Thereafter the remaining warlords and Chiang Kai-shek's government agreed to tolerate each other. China was far more unified, but a new military struggle was opening up between the Kuomintang and the communists. Simultaneously Japan took advantage of China's weakness to seize Manchuria in 1931. In the end Chiang Kai-shek, faced with the Japanese war and simultaneous civil conflict with the communists, failed to create the national unity of China which was Sun Yat-sen's testament to his followers.

CHAPTER 11

The Emergence of Japan, 1900–1929

The continent of Asia can be divided into three regions, each in a different relationship to the West. Southern and south-east Asia was, by the close of the nineteenth century, partitioned by the European powers and the United States and constituted the most populous and important parts of the Western world empires. In eastern Asia, China had fallen under a different kind of Western control, remaining semi-independent, but with large areas under foreign economic control, while some parts of China had also fallen under foreign territorial control. Also part of eastern Asia were the islands of Japan.

Japan's history is strikingly different from the rest of Asia. Japan had been forced open by the American warships of Commodore Perry in the mid-nineteenth century and exposed to the pressures of the Western powers backed by guns. They refused to permit Japan to follow her own course in isolation and demanded, as a Western right, that Japan open her markets to trade with the West. The rulers of Japan, the Tokugawa Shoguns, could not match the military power of the West and so had to concede. After 200 years of virtual isolation, imposed by the Shoguns to protect her from Western influence, Japan then lay exposed and virtually helpless. Like China, she was forced to accede to 'unequal treaties', providing Western merchants with economic advantages and special territorial privileges which set aside Japan's sovereign rights, but unlike China, she was allowed to ban opium. Half a century later, by the early twentieth century, the Western powers agreed to abrogate the 'unequal treaties' and Japan developed a military power not only capable of defeating her much larger neighbour, China, but also one of the Western great powers, Russia. The foundations of a modern state had been laid and Japan stood on the threshold of replacing Western dominance in eastern Asia. By the fourth quarter of the twentieth century, though her military power was modest and her Asian territorial empire broken by the West, Japan had become an industrial superpower second only to the United States.

Japan was the only Asian nation to achieve this astonishing transformation within the short span of a little more than a hundred years from the 1860s to the 1990s. But the perspective of the 1990s should not lead us to the conclusion that Japan represents a unique progressiveness among the otherwise stagnant and overwhelmingly peasant societies of Asia. Today, for instance, Taiwan, Singapore and South Korea are showing that they are capable of following Japan's industrial 'miracle', mainland China's growth is also accelerating. In the later nineteenth century the Japanese reformers, reacting to the West, tended to think of 'Western' as one overall formula for human progress and national power. Everything was seen as part of this same phenomenon and there was at first little understanding of what differentiated the Western nations from each other socially, politically or economically. So too, the West used to think of Asia's history in an undifferentiated way. The 'slowness' of

China's 'modernisation' was sometimes compared with the speed of Japan's, thereby applying the same Western yardstick to two totally different societies, the one a vast land empire of 420 million people at the turn of the century, the other a group of compact islands with a population of some 30 million. The contrast of physical conditions, even leaving aside questions of culture and historical development, is far greater than that between the British Isles and Russia. Even to compare Russia and China is likely to lead to fog rather than illumination. That is not to deny that there are common cultural influences which affected Asia, just as there are common features of Western culture.

Japan from the sixth century onwards owed much to the Korean and Chinese civilisations adopting and adapting the religions of China – Buddhism of Indian origin and Chinese Taoism – and the philosophy of Confucius. Indeed some aspects of Confucianism, with its emphasis on hierarchical family relationships and the obligations owed to those more senior, retained a stronger hold in modern Japan than in China. The Tokugawa shoguns had been the real rulers of feudal Japan since the early seventeenth century with the emperors fulfilling largely ceremonial functions. The shoguns sought to preserve a static, hierarchical society dominated by the warrior caste of *samurai*, a Japan free from the contagion of the outside world. For two and a half centuries they appeared to succeed. Confucianism with its emphasis on the duty inferiors owed to their superiors and the ideal of harmony in a hierarchical society was an ideology well suited to the shogunate. According to the Confucian ideal the officials' task was to enrich and enlighten the people; in practice they acted as the bureaucracy of an authoritarian state. At the same time the ruling elites of Japan, though imbued with the conservative Confucian beliefs, also showed themselves open to new ideas where they demonstrably contributed to the increase of wealth. Economic and social change from the early nineteenth century on, however, eroded the orderly traditional society. To internal strains were added external ones all pointing to the need for a stronger state, an ending of the shogunate era and a centralised nation built around a restored monarch.

The urgent need for such strengthening was brought home to the Japanese by the forcible appearance of the West. Japan's response under the last of the Shoguns was to make an effort to catch up with Western military technology. The industrialisation of Japan had its beginning not in the setting up of a textile mill, but in a shipyard in 1863 capable of building steam warships. The process was much accelerated after the 1868 revolution known as the Meiji Restoration. The requirements of armaments and attempts to gain self-sufficiency created the Osaka Ironworks (1881) and at about the same time steel-making by the Krupp method was started. Heavy industry was expanded originally to meet these national defence needs before a single railway line was constructed. National defence never lost this primacy of concern in Japan, at least not until after the Second World War. Her population lived in compact territories which made arousing a sense of national consciousness and patriotism easier than in the vast area of China. The revolution which overthrew the Shogunate and started the Meiji era was a turning point in this respect too, as in other aspects of the modernisation of Japan. The great feudal domains were abolished and the people were now subject to the imperial government, which strengthened its central authority in many ways in the 1870s and 1880s.

The rapid progress achieved by Japan had its origins nevertheless in the period before 1868. There already existed large groups of educated people – the former warriors (the *samurai*), merchants and craftsmen, who had obtained some Western technological knowledge through contacts at the port of Nagasaki, where the Dutch merchants were allowed to remain under rigid supervision – and they formed a reservoir of people with a capacity to learn and adapt to new Western skills. The revolution of 1868 brought to power a remarkable group of *samurai* statesmen. They restored the monarch to his ancient pinnacle; but the emperor was no mere figurehead. He was advised by a small group, later a council of elders, or *genro*, who wielded enormous power. He listened to their advice, but at times of differences between his *genro* his own views were decisive, and at critical moments of Japanese history the emperor actively used his prerogative as final arbiter. Below the emperor and the *genro* council, which had no formal place in the constitution, a Western structure of government with a prime minister, cabinet and an elected parliament was set up in the last decades of the nineteenth century. Despite the outward style of Western government, Japan was not democratic but was ruled by a few prominent leaders. The Meiji Restoration was no social revolution but a revolution from above.

These Meiji oligarchs presented to the world a picture of a close group acting behind a faceless, godlike emperor. In reality they were men of powerful personality and sometimes fundamentally clashing policies who fought each other when critical decisions, especially on Japan's relations with the rest of the world, had to be reached, both in the *genro* council and through their nominees in the government and in the army and navy. Once the emperor's decision was made, the ruling group accepted this resolution of their conflict. During the last three decades of the nineteenth century some six oligarchs, mainly members of two clans of the Choshu and Satsuma, transformed Japan by introducing widespread changes, military, naval, industrial, economic and educational. The increasing government expenditure and beginnings of industrialisation nurtured by the state, the construction of railways, were all based on the improving productivity of the Japanese farmer. His standard of living was held back, however, to provide the margin of capital for this early industrial modernisation.

By the turn of the century, the young reformers of the 1860s had become elder statesmen. Pre-eminent among this small group were Ito Hirobumi and Yamagata Aritomu. Ito was Japan's elder statesman and the best-known Japanese in the West. He had travelled and studied in the West and was responsible for Japan's representative constitution. Field Marshal Yamagata had created the modern Japanese army, which proved victorious in the wars with China in 1894–5 and with Russia in 1904–5. He was opposed to Ito's policies at home, and Ito's more pacific approach to foreign affairs. In 1909 Ito was assassinated in Korea; soon Yamagata's influence also weakened when after 1914 the surviving *genro* grew old and were replaced by new power groups.

One feature of Japan's emergence as a world power can be discerned from early on: a ruthless disregard for personal pride when it conflicted with the higher interests of national defence and survival in the face of Western pressure. The natural reaction of peoples treated as inferior by the Westerner is to become assertive, even over-assertive, of the worth of their own race. The Japanese became deeply sensitive to issues of race and reacted with anger to American discrimination against Japanese immigration. It was seen as a humiliating slight. Nor did it help when later Hollywood portrayed 'orientals' as crafty and cruel villains. But in the 1880s a Japanese official could write that, if Japan were to survive as a nation, then:

> having accepted the hypothesis that the physical and mental constitution of our Japanese is inferior to that of European peoples, it follows that in the event that we persist on an inferior racial level there is a danger that we may soil the historical record of our blameless Empire. What, then, can we do? The only solution is to improve our racial quality by means of intermarriage [with the white race]. When we marry European women there is an additional benefit in the custom of following a meat diet.

Ito wished to have the expert opinion of the famous Social Darwinist, Herbert Spencer, who tactfully advised against intermarriage since, as he explained, it destroys racial characteristics and breaks down the integrity of personality. (Needless to add, this was all part of the pseudo-racial science of the nineteenth century, an unwarranted extension to human beings of Darwin's theories about animals, the survival of the fittest, namely those best able to adapt to the changing conditions of their physical environment. To seek falsely to apply such observations to human qualities helped to lead to some terrible perversions in the twentieth century.) What Japanese concerns do illustrate is the length to which Japan's leaders were prepared to go to ensure that the Japanese nation should not succumb to the West. This was the mainspring of Japanese thinking and of the policies adopted during the Meiji Restoration and after.

In foreign relations 1895 is a year of great importance for Japan. During the period from the first diplomatic contacts down to 1894 the Japanese had preserved their independence from the West. Indeed a start was made in negotiating treaties with the European powers that would lead in due course to the abrogation of the wounding special treaties. The treaties had placed the Europeans in Japan beyond Japanese authority on the grounds that the Japanese lacked the civilisation to be entrusted with applying their laws to Europeans. But one reason why the West did not attempt to carve out spheres of interests or colonies in Japan as in China is to be found in the fact that the Europeans were impressed by Japanese progress in adopting

Western ways and by their consequent growing strength. But what was more important during these critical early decades was that the West did not regard the commercial possibilities and the market of Japan as nearly as important as China's for the future. Japan's neighbour, tsarist Russia, deliberately rejected a policy of penetrating Japan in favour of the exploitation of China. The same was true of the other Western powers. At the turn of the century the scramble for European concessions was reaching its height in China, and Britain's place as the paramount power in eastern Asia was being challenged. The Colonial Secretary, Joseph Chamberlain, declared, 'our interests in China are so great, our proportion of the trade is so enormous and the potentialities of that trade are so gigantic that I feel no more vital question has ever been presented for the decision . . . of the nation'. The West's image of China protected Japan and contributed to the very different development of the two nations after the incursion of the West into eastern Asia.

In 1895 Japan had just brought to a victorious conclusion a war with China over the question of the suzerainty of Korea. As part of her peace terms she had forced China into territorial concessions. This step by the Japanese into what the European powers wished to keep as their preserve led to an angry reaction by France, Germany and Russia, which demanded that Japan give up her territorial spoils in China. It was with a national sense of humiliation that the Japanese rulers bowed to this pressure.

The Japanese, who had lived at peace with China for close on a thousand years, had learned from the West that a great power must acquire an empire and exercise power beyond the national frontier. But Japan was not treated as an equal. This realisation marks a turning point in the Japanese outlook. It was necessary carefully to study every move; Japan would succeed only by the judicious use of force coupled with guile and then only if the Western powers were divided and so could not combine against her.

A complex two-tier decision-making process developed from 1901, after which time no individual *genro* led the government; policy was first discussed between the different groups in the government and then by the *genro*. This reinforced the tendency to discuss fully all aspects, advantages and disadvantages, of every important policy decision. The Emperor was the supreme authority. The *genro* were expected in the end to submit to him an agreed decision for his formal consent. But in the Meiji era the Emperor's influence was considerable and he could to some degree steer and prolong *genro* discussions on important issues on which there were differences of opinion. In its fullest and most constructive form this deliberate way of reaching group decisions after long and careful discussion lasted until about the First World War, when the advancing age of the surviving *genro* weakened their influence. The influence of Emperor Meiji's descendants did not match his own. His son, whose reign lasted from 1912 to 1926, was weak in health and mind; his grandson, Emperor Hirohito, was supreme only in theory but followed until 1945 the advice of Japan's military and political leaders. The post-Meiji emperors were kept aloof from any real role in the making of decisions. In later decades the Japanese looked back on the Meiji era as a period of brilliant success abroad as well as at home, a golden age.

Japan's policy towards the eastern Asian mainland from 1900 until the outbreak of the Great War in Europe illustrates both circumspection and ultimately boldness. There was an attempt to steer a middle course between the exponents of expansion and the more cautious groups who wished to strengthen Japan in Korea by means of commerce and influence rather than outright territorial control. With the acceptance of the alliance Britain offered in January 1902 – after long debate and scrutiny – the Japanese leaders knew that, if it came to war with Russia, Japan could count on Britain's military help if any other power joined Russia against her. By diplomacy the Japanese had ensured that they would not be blocked by a united European front aligned against her as in 1895. The *genro* decided for war in February 1904. But in launching a war against Russia the mood was not one of arrogance. The Japanese leaders knew they were taking a carefully calculated risk. They hoped to do well enough to gain Japan's most important aims: expansion of territory on the Asian mainland and security for Japan and her empire. Specifically the Japanese were determined to achieve dominance over Korea and southern Manchuria.

The *genro* at the time they decided on war were already considering how the war might be ended in good time. There was no expectation that Russia could be completely defeated. Russia was not

The Russo-Japanese War of 1904–5 as seen from opposing sides. Before the conflict began, the Russians were confident that they would crush the 'yellow devils' easily (left). *The Japanese woodcut* (right) *celebrates a more tangible triumph, the naval victory in the Straits of Tsushima on 27 May 1905.*

brought to the point where she could not have continued the war, although her navy was annihilated and Japan also won spectacular successes on land (page 58). Yet the Japanese too were exhausted by the war and, through President Theodore Roosevelt's mediation, secured a peace treaty which brought them great gains. These gains, however, fell short of their expectations. There were riots in Japan when the peace terms became known in September 1905. The Japanese people wanted Russia to acknowledge defeat by paying reparation. The Russians refused to do so and the *genro* knew that Japan, her financial resources weakened, was in no position to continue the war in the hope of exacting better terms. On 5 September 1905 the Peace of Portsmouth was concluded.

Japan did not use military force again for a quarter of a century and thereby risk all she had gained in her wars with China and with Russia. By the time of the Meiji Emperor's death in 1912, Japan had won international recognition as a great power. Her alliance with Britain was renewed, her 'special' position in northern China acquiesced in, as well as her outright annexation of Korea. Internally too, Japan had made great strides during the forty-five years of the Meiji Emperor's reign.

But on the negative side there were tensions building up in Japan. There was pressure from below among the more prosperous and influential merchants, administrators, landowners and the educated elites, all desiring some share in power; they resented the fact that an entrenched oligarchy ruled Japan from behind the scenes and monopolised all the important positions in the state. Within the oligarchy too there was growing conflict between the party-based governments demanding independence of the *genro*, and the *genro* who advised the emperor on all questions of importance. For a time the *genro* continued to exercise their traditional function. But the army, its prestige raised by success in the Russo-Japanese War, won a new place with the right to present its views to the emperor directly, so bypassing the civilian governments. The remarkable unity that had been achieved during the founding years of the Meiji era under the leadership of the emperor and the *genro* existed no longer in the 1920s and 1930s. Instead, powerful rival groups sought to dominate policy. In the absence of the *genro* and a strong emperor, Japan lacked any supreme body to co-ordinate her domestic and foreign policies. The beginnings of strife between labour and employers was also making itself felt as Japan became more industrialised in the early twentieth century. The educated Japanese became vulnerable to a cultural crisis of identity. Should Japanese ways be rejected totally? Western dress and conformity with Western customs became general among the progressives. There also occurred a nationalist–patriotic reaction. The Japanese elites were obliged to choose between Japanese tradition and Western ways, or to find some personal compromise between the two.

The First World War and its consequences brought about a decisive change in the international power relations of eastern Asia. The period was also one of economic industrial boom for Japan, whose earlier development provided the basis for rapid expansion. Japan benefited, second only to the United States, from the favourable conditions created by the Allies' needs at war and their disappearance as strong competitors in Asian markets. The First World War enabled Japan to emerge as an industrial nation.

Japan joined the Allied side in the war in 1914 after careful deliberation. China, after the revolution of 1911, was showing increasing signs of losing her national cohesion (pages 81–83). For Japan, the war in Europe provided an opportunity to strengthen and extend her position, especially in Manchuria. But behind Japanese expansion there was also a 'defensive' motivation similar to the earlier imperialism of the West and similar as well to fears expressed by American strategic planners (page 49). What would happen when the war was over? The *genro* Yamagata was convinced that the great war among the Western powers would be followed by a global racial struggle, a struggle between 'the yellow and white races'; Japan would therefore have 'to make plans to prevent the establishment of a white alliance against the yellow races'. He looked to friendly relations with Russia and the avoidance of hostility with the United States. Critical was the relationship with China. Here Yamagata sought the best of all worlds: the practical establishment of Japan's senior partnership in a friendly alliance. Japan should seek to 'instil in China a sense of abiding trust in us'. China and Japan, 'culturally and racially alike', might then preserve their identity when competing with the 'so-called culturally advanced white races'. When the Japanese made their Twenty-one Demands on China in 1915, the Chinese naturally regarded the Japanese from quite a different point of view – more as enemies than friends (page 81). In their first form the demands amounted to a claim for a Japanese protectorate, including insistence on employing Japanese 'advisers' in financial, military and administrative affairs in the Chinese government. Until the close of the First World War there was little the Western powers could do to restrain Japan, beyond diplomatic pressure.

In the Taisho (meaning 'great righteousness') era from the Meiji Emperor's death in 1912 until the death of his son in 1926, it seemed that, despite Japanese assertiveness in China during the Great War, the overall trend would be towards greater liberalisation and peace. The *genro* were ceasing to play so critical a role, especially after Yamagata's death in 1922, and one great obstacle towards constitutional parliamentary development was thereby removed. The new Emperor was weak and the powers of the government increased. Yet, as developments after 1926 were to show very clearly, in the end the 'liberal' Taisho period marked only a transition to a more illiberal and authoritarian state than had developed in the Meiji era. There were signs too that Taisho was 'liberal' only in a very restricted sense. Industrial expansion, first fostered by the state, was later handed over to a few large business enterprises still pre-eminent today. These huge business empires, the *zaibatsu*, were conducted paternalistically and required loyalty from their employees from the cradle to the grave. Links between big business and the state remained unusually close. There was no possibility of the growth of a strong and independent democratic labour movement under such industrial conditions.

Distress arose in Japan at the end of the war due to the phenomenal rise in the price of rice, the country's staple food; this led to serious riots all over Japan in the summer of 1918. Troops repressed the violence in the towns and villages with great severity. Hundreds of people were killed and thousands more arrested. The collapse of the war boom in 1921 led to further repression of any signs of socialism or of attempts by labour to organise. The devastating Tokyo earthquake in September 1923 became the pretext for arresting Koreans, communists and socialists who were accused of plotting to seize power. Many were lynched by 'patriotic gangs'. The police were given authority to arrest and imprison anyone suspected of subversive thoughts, and many were brutally treated. Compulsory military training of Japanese youth was seen as a good way to counteract 'dangerous thoughts'. Thus the 1930s cannot be seen as a complete reversal of the Taisho period.

In Japan's relations with the world too there is more continuity than at first appears. On the one hand the Russian Revolution of 1917 and the emergence of the United States as a world power had repercussions of enormous importance in eastern Asia. The Soviet leaders succeeded for a time in forging an alliance with Chinese Nationalists in a joint drive against Western and Japanese imperialism (page 179). On the other hand, the United States was calling for a new deal for China and an end to the pre-war power alliances, particularly the Anglo-Japanese alliance, which had enormously

The aftermath of the Tokyo earthquake of 1 September 1923. Strong winds had fanned the fires and made two-thirds of the population homeless. Some 74,000 people are believed to have lost their lives.

strengthened Japan's position in Asia. But the Japanese government, beset by severe economic problems in the 1920s, and dependent on American trade, was in no position to resist the United States. This became clear at the Washington Conference in 1921–2. Several treaties were signed, placing the security of the eastern Pacific and the integrity of China on a multinational basis. The Japanese were obliged to return to China the Shantung province gained at the Paris Peace Conference (page 81). A naval limitations treaty placed Japan in a position inferior to Britain and the United States, which were allowed a ratio of five battleships each to Japan's three. Finally, Japan became a co-signatory to the nine-power treaty to seek to uphold the unity of China. It is true that Japan also received private assurances recognising her special interests in Manchuria; nevertheless the Washington Treaties placed a considerable check on any Japanese unilateral action in China.

The 'spirit of Washington', as the great-power co-operation in eastern Asia came to be described, proved as unsuccessful in the long run as the 'spirit of Locarno' in Europe (pages 145–6). Foreign Minister Kijuro Shidehara became identified with Japan's pacific policy in Asia and he loyally did his best to act in its spirit. But there were ominous signs of the troubles to come. With the passing of *genro* control the army became more independent and chafed under the consequences of Japan's new foreign policy. Great-power co-operation proved singularly ineffective in China and certainly did not reduce either that country's internal conflict or its anti-imperialist feelings. Good relations with the United States were seriously harmed by the passage of an immigration law in 1924 which excluded the Japanese, further strengthening the military view that the United States had become Japan's most likely enemy. The rise of Chinese nationalism and Chiang Kai-shek's thrust to the north in 1926 were seen as threats to Japan's position in Manchuria.

The new Emperor Hirohito, whose reign began in December 1926, chose Showa, 'enlightened peace', as the name of his era. But the domestic and international difficulties besetting Japan were to make the coming years a period of war and violence.

PART III

The Great War, Revolution and the Search for Stability

CHAPTER 12

The Great War – I: War without Decision, 1914–1916

The shape of the future world after August 1914 would now be decided by force. At the outset of the war all the major nations launched offensives to knock out the enemy quickly, and every one of these offensives had failed by the autumn of 1914 with great loss of life. War ended four years later not by defeat of the armies in the field alone, as in the wars of the nineteenth century, but with the breakdown of the political and economic structure of the defeated, their societies weakened or shattered.

On the eastern war-front in August 1914 the two Russian armies assigned to invade East Prussia were badly led. Fulfilling their undertaking to the French, the Russian armies, superior in numbers, invaded East Prussia. After some initial Russian success General von Hindenburg was called from retirement to take command of the German defence and he selected General Ludendorff as his chief of staff. The myth of Hindenburg the heroic war leader was born. At the battle of Tannenberg on 28 and 29 August one Russian army was practically destroyed; the other was mauled in a subsequent engagement – the battle of the Masurian Lakes – but was able to withdraw to Russia in good order. Tannenberg is celebrated by the Germans in the tradition of the ancient Teutonic knights defeating hordes of Slavs. What followed was as important as the battle itself and is less heroically Wagnerian. The pursuing German army of the second Russian army was in its turn thrown back by the Russians. The end result of the year's fighting was heavy casualties on both sides and neither a German nor a Russian decisive victory but a stalemate.

Farther south, the Russians more than balanced their defeat in Prussia by proving their military superiority over the Habsburg armies. Austria–Hungary had launched an offensive into Polish Russia and in September suffered a crushing defeat; almost half (400,000) of the Austro-Hungarian army was lost and the Russians occupied Galicia. Russia also suffered heavy casualties, a quarter of a million men. The 'forgotten' war in the east for three long years from 1915 to 1917 sapped Germany's military strength by forcing a division of Germany's armies between the two major fronts east and west. German victory came too late in the east to save her.

Another military campaign which is forgotten, though it cost France 300,000 casualties, was the 1914 French offensive into Lorraine. The French initiative came to be overshadowed by the German breakthrough in north-west France. In accordance with the (modified) Schlieffen Plan the German armies attacked Belgium and were pouring into France in a great enveloping move. At the frontier the French armies were beaten and the small British army, right in the path of the Germans, withdrew from Mons having suffered heavy casualties. The French Commander-in-Chief, General Joffre, did not lose his nerve despite these almost overwhelming reverses. The French armies withdrew in good order and escaped encirclement.

As the Germans rapidly advanced, their offensive

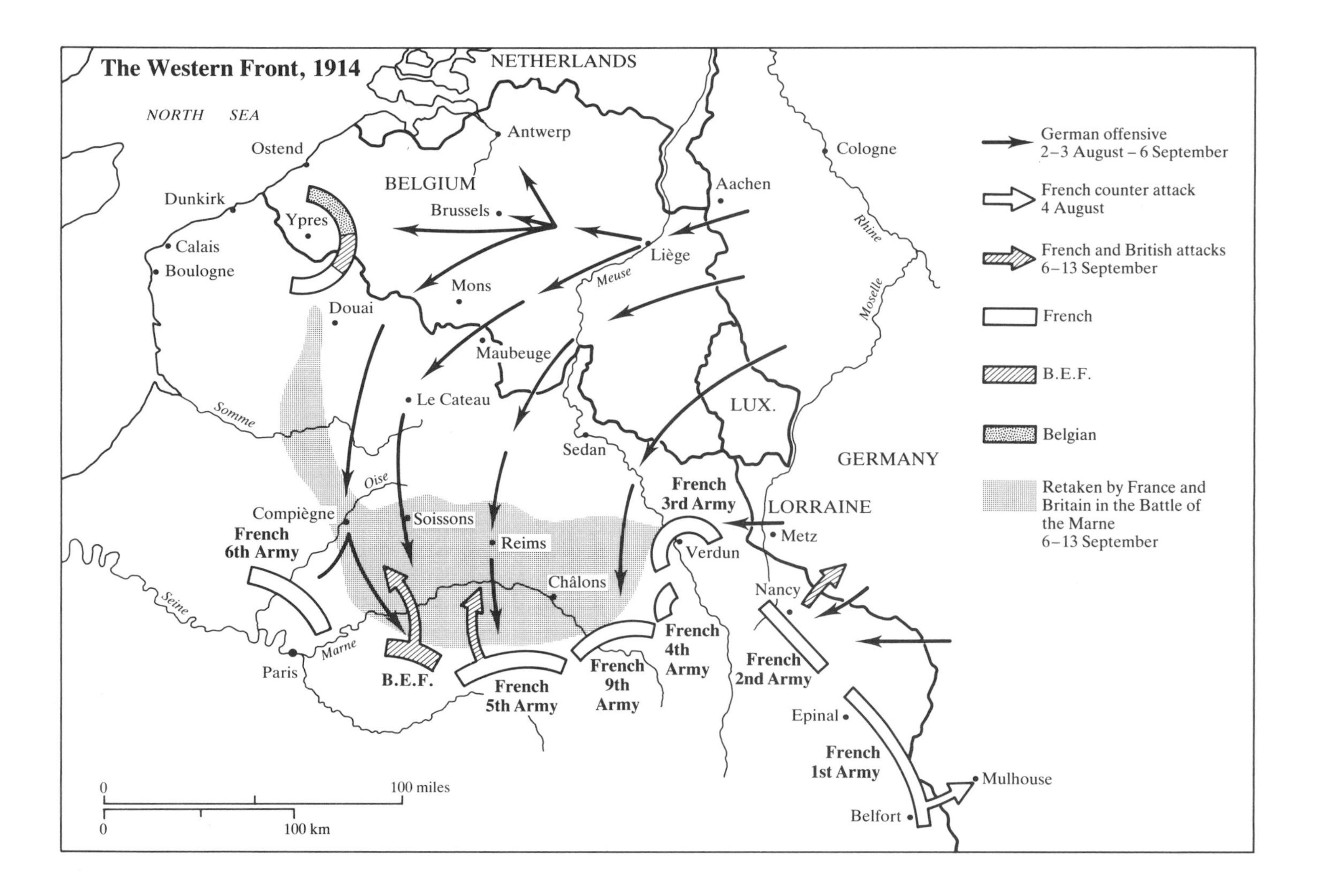
The Western Front, 1914
NETHERLANDS
NORTH SEA
Ostend
Antwerp
BELGIUM
Brussels
Dunkirk
Ypres
Calais
Boulogne
Cologne
Aachen
Liège
Meuse
Rhine
Moselle
Mons
Douai
Maubeuge
Le Cateau
LUX.
Somme
Sedan
GERMANY
Oise
Compiègne
Soissons
Reims
Châlons
French 6th Army
French 3rd Army
LORRAINE
Metz
Verdun
Seine
Nancy
Paris
Marne
B.E.F.
French 5th Army
French 9th Army
French 4th Army
French 2nd Army
Epinal
French 1st Army
Mulhouse
Belfort
0
100 miles
0
100 km
German offensive 2–3 August – 6 September
French counter attack 4 August
French and British attacks 6–13 September
French
B.E.F.
Belgian
Retaken by France and Britain in the Battle of the Marne 6–13 September

Enlisting Patriotism. Wartime posters – a British one of 1914 (right); *a German one urging 'Keep At It!'* (left).

ran out of steam. General Gallieni, appointed to defend Paris, now conceived of a counterstroke. The Germans had wheeled in before Paris. Joffre and Gallieni halted the retreat and counterattacked. The outcome was the battle of the Marne, won by the French during the period 6 to 13 September. Now it was the German turn to withdraw; they halted 100 kilometres from Paris having established a firm defence. The battles spread and raged to the west, all the way to Flanders, in a 'race to the sea' as the armies attempted to outflank each other. The British, French and Germans suffered heavy casualties in these epic struggles around Ypres. By the end of November 1914, the machine gun, the trenches and barbed wire finally proved the strength of the defensive. The western front was now deadlocked. The French had already suffered heavy casualties in the fighting in north-west France, with 380,000 killed and 600,000 wounded. This was matched by casualties on the German side. Yet it was only a beginning. The war in the west would from now on be won not by superior strategy, nor by movement and rapid encirclement, but by the slow process of attrition. The Great War had turned into the first 'industrial war' to be won as decisively on the home front, producing ever vaster quantities of guns and munitions, as in the field.

In Britain the Liberal government of Asquith at first preserved most civic freedoms. There was no conscription. Two million men volunteered in response to Kitchener's appeal for a New Army. But soon there were doubts whether the war could be won by peacetime-style government. In the spring of 1915 the government was being blamed for a shortage of munitions. Asquith strengthened the government by bringing in the Conservatives; Labour, too, was found a place. A small War Committee took over a tighter direction. Lloyd George, the new Minister of Munitions, built up a network of control over raw materials and manufacturing industry. War supplies improved and national economic planning was seen to work, which after the war boosted the claims of the socialists. The war could not be fought in the traditions of previous victorious struggles. That became clear when conscription for military service was introduced early in 1916. Even so 1916 did not bring the expected victory. The politicians sought a new leader to direct the war with more ruthless purpose and energy. In December 1916 the fiery and charismatic Welshman, Lloyd George, replaced Asquith and headed a coalition government for the remainder of the war.

During the years of the war the individual lost many rights as hope of a quick victory vanished. In accepting state direction, organised labour co-operated with the national government, and a political 'truce' was proclaimed in Britain as in other belligerent countries. Due in no small measure to Lloyd George's skill, the dominant style was that of co-operation rather than coercion, of preserving constitutional parliamentary government rather than resorting to authoritarian rule.

In France President Poincaré called for a 'sacred union' in defence of the fatherland. Patriotism for the anti-clerical republic was sanctified. Political and social issues which had rent the republic before were now subordinated in face of the common enemy invading France for a second time. Symbolically the veteran socialist leader, Jean Jaurès, who had so fervently denounced militarism and had worked for Franco-German reconciliation, was assassinated by a nationalist fanatic on the very eve of the war. He too would have joined with his fellow socialists in the defence of France.

For France, invaded and losing large tracts of the country right at the beginning of the war, it could not be 'business as usual' – the inappropriate words of calm coined by Winston Churchill across the Channel – because from the start France was in imminent danger of defeat. That is why the French were the first to establish a government of national unity representing all parties from left to right.

Although the war was fought on French soil, and the loss of industrial north-western France was serious, the French improvised war production and relied on financial and material aid from Britain and the United States. Shortages of food and of necessities sent prices soaring. Increasingly authoritarian control of production, allocation of labour and distribution had to be undertaken by the state.

The first of the belligerents to organise their production and manpower, however, were the Germans. The British naval blockade reducing essential supplies from overseas – though war materials continued to pass through neutral ports, Scandinavian and Dutch – made careful planning all the more essential. Substitute (*Ersatz*) materials were invented with scientific skill and ingenuity. As the general staff, with an almost characteristic lack of prudence, had made no plans for a long-drawn-out war, the war the Germans had to fight, it was a 'civilian', Walter Rathenau, in August 1914, who was responsible for setting up a centralised organisation to ensure the supply of essential raw materials.

In Germany too the political parties closed ranks to support the nation at war. Only a small minority of socialists continued to oppose the war. The Kaiser responded emotionally, declaring that 'I do not know parties any more, only Germans.' He actually received the Social Democratic leaders in his palace and they were happy to shake hands with their Kaiser. Who would have believed a year earlier such a thing would happen? Until 1916 the *Burgfrieden* (literally 'Courtpeace', another typically Wagnerian phrase) held, but then tensions began to appear and a larger group of socialists began to oppose the war. The Reichstag, unfettered, debated war aims and the conduct of government, culminating in the famous peace resolution of July 1917: 'The Reichstag strives for a peace of understanding and lasting reconciliation of nations. Such a peace is not in keeping with forcible annexations of territory . . .' But it turned out that, if German armies were to prove victorious, the Reichstag did not expect its resolution to be taken too literally.

In any case, the Chancellor was dependent not on the Reichstag but increasingly on the High Command. The Kaiser, too, became more and more of a shadow. After Hindenburg and Ludendorff had been appointed to the High Command, they demanded in 1917 the dismissal of the Chancellor Bethmann Hollweg. He was too independent. His successors were nonentities and Germany practically fell under a Hindenburg–Ludendorff military dictatorship during the last year and a half of the war.

If Austria–Hungary had been on the verge of dissolution through the disaffection of the Habsburg's Slav subjects this would certainly have shown itself when the Monarchy's Slav neighbours – the Russians and Serbs – went to war. In Vienna and Budapest there was much concern. The Serb, Ruthene and Czech populations were lukewarm in their war effort. Some Czechs and Poles formed their own Legions, which fought for the Allies. But there were no large-scale defections, let alone national uprisings. Croats, Slovenes, Italians, Romanians fought bravely side by side with Germans, Austrians and Magyars, and so did many Poles and Czechs.

The Austro–Hungarian army was a unique multinational force. But in one respect it was not unique: the incompetence of its leadership. The ordinary soldiers suffered appalling hardships, and

News of the sinking of the passenger liner, Lusitania, *on 7 May 1915, reaches England. Relatives await news of survivors at the Cunard shipping line's London offices.*

casualties during the first nine months of the war exceeded 2 million. Even so, new conscripts allowed fresh armies to be formed. In 1915, facing war on three fronts with Russia, Romania and Italy, the Monarchy was too weak to meet all her enemies, and substantial German armies were needed to sustain the ally. The 'national' division between Austria and Hungary also impeded the war effort. The Hungarians refused to go short of grain and profited by raising prices to the Austrian half of the Monarchy, which went hungry. War production, concentrated in Bohemia, was inefficient. But the multinational army fought on doggedly, though new recruits failed to maintain its strength, sapped by the losses in the field. In 1916 the aged Emperor Francis Joseph died. His successor Charles believed the Monarchy was close to collapse, having overtaxed its strength, and he was soon secretly trying to make peace. The army remained loyal to the dynasty virtually to the end.

New weapons killed in new ways: attacks from Zeppelins from the air and poison gas on land. Far more serious in its effect of spreading war to non-combatants was the conflict on the oceans. Germany attempted to break the effects of the British-imposed blockade by ordering in 1915 her submarines to sink all belligerent and neutral ships which entered a 'war zone' around the British Isles. To avoid capture the submarines torpedoed, without warning, boats bound for Britain. On 7 May 1915 the Germans sank the British passenger liner *Lusitania*; almost 2000 crew and passengers, including women and children, lost their lives. World opinion, especially in the United States, was outraged. 128 Americans had been among those who had lost their lives. Germany's excuse that starving women and children in Germany were victims of Britain's food blockade was always flimsy. The submarine campaign failed completely in its objective. It failed to cut off vital supplies from reaching France and Britain and it failed to frighten the neutral countries from continuing to expand their trade with the Allies.

Germany launched a propaganda campaign of hatred directed especially against Britain. This had little effect on those actually engaged on the battlefronts. Much to the embarrassment of the generals on both sides, the German and Allied troops on the western front spontaneously stopped fighting on Christmas Day 1914, exchanged gifts and even played football between the trenches. There was little hatred, even a good deal of fellow feeling. The soldiers knew that there was no way out of the war except through death or injury or victory.

The Great War differed from the Second World War in one very important respect. There were no planned atrocities committed by the military on prisoners of war or on civilians. Wartime propaganda was, for the most part, lies. There were no savage Huns killing Belgian priests, nuns and babies, nor Belgian civilians behind the lines gouging out the eyes of wounded Germans. The Red Cross was respected in all countries, including tsarist Russia. Brutalities no doubt occurred but they were isolated. The record of the Germans in Belgium, Russia, Poland and elsewhere during the First World War in no way supports the conclusion that the Germans did not respect human rights or regarded the conquered peoples as inferiors. There were no mass murders of civilian populations as occurred during the Second World War. There was this much substance to early Allied propaganda that during the first two months of the war trigger-happy German troops did kill several hundred innocent Belgian civilians who were falsely accused of atrocities which German propaganda had led the troops to expect. The German Army Command in Belgium quickly brought the situation under control and the occupation was humanely conducted by the German military authorities, though there was undeniable hardship. The blot on this record was the forced deportation of some 60,000 Belgians in 1916 to work in German factories. Though it was wartime, the socialists in the Reichstag loudly protested; the deportations ceased, and by the summer of 1917 the great majority of the Belgians had been sent home again. In Belgium herself no coercion was exercised to force Belgian industry to work for the German war effort, though factories were dismantled. Only the miners, with the permission of the Belgian government, continued to produce coal.

Both among the Belgians and in occupied Russian Poland, the Germans and Austrians attempted to win over the population to their cause. The Poles were promised an independent state at least in form, though in practice such an independent Poland would have become a German satellite. There was no maltreatment. The Poles of Prussia and of the Habsburg Monarchy fought with much loyalty for Germany and the Habsburgs, seeing tsarist Russia as the oppressor.

Unquestionably the worst atrocity against defenceless civilians occurred in Turkey against the Christian Armenian people in 1915 and 1916. When the war went badly for the Turks in 1915 and the Russians were pushing into Anatolia, the Russians attempted to inflame and exploit Armenian nationalism against the Turks. An Armenian Legion fought for the Russians and an Armenian puppet government was set up. The Turks, uncertain of the loyalty of the Armenian population in Asia Minor, committed the worst atrocity of the war by ordering the wholesale deportation of the Armenians from the lands adjoining the battlefront to Syria. Armenian historians accuse the Turks of genocide against their people. Turkish historians admit that huge massacres took place but deny that the Turkish government intended them to happen. Sporadic large-scale massacres had already taken place before 1914, shocking Western Europe. What is certain is that the tragedy of 1915 and 1916 was on an ever greater scale. The forced deportation of men, women and children caused the deaths of tens of thousands through starvation and disease. Some (by no means all) of the Turks reverted to outright massacres on the spot. There are no reliable figures for those who perished. They vary, according to whether the sources are Turkish or Armenian, from 200,000 to more than 2 million. Of the 1.6 million Armenians between a half and three-quarters of a million perished. In the 'progressive' twentieth century the Armenian massacres were a precursor of even more extensive and cold-blooded massacres.

The five great nations of Europe went to war in 1914 not for any specific territorial gains. It was not a 'limited' war in the post-Napoleonic nineteenth-century manner. The war was a gigantic contest between them to determine their power in Europe and the wider world. It belongs with the wars of international insanity of the first half of the twentieth century. When that contest was decided, it was widely believed, it would inevitably bring about also the ruin of the imperial world ambitions of the defeated and provide new imperial prospects of conquest and influence for the victors. The illusion was fostered that this contest would settle the power struggle for ever. Hence the phrase 'the war to end wars'.

For two small nations there was no choice. Serbia was guilty of provoking Austria–Hungary and then in 1914, when faced with the Austrian ultimatum, fought for her independence. The Belgians were guilty of nothing. Their misfortune was their strategic position between France and Germany. Both French and German military planners wanted to march through Belgian territory, but Britain had prevented France from taking the initiative. Belgium wished to preserve her neutrality. The King of the Belgians, even after the invasion of his country, remained suspicious of both sides. He claimed he was defending the little bit of Belgium still free from German occupation as a neutral and not as an ally of Britain and France.

In the Balkans another small nation, Greece, was finally brought into the war in 1917 by France and Britain against the wishes of the King of Greece. Britain and France sent a military expedition to Salonika in October 1915 and then attempted to coerce the pro-German King Constantine into war on the Allied side. Although not as blatant as German aggression in Belgium, it was another violation of the rights of a small nation.

A number of European countries chose and were allowed to remain neutral throughout the war: the Netherlands, Denmark, Sweden, Norway, Switzerland and Spain. Their sympathies between the contestants were divided. They had benefited from the balance of power and so they would have preferred to see the war ended in the way that President Wilson, who led the most powerful of the neutrals, the United States, hoped, with the conclusion of a compromise peace. The European neutrals were too weak to insist on their 'neutral rights', the freedom to trade. The Dutch government, for instance, had to guarantee that the goods imported to the Netherlands from across the seas and passing through the British blockade would not be re-exported to Germany. In fact the neutrals did well as centres of trade to the belligerents during the first three years of the war. The 'illegal' trade between the Scandinavian countries, the Netherlands and Germany was enormous. It was no secret to the British and French authorities that a profitable trade even from their own countries by way of neutral countries was being conducted with Germany.

Some industries in neutral countries experienced a great boom. The Spanish coal mines in Asturias and textile mills in Catalonia supplied the French. Dutch industry developed; the Swiss found a ready market for clocks, machines and textiles. The shortage of food made farming highly profitable. But in the last two years of the war, while the farmers and some industrialists continued to do well, the standard of living of the mass of the workers in the neutral countries of Europe fell with soaring food prices.

The United States was by far the most important and powerful of the neutrals from 1914 to 1917, the only great power in the world not at war. The feeling of most Americans was that the war in Europe was but one further chapter in the history of the folly of European nations; it reinforced in their view the wisdom of the Founding Fathers in establishing the American Republic and separating her destiny from the rivalries of Europe. In Europe, Frenchmen, Englishmen, Italians and Russians were fighting the Germans, Austrians and Hungarians. During the Easter rising in Dublin in 1916 some Irishmen were fighting the English too; in the United States their descendants lived at peace with each other. Americans were convinced that they were building a higher civilisation and from this stemmed a genuine desire to help her neighbours on the American continent and in the world attain the blessings of liberty. This too was the faith of President Wilson. It helps to explain the missionary style of American diplomacy.

Wilson's moralising certainly led to some decidedly contradictory behaviour. The United States intervened on her own continent, sending troops to the countries of weaker neighbours in Mexico, Haiti, Santo Domingo and Nicaragua to establish American supremacy and naval bases in the Caribbean. But this was not seen as anything at all like European 'imperialism'. The purpose of the United States was 'pure': to teach her badly governed neighbours the benefits of American democracy. If people were enlightened and were given a free choice then Americans believed they would choose the American way.

In August 1914 Wilson issued a neutrality proclamation. Both Allied and German propaganda sought to persuade the American people that right and justice were on their side. The Germans emphasised that they were fighting a despotic and cruel regime in Russia, whose persecution of the Jews had already led to a great exodus of immigrants to the United States. The British dwelt on the rights of small nations and the dangers to a peaceful Europe if the Kaiser and Prussian militarism were to get away with breaking treaties and attacking weaker neighbours. The behaviour of the countries at war made a deep impression on the United

States and nothing more so than Germany's warfare against defenceless merchant vessels and even passenger liners. The President took his stand legalistically on 'neutral rights', the right of Americans to travel the oceans safely and of American merchant ships to trade with Europe. Wilson protested at Britain's conduct of the blockade and Germany's ruthless submarine warfare designed to cut off the British Isles from the world's arteries of trade essential to her war effort. Wilson's protests were effective. Rather than risk an American declaration of war, the German government desisted from attacking American ships in 1915 and on 1 September also pledged not to sink any more Allied passenger liners, which had also led to the loss of American lives. But meanwhile the loss of American lives and the ruthlessness of German warfare had swung the majority of American opinion in favour of the Allied cause. But this was sentiment, not action; the Americans also stood behind their President in wishing to keep out of the war.

The Americans saw no reason, however, why they should not profit from the huge increase of trade brought about by the war. While Germany was just about able to maintain her trade with the United States through neutrals, US trade with the Allies increased fourfold. By 1916 that trade was calculated at a staggering $3214 million, whereas trade with Germany and the neutrals amounted to a little over $280 million. The war resulted in a great expansion of American industry. During the war years Ford developed a mass market for motor cars and trucks. It was the beginning of the motor revolution, which matched in importance the earlier railway revolution in transport. Free from the burdens of war, the United States developed new technologies and more efficient methods of industrial manufacture, outdistancing the European nations more and more. As the Allies used up their capital to purchase from the United States, America herself replaced Britain as the principal source of capital to other nations. American prosperity came to depend on Allied purchases and, when these could no longer be met by payment, the prohibition against loans to the belligerents was relaxed. However, Britain's command of the sea prevented the Germans importing goods directly through their ports from overseas, though supplies did reach them through neutral ports (page 97). America's response to Allied needs meant that her economic strength was thrown predominantly behind the Allied cause long before she formally abandoned neutrality.

There was no reason for the United States to go to war. She was still safe from European attack and was constructing a navy designed to be as powerful as any in the world to guarantee that safety in the future. She coveted no more territory. But already Americans perceived weaknesses in their position. The growth of Japanese power in Asia, no longer checked by the Europeans, threatened American interests in Asia. Even more worrying appeared to be the prospect of the European conflict ending in the complete victory of one side or the other. That would destroy the global balance of power. Would not the United States then be faced with the threat of a European superpower? American naval war plans before April 1917 were intended to meet that danger and not the possibility of joining on the Allied side. It made sense that Wilson would attempt to preserve the European balance by attempting to persuade the belligerents to conclude a compromise peace. But all his efforts in 1915 and 1916 failed. They failed for a simple reason. As long as the Germans occupied Belgium and northern France, they felt themselves at least partially victorious, but the Allies would contemplate no peace unless Germany gave up all her conquests. This would have made the sacrifices of Germany all in vain. In truth, neither side was ready to conclude a peace that might prove merely temporary. The only way they could conceive of ensuring a durable peace was through total defeat of the enemy.

When the first two months of the war did not lead to the expected decision, France, Britain and Russia and Germany and Austria–Hungary hoped to strengthen their position by winning new allies and opening up new war-fronts to threaten their enemies. The Germans were the first to be successful in this respect, persuading the Turks to attack Russia and enter the war in October 1914. The Turkish decision not only widened the area of conflict but also profoundly changed the history of the Middle East. The future of the Middle East became a bargaining counter between the powers at war. Britain invaded Mesopotamia to secure the oilfields, and supported an Arab revolt. Less successful was a British and French naval attack on the Dardanelles repelled by the Turks in February and March 1915. However an attack on Turkey was still seen by Churchill and Lloyd George as the best way of striking a decisive blow in a war deadlocked in the west but immensely costly in human life. In April 1915 British and French troops landed on the Gallipoli peninsula with the object of capturing Constantinople. But the Turks defended resolutely, and the Anglo-French campaign was a failure. Turkish and Allied losses were heavy before the Allies finally decided on evacuation, which they completed in January 1916. The Ottoman Empire did not play a decisive role in the war: the Turkish participation on the losing side resulted in her dismemberment and the dramatic growth of Arab nationalism.

Ottoman territory was held out as a bait during the war in order to keep one ally, Russia, in the war. In the famous 'secret treaties', Britain and France in 1915 promised Constantinople and the Straits to Russia. Other portions of the empire were promised to Italy as colonies by the treaty of London (April 1915) to induce the Italians to join the Allies and attack Austria–Hungary to the north.

Though nominally partners of the Triple Alliance with Germany and Austria–Hungary, the Italians had declared their neutrality in August 1914. They were for the next nine months wooed by both sides. The Italian government in the end chose war for territorial gain alone, though the politicians were divided whether or not to go to war. The government blatantly sought to extract the best bid, an attitude dignified by Prime Minister Salandra as conforming to *sacro egoismo*. What was decisive for Italy was a determination to complete her 'liberation' and to wrest from Austria–Hungary the Italian-speaking lands of the Trentino and Trieste. But her appetite was larger than this; the Italian government hoped also to acquire the German-speaking South Tyrol, as well as influence and territory in the Balkans and Ottoman territory in Asia Minor. The Austrians felt they were being blackmailed. 'Against brigands such as the Italians are now, no diplomatic swindle would be excessive,' secretly wrote the Austrian Prime Minister. The Allies offered the most. In May 1915 the Italians declared war on Austria–Hungary and so quite unnecessarily entered a war that was to prove for the Italians immensely costly in human life and material resources.

For the Balkan states the Great War provided an opportunity to start a third Balkan war for the satisfaction of Balkan territorial ambitions. Bulgaria in September 1915 joined the war on the side of Germany and Austria–Hungary with the promise of large territorial gains, including Serbian Macedonia. A year later, in August 1916, Romania was promised by the Allies Romanian-speaking Transylvania and part of the Austro–Hungarian Empire as well as other territories, and she declared war to secure them.

In eastern Asia, Japan's chosen policy was to strengthen her position in China. She declared war on Germany in August 1914, captured Germany's Chinese colonial sphere and then presented to China the Twenty-One Demands to assure herself a predominant position (page 89). The war begun by Germany, Austria–Hungary, Russia, France and Britain for one set of reasons widened to include other nations, all of whom, with the exception of the United States, saw in it an opportunity for extending their territorial empires.

In each of the belligerent countries there were some politicians who after the failure to win the war in 1914 looked towards the conclusion of a compromise peace. But, despite President Wilson's efforts to build a bridge between the combatants through mediation, the generals and the governments conceived only of a peace ended on the victor's terms. This attitude, as much as the outbreak of the war itself, changed the course of world history. In Berlin, Chancellor Bethmann Hollweg at times viewed the unfolding drama in terms of Greek tragedy; it would be disastrous for civilisation whether Germany won or lost. In victory, would he be able to keep in check crude concepts of military conquest?

In the plans for a peace following a German victory which Bethmann Hollweg drew up in September 1914, he tried to create a new Europe, at least a new continental Europe, because he could not conceive defeating Britain, only of isolating her through the defeat of Russia and France. He said he wished to conclude a so-called 'Bismarckian' peace of limited annexation. On the other hand he was convinced that France and Russia must be so weakened that they would never be able to threaten Germany again. Belgium, and even a coastal strip of northern France, would have to fall under direct or indirect German control. Through the creation of autonomous states, carved out of the Russian Empire, but made dependent on Germany, Russia would be pushed far to the east. A continental economic custom union would bring prosperity to all, and reconcile continental Europe to German hegemony while excluding Britain. All this he called 'Middle Europe'. To satisfy imperial ambitions, the German African colonies would be augmented with French and Belgian colonial possessions to form German 'Middle Africa'. The base of Germany's political and economic power would, however, have lain in her domination of continental Europe. There was to be no return to the balance of power. This meant in practice the destruction of Russia and France as great powers and a compromise peace with Britain which would acknowledge Germany's continental domination – hardly a limited Bismarckian peace!

Russian aims were both specifically territorial and absolute. The Russian government wished to fulfil what it regarded as Russia's 'historic mission' of acquiring Constantinople and control of the Straits. What this involved was the final destruction of Ottoman power and its replacement by a Russian domination of the Balkans, Asia Minor and as much of the Middle East as France and Britain would allow.

All Allied war aims were dependent on defeating Germany. With Germany eliminated as a great power, the reduced Habsburg Empire and the smaller Balkan states presented no problem to Russia. The rivalry of allies would be more serious than the ambitions of former enemies. We can gain a glimpse of Russian aims. According to the French Ambassador's memoirs, the Russian Foreign Minister, Sazonov, told him on 20 August 1914 that the 'present war is not the kind of war that ends with a political treaty after a battle of Solferino or Sadowa'; Germany must be completely defeated.

> My formula is a simple one, we must destroy German imperialism. We can only do that by a series of military victories so that we have a long and very stubborn war before us.... But great political changes are essential if... the Hohenzollern are never again to be in a position to aspire to universal dominion. In addition to the restitution of Alsace-Lorraine to France, Poland must be restored, Belgium enlarged, Hanover reconstituted, Slesvig returned to Denmark, Bohemia freed, and all the German colonies given to France, England and Belgium, etc. It is a gigantic programme. But I agree with you that we ought to do our utmost to realise it if we want our work to be lasting.

It is a commonplace to compare the peace of Brest-Litovsk of March 1918, which the Germans imposed on the hapless Russians, with Versailles, and to conclude that the Germans only justly received what they had meted out to others. The reverse is also true. The Russians had every intention of treating the Germans as harshly as the Germans treated Russia in defeat. When we compare the 'war aims', it becomes rather hazardous to pass comparative moral judgements on them.

The French government also wanted to impose conditions on the defeated so that they would remain victors for all foreseeable time. The French, alone among the great powers, were fighting the same enemy for the second time for national survival. French territorial demands were limited to Alsace-Lorraine and colonies. But French requirements went far beyond that, beyond the restoration of Belgium, to the imposition of terms that as Viviani, the French Prime Minister, declared to the Chamber of Deputies in December 1914, would destroy Prussian militarism. The economic imbalance between Germany and France was to be righted by territorial cessions and by forcing the Germans to transfer wealth – gold – to France under the heading of 'reparations'. Germany would be made to 'pay for the war', to weaken her and to strengthen her neighbours.

The British approach was more pragmatic, avoiding commitments as far as possible. There was no desire whatever to reconstitute Hanover! Indeed there were no war aims formulated at all during the first two years of the war, except for the restoration of Belgian independence, since this had been the principal ostensible reason for going to war. Little thought was given to the terms to be imposed on defeated Germany, far more on what favourable inducements might entice Germany's allies to abandon her. There was no desire to break up the Habsburg Empire. But the one recurring theme, the destruction of the war spirit of the principal enemy, was frequently proclaimed. General Sir William Robertson, Chief of the Imperial General Staff, in a speech to munition workers in April 1917, summed up this uncompromising outlook: 'Our aim is, as I understand it, to deal German despotism such a blow as will for generations to come prevent a recurrence of the horrors of the last two and a half years.' But this did not mean exactly what the Russians and French had in mind. Britain's prime minister, Lloyd George, as well as

Arthur Balfour, the Foreign Secretary, were convinced that Germany's great power on the continent could not be permanently diminished. The best hope for peace was the emergence of a peaceful democratic post-war Germany. Thus Germany should not be driven to seek revenge to recover territory won from her. Unjust and harsh treatment of defeated Germany would only sow the seeds of future conflict. Britain's leaders looked to a close alliance with the United States to guarantee the maintenance of peace. Later differences which emerged with France over the right policy to adopt are clearly foreshadowed in British war aims. These were only 'absolute' on one point: the security of the British Empire from any future German challenge. Germany would not be permitted again to compete with Britain's naval supremacy. As for other war aims, they were to be formulated by Britain during the war in response to the demands of allies, or would-be allies, or in pursuit of military objectives. The latter led to the encouragement of the Arab revolts against the Turks, for instance, and so to the post-war transformation of the Middle East.

Were these war aims only formulated during the course of war to justify to the people an increasingly bloody, but basically irrational, war, as has so often been asserted? Or do they represent a continuity of assumptions held since before the war? They are indeed all of a piece. That is not to say that France would have gone to war for Alsace-Lorraine, or Germany in order to dominate Belgium, or Russia for Constantinople. The territorial aspirations were but a reflection of a more deep-rooted belief: that the balance of power could not last, that either Germany and her allies or Britain, France and Russia must dominate, that sooner or later a supreme struggle between the powers on the continent would be inevitable. Russia was convinced that either she or a Habsburg Empire supported by Germany would dominate the Balkans. The struggle could not be avoided. No one 'stumbled' into war. Nor would any power stumble out of it. The end would be brought about by military imperatives.

The attempts of the belligerent nations to win a decision in 1915 and 1916 all failed at a cost in human life never before experienced. Both sides on the western front attempted to break through the other's carefully prepared defences. For the soldiers this meant leaving the security of their own trench and advancing across a 'no-man's land' raked by machine-gun fire to the enemy trench protected by barbed wire and bayonets. If you were lucky artillery had cleared something of a path before you and disorganised the defence, but it was rarely totally effective. If good fortune favoured you, you actually reached the enemy trench; others only moved a few yards beyond their own trench before falling to the enemy fire. French and British offensives were launched by Joffre and Haig in the spring of 1915. No breakthrough was achieved; the little territory gained was no compensation for the appalling losses. In the autumn of 1915 the Allies renewed their offensive, ending again without any worthwhile gain; 242,000 men were lost by the Allies in that autumn offensive alone. New recruits were nevertheless still increasing the size of the armies.

On the eastern front German troops in 1915 were now essential to sustain the Austro-Hungarian front as well as their own. In successive Austrian and German offensives from January to September 1915 the Russians suffered heavy defeats, were driven from all German territory as well as Habsburg Galicia and gave up a large area of the Russian Empire including Russian Poland. The Russian retreat demoralised the army. The Germans and Austrians captured more than a million prisoners and the Russians had lost another million men. But the Russian war effort was not broken. By enormous effort on the home industrial front and by the raising of new troops the Russian front-line strength reached 2 million once again in 1916. Some 4 million men had by then been lost. The tsarist government, despite the vast reserve of population, was incapable of doing more than making good the losses. The Russian armies that would by sheer numbers steamroller over Germany and Austria–Hungary never materialised in the First World War as they were to in the Second. That nightmare vision for the Germans which had been so powerful an influence on them in deciding for war in 1914 was illusory.

Before 1915 was ended the first of the nations to have gone to war in August 1914 was crushed. Serbia was overwhelmed by a joint Bulgarian, German and Austrian attack.

The new front created by Italy's entry into the war in May 1915 resembled the fighting in France rather than in Russia. Although the Italians enjoyed a superiority over the Austrians, they suffered heavy

Images of War. Thoughts of home on the Russian front (left). *The imperial Austro-Hungarian army suffers casualties after an unsuccessful assault* (right). *The Kaiser's troops attempt one last onslaught at Villers Bretonneux on the western front in March 1918 – without success* (top right). *Will new men and weapons bring victory? A Canadian division is supported by a Mark IV tank* (top left).

casualties in a series of offensives during the course of 1915 without coming near to winning any decisive battles or achieving a breakthrough. Here too the short glorious war that was expected proved an illusion and Italy was locked in costly battles of attrition. It was easier to enter the war than to leave it with profit.

The central powers (Germany, Austria–Hungary, Turkey and Bulgaria) planned to carry on the war in 1916 so that through attrition the enemy would be exhausted. The German commander in the west, General Falkenhayn, calculated that if the Germans attacked the fortress of Verdun, then the French would sacrifice their manpower to hold on to it. This would break France's military morale.

Verdun became associated with the doggedness of its French hero defender Pétain, who, like Hindenburg, was to play a critical political role in post-war Europe for which he was unsuited. Falkenhayn failed to take Verdun or to limit German casualties by the use of artillery as he had planned. By the year's end German casualties – a third of a million men – were almost as heavy as the French losses of 362,000 men.

During the summer months until the autumn of 1916 the British and French armies not committed to Verdun launched their great offensive on the Somme intending to bring victory. The casualties suffered in hurling men against well-prepared positions were horrifying. The German army was not beaten but, refusing to yield territory in tactical withdrawals, also suffered enormous casualties. The French, British and Germans sacrificed more than a million men. British casualties alone exceeded 400,000, French 190,000 men, and the Germans around 500,000. Still there was no decision.

The Somme offensive in the west was part of a co-ordinated inter-Allied plan to attack the central powers. Only the Russians in 1916 gained a great victory. General Brusilov's summer offensive was an overwhelming success, destroying the independent Austro-Hungarian war effort. The Austro-Hungarian army lost more than 600,000 men in casualties or as prisoners, the Germans 150,000. But Russia, too, failed to defeat Germany in the east. Russian casualties were heavy and multiplied during the fighting from August to September. As it turned out, though no one expected it at the time, the Brusilov offensive was to be the last major Russian military effort before the outbreak of the revolution in Russia. The central powers did score one easy military success in the east in 1916 after the halting of the Russian offensive: the defeat of Romania. Her supplies of foodstuffs and oil now became available to the central powers.

While the war was being fought, during the winter of 1916 and the following spring of 1917, new forces were at work which changed its course fundamentally: American intervention and the Russian Revolution.

CHAPTER 13

War and Revolution in the East, 1917

The upheavals in Russia during 1917 changed the history of the world. Russia broke with the evolutionary Western path of national development. The birth of communist power was seen by Lenin, its founder, as the means by which not only the vast lands and peoples of Russia would be transformed but also the world. For seven decades Lenin was revered by half the world as its spiritual guide despite the bitter dissensions among communist countries as to which was the rightful heir. His vision of communism as a world force was realised less than twenty-five years after his death.

One of the fascinations of history is that it shows how a man, in many ways very ordinary, with ordinary human weaknesses, making mistakes and bewildering his contemporaries with the inconsistencies of his actions, can exert enormous influence on his own times and on the world decades later. Napoleon and Hitler caused devastation. Napoleon left some good behind him; Hitler, nothing but destruction. Lenin's reputation today has suffered with the demise of the Soviet Union, once elevated by propaganda he is now stripped of myth, but the impact of his ideas was enormous.

The success of Lenin's revolution, and the birth and growth of Soviet power, exercised great appeal as well as revulsion. Lenin's achievement was that he gave concrete expression to the theories of Karl Marx. The Russian Revolution appeared as the beginning of the fulfilment of Marx's 'scientific' prophecy that capitalist society was heading for its inevitable collapse and that the 'proletariat', the workers hitherto exploited, would take over and expropriate the exploiters. The poor shall inherit this world, not the next. That was obviously an intoxicating message. Of course Marx had written his great works in the mid-nineteenth century. Some 'adjustments' of his predictions were necessary to square them with the realities of the early twentieth century.

In Germany, where Marx's teachings had the largest political following, and where a powerful Social Democratic Party emerged, the lot of the working man was improving, not getting worse as Marx had predicted. The collapse of capitalism did not after all seem imminent. Some German socialists asked whether the party should not concentrate on securing practical benefits for the workers and accept the political system meanwhile. This became the policy of the majority of the party. The British Labour movement was clearly taking this direction too. In France the doctrine of industrial and class strife leading to revolution had limited appeal outside the towns. Marx's apocalyptic vision of capitalism in its last throes bore little relevance to conditions in the most industrialised countries. But Lenin was not disconcerted. He sharply condemned all the 'revisionists' and compromises with the 'exploiting' bourgeois society. He found much later the answer to the paradox in the book of an English radical on the nature of imperialism. J. A. Hobson believed that the drive for empire by the European states was caused by the need of advanced Western countries to find new profitable markets for investment. Lenin elaborated and went further. Imperialism, he wrote, was the last stage of capitalism. It postponed the fulfilment of Marx's prophecy. Because the Asiatic and African labourer was cruelly exploited, employers could afford to pay their European workers more. But the extension of the capitalist world could only postpone, not avert, its collapse. The proletariat must steel itself for the ultimate takeover and not compromise. The class struggle, as Marx taught, was the driving force of historical evolution. Anything that lessened the class struggle was treachery against the proletariat.

Lenin's views were so extreme, ran so much counter to the world in which he lived, that the majority of socialists ridiculed him when they were not accusing him of seeking to divide the socialist movement. Those who were not socialists did not take him seriously. His following, even among Russian socialists right up to the revolution of November 1917, was only a minority one.

This fanatical believer in the victory of the proletariat and castigator of bourgeois capitalist society and its intelligentsia of professors, lawyers and administrators had himself been born into the strata of society he virulently condemned. More important, its privileges had given him the education and freedom indispensable to his early success. The founder of communism indubitably sprang from the Russian tsarist middle class, to the embarrassment of some of his Soviet biographers. His real name was Vladimir Ilyich Ulyanov. He assumed the name of Lenin later to confuse the tsarist police. He was born in 1870. His mother was the daughter of a retired doctor who had become a small landowner. His father exemplified success and social mobility in nineteenth-century Russia: he had made his way from humble origins to the post of provincial director of schools, a position in the Russian civil service entitling him to be addressed 'Excellency'. Lenin was not 'of the people'.

Lenin was only sixteen when his father suddenly died. A year later an unnatural tragedy blighted family life. The eldest son of this eminently respectable family, Alexander, a student in St Petersburg, had become involved in a terrorist conspiracy to assassinate the Tsar. Apprehended, he was tried and hanged. Lenin now began to study and enquire into his brother's beliefs and actions, which were a naive and violent response to autocracy in the tradition of Russian terrorism. But in Russia there was not yet guilt by association. The family was treated with consideration. Lenin was accepted to study law in the University at Kazan. However, he was soon involved in student protests and was expelled. For three years he read and studied and became engrossed in the radical writings of his time.

It was during this period that he first discovered in Karl Marx's writings a revolutionary philosophy and a goal which, according to Marx, was a scientific certainty. He spent his life working out the right policies and tactics for Marxists to follow in order to realise the goals of the proletarian revolution. Unlike many other socialists, his faith in Marx's prediction was absolute, akin to that following a religious revelation. This faith and certainty gave him strength, but Lenin saw no point in martyrdom. His brother's gesture had been heroic but useless. The leader must preserve himself and avoid danger. It was an aspect of Lenin's ice-cold rationality – despite his attacks on the intelligentsia – that he ignored taunts that he sent others into danger while he himself enjoyed domesticity and safety abroad in London, Geneva and Zurich.

A remarkable feature of tsarist Russia at this time is that despite police surveillance of political suspects – and Lenin was undoubtedly a suspect – no political opponent was condemned for his thoughts, as later in communist countries, but only for his deeds. Even then punishment by later standards was frequently lenient. The death penalty was limited to those involved in assassination, political murders or plotting such murders. If sentenced to dreaded fortress imprisonment a man's health could be broken. The lesser sentence of exile to Siberia bears no relationship to the labour camps of Stalin's Russia. The inhospitable climate was a hardship but there was no maltreatment. Lenin, for instance, when later on he was sentenced, was free to live in a comfortable household and to study and read.

But before this he was allowed a second chance and after three years of waiting and petitioning was readmitted to Kazan University. He was thus able to complete his university studies before moving as a fully fledged lawyer to the capital, St Petersburg. Here he plunged into political activities and became a leading member of a small group of socialists. Adopting the agitational techniques of the Lithuanian Jewish socialist organization, the Bund, the St Petersburg socialists determined to spread the message of Marxism by involving themselves in trade union agitation on behalf of workers. Lenin and his associates agitated successfully among the textile workers. The police stepped in. Eventually Lenin was sentenced to three years exile in Siberia. In 1900 he was permitted to return to European Russia. He had matured as a revolutionary. He believed he could best promote the revolution by leaving Russia, as so many socialist émigrés had done before him, and to organise from safety in the West. Perhaps the police authorities were happy to get rid of him. In any event, Lenin in 1900 received the required permission to leave his country. Except for a few months in Russia after the outbreak of the revolution in 1905, Lenin spent the years before his return to Russia in April 1917 mainly as an exile in Switzerland.

Abroad, he developed the organisation of his revolutionary party based on his own uncompromising ideology. In the process he quarrelled with the majority of Russian and international socialists and finally split the Russian Democratic Socialist Party. His faction, which at the Second Party Congress in Brussels and London in 1903 managed to gain a majority, became known as the 'majority' or Bolsheviks, and the minority took the name of Mensheviks, although soon the fortunes were reversed and until 1917 the Mensheviks constituted the majority of the party. It is easier to define the Bolsheviks' ideas than the Mensheviks'. The Bolsheviks thought that leadership was established by the power of Lenin's personality and the hardness and sharpness of his mind and at each point of crisis had to be re-established. Lenin imbued the Bolsheviks with his own uncompromising revolutionary outlook. There was to be no co-operation with the 'bourgeois' parties, unless for tactical reasons it were expedient to support them briefly and then only as 'the noose supports a hanged man'. Lenin believed a broadly based mass party run by the workers would go the way of the Labour Party in Britain and weakly compromise. Only a small elite could understand and mastermind the seizure of power by the proletariat. The party must be centralised and unified. Lenin therefore sought to build up this party of dedicated revolutionaries who would agitate among the masses and take advantage of all opportunities, having but one goal, the socialist revolution.

The Mensheviks were never as united as the Bolsheviks nor were they led by any one man of commanding personality. In turn they accused Lenin of dictatorial behaviour. The Mensheviks developed their own Marxist interpretations. Accepting Marx's stages of development, they believed that Russia must pass through a bourgeois capitalist stage before the time would be ripe for the socialist revolution. And so when Russia embarked on the constitutional experiment after 1905, they were prepared to support the constitutional Kadet party in the Duma (page 56). Despite their Marxist authoritarian revolutionary ideology, the leadership in practice softened the line of policy. Lenin was never very consistent about his tactics, but his driving passion for the socialist revolution, his ruthless pursuit of this one goal when others in the party wavered and were distracted, gave him ultimate victory over the Mensheviks, who endlessly debated and advocated freedom of speech for all – even for Lenin, who was determined to undermine their authority. What true revolutionary in any case cared for 'majorities' and 'minorities'? Rule by the majority Lenin contemptuously regarded as a liberal bourgeois concept.

Within Russia herself the adherents of the supporters of the Social Democratic Party had little appreciation of why the Mensheviks and Bolsheviks were quarrelling in face of the common enemy of autocracy. It was not among the rank and file, small in Russia in any case, that their differences mattered. The Bolsheviks had no more than 20,000 members as late as February 1917. In any case it was neither Mensheviks nor Bolsheviks who won the greatest popular support but the Socialist Revolutionaries. Formed in 1901, they looked to the much more numerous peasants rather than to the urban workers. Some carried on the tradition of terror; a special group organised assassinations and thereby satisfied the demand for immediate revolutionary action. In the long run the revolution of the peasantry would occur. Other Socialist Revolutionaries, acting as a reforming party, would press for liberal constitutional reforms and laws to protect the peasants. These liberal reforms would pave the way to socialism later. The Socialist Revolutionary terrorist and party wings were never really co-ordinated. The phenomenon became evident in Ireland too.

The revolution of 1905 took the Bolsheviks and Mensheviks by surprise. At the outset they had only a small following among the workers, the Bolsheviks probably only a few hundred. Lenin did not affect its course. Nine years later, the outbreak of the

First World War appeared to mark the end of international socialism as one after the other the national socialist parties placed their countries before the brotherhood of the proletariat. Some socialists formed a pacifist wing; with them Lenin had nothing in common. Only a small band of revolutionaries gathered around Lenin. He was briefly imprisoned as a Russian spy in Austrian Poland at the outbreak of the war but was released to rejoin the other socialist exiles in Switzerland. The Social Democrat Party in Russia had dwindled from its peak of some 150,000 members in 1907 to probably less than 50,000 in 1914 and only a small minority of them were Bolsheviks. But Lenin's supreme self-assurance and confidence in Marx's analysis enabled him to survive disappointments and setbacks. For him the conflict among the imperialists was the opportunity the socialists had been waiting for. He hoped for the defeat of Russia and the exhaustion of the imperialists. Then he would turn the war between nations into a civil war that would end with the mass of peoples united in their aim of overthrowing their rulers and establishing the 'dictatorship of the proletariat'.

Lenin's view of the war and of the role of the socialists did not persuade even the left wing of the socialists who met in conferences in Switzerland at Zimmerwald in 1915 and Kienthal in the following year. The majority wished to bring the war to a compromise end, with international friendship and no annexations, and so espoused a pacifist stand. Lenin attracted only a handful to his side, among them the brilliant and fiery young Trotsky, who had inspired the workers' councils – the soviets – which had sprung up during the 1905 revolution. Trotsky believed in revolutionary action, in a 'permanent revolution'. He forecast that the bourgeois first stage would flow into the socialist second stage. Lenin closely shared Trotsky's views, believing he would witness the socialist revolution in his lifetime. When the new revolution did occur, however, in February 1917, the events took him once more by surprise.

The overthrow of tsarism took place with startling speed. For the army of 6.5 million men in the field, 1916 had closed with hope for the future. The Russian army, after suffering some 7 million casualties, had nevertheless proved more than a match for the Austrian army. Indeed, only the great power of the German army had stood in the way of total Habsburg disaster. The Germans proved formidable foes, but they were now outnumbered and the plans for a co-ordinated offensive east, west and south on the Italian front held out the promise that the central powers could be overwhelmed in 1917. The severe problems of weapons and munitions for the Russian army had been largely overcome by a prodigious Russian industrial effort during 1916 After the heavy losses sustained in the third year of war the rank and file in the army viewed war with stoicism and resignation rather than with the *élan* and enthusiasm of the early months. But it was not an arms demoralised and ready to abandon the front. The 'home front' was the first to collapse.

The hardship suffered by the workers and their families in the cities swollen in numbers by the industrial demands of the war effort was felt in the winter of 1916/17 to be becoming insupportable. The ineffectual government was being blamed. The Tsar had assumed personal responsibility for leading the armies and spent most of his time after the summer of 1915 at army headquarters. He had left behind the Empress Alexandra, a narrow-minded, autocratic woman. The 'ministers' entrusted with government were little more than phantoms. The infamous Rasputin, on the other hand, was full of energy until murdered in December 1916 – an event greeted with much public rejoicing.

The rioting that spontaneously broke out in Petrograd – formerly St Petersburg – early in March (23 February by Russian dating) 1917 was not due to the leadership of the socialist exiles. Their organisation within the country had suffered severely when early in the war the tsarist government smashed the strike movement. Yet unrest in Petrograd and Moscow had been growing. Only a proportion of the workers in war industries had received wage rises to compensate them for the rapid rises in the price of food and other necessities. Other workers and the dependent families of the soldiers at the front were placed in an increasingly desperate position. The peasants were withholding food from the towns and were unwilling to accept paper money, which bought less and less. The railway system was becoming more inefficient as the war continued, unable to move grain to the towns in anything like sufficient quantities. Dissatisfaction turned on the supposedly 'German' Empress and the administration and government which permitted such gross mismanagement. The revolution in March 1917 succeeded because the garrison troops of the swollen army were not loyal and would not blindly follow the command of the Tsar as they had done in peacetime.

Quite fortuitously the Duma had begun one of its sessions at the very time when this new unrest began. Among the professional classes, the gentry and the army generals, the Duma leaders had gained respect, even confidence, as faith in the Tsar's autocracy and management of the war rapidly diminished. The feeling of country and towns was still patriotic. Everyone was suffering – gentry, workers, peasants and the professional classes. The war against the invader should be won. But at the same time an alleviation of the hardships that the population was suffering especially food shortages, must be dealt with now, without delay. There seemed no contradiction. The Duma was the one institution which provided continuity and embodied constitutional authority. Under the pressure of striking workers and increasing anarchy in Petrograd, the Duma attempted to gain control over the situation. Its leaders advised the Tsar to abdicate. The Tsar, lacking all support, hesitated only a short while before giving up his throne. His brother declined the poisoned chalice when offered the crown. Once the decisive break of the Tsar's abdication had been achieved there could be no saving of the dynasty. The Duma also gave up meeting, handing over all authority to a small group of men who became the provisional government, composed of mainly moderate liberals and presided over by a benign figure of the old school, Prince Lvov. The new government contained one Socialist Revolutionary, Alexander Kerensky, whose co-operation, however, was sincere and who set himself the goal of revitalising the war effort by winning over the Russian people with a programme of broad reform and freedom.

From the start, the provisional government did not enjoy undisputed authority. In Petrograd, as in 1905, a Council of Soviets of Workers' and Soldiers' Deputies sprang up, claiming to speak on behalf of the workers and soldiers throughout Russia. They were not ready to rule. But they asserted the right to watch over the provisional government and to act as they pleased in the interests of 'political freedom and popular government'. The provisional government sought the co-operation of the Petrograd Soviet and had to agree to permit the garrison troops, who had taken the side of the revolution, to remain in Petrograd. Henceforth this disaffected force was under the control of the Petrograd Soviet and could not be moved. The provisional government also agreed to the establishment of soldiers' councils throughout the army, and the Soviet published their famous 'Order number one' decreeing that they should be set up in every army unit by election. But the Soviet, dominated by Mensheviks and Socialist Revolutionaries, was quite incapable of providing for the coherent government of Russia and had no intention either of replacing the provisional government or of seeking an early end to the war other than through a Russian victory. Two leading Bolsheviks at this time, Lev Kamenev and Joseph Stalin, were ready to co-operate with the 'bourgeois' revolution.

The Soviets of Workers' and Soldiers' Deputies and the Soviets of Peasant Deputies were dominated by the Socialist Revolutionaries and had no thought of ruling the country. However, the provisional government also found it increasingly difficult to prevent the country sinking into anarchy. Only the army at the war-fronts stood firm. At home the provisional government spoke of agrarian reform, order, freedom and victory. A new, freely elected parliament would be called to decide on Russia's future and provide a government based on the democratic wishes of the people. But meanwhile the provisional government lacked the power and the means to improve the conditions of the people. In the worsening situation in May 1917, the provisional government insisted that rivalry with the Soviets must cease and that socialist representatives of the Soviets enter the 'bourgeois' government. The Soviets agreed to share power in a coalition and the fusion seemed to be consummated when Alexander Kerensky, as war minister, became its leading member.

These developments were anathema to Lenin. With the assistance of the German High Command, who naturally wished to further the disintegration of Russia, Lenin reached Petrograd in April, having travelled from Switzerland by way of Germany. Lenin had no scruples about accepting the aid of the German class enemy. Soon, he believed, revolution would engulf Germany too. What mattered now was to win back the Russian socialists to the correct revolutionary path, even though he led the minority Bolsheviks. The socialist revolution, Lenin believed, could be thwarted by the collaboration of socialists and the bourgeois government. With relentless energy, overcoming what proved to be temporary failures, he changed the revolutionary tide.

For Lenin the mass upheaval taking place in Russia was more than a 'bourgeois' revolution. He believed the revolutionary upsurge would pass beyond the bourgeois to the socialist stage without pause. In his 'April theses' Lenin argued that the provisional government was the great antagonist already of the 'republic' of Soviet workers and poor peasants taking shape among the grass roots of society. This view was rejected by the Socialist Revolutionaries, by the Mensheviks and at first by many of the Bolsheviks as well. But Lenin won the Bolsheviks over and thereby became the principal architect of the course that the revolution took in November. Lenin's first aim was to destroy the provisional government. With agitation of 'all land to the peasants' and 'all power to the soviets', he helped the revolutionary process along. But Lenin was not the actual cause of the increasing lawlessness; he could only fan the already existing flames. The economic situation was daily getting more out of hand. Inflation was increasing by leaps and bounds. The provisional government was entirely ineffectual in halting the slide into chaos at home. The one hope left for it was the army.

Kerensky appointed a new commander-in-chief, General Kornilov, and ordered a fresh offensive in Galicia. The army responded, made some progress at first, but was then routed when facing an attack in turn. Meanwhile, in July, while the offensive was still in progress, fresh disorders in Petrograd, supported by thousands of sailors from Kronstadt, looked like the beginning of the new revolution. Lenin, however, regarded an uprising at this time as premature. The Bolshevik leadership was divided in its response and hesitated to give a lead to the masses. The rising proved a total failure. The provisional government branded Lenin a German spy and ordered his arrest. He was forced into hiding and later fled to Finland. The prospect of an early Bolshevik revolution now seemed remote. Yet despite the ruin of his hopes, Lenin's diagnosis that Russia was in the grip of a continuing revolutionary ferment proved, in the end, to be correct.

The turn of events in September aided the Bolsheviks. General Kornilov was marching on Petrograd with troops with the avowed intention of destroying the Bolsheviks and dissension and defeatism in the armies' rear. Kerensky ordered Kornilov to lay down his command. Kornilov refused and proclaimed himself the saviour of the nation. Kerensky now appealed for armed help from all the people, including the Bolsheviks. Kornilov's march on Petrograd ended in fiasco, but the Bolshevik militia, the Red Guards, retained their arms. Lenin now set about the overthrow of the provisional government. In the Petrograd Soviet the Bolsheviks in September 1917 at last enjoyed a majority. Lenin returned to Petrograd in October in disguise. He won over the Central Committee of the Bolshevik Party to his view that the time was now ripe for an armed insurrection. The task of organising the rising was assigned by the Petrograd Soviet to a military revolutionary committee. Trotsky was its leading spirit. To this threat, Kerensky and the provisional government reacted complacently and too late.

On the Bolshevik side there was not much confidence either. Trotsky's armed men were largely untrained. Nevertheless Trotsky organised them to seize power on 25 October (Russian date), 7 November (Western). Bolshevik strength, feeble as it was, proved enough. Kerensky could not find sufficient troops to defend his government.

With the seizure of the Winter Palace, where the provisional government was in session, the virtually bloodless revolution was over. The insurrection had been deliberately timed so that it coincided with the assembly of the second All-Russian Congress of Soviets of Workers' and Soldiers' Deputies. The Bolsheviks, who were in the majority, dominated the proceedings. Until the time when a constituent assembly was elected and met, the Congress entrusted the executive to a provisional workers' and peasants' government, thus regularising the power won by Lenin and his associates. But the hold of power by the Bolsheviks was precarious. It might last a day, a week or longer. They could be overwhelmed by a few hundred troops or outside powers. Lenin's achievement was to solidify Bolshevik power until it embraced the greater part of the former Russian Empire.

Had this birth of communist power fulfilled the 'scientific' forecasts of Karl Marx as Lenin believed? Was it a realisation of the inevitable historical process of class conflict according to Marxian theory? Lenin had to adapt Marx to fit the fact that the revolution had first succeeded in an overwhelmingly peasant country. But he believed, thus squaring these facts with Marx's analysis, that the revolution in backward Russia would not survive

Revolutionary Russia. Top: *July 1917, demonstrators scatter outside the Duma in Petrograd as the Provisional Government seeks to hold on to power. In the confusion a Bolshevik regiment standing guard at the Taurida Palace fires on other Bolsheviks trying to seize it.* Opposite: *Lenin's urban supporters, Petrograd, 1917.* Above: *after the October Revolution, the Bolsheviks take the plaudits of the crowd. Stalin is at the extreme right of the photograph; Trotsky is the second from the left.*

without the international socialist revolution, without the proletarian revolution, especially in neighbouring Germany. Russia had but provided the spark. The advanced industrialised West, with its large proletariat would, so he thought, take over the leadership of the world revolution. In fact, the Russian crisis had its immediate cause in the war – not in a general world crisis of capitalism, but in the specific failing of Russian autocracy and of the provisional government to provide for the successful economic and military management of the war. Tsarism first and Kerensky next were destroyed by inflation, by lack of food in the towns and by the general hardships inflicted on a people without an end to war in sight or sustained victories to show for their immense sacrifices.

The second All-Russian Congress of Soviets had called for a just and democratic peace without annexations and indemnities, and had also abolished the landlords' ownership of land. Bolshevik propaganda in the army and the lawless state of the countryside, where the peasants seized the land, added to Russia's state of anarchy. The invading German armies, with their appeal to the subject nationalities, Ukrainians, Georgians, Poles and the Baltic peoples, threatened Russia with territorial disintegration. Lenin's insistence on peace with the Germans at any price appeared suicidal even to his closest collaborators. Fighting ceased and armistice negotiations were formally completed early in December 1917. Meanwhile, Lenin in November had permitted elections for the Constituent Assembly to be held. When it met in January 1918 the Bolsheviks found they had not obtained a majority. Out of a possible 520 deputies the Bolsheviks had only gained 161, and the Socialist Revolutionaries, with 267 deputies, held an absolute majority. Lenin now turned his back on this 'sovereign' assembly and the whole democratic process. The assembly was adjourned and prevented from gathering again.

Trotsky was sent to negotiate peace terms with the Germans. At Brest-Litovsk he prevaricated and made fine speeches. Lenin and the Bolshevik leaders pinned their hopes on the coming German revolution, spurred on by revolutionary propaganda among the German troops. The Germans lost patience with Trotsky's intoxication with his own intellectual brilliance and occupied large regions of western Russia virtually without resistance. Trotsky thereby almost destroyed the revolution in its infancy. On 3 March 1918, the Russians, on Lenin's insistence, and overruling Trotsky's tactics, accepted the peace terms of Brest-Litovsk which

Treaty of Brest-Litovsk, March 1918
0
300 miles
0
300 km
Murmansk
Archangel
SWEDEN
FINLAND
Petrograd
RUSSIA
Stockholm
ESTONIA
(Livonia)
Riga
(Courland)
Volga
Moscow
BALTIC
SEA
LITHUANIA
Danzig
GERMANY
Vistula
Brest-Litovsk
Don
Warsaw
POLAND
Kharkov
Kiev
Dnieper
Cracow
Donets
Lvov
UKRAINE
Vienna
Danube
Budapest
Odessa
AUSTRIA – HUNGARY
ROMANIA
Belgrade
Bucharest
BLACK SEA
SERBIA
Territory lost by Russia

Lenin, November 1917.

dispossessed Russia of a large part of her former Empire. Lenin had cajoled and bullied his colleagues on the Central Committee into accepting the harsh terms. Then he had to fight again to achieve its ratification by the Congress of the Bolshevik Party.

Peace with Germany gave Lenin and the Bolsheviks a breathing space, and saved the Bolshevik revolution. Lenin still confidently expected the war among the Western nations to turn into the great civil war and victory for the proletariat. But meanwhile the revolutionary spark had to be kept alive. It was now threatened by anarchy and by civil war from the opponents of the Bolsheviks, aided by Russia's former allies, who hoped somehow to bring her back into the war. In the succeeding years of war and famine, the Russian people were to suffer even more than they had suffered during the course of the First World War itself. But at the end of this period, the first communist nation was firmly established in a world very different from the one imagined by Lenin at the time of revolution and one which presented problems of a kind entirely different to those for which the two chief founders of communist power, Lenin and Trotsky, had prepared themselves in rigorous Marxist analysis.

CHAPTER 14

The Great War – II: The End of War in the West, 1917–1918

If the war had come to an end in 1917, if the conflict had been decisively won by either the Allies or the central powers eighteen months earlier, then for certain the history of the world would have been very different. Instead the war went on. Neither a compromise peace nor a decision on the western front could be attained. European society had withstood the strains of war for more than two and a half years extraordinarily well, much better than anyone thought likely in the beginning. In the third year, the toll of destruction finally began to crack the political and social cohesion of Russia, the largest of the European powers; nor could even the militarily stronger Western countries escape the consequences of the conflict. The year 1917 marked as great a change in the direction of world history as did 1914.

From the start the war had not been entirely European. With the entry of Turkey into the war in 1914 the destiny of the Middle East was bound up in the war's outcome. In what, from the point of view of the war itself, was a sideshow, the British launched offensives in 1916, 1917 and 1918 against the Turks and at the end of the war became the predominant military power in this region of the world. They were now bound to agreements and promises to the French (the Sykes–Picot agreement) to divide influence with them after the war; to the Arabs they had held out prospects of independence; and to the Zionists, who under Chaim Weizmann's leadership were working for a Jewish State, 'a National Home of the Jewish People' in Palestine. From these origins in the First World War developed the Middle East conflicts which have continued down to the present day.

From the start, too, eastern Asia was involved in the war. On the pretext of pursuing the war against Germany, Japan began by occupying the German colonial sphere in China in 1914, and went on to attempt to gain predominance over a much greater part of China while the European powers were locked in devastating conflict thousands of miles away. On the continent of Africa the war seemed only to result in a rearrangement of colonies: a further chapter in the history of imperialism. Yet the new 'mandates' of the League of Nations over former German colonies held out eventual promise of independence for the African people. Peace treaties did not end these worldwide repercussions of the war. National aspirations which were intensified during the war continued to ferment when the war was over.

Nineteen-seventeen was a momentous year in world history. Two events almost coincided: the Russian Revolution and the United States' entry into the war. By becoming a belligerent and assuming world commitments, the United States was in decisive breach of the advice of George Washington and the Founding Fathers of the Republic. After the war, the American people tried to treat this as an aberration and return to normalcy and 'isolation'. But Americans could not escape involvement in global affairs in the twentieth century as they perceived their security and prosperity threatened by events elsewhere in the world.

Because of the realities of American politics, the decision for war rested on the shoulders of one man, President Wilson. Wilson's Secretary of State, Robert Lansing, was a convinced interventionist on the Allied side long before Wilson reached the same conclusion. He saw the war in Europe as a fight for democracy against the warlike Prussian Junker spirit. Lansing's views did not much affect the President one way or the other. He listened more to his friend and personal emissary, Colonel Edward M. House. But Wilson was very much his own man, supremely confident of his good judgement at a time when in questions of foreign policy, of peace and of war, the presidency was virtually supreme. There can be no doubt that his personal sympathies lay with the democracies. The overthrow of the Tsar in March 1917 therefore removed one obstacle to the United States' siding with the Allies. Nor can there be any doubt that from the start of the war in Europe the actual interpretation of American neutrality enormously favoured the Allied cause in providing financial credit and war supplies, even though Germany managed to secure some American imports through the neutral Scandinavian ports and Holland. Still, US policy was not even-handed and did not exemplify Wilson's own call to the American people to 'act and speak in the true spirit of neutrality'. In November 1916, Wilson narrowly won a second term as president, using such slogans as 'He kept us out of war'. Was Wilson cynically playing politics when during the campaign he declared, 'I am not expecting this country to get into war,' although five months later he led the United States into war?

The charge of insincerity cannot be simply dismissed. Wilson's change of stance in April 1917, his public enthusiasm for the rightness and justice of the noble cause of war, was not what he felt; he hated war, and his efforts to keep the United States out of the war before February 1917 were genuine. To claim that the United States did not behave as a proper neutral from 1914 to 1917, that Wilson hoped to frustrate a German victory by assisting the Allies, that he legalistically stretched the concept of America's neutral rights, condoning British infractions and harshly condemning German violations of these rights, does not prove that Wilson desired or expected the United States to enter the war and was willing to sacrifice American lives for the Allied cause. Wilson knew there was a risk of war. From the outset the Germans had been left in no doubt, and were indeed themselves in no doubt, that to resume unrestricted submarine warfare against American ships supplying the Allies would lead to war with the United States. Expecting to win the war before America could carry military weight in Europe, the Kaiser, urged by the German military, nevertheless on 9 January 1917 finally chose to use this weapon.

Wilson had wished to save America's strength so as to ensure a just and permanent peace after war was over. The war, he believed, would leave the world exhausted, ready to listen to his words of reason. To gain his end, he had attempted as a first step to lead the warring nations to a compromise peace through his personal mediation. But war was nevertheless eventually forced on him by the German military leaders.

On 22 January 1917, after the failure of his last effort to mediate, Wilson still proclaimed a vision of a 'peace without victory' and a new world order or League of Nations to ensure that peace would prevail. Nine days later the Germans publicly announced their intention to attack all neutral shipping. Wilson could not ignore the challenge, but his reaction stopped short of war. The next blow to his attempt to keep out of war was the revelation of the so-called Zimmermann Telegram, a message from the German Foreign Minister to the Mexicans encouraging them to go to war with the United States and to recover their lost territories in alliance with Germany. The telegram had been intercepted by British intelligence and published on 1 March. Anger and indignation swept America. A few days later American cargo ships were sunk without warning by German submarines. Still Wilson hesitated. In the confidential documents and private papers of this time there is no hint of enthusiasm for war on Wilson's part, though his Cabinet were now unanimously in favour. But on 2 April 1917 Wilson submitted to Congress a request to recognise that Germany had made war on the United States, which both Houses of Congress approved on 6 April 1917.

Even so, President Wilson still maintained a separate status on behalf of the United States. He did not simply join the alliance; the United States became an 'associated power', Wilson thereby retaining a free diplomatic hand. He would pursue his goal of arriving at a just peace by other means. The American people were not making war on the

German people but on their militarily crazed rulers. Wilson's faith in American democracy made him believe rather naively that he could appeal to the peoples to follow his ideals if the governments of the Allies or former enemies should place obstacles in the way of the just peace he envisioned.

The United States was not ready for war in April 1917. Her military preparations, especially her great naval expansion, as well as her war plans, had been designed to secure American safety against the eventual victors of the First World War, whether led by Britain or Germany. Some military men believed the Germans could land more than a million men in the United States should they decide to invade her; the navy estimate was a more sober 200,000. The US Navy thus built a great battleship fleet 'second to none' – that is, equal in size to the British – to protect the United States from invasion after the First World War had ended. America's military preparations were particularly ill-suited for the war she now joined. The Allies did not need any more battleships, but they were desperately short of troops on the western front. Wilson had forbidden war plans of intervention in the First World War before April 1917; now everything had to be improvised.

The impact of American military intervention in Europe was not felt for a year. Not until May 1918 were American forces, under General John Pershing's command, strong enough to affect the fighting on the western front. It was just such a breathing space the German High Command had counted on to force Britain and France to their knees.

Along the battlefields of France the year 1917 again brought no result but continued to grind up hundreds of thousands of men and their weapons. General Robert Georges Nivelle, who had replaced Joffre in all but name as French commander-in-chief, planned a great spring offensive to be co-ordinated with Russian and Italian offensives. The British army had now grown to 1,200,000 men and the French to 2,000,000; together with the Belgians the Allies now enjoyed a superiority of 3,900,000 over 2,500,000 Germans. The Germans stood on the defensive in the west but frustrated the French and British efforts in the spring and summer of 1917 to break through their lines and rout their armies. Nivelle's failure resulted in widespread demoralisation among the French troops. The French nation which had withstood so much in two and a half years of war appeared, during the spring of 1917, to lose her cohesion and unity of purpose. Soldiers mutinied, bitter at the spectacle of Paris, with its cafés and boulevards and smart ladies untroubled by war. Bitterness and despair, fear of mutilation and death, reopened old wounds of social schism.

The collapse of French morale was localised and General Henri Philippe Pétain's skilful handling of the situation, and the belief he instilled that the war would in future be fought with more consideration for the value of human life, brought the mutinies under control. Of the 30,000 to 40,000 mutineers forty-nine were shot to serve as an example. In the summer of 1917 the 'sacred union', the French political truce, ended. Following the lead of Russian Bolsheviks, French socialists now spoke of compromise peace. At this critical juncture President Raymond Poincaré chose as head of government, hated though he was by the socialists, the seventy-six-year-old veteran politician Georges Clemenceau, who embodied the spirit of fighting the war to victory. The country responded once more.

For the British and Canadians who bore the brunt of the fighting during the summer and autumn of 1917 it was a bitter year, and their commander Field Marshal Lord Haig was criticised for the unprecedented losses sustained in the offensives in Flanders. In November he reached the deserted village of Passchendaele less than ten miles from his starting point. Passchendaele came to symbolise the apparently pointless slaughter. There was no longer any romance in war.

By the autumn of 1917 three of the now six great powers at war were on the point of military and economic collapse. The Austrian half of the Dual Monarchy was desperately short of food; the Habsburg army could not without German help sustain the war on all fronts. The new Emperor Charles I was secretly seeking a way out of the war. On the other side, the Italians were also soon in desperate plight. Suffering 340,000 casualties, the Italian army was defeated at the battle of Caporetto in October 1917, but with some British and French help recovered to man a new line of defence.

One of the great powers, Russia, did collapse. The revolution that overthrew the Tsar in March 1917 had not taken her out of the war immediately. The new provisional government intended to fight it more energetically and successfully than before. But Alexander Kerensky, War Minister of the government and later its leader, could not with fine speeches make up for Russia's exhaustion and the mismanagement of the 'home front'. The Russian summer offensive which he ordered turned into a rout. In November 1917 the Bolsheviks seized power and called for peace immediately 'without annexations and without indemnities'. Russia was out of the war, a stunning blow for the Allies.

Nineteen-seventeen was a disastrous year for the Allies. Only on the oceans did they win what for Britain and France was a battle for survival. The Germans only once seriously challenged the battleship might of the British navy. The resulting battle of Jutland in May 1916 was claimed by both sides as a victory, but the German fleet did not again challenge the British navy whereas Britain continued to rule above the waves and maintain her blockade of Germany. The real danger to the Allies was the 'blockade' imposed below the water's surface by German submarines. At first it looked as though the Germans would sink enough ships to knock Britain and France out of the war by cutting the Atlantic supply line, for they sank 212 ships in February 1917 and a record 335 ships, totalling 847,000 tons, in April. By convoying ships losses were reduced to 107 ships by December. This was the damage that some 100 German submarines inflicted. What would have happened if the Germans had before the war concentrated on this effective offensive weapon instead of wasting resources on the prestigious German battleship fleet? They were to repeat the error in the Second World War.

During the grim winter of 1917 and 1918, widespread disaffection and doubts whether the war could ever be won led to new calls for peace from all sides. Lenin had nothing to lose by calling the labouring masses in Europe to revolution and to bring to an end the capitalist imperialist war of their masters. Lloyd George, determined to fight until the German rulers were defeated, responded, to still the doubts in Britain, by delivering a speech in January 1918 to the British Trades Union Congress. Its keynote was moderation and an insistence that the central powers give up all their conquests so that the sanctity of treaties be upheld. Lloyd George's speech was overshadowed a few days later, on 8 January 1918, by President Wilson's famous Fourteen Points setting out in a similar way the basis of peace. The worldwide appeal of the Fourteen Points lay in their lofty design for a new era of international relations. The world led by the United States and Wilson's 'new diplomacy' would 'be made fit and safe to live in'; every nation would 'determine its own institutions, be assured of justice and fair dealing by the other peoples of the world as against force and selfish aggression'. But the specific Russian, British and American peace proclamations, with their insistence on the restoration of conquered territory, all presupposed the defeat of Germany. No German could regard as a 'compromise' giving up all the territory still firmly occupied.

In 1918 it appeared likely that the Allies would be defeated rather than Germany. The generals Hindenburg and Ludendorff had established a virtual dictatorship in Germany and marshalled all resources in a country exhausted by war. In March 1918 Ludendorff mounted a tremendous offensive in the west; during April, May and June German troops broke through and once more came close to Paris. The cost in casualties was again huge: 800,000 Germans and more than a million Allied troops. This turned out to be imperial Germany's last bid for victory, though the Allies, commanded now by Marshal Ferdinand Foch, did not know it.

The Allied counter-offensives found a weakened enemy losing the will to fight. The greatest defeatism was not, however, to be found on the battlefront but among the so recently revered German generals, Hindenburg and Ludendorff. Germany's allies were collapsing in September 1918. The Turkish army was defeated in Palestine. The Bulgarians could not resist an Allied advance from Greece and requested an armistice. Though Austrian troops were still stoutly defending the Italian front, the Dual Empire was disintegrating and its various nationalities were proclaiming their independence. In France, the arrival of new masses of fresh American troops had not only blunted Germany's earlier thrust against Paris, but filled the German High Command with a sense of hopelessness. Successful Allied offensives broke their last will to resist.

Ludendorff, towards the close of September 1918, demanded that the government in Berlin should secure an immediate armistice to save the army. In Berlin the politicians tried to win a little time. Later Ludendorff propagated the lie, so useful to the Nazis, that the army had been 'stabbed in the back'. The truth is that Ludendorff wished to end a war that was militarily lost while the army still preserved its discipline and cohesion. He got his way. On 11 November 1918 the last shot was fired in France.

CHAPTER 15

Peacemaking in an Unstable World, 1918–1923

The history of the period from the armistice in November 1918 until the conclusion of the majority of the peace treaties a year later has a dual aspect. On the one hand the victors, assembled in Paris, argued about peace terms to be imposed on Germany and her allies; they knew that after four years of war and all the changes it had brought about, the people of the West longed for an immediate and a stable peace. At Paris too, decisions would be taken to reconstruct the map not only of Europe, but also of the Middle East, Africa and China. A new framework of conducting international relations would be created by establishing the League of Nations. All this represents just one side of the historical development of this critical period.

The other side of the picture was that eastern, central and southern Europe was daily becoming more disorganised; in Turkey a nationalist revolution would reject the peace terms altogether; China continued to disintegrate, rent by internal dissension and the pressure of the Japanese and the West. The future of Russia and the ultimate size of the territories that would fall under Soviet control was one of the biggest uncertainties of all. With the end of the war and the collapse of the defeated rulers there was a threat of anarchy. National and social conflicts erupted in revolution. In Russia the war had not ended in time to save the country from internal violence. For how much of the rest of Europe was it now too late as well? No previous war had ended in such chaos. The peacemakers thus did not preside over an empty map of the world waiting for settlement in the light of their decisions reached around the conference table.

The great powers no longer disposed of huge victorious armies. These were being rapidly demobilised and war-weary peoples were not ready to allow their leaders to gather fresh mass armies. The leaders who mattered, the 'big three' – Wilson, Lloyd George and Clemenceau – as the representatives of democracies were dependent on assemblies and electorates and became increasingly conscious of the limits of their ability simply to follow the dictates of their own reasoning. Another 'Europe' and 'Asia' was taking shape beyond the control of the victors at Paris. It was shaped by its own local antagonisms.

When the peace conference opened on 18 January 1919, just two months after the signing of the armistices with Turkey, Austria, Hungary and Germany, obviously the problem that most weighed on Wilson, Clemenceau and Lloyd George was the future of Germany. The armistice terms had been harsh, but fell short of demanding unconditional surrender. The German government had applied to Wilson for an armistice on the basis of the Fourteen Points, after Ludendorff and Hindenburg had suddenly declared that the army was in no condition to hold out a moment longer. In accordance with Wilson's clearly expressed reply that the terms to be imposed on Germany would be harsher still if the Kaiser remained in power, the generals themselves had co-operated in persuading the

Kaiser to abdicate and depart for exile in the Netherlands. And they were also ready to co-operate with the new government of Social Democrats in Berlin headed by Friedrich Ebert. Hindenburg and his generals brought the German armies home from France and Belgium in excellent order. They were received more as victors than as defeated troops by the German population. But, once on German soil, these once great armies simply dissolved; they did not wait to be demobilised according to plans which did not exist. They just went home. Only in the east, in Poland and the Baltic, were there still army units left, sufficiently powerful in the chaotic conditions of this region of Europe caught up in civil wars and national conflicts to constitute a decisive military factor. To combat Bolshevism the Allied armistice conditions actually required the Germans to remain in occupation of the eastern and Baltic territories until Allied troops could be spared to take over their responsibilities as guardians against the 'reds'.

Despite the changes in Germany and the proclamation of a republic, the Allied attitude in Paris did not noticeably alter. Whether 'Junkers' or 'Social Democrats', the Allies continued to regard them as arrogant and dangerous Germans and treated them accordingly. But they also dealt with the Germans at a distance, rejecting the responsibility of occupying the country and confining themselves to the strategic occupation of part of the Rhineland alone. Considering the condition of threatening anarchy, the Allies continued to be haunted by the fear that the Germans only wanted to use the armistice as a breathing space to reorganise and resume the war. Such thoughts had indeed crossed Ludendorff's now disordered mind and the possibility of resisting should the peace terms prove unacceptable was discussed by Hindenburg and the Social Democratic government. The answer was obvious. There were no German armies any longer in existence in 1919 that could hope to put up a defence even against the reduced strength of the Allied armies. Yet the Allies kept up the fiercest pressure during the weeks of the armistice. The blockade was maintained from November 1918 through that winter until March 1919; later this proved a good propaganda point for the Nazis, who exaggerated Allied callousness.

During that first winter and spring of 1918/19, Germany was left to survive as best as she could. The new democratic republic, soon known as the Weimar Republic after the town in which its constitution-making parliament met, could not have had a worse start. Within Germany herself, a vacuum of power, similar to that in Russia in 1917, which rival groups sought to fill, threatened stability. Everyone was aware of the parallel, not least the new chancellor Ebert. But Ebert, once a humble saddle-maker, was a politician of considerable experience and strength. He was determined not to be cast in the role of the Russian Kerensky. For Ebert, the most important tasks ahead were to establish law and order, revive industry and agriculture so that the German people could live, preserve German unity and ensure that the 'revolution' that had begun with the Kaiser's departure should itself lead to the orderly transfer of power to a democratically elected parliamentary assembly. Ebert was tough, and determined that Germany should become a parliamentary democracy and not a communist state. This was a programme which won the support of the army generals, who recognised that the Social Democratic republic would be both the best immediate defence against anarchy and Bolshevism and a screen acceptable to the Allies behind which Germany's traditional forces could regroup.

The compact reached between the army command and the Social Democratic government of the Republic in order to counter the danger of a Bolshevik revolution has been much criticised. Why did the Social Democrats leave the revolution half-finished, retain the army and the imperial administration, and leave society and wealth undisturbed? Did they not thereby seal their own doom and pave the way for the Nazis a decade later? With hindsight one may legitimately ask would Germany's future have been better with a 'completed' communist revolution? The question is deceptively simple. It is unlikely that the Allies would have allowed the communists to retain power in Germany; an extensive Allied occupation might then have resulted after all. The breakdown of order within Germany left the sincerely democratic socialists isolated and so forced them to seek co-operation with the forces that had upheld the Kaiser's Germany hitherto. They had no other practical alternative.

There can be no doubt, either, that a communist seizure of power would have represented the will of only a small minority of Germans; the great majority, including the workers, did not desire to emulate Bolshevik Russia. All over Germany in

Revolution Infects Germany. Left: *Karl Liebknecht, founder, with Rosa Luxemburg, of the Spartacus League, which in 1919 became the German Communist Party.* Right: *Rosa Luxemburg herself, the fiery Polish revolutionary with a humane vision. She was taken prisoner with Liebknecht and murdered on 15 January 1919. A third prisoner was more fortunate: Wilhelm Pieck survived to become first president of the German Democratic Republic (East Germany) in October 1949.* Above: *street fighting in Berlin during the Spartacist rising in January 1919.*

November 1918 'workers' and soldiers' councils' formed themselves spontaneously; the Russian model of the 'soviet' was quite consciously followed by those who organised these bodies. The movement began in Kiel where sailors of the imperial navy mutinied, unwilling at the end of the war to risk their lives senselessly to satisfy their officers' sense of honour. The officers had planned to take the High Seas Fleet out to sea to engage the British in one last glorious suicidal battle. From Kiel the setting up of German soviets spread to Hamburg and other parts, then to Berlin and the rest of Germany. But not all these self-proclaimed soldiers' and workers' councils, which claimed to speak for the people, were in favour of a Bolshevik state. In many, the more moderate socialists predominated and those who before the armistice had been opposed to war (Independent Socialists) now joined with the majority who had supported war. In others the Independent Socialists allied with the Spartacists, the name the communist faction led by Karl Liebknecht and Rosa Luxemburg had assumed.

In Berlin, the capital, the crucial struggle between the socialist factions was decided. Ebert had assumed the chancellorship, constitutionally accepting this office from Prince Max von Baden, the last imperial chancellor. His fellow socialist, Philipp Scheidemann, in the confusion that followed proclaimed a republic to anticipate Liebknecht. Liebknecht simultaneously proclaimed the 'socialist republic' to his followers. Ebert would have preferred a constitutional monarchy, but now the die was cast. Ebert and Scheidemann won over the Independent Socialists with concessions that would allow the Berlin Soldiers' and Workers' Council 'all power' until the constituent parliament met. The constituent parliament was elected early in January 1919 and assembled in Weimar in February to begin its labours of drawing up one constitution for the whole of Germany.

All this gives a false impression of orderliness. During the winter and spring following the armistice it was uncertain whether Ebert would survive. Germany was torn by political strife of unprecedented ferocity, and separatist movements in several regions even suggested that Germany might disintegrate and so follow the fate of the Habsburg Empire. In the second-largest state, Bavaria, political strife was unfolding. The Independent Socialist leader Kurt Eisner had led a revolution of workers and soldiers in Munich, proclaimed the republic of Bavaria, and deposed the royal house of Wittelsbach. All over Germany the princes disappeared. They had counted for so little, their disappearance made little impact now. Eisner's republic was not communist. Though he had been opposed to the war, he was at one with Ebert in desiring a democratic Bavaria, in a Germany of loosely 'federated' states. Elections duly held in January and February 1919 in Bavaria resulted in the defeat of Eisner's Independent Socialist Party. On his way to the Bavarian parliament to lay down office, Eisner was brutally murdered in the street. This was the signal for civil war in Bavaria, which slid into anarchy and extremism.

December 1918 and January 1919 were the decisive months in Berlin, too. There the Spartacists decided to carry the revolution further than the Social Democrats were prepared to go. The Spartacists attempted an insurrection in December, seizing Berlin's public buildings, and the Social Democrats, still having no efficient military force of their own, appealed to the army. Irregular volunteer army units were formed, the so-called Free Corps; all sorts of freebooters, ex-officers and men enjoying violence joined; there were few genuine Social Democrats among these paramilitary units. The scene was set for fighting among the factions, for bloodshed and brutality. The Spartacist rising was put down and Liebknecht and Rosa Luxemburg were murdered as they emerged from their hiding place. The rising followed by strikes and fresh disorders seriously threatened Ebert's government in the new year of 1919 (page 134).

In Bavaria there were three rival governments – two Bolshevik and one majority Socialist. The showdown came in Bavaria in April 1919. The moderate Socialists called on the Free Corps units in Bavaria for military assistance. The Bolsheviks were bloodily suppressed and in Munich many innocent people lost their lives. It was a tragedy for Germany and the world that the Weimar Republic was founded in bloodshed, that the Social Democrats had to call on the worst anti-democratic elements in the state for support. This left a legacy of suspicion and bitterness among the working people, split the Socialists and so in the end helped the right-wing extremists to power. The communists blamed the Social Democrats, the Social Democrats the communists. Democracy had triumphed but at what proved to be a heavy price.

*

In Paris there was a keen awareness that to delay the making of peace would endanger stability even further. Germany should be presented with the terms and given a short period for a written submission embodying their reply. There should be no meaningful negotiations with the Germans. Better a 'dictated' peace quickly than a long-drawn-out wrangle that allowed the Germans to exploit Allied differences. It was a remarkable achievement that despite these serious differences – the French, in particular, looked for more extensive territorial guarantees and reparations – in the short space of four months an agreed treaty was presented to the Germans on 7 May 1919. This represented the compromises reached by Wilson, Lloyd George and Clemenceau. The Italians took little part, deeply offended and dissatisfied with their territorial gains in general and the rejection of their claim for Fiume in particular. There was no set agenda for the negotiations in Paris. The crucial decisions were taken by Wilson, Lloyd George and Clemenceau and then the details were left to the experts who accompanied the statesmen in large numbers.

Clemenceau was aware of France's basic weakness, inferior in population and industrial production to a Germany that was bound to recover. How to provide then for French security? The break-up and partition of Germany were not seriously considered, though a separate Rhineland would have served French interests. Germany, albeit deprived of Alsace-Lorraine and of territory in the east, remained intact as potentially the most powerful European continental state.

One of the few undertakings of the Allies, and incorporated in the Fourteen Points, was to reconstitute an independent Polish nation and so to undo the eighteenth-century partition of Poland by Russia, Austria and Prussia. The carrying out of this pledge created great difficulties in redrawing Germany's eastern frontier. The German city of

Left: *Lloyd George, Orlando, Clemenceau and Wilson at the Versailles conference, 1919.* Below: *Parisians celebrate the news of the armistice, November 1918.*

Peace Settlements, 1919–1923

Danzig was separated from Germany and turned into an autonomous free city for which the League of Nations accepted certain responsibilities and over which Poland enjoyed specific rights. The wedge of Polish territory to the sea created the 'Polish corridor' which henceforth separated Germany from East Prussia. In parts of Silesia a plebiscite in March 1921 and the League decision in 1922 decided where the precise frontier with Poland ran. But the peace treaty placed several million German-speaking peoples under foreign rule. In the west, apart from Alsace-Lorraine and two small territories which became Belgian, Germany lost no territory; the Saarland, with its valuable coal, was placed under the League, and the French were granted the rights to the mines with the provision that after fifteen years a plebiscite would allow the population to choose their own future.

An important guarantee of French security was the requirement that the Germans were not permitted to fortify or station troops in the Rhineland; all the German territory west of the Rhine and bridgeheads across the Rhine, moreover, were occupied by the Allies for fifteen years and evacuation would only occur in three stages every five years if Germany fulfilled the treaty conditions of Versailles. But Clemenceau never lost sight of the fact that France remained, even after these German losses, inferior to her neighbour in population and industrial potential, and therefore militarily as well in the longer term. Clemenceau realised that France would need the alliance of Britain and the United States even more after 1918. France had been gravely weakened by the war. With Bolshevik Russia no longer contributing to the balance of Europe as tsarist Russia had done before 1914, German preponderance on the continent of Europe had potentially increased. Clemenceau understood, and some basic facts bear out what he foresaw.

Population (*millions*)

	1920	1930	1940
France	38.8	41.2	41.3
Germany	59.2	64.3	67.6(1937)
Britain	44.3	46.9	48.2
Russia	155.3	179.0	195.0
Poland	26.0	29.5	31.5
Czechoslovakia	12.9	13.9	14.7
Yugoslavia	12.4	14.4	16.4
Austria	6.5	6.6	6.7
Hungary	7.9	8.6	9.3

But Clemenceau struggled in vain with Wilson and Lloyd George in Paris to secure more permanent guarantees than were provided by the occupation of the Rhineland, which remained sovereign German territory. He accepted in the end that Germany could not be diminished further in the west; that France could not attain the Rhine frontier. He feared that, if he refused, Britain and the United States would cease all post-war support of France. In place of 'territorial' guarantees, France was offered a substitute: the promise of a post-war alliance with Britain and the United States. This treaty, concluded in June 1919, was conditional upon the consent of the Senate of the United States. As it turned out, Clemenceau had received payment with a cheque that bounced, though Wilson at the time was confident that the Senate would approve.

It became from the French point of view all the more vital to write into the treaty provisions for restricting the German army and armaments and

Coal including Lignite and Steel Production, 1920–1939
(*million metric tons*)

	Coal and Lignite				Steel			
	1920	1929	1933	1939	1920	1929	1933	1939
Britain	233.0	262.0	210.4	235.0	9.2	9.8	7.1	13.4
France	25.3	55.0	48.0	50.2	2.7	9.7	6.5	8.0
Germany	220.0	337.0	237.0	400.0	7.8	16.2	7.6	23.7

to have the means of supervising these provisions to see that they were carried out. But for how long could this be maintained? The German army was reduced to a professional force of 100,000 men, a size appropriate for only the smallest of European states. Such a force was not even adequate to ensure internal security. Add to this a few obsolete warships, the High Seas Fleet having under the armistice conditions been already interned in British waters, a prohibition to build an air force, an Allied control commission to supervise the production of light armaments that the Germans were permitted to manufacture and the total picture is one of Germany reduced to military impotence. Finally, Germany lost all her colonies.

In Germany there was a tremendous outcry. But already in 1919, among the military and the more thoughtful politicians, it was realised that the sources of Germany's strength would recover and her industries revive. As memories of the war receded, opportunities would arise to modify or circumvent the restrictions imposed on Germany by the 'dictated' Versailles Treaty. The German public especially focused their anger on the 'war guilt' article of the treaty. It was misunderstood and considered out of context. It stated that Germany had imposed war on the Allies by her aggression and that of her allies. Today, looking at the July crisis of 1914, there can be no real doubt that Germany and Austria–Hungary were the 'aggressors', though their motives and justification can be debated still. What the Germans could not be expected to know was that this article (231) and the one that followed represented a compromise between the Allies on the question of reparations.

The French and British wished the Germans to pay the 'whole cost' of the war. North-eastern France, once France's industrial region, had been devastated while Germany was untouched. Britain and France had incurred heavy war debts which the United States insisted had to be repaid. France and Britain had to be satisfied with the controversial article 231 whereby Germany and her allies accepted responsibility for causing all the loss and damage because of her aggression. But in article 232 the Germans were not required actually to pay for all these losses and damages, that is 'the whole cost of the war'. The Germans would have to pay only for losses caused to civilians and their property. This represented a victory for Wilson; Allied public opinion would be appeased by the 'war guilt' clause. Little thought was extended to German public opinion. No agreement on a total sum was reached. This was left for a Reparations Commission to determine by May 1921. The Germans were presented with the treaty draft on 7 May 1919. Their voluminous protests and counter-proposals delivered on 29 May were considered, a small number of concessions made. They were then presented with the unalterable final draft in the form of a virtual ultimatum on 16 June. Unable to resume the war, the Germans formally accepted and signed the treaty on 28 June 1919. They began as they were to continue: evading its terms. A week earlier, the German fleet, interned in Scapa Flow, was scuttled by the crews.

Had the Allies acted wisely in their treatment of Germany? The financial thinking of the Allies, led by the United States, lacked realism. Reparations and war debts, the growth of trade and employment were international and not purely German problems. John Maynard Keynes, the distinguished economist, who had been sent to Paris to serve as one of Britain's financial experts, later in his famous book on the peace treaty, *The Economic Consequences of the Peace*, condemned the financial provisions. The total amount of reparations payable by Germany fixed in May 1921 – 132,000,000,000 gold marks – was actually not so excessive. But only a prosperous, stable Germany in a relatively free international market could contribute to general European prosperity. Lloyd George understood that to 'punish' Germany financially would create a powerful competitor in export markets as Germany sought the means to pay. If there were to be security from Germany in the longer term, then one way was to reduce German power by dividing the country; but this offended prevailing views of nationality. The other way was to ensure that Germany's political development would lead to a fundamental change of attitudes: genuine democracy coupled with a renunciation of nationalist aspirations. Instead the peace weakened the democratic movement and heightened nationalist feelings.

Besides Germany and Austria–Hungary the other great power defeated in war was Russia. The West was perplexed by the Russian problem. Lenin's Russia was openly hostile both to the victors and the vanquished of 1918. They were all, in Lenin's eyes, imperialist bourgeois powers ripe for revolution. There were voices in the West which called for an all-out effort to kill the poisonous influence of Red Russia from the outset. But there was also sympathy for her plight. Confused attempts were made by France, Britain and the United States to provide support for the anti-Bolshevik forces in Russia and so the West became embroiled, though only feebly, in the chaos of the Russian Civil War (page 179).

The communist seizure of power in November 1917 had initially gained control only of Petrograd and Moscow. That seizure was not given the stamp of approval by the rest of Russia. Lenin had allowed elections for a constitutional parliament, arranged by Kerensky's provisional government. This 'constituent assembly' which met in January 1918 was the most representative ever elected, and the mass of the peasantry turned to the Socialist Revolutionaries who constituted the majority of the elected representatives. Only a quarter of them were Bolsheviks. Lenin had no intention of allowing the assembly to undo the Bolshevik revolution. The assembly was forcibly dispersed on his orders. It was the end of any genuine democratic process. During 1918 Lenin was determined that the Bolsheviks should seize power throughout Russia, and dealt ruthlessly with opposition and insurrection against Bolshevik rule. Lenin was not held back by any moral scruple. He saw as the greater goal the success of the communist revolution, even though a majority of the people were too backward to understand it. Every other consideration had to be subordinated then to the secure achievement of Bolshevik power, which would act as a torch to set alight revolution in the more advanced West. Lenin's eyes were fixed on the world. Without a world revolution, he believed, the purely Russian Revolution would not survive.

Lenin met the force of opponents with force and terror. The terrorist police which Lenin set up in December 1917 was called the Cheka. This organisation was given the right to kill opponents and even those suspected of opposition, without benefit of trial, by summary execution. The authority of the state now stood behind the exercise of brute lawless power. No questions would be asked and the killing of some innocents was accepted as inevitable in the interests of the consolidation of communist power in Russia – 'the great goal'. Lenin's successors were to accept such exercise of terror, which reached its climax under Stalin in the 1930s, not as a temporary necessity in conflict but as a permanent part of Soviet control over the population.

Soviet terror included the killing of the Tsar and his family in July 1918. Soviet ferocity was partly responsible for resolute centres of opposition to the Bolsheviks. Already before the peace of Brest-Litovsk some of the non-Russian peoples around the whole periphery of the old Russian Empire had shown a desire for independence. With German help in 1918, states were being formed in the Baltic (Lithuania, Latvia, Estonia); Finland became completely independent and the local Bolshevik forces were defeated; the Ukraine became an independent state; in central Asia independence was claimed by the peoples living in these regions; only Poland had been promised her independence and sought to make good her claims and, much more, to create a large Polish nation by carving out territories from Russia proper. In opposition to 'Red' Petrograd, to Moscow and the central region controlled by the Bolsheviks, other Russian forces, led by tsarist generals, formed in many parts of Russia, sometimes in co-operation but also sometimes in conflict with local nationalist forces. These disparate military groups and armies became known collectively as White Russians, which suggested they possessed more coherence than was actually the case. In many regions there was a complete breakdown of law and order and independent brigand armies looted and lived off the countryside.

Among these independent and lawless armies one of the strangest was the Czech Legion (of some 50,000 officers and men) which had been formed in Russia from prisoners of war to fight for the Allied cause. After the Russian peace with Germany the Czech Legion attempted to leave Russia by way of the Trans-Siberian railway and the port of Vladivostok in Siberia. Fearing Bolshevik intentions, they came into open conflict with the Bolsheviks sent to disarm them. In Siberia they then formed a nucleus around which White Russian forces gathered. The self-proclaimed Supreme Ruler of Russia at the head of these partly disciplined and frequently insubordinate troops was Admiral Kolchak. The Allies had first intervened in Russia in the hope of reopening a war front in the east in order to relieve pressure on the western front. After the conclusion of the war with Germany, Britain and France were unsure whether the Bolsheviks or the Whites would ultimately gain power. Lloyd George's instincts at Paris were sound in that he did not wish to make an enemy of the Bolsheviks. He proposed Allied 'mediation' between the Russians fighting each other quite irreconcilably. British intervention was small and limited. The French made a more determined but useless attempt, co-operating with White forces in the Ukraine from a base in Odessa. The Japanese landed a large force in Siberia, pursuing imperialist ambitions of their own; and the Americans a smaller force at Vladivostok, ostensibly to rescue the Czech Legion but really to watch the Japanese. Allied intervention was too small to make a significant impact on the outcome of the civil war in Russia.

Lenin left it to Trotsky as commissar for war to create a Red Army to complete the conquest of the former Russian Empire and defeat all the opposing forces. Their disunity made it easier for Trotsky to defeat first one opponent and then the next. Nevertheless his achievement in recreating an army for the revolution was remarkable. Army discipline was reintroduced, as was the death penalty. Trotsky was no less ruthless than Lenin in the draconian measures he was ready to take to achieve discipline. Former tsarist officers were recruited to provide the necessary expertise and 'political commissars' were attached to the units to ensure that the armies would continue to fight for the right cause.

Lenin ended the period of civil war in 1920 partly by compromise and partly by conquest. He recognised the independence of the Baltic states of Finland, Estonia, Latvia and Lithuania. Poland was for communist Russia the most critical region. Poland was the gateway to Germany, and so, Lenin believed, the gateway to world revolutions. But the Poles proved too strong for the Red Army, though not strong enough to defeat it decisively. The war between Poland and Russia lasted from the spring of 1920 until the following October. Given only limited Allied help, the Poles were really left to win or lose by themselves. At first they succeeded spectacularly and reached Kiev in the Ukraine. The Red Army then drove them back and for a time Lenin hoped to overrun Poland altogether and to instal a puppet communist government. But at the gates of Warsaw the Red Army was defeated in turn and Lenin in 1921 accepted Polish independence. The remainder of the Russian Empire was successfully brought under communist control and the short-lived independent states of the Ukraine, Georgia and Transcaucasia were forcibly incorporated in the Soviet Union.

Communist Russia had failed to spread the revolution. The sparks that led to short-lived communist takeovers in Hungary and Bavaria were quickly extinguished. Russia had also failed to thrust through Poland to the West. Equally the West had failed either to overthrow the Bolsheviks or to befriend them. For two decades from 1921 to 1941 the Soviet Union remained essentially cut off, a large self-contained empire following her own road to modernisation and living in a spirit of hostile coexistence with the West.

Up to the last year of the war the Allies did not desire to destroy the Habsburg Empire, which was seen as a stabilising influence in south-eastern Europe. Wilson's Fourteen Points had promised 'autonomous' development to the peoples of the empire, not independence. Reform, not destruction, was the aim of the West. Within the Monarchy itself the spirit of national independence among the Slavs had grown immensely, stimulated by the Bolshevik revolution and the Russian call for the national independence of all peoples. Now the Czechs and Slovaks wished to form a national unit within a Habsburg federal state where each nation would enjoy equal rights. The Slovenes, Croats and Serbs of the Monarchy wished to form an independent Yugoslav nation and the Ruthenes demanded freedom from Polish dependence. The Habsburg dynasty and ruling classes could not respond adequately to these aspirations even in the Austrian half of the Monarchy; it was unthinkable that the Magyars would accept a sufficiently liberal policy to win over the Slavs, or even that they could have done so as late as 1917. The Monarchy was tied to dualism. Outside the Monarchy, émigrés were winning the support of the Allies for the setting up of independent nations. As the Monarchy weakened under the impact of war, so these émigré activities grew more important.

In 1918 Wilson became gradually converted to the view that the Czechoslovaks and Yugoslavs were oppressed nationalities whose efforts for freedom deserved sympathy and support. Before the conclusion of the armistice, the Czechoslovaks had won Allied recognition as an 'Allied nation', Poland had been promised independence, and the Yugoslav cause, though not accorded the same recognition, had at any rate become well publicised. When Austria–Hungary appealed to Wilson for an armistice on the basis of the Fourteen Points in October 1918, Wilson replied that the situation had changed and that autonomy for the other nationalities was no longer sufficient. This was strictly true. With defeat, the Hungarians and the Slavs all hastened to dissociate themselves from the Germans. Poland and Yugoslavia declared their independence as did the Hungarians. The German Austrians only had one option left, to dissociate Austria from the dynasty, and declare German Austria a republic. The revolution in Vienna was bloodless as Charles I withdrew.

The Habsburg Empire broke apart before the armistice on 3 November 1918 and there was no way the Allies could have brought her together again. But in no other part of the world was it more difficult to reconcile Wilson's ideals of national self-determination and national frontiers as the different peoples of the Balkans did not live in tidily delineated lands. There would always be people who formed majorities and minorities. The defeat of the dominant Austrians and Hungarians now determined that they and not the Slavs, Romanians and Italians would constitute new minorities within the 'successor states' of the Habsburg Empire.

The Allies at Paris modified the central Europe that had been created by strong national leaders in respect to frontiers, attempted to ensure good treatment of minorities and enforced punitive conditions on the defeated Hungarians and German Austrians; in its essentials, however, power had been transferred to the new nations already. Austria was reduced to a small state of 6.5 million inhabitants. The peace treaties forbade their union with Germany. The principle of national self-determination was violated as far as the defeated were concerned. The Italians had been promised the natural frontier of the Brenner Pass, even though this meant incorporating nearly a quarter of a million German-speaking Tyrolese into Italy. The new Czechoslovak state was granted its 'historic frontiers' which included Bohemia, and another 3.5 million German-speaking Austrians and also Ruthenes were divided between the Czechs and Poles and separated from the Ukraine. Hungary was reduced to the frontiers where only Magyars predominated. Hungary was now a small state of some 8 million, nearly three quarters of a million Magyars being included in the Czechoslovak state. The Hungarians remained fiercely resentful of the enforced peace, and their aspirations to revise the peace treaties aroused the fears of neighbouring Romania, Czechoslovakia and Yugoslavia.

A peace settlement in the Near East eluded the 'peacemakers' altogether. With the defeat of the Ottoman Empire and the Turkish acceptance of an armistice on 30 October 1918, the Arab people had high hopes of achieving their independence. The Americans, British and French were committed by public declarations to the goal of setting up governments which would express the will of the peoples of the former Turkish Empire. But Britain and France had also during the war secretly agreed on a division of influence in the Middle East. To complicate the situation still further, the British government had promised the Zionists 'the establishment in Palestine of a National Home for the Jewish people' in what became known as the Balfour Declaration (2 November 1917). How were all these conflicting aspirations now to be reconciled? Wars and insurrections disturbed Turkey and the Middle East for the next five years.

The Arabs were denied truly independent states except in what became Saudi Arabia. The other Arab lands were placed under French and British tutelage as 'mandates' despite the wishes of the inhabitants. Iraq and Palestine became British mandates and Syria and Lebanon, French. Within a few years, the Arab states of Syria, Lebanon, Transjordan and Iraq emerged but remained firmly under British and French control.

Peace with Turkey proved even more difficult to achieve. The Sultan's government had accepted the peace terms of the Treaty of Sèvres in August 1920, but a Turkish general, Mustafa Kemal, the founder of modern Turkey, led a revolt against the peace terms. The Greeks, meanwhile, were seeking to fulfil their own ambitions and landed troops in Turkish Asia Minor. The disunity of the Allies added to the confusion and made the enforcement of the Treaty of Sèvres quite impossible. By skilled diplomacy – by dividing the Anglo-French alliance, and by securing supplies from the French and Russians – Kemal gathered and inspired a Turkish national movement to free Turkey from the foreign invasions. He defeated the Greeks in September 1922 and then turned on the British troops stationed in the Straits of Constantinople. In October 1922 Lloyd George, unsupported by his former allies, was forced to accept Kemal's demands for a revision of the peace treaty. This was accomplished by the Lausanne Conference and a new treaty in July 1923

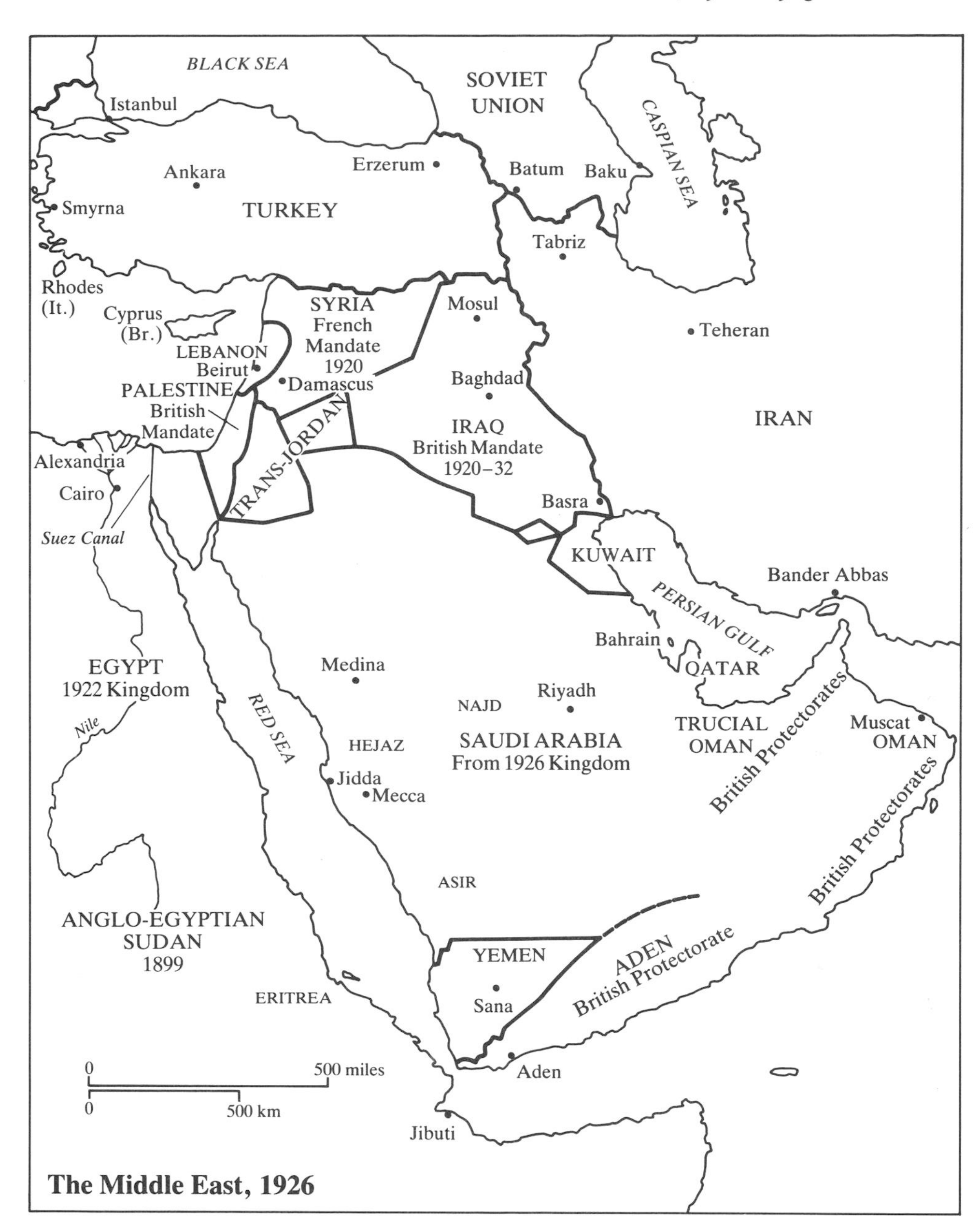

The Middle East, 1926

which freed Turkey from foreign occupation and interference. Shortly afterwards Turkey was proclaimed a republic and Kemal became the first president. Of all the defeated powers, Turkey alone challenged successfully the terms of peace the Allies sought to impose.

It was clear to President Wilson that the effort of reaching peace had involved unsatisfactory compromises and that Allies and former enemies were both deeply dissatisfied with some of the terms. One ally, Italy, had left the conference over the decision not to yield the port of Fiume to her, and the Italians returned only for the formal concluding ceremonies. The Japanese were offended by their failure to have a 'racial equality' clause incorporated in the Covenant of the League of Nations. The Hungarians and Germans did not regard the treaties as just and were determined to revise them. Wilson nevertheless pinned his hope for the future on the League of Nations.

The real purpose of the League of Nations was

to find a better way of solving disputes that could lead to war than by the kind of devastating conflict through which the world had just passed. In the League great states and small states were to find security with justice. Within ten years of its founding, these high hopes seemed unlikely to be fulfilled. Britain, France and the United States would not risk war in the 1930s to uphold the League's ideals when the aggressors were other great powers – Japan, Italy and Germany and the Soviet Union. The strength of the League depended on its members and not on the rules and procedures laid down; to be sure, if these had been applied and observed they would most likely have preserved peace. At the heart of the Covenant of the League lay article Ten whereby all the members undertook to preserve the existing independence of all other members. Furthermore, if there were aggression against a member or a threat of such aggression, then the Council of League would 'advise' on the best way in which members could fulfil their obligations. Possible sanctions of increasing severity were set out in other articles which, if adopted, would hurt the aggressor. The weakness of the League was that each member could in effect decide whether or not to comply with a Council request to apply sanctions. Furthermore the Council, consisting of permanent great-power members, together with some smaller states, could act only unanimously, so that any one of its members could block all action. The League was not a world government, lacked all armed force and remained dependent on the free co-operation of its members to behave according to its principles and to join with others in punishing those states that did not.

It was a heavy blow to the League when the United States in the end repudiated Wilson's efforts. Before a treaty to which the United States is a party can be valid, a two-thirds majority of the Senate has to vote in its favour. There were genuine misgivings about the wide-ranging but unique commitment of article X, whereby the United States would literally be obliged 'to preserve' the independence of every nation in the world. The President might have won the necessary majority if he had dealt tactfully with the opposition. But he would not admit the obvious gap between the utopian aims of the League and realistic national policies. Wilson rejected the compromise of accepting Senate reservations to the treaty and toured the country in September 1919 to appeal over the heads of the Senate to the people. On his return to Washington, he suffered a severe stroke. The chance of compromise with the Senate was now lost for certain. The treaty without amendments was lost twice when the Senate voted in November 1919 and March 1920. But this did not mean that the United States was as yet 'isolationist'. The United States would have joined the League with no more reservations than in practice the other great powers demanded for themselves. The treaty of alliance with France signed together with Britain at Paris in 1919 (page 126) is often lost sight of in Wilson's débâcle over the League. It was Wilson who lost all interest in it. For him it was a question of the League or nothing. The alliance treaty between the United States, France and Britain, if it had been ratified by the Senate, could have altered subsequent history. Opponents of universal and vague commitments to the League, like the powerful Senator Henry Cabot Lodge, were in favour of this treaty of alliance or, as it was called, Guarantee. But the treaty was never submitted to a Senate vote.

The presidential elections of 1920 reflected the new mood of the people. With the slogan 'Return to Normalcy' the Republican candidate Warren Harding won by a large margin over the Democratic candidate. The American people turned their backs on Wilson's leadership and Wilson's vision of America's mission in the world.

The conditions for a stable peace had not been laid by 1920. The French, deprived of the treaty of Guarantee, were well aware how far Europe was from achieving any balance of power, which hitherto had kept the peace. Much now depended on the attitude which the British would take to the issues of the continent; much, too, would depend on the course of German history. Nor had any reconciliation of conflicting interests been achieved in Asia (page 205). The Japanese had secured Germany's former rights in China in the province of Shantung and so incensed the Chinese delegation in Paris that it refused to sign the treaty of Versailles. The sure foundations of peace had thus not been achieved at Paris in 1919. Perhaps it was unrealistic to expect they would be.

CHAPTER 16

Democracy on Trial: Weimar Germany

Even before the outbreak of the war, the more discerning conservatives such as Bethmann Hollweg recognised that imperial Germany must move in the direction of a more broadly based constitutional monarchy. The Kaiser, the big landed and industrial interests and the powerful military frustrated progressive constitutional policies. Then it happened with the imminence of defeat facing Germany in November 1918: the Social Democrats joined the cabinet of Prince Max von Baden; government, it was intended, should in future be dependent on a Reichstag majority. The great change from a semi-authoritarian to a parliamentary democracy had taken place without a revolution. The revolution had been anticipated and made unnecessary. The Kaiser had left for exile in Holland with his little-loved family and the consequent vacuum of power had to be filled.

The peaceful transfer of power was almost successful and there can be no doubt that this is what the vast majority of the German people desired. They did not want to suffer a civil war and bloodshed on top of the defeat. They feared revolution, especially of the kind that had occurred in neighbouring Russia. Indeed, deeply disillusioned by the suddenness of defeat, they cared little about politics altogether, wanted law and order and to keep their possessions. This 'silent majority' showed an extraordinary capacity to get on with their own lives regardless of the wild men, the battalions of mutinied sailors and armed bands of various political persuasions rushing around in lorries. Life in Berlin during the early days of the republic went on with everyday orderliness. If shooting occurred, people sheltered in doorways, while in neighbouring streets others shopped, ate and amused themselves as usual. Prussia had been renowned for her public orderliness. No one in their lifetime had experienced violence on the streets. Now the ordinary German coped with the breakdown of his orderly world by simply ignoring the disorder and turning the other way. It was admirable in one sense. In another, this lack of interest was a dangerous omen for the building of a democratic state. A few years later the majority of Germans would equally easily avert their eyes from Nazi and communist thuggery in the streets and from violence to the rights of their fellow citizens in Hitler's time.

Political democracy requires that the majority feel a concern for their rights and the rights of others and are ready to defend them. In Germany in the early years of the Weimar Republic it was possible for the committed few who did not shrink from using force to threaten to take over control of the state, jeopardising peaceful change. When on 9 November 1918, Prince Max von Baden announced the abdication of the Kaiser and handed over his office to Ebert who thereby became chancellor 'on the basis of the constitution', the German people were pleased to learn not that there had been a 'revolution', but that the revolution had been pronounced as having occurred unbeknown to all but a few. The Social Democrats had long ago given up any real intention of seeking revolution. Like the British Labour Party they were intent on gradual parliamentary and democratic change. They had become the true heirs of the liberals of '1848' including taking pride in German nationalism. They had supported the war. No less a personage than Field Marshal von Hindenburg, who represented the traditions of the Prussian army, testified that Ebert was sound and 'loved his fatherland'.

But this kind of 'tame' revolution did not satisfy the more politically active. In imitation of the Russian example, 'soldiers' and workers' councils' sprang up all over Germany (page 123). Ebert humoured them, knowing that the parliamentary constituent assembly he planned would soon give the government of the Reich a solidly based and legal foundation. Then, too, the Social Democratic government was so weak that it had no military forces of its own to resist any group seeking to wrest control from it. The Spartacists' insurrections in December 1918 and January 1919, followed by political strikes and disorders, although fomented by a revolutionary party with only little support among the workers, nevertheless posed a serious threat to the Ebert government. With the support of the army command and irregular Free Corps bands of soldiers the violence of the extreme left was met with counter-violence and lawless terror. The two Spartacist (communist) leaders, Rosa Luxemburg and Karl Liebknecht, were murdered. Violence continued in other parts of Germany especially in Berlin and Munich. The Free Corps units, fanatical opponents both of democracy and of Bolshevism and the forerunners of those who were to support the Nazis, everywhere, with excessive brutality, suppressed the militant left.

The Social Democratic government and the Republic survived. What had maintained it in power was the tacit alliance between Field Marshal von Hindenburg and General Wilhelm Groener, the army Chief of Staff, with Ebert and his government. Their motives for co-operating with the socialist government were to maintain German unity and to prevent the 'patriotic' German Social Democrats from being driven from power by the Bolshevik 'internationalists'. They also believed that the traditions of the Prussian army represented the 'best' of Germany and that the new emerging Germany could be imbued with these qualities provided the Reichswehr retained a position of power in the state.

It was a misfortune that the Social Democrats were inevitably stained by the misdeeds of military excess. The communists had not been suppressed, only prevented from seizing power. The communists were never to gain as many votes as the Social Democrats, but as the Social Democrats weakened from their high-water mark of support of 38 per cent of the electorate in 1919, the Communist Party, benefiting from the depression, recovered to secure 13 per cent of the vote in 1930, which in the last free elections in November 1932 rose to 17 per cent. By then the Social Democratic support had sunk to 20 per cent. Figures do not fully reveal how this split of the socialists handicapped the strengthening of the democratic parliamentary Republic in the 1920s. The growth of the Communist Party to the left of the Social Democrats competing for the working man's vote sapped the will of the Social Democratic politicians to lead the governments of the Republic boldly, even though they formed the single largest party in the Reichstag throughout the 1920s. After 1919 they enjoyed no absolute majority, so had they wished to govern they would have had to form coalitions with the 'bourgeois' parties of the centre and moderate right. This, of course, they feared would lay them open to the cry of having 'betrayed' the working class. The early experiences of the Republic also reinforced their conclusion that the danger to her democratic existence arose from an extreme left, that is, a communist takeover.

We know better now; but the sudden and huge expansion of the Nazi vote between 1928 and 1932 was entirely unforeseen. The Social Democrats were afraid of losing votes to the political left by collaborating with the 'bourgeois' parties in coalition governments; only one of the sixteen chancellors after 1920 was a Social Democrat. Between November 1922 until June 1928 (except for a brief period of three months in 1923) – that is, for the greater part of the life of the parliamentary Republic they had done so much to create – the Social Democrats refused to participate in government at all. The parties of the centre and moderate right formed the basis of all the coalition governments, sometimes seeking to strengthen their position in the absence of the Social Democrats by seeking the more extreme-right support of the Nationalists. Even so, every one of the coalitions without the Social Democrats was a minority government. They generally lasted only a few months. The major political parties from the Conservatives to the Centre Party were either hostile or lukewarm about the new Republic even before the National Socialists became significant. The only genuine parliamentary party fully supporting democracy among the non-socialist 'bourgeois' parties was the German Democratic Party, whose support significantly dwindled during the 1920s. Though the Social Democratic leaders recognised that they had most to lose from the destruction of the democratic Republic, their own shortsighted political attitude contributed to the spectacle of government instability which lowered the esteem of parliamentary government in the eyes of the German people when that esteem was already being constantly assailed by the anti-democratic political parties.

The difficulties under which the Weimar laboured during its early years were very evident. It is therefore all the more remarkable how much was nevertheless constructively achieved. The constituent assembly met in February 1919 in Germany's capital of culture, the little town of Weimar, where Germany's two greatest poets, Goethe and Schiller, had lived. Berlin was politically too unsettled and dangerous for lengthy parliamentary deliberations. The majority of the National Assembly belonged to the Social Democratic Party, the Centre Party and the successors of the old Liberal Party.

The constitution-making was completed by August 1919. In the spirit of '1848', the inalienable rights of the individual to basic freedoms – free speech, equality before the law, freedom of religion – were set out; so were political rights of free speech and assembly, but the latter could be set aside, for the president was given emergency powers to restore public order if it were seriously disturbed or threatened. The legislators were still living under the shadow of the danger of communist coups and the ability of the president to act quickly and decisively seemed essential. Only later did it turn out that the considerable powers granted to the president would pave the way for the destruction of the democratic republic. The president himself was to be elected every seven years by a direct popular vote, like the president of the United States. There was no separation of powers as in the American constitution, yet his powers, which included that of appointing the chancellor, meant that the Weimar constitution also differed from the British form of parliamentary government. The chancellor had to win the majority support of the Reichstag; if he failed, the president could dissolve the Reichstag and call new elections. The introduction of proportional representation was one of the most significant features of the constitution. It led to a multiplicity of parties and inevitable coalition governments. The old pre-1918 states – Prussia, Bavaria and the smaller states – retained their own governments but with lesser powers. The constitution emphasised the sovereignty of the people and the right of all adult men and women to vote. There could be no doubt that the intention of the constitution was to replace the old authoritarian state with a 'scientifically' constructed democracy.

The flaws of the constitution have been touched on here and are frequently stressed. But they were not the real reason for the failure of political democracy in Germany. The reasons for this failure are not to be found in the shortcomings of legal documents but in the shortcomings of the politicians of the Weimar period and in the reactions of the German people to the problems that faced them. It is perfectly true that the army remained profoundly anti-democratic in attitude despite its oath of loyalty to the republic. So was the higher civil service on the whole. No doubt many judges were politically biased when dealing leniently with the many political crimes of the right and harshly with the few of the left. But they did not play an active role in seeking the overthrow of the republic. During its brief years, Weimar also appointed and promoted to high administrative and judicial positions sincere democrats who would never have secured such appointments in imperial Germany. All discrimination on grounds of politics or religion was ended. Given time, these newcomers would have increased and enjoyed a growing influence in the state. But time was too short.

The army was a special case. The Social Democrats treated the army High Command and the officers as indispensable pillars of the republic. They shared as patriotic Germans a false veneration for the gods of yesterday such as Hindenburg. There was little excuse for this after the behaviour of the Chief of the Army, General Hans von Seeckt, in the spring of 1920. A right-wing plot to overthrow the Republic, supported by Free Corps units near Berlin, came to fruition in March 1920. Led by a General Lüttwitz, the troops actually entered Berlin and installed a Prussian bureaucrat, Wolfgang Kapp, as chancellor. Why was the government of

Ebert so weak? It had at its disposal the regular army. To Ebert's astonishment, Seeckt refused to defend the government, declaring that the 'Reichswehr does not shoot on the Reichswehr'. Ebert and the government ignominiously fled from Berlin to the safety of southern Germany. The trade unions ordered a general strike. In Berlin some civil servants continued to function, others obeyed the government's call and refused to work under the new, self-appointed Chancellor. But the banks supplied no funds. While there was no military opposition to Kapp's seizure of power, the country was industrially paralysed, and few people would positively co-operate, though the army continued to remain 'neutral'. Nevertheless Kapp quickly recognised that he could not govern in such circumstances. A few days after his arrival in Berlin, he 'resigned' and withdrew with his troops. Ebert returned. The weakness of the Social Democrats was now shown clearly, for they neither dismissed the disloyal head of the army, nor attempted to remove from the service of the Republic those who had disobeyed the government's call to strike. The whole affair was quickly dismissed as a ridiculous adventure. But the extremists on the right did not abandon their war against the Republic of 'traitors'.

Why did the army not back the right-wing insurrectionists like Kapp? It was not for love of the Republic, or of the Social Democrats, that is clear. For the army, the Republic was necessary to deal with the Allies, who were in occupation of the Rhineland. The French still enjoyed overwhelming military strength and could occupy parts of Germany at will, as they did in 1920, 1921 and 1923. Seeckt and the army High Command knew that the French would certainly not stand idly by if the legal democratic German government were overthrown by the generals. That would be the signal for intervention. It was therefore as unrealistic to support a man like Kapp as it would have been to bring the Kaiser back.

Besides attempted coups and violence from left and right, every German was affected by the unprecedented experience of hyperinflation. The murder in June 1922 by a young nationalist of the 'Jew' Foreign Minister Walter Rathenau undermined internal and foreign confidence in the political stability of Weimar Germany with inevitably disastrous consequences for Germany's financial standing as well. The final blow to German financial stability was delivered by the Germans themselves. It was due not to reparations payments made by Germany but to the decision of the government to organise passive resistance when the French, in response partly to the threatened political disintegration of Weimar Germany and evasion of reparations, occupied the Ruhr in January 1923 (page 144). The consequent industrial standstill in the Ruhr and the relief paid by the government to the Germans who had no income now could be met only by printing more money since the government was reluctant to increase taxation sufficiently to meet the bill. By the autumn of 1923 paper money was practically worthless. A tram ticket cost millions of marks. All goods, including food, became scarce. No one wanted paper money that might lose half its value in a day. Somehow people survived with ingenuity. The pensioner and the weakest members of society suffered the most. Unemployment soared. Only those who had property and understood how to manipulate credit became rich. Industrialists like Hugo Stinnes amassed factories

Germany suffered hyper-inflation in 1923; this woman is finding banknotes more profitable to burn as *fuel than to spend* on *fuel.*

and mines paid for in worthless currency. The inflation left an indelible impression.

For ordinary people the effect was as bad as the communism they had so feared and resisted. Their savings were wiped out. The middle classes saw their modest accumulation of wealth, saved from the war years, being lost. The long-term consequences of the war were now really felt. And more and more people were saying that it was all the fault of the republic, both the lost war and the lost money. The general misery provided fertile soil for extremists. In the autumn of 1923 the attitude and questionable loyalty of the Chief of the Army, Seeckt, was perhaps the most disturbing feature of the situation. The communists believed Germany to be ripe for revolution and attempted to start it in Saxony and Thuringia. Separatism was still a potent force in Bavaria and a new name, Adolf Hitler, came to national attention when he attempted and failed to seize power in Munich. But in this hour of crisis for democracy and the republic, Gustav Stresemann, a political leader of the more moderate right, an ex-monarchist, an ex-supporter of the war of 1914 and of Germany's plans to achieve continental European hegemony, was entrusted with guiding Weimar's foreign relations.

Stresemann led the small People's Party. The Social Democrats agreed to his appointment as chancellor in August 1923 and joined the parties of the centre and moderate right in briefly forming a grand government coalition. In November, he became foreign minister in a new government and remained in this post through every successive government until his death. Historical controversy surrounds the evaluation of Stresemann's role in the Weimar Republic. Was he a blatant nationalist, even still an expansionist? There can be no doubt that he did wish to free Germany from the remaining restrictions of the Versailles Treaty: reparations, foreign occupation and military limitations. He followed pacific policies openly, yet was ready secretly and deceitfully, by any practical means, to reach his goals in making Germany respected and powerful. His aims included the restoration of German territory lost to Poland in the east, and the former colonies too: in short a return to pre-1914 Germany before the folly of the German leaders and the lost war threw away Germany's peaceful ascendancy in Europe. But it is mistaken to see in Stresemann a precursor of Hitler. He was at heart a conservative and an old-fashioned nationalist. He learnt from the war experience that Germany could not 'conquer' Europe. To attempt this would create another coalition against her. He was realistic and accepted limits to German power. His powerful and respected Germany would be one of Europe's great powers, not the *only* great power. Germany in the aftermath of defeat he compared to Austria after the defeat of Napoleon. Like Metternich, he would recover his country's position and prestige. He succeeded in doing so during the course of the next six years until his untimely death in October 1929.

Stresemann had the courage to do the politically unpopular. Despite the nationalist patriotic clamour against the French and the diktat of Versailles, he recognised that Germany was only ruining her economic recovery at home and her reputation abroad. His policy was that of sweet reasonableness, a policy of 'fulfilment', as it became known. Germany would now freely accept the Versailles Treaty, seek peace and friendship with France and renounce any future claim to recover Alsace-Lorraine and any part of territory lost in the west. The French should feel secure and so, to prove their own acceptance of the entirely new spirit of reconciliation, would show their confidence by giving up the remaining guarantees of her security – the occupation of the Rhineland and the Allied commission supervising German disarmament. He called off passive resistance and allowed the French President, Poincaré, the illusion of victory and German submission. The French were not so naive as to accept all these protestations of love at their face value. But the British were delighted at this promising turn of events. They wanted the war to be over and peace and goodwill instantly to reign. British foreign secretaries were more suspicious of the French than of the Germans, though one of them at least, Austen Chamberlain, recognised clearly enough that French militancy was the result of their feeling of insecurity. Yet he too grasped at the opportunity of avoiding an Anglo-French alliance. Instead he underwrote a general Western European security treaty suggested by Stresemann to head off any possibility of an Anglo-French alliance and drafted with the help of the British Ambassador in Berlin. The outcome was the Locarno Treaties of 16 October 1925. France and Germany undertook to respect each other's territories and frontiers and to accept them as final. This treaty of Mutual Guarantee, which included Belgium, was also signed by Britain and Italy. Britain

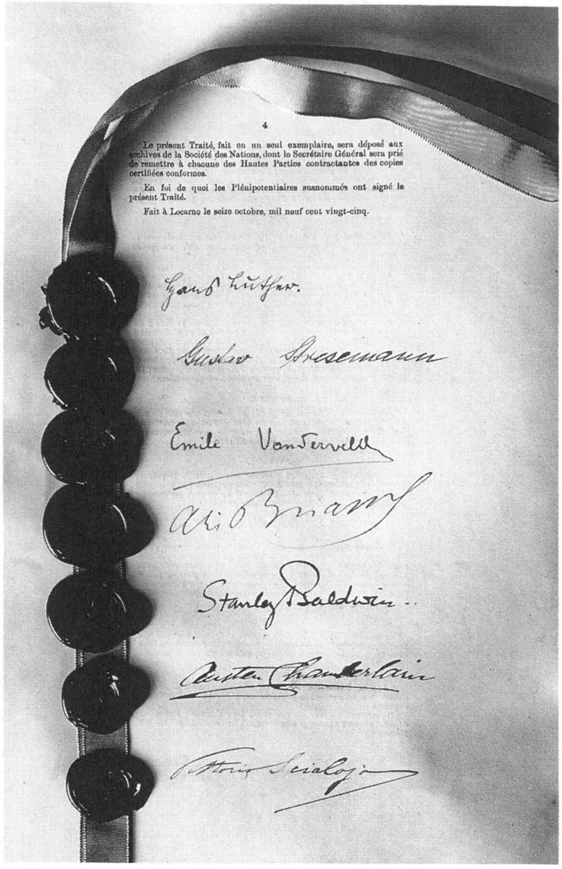
4

Le présent Traité, fait en un seul exemplaire, sera déposé aux archives de la Société des Nations, dont le Secrétaire Général sera prié de remettre à chacune des Hautes Parties contractantes des copies certifiées conformes.

En foi de quoi les Plénipotentiaires susnommés ont signé le présent Traité.

Fait à Locarno le seize octobre, mil neuf cent vingt-cinq.

The Treaty of Locarno, signed on 16 October 1925 by Stresemann, Briand and Baldwin, amongst others. The new spirit of peace it engendered proved less than durable.

and Italy guaranteed that they would come to the immediate aid of any country attacked by the other signatories of Locarno. But Stresemann had refused to extend Locarno to cover Germany's eastern frontiers with Czechoslovakia and Poland, nor would Britain guarantee the post-Versailles frontiers in the east as she had done in the west. Although Germany also signed arbitration treaties at the same time with Poland and Czechoslovakia, they did not form part of the Locarno security system. Stresemann's hardly realistic long-term aim was to revise the eastern frontier peacefully making use of Germany's economic preponderance.

In return for renouncing territorial changes at the expense of France Stresemann won concessions from the Allies. Reparations were scaled down in 1924 and 1929 (page 145). Stresemann aimed to get rid of them altogether. Germany was admitted to the League of Nations in 1926 and given a permanent seat on the Council. Stresemann joined on condition that Germany too need never fight to back up the League if she chose not to do so. The Allied commission supervising German disarmament was withdrawn. Stresemann never lived to see the fulfilment of one of his most cherished objectives – the complete Allied evacuation of all German territory – but before his death he had secured agreement that the Rhineland would be evacuated in 1930. With his French opposite number, Aristide Briand, Stresemann gave publicity to the new Franco-German friendship, the essence of the so-called 'spirit of Locarno', even though in private Stresemann was continually demanding more concessions than France would grant. As for Briand, he believed the French had no alternative but to make the best of German protestations and promises.

At home, too, the years from 1924 to 1927 were a brief golden period for the Republic. The currency was stabilised. The promise of peace at home and abroad enabled the hardworking Germans to attract large American loans which covered the cost of reparations. American efficiency and methods of manufacture were successfully adopted by German industry. Business concerns combined and formed themselves into huge cartels in steel, chemicals and the electrical goods industries. Export flourished. Trade unions, too, enjoyed freedom and for the first time the positive protection of the state. These were the brief years of prosperity and had they continued the German people might well have come to value more their new republican democracy. Instead, as the economic crisis which began among the farmers and spread to industry hit Germany, a majority of the electorate in the early 1930s turned to parties which sought totalitarian solutions.

CHAPTER 17

Britain, France and the United States from War to Peace

The democracies of the West were tested in the period after the war. If they failed to retain the active support of the people, then others were ready to take over power. To the right, fascist movements and later the Nazi movement developed, promising new solutions. To the left, the communists pointed to the Soviet Union and the new society being created there as the right goal for all progressive peoples.

Before the Great War the triumph of liberal democracy had seemed certain in the West. Even Russia had begun to establish embryonic parliamentary institutions, and Italy had extended the vote to all adult males. The war, that ended with the victory of the democracies, might have been expected to confirm the superiority of the parliamentary form of government. The tide first turned against democracy in Russia after the revolution of 1917, in Italy in the 1920s with Mussolini and the emergence of the fascists. Forms of fascism spread to a number of the new Balkan successor states of the Habsburg Empire. Czechoslovakia was the shining exception, a bastion of Western liberal ideas and institutions in Eastern and central Europe. The most critical question was whether Germany would become a liberal democracy (Chapter 16).

The immediate danger from the Bolsheviks faded. The Polish defeat of the Red Army in 1920 halted any dream of spreading revolution with the Red Army in the vanguard. Lenin and Stalin did not lose their sense of isolation and insecurity. On the contrary, they expected the capitalist West to turn on communist Russia and crush her. In foreign relations the initiative nevertheless passed out of the hands of the Kremlin. Soviet policy in the 1920s was directed to increasing the difficulties of 'imperialist' Britain by encouraging the colonial peoples, especially in Asia, to struggle for independence. Another objective was to divide the Western democratic nations from each other; separate agreements of technical and military co-operation were concluded with the government of Weimar Germany (Rapallo, 1922; Berlin, 1926). Even while co-operating, however, the third prong of Soviet policy, surreptitiously masterminded by the Comintern, was to promote internal disruption within the Western democracies with the objective of weakening them and so making it a safer world for the first and only communist state – Russia. In Weimar politics the German Communist Party exerted a harmful influence on the attempts to construct a parliamentary democracy. Thus although the Soviet Union lacked the strength to endanger peace in Europe *directly*, communist tactics in the democratic states and fear of communism were among the formative influences of the 1920s.

The communists were weakest in the country which they had mistakenly believed would lead the 'capitalist assault' on the Soviet Union one day. There was never any danger between the two world wars that Britain would deviate from her evolutionary democratic path. The tradition of parliament, the impartial administration of the law and civic freedoms of the individual were too deeply embedded in the British way of life to be overthrown by any authoritarian movement. But, within the constitutional framework accepted by all except small minorities, the struggle for what came to be called 'social justice' increased. Working people demanded the satisfaction of basic economic rights; they called for state intervention to assure them of these rights should this prove necessary; they wanted work, a decent wage and adequate support for themselves and their families when out of work or unable to work due to sickness; they expected the ending of bad housing and, as they became increasingly aware of their disadvantaged position in society, a better future for their children. Industry, the manufacturers and the mine owners all looked back to before the war and wanted to be rid of all wartime government control and direction, though not subsidies when forthcoming.

What government wanted depended on party. The majority of the Conservatives believed in market forces to remedy the economic difficulties, in sound money and in a balanced budget. Government's business in the direct control of industry, they believed, was to divest itself as rapidly as possible of such controls as had been brought in during the war. The Labour Party had scarcely begun in the 1920s to translate socialist aspirations into practical policies. That work was not done until the 1930s. Meanwhile the Labour Party knew clearly what it did not want: communism on the Russian model. The small British Communist Party was refused affiliation to the Labour Party and in the mid-1920s communists could no longer be individual members of the Labour Party. The Labour Party, supported by the Trades Union Congress, sought power within the constitution knowing that to be tainted with communism would drive away moderate political support and so condemn the party in British politics to a minor role. The Labour Party was successful in becoming the main opposition party, and held office on its own twice during this period, briefly in 1924 as a minority government and from 1929 until the financial débâcle of 1931.

Labour prospered on the decay of the once great Liberal Party. The Liberal Party had simply lost its identity, its reforming policies absorbed by the Conservatives to the right, with Labour to the left offering a more plausible dynamic alternative to Conservative rule. The working man's vote in the industrial towns swung to Labour; many Liberal supporters deserted liberalism for the Conservatives, giving the latter an almost unbroken hold of power in the inter-war years. The Liberals in the post-war years had neither great national causes nor political leaders who could command a mass personal following as Gladstone had once done. Lloyd George appeared the obvious candidate; the man through whose energy and leadership Britain's war effort had been galvanised to victory; Lloyd George had then become a leader on the world stage at the Paris Peace Conference. His standing in 1919 was indeed high. As prime minister of a coalition government of those Liberals who followed him and the Conservatives, the elections of December 1918 gave the Conservative-Lloyd-George-Liberal coalition parties a landslide victory. The Liberals under Asquith, who opposed them, won no more than twenty-eight seats. Labour, with 2.3 million votes and sixty-three seats, for the first time became the main opposition party. This election marked a profound change in British politics. The results, moreover, reflected a greatly enlarged electorate. For the first time the vote was exercised by women over thirty; having proven during the war that they could do a man's job on the land and in factories, women could no longer be denied the vote.

For a time Lloyd George's personal ascendancy obscured the collapse of Liberal support in the country. He had agreed with his coalition partner, Andrew Bonar Law, the leader of the Conservatives, that the Conservatives would support 159 Liberal candidates, and the majority, 133, were elected as a result. Nevertheless the Conservatives predominated over Lloyd Georgian Liberals in the coalition by almost three to one. This meant Lloyd George was at the mercy of Conservative support. They would drop him for a Conservative leader when he ceased to be an electoral asset. And that is what they did in 1922.

An immediate problem facing post-war Britain was Ireland. 'Home Rule' was no longer enough for the Irish nationalists, whose cause had been spectacularly enhanced by the Easter rising in Dublin in 1916. The Sinn Fein fought the general election of December 1918, won all but four seats outside Ulster, and met in Dublin – those members not in prison – in a self-constituted Irish parliament which promptly declared the whole of Ireland an independent republic. Bloodshed, guerrilla war and the breakdown of law and order followed. The

Irish Republican Army rebels take to the streets of Dublin in July 1922 to show their strength.

Troubles began in 1919. Allied with Sinn Fein was the Irish Republican Army which attacked the armed police (Royal Irish Constabulary), and the British volunteer troops known as the Black and Tans. The IRA attempted to force the British government in London to recognise Irish independence. It was the worst sort of violent conflict – civil war, without battle lines, carried on by ambush, assassination and murder on both sides.

Two problems stood in the way of a solution: Lloyd George's refusal to grant total independence without any link with Britain, and the attitude of the six counties of Ulster, where a majority of Protestants fiercely defended the integrity and union of the British Isles, refusing to be merged with the predominantly Catholic south. An attempted British solution of December 1920 did not satisfy the south. Atrocities on both sides multiplied. But an appeal by the King in June 1921 led to a truce and a negotiated settlement that December. The Irish Free State became a Dominion and so remained within the British Empire, and six counties of Ulster were granted the right to vote themselves out of independent Ireland and so remain a part of the United Kingdom. But the Irish leaders in London, in accepting partition, brought about a new civil war in Ireland in 1922 with those who rejected the treaty. Not until the spring of 1923 was Ireland at peace, with partition a fact. Yet the seeds of conflict tragically remained.

Dominion status in practice meant independence. The other British Dominions asserted their own independence, though the personal links between Dominion leaders such as South Africa's General Smuts and the British political leaders remained close and every Dominion except the Irish Free State independently joined Britain in declaring war on Germany in September 1939. As significant as this insistence of the right of the 'white Dominions' to exercise independence was Britain's declared intention to extend dominion status to the 'brown empire'. During the war, in 1917, the British government had declared that its aim was 'responsible government' for India. Fourteen years later, in 1931, a viceroy of India had advanced this to 'Dominion status' for India eventually. No one in Britain believed this would come about for a generation or two. But the major Indian independence party, the Congress Party, agitated for independence to be conceded quickly.

During the 1930s Mahatma ('great-souled') Gandhi had launched his remarkable movement of non-violent passive resistance to the British–Indian authorities. He served notice to the Raj that India could not be ruled in the long run without the consent of the Indian masses. And these masses of the poor of India were responding to a Western-educated lawyer, now turned into a holy man and skilled politician all in one, walking the length and breadth of India with little more than a loincloth and a stick. The emaciated figure of the frail Gandhi was as powerful a symbol for change as the strutting militaristic dictators of Europe. His teaching of how the poor and powerless could force the hand of the powerful and armed has proved to be one of the most potent influences in the world of the twentieth century.

Violence in Ireland and mass protest movements in India did not complete Britain's difficulties. Nearer home British governments from 1920 down to the present day became preoccupied with Britain's relative industrial decline, the threat of falling living standards and, most of all, the miseries of unemployment. Britain was not a happy land between the wars. The problem was deep-seated and arose from a combination of changes. Britain had increasingly derived earnings from trading as well as manufacture to offset the cost of importing food and raw materials. After a short post-war boom world trade contracted, particularly in the 1930s, and the earnings from carrying the world's trade fell correspondingly. There was no demand for more ships, and the shipyards of Scotland and north-eastern England became symbols of the deepest depression and unemployment.

World patterns of trade were also changing. Britain's traditional trade in textiles and other goods to the empire suffered as the poor of the world became even poorer. As raw material prices fell with slackening industrial activity so the poorest parts of the world earned less and less; this in turn gave them less to spend on British goods. Then textile factories, the first stage of industrialisation, were springing up in India and Japan and with their low labour costs drove Britain out of many traditional markets. Actually Britain was remarkably successful in developing the industries of the second industrial revolution, the chemical, electrical and motor industries. But these successes could not take up the slack of Britain's pre-war traditional exports.

The coal industry was one of the worst affected. The mines were not efficient, and demand for coal slackened with declining industrial activity in Europe and the competition of oil. The powerful miners' union saw nationalisation as the solution which would enable the numerous privately owned mines to be developed on a national basis. The mine owners, faced with declining profits, argued for increasing hours and cutting wages. But the owners' case was weakened by the fact that they had not used their large profits of the war years to modernise the mines. The mines had then been under state control and the miners were embittered when Lloyd George returned them to their owners' control in 1921. A miners' strike failed to win better terms. In 1925 a strike was narrowly averted when the government paid a temporary subsidy to the mines to prevent wage cuts and set up an inquiry. The report of this inquiry (the Samuel Commission) the following year found much in favour of the miners' view but rejected nationalisation and suggested that less drastic cuts in wages were probably inevitable. The miners were anxious to avoid a strike which would bring hardship to themselves, but in negotiating with the owners refused to countenance any further cut in wages or increase in hours. At the end of April 1926 the government subsidy came to an end and the mine owners now locked out the miners.

The importance of the dispute with the miners lay in the fact that it led to the General Strike of 1926, the most widespread and dramatic breakdown of Britain's industrial relations for a century. It lasted only nine days from 3 to 12 May 1926. But these days manifested Britain's division into the labouring class and the middle and upper classes, who for the main part wished to break the strike. There was more involved than a strike of miners. The Trades Union Congress involved itself and in doing so involved organised labour on the one hand and the Prime Minister Stanley Baldwin and the British government on the other. Its sincere intention was to facilitate a compromise settlement between the mine owners and the miners. When these efforts foundered the TUC used its industrial muscle to call out on strike key industries, including transport. The government countered by putting into practice carefully worked-out emergency measures to keep the essential services going. The TUC's attempt to force the government to coerce the mine owners failed, though the rank and file overwhelmingly supported the call to strike. What was the strike really about then? It certainly was not an attempt to bring about a revolution. It was not purely industrial either. At the end of the General Strike, which the TUC called off, the miners were left to fight their own battle, which lasted several bitter months.

In the 1920s and 1930s Conservative-dominated

The British General Strike of 1926. Armoured cars escort a food convoy down the East India Dock Road in London.

governments of the Lloyd George, Baldwin and Chamberlain era were socially conscious and anxious to pass measures which would protect the sick and unemployed and help the poor. Their finance was orthodox, believing the country was best served by sound money and balanced budgets but not by direct control of industry. The minority Labour government of 1924 was just as orthodox in financial questions as the Conservatives. Neither Conservatives nor Labour followed policies of confrontation and even the General Strike was not a confrontation that either side had been keen to invite. What would be held against the governments of the inter-war years was the persistence of 1 million unemployed, and much higher numbers during the most severe years of depression, concentrated above all in the north of the country. No government knew how to 'cure' this unemployment in the prevailing international conditions. It was the biggest argument against 'democracy', yet the great majority of the British electorate turned neither to fascism nor to communism.

France emerged the victor from the Great War, but no country, excepting Russia, had suffered more physical damage, human and material. In the struggle for power on the European continent,

Prime Minister Stanley Baldwin of Britain, an adept at pouring oil on troubled water.

France was the loser. Population losses had been such that there were now three Germans for every two Frenchmen. French industry had been devastated in northern France. The war had deeply scarred the towns and countryside of this region, whereas no battles, apart from the early encounters in East Prussia, had been fought on German soil. One in every five Frenchmen had been mobilised during the war (one in eight in Britain), 1.4 million killed and another three-quarters of a million permanently invalided. Put another way, it has been calculated that for every ten men between the ages of twenty and forty-five, two were killed, one was totally invalided and three were incapacitated for long periods of time, leaving only four available for work. The French governments faced the common problems of demobilisation and changeover from wartime and industrial controls to a peacetime economy. In addition the French had to cope with the task of reconstruction in the war-torn regions of France.

The acquisition of Alsace-Lorraine and the utilisation of the Saar mines were important compensations for the losses suffered, but did not cancel them out. Financially France was in a difficult plight. The government had financed the war not by taxes but largely by making loans at home and receiving loans from Britain and the United States. After the war, yet more money had to be found for reconstruction and invalid or widows' pensions. France was dependent on the goodwill of the United States and Britain. She was also dependent on receiving reparations from Germany to cover the gap between what she could earn and what she spent. French needs and policies in the 1920s have not received the understanding and sympathy they deserve. In British judgement, the French were acting vindictively and arrogantly towards defeated Germany, and thus were responsible in part for Germany's fervent nationalism and for delaying a 'normalisation' and pacification of Western Europe. Britain came to see her role not as an ally of France so much as a mediator between France and 'helpless' Germany in the interests of creating a new balance of power. This British attitude of 'conditional' support could only strengthen France's anxieties about her long-term security once Germany had revived her strength.

For France the 'German problem' was insoluble, because France *alone* could not enforce any solution in the long run. Britain and the United States could express their disapproval effectively by applying financial pressure on a weakened French economy. But the exaction of reparations from Germany was for France not only a necessary financial operation. Far more was involved. Nothing less than the question of whether Germany would be required, and if necessary forced, by the Allies to abide by all the terms of the Treaty of Versailles. On that issue depended the security of France. If Germany could set aside reparations with impunity, then why not also the military restrictions and finally the territorial clauses of Versailles? Marshal Foch had expressed these deep fears when he called the Treaty of Versailles no more than a twenty-year truce. France had already lost one pillar of her security when the Senate of the United States failed to ratify the treaty of Guarantee (page 132), and Britain, too, according to its original terms, had backed out. The second pillar of her security was the Allied (including her own) right to occupy the Rhineland zones and to continue to do so beyond the five-, ten- and fifteen-year periods specified if Germany did not fulfil her obligations under the Treaty of Versailles. After the failure of the treaty of Guarantee, the French were naturally all the more determined to maintain their rights. In the third pillar, the League of Nations, the French realistically did not place much faith.

In March 1921, with the Germans appearing to be evading the military and financial obligations placed on them, the French, with Britain's blessing and co-operation, occupied three industrial German towns. Almost immediately afterwards the Germans were presented with the total reparations bill of 132 billion gold marks (£6600 million) and a method of payment. The Germans gave way. Reparations were regularly resumed until the end of 1922. Then the Germans defaulted once again and disputed with Poincaré, by then prime minister, the amounts due and already delivered. Despite British disapproval, French and Belgian troops occupied the industrial Ruhr in January 1923, ostensibly with the object of collecting what was due. The more important objective was to weaken Germany's reviving power by occupying her most important industrial region. French uncertainties about Germany's ultimate intentions had been increased by the murder of Rathenau, by the political instability of the country and by what appeared to be deliberate attempts to evade her obligations (page 136).

The French move was no sudden reaction but the result of a carefully thought-out policy. It separated her from Britain, as the Germans could not fail to note, and they exploited the split successfully in the 1920s. The German government called an industrial boycott in the Ruhr, thereby providing the French with a reason for staying there; only the German coal owners refused to behave so patriotically and continued delivering coal to the French. The ruin of German finances, which was the consequence of Germany's decision to order industrial passive resistance in the Ruhr, was a victory of sorts for Poincaré. In outward appearance his resistance to British mediating pressure seemed justified too. He demanded that the Germans call off their industrial boycott before fresh negotiations over reparations could be started to resolve the underlying problem that had led to the occupation. In September 1923 the new Stresemann government abandoned resistance and agreed to resume reparations payments (page 137).

All along, however, reparations had been only part of the reason for the conflict. The French felt too weak to control the Germans single-handed. The year 1923–4 marked France's last effort to attain what she had failed to secure at Versailles, a means of checking the future threat of German preponderance in Europe. France failed in 1924 and had to bow to the pressure of the United States and Britain. This was marked by her agreement that experts should work out a new reparations settlement which, when accepted by Germany, would leave France no excuse to stay in the Ruhr. The American expert Charles G. Dawes gave his name to the reparations plan of 1924; it did not fix a final total but, as expected, scaled down the immediate annual payments and coupled payment to a loan to the Germans. The Germans accepted the plan and with the restoration of the value of their currency became internationally creditworthy. Poincaré fell from power. Briand, who returned to power, had no option but to end the occupation. All efforts meanwhile which the French had made to encourage separation in the Rhineland failed.

The French had to make the best of the situation. The outcome was the European reconciliation of Locarno. Briand and Stresemann to all outward appearances had buried wartime enmities. In the Locarno Treaties, signed on 16 October 1925, the Germans renounced any desire to change their western frontier with France and so accepted the loss of Alsace-Lorraine. Britain and Italy guaranteed the western frontiers and the continued demilitarisation of Rhineland against a 'flagrant breach', and engaged themselves to aid the victim of aggression whether France or Germany. The British congratulated themselves that their original Versailles obligations were now lessened, since 'flagrant' was an adjective open to different interpretation. The French sadly noted that they had secured British support not in an equal Anglo-French alliance but with Britain in her new role as mediator and arbitrator. Much would therefore depend on the view Britain took of any particular situation.

France was left with no secure allies. Her position was worse than in 1914 when Russia, militarily, had been a powerful and reliable ally. She had a new alliance with Poland and Czechoslovakia, but these two countries could not be relied on to fight for French security nor France for theirs, for there was a 'catch' in the European security arrangements. The Germans had refused to include their eastern frontier with Czechoslovakia and Poland in the Locarno Treaties package (page 138). Britain and Italy did not act as guarantors of these frontiers, either. The Germans had signed arbitration treaties with Czechoslovakia and Poland separately, but they were worth little. The Germans could still resort to force if arbitration did not give them what they wanted. Only the separate alliances of Poland and Czechoslovakia with France might deter Germany. But now by the terms of the Locarno Treaties France would be arraigned as the aggressor if the French army sought to come to the aid of their eastern allies by the only means available to them – an attack on Germany. Britain was to exercise this 'leverage' to the full when, thirteen years later, France declared herself ready to aid her Czech ally against Germany in 1938. Britain then insisted that, should such an eventuality lead to war with Germany, she was not bound to help France (page 242).

In the new spirit of conciliation, France also relinquished prematurely her territorial guarantees permitted by Versailles, the occupation of the Rhineland zones. In order to prove their goodwill, Britain and France had pulled out their last troops by 1930. The 'goodwill' and 'faith' were not justified, as the later experience of the 1930s was to show. Briand played this last card of defusing the

German problem by seeking to make Germany and France the nucleus of a 'new Europe', but in vain.

Where, then, was the most serious single flaw in the way in which Britain and France, with American financial connivance, dealt with Germany? Was the right policy coercion or conciliation? Both were tried, with some good results and some bad. We cannot rerun history to discover what would have happened if there had been greater or less coercion. But the basic fault of Allied policy lay in not maintaining Anglo-French unity after the war. Allied policy of either coercion or conciliation should have been based on strength, on the capacity and determination to preserve peace if ever again threatened by Germany. The French realised this and tried to act as if they were strong. It was Britain which basically undermined this stance. Horrified by the Great War and the millions of dead and maimed, she attempted to withdraw and limit her European commitments. At Locarno she had refused to guarantee the frontiers of Poland and Czechoslovakia, an open invitation to German revisionism. This was true even in Western Europe. While Britain acknowledged that her strategic 'frontier' now ran along the Rhine, the British Cabinet was not willing to match this concept militarily by maintaining a British army capable of defending this supposedly 'joint' frontier. France alone stood as guardian of the European frontiers of Versailles, and France by herself was too weak for that role. Briand's policy of reconciliation was sincere enough; it seemed also the only way left to achieve French security.

Despite the grave uncertainties of France's European position, and weakness of her international financial position, she achieved a spectacular domestic recovery in the 1920s. The majority of Frenchmen resisted the siren call of those on the right, the fascist Action Française, or the Communist Party on the extreme left, who sought to overthrow the institutions of the Third Republic.

The elections of November 1919 were won by groups of the conservative right allied in a Bloc National. Led by an ex-socialist, Alexandre Millerand, its commanding figure was Clemenceau, the 'father of victory'. Behind the Bloc stood big business interests and the mass of voters, especially the peasantry frightened by the Bolshevist bogey. They approved of a policy of dealing sternly with Germany; exacting reparations rather than paying taxes. Once elected, the Bloc National reverted to the tradition of the Third Republic in denying the presidency to Clemenceau in 1920. They preferred a weak president, only this time overdid it in electing a man who a few months later had to retire into a mental home. Clemenceau's career too was ended.

The work of reconstruction was begun in north-eastern France and with government credits there was enough to do to ensure full employment in the 1920s. Some concessions were also made to the workers in legislating for an eight-hour day and conceding collective bargaining. But control of industry was handed back to the owners. The government was firmly opposed to nationalisation and socialism. Among industrial workers after the war there was much discontent. Their wages had not kept pace with rising prices. The main French trade union – the Confédération Générale du Travail – was determined to challenge the government in a series of large, well-organised strikes. The socialist-inspired strikes were as much political as economic. Confident of the army and of majority electoral support, the government would not yield; the unions had no chance and lost. In 1920 French socialism split, as it did elsewhere in Europe. The communists formed their own party and separate trade union. The 'democratic' socialists, led by Léon Blum, and democratic trade unions organised themselves also. The split of the 'left' was mirrored by a split on the right, Poincaré's policies having failed to produce the expected results in 1923.

The elections of 1924 gave power to a grouping of centre radicals and socialists, the so-called Cartel des Gauches. The Bloc National formed the main opposition to the right, and the small Communist Party to the left, but the presence of the communists to their left, bitterly critical, had the effect of inhibiting the socialists from collaborating with the radicals of the centre. The split of French socialism thus deprived the large socialist electorate from exercising an influence in the government of the Republic commensurate with their strength. It was a formula for sterility. Meanwhile the undoing of the Cartel government was its inability to master the financial situation. The franc fell precipitously in value. While American loans were reaching Germany, the French inability and refusal to negotiate a debt settlement with the United States closed the American money market to the French. In 1926, the Chamber turned once more to the strong man of French politics, Poincaré. Poincaré was granted special powers to restore France to financial health, which he promptly succeeded in doing by raising

Passengers crowd on to a Parisian locomotive during a rail strike in May 1920.

taxes and cutting expenditure. France now experienced a few golden years of progress and prosperity until the effects of the worldwide slump made themselves seriously felt in France in 1933.

In industrial strength and influence the United States had emerged as a world power by the close of the First World War. But victory left the American people disillusioned with the role of world leadership which Wilson had sought to thrust upon them. Yet during the 1920s and 1930s there was no way in which the Americans could opt out of world affairs and return to what appeared only in retrospect as a golden past of American self-sufficiency.

The immediate post-war mood favoured a rapid return to freeing the individual American from all constraints of wartime control and freeing business too to get on with the job of expanding American prosperity. An amiable conservative Republican politician, Warren G. Harding, had been elected to the White House in November 1920 on a campaign slogan which reflected the public mood precisely: 'less government in business and more business in government'. Businessmen were no longer depicted as the 'robber barons' ruthlessly amassing wealth but as the new patriotic leaders who would benefit the average American. On 4 March 1921 Harding was inaugurated. Big business was brought into government with the appointment of Andrew Mellon, one of the richest men of the United States, whose wealth was exceeded only by Rockefeller and Ford, as secretary of the Treasury. Mellon's fortune was founded on banking, channelling money into steel, railroads and a wide range of industry. There were other appointments of men of proven ability: Herbert Hoover, Henry Wallace and, as secretary of state to take charge of foreign affairs, a brilliant lawyer, Charles Evans Hughes. Unfortunately Harding made grave errors too in rewarding political cronies of his own state, Ohio. The 'Ohio gang' were to surround Harding in 1923 during the last months of his administration with some of the worst and most spectacular scandals of corruption in the history of American government.

The early boom which had absorbed the ex-servicemen in 1919 collapsed in 1920 and the depression lasted until 1922. But then followed seven years of remarkable economic expansion and rising industrial prosperity led by the growth of the automobile industry, electrical machinery and appliances and building. Yet the decade was to close with the most severe and longest-lasting economic collapse in American history. The 1920s did not turn out to be the new era of never-ending prosperity.

With hindsight the weaknesses of the 1920s can be discerned. Industry, enjoying the protection of a high tariff, had over-expanded as its productivity had increased. Wages had failed to keep pace with the increases in production. Big business had successfully defeated the great waves of strikes that spread across the country in 1919 by characterising the strikers and their leaders as Bolsheviks. Acts of terrorism in the cities were blamed on the 'radicals' and communists. Anti-labour hysteria swept the country. Aliens were arrested as suspected communists though few were actually deported. The most celebrated case of prosecution of suspected radicals arousing worldwide interest was the arrest and conviction in 1920 of two anarchists, Nicola Sacco and Bartolomeo Vanzetti, for robbery and murder. Liberals insisted that their trial was a travesty of justice and called for their release. They were executed all the same in 1927.

Intolerance and hysteria extended to other minorities: the vulnerable blacks as well as Jews and Catholics. The racial prejudice of the whites and competition for work in the cities exploded in racial riots in some twenty cities in 1919. Before the Great War the great majority of blacks had lived in the South. During the war half a million blacks sought an escape from poverty by migrating to the industrial cities of the North. Wilson's efforts to establish democracy and self-determination in Europe stood in glaring contrast to intolerance and discrimination at home. In the south the Ku Klux Klan greatly expanded its violent activities.

One of the most extraordinary aspects of American government in the era of financial and industrial 'freedoms' of the 1920s was the invasion of people's privacy and right to lead the life they chose through the enactment of Prohibition. Congress had passed the law in 1919 over Wilson's veto. The law could never be properly enforced as ordinary citizens constantly broke it by surreptitiously consuming liquor. On the now illegal manufacture and transportation of alcoholic drinks gangster empires flourished. The most notorious, Al Capone's, in Chicago, with its aura of violence and series of street murders undertaken by rival gangs, became as much a symbol of America in the 1920s as jazz and the stolid respectability of President John Calvin Coolidge, who had succeeded to the presidency in August 1923 on the death of Harding. Related to the attitude of intolerance was the change in immigration laws. They too exhibited a racial aspect of discrimination. Immigration from eastern Asia was cut off. Quotas for immigrants were now established, which favoured the British, Germans, Irish and Scandinavians as against the 'new immigrants' from central and southern Europe. The era of virtually free entry to the United States from Europe was over. Something special which the United States stood for – a haven from persecution – was ended.

The St Valentine's Day Massacre of 14 February 1929. Mobsters mow down mobsters, and Chicago's name is mud world-wide.

American soldiers returned from Europe believing they had won the war for the Allies, and their President sailed home believing he had put the world on the road to peace and prosperity. Dreams turned sour. The American people now wanted to get on with their own lives, to own a home, a Model-T Ford and a refrigerator. The Hollywood dream industry started on its phenomenal growth. In the inter-war years more and more Americans questioned why the United States had involved herself at all in the war. The overwhelming feeling was that the American continent was far enough away from the storm centres of Europe and Asia to enjoy geographical security. There was thus no reason why Americans should again sacrifice their lives for other nations. They needed no large army. Their security could be guaranteed by a navy powerful enough to meet any challenge.

Beer is poured down the drain during the Prohibition years in the USA. Even the children here look displeased.

International naval disarmament was welcomed as it would allow less to be spent on the United States Navy. President Harding bowed to the public revolt on armaments expenditure. Secretary of State Hughes was spectacularly successful in hosting a naval disarmament conference in Washington. The British too were anxious to turn their backs on the war and reduce armaments expenditure. The outcome of the conference was a treaty in which Britain and the United States agreed to limit their battleship strength to 500,000 tons each and Japan to 300,000 tons. It was said that the Washington Conference between November 1921 and February 1922 sank more ships than all the naval battles of the war put together. As there were no American or British naval bases anywhere close to Japan and American and British naval defences spanned the Atlantic and Mediterranean too, the apparent Japanese inferiority was not so real. At that same conference, in further treaties, the Americans hoped to ensure that China would remain free and independent. More important, the Japanese government itself decided to withdraw from Siberia and China. The treaties provided the illusion of peace in eastern Asia without solving the underlying conflicts, just as the later Locarno Treaties created the illusion of peace in Europe. The climax came in 1928 with the Briand-Kellogg treaty 'outlawing' war. They could be dismissed as harmless were it not for the fact that they lulled the West into a false sense of security. No doubt many people wished to be lulled.

Americans did not speak of 'isolationism' in the 1920s, but of 'America first'. Even the mid-westerner knew that the United States could not be separated from the rest of the world. What Americans demanded was that in dealings with the rest of the world it was the duty of Congress and the administration to take care of American interests and not to meddle in the world concerns of the League of Nations. Above all America should not be dragged into conflicts by concluding a military alliance with any other country but should preserve a 'free hand' confident in her ability to defend her interests. It was an attitude based on confidence.

Principal Allied Debtors and Creditors, November 1918
(millions of dollars)

	Owed to USA	Owed to Britain	Owed to France	Total debt	Total due
United States	–	–	–	–	7,078
Britain	3,696	–	–	3,696	7,014
France	1,970	1,683	–	3,653	2,237
Russia	188	2,472	955	3,615	–
Italy	1,031	1,855	75	2,961	–
Belgium	172	434	535	1,141	–
Other states	21	570	672	1,263	–

In fact the American administrations involved the United States more in problems of international diplomacy than the American people would have approved of.

One aspect of 'America first' was the insistence on collecting all the moneys lent mainly to France and Britain but also to the other Allies, during the Great War. Since Europe remained in desperate need of American loans, the administration could pressurise the wartime allies by closing the American money market to those nations which defaulted. One of the curious results of this outlook was the treatment of Germany. When the United States at length concluded a separate peace with her former enemy only token reparations were demanded. Consequently Germany had free access to the American money market. American financial orthodoxy in the 1920s had the effect of dragging out the reparations problem which did so much to unsettle Europe.

Americans did play a major role in 1924 and 1930 and gave a lead in sorting out the reparation question, but rejected the British suggestion that German reparations should be linked to Allied indebtedness. It would have created a very much healthier international financial climate if both large reparations and large debts had been cancelled altogether. Many of these lessons were learnt only after the Second World War. A narrow, nationalistic approach to international finance and trade in the end harmed the United States as much as it did any other country; for it contributed to the great collapse of 1929 and to the depression of the 1930s and so, indirectly, to the rise of Hitler and the outbreak of the Second World War.

CHAPTER 18

Italy and the Rise of Fascism

The world of the twentieth century sharply differs from that of the nineteenth. The twentieth century is the age of the masses. Those who govern have the opportunity for the first time to communicate directly with those they govern. The mass-circulation newspapers, the radio, the cinema and, after the Second World War, television created entirely new conditions of government. Contemporaries were not slow to recognise this. Those who ruled could create images of themselves, of their policies and objectives, of society and the world around them and so seek to lead and manipulate the masses. Mass persuasion became an essential ingredient of government; and the techniques of the art were seriously studied and consciously applied by elected governments and totalitarian regimes alike; the British Prime Minister Stanley Baldwin used the radio effectively during the General Strike of 1926 by broadcasting to the nation; President Roosevelt started his famous 'fire-side chats'; and the totalitarian leaders, Stalin, Mussolini and Hitler, put on gigantic displays which could be 'witnessed' by millions through the cinema. Mussolini's and Hitler's raucous speeches became familiar to every Italian and German; they were amplified by loudspeakers erected in public places in case anyone turned off their radio at home. Mass participation in politics was a fact in the post-war world.

The minority of the politically and economically privileged not unnaturally felt alarmed and threatened by this new age which was dawning. In countries with strong traditions of representative government and democratically inspired institutions this new force of the 'masses' might be won over and representative institutions so adapted to win their allegiance to them. This is essentially what happened in Britain and the United States in the 1920s and 1930s and, less convincingly, in France too. In the Soviet Union the mass of people were brought into harmony with the rulers by propaganda, appeals to communist idealism and, where this did not suffice, by force and terror. The revolution created an entirely new class of privileged and bound these to the regime. But those who had possessed social, political and economic privilege in pre-war Russia overwhelmingly lost it. It was a total revolution, and its spectre haunted the majority of Western societies where communist parties only gained the allegiance of a determined minority of society. The communist appeal to the masses, and their use of the masses, had to be effectively countered if communist revolutions were to be avoided. But how far were existing institutions strong enough to cope with this onslaught? The danger from the extreme left was generally exaggerated as it was unknown and could not therefore be measured. The weaknesses of existing representative forms of government to deal with national problems, however, became glaringly clear to everyone. The soldiers returning from the hardships of a long war to the unsettled conditions of post-war Europe, with its endemic under-employment as economies readjusted from war to peace, were disillusioned.

Besides the unsettled post-war conditions, the fears of Bolshevik revolutions and mass participation in politics, there is a fourth new element in the post-war situation: the expectations of expanding national frontiers and financial reparations that would follow victory and recompense the people for the sacrifices of war. The victors did not experience such rewards. Neither territorial increases nor reparations could compensate for the immense human loss and material damage of the war. The defeated in any case lacked the means to compensate the victors adequately. Among the defeated powers the sense of loss now suffered made the sacrifices of war seem all the more unbearable. Unrequited nationalism was a powerful destabilising force in post-war Europe. It differed from the pre-1914 variety in that it was not just expansionist; it also was fed by the fury felt at the injustices real and imagined of the outcome of the Great War and the peace settlements. That the defeated powers should harbour such resentments was to be expected.

Among the victorious nations the Italians particularly suffered from this malaise. They referred to the 'mutilated' peace that had not given them what they believed they deserved. The Ottoman Empire had been defeated by the Allies, but the Greeks, British and French were the intended principal beneficiaries. The sorest point of all was that Italy, despite her sacrifices in the war, had not replaced the Habsburgs as the paramount Balkan power. At the peace conference the flashpoint of Italian resentment came when Italian claims to the Italian-speaking port of Fiume, formerly in the Habsburg Empire, were rejected by her allies. Gabriele D'Annunzio, poet and professional patriot, thereupon took the law into his own hands and with government connivance and indications of royal support in 1919 seized Fiume at the head of an army of volunteers. The outburst of super-patriotism, bravado and violence, the dictatorial rabble-rousing techniques of balcony-oratory which D'Annunzio adopted made him the Duce on whom Mussolini modelled his own political style.

Whenever representative institutions had no established hold there was a tendency towards authoritarian forms of government which promised to meet the multiplicity of problems. The particular movement which became known to the world as fascism first reached power in post-war Italy. There are a number of general reasons for its rise: it developed in response to problems and opportunities facing the West in the twentieth century and arose out of the Great War. But its success at the same time has to be studied in purely Italian terms. The form that fascism later took varied so much from one country to another as the movement spread in the 1930s to Austria, Hungary, Romania, France, Portugal and Spain that historians dispute the usefulness of applying a common label. Today fascism as a description has been further debased by being applied to almost anything of which the Marxist left disapproves.

What can it be said to have had in common before the Second World War? Fascism was a movement designed to secure the support of the masses for a leader without the intermediary of a democratically elected parliament. It was a substitute for democracy, giving the masses the illusion of power without the reality. Thus, though violently anti-communist, fascism appeared to support the existing social and economic hierarchy of society and so appealed to the right. Fascism made a virtue of destroying the powers of parties and divisions in the state. It stood for 'strength through unity' at the expense of civil liberties. The cult of the leader was fostered by the leader above all and his principal lieutenants. Fascism was a chauvinist male-oriented movement assigning women to the role of child-bearing and raising a family. It was stridently nationalist. The leader, with virtually unlimited powers, stood at the apex of a party, a private army and a bureaucracy. Violence against opponents cowed possible opposition. The fascist army and bureaucracy of course ensured that tens of thousands would have a vested interest in preserving the fascist state. Here loyalty to the movement, not social standing, provided an avenue of advancement to the unscrupulous and the ambitious.

In Italy, as elsewhere, fascism derived its strength as much from what it was against as from what it was for. In detail this varied according to the tactical need of the movement to attain and then retain power. It was a totalitarian response to new social forces and to change and to discontents real and imagined, both personal and national. Parliamentary government had functioned very imperfectly already before the war (pages 31–2). The conduct of the war did not enhance parliament's prestige. The disaster of the battle of Caporetto was blamed on civilian mismanagement. The mass of impoverished Italians in the south, and the agricultural and the urban workers in the north, half a century after unification still did not identify themselves with the parliamentary state set up by Piedmont, depending as it did on local favours and corruption.

Government was by personalities rather than by leaders of parties. Manhood suffrage, introduced in 1912, and proportional representation in 1919, undermined the way in which parliament and government had previously been managed. The two biggest parties which emerged from the elections of 1919 with more than half the seats between them, the Catholic Popular party (100 seats) and the Socialists (156), were both incapable of providing the basis of a stable coalition with the Liberal and Nationalist Parties to the left of centre or the right of centre. The Socialists were divided between the communists and the more moderate socialists in 1921. Since 1919 neither wing wished to collaborate with government and both spoke the language of revolution. The Catholic Popular Party had been formed with the tacit support of the Pope to fight socialism. But it was not a class party. The majority were genuinely reformist, advocating the distribution of the landed estates to the peasantry. It was a mass party relying on the support of the agricultural labourer in the south, just as the Socialist strength lay in the industrial towns of the north. But the Popular Party also included conservative and extreme-right supporters. Their support of government policies was accordingly unpredictable. The five governments between 1918 and 1922 were consequently faced with parliamentary paralysis and no sound base on which to build a majority. Giovanni Giolitti dominated the last years of Italian parliamentary life.

Benito Mussolini. Oratorical flourishes and heroical posturing on the doorstep; sexual frolics indoors.

Against the Catholics and Socialists, Giolitti enlisted the help of Mussolini's fascists, who in the elections of May 1921 with his electoral support gained thirty-five deputies out of more than 500. It was a modest parliamentary beginning for the fascists. But, without Giolitti, Mussolini and his party would have remained a negligible constitutional force. In the streets, however, the fascists had already made their violence felt. They flourished on the seed-bed of industrial and agricultural discontent. There was large-scale post-war unemployment. On the land the peasantry took possession of uncultivated parts of the large landed estates. In the towns militant unionism demanded higher wages and in some instances in 1920 occupied factories. It was not the beginning of revolution. Higher wages were conceded, the standard of living of the urban worker rose appreciably despite higher prices. Real wages were between a quarter and a third higher in 1922 than in 1919, and by the autumn of 1922 unrest subsided. It was at this point that Mussolini came to power, claiming to have saved the country from the imaginary threat of Bolshevism and offering fascism as an alternative.

Mussolini succeeded in attracting attention to himself in his pose as statesman and Duce. He made Italy seem more important in international affairs than her weak industrial resources and military strength warranted. It was an image built up with skill to mislead a gullible world until the image was shattered when the ineptitude of Mussolini's armies were revealed on every front during the Second World War. The success of fascism lay largely in creating such myths, which after 1925 become identified with the public personality Mussolini created of himself.

Benito Mussolini was born to genuinely 'proletarian' parents on 29 July 1883 in the small town of Predappio in the poor east-central region of Italy, the Romagna. His father was a blacksmith and named his son Benito after the Mexican revolutionary leader Juarez. From youth onwards, Mussolini admired rebellious violence against the 'establishment' of schoolmasters; and as he became older he rebelled against the better off and privileged. He experienced poverty, and his hatred of privilege turned him into an ardent socialist. He left Italy and spent some time in Switzerland under socialist tutelage. He then accepted both the internationalist and pacifist outlook of the socialists. Yet in 1904 he returned to Italy to serve his obligatory time in the army and clearly enjoyed army life and discipline. It was the first and not the only inconsistency in his development. For a time he took a post as a teacher. But above all Mussolini saw himself as a socialist political agitator. He rose to prominence in the pre-war Italian Socialist Party, belonging to the most extreme revolutionary wing. He denounced nationalism as a capitalist manifestation and was briefly imprisoned for his activities in seeking to hinder the war effort during Italy's Libyan war with Turkey, 1911–12 (page 35). His imprisonment brought him into favour with the revolutionary socialists who controlled the Socialist Party in 1912. They appointed Mussolini to the editorship of *Avanti*, the socialist newspaper.

Consistency and loyalty to friends and principles was not a strong trait in Mussolini. War, that is international violence, later attracted him. Mussolini was no pacifist by nature. So all went well with his efforts as a socialist editor until shortly after the outbreak of the Great War. Then, to the anger of the Socialists who condemned the capitalist war and demanded non-intervention, Mussolini switched and started banging the drum of nationalism and patriotism in *Avanti*. The Socialists thereupon ousted him from the editorship. Mussolini then founded his own paper in November 1914, the *Popolo d'Italia*, and campaigned for intervention. Without political connections his influence, however, was negligible. He served in the army from 1915 to 1917, was wounded and, on release from the army, returned to patriotic journalism.

Mussolini observed the impotence and weakness of parliamentary government after the war and saw it as an opportunity for him to form and lead an authoritarian movement; with its help he might then play an important role in the state, something he had so far failed to do.

A meeting in Milan addressed by Mussolini of some 200 of his followers in March 1919 marks the formal beginning of the fascist movement. The movement in the beginning expressed its hostility to property and to capitalist industry and followed the line of French syndicalism in advocating worker control of industry – 'economic democracy' – and so tried to win the urban workers' support. Yet in its early years the money flowing in to support it, and to fund Mussolini's own newspaper, came from Milan industrialists. The landowners too intended to use his bands of ruffians – the *squadristi* – against peasants. Mussolini's personal inclinations were probably socialist still in 1919, but in his bid for power he was ready to trim his sails and operate in the interests of property to secure the support of industrialists and landowners. He had become a pure opportunist and adventurer.

Fascism was the main beneficiary of the ineffectual trade union activities, the occupation of the factories in the summer of 1920 and the Socialists' appeals to workers to engage in a general strike. During the winter of 1920 and the following spring, bands of fascists in their black shirts both in the towns and in the countryside attacked all forms of labour organisations, socialist councils, socialist newspapers, even cultural societies. Opponents were beaten and tortured. The 'red shirts' offered resistance and street battles ensued. Liberal Italy and the Church, while condemning all violence, connived at the destruction of socialist organisations by the fascists. Since the government appeared powerless to restore law and order, the fascists came to be regarded as the protectors of property by the middle classes and not as the principal disturbers of the peace, which they were.

The rapid growth of violent bands of fascists, swelled by the followers of D'Annunzio, whose escapade in Fiume had collapsed, could no longer be effectively controlled by Mussolini and at this stage, in 1921, was unwelcome to him. Mussolini had entered parliament as the leader of a small party and sought power in alliance with either one of the two large parties, the Catholic Popular Party or the Socialists. He chose the Socialists temporarily to capture the mass votes of the urban workers. But the leaders of the fascist bands were outraged at this 'betrayal'. Mussolini even lost the leadership of the party for a short time. The fascists continued their violence in the cities and the countryside. Mussolini also nourished the belief of the parliamentary Liberals that he would co-operate with them against the socialist left.

Mussolini played the anti-Bolshevik card for all he was worth. The call by the Socialists in July 1922 for a general strike in a bid to stop the increasing lawlessness and drift to the right provided a semblance of justification for Mussolini's claims. The strike call was a failure but increased the desire for tough measures against the workers. The support the fascists were given was particularly strong from those groups – artisans, white-collar workers and shopkeepers, the lower-middle class – who saw their status threatened and usurped by the demands of the workers. The army despised the parliamentary regime, which was obliged to reduce their swollen wartime strength. Mussolini's strident nationalism naturally appealed to them. Prefects and civil servants in the provinces too connived at fascist violence and were hedging their bets in case the fascists should one day come to power. Giolitti's policy of non-interference in disputes which he believed would blow themselves out was a clever tactic as far as weakening the strength of the trade unions and socialists was concerned. Strikes diminished. Any danger the left had posed was rapidly vanishing. But the low government profile also created a power vacuum which the fascists filled until they themselves openly defied law and order and even threatened the state itself. Without government weakness, without the parliamentary paralysis which prevented the liberal centre from forming a stable coalition, the fascists could never have gained power. While the politicians connived and jockeyed for power, divided as much by ambition as policy, administration throughout the country was becoming anarchic.

The fascists chose the month of October 1922 to seize power from the unstable liberal administrations. Their plan was first to stage uprisings in the provinces which would capture prefectures and post offices and cut off Rome from the surrounding countryside thus paralysing government, and then to march on Rome with armies of 'blackshirts' and throw out the government by force if intimidation did not suffice. Conveniently for Mussolini his one rival Duce, D'Annunzio, who might have claimed the leadership, fell on his head from a balcony after quarrelling with his mistress. It was rumoured that the poet's fall had been assisted. A touch of opera was never entirely absent from the dramatic moments of Italian history.

Yet a fascist victory was far from certain. It was a great gamble, as Mussolini knew while he waited in Milan, a fascist stronghold not too far from the Swiss frontier, in case of failure. The King, Victor Emmanuel III, held the key to the situation. Loyalty to the dynasty was strong and it seems most probable that the army, though infiltrated by fascists from the highest-ranking officers to the most junior, would have responded to his lead and command. But there was nothing heroic about Victor Emmanuel. He did not put army loyalty to the test. Although a constitutional monarch, he must increasingly have lost confidence in the jockeying politicians and in the corruption of the electoral system. When his ministers finally found the courage to resist the threats of the fascists, the King refused them his backing and in doing so handed Italy over to Mussolini.

The government in Rome, after receiving news of the fascist uprising, of the seizure of government buildings in the provinces, was at first undecided how to act. It had already resigned in the process of another reshuffle but in the interim remained in charge. After a night of alarm, Luigi Facta, the temporary Prime Minister, having secured assurances of the loyalty of the army garrison in Rome, decided with the support of his ministers on a firm stand. The army was ordered to stop the fascist attempt to seize Rome. Early on the morning of 28 October 1922 an emergency decree was published which amounted to a proclamation of martial law. To this decree the King refused his assent and so it was revoked. The way was now open to Mussolini to state his terms. He demanded that he be asked to head the new government. The King's action had left the state without power at this critical moment. The government was discredited and so was the Crown when Mussolini, arriving comfortably in Rome in a railway sleeping-car on the morning of 30 October, accepted from the King the commission to form a new government. Thus the march on Rome occurred *after* and not before Mussolini's assumption of the premiership. There was never in fact a 'seizure' of power – though fascist historiography embroidered and glorified the event – only a *threat* to seize power. The fascists also did not *march* on Rome but were conveyed in special trains to the capital and there reviewed by the King and the Duce before being quickly packed off home on 31 October. Yet without the threat of seizing power Mussolini would not have achieved his ends. The threat was real, though whether he would have succeeded if he had attempted to seize control of Rome is another, much more debatable, question.

Now that Mussolini was in power he had no programme to place before parliament. He had concerned himself solely with the problem of how to attain power. Should he complete the 'revolution' now, as the fascist militants expected, or should he manipulate the parliamentary system and seek to govern at least pseudo-constitutionally? Should the Fascist Party replace the state or should it be subordinated to the state? These important questions, often asked, are in fact somewhat unreal. What mattered to Mussolini now that he had attained power was to retain as much of it personally in his hands for as long as possible. He had no principles or methods and despite talk of a new corporative state all relationships with existing institutions and organisations possessing some power in the state were subordinated to his will. His own fascist backers in this sense posed as much of an obstacle to him as political opponents, the monarchy, the papacy, the army and the bureaucracy. 'Policy' was what Mussolini felt best served his interests in dealing with every group.

Did Mussolini establish a 'totalitarian' regime? The monarchy was preserved, and the Church and the armed forces enjoyed some independence, while the independence of parliament was virtually destroyed. But Mussolini avoided a sudden revolutionary break; he allowed some degree of independence, believing this to serve his interests. He lacked in any case the iron will, utter ruthlessness and total inhumanity of Hitler. Rather than make the Fascist Party supreme, Mussolini preferred to leave some delegated power in the hands of rival interest groups so that his task of domination would be made easier. Mussolini understood in his early years before self-delusion blinded him that some voluntary limits on his exercise of power would make him more acceptable and so strengthen his hold over government. The Duce was a complex character whose undoubted arrogance and insensitivity was complemented by intelligence and unusual political skill.

In October 1922 Mussolini made himself the head of a government which looked not so different to previous government coalitions based on personal bargaining. Included were the Catholics and Conservatives. Mussolini, in addition to holding the premiership, was also minister of the interior and his own foreign minister. He won an overwhelming vote of confidence in parliament for this government. His objective of breaking the political power of other parties by inveigling the majority to co-operate with him in national tasks was attained slowly but surely. When he felt sufficiently strong and secure, he backed a fascist bill for parliamentary 'reform', the Acerbo bill. In place of proportional representation this bill established that the party gaining most votes (as long as these amounted to at least 25 per cent of the total) should automatically secure two-thirds of all the seats in the Chamber of Deputies. Since the fascists were infiltrating and taking over the provincial administrations, they would be able to ensure in any case that more than a quarter of the votes were cast for the list of government candidates. The bill passed in November 1923 made certain that Mussolini would have at his disposal a permanent majority of deputies ready to do his will. The morale of any intending opposition parties was consequently undermined. Intimidation played its part in persuading the deputies lamely to consent to Mussolini's retention of power by legal and constitutional means. He always hinted he could act differently, especially as he now had a private army, the former fascist bands, which had been transformed into a voluntary militia of national security paid for by the state and swearing allegiance to the Duce, not the King.

The elections of April 1924 were a triumph for Mussolini. Intimidation and corruption to a degree not practised before secured for his candidates two-thirds of all the votes cast. The year 1924 was the last, nevertheless, in which Mussolini could have been driven from power. There was a revulsion of feeling in the country when a socialist deputy, Giacomo Matteotti, was murdered by a fascist gang after he had attacked the corrupt elections in parliament. Mussolini was taken aback by the sense of outrage; he was accused in parliament in June 1924 of being an accomplice of murder, and a group of opposition deputies withdrew in protest. But the King did nothing. Mussolini rode out this, his first and last serious storm before his fall in 1943. In 1926 his regime became more openly totalitarian with the suppression of the free press.

Just as Mussolini did not wish to be dependent on a genuine representative assembly, so he did not intend to be at the mercy of fascist followers more revolutionary than he. In December 1922 he created a Grand Council of Fascism over which he presided and which he dominated. In October 1926 it was the turn of the independence of the Fascist Party to be undermined; all elections within the party were henceforth ended; the party was organised from above with Mussolini as its supreme head. Within two years the party was bureaucratised and its violent activities outside the law curbed.

The Pope and the Catholic Church were another powerful and independent focus of power in the state. With remarkable skill, Mussolini, an avowed atheist, succeeded in reducing the political influence of the Church. It had not been so hostile to fascism as might have been expected, since it saw in fascism a bulwark against atheistic communism and socialism. The threat of socialism had already brought the Church back into the politics of the Italian state before the war (page 33). Mussolini built on this reconciliation of state and Church. The outcome of long negotiations from 1926 to 1929 was the Lateran Accords; by recognising papal sovereignty over the Vatican City, the state returned to the papacy a token temporal dominion in Italy; furthermore Catholicism was recognised as the sole religion of the state, and much of the anti-clerical legislation was repealed. The treaty won for the Church a position in Italy it had not enjoyed since unification. Judged as *Realpolitik* Vatican diplomacy was successful. But what of the moral standing of the Church? It was to be compromised even more when the Vatican attempted to preserve Catholic interests in Germany by concluding a concordat with Hitler in 1933. Temporary advantages led to long-term damage. The Church was inhibited from taking a clear moral stand and from condemning outright the crimes against humanity which the dictators in the end committed. Official Catholic protest tended to be muted (more so under Pius XII after 1939 than under Pius XI) though individual priests, including the Pope, sought to protect persecuted individuals.

The positive contribution of fascism was supposed to be the introduction of the 'corporate state'. This was based on the idea that, instead of being fought out, conflicts of interest were to be negotiated under the guidance of the state in bodies known as corporations. Thus in 1925 the employers' federation and the fascist trade unions recognised each other as equal partners, and corporations to settle differences in many different branches of industry, agriculture and education were envisaged. A huge bureaucratic structure was built up under a Ministry of Corporations. The industrialists nevertheless largely preserved their autonomy from the state. Not so the representatives of labour – labour was now represented in the corporations by fascist bureaucrats. The workers were exploited and even their basic right to move from one job to another without official permission was taken away. Real wages fell sharply, and fascism, despite some spectacular schemes such as the expansion of wheat-growing in the 1930s, and drainage of marsh land, could not propel the under-developed economy forward. Economically, Italy remained backward and labour ceased to make social advances. The increasing fascist bureaucracy, moreover, was a heavy burden to bear. Massive propaganda showing happy Italians and the Duce stripped to the waist in the fields might fool foreigners but could not better the lot of the poor.

The cult of the Duce was substituted for genuine progress. He posed as world leader, as the greatest military genius and economic sage, as the man who had transformed the civilised Italian people into conquering Romans. His conquests in the 1920s were meagre, however. In Libya and Somalia his troops fought savagely to reduce poorly armed tribesmen. After ten years of fighting they were subjected. In no way was this a glorious military episode. In the Balkans and the Middle East there was little he could do without British and French acquiescence. He tried in 1923, defying the League of Nations by seizing the island of Corfu from the Greeks, using as a pretext the murder of an Italian in Greece. But Britain and France intervened and, after finding a face-saving formula, Mussolini had to withdraw. He did, however, secure Fiume for Italy in the following year. All in all it was not very heroic. For the rest, Mussolini unsuccessfully tried to exploit Balkan differences and sought the limelight by signing many treaties. Before the rise of

Hitler, Mussolini had few real opportunities to exploit Western differences in order to fulfil his designs of imperial grandeur. So he was misjudged abroad as a sensible statesman in the 1920s. Conservatives even admired the superficial order he had imposed on Italy's rich and varied life. The 1930s were to reveal to the world what his opponents in Italy and the colonies had already learnt to their cost – the less benevolent aspects of Mussolini's rule.

PART IV

The Continuing World Crisis, 1929–1939

CHAPTER 19

The Depression, 1929–1939

The despair of poverty is hard to imagine for those who have never suffered it. A decade after the conclusion of the Great War the era of the great depression began, reducing millions of people in the advanced Western world to the levels of grinding poverty suffered throughout the twentieth century by humanity in Asia, South America and Africa. The peoples living in the empires of the West now fell even below the barest subsistence levels as the price they could obtain for their raw materials dropped precipitously. Their economies were dependent on the demand of the West. Whatever befell the industrialised West, the effects on the poor of what we now call the Third World were even more catastrophic. The great depression, usually considered solely in terms of the ills affecting the industrialised countries, should be seen in its worldwide setting. At the time only one country appeared immune – the Soviet Union, where industrial production increased. It was a persuasive argument to some that communism provided the only solution to the periodic booms and depressions which bedevilled the trade cycle. But in the Soviet Union, Stalin's state planning actually imposed hardships as great and greater than anything happening in the West (Chapter 20).

The impact of the economic crisis on politics and society was immense in the West, second only to that of the Great War. The effect of the depression was aggravated by its occurring before the trauma of the Great War had been overcome. It is the shortness of time that elapsed between one shock and the next that gives the years from 1919 to 1939 their particular characteristic when compared with the long period of growing prosperity in the West before 1914 and the growth that occurred during the thirty-five years after 1945. In contrast, 1919 to 1939 came to be viewed as a 'continuing world crisis'. The industrial depression that began in 1929 had been preceded by an agricultural depression dating from 1921, not really overcome in the mid-1920s, and then rapidly deepening after 1926. The 'boom years' of industrial expansion of the 1920s thus were not as uniformly prosperous as often supposed. For all its startling psychological repercussions, the Wall Street crash on 'black Tuesday', 29 October 1929, did not cause the depression. The Western world, despite its attempts to return to the 'normality' of the pre-1914 years, was unable to do so after the Great War. Indeed, in this desire to return to the past there was an insufficient recognition of how enormously the war had dislocated the workings of the world economy. No radical new international financial initiatives were believed to be required to cope with the situation. Instead each nation sought to return to pre-war practices, some like Britain to the gold standard, sound money and balanced budgets.

The new problem of Allied war debts and German reparations did necessitate a fresh approach and international discussion and co-operation. During the 1920s, before 1931 when all these payments came practically to a halt, the international settlements followed a circular route of German

The Global Depression. Left: *in China, as everywhere, the common denominator is destitution.* Right: *an unemployed war veteran in Hanover in 1932 has little to thank Weimar democracy for.* Below left: *an American family escapes the Oklahoma 'dust bowl' in June 1938.* Below right: *a French soup kitchen at Ivry in 1934.*

Anxious New Yorkers mill around Wall Street during the Crash of October 1929 wondering how bad it's going to get.

reparations payments constantly scaled down, making possible the payment of Allied debts to the United States also scaled down, while American loans to Germany, exceeding German reparations payments, completed the circle. This was not very sensible financially, but the actual sums involved, though not the principal cause of the breakdown of world trade, contributed to the disruption of international finance by the end of the decade. The causes of the depression are so complex that they remain a matter of lively debate among experts. It is best here to make a number of brief points.

Study of the economic development of each Western nation reveals how far the depression of the 1930s had causes going back even before the First World War. As has been seen, Britain, for example, continued to rely on textile, coal and shipbuilding industries of the first industrial revolution, and was shifting only slowly, too slowly, to industries of the more advanced technology of the twentieth century. This lack of progress caused continuous and heavy unemployment even during the 1920s, when only in one year did unemployment drop below 10 per cent of the workforce.

The United States provided a contrast with the massive growth of new consumer industries such as the automobile industry and with unemployment at around only 4 per cent. The problem here was that these new industries did not produce necessities and the decision not to buy a new car because of a lack of faith in the future could produce a sudden reversal of fortunes in manufacturing industry. But it was not until 1931 that unemployment became the serious kind of problem that it had been in Britain throughout the 1920s. The French economy was different again, with half the population engaged in agriculture. But post-war reconstruction favoured the rise of new industries (as in Germany after the Second World War) and by 1930 France had emerged strengthened, even requiring foreign labour to augment the native labour force. The effect of the worldwide depression was stagnation throughout the 1930s.

In Germany the impact of the world economic crisis was conditioned by the particular experiences of Germans since the lost war. Having once experienced hyperinflation which made money worthless (page 136), the German government was determined to preserve sound money regardless of the cost in terms of unemployment. Agricultural prosperity had suffered a serious setback some two years before in 1929, while German industry boomed. The later 1920s saw the formation of large industrial cartels and the introduction of new technology. Germany not only financed this modernisation by attracting loans from the United States but also paid off reparations from loans. Other American loans financed unproductive municipal projects such as town halls and swimming baths. Much of this loan capital could be recalled at short notice and when this happened in 1929 the German economy, already affected by declining international markets, threatened to spin out of control. The largest Western percentage of unemployed was Germany's in 1932 with 30 per cent out of work.

The state of the United States economy was the common denominator in the world economic crisis. The American economy had assumed such importance that the other Western economies depended on its good health. There is thus pretty general agreement that the origins of great worldwide depression are to be sought in the United States. With the American economy running down, the prices of raw materials slumped; markets all over the world contracted as a result. When the United States reduced the flow of capital abroad, and in 1930 created a prohibitive tariff which prevented the European powers from selling their goods in the United States, the rest of the world could no longer cope.

There were weaknesses in the economic structure of European nations which had already made themselves felt, as in Britain, before 1929. The American recession turned these problems into one of the most severe crises these countries had ever experienced. The depression proved to be not just a short downturn in the business cycle, as had been expected. The bad year from 1929 to 1930 was followed by an even worse year in 1931. When 1932 brought no relief, hope of an automatic upturn collapsed. World economic conditions did improve from the low point of 1931–2 but only gradually. The world depression continued down to the Second World War, which, like the First, transformed economic activity and absorbed the unemployed to feed the war machine. So long and deep a depression was a new experience and governments were frequently at a loss as to how best to handle the economic problems of their day. Sometimes, as in Germany from 1931 to 1933, they made matters worse.

The depression also provided a test for the different forms of government by which the peoples of the world were ruled. The performance of different governments was inevitably judged by ordinary people according to how effective they perceived them to be in finding remedies for the ills of depression, unemployment foremost among them. In people's minds, the communist, the various fascist and Nazi 'models', the conduct of the democratic governments, as well as colonial rule, could in these circumstances be uniquely compared.

Any government and political system which happened to exist during the early depression years was bound to be blamed for the widespread misery. But those authoritarian governments that were already firmly established by 1929 were in a better position to maintain themselves by brute force and to manipulate the attitudes of the masses through propaganda. Popular discontent could no longer threaten the Soviet system of communist rule. The Western colonial empires were under firm military control. Mussolini stifled protest: strikes were prohibited by law; the Italian state set low rates of interest; and the Institute for Industrial Reconstruction was created in January 1933 to assist Italian banks, which in turn led to the state assuming direct responsibility for a range of industry from shipping to steel. Unemployment in Italy nevertheless remained stubbornly high in the early 1930s and the standard of living persistently low. Yet there was no open criticism as Mussolini advertised himself, photographed stripped to the waist with spade in hand and working on public works projects such as draining the marshes or extending land for wheat cultivation.

Hitler came to power during the most serious period of depression and he quickly consolidated dictatorial power. Nevertheless it was his evident success in reducing unemployment in Germany from 6 million in October 1933 to just over 4 million a year later and 2.8 million in 1935 that so increased national popular support for him. Rearmament and army expansion after 1936 virtually eliminated unemployment in Germany. Whatever evils came to be associated with Hitler's rule in the eyes of the German people, they gave Hitler credit for 'curing' unemployment. Hitler recognised that he could turn the prevailing despair to his advantage if he could infuse a spirit of action, convey his understanding and concern for the plight of the unemployed and actually put people to work. His success was not instantaneous; it was achieved, moreover, by forcibly destroying the independence of labour. It was achieved, too, in the face of traditional banking advice. Hitler listened to the Keynesian-type economists in Germany who had met with rejection by Brüning (page 199). Hjalmar Schacht, who returned as president of the Reichsbank, created large paper credits. Money was spent on new super-highways – the *Autobahnen*, which had military value – on expanding rearmament and on support for agriculture. The Nazi economy was tightly controlled by the state in order to achieve self-sufficiency in agriculture – and as far as possible in industry – without replacing the actual private ownership of industry or the land.

At the price of liberty, the Nazi economy from 1933 to 1939 was remarkably successful in maintaining stable prices, full employment eventually and a modest rise in the standard of living of the working man. Rearmament was not allowed to cut standards of living drastically. Hitler was anxious to win and retain German support by providing economic and social benefits, and used violence only against open opponents from the beginning and against the Jews from 1938. The authoritarian models' good points, which were proclaimed by their own captive press, radio and film, impressed the unemployed in the democracies more than the bad. Democratic governments requiring the co-operation of parliament looked less effective and more cumbersome by comparison.

Poincaré's government of national union had restored French finances to health in 1926 (page 146). The elections of 1928 had given the right a great victory, but his retirement a year later, sick and worn out, marked the end of an era in which France had attempted to reassert her standing as a great power in Europe, and coincided also with the time when the depression became more serious worldwide. French governments after Poincaré lost their stability once more: between 1929 and 1934 they lasted an average of three or four months. Albert Lebrun, elected president in 1932, remained until the fall of France in 1940, but he was a colourless politician who gave no kind of lead. At first the strength of France's financial position seemed to make her immune, alone among the Western nations, from the débâcle following the crash in October 1929 in the United States. Throughout 1930 unemployment remained low. But in the autumn of 1931 the slump and unemployment finally spread to France. French governments now sought by financial 'orthodoxy' to meet the crisis, simultaneously cutting pensions, salaries and public expenditure. The cessation of German reparation payments in 1931, coupled with the Americans' continuing insistence on repayment of debts, compounded the difficulty. Despite devaluing once in 1928, successive governments until 1936 added to France's problems by refusing to devalue an overvalued franc which made the task of exporting increasingly hard. During the worst years from 1933 to 1934 the survival of the Republic herself seemed very doubtful. Big business and the extreme right admired the fascist model as an authoritarian solution behind which they could operate profitably. Among politicians of the right, Pierre Laval and André Tardieu as well as Marshal Pétain, the hero of Verdun, inclined towards some sort of authoritarian resolution for the troubles and divisions of the Republic.

The unpopular measures of successive French governments in a parliamentary Chamber of predominantly centre and left-wing parties, as well as fear of communism, played into the hands of the right. The socialists led by Léon Blum would not join any coalition government which included the 'bourgeois' Radical-Socialists, whose main support came from the conservative peasantry and the middle classes and whose aims were not in the least socialist. The communists under Maurice Thorez meanwhile followed the Moscow line of the Comintern, which ordered them to regard the Democratic Socialist Party as their greatest enemy. So governments were formed mainly by the Radical parliamentary leaders seeking alignments to the right. The impact of the depression gravely weakened and divided the left, with the communists until 1934 pursuing an apparently insane tactic of undermining the stability of the Republic that might well have helped fascism to power in France as it had done earlier in Germany. The realisation of the folly of the Moscow course dawned on Thorez and in 1934 he became a leading and successful advocate of changing it.

The years 1933 and 1934 also saw the growth in France of paramilitary fascist 'leagues' whose bands of rowdies brawled in the streets of Paris like Nazi stormtroopers. There was the royalist Action Française, the oldest of the leagues founded before the First World War. Another was the Jeunesses Patriotes composed mainly of students. François Coty, the perfume millionaire, financed the Solidarité Française and a fascist journal, *L'Ami du peuple*. The most important of these leagues was the Croix de Feu, made up of war veterans led by Colonel de la Rocque, whose main aim was the negative one of overthrowing the parliamentary Republic. Royalism, extreme Catholicism, anti-Semitism, other movements inspired by Mussolini's and Hitler's example, all had little in common except a determination to undermine the Republic. With this aim the politically opposite Communist Party at first also agreed, and the communists were even ready to work in parallel with fascists to achieve this object. The leagues were supported by numerous vicious Parisian newspapers which were constantly stirring up popular hatred against the legislators.

At the worst possible moment, with the government discredited by its instability and inept handling of the depression, with financial hardship deepening and polarising class antagonism, the politicians were smeared with the taint of corruption by what became known as the Stavisky scandal. Stavisky was a swindler who had through the years floated a number of bonds and shares which defrauded the investors. Although arrested, he had enjoyed a strange immunity from trial, in the meantime making more money from shady deals. In January 1934 he had finally shot himself and the police, who could have saved his life, allowed him to die. It was rumoured that his death had shielded highly placed politicians and the police from the revelation of their involvement in his crimes and in these allegations there was undoubtedly some truth. All the anti-parliamentary forces seized on the scandal to make a concerted effort to overthrow not only the government but the Republic. The members of the various leagues were summoned in their thousands on to the streets of Paris to oust the politicians. The climax was reached during the night of 6 February 1934 when street battles raged in Paris, the police and Garde Mobile narrowly gaining the upper hand. Hundreds of demonstrators were wounded, some seriously, and it is surprising that the death toll – some eighteen people – was relatively small. The supposedly strong government under the Radical Prime Minister Édouard Daladier turned out to be weak after all and promptly resigned. The Republic was saved by a few of its resolute defenders among the Paris police, by luck and above all by the total disunity of the leaders of the right. There was no Hitler or even Mussolini among them.

Weak French governments which could find no solution to the political, social and economic problems succeeded each other during the next two years. The elections of May 1936, however, seemed to herald a turning point: the parties of the left – the Socialists and communists – together with the Radicals had by then formed an electoral alliance, the Popular Front. This extraordinary change had been made possible by the *volte face* of the French Communist Party. In June 1934 the communists and Socialists had overcome their mutual suspicions to join in a United Front to fight fascism. The reasons for the change have fascinated historians, for the communists had regarded the Democratic Socialists, or 'social fascists' as they called them, as their worst enemies. They accused them of leading the proletariat away from the true goal of communist revolution under the guise of representing the working people's class interests. The fascists, on the other hand, could be recognised as the enemy of the proletariat and were but a passing phenomenon associated with the later stages of capitalism before its inevitable demise.

Outside the Soviet Union, some of the communist parties which subscribed to the Soviet-controlled Comintern began to question these doctrinaire views. How could all Social Democrats be regarded as enemies when they were fighting the same foe as in Austria, where the Social Democrats forcibly resisted the authoritarian clerical Dollfuss government and were in 1934 bombarded in Vienna into submission (page 219)? In Germany Hitler's Nazis looked like consolidating their power. Communists languished in concentration camps, their party organisation smashed up. There was a serious danger that fascism would win power in other European countries. The French communist leader, Maurice Thorez, became especially fearful of a fascist triumph in France. The French Communist Party took the lead in creating a new United Front with the socialists. They could not have openly disobeyed the Comintern in Moscow. But the Soviet leadership was divided and persuaded by the brilliant Bulgarian communist leader, George Dimitrov, the hero of the Reichstag fire trial,[1] to allow some latitude and experimentation of tactics. From the summer of 1934 onwards Thorez pushed on, the Soviet leaders acquiescing. The socialist and communist trade unions merged. Not satisfied with a socialist alliance alone, Thorez

[1] For the Reichstag fire, see page 201. Dimitrov was among those in Berlin accused of organising the fire; he defied and taunted the Nazis and was acquitted.

Riots in Paris on 6 February 1934 on the Place de la Concorde. But the republic survives.

extended the alignment even further to include the 'bourgeois' Radicals, and so turned the United Front into the much broader Popular Front. The electoral pact of the three parties – Socialist, communist and Radical – gave the Popular Front electoral victory over the right in the spring of 1936 and brought Léon Blum to power as prime minister. Though the Radicals did least well, the communists gained greatly and the three parties together won 378 seats against the right's 220. The electoral arrangements, rather than a large shift in the voting, had achieved this result. But French society remained more divided than ever. This polarisation was as important as the election results. Léon Blum had taken no part in the elections. He had been nearly beaten to death in the street when fanatics of the Action Française had set upon him. He was fortunately rescued by building workers who happened to be nearby. That was the other side of French politics.

The right now assailed Blum, who headed the Popular Front government, not only for serving as a cover for the communists, but also as an alien, as a Jew. In few countries outside Nazi Germany was anti-Semitism as crude and virulent as in some sections of French society. Blum was sensitive to these attacks; he followed in the socialist traditions of pacifism and humane consideration for the poor. He could never quite rise above the viciousness of the onslaught on him and too self-consciously sought to prove himself a patriot and conciliator. In his Cabinet when facing opposition he was prone to indecision and weakness, as became very clear when the Popular Front government in Madrid appealed to France for help at the outset of the Spanish Civil War (page 225). There was every reason why the French Popular Front government should help republican Spain with arms, not only on ideological grounds but also because a fascist victory threatened to encircle France. This too was Blum's view. But the outcry of the right and the weakness of his Radical and Socialist ministerial colleagues changed Blum's mind and he reversed his earlier decision to respond to Madrid's appeal.

In domestic affairs, Blum's government scored one spectacular success. At the time that he took office, France was hit by a huge wave of strikes and factory sit-ins. Discontent with low wages and poor working conditions in industry and on the land had finally led to this confrontation which served notice to the politicians that as in other Western countries – except, of course, in fascist Italy and Nazi Germany – organised labour demanded basic rights and higher wages. The employers and propertied were thoroughly frightened. Blum brought the employers and the trade unionists – the Confédération Générale du Travail – together at his official residence, the Hôtel Matignon on Sunday, 7 June. After a night's discussion there emerged a package: a substantial wage increase, two weeks' paid holiday, a forty-hour week and, most important of all, the employers' acceptance of the trade unions' bargaining rights; in return the unions would persuade the workers to end their sit-ins and the strikes. Believing themselves on the verge of social revolution, parliament rushed this constructive legislation through in a few days – an uncharacteristic show of good sense and urgency. Industrial peace was restored for a time. But the impact of the Blum government on the health of the economy was small, despite the belated devaluation of the franc in October 1936. Blum was determined to work pacifically, by seeking the co-operation of big business and high finance, which loathed all his government stood for. There was to be no enforced socialism. After a year, the stagnating economy and price rises had wiped out much of the advantage the workers had gained by wage rises.

Premier Léon Blum with his wife, among friends, in July 1936.

Soon after coming to office, Blum banned the 'leagues'. This proved as ineffectual as in Germany in 1932. The leagues assumed a new 'legitimate' political garb – but the street brawling continued as before. A particularly violent clash between the communists and the right in March 1937 ended in bloodshed; it horrified Blum and damaged the reputation of the Popular Front. Blum was ready to resign immediately but carried on in the end. He resigned three months later, in June 1937, disillusioned and frustrated in his domestic and foreign policies, when a hostile Senate, dominated by the Radicals, refused to give him the powers he had asked for so that his government could deal with the financial crisis. For a further year a hollowed-out Popular Front continued. The disunity of the left, its weakness, the bitterness of class war, which even took the form of making it fashionable on the right to mouth 'better Hitler than Blum', allowed government to fall into the hands of a coalition of the disunited Radicals and the right. Édouard Daladier in April 1938 emerged as another supposedly 'strong' man whose actual performance belied his reputation. His finance minister, Paul Reynaud, tried to restore the economy by increased taxation and a longer working week. The employers, recovered from the early days of the Popular Front, were able to redress the balance again in their favour but at the expense of social bitterness. The repercussions for world peace of France's feebleness were immense. It was a misfortune that all this occurred when across France's eastern frontier a determined and ruthless dictator was taking full advantage of the French political and social crisis.

Political division at the centre of government in the years between the wars did not lie at the root of Britain's social and economic difficulties. Indeed it is difficult to think of any two decades of British history where there was such unanimity. The Liberal Party never recovered sufficiently to provide an alternative government. The role was taken over by the Labour Party. Labour had briefly formed a minority government in 1924, and then again from 1929 to 1931. Just three years after the conclusion of the General Strike, Baldwin in May 1929 went to the country confident of electoral victory. The total Labour vote (8.4 million) was slightly lower than the Conservative (8.7 million), but the constituency electoral system gave Labour more seats, 289 against the Conservatives' 260, while lack of proportional representation penalised the Liberals who, despite their 5.3 million votes, gained only 59 seats. But the really perverse fact of the election of 1929 was that there was less practical difference between Ramsay MacDonald's brand of Labour policies and the policies of the Conservatives than between the policies of either party and those of the Liberals. It was the Liberals who put forward a radically different economic strategy masterminded by the most famous economic thinker of the age, John Maynard Keynes. He and others produced the pre-election plan *Britain's Industrial Future*, which advocated government spending as the spearhead to industrial revival. 'We Can Conquer Unemployment' was Lloyd George's more popular election version of this plan. Lloyd George, with his own 'brains trust' behind him, was ready to provide the British people with their 'New Deal'. But there was to be no political comeback for Lloyd George. His new remedies were never tried, at least not until after the Second World War.

Labour became the alternative to the Conservatives. Its leadership was anxious not to present the party as too socialist, let alone as revolutionary, as the communists had no electoral appeal. The left wing of the Labour movement found itself isolated, shunned both by the communists who were following the Comintern line of fighting the 'social fascists' and by the bulk of the trade unions and the moderate Labour right. Despite Ramsay MacDonald's commitment to a Labour Party whose theoretical aim was to transform capitalism into socialism, as leader of the party he saw this as some very distant objective, certainly not practical politics in 1929. From that day to the present, the precise definition of what should constitute the Labour's definition of 'democratic socialism' rent the party. The predominant majority of the Labour Party always stood behind leaders who warned that to embrace far-reaching socialist measures, such as bringing the greater part of industry under state control, would alienate the electorate and condemn the party to permanent opposition. The move to the left needed to be gradual and pragmatic.

In fact the Labour minority government which MacDonald formed in June 1929 largely excluded the Labour left. The electoral programme had soft-pedalled socialism and the whole issue of public ownership, except for the coal industry (and even the Conservatives were to move eventually towards some form of state supervision over the coal industry); quite likely Labour owed its electoral success to this stance of 'respectability'. Philip Snowden, Chancellor of the Exchequer; was as orthodox, as sternly opposed to unbalanced budgets and as fearful of inflation as any Conservative chancellor. It is true that MacDonald's government might have been ousted if it had followed policies on which the Conservatives and Liberals would have combined against Labour. The survival of the government was his first priority. But it must also be noted that MacDonald held back from radical policies – such as new measures for dealing with unemployment – which would have secured Liberal support.

The single biggest problem facing Britain at home throughout the 1920s was unemployment, which persisted at over 1 million, more than 10 per cent of the labour force. This average for the whole country does not reveal its full seriousness, since unemployment was far more severe in the Clydeside of Scotland and Tyneside in north-east England where shipbuilding was in the doldrums, in the coal-mining valleys of South Wales, in Ulster and in the textile region of south Lancashire. Whole regions were blighted, sunk in poverty with unemployment persisting year after year. The famous hunger marches to London in the 1930s helped to draw the 'forgotten ' regions to the attention of the more prosperous Midlands and southern England. It brought home to the man in the street the desperate and seemingly hopeless plight of the unemployed. The coming to power of the Labour government was followed within a few weeks by the Wall Street crash. The effects of the American depression soon spread to Britain. Unemployment rapidly rose. The government attempted nothing that might have stemmed this rise. Within the government Oswald Mosley, taking his cue from Keynes, recommended radical measures to deal with unemployment. He resigned from the government in May 1930 having failed to persuade his colleagues, and eventually left the party after his motion against government unemployment policies was defeated at the party conference in October and further efforts to change the party's policies proved fruitless. His authoritarian inclinations have obscured the question whether his economic judgements were sound. Once considered a potential leader of the Labour Party, he came to lead instead the British Union of Fascists and left the mainstream of British politics.

The indomitable British MP Ellen Wilkinson leading the Jarrow hunger marchers on the road to London, October 1936.

Labour's meagre legislative record, with unemployment rising to 2.8 million by the summer of 1931, had severely weakened MacDonald's standing in both the country and in the Labour Party when the financial crisis hit London. The Labour government had sought to follow financial policies acceptable to the orthodox bankers and adopted a course above parties – thus diminishing its independence of action. Policy recommendations were left to commissions and committees of experts. These orthodox financiers now recommended that government expenditure be cut by lowering wages of government employees, by reducing unemployment benefits and by raising new taxation. MacDonald's colleagues baulked, but eventually agreed to most of these measures. They went much against the grain even of the Labour moderates. When MacDonald insisted, on the advice of the bankers, on the full cuts, a minority of the Cabinet backed by the General Council of the Trades Union Congress, which opposed all cuts, would not accept further economies. The realisation was growing that the government in simply giving in to the financiers would separate itself from the bulk of the Labour movement. If the policy were necessary, would it not be better to have left it to the Opposition?

At the suggestion of the bankers, who urged MacDonald that the prime need was to restore international confidence in the government – a loan from the United States was said to be conditional on sufficiently stringent government economies – MacDonald and Snowden had already conferred with the leaders of the Opposition. At the height of the crisis King George V played a leading role in persuading MacDonald, Baldwin and the Liberals to join in a new 'national government'. Lloyd George, who might have blocked a coalition led by MacDonald, was in hospital. On 24 August 1931 the King's personal appeal was 'loyally' acceded to, such was still the inherent influence of the Crown. MacDonald on the next day headed a new national government with Baldwin serving under him. Only three Labour Cabinet ministers, including Snowden, followed MacDonald. The Labour Party formally rejected the national government and voted for a new leader. At the general election which followed in October 1931 the Labour Party suffered a devastating defeat. They could hold only fifty-two seats. The Conservatives won a corresponding victory of 471 seats and so an absolute majority. The Liberals were soon as badly split as Labour; after supporting the national government for a time about half the sixty-eight MPs in 1932 turned against it. MacDonald's National Labour following was reduced to thirteen. In all but name, Britain was ruled by the Conservatives until 1940. MacDonald had genuinely believed in a financial crisis and had been panicked into action which the Labour Party regarded as a betrayal.

What was the domestic record of the Conservative-National administrations, MacDonald's (1931–5), Baldwin's (1935–7) and Neville Chamberlain's (1937–40), in meeting the social and industrial ills of Britain? There can be no doubt that these governments followed policies which they believed would most effectively alleviate the distress of unemployment and would cure the sickness from which the British economy suffered. They did care. But their political philosophy and economic thinking precluded them from following the communist or fascist totalitarian remedies. They also rejected the notion that government could initiate public spending sufficiently large to mop up unemployment regardless of other harmful effects on the economy such spending would have had. The fact that the national government with its tiny Liberal and Labour components in parliament but backed by the overall Conservative majority could act decisively without fear of parliamentary defeat in itself helped to restore confidence. MacDonald, followed by Baldwin in 1935, presided over their cabinets as prime minister, but the rising star was Neville Chamberlain, who became chancellor of the Exchequer in the depth of the depression in November 1931. Winston Churchill might have become the real force in these governments of the 1930s had he not quarrelled with Baldwin and the Conservative majority when the Conservatives were still in opposition over how to deal with the problem of Indian nationalism. The Labour government supported by Baldwin wished to make concessions; Churchill thundered against appeasing Indian nationalism and resigned from the Conservative shadow Cabinet. It was a tragic misjudgement not only as regards India but possibly in its effect on world history. Churchill was politically isolated in the 1930s and when he warned against appeasing Hitler, most of the Conservatives did not listen.

The later 1930s belonged to Chamberlain not Churchill. Chamberlain tackled the economic problem with the characteristic vigour he had already displayed as minister of health in the 1920s. Nevertheless government policies were pretty cautious. They were less spectacular, but arguably more effective, than Roosevelt's in America. Chamberlain sought to create conditions which would allow British industry to revive. Recovery was not, however, all a matter of government economic planning. Equally important was the behaviour of the British people – those in employment – who by their spending gradually helped to lift Britain out of the slump.

Already in September 1931 Britain had gone off the gold standard and devalued her currency by a quarter so as to make British exports more competitive. She followed the United States in adopting a protective tariff to discourage competitive imports from abroad; a limited degree of imperial preference was agreed by the Imperial Economic Conference at Ottawa of July/August 1932, which lowered mutual tariffs in the Commonwealth, stimulating empire trade. Currency control was introduced and not eased until 1979 (it was abolished soon after). Cheap credit stimulated the domestic economy, especially in the house-building trade. Schemes of direct government subsidies and marketing boards also greatly aided the British farmer. The government sought to rationalise and produce a more uniform system of unemployment benefits. The intentions were good, but the resulting family 'means tests', which investigated whether a whole family had sufficient for its needs even if one of its members was out of work, came to symbolise the heartless bureaucracy of what was intended as a sensible policy. The echoes of the resulting bitterness made themselves felt for decades.

Class distinction was more acceptable to the man in the street in good times, or in the war when common hardships and dangers were being shared by the upper and lower classes in the trenches. In the 1930s the increasing division between rich and poor, employed and unemployed, left bitter memories of Conservative rule that not even Winston Churchill's personal popularity could overcome in 1945. The Prince of Wales, by his well-publicised concern for the misery of the unemployed, did something to bridge the gap. The abdication crisis of November and December 1936, which forced Edward VIII to renounce the throne unless he gave up his proposed marriage to the divorced Mrs Simpson, was seen by some embittered working men as a manoeuvre to get rid of a king who sympathised with them.

Unemployment, nevertheless, in the mid-1930s

was slowly declining. It never reached the proportions of German and American unemployment at their peak in 1932–3, and fell steadily from 1933 to 1937 from just under 3 million to 1.7 million. Even with rearmament getting under way thereafter, it did not fall below 1 million and since it was heavily concentrated in the depressed areas it actually varied from 26 per cent in Northern Ireland and 24 per cent in Wales to 6 per cent in the Midlands. Such gestures as subsidising the completion of the liner *Queen Mary* on the Clyde and other limited public schemes could not touch the hard-core unemployment problems of these regions. This, rather than the fact that total production in 1934 exceeded the level of 1929, was what made the deepest impact on the public mind in the 1930s.

Unemployment *(percentage of total labour force)*

	Britain	Germany	United States
1923	8.1	9.6	2.4
1930	11.2	15.3	8.7
1931	15.1	23.3	15.9
1932	15.6	30.1	23.6
1933	14.1	26.3	24.9
1934	11.9	14.9	21.7
1935	11.0	11.6	20.1
1936	9.4	8.3	16.9
1937	7.8	4.6	14.3
1938	9.3	2.1	19.0

One serious consequence of the depression was that the democracies became preoccupied with problems at home. Chamberlain saw rearmament as a waste of national resources. Gradually recovery was proceeding. For those in work living standards were rising rather than falling. War threatened the better way of life governments were seeking to achieve for their peoples. But it was the war effort that alone 'cured' unemployment in Britain and the United States.

The social consequences of the depression, the despair of the unemployed, the failure to provide adequately for the poor and the sick, the undernourishment of millions of children, unhealthy slum housing and many other ills in the early years of the 1930s turned the mass of people on the continent of Europe towards a search for new solutions. Since Stalin's Russia appeared to have found the answer to banishing the capitalist trade cycle, communism attracted millions. Their support was given not only for materialistic but also for idealistic reasons. Communists fought fascism and in claiming to provide a better and healthier life for the poor acted in a way that seemed ethical and good. The realities of Stalin's tyrannical regime were unknown to many, overlooked or explained away. Mussolini and Hitler were seen by other millions as the saviours who would restore a sense of national unity, orderly government and employment to their people. They had many admirers outside Italy and Germany, even some in Britain. The deep divisions and the turmoil in France discredited parliamentary government in this part of Europe too. In Britain, the Labour government had ignominiously fallen, though Parliament itself survived the crisis. Humane and democratic socialism was everywhere the main victim. Such desperate conditions, millions of people felt, demanded not compromise but radical remedies. The left battled the right politically, in Spain even on the battlefield. But there was at least one country in Europe where humanity, democracy and social progress were safe and which did not follow the pattern of most of the rest of the continent.

Sweden had not bypassed the depression, but the economic slump led to the establishment of a democratic form of government which determined the social and economic policies of the country for almost six decades. Before 1932, the socialist parties on the one side and the liberals and conservatives on the other were evenly divided, and coalition governments frequently had to make do with parliamentary minorities. The same weakness, however, was not evident in the strong economic development of Sweden during the second half of the 1920s. She was ceasing to be a predominantly agricultural country: her steel, ballbearings and other advanced industrial products like telephones were in worldwide demand, in addition to her older exports such as woodpulp and matches. Nonetheless, in this large, under-populated northern region of Europe, farming continued to play an important role in the 1930's.

Modernity on Endless Trial. Sweden has, for most of the twentieth century, been the quintessentially modern collectivist European nation-state. In the 1930s this formerly tradition-bound and orthodox country transformed itself into a model of innovation, organization and liberty. The state positively encouraged healthy living (top right), *new freedoms* (right), *less divisive, punitive punishment – as in this hotel-like prison* (left), *and a minimum standard of living for all, which included durable, comfortable modern housing* (top). *But the* fin-de-siècle *mood brings re-evaluation, even here.*

The impact of the depression, at its height in 1932 and 1933, was devastating. One in three of the workforce was unemployed; many farmers could no longer meet their mortgages and were forced to sell. But Sweden recovered relatively quickly from the crash compared to the rest of Europe and she was politically strong and stable. The credit for this must go largely to the coalition administration of the Farmers' Party and the Social Democrats, led by the Social Democrat Per Albin Hansson. Hansson, born in 1885, was self-educated, having left school at the age of twelve. At eighteen he founded the Social Democratic Youth Movement. Prime minister in September 1932, he proved himself an outstanding parliamentary tactician and an able national leader, remaining continuously in office until his death in 1946. The compromise reached with the Farmers' Party was to abandon free trade and to promise minimum farm prices and other supports. For the industrial unemployed, relief works were launched and industrial revival encouraged. In the first three years of the administration, bills to promote active state intervention were passed, regulating the working hours of agricultural labourers, statutory holidays and unemployment insurance. The simple slogan was to make Sweden 'a home for all her people' and so to create social harmony.

By 1939 Sweden's unemployment problem had been solved and the plans for a welfare state had been worked out. The Social Democrats, since their election victory in 1936, had become the dominant political force in the country. The war postponed the extension of social welfare, but from 1946 to 1950 the reforms were enacted, including comprehensive old-age pensions, child allowances, health insurance and educational reforms. The Swedish people were to be safeguarded from 'cradle to grave', in sickness and in health. The socialist element of the government policies was to tax the better-off heavily to pay for the welfare state and to redistribute income, rather than to try to nationalise private industry. For once a utopian vision seemed to correspond to reality. Sweden and her people prospered. Swedish research, technology and design were second to none. After the death of Hansson, Targe Erlander succeeded to the premiership (1946–69). The Social Democratic dominance for all but six years since 1932 came to an end only in 1992.

Sweden exemplified a distinctive and much admired social, political and cultural way of life. The emphasis on closeness to nature and on individual choice and liberty extended to the sphere of sexual permissiveness long before it did so in the rest of Europe. In many areas of social reform Sweden was the pioneer. The Swedes enjoyed one of the highest standards of living in Europe, along with the Swiss, the Norwegians, the Finns, the Germans and the people of Luxembourg. Swedish society was egalitarian and unshakeably democratic, although it had to make readjustments in the early 1990s.

On Franklin Delano Roosevelt came to rest the hopes of those who continued to pin their faith on liberalism and democracy in the 1930s as providing a better answer to the world's ills than totalitarian leadership. Roosevelt's New Deal was to be the answer to those who in the crisis despaired of reconciling freedom with the measures necessary to bring about economic recovery. Keynes wrote in December 1933 that Roosevelt had made himself 'the trustee for those in every country who seek to mend the evils of our condition. If you [Roosevelt] fail, rational change will be gravely prejudiced throughout the world, leaving orthodoxy or revolution to fight it out.' The shortcomings of the New Deal are very evident to historians today. Unemployment remained obstinately high. It fell from some 13 million in 1933 to under 8 million in 1937 but it rose again to 9.5 million in 1939. In fact Roosevelt's administrations failed to 'cure' the blight and waste of human resources until the United States geared industry to war. But the attitude of the President and administration, brilliantly publicised, gave renewed hope to the nation and provided leadership without the destruction of democracy. There is thus a stark contrast between the general psychological impact of the New Deal and the real success of the many different laws, special agencies and programmes which constituted it.

The depression provided Roosevelt with the opportunity of attaining and retaining political power for more than a decade until his death in 1945. But its onset destroyed the political power of his predecessor at the White House, Herbert Hoover. Hoover in 1929 had begun his term at the moment of highest confidence. The failure of his economic policies to halt the steep rise in unemployment shattered his reputation. He had a clear concept of the role of the state. He wished to limit federal powers, which he warned would throttle individual initiative. He was by conviction a conservative, though he was willing to adopt new ways to stimulate business. His inability, nevertheless, to halt the steep slide into depression did more than discredit him personally, it also discredited the whole philosophy of minimal state intervention. But Hoover did act to contain the effects of the onset of the depression. He appealed to businessmen not to contract their activities and to maintain their workforce. He appealed to the banks to extend credit. Besides such exhortations, federal policies were limited – though in the right direction. The nation should help herself by enlightened *voluntary* co-operation between the different interest groups. Prosperity 'lay just around the corner'.

When the voluntary approach did not work, Hoover took more energetic steps to influence the economy. He persuaded the bankers to establish a National Credit Corporation in October 1931; the strong banks were to assist the weak and failing ones. But banks continued in their thousands to close their doors. Business confidence was not restored. In 1931 Hoover belatedly halted international financial chaos for a time by calling for a year's moratorium of Allied debts to the United States; German reparations also ceased in practice. Hoover broke with his traditions by establishing the Reconstruction Finance Corporation in 1932, empowered to make loans to banks and financial institutions. That summer he accepted a Congressional bill to advance federal loans to individual states to provide unemployment reliefs and public works. The federal budget, despite his misgivings, allowed for more state expenditure than income. But the funds thus pumped into the economy were overshadowed by the stringent credit policies followed by the banks, paradoxically because they were better supervised and receiving financial support. The net result was that from 1929 to 1934 the American money supply contracted by nearly a third, inevitably deepening the depression and increasing unemployment.

Roosevelt had no basic understanding of the overall management of the economy and in the election campaign of 1932 attacked President Hoover for his unbalanced budgets, promising as one of his remedies for the depression to cut federal spending by a quarter! Roosevelt's electrifying inaugural address of 4 March 1933 reveals the other, psychological side of his mixture of ideas together making up the promised New Deal. He

The Great Communicator. US President Franklin D. Roosevelt about to speak to the people in 1937 during one of his 'fireside chats'.

cautioned against unnecessary fear, attacked the 'unscrupulous money changers' and vigorously promised action: 'our greatest primary task is to put people to work'. He was now determined to put into practice what a year earlier he had called 'bold persistent experimentation'. If something fails, he declared, admit it frankly and try something else, but 'above all try something. The millions who are in want will not stand by silently forever while the things to satisfy their needs are within easy reach.'

Roosevelt spoke to the ordinary people and they were at last convinced that the new president was not prepared to capitulate to seemingly uncontrollable economic forces, to the inexorable workings of the business cycle. Roosevelt exuded confidence, charm and sincerity. There was something else about him. Crippled by polio in 1921, he had lost the use of his legs. Now, as president, he personified the fact that adversity could be triumphantly overcome. Quite possibly one consequence of his serious disability was that he developed a new homely touch in politics, a charisma in the eyes of the mass of the people that became an invaluable asset to him. The pampered child of wealthy Americans, privately educated at the best schools and at Harvard, Roosevelt bore a famous family name. And indeed he modelled himself on his famous relative Theodore.

His early political career advanced by easy progression from the Senate of the state of New York, to a junior place in the Navy Department in Wilson's administration. Then to the governorship of New York State when already stricken with polio. The Republicans seemed firmly in power in the 1920s, but the depression gave the Democrats their chance and Roosevelt secured the nomination in 1932. Roosevelt was happiest when active. During the first Hundred Days of his own administration he initiated measure after measure, backed by a bevy of academics and politicians who served as his think tank, or brains trust as it was then called. One associate who knew him well described Roosevelt's mind as 'fly-paper'. There was a tremendous array of New Deal policies, Washington became the centre and source of new federal powers hitherto undreamt of, and a vast sprawling bureaucracy administered the programmes. The public's thirst for action was satisfied. Thirst too was slaked by the Twenty-first Amendment in February 1933, ratified by the States in December. It was the end of Prohibition. 'Happy Days are here again'.

An emergency banking act restored confidence in the banks and in June 1933 deposits were insured by the Federal Deposit Insurance. In May 1933 the Agricultural Adjustment Act (AAA) tried to raise farm prices by paying federal subsidies to farmers for reducing production; marketing agreements were supervised by the federal authorities. In June 1933 the National Industrial Recovery Act (NIRA) created corporate committees representing the public, management and labour to establish codes on production, prices and competition. Labour was aided by the laying down of maximum hours and minimum wages and by being conceded the right to join a trade union, which at last gave a great impetus to the unionisation of the less skilled workers. Underlying NIRA was a belief in national planning. But the biggest businesses dominated the codes, as government supervision was small.

Among the most celebrated early measures was the creation of the Tennessee Valley Authority (TVA) in May 1933, which established government authority over a vast impoverished region containing a hydroelectric dam and fertiliser factories. The Authority promoted scientific agriculture, prevented flooding and engaged in a variety of social programmes to aid the poor. Another part of the NIRA Act established the Public Works Administration with a fund of $3.3 billion. Under the Secretary of the Interior, Harold Ickes, it was set up to promote construction which was in the public interest, and employed during its first year 1 million men. But Ickes was cautious in his approach; not so ex-social worker Harry Hopkins. Hopkins worked for speedy aid to restore the morale of the unemployed. The Civilian Works Administration run by the indefatigable Hopkins employed 4 million people on public works schemes and cost $2000 million in 1933 to 1934. Roosevelt thought this was too much and abolished it in the spring of 1934. His own programme in 1933 was the Civilian Conservation Corps, which offered American unemployed young men from the cities work in army-style camps in the countryside. 300,000 lived in over a thousand camps planting trees and working in rural areas. Other New Deal measures sought to supervise and regulate Stock Exchange dealings and financiers.

The work of many minds, the New Deal measures were not intended to introduce 'socialism'. Roosevelt attempted to make capitalism work better, to use the power of representative democratic government to secure social justice for all the people. Despite the measures comprising the New Deal, the United States' unemployment figures disappointingly showed only gradual improvement. The reason for this is not now difficult to find. Congress and the President in 1933 and in 1934 were not prepared to tolerate large deficit budgets. Funds spent on the programmes of the New Deal were balanced by savings secured by reducing veterans' allowances, curtailing unemployment reliefs and discharging government employees. What one hand gave, the other took away, and federal deficits increased only gently in 1933 and 1934. The federal government had played a larger role and Roosevelt was genuinely responsive to the needs of the poor; but in the end practical achievements when seen against the vastness of the problem proved insufficient to 'cure' unemployment.

The New Deal policies ran into trouble in 1935. While the Congressional elections of 1934 had strengthened the reformers, the Supreme Court took a conservative view of constitutional rights. In May 1935 the Court invalidated the National Industrial Recovery Act as an unconstitutional delegation of power and regulation of business. Roosevelt's administration was already moving towards changes in the New Deal and so did not

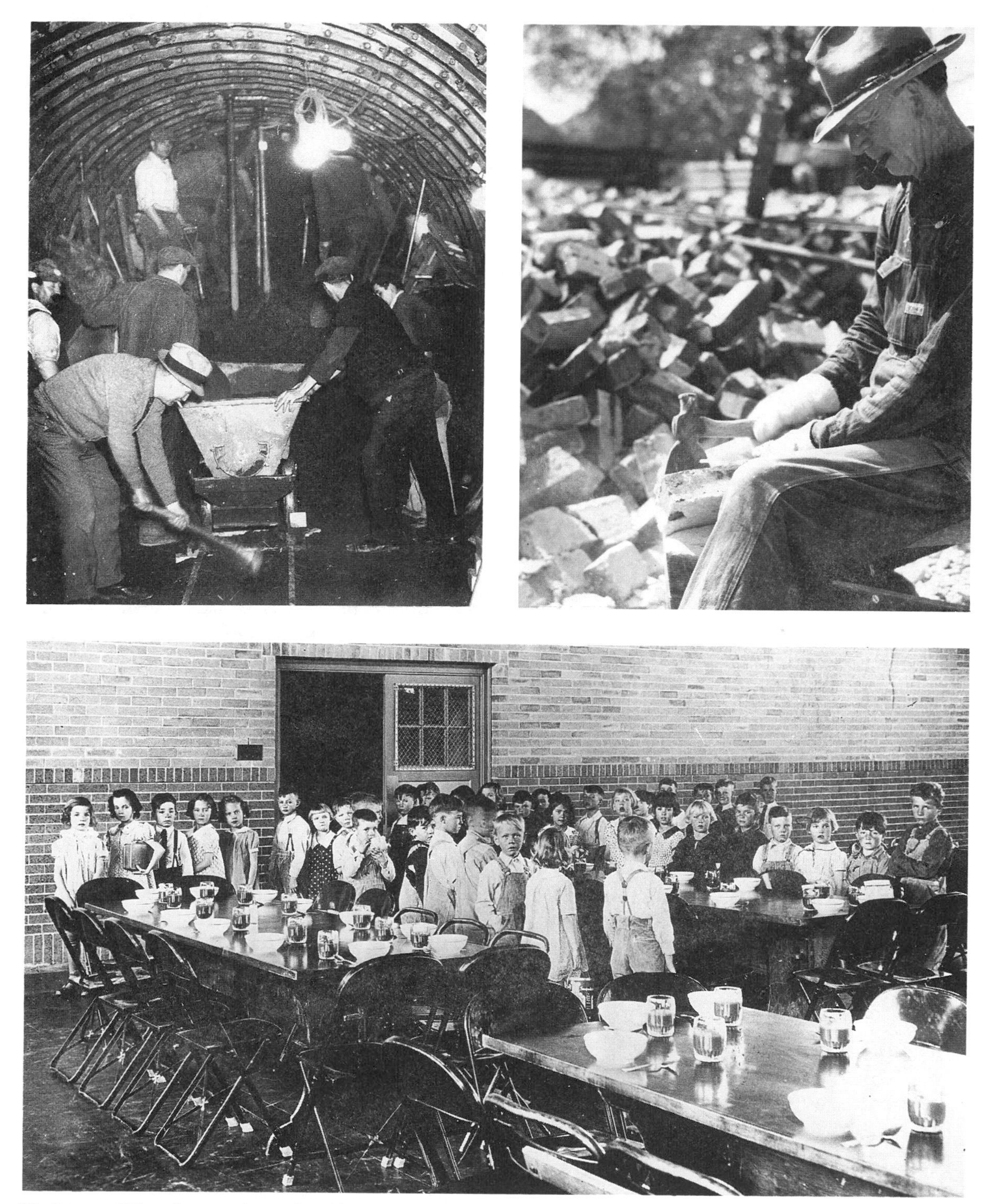

The Scourge of Unemployment. Among the public works programmes authorized by the Emergency Relief Appropriation Act passed by the US Senate in 1935, the Works Progress Administration (WPA) was one of the most successful. It spawned almost a million and a half individual projects as varied as building highways, financing vaudeville shows and circuses, and hiring writers and artists. By the time the scheme ended in 1943 more than eight million had been in its employ. Pictured are: below, *a free lunch project in Utah;* left, *sewer construction; and* right, *brick-making.*

attempt to re-enact any parts of the National Industrial Recovery Act. The attempt to co-operate with business had not led to the expected beneficial results. The New Deal legislation of 1935 to 1936 sought to reform business practices and to destroy concentrations of business power. Another important decision was to create many more jobs – 'work relief' – by setting up the Works Progress Administration under Harry Hopkins and providing it with large funds, $1.47 billion on average in a full year (1936–40). Besides public works, Hopkins created projects for out-of-work artists and writers. The latter collected information and wrote guide books. Many suddenly discovered a new vocation for writing. Nearly one and a half million projects were set up which at different periods of time employed a total of more than 8.5 million people, during its years of operation. Even so, all these programmes absorbed only one-third of the unemployed.

One of the most significant reforms of the New Deal era was the introduction – belated in comparison to other Western nations – of basic welfare policies such as old-age pensions. The passage of the Social Security Act in August 1935, inspired by the efforts of Frances Perkins, provided – besides federal old-age pensions – unemployment insurance and help to the less privileged. Many of the poorest sections of American society were still excluded, but the act marked a beginning on which later expansion could be built. The growth of labour unions and recognition of their rights by the National Labor Relations Act (Wagner Act) further limited business power. All in all, the New Deal had redistributed power in the community and greatly increased that of the federal government.

In November 1936 Roosevelt was re-elected to a second term by a bigger victory than in 1932, gaining 61 per cent of the popular vote. He represented the non-revolutionary change the majority of voters wished to see. His biggest personal political setback occurred soon after the election, when he attempted to change the composition of the Supreme Court, which threatened his New Deal legislation. He requested Congress to legislate that the Supreme Court could be enlarged by the president appointing an additional supplementary justice for every existing justice over the age of seventy who did not wish to retire. But Congress refused to tamper with the Court in this way. Nevertheless Roosevelt's complaints of the Court's unresponsiveness to social needs seems to have produced a change of attitude; the Court ceased to be the conservative obstacle to New Deal legislation after 1936. In any case, gradually Roosevelt's nominees came to predominate as the older judges retired.

That the New Deal was not even larger in scope was not so much due to the attacks of its opponents as to the policies of the administration itself. Roosevelt never could abandon his belief in a 'sound money' policy. He favoured keeping spending within well-controlled limits. A recession in 1937 was followed by a slow recovery, but even in 1940 15 per cent of the workforce remained jobless. Yet America in 1940 was very different from when Roosevelt first entered the White House. He had sought reform and change, but not a revolution of the capitalist system. His bold approach, his faith in democracy and his desire to help the ordinary people, the disadvantaged and the poor, not only brought hope where there had been despair, but significantly changed American society and attitudes.

CHAPTER 20

Soviet Russia: 'Communism in Transition'

The Soviet leadership, after the departure in 1922 of the Japanese, the last foreign troops on Soviet territory, was able to fashion and create Soviet society free from outside interference. The Allies had withdrawn. The Whites were defeated. Bolshevik armies had established control over the Caucasus region, central Asia and the whole of Siberia during 1920 and 1921. With the end of the Civil War, and Russia's own foreign war with Poland – fighting stopped in October 1920 – not only was Soviet revolutionary power established, but for two decades, until Hitler's invasion of 1941, the expected concerted capitalist attack did not materialise. It never in fact materialised as the Soviet Union eventually fought Germany in alliance with capitalist Britain and the United States. But the fear that the halfhearted Allied intervention immediately after the revolution was not the end but the precursor of an attempt by the capitalist world to liquidate the first communist state powerfully influenced the Soviet Union's foreign policy throughout the period. It placed her, according to such calculations, in a desperate situation of weakness and inferiority.

To preserve Soviet power every weapon appeared to be justifiable. Britain and the West were to be weakened by pursuit of a vigorous anti-imperialist policy in Asia and the Middle East. Western communist parties, members of the Comintern (the First Congress of the Third International was convened by Lenin in Moscow in March 1919) were to join the struggle for the survival of the Soviet Union, however much such a policy might conflict with a purely national interest. Simultaneously, foreign relations with the West were conducted so as to exploit divisions between them. Arrangements for mutual military and technical aid were developed with Weimar Germany after the signature of the Treaty of Rapallo in April 1922. Such a policy was combined with the apparently contradictory support for the German Communist Party's attacks on the 'social fascists' which contributed to the fall of Weimar and the coming to power of the Nazis. Even when the German communists became the first victims of Nazi violence, they held to the doctrinal correctness of the analysis that the overthrow of bourgeois socialists had brought the communist revolution a step closer.

The imminent danger of foreign intervention was thus as much an illusion of the Soviet leaders in the 1920s as the expectation of communist revolution spreading in the West which, as late as 1921, the Soviet leadership still believed was the only hope of Russia's survival. But, for anyone living in Russia in the winter of 1920/1, there could be no illusion about the country's virtually total collapse after six years of war and civil war. Then a new disaster struck: in the summer of 1921 the grain crop failed. Added to the millions killed in war, countless more millions now died of starvation and disease. This time the West 'intervened' in a humanitarian mission of relief. In March 1921, even before the actual famine, Lenin told the Tenth Congress of the Communist Party, 'We are living in such conditions of impoverishment and ruin that for a time everything must be subordinated to this fundamental consideration – at all costs to increase the quantity of goods . . .' Principal among them were food and medicine. The aid of Hoover's American Relief Administration was therefore later accepted. Yet all such efforts had only a limited effect in the face of the scale of the disaster. No understanding of the early years of Soviet rule is possible without an appreciation of the suffering of the Russian people amid mounting chaos such as had not occurred in the history of Europe in modern times. Foreign military intervention, albeit halfhearted, contributed to the general breakdown.

Lenin, whose authority towered above that of his frequently arguing lieutenants, heading a Communist Party which at first was only small, sought to establish some sort of stable basis on which communism could be built. Between 1919 and 1922 the Bolshevik Party became a mass movement of 700,000 members, by no means all of whom were still revolutionary. In Lenin's policies there was little consistency – they were more reactions to successive emergencies. During the Civil War the Red Army of 5 million men as well as the workers in the cities had to be fed. The term 'war communism' is used to decribe the measures taken during the years from July 1918 to 1921 which were as extreme as was the situation facing Lenin. A Supreme Council of National Economy had already been created in December 1917 to take over such industry and finance as it considered necessary and to plan centrally the Soviet economy. After June 1918, industrial enterprises were rapidly nationalised and workers and managers subjected to rigid control. As money became virtually valueless with the collapse of the economy, theorists saw one advantage in the misfortune: communism might be attained not gradually but in one leap; state industries could now be 'purely' planned – the money economy abolished and with it all private enterprise and trade.

The key problem of the war-communist period was how to secure food from the peasants, whose alliance with the urban proletariat Lenin had declared to be essential to the success of the revolution. The value of money had been reduced to almost nothing; the factories were not producing goods that could be bartered. The peasants obstinately clung to the ownership of their land and refused to join state farms. Lenin at first attempted to divide the peasants, the poor from the better off – the kulaks, or exploiters, as they were called. This no doubt succeeded in spreading hatred in the villages but it did not yield grain. Then he wooed the so-called 'middle peasants' – the supposedly less poor (these categorisations corresponded to policy tactics rather than realities: only one in a hundred peasant households employed more than one labourer). Force was applied since the state could give nothing to the peasants in exchange for what were defined as 'surpluses'. With the utmost ruthlessness, detachments were sent into the countryside to seize food. Peasants were shot for resisting expropriation. Villages were searched, peasants left destitute. Bolshevik punitive expeditions attempted to overcome peasant resistance and violence. The excesses of war communism were encouraged by Lenin. The only answer he could find as the crisis deepened in early 1920 was even more ruthless pressure on the peasants. Those who were accused of retaining food were condemned as 'enemies of the people'. The Civil War above all, and the policies of war communism resulting from it, led, however, to the total collapse of what remained of the Russian agricultural and industrial economy. Transport had broken down and there was a large exodus from the starving towns and idle factories back to the country.

During his years of power, Lenin never wavered from his insistence on the supreme authority of the party and centralised control. No sectional interest of workers or peasants organised in the form of trade unions should act as a counterpoise to the party. Power was to be retained by the centre with iron discipline. In this he was strongly supported by Trotsky, who wished to rebuild Russia by mobilising the people under military discipline. Under the harsh realities of the Civil War and its aftermath Lenin had given up his earlier views that once the revolution had succeeded the state would begin to wither away and socialism would evolve by the spontaneous enthusiasm and work of the masses. He convinced himself that it was necessary to replace the revolution with a one-party state. But as he conceived it there was flexibility; especially after 1921 'non-party' specialists were encouraged. The bureaucracy was an inevitable outcome of the centralised state, though it deeply worried Lenin during the last months of his life. He began to alter course in 1921–2 and simultaneously government employees were drastically reduced. It was also Lenin who urged the use of force and terror where other means failed to achieve the desired ends. However much he criticised the consequences of the direction of state policy, the foundations of the Soviet state had been laid by Lenin.

While it is true that Lenin permitted debate within and outside the higher echelon of the party as in newspapers, men of the old guard, such as Lev Kamenev, Grigori Zinoviev, Aleksei Rykov, Nikolai Bukharin and Leon Trotsky, who differed on the right policies to be followed, ultimately had to obey the party line once Lenin had reached a decision. On the issue whether there could be any but a one-party state no debate was possible. The Tenth Party Congress, held in March 1921, passed the resolution 'On Party Unity', which though it did not stifle all debate and criticism forbade the formation within the party of any political groups 'with separate platforms, striving to a certain degree to segregate and create their own group discipline' and then to publish views not authorised by the party. The famous Paragraph Seven of this resolution empowered the Central Committee by two-thirds majority to expel from the party members of the Central Committee who diverged, and so to banish them into political exile. The weapon for stifling any dissident view not favouring the leader or group of leaders in power had been forged. Stalin later made full use of it to eliminate anyone he chose to accuse of factionalism.

In March 1921, simultaneously with the resolution on party unity, came the about-turn of Lenin's policy – the inauguration of the slogan New Economic Policy (NEP), coined to cover the dramatic reversal. The conviction that ever-increasing ruthlessness, especially in extracting food from the peasantry, was threatening the whole country's coherence must have been taking shape for some time. It was a mutiny of the sailors in the fortress of Kronstadt early in March 1921, bloodily repressed, which Lenin claimed 'was the flash which lit up reality better than anything else'. But the decision had already been taken by him following peasant riots and workers' strikes in the previous months.

The New Economic Policy began when the Tenth Party Congress passed a resolution replacing the seizure of surplus food with a less onerous and a properly regulated 'tax in kind'. Any further surplus the peasant could market freely. Three years later in 1924 the tax in kind became a money payment. Free trading and, with it, a money economy revived. Small-scale production by not more than twenty workers was allowed once again. Large industries continued under state ownership with few exceptions. The vast majority of production was by state enterprises or by individual artisans. Between 1921 and 1926, the mixed industrial economy, part private part state, recovered so that by 1926 the level of production of 1913 had been reached. In agriculture, individual peasants farmed more than 98 per cent of the land sown. Agriculture recovered from the low levels of 1921 and 1922, but the amount left over from peasant consumption was less than in 1913; yet the need for grain to feed the expanding urban population and for export to provide capital grew much faster than the traditional peasant agriculture supplied. Nor were the peasants imbued with enthusiasm for socialism despite attempts to arouse a sense of common solidarity against the better-off peasants, the kulaks. A peasant farming his land traditionally, and encouraged to improve his standard of living by having stimulated in him a desire for profit, was not likely to accept the ideals of communism. The more successful a peasant, the less socialist he became. NEP on the land helped to save Russia from starvation, but did not provide the surplus to allow the economy to advance rapidly.

A complementary element of the more liberal economic approach of NEP in the 1920s was the tightening of party discipline and centralism. Cultural concessions, for instance, were made to the non-Russian nationalities, but not at the expense of centralised party and military control. The Tenth Party Congress of March 1921, which saw the beginnings of NEP, also, as has been noted, passed the resolutions against factions within the party. The swollen Communist Party itself was purged of some 200,000 members considered unreliable to the Bolshevik ideals. Lenin warned that the revolutionary old guard must hold together through all the transitional phases of communism, even those like NEP which marked a retreat from socialist objectives. How temporary would the retreat have to be? That was a fundamental and contentious issue. As long as Lenin remained the indisputable leader, however much debate and individual criticism took place within the party, great changes of policy were still possible without destroying the cohesion of the party or without producing a savage fight, literally to the death, between Lenin's lieutenants. Lenin's own premature death so early in the formation of the state was therefore of enormous significance.

The struggles of the revolution and war had sapped Lenin's strength. Towards the end of 1921 he fell seriously ill. In May 1922 at the age of fifty-two he suffered a serious stroke which paralysed his right side. By October he had recovered sufficiently to resume a partial workload. In December 1922 his health again deteriorated and on 21 January 1924 he died. Of particular interest during his last weeks of active work from the end of 1922 to 4 January 1923 are the notes he dictated which together comprise what was called his 'testament'. In these memoranda he stressed the need to strengthen the unity of the Central Party Committee, and characterised the strengths and weaknesses of six leading members of the party. The characterisation of Stalin, who having 'become the General Secretary has accumulated enormous power in his hands and I am not sure whether he will be able to use this power with due care', was especially important in view of the question who should succeed Lenin. During his illness he was outraged by Stalin's attempt to cut him off from influence in January 1923, a year before his death. He urged Stalin's dismissal and replacement by a new general secretary 'more tolerant, more loyal and less capricious'. It was too late. Lenin was too ill to act as unquestioned leader any longer. He had also criticised Trotsky, though describing him as the other leading personality of the party, for 'non-Bolshevism', for 'his too far-reaching self-confidence' and as too much attracted to pure administration. What was the purpose of this critical testament? Lenin was preoccupied by what would happen after his death. He concluded that no single one of the Bolshevik leadership could be designated as his successor. By his frank criticisms of all his lieutenants he was arguing for his own solution to the succession. This was to increase the Central Committee to fifty, even a hundred persons, by adding industrial workers and peasants close to the feeling of the rank and file of the party and for this body to control and supervise the collective leadership.

But following Lenin's death no stable collective leadership in fact took over. Stalin, who had been appointed general secretary with Lenin's support in 1922 to bring order to the organisation of the party, transformed this important but secondary position into a vehicle for the advancement of his personal power. His work for the party before this elevation had shown him to be ruthless and a good organiser. To these qualities he added cunning and a sense of timing in political intrigue. Using his powers to the full, he promoted to key posts men who would follow him and strengthened his position further by removing others who supported rivals. Among the old guard, Trotsky was widely disliked for his arrogance, intellectual brilliance and showmanship. Stalin aligned himself with Zinoviev to undermine Trotsky's influence. In a little more than five years, he had ousted all the prominent former leadership. But he was not Lenin's undisputed heir; nor did he enjoy the veneration granted to the late leader. Stalin encouraged a Lenin cult. He then kept himself at the top by the ruthless liquidation of all real and potential rivals who might conceivably challenge his control. Not until the end of the Great Terror in 1938 did any challenge to Stalin's supreme control become unthinkable. Yet his paranoid fear of plots and conspiracies beset him to the end of his life.

Lenin tolerated party discussion; Stalin could not stifle it in the 1920s as the better-known, more prominent Soviet leaders still overshadowed him. He supported a moderate internal economic policy, upheld NEP and identified himself with Lenin's policies after his death. Appealing to party unity, while packing key positions with his supporters, Stalin was ready to take on the most prestigious of the old Bolshevik leaders. The big quarrel with Trotsky occurred at the end of 1923 and early 1924 after Trotsky's attacks on the old guard. Trotsky was effectively defeated at the Thirteenth Party Congress in January 1924. Together with Zinoviev, president of the Comintern, whose power base was the Leningrad party, and Kamenev, chairman of the Moscow Soviet, Stalin had already made himself the leading member of the triumvirate controlling the party, the key to controlling the country. Trotsky had published a book, *Lessons of October*, in which he bitterly attacked the credentials of Zinoviev and Kamenev, who had been 'Right' Bolsheviks opposed to the October Revolution in 1917. In his denunciation Trotsky implied that such shortcomings were responsible for the failure of revolution beyond the Soviet Union, for instance in Germany. The triumvirate countered by stressing the long-standing quarrel between Trotsky and Lenin about 'permanent' revolution, which Trotsky had fervently advocated; and Stalin enunciated the slogan 'socialism in one country'. Stalin declared more realistically that the Soviet Union *had* survived and claimed that the conditions existed in Russia for the complete construction of socialism; this he saw as the primary task. The policies of communists in other countries too were therefore expected in practice to make this their primary objective, subordinating national considerations to the strengthening of the Soviet Union.

Trotsky and Stalin were not so far apart as their polemics made it appear. At moments of great danger, such as the Soviet leaders believed existed in 1927 and 1928, Trotsky was just as ready as Stalin to place the safety of the Soviet Union first. In this respect they were both heirs of Lenin's *Realpolitik*. In the power struggle in the top echelon of the party, Stalin calculated that a moderate line would be the most successful, while Trotsky assumed the mantle of the ardent, unquenchable revolutionary and the champion of 'democracy' within the party. The genuineness of Trotsky's democratic sentiments was never tested, for he never wielded supreme power. He was certainly no less ruthless than Stalin in his readiness to subordinate means to an end. But Stalin's control of the party machine secured Trotsky's gradual elimination. In January 1925 Trotsky lost the argument of his *Lessons of October* and the Central Committee deprived him of his nominal leadership of the Red Army.

Stalin now pushed from key control two other members of the Politburo, his fellow triumvirates, Kamenev and Zinoviev. Instead he allied with those who fully backed the NEP, Nikolai Bukharin, a long-standing companion of Lenin and editor of *Pravda*, and two other Politburo members, Aleksei Rykov and Mikhail Tomsky. But Trotsky, Kamenev and Zinoviev still retained their places on the Politburo, at least until 1926. That year the three men, calling themselves the United Opposition, mounted attacks on Comrade Stalin's capacity to unite the party and on the economic state of the country and bureaucracy. Stalin expelled all three from the Politburo and purged their supporters Trotsky's further attacks on Stalin and the organisation of an open demonstration against the leadership in November 1927 led to his and Zinoviev's and many of their followers' exclusion from the party in December 1927. A year later Trotsky was expelled from Russia.

Two years later it was the turn of the 'Right' opposition. Bukharin lost control of the Comintern at the end of 1928 and in 1929 and 1930 Tomsky and Rykov were replaced (page 186). All eventually died violently, victims of Stalin's purges of the mid-1930s. But it is simplistic to reduce the struggles at the centre of power to Stalin's completely cynical manoeuvrings to reach the top. Three deep concerns formed just a part of the immense nexus of problems associated with 'communism in transition': transforming a predominantly peasant society into an industrial power capable of catching up with the capitalist West, while keeping the goal of a communist society in view; at the same time the leadership was anxiously scanning the international horizon for an impending attack by the capitalist nations; as disastrous was the possibility that their own imperialist rivalry would start a second world war involving Russia in the maelstrom. Any one problem was in itself gigantic; together they were truly baffling. And there were no models to follow. Marxism was based on revolution in an advanced industrial nation, not an overwhelmingly peasant society. Lenin, when confronted with practical problems, had made bewildering changes of policy, justifying each with fresh doctrinal pronouncements. The mark of the dominant leader was his capacity radically to change policy and *retain* power. After Lenin, only Stalin as it turned out could do that. But this does not mean that he changed policy merely for the sake of discrediting his rivals or that he had plotted in advance first a policy to the 'right' and then to the 'left'.

Stalin's own uncertainty about his ability to hold on to supreme power in the face of the policies he felt it necessary to pursue is indeed the basic explanation of his murderous purges of the 1930s. He linked the survival of the communist regime with his own survival as undisputed leader. He wanted to be regarded as infallible; for proof he presented an unending stream of wrongdoers who in public trials confessed their errors and were shot. Their confessions to foreign conspiracies were intended to underline the mortal dangers to which the Soviet Union was exposed, but saved from by Stalin's vigilance. At the same time an understanding of Soviet policies is not possible without the assumption that there were deep and genuine problems, that more than one plausible option of action presented itself; and even granted that Stalin never lost sight of his tenure of power and would stop at nothing to maintain it, he was also concerned to discover the *right* policy to follow.

Stalin had reached the leadership group through Lenin's own selection and Lenin had an eye for remarkable men to act as the founding members of the new state. Unlike Lenin and the rest of the Bolshevik leadership, Stalin spent the years of preparation not in comfortable and argumentative exile, but in Russia herself, in constant danger and engaged in organizing the party when not in tsarist prison or Siberian exile. In Stalin, the cobbler's son born in Georgia in December 1879, Lenin saw a hardened, totally dedicated revolutionary leader, painstaking, and an effective organiser. Stalin showed a total disregard for 'conventions' of the law and civil rights when they impeded what he deemed necessary. As a young revolutionary in tsarist days he was lawless in a cause; in power he became lawless without restraint, filling the prisons, the places of execution and the labour camps in the 1930s and later with millions of people innocent of any crime except to arouse Stalin's suspicions. The apparently benign, modest and down-to-earth leader – it was easy for the Stalin cult to portray him as the father of his people just as the tsars before him had been – had turned into a monstrous tyrant.

Stalin was a consummate actor who could hide his true nature and if he chose charm those who had dealings with him, just as he was to charm Churchill and Roosevelt when the three leaders met during the Second World War. He was capable of carefully weighing alternatives, of calculating the risks and proceeding rationally, of outwitting his enemies at home and abroad. Secretive, suspicious, malevolent and lacking Lenin's intellect, he made himself into Lenin's heir and saw himself as such. His crimes were immense. His mistakes brought the whole country close to catastrophe in 1930 and in 1941, yet both he and the Soviet Union survived. During the Stalin era, there occurred the decisive shift that was to propel the Soviet Union from being a backward country to a state capable of grinding down and, during the latter part of the Second World War, overwhelming Germany. The industrial and military transformation of Russia, the creation of tens of thousands of technically proficient men, of administrators and doctors from a backward peasant society. The other legacy of the Stalin era was millions of dead; victims of collectivisation, deportation and the Gulags.

*

That the New Economic Policy had to be a 'transitional' phase in the construction of communism was obvious, unless communism itself was to abandon its Marxist goals. NEP had brought about an amazing recovery but was it capable of continuing at its previous pace of growth, after the first five years, given the low base from which it had started? Would the Soviet Union not merely catch up with tsarist pre-war production but decisively move beyond it? Then how could NEP enable the Soviet Union to acquire the sinews of the modern industrial state with an iron and steel industry, machinery and armaments, improved transportation and adequate power? A vast network of electric power stations was one of Lenin's pet dreams. With a 'mixed' economy would too many resources be swallowed up in providing the consumer with his needs rather than investing for the future? Had the essentially tsarist agricultural methods reached the limit of their productive capacity? On purely economic grounds, leaving aside ideological considerations, there were powerful arguments for a change of policy at the point when NEP failed to provide for the economic growth desired by the Bolshevik leadership.

During the winter of 1927 and 1928 the peasants reacted to increased taxes, low official prices, threats against the offence of hoarding and simply a lack of goods to buy by hanging on to their grain. Industrial investment had already speeded up industrialisation, the 'selfishness' and 'petty-bourgeois' behaviour of the kulaks in Stalin's judgement threatened the whole economy. Violence against the peasant to extract the grain needed to feed the towns was again resorted to in 'emergency' measures. The peasantry from rich to poor were hard hit in 1928 and alienated from the Soviet regime, though it was obviously the kulaks and better-off peasants who had most grain and so suffered the most. After the summer of 1928 Stalin faced the prospect of annual crises to purchase sufficient grain unless some fundamental changes were effected in dealing with the peasantry and agricultural productivity. Stalin had little love for the Russian peasantry, which he believed was holding the country to ransom.

Industrial expansion was jeopardised by the crisis in agriculture. If the peasantry were to be appeased, more goods would need to be released for their consumption. This was in contradiction to a policy of catching up rapidly with the advanced capitalist countries. No Soviet leader ever lost sight of

Russia's comparative weakness, which was believed to offer a temptation to the capitalist nations to attack her. The more relaxed attitudes of the mid-1920s, which also affected foreign policy – the slogan here used to describe Soviet aims was 'peaceful coexistence' – came to an end in 1927 and 1928. The Soviet leadership was beset by acute new fears that some concerted onslaught on the Soviet Union was imminent. The Soviet policy in China of supporting the nationalist revolution of Chiang Kai-shek had collapsed when Chiang turned on his former communist partners (page 83). Relations with Britain had deteriorated, and Britain, France and Poland were credited with plans to launch an offensive against the Soviet Union. There was a sense that the breathing space in Europe and the Far East could be short. The world-wide depression added a new element of uncertainty.

We have little indication of Stalin's thinking during this or any other period. One can plausibly surmise that in 1928 and 1929 he was still much concerned with rivals and criticisms of his policies and economic developments, which were certainly not going well. The problem of the change of course of the economic and social policies of the Soviet state has been debated by historians and we may never be able to fathom what perceptions and plans were Stalin's at any precise moment. Certainly a vociferous group of his supporters was calling for rapid industrialization and Stalin leant on them in his struggle with opponents of the policy. At what point in particular did he regard NEP as an obstacle to be cleared away if the pace of Russian industrialisation and its direction were to conform to his own objectives? If industrialisation were to be pushed ahead rapidly, the necessary investment would not significantly come from foreign loans, or even significantly from exports of grain, but from the higher productivity of workers and peasants and a holding back of consumption by them. In plain English, the industrial advance was achieved at the sacrifice of their own living standards, the work being rewarded with only low real wages. Long-term state planning by the State Planning Commission was certainly well under way and resources were increasingly transferred to large-scale industrial projects. By 1926 the increasing shortages of goods led to multi-pricing of the same goods in 'commercial' shops or at artificially low prices but strictly rationed. Despite rises in wages the actual cost of living rose much more steeply and in the opinion of one economic historian, Alec Nove, the 'fact still seems to be clear: 1933 was the culmination of the most precipitous peacetime decline in living standards known in recorded history'. While there was none of the unemployment that plagued Western economies at the time, the great industrial leap forward was accompanied by mass misery and hunger.

A 'maximum' version of the First Five-Year Plan was adopted by the Sixteenth Party Congress in 1929. Industrial output was intended to increase more than twofold and agricultural output to rise by half. The industrial growth actually achieved fell far short of such unrealisable targets. In trying to fulfil them there was huge waste and confusion. Coercion and regulation were necessary means to drive industrialisation forward especially in the primitive regions of Russia, the Urals and Siberia, where for military strategic reasons new industrial complexes were set up. The emphasis was on heavy industry, iron and steel, and machinery. The First Five-Year Plan, declared to be fulfilled a year in advance, actually fell short of its target in most industrial sections. But great iron and steel works were being constructed, the gigantic Dnieper dam was built and the engineering industry greatly expanded. The basis of a modern industry had been constructed.

The Second Five-Year Plan (1933–7) brought improvements for the Russian people. The economic sacrifices demanded of the people were not as harsh and there was greater emphasis on producing goods for consumption. Planning became more efficient and a greater self-sufficiency was achieved. After 1937 the massive switch to arms production once more created new bottlenecks and shortages. Control over the labour force became much harsher. Workers were tied in 1940 to their place of work and absenteeism became a crime. Industrially the Soviet Union in a decade and a half had been transformed and proved strong enough to withstand the shock of the German invasion. Statistics should always be considered with caution and this is especially true of Soviet statistics. But the figures shown in the table indicate and reflect the change of Soviet Russia's industry. Whether Soviet statistics are to be relied on is an open question.

The results were in any case impressive, the human cost equally enormous. Enthusiasm for building socialism was replaced by terror and

Soviet Russia's Industrial Growth

	1928	1940	1950
Electricity (*milliard Kwhs*)	5.0	48.3	91.2
Steel (*million metric tons*)	4.3	18.3	27.3
Oil (*million metric tons*)	11.6	31.1	37.9
Coal (*million metric tons*)	35.5	166.0	261.1
Machine-tools (*thousands*)	2.0	58.4	70.6
Tractors (*thousands*)	1.3	31.6	116.7
Mineral fertiliser (*million metric tons*)	0.1	3.2	5.5
Leather footwear (*million pairs*)	58.0	211.0	203.0

coercion. Ideals of socialist equality did not inhibit Stalin from decreeing differential rewards. With much stick, and the carrot of high rewards for successful skilled piece-work, he drove the mass of new peasant workers in industry to pull Russia out of the morass. Socialism could not be built in a society predominantly peasant and backward, Stalin believed. Nor could a backward Soviet Union survive, surrounded as she was by enemies. But the arbitrary murderous excesses of Stalin's rule in the 1930s bear no relation to the achievement of such goals. On the contrary, they gravely jeopardised progress. In dealing with the peasantry and agriculture his policies led to disaster. Here the 'revolution from above' not only inflicted enormous hardship on the majority of the population, the peasantry, but also failed in its purpose to 'modernise' agriculture on a scale similar to industry.

Stalin's cure for Russia's backward agriculture was to transform the small scattered peasant holdings into large farms collectively and co-operatively farmed. In theory this was sound. In practice productivity slumped when the individual peasant's personal ownership of his lands and his livestock was abolished. The peasants did not voluntarily give up their land and join collective farms. By 1928 less than three acres in a hundred of sown land were cultivated by collective or state farms. At the beginning of that year Stalin organised from his own secretariat the forcible seizure of grain as the peasants were unwilling to part with it for the artificially low prices laid down. It was a return to the methods of war communism. Bukharin, Rykov and Tomsky, once Stalin's allies against the Trotsky 'left', as has been seen, attacked Stalin from May 1928 onwards when they realised he intended to continue the emergency measures. Bukharin in particular condemned Stalin's dictatorial pretensions, declaring, 'We stand by the principle of collective action and refuse to accept the principle of control by a single individual, no matter how great his authority.' Stalin countered by savagely attacking Bukharin as a right-wing deviationist. Between February and July 1929 the political standing of the three leaders was progressively undermined and the expulsion from the Politburo of Tomsky and Bukharin in November 1929 marked the elimination of their opposition to Stalin's industrial and agricultural plans. (Rykov retained his membership of the Politburo until 1930.)

From the summer of 1929 Stalin issued party directives to secure more grain for state purchase at low prices. The kulaks were singled out as the most prosperous and therefore pressure on them would, it was thought, yield a good return. Not only their grain but their farms too began to be seized. NEP was breaking up. On 7 November 1929 Stalin signalled the drive for forcible collectivisation at the greatest possible speed. He characteristically declared that the middle peasants as well as the poor peasants had turned to the collective farms. The continuing crisis caused by the difficulty of getting grain was a crucial reason for the sudden urgency, but behind Stalin's assault also lay a long-felt suspicion of peasants as reliable allies of the urban proletariat.

Between the Bolsheviks and the peasants there was a large gap. The notion of petty-peasant proprietorship simply did not fit into the communist model of the future classless society. Stalin saw even the poorest peasant defending his possession of land and animals as exhibiting the characteristics of the 'petty-capitalist class'. As long as the landed peasant persisted in Russian society, Stalin believed, a communist state would never be built. He may have calculated that by ruining the more prosperous peasants, the kulaks, by defining them as a class to be destroyed, all the peasants would be taught the lesson that successful private enterprise held no future for them. Certainly party leaders believed that they could stir up class war between the poor peasant and the kulak and so gain some peasant support. 'Kulak' was, moreover, an entirely elastic definition and could be extended to any peasant; those too obviously poor could simply be labelled as kulak sympathisers. Under the cover of the supposed kulak enemy, land could be seized, peasants expelled and sent by cattle trucks to Siberia, and the whole peasantry could be terrorised. Without forcible measures to overcome the agricultural crisis, Stalin believed, the *acceleration* of industrialisation would fail, and one of his close supporters improbably claimed that all industrial growth would come to a standstill halfway through the Five-Year Plan if industrialisation was not accelerated.

Plans for the acceleration of industrial production went hand in hand with plans for the acceleration of collectivisation of the peasant farms. From the summer of 1929 onwards the peasants were being pressurised by party representatives in the villages to join the collective farms. The peasants reacted with suspicion or outright hostility. Although progress was made, the attitude of the bulk of the peasantry undoubtedly remained negative. Nevertheless by October 1929 collectives were farming almost one acre in eleven of sown land. Forcible procurement of grain meanwhile by party task forces over the whole country were securing results. In the autumn of 1929 Stalin, supported by Molotov and Kaganovich, determined to break all resistance to a great leap forward and to the mass discontent that coercion in the procurement of grain was producing.

It was in part wishful thinking and in part a command that collectivisation was to be quickly achieved regardless of what resistance remained. In December 1929 mass 'dekulakisation' began. Stalin decreed their 'elimination as a class'. Elimination of the individual peasant defined as kulak did not yet mean death, except in the case of those categorised as the most active counter-revolutionaries, but meant the confiscation of his property and imprisonment or the deportation of the whole family to Siberia, where with a few tools they began to farm again. Some kulaks were allowed to remain in their locality and were integrated into the collective system. The whole programme was carried through with the utmost violence and barbarity; six million peasants were the victims. Many perished through deprivation or suicide. It was an enormous tragedy almost totally hidden from Western view. The miseries of the depression do not compare with the human disaster in Stalin's Russia.

The result in the countryside was chaos. More than half the peasant farmers had been collectivised by the spring of 1930. As the time for spring sowing approached, reports from the countryside came back to Moscow that the forcible collectivisation was preparing the way for an unparalleled disaster. There was much peasant resistance, including uprisings. The new collectives were unlikely to produce a fraction of the food produced by the

Farming like machines without machines in the Soviet Union: a collective in the Volga basin, c.1930.

individual peasants before collectivisation. Stalin, faced with disastrous failure, compromised. In the face of so great a failure, his own standing could be jeopardised. He published an article, 'Dizzy with Success'. Local party workers were blamed for the excesses; coercion was wrong; those peasants who wished to leave the collective farms could do so. But instead of the expected few there was a mass exodus; more than half the peasants left the collectives and took back some of their land to farm. The best land the collective farmers retained.

To counter this unexpected turn of events, Stalin in the summer of 1930 ordered a resumption of forcible collectivisation. There was no let-up this time. By 1935, 94 per cent of the crop area of land was collectivised. The results in productivity were appalling. The peasants slaughtered their animals; the collectives were inefficient; the yield of crops dropped and party purges and coercion could not relieve the food shortages. The conditions of the early 1930s revived the experiences of the early 1920s. There were widespread famines and millions perished. The situation would have been even worse if Stalin had not learnt one lesson from the winter of 1929/30 and the widespread peasant violence and resistance to collectivisation. The collectivised peasants were permitted small plots and to own a few animals from 1930 onwards. After 1932 they were even allowed to sell food privately over and above the quota to be delivered to the state at state prices. The private peasant plot became an important element in the supply of milk and meat. Agriculture recovered slowly from the onslaught, but there was no leap forward as occurred in the industrial sector. The pre-1928 levels were only just attained again, though the population had grown in the meantime. Economically Stalin's collectivisation did not solve Russia's need for growth of agricultural production before the German invasion in 1941 dealt a devastating blow. Even Stalin had to compromise with the peasantry in allowing some private production and sale or face the prospect of permanent conditions of famine.

The enormous tensions created by Stalin's industrial and agricultural policies from 1929 to 1934 were accompanied by a policy of terrorisation to thwart any possible opposition. Propaganda sought to raise Stalin to the public status of a demi-god, the arbiter of every activity of society – art, literature, music, education, Marxist philosophy. Terror tactics were not new under Soviet rule. Show trials, which turned those who were constructing the new Russia into scapegoats for failures, had begun in 1928. We know so little of the inner workings of Soviet government that historians have been reduced to surmise. It appears that Stalin's power was not absolute between 1928 and 1934 and that the failures, especially in agriculture, were weakening his position. Perhaps a straw in the wind was the curious fact that the Seventeenth Party Congress early in 1934 changed his title from that of 'General Secretary' to just 'Secretary' of the party. Was this a rebuke against his attempt to gather all power in his hands? Was the leader of the Leningrad party, Sergei Kirov, who was also a member of the Politburo and hitherto a Stalin supporter, among those who attempted to clip Stalin's wings? That December 1934 Kirov was murdered and Western experts suspect that Stalin was implicated. That he acted as pallbearer at Kirov's funeral is no evidence to the contrary. The first mass terror-wave of arrests and executions followed. Then there was a pause, just as there had been with collectivisation. Stalin in 1936 even promulgated a constitution guaranteeing every conceivable human and civic right! It was no more than a façade that misled only the most gullible. Then the arrests and executions were resumed. The years from 1936 to 1938 are known as the Great Terror. At the end, Stalin emerged as the undisputed dictator whom none could resist.

Stalin turned on the elite of communist society, the party functionaries, the army officers from the junior to the commander in chief, the technocrats and managers. The world learnt only a little from the show trials of the prominent leaders, the 'fathers' of the revolution, who were now paraded to confess publicly their sins, confessions secured beforehand by torture and threats. Not only they, but also their wives and associates, were murdered. Nothing like this had ever occurred before. Behind the benign façade of Stalin's smile there existed a paranoiac tyrant who had convinced himself that he alone could lead Russia and who disregarded all human cost. Stalin may have been 'mad' according to some definitions, but he acted with cold and ruthless calculation. The victims of these purges have never been counted. Dekulakisation, the famine and the purges claimed millions of victims. No one was safe. Death, exile or incarceration in the huge complex of labour camps was the fate of anyone who fell under suspicion. The material loss to Russia of

Above: *in 1935, the benign dictator, Stalin, suffers the adulation of two grateful subjects from a collective farm in Tajikistan, while the purges continue apace.* Right: *At Kirov's funeral, December 1934, Stalin, implicated in Kirov's murder, is pre-eminent amongst the mourners, among them the equally hypocritical Molotov, Voroshilov and Kalinin.*

skilled people was incalculable. The grip of the secret police under the hated Beria was not loosened until after Stalin's death. There were thousands willing to do Stalin's bidding and commit all these crimes. He justified them by claiming there were conspiracies with outside Western powers, with Japan, Germany, Britain and France, to sabotage and attack the Soviet Union. Did he believe it? Stalin thought it theoretically possible and that was enough.

Stalin had little experience of foreign travel. Behind his notion of Russia's correct foreign policy two assumptions or principles can be discerned: Russia's defence in a hostile capitalist world must come first at all costs; secondly, the behaviour of other powers could be deduced by a Leninist analysis. Not only were these powers motivated by a joint hostility to the only communist state, but they were also locked in an imperial struggle for supremacy among themselves. Thus Soviet theoreticians, including Stalin in the 1920s, believed in the likelihood of war between Britain and the United States. But this was not seen, as might be expected, as benefiting the Soviet Union, for a great war anywhere might force Soviet involvement against her will. Later in the early 1930s, Stalin hoped that rivalry in eastern Asia would lead the United States to check Japanese expansion in China. But Soviet hopes were disappointed by American non-intervention during the Manchurian crisis of 1931–3 (page 213).

The Soviet view of the West was grotesquely distorted. The Western social democrats were cast in the role of 'right deviationists' or 'social fascists' from 1929 to 1934, more dangerous than the real fascists. The Nazis were seen as a short-lived right-wing excess against which the workers would soon react. There was a lingering fear of Poland and her ally, capitalist France, and of 'hostile' Britain. Thus from the West as well as from Asia, the Soviet Union appeared to be in continuing and great danger.

From 1934 to 1938 there was some readjustment of Soviet policy and a rapprochement with the

Western democracies. The Soviet Union was accepted finally by the United States when Roosevelt agreed to establish diplomatic relations in 1933. In 1934 the Soviet Union joined the League of Nations, and the Commissar for Foreign Affairs, Maxim Litvinov, now preached the need for collective security against Hitler's Germany and Mussolini's Italian expansionist policies. The genuine search for peace did not mean, however, that the Soviet Union was ready to go to war in alliance with the Western democracies against Germany. Rather, the Russians wanted to avoid a war breaking out altogether, and believed a firm stand would deter Hitler and Mussolini. If it did not, as it did not in September 1939, the Soviet leaders were determined to avoid being involved in war themselves. If there had to be a war – a situation full of danger for Russia – then at least it should be confined to a war between the Western powers. As long as Nazi Germany could be prevented from turning *first* on Russia, then the Soviet Union would remain neutral and appease Germany to any extent necessary to preserve peace. But the nightmare of the Soviet leadership was a reverse of that situation, that France and Britain would stand aside while Hitler conquered *Lebensraum* in the east. What is more, would the Ukrainians and Georgians and other non-Russian nationalities fight for Russia, when the people were suffering from such terrible communist repression? While socialism was still in transition, Russia could not afford war without risking the very survival of socialism.

The Soviet Union attempted to create a 'barrier of peace' by signing non-aggression treaties with her neighbours, of whom the most important was Poland. Until the autumn of 1938 Hitler employed no direct violence near Russia's borders. In eastern Asia the threat of war was met by a combination of policies, in the first place by appeasing Japan: in 1935 Russia sold her interest in the Chinese Eastern Railway to the Japanese puppet state of Manchukuo. It was lessened, furthermore, by encouraging Chiang Kai-shek's nationalist resistance to Japan in the hope that Japan would then be too busy fighting China to turn on Russia as well. When necessary, however, the Soviet Union did not hesitate to resist militarily any direct Japanese attacks on Soviet spheres of influence, on the People's Republic of Mongolia and along the Russo–Chinese frontier. There was full-scale fighting between Soviet and Japanese troops in 1938 and in the summer of 1939. These were no mere 'incidents'. Marshal Zhukov in 1939 had the advantage of modern tanks and troops far better armed than the Japanese. The Japanese suffered a severe defeat and left behind 18,000 dead. Thereafter they avoided open conflict with Russia. The Soviet Union and Japan in fact remained at peace until it suited Stalin, shortly before Japan's surrender, to attack the Japanese in China in 1945.

In the West, the Soviet Union did what she could to persuade France and Britain to stand up to Hitler and Mussolini. The menace they presented to peace and so to the Soviet Union was belatedly recognised in 1934. The Soviet Union then signed a treaty of mutual assistance with France in May 1935 to strengthen the deterrent alignment. The Soviet Union also joined in the League's ineffectual sanctions to deter Mussolini from conquering Abyssinia. In 1934 the new United Front tactics were acquiesced in when France herself seemed in danger of succumbing to fascism (page 165). But at the same time the communist leadership was always conscious of and never wished to repeat the experiences of the First World War when Russia was cast in the role of providing military relief to the West and in the effort went down in defeat. Russian policy aimed to maintain a careful balance and to avoid war by encouraging the will of France and Britain to resist. In line with this overall strategy the Russian help afforded to the Republican side during the Spanish Civil War was carefully limited to exclude any possible risk of war. It was left to the Comintern to organise the International Brigades to fight as volunteers on the Republican side. But Soviet technical advisers, tanks, aircraft and supplies played a crucial role in the war (page 230).

The year 1937 saw Stalin's military purge at its height. Russia was more unready than ever to face military attack from the West. The Soviet Union almost frantically attempted to construct a diplomatic peace front in 1938. It failed. Britain and France went to Munich in September and consented to the partition of Czechoslovakia (page 244). The Russians meanwhile had promised to support the Czechs only to the extent of their limited treaty obligations. Whatever Russian aid might have been forthcoming if the Czechs had fought, it appears certain that Stalin would not have risked war with Germany. The tendency of the Western powers to give way to the Nazis did not alter Soviet policy but reinforced its objectives to avoid war;

simultaneously Soviet diplomats sought to stiffen French and British resistance to Hitler by warning their governments that Hitler meant to defeat them. Stalin's faith in 'collective security', probably never strong, did not survive after the German occupation of Czechoslovakia in March 1939. It was unlikely that peace could much longer be preserved between Hitler and his neighbours and his prime objective remained to stop the Soviet Union from going to war. And so after simultaneous and secret negotiations with France and Britain on the one hand and Germany on the other – a double insurance policy – Stalin, having delayed as long as he dared, concluded a non-aggression pact with Germany on 23 August 1939. There were a few anxious days while Stalin waited to see whether Britain would actually fulfil her alliance obligations to Poland. Stalin had calculated correctly and kept the Soviet Union at peace. The Germans extracted a price in requiring supplies from the Soviet Union. To that extent Stalin became the most active proponent of appeasement. The war that began in September 1939, Stalin believed, afforded the Soviet Union a long breathing space during which communism would strengthen the Soviet Union's capacity to meet the dangers still to come. But the breathing space he had actually won lasted barely two years.

CHAPTER 21

The Failure of Parliamentary Democracy in Germany and the Rise of Hitler, 1920–1934

In retrospect there can be no minimising the importance of one historical date – 30 January 1933, when Adolf Hitler was appointed chancellor of Germany by President von Hindenburg. Within eight years of his coming to power, Germany had conquered continental Europe from the Channel coast to the gates of Moscow. It was not a conquest and occupation such as had occurred in the Great War. In German-occupied Europe some 10 million people, including 2 million children, were deliberately murdered. Hitler's Reich was a reversion into barbarism. Racism as such was nothing new, nor was it confined to Germany. These doctrines attracted groups of supporters in most of Europe, including France and Britain, in South America and in the United States. But it was in Germany that the resources of a modern industrial state enabled criminal leaders to murder and enslave millions. Until the concentration camps revealed their victims the world was inclined to believe that a country once in the forefront of Western culture, the Germany of Goethe, could not so regress. This faith in civilisation was misplaced. How was it possible? For just one of the more easily discernible parts of the explanation we must turn to the politics of Weimar Germany, which failed to provide stable governments until political democracy ceased to function altogether after the onset of the economic crisis of 1929.

From 1920 to 1930 no party was strong enough on its own to form a government and enjoy the necessary majority in parliament. But until 1928 a majority in parliament either favoured or at least tolerated the continuation of the parliamentary system of government. The Communist Party was too weak in its parliamentary representation to endanger the Republic during the middle years of Weimar prosperity from 1924 to 1928; its strength was appreciably smaller than that of the deputies of the moderate Socialist Party. Indeed the Socialists steadily gained votes and deputies in the Reichstag. From 100 in May 1924 their representation increased to 153 in 1928. Significantly the Communist Party fell in the same period from 62 to 54 Reichstag deputies. On the extreme anti-democratic right the Nazis did even worse in parliamentary elections; in May 1924 there were 32 Nazis elected to the Reichstag and in 1928 only 12. Even the conservatives, the Nationalist Party, who formed the opposition for most of the time from 1918 to 1930, declined from 95 to 73.

Weimar Germany appeared to gain in strength. This was not really so. The Nazis were winning adherents wherever there was distress. Even during the years of comparative prosperity, many of the farmers did not share the benefits of industrial expansion. Then governments were discredited by their short life-spans – on average only eight months. Parties appeared to be locked in purely selfish battles of personal advantage. The Social Democratic Party must share in the blame for the instability of the Weimar coalition governments. It preferred to stay in opposition and not to participate in the business of ruling the country. The difficulties

Prussian honour is allied to the new barbarism at the official opening ceremony of the first sitting of the Reichstag during the Thousand-Year Reich, 21 March 1933. Hitler and Hindenburg sit side-by-side at the Garrison Church of Potsdam; as ever, Hitler eschews uniform when appearing alongside the bemedalled Field Marshal.

of any party with socialist aspirations joining a coalition were genuinely great. Coalition meant compromise on policy. In any coalition with the centre and moderate right the Social Democrats could not hope to pass socialist measures and they were afraid that co-operation with the 'bourgeois' parties would discredit them with their electoral base, which consisted mainly of urban workers and trade unionists. From an electoral party point of view these tactics appeared to pay off as their increasing representation in the Reichstag shows. But the price paid was the discrediting of parliamentary government, for the exclusion from government of both the Nationalists and the communists and the absence of the Socialists meant that the coalitions of the centre and mainly moderate right were minority governments at the mercy of the Socialists.

In government there was thus a permanent sense of crisis, the coalition partners who formed the governments, especially the smaller parties, becoming more concerned about how the unpopularity of a particular government policy might affect their own supporters than about the stability of government as a whole. This situation imperilled the standing of the whole parliamentary democratic system. After 1925 there seemed to be only one method by which the parties of the centre and moderate right, saddled with the responsibility of government, could logically attain stability and a majority and that was to move further to the right. So its right wing came to predominate the Centre Party, enabling the conservatives, the Nationalist Party, to join coalition cabinets with them. The coalition cabinets were also very much cabinets of 'personalities' relying on presidential backing and only loosely connected with, and dependent on, the backing of the Reichstag parties. The close link between party and government, as existed in Britain, was lacking in the Weimar working of the constitution. Indeed it did not so much 'work' as function by one expedient after another.

When in 1928 the Socialists at last joined a broad coalition excluding the more extreme right they seemed to be remedying their earlier mistaken policy; but it was very late in the history of the parliamentary Republic. The coalition partners, especially the Centre Party, had already moved so far to the right that they now felt ill at ease working with the Socialists under a Socialist chancellor. This so-called grand coalition had the utmost difficulty holding together for the two years (1928–30) the government lasted, plunging from one internal crisis to the next. The influence of the brilliantly successful Foreign Minister, Gustav Stresemann, just managed to keep the right wing of the coalition in government. To carry through his diplomacy of persuading the Allies to relax their grip on Germany, he needed a stable government behind him. But the coalition did not survive his death in October 1929.

The three years from 1928 to 1930 were critical in the decline of Weimar Germany. Economic distress was becoming severe among the small farmers. Then followed the Wall Street crash and its chain reaction in Europe. Industrial output contracted and unemployment soared (page 164). The Nazis were able to capitalise on the grievances of the small farmers and then as the depression widened and deepened they exploited the resentments of the lower-middle classes, the shopkeepers and white-collar workers who were facing uncertainties and financial hardships and who feared a Bolshevik revolution from the unemployed industrial workers. On the political scene, the conservative Nationalist Party was excluded from power by the 'grand coalition' which in 1928 supported a broader-based government. The Nationalists in that year had fallen under the leadership of a wealthy industrialist and publisher, Alfred Hugenberg, who hated Weimar democracy and socialism equally. The Nationalists had not done well in the elections of 1928. The effect of their setback was to encourage Hugenberg to look to the more extreme right for votes. In the wings, the small, violent and racialist Nazi Party stood on the threshold of achieving mass support.

The first opportunity for the Nazis to make a significant electoral impact in the Reichstag elections came in 1930. The economic crisis had broken up the Socialist-led grand coalition. The partners of that coalition could not agree whether employers or the workers should suffer from the government's only remedy to the crisis, the cutting back of expenditure. Like the majority of the Labour Party in Britain, the Social Democrats could not remain in a government which reduced unemployment benefits. President von Hindenburg now called on the leader of the Centre Party, Heinrich Brüning, to lead a new government. There were threats that the President would dispense with the Reichstag's approval and resort to emergency decrees provided for in the constitution if it rejected Brüning's savage deflation. This happened within a few weeks and Brüning now staked his future on dissolving the Reichstag and on a new election. Its unexpected result and its political consequences ushered in the final phase of Weimar democracy. The vote of the Nazis increased from some 810,000 in 1928 to nearly 6.5 million in the September 1930 election. They increased their representation from 12 to 107, just behind the Socialists, who had 143, and nudged ahead of the Communists, who had 77, to become the second largest party. The conservative Nationalists lost half their support.

It would still perhaps have been just possible to stabilise the political fortunes of Weimar, but Brüning's financial 'cures' killed any chance of this happening. Confidence throughout the country in the ability of the politicians to solve the crisis ebbed away. Economists of the Keynesian school of thought met with complete rejection in the Brüning era. (The Nazis lent them a more ready ear.) There was an alternative policy of expansion and of credit and of state help to put the unemployed to work. Financially the country was sliding into a position where administrators felt that something had to be done. In parliament, the Social Democrats, under the great shock of the National Socialist landslide, backed the minority Brüning government from the benches of the opposition as far as they could. Brüning's preference was for authoritarian, austere government, and with Hindenburg's backing he governed by emergency presidential decrees.

Hindenburg did not want Hitler to come to power. He felt a strong antipathy for the 'Bohemian corporal' (he was actually a Bavarian corporal), a violent uncouth Austrian who shared none of Hindenburg's own Prussian Junker qualities. When Hindenburg was elected president in 1925 by a narrow margin over the candidate of the Socialists and Centre, the spectacle of an avowed monarchist and legendary war hero, the most decorated and honoured of the Kaiser's field marshals, heading a republic seemed incongruous indeed. But the seventy-seven-year-old symbol of past glories did his job decently enough, even raising the respectability of the Republic by consenting to serve as her head. But all his life he had been trained to believe in command and leadership, and the spectacle of parliamentary bickering and the musical chairs the politicians were playing in and out of government appeared to him a travesty of what Germany needed.

Nevertheless the Field Marshal could be relied on to honour his oath to the republican constitution. This gave him the constitutional right to act in an emergency, and he believed, not without justification, that the destructive behaviour of the political parties during the economic crisis of 1929 to 1930 had created a crisis of government. The Young Plan, which fixed the total amount of reparations at 121 thousand million Marks to be paid in instalments over fifty-nine years, was assailed by the Nazis and the right. In 1932, however, at Lausanne, the amount was reduced to 3000 thousand million Marks. Brüning's attempt to court Nationalist opinion and aid the stricken economy by announcing an Austro-German customs union in 1931 failed because the Allies declared that it broke the Versailles Treaty, which prohibited the union of Austria and Germany. Thus dissatisfied, German nationalism was further increased. The army now enjoyed great influence and the attention of historians has been especially focused on the few men, including Hindenburg's son, who increasingly gained the old gentleman's confidence and influenced his decisions.

Brüning governed with austere authority, complete integrity and disastrous results. Raising taxes and reducing salaries was naturally unpopular, all the more so as the economic crisis deepened. Unemployment rose from 2.25 million in 1930 to over 6 million in 1932. Brüning in April 1932 tried to curb street violence by banning all the private armies such as the SA, the SS and the Stahlhelm. His intentions were good but this measure too was largely ineffectual as the organisations survived without openly wearing uniforms. At the depth of the crisis in 1932 the presidential term of office expired. Hindenburg was deeply chagrined not to be re-elected unopposed. Hitler chose to stand against him and lost, but more significant than his failure was the fact that more than 13 million had voted for him. Hindenburg had secured over 19 million votes but was so old that he could not last much longer. Shortly after the presidential elections in May 1932 Hindenburg dropped Brüning. Franz von Papen became chancellor, enjoying no support in the Reichstag or the country. Less than a year was left before Hitler assumed power over Germany. How had he, a complete unknown only eleven years earlier, achieved this transformation? To understand Hitler's rise we must now look at this aspect of Weimar Germany's politics: how Hitler managed to challenge successfully the whole democratic basis of the state.

Fewer than three out of every hundred Germans voted for the Nazis at the national election of 1928 and that was after seven years of unceasing Nazi propaganda. But the Nazis had built an organisational base and increased the party's membership significantly. Nazi ideology was no consistent or logically developed theory such as Marxism claimed to be. There was nothing original about any of its aspects. It incorporated the arrogant nationalistic and race ideas of the nineteenth century, specifically the anti-Semitic doctrines and the belief in German uniqueness and Germany's world mission, together with elements of fascism and socialism, for in its early days the National Socialist Workers' Party wooed the urban worker.

The National Socialists, or Nazis for short, had grown out of one of the many small racialist and nationalist groups already flourishing in Germany – one organised in Munich by a man called Anton Drexler. His name would have remained insignificant but for Hitler's association with the group. Under Hitler's leadership from July 1921 onwards, the party was opportunistic, seeking to grow strong on all the resentments felt by different sections of the German people: the small farmers, who suffered from the agricultural depression and, later, inflation; the middle class, whose status was threatened and whose savings had been wiped out; unemployed workers; those industrialists at the other end of the scale who were the declared enemies of socialism even in its mildest form; theologians, mainly Protestant, who saw in Nazism a spiritual revival against Weimar materialism. The extreme nationalism of the Nazis made a strong appeal.

Few of those who were early supporters accepted all the disparate objectives that Nazism purported to stand for, but every group of supporters was prepared to discount, overlook or accept as the 'lesser evil' those things it inwardly disapproved of. They saw in Hitler and his movement what they wished to see. This same attitude also accounts for the still widely held view that there was a 'good Hitler' who cured unemployment and unified Germany, and a 'bad Hitler' who persecuted the Jews, made war and ignored justice when dealing with individuals and minority groups. That attitude expresses the feelings of those who brought the Nazis to power and maintained them; it assumes that one does not have to judge the 'whole' but can accept the evils for the sake of the benefits.

Nazism exploited the backward-looking conservatism that flourished in Germany after the disillusionment of defeat in 1918. Paradoxically

Hitler imposed a revolution of values and attitudes that plunged German society into accelerating change after 1933. But what some of those Germans who supported him saw in Hitler in the 1920s was a return to an old virtuous Germany, a simpler Germany that had never really existed. Part of this turning back can be seen in Hitler's emphasis on the need for a healthy people to live close to the land. It was erroneously argued that modern Germany lacked land and space for a 'healthy' expansion of the people. Hence the obsession with gaining *Lebensraum*, and Hitler's plans for satisfying these 'needs' in the east. Hitler, too, dwelt obsessively on the medieval image of the Jew as an alien, a parasite, who produced nothing but lived on the work of others. 'Work' was ploughing the land, the sweat of the brow, not sitting in banks and lending money. Yet he also had sound instincts which led him to accept some modern economic concepts as a way out of the miseries of the last Weimar years. The discredited race doctrines of the nineteenth century were reinforced and amplified in the study of a new race biology. The ideology of race lent a spurious cohesion to all the Nazi policies.

This was a turning back on the age of reason. Numerous organizations from the large veteran association, the Stahlhelm, to small so-called *völkisch* groups embraced strident nationalism and a mystical Teutonic secular faith. None saw in Weimar's parliamentary democracy anything but a shameful subordination of the German nation to alien foreign domination. It was identified also with the Jews, who played a small but distinguished role in its constitutional, administrative, economic and artistic life, although they formed only 1 per cent of the nation's population. They were besmirched by Nazi calumnies that they were war profiteers and corrupters. More significant than the slanders themselves is the wide credence which lies won in Germany.

The counterpart to this support for right-wing extremism in its various forms was the lack of positive support and understanding by the majority of Germans for the spirit of parliamentary democracy. In the 1920s anti-democratic ideas were not only propagated by the communists and by the ignorant and ill-educated, but found strong support among the better-off, middle-class youth, especially within the student unions and universities. Stresemann's success in dismantling the punitive aspects of Versailles won no acclaim because his methods were peaceful and conciliatory, as they had to be if they were to succeed in the years immediately after the war. The notion that a democracy tolerates different ideas and different approaches to solving problems was instead condemned as disunity, as the strife and chaos of parties. The parties themselves – apart from the totalitarian-oriented Nazi and Communist Parties – rarely understood that they had to place the well-being of the whole nation before narrow party interests, that even while they attacked each other they had to acknowledge a common framework and defend above all parliamentary democracy itself. Democracy was regarded as representing the lowest common denominator of politics, the rule of the masses. Fascism and Nazism also appealed to the elitists, who saw themselves as leading the masses.

The educated and better-off followers feared above everything 'social revolution'; they preferred the Nazi promise of 'national revolution' which would, they thought, enhance their career opportunities. What made the Nazis so successful was precisely the combination of physical force in the streets, which was welcomed by anti-communists, and the support of the 'professionals' in the army, civil service, the Churches and education. They, the supposedly educated elite, had helped to undermine Weimar democracy even in the years of prosperity and made Nazism respectable. In the absence of strong positive support, democracy – and with it the rule of law – is dangerously exposed. It could not survive the economic blizzard of 1929 to 1932, which was not the root cause of its downfall but more the final blow. Nevertheless there were regions of Germany that did not succumb to the tidal wave of Nazism even in 1933; this is true of the strongly Catholic Rhineland and Bavaria. In the big industrial cities, too, such as Berlin and Hamburg, most factory workers in the beginning continued to support the Social Democrats and the communists. The rise of the Nazis to power was not the inevitable consequence of the lost war, of inflation and depression. It was not automatic, the result of the inexorable working out of the disadvantages besetting Germany after 1918. Hitler succeeded because a sufficient mass of German people, including many in leading positions of society, chose to support what he stood for. While he did not reveal all his aims, he did reveal enough to be rejected by anyone believing in democracy and basic human rights. Among mainly young Nazi thugs there were many fanatical and warped idealists. Other supporters were opportunists joining a bandwagon for reasons of personal gain. Many saw in Hitler a saviour who would end Germany's 'humiliation' and the 'injustices' of Versailles.

No preparation for power was stranger or more unlikely than Adolf Hitler's. He lived for fifty-six years, from his birth in the small Austrian town of Braunau on 20 April 1889 until his suicide on 30 April 1945 in his bunker under the Reich Chancellery in Berlin. During the last twelve years of his life he dominated first Germany and then most of continental Europe. His impact on the lives of millions was immense, responsible as he was for immeasurable human misery. He believed mankind to be engaged in a colossal struggle between good and evil and he made this hysterical fantasy come true more nearly than any single man had done before. Yet nothing in the first thirty years of his life pointed to the terrible impact he would make on history. The historian searches in vain for anything extraordinary in his early life.

Mein Kampf 'My Struggle', which Hitler wrote during his short spell of imprisonment in 1924, glamorised his past, and recent research has shown his account to be unreliable. Hitler suffered no hardship other than the consequences of his own early restless way of life. His father was a conscientious customs official who died when he was fourteen years old; his mother was devoted and did her best for her son, whose attachment to her was deep. But Hitler could not accustom himself to regular work, even during his secondary school days. Supported financially by his mother, he drifted into a lonely way of life, avoiding all regular work, aspiring to be an artist. He attempted to gain entrance to the Academy of Fine Arts in Vienna but was rejected, as were the majority of applicants. Nevertheless, in his nineteenth year he moved to the Habsburg capital. His mother had recently died from cancer; Hitler had cared for her during the final traumatic phase, aided by a Jewish doctor to whom he expressed his gratitude.

For the next two years the money left him by his parents and an orphan's pension provided him with an adequate income. He could indulge his fancies; he read a great deal and impractically designed grandiose buildings in the backroom of his lodgings. He continued in this lonely and irregular lifestyle; soon all the money he had inherited was spent. There is little reliable information about his next two years. He disappeared from view, living in poverty without attempting regular work, relying on charity and boarding in cheap hostels. It would seem probable that he still dreamt of becoming an architect, and more importantly imbibed the crude anti-Semitic and racialist ideas current in Vienna at that time. In May 1913, in his twenty-fourth year, he moved to Munich, Bavaria's artistic capital. He lived there by selling sketches and watercolours, executed with care and photographic accuracy, pleasing pictures of no great artistic merit. He could, then, be fairly described as self-educated but without discipline, with sufficient artistic skill to have earned his living as an engraver or poster designer had he desired regular work. He was essentially a loner, who had established no deep relationships, and he was already filled with resentments and hatreds which came to be centred more and more on the Jews.

The outbreak of the Great War he later regarded as the turning point in his life. He volunteered for the Bavarian army with enthusiasm. He already saw himself as a Pan-German, and not a loyal subject of the multinational Habsburgs, whom he detested. During the war he was wounded and awarded the Iron Cross First Class; he served as a despatch messenger, though in those days communications were passed mainly on foot along the small distances from trench to trench or from one command post to another. It is notable that he was never promoted beyond the rank of corporal, despite the desperate need for NCOs, a reflection of his superior's view that Corporal Hitler was not a suitable leader of men. When he returned to Munich after the war at the age of twenty-nine, his lack of formal qualification and education was typical of millions for whom the future looked grim. But it is from this point on that his hitherto insignificant and unsuccessful life took a fantastic new turn.

For a start, his interest in politics and loyalty commended him to the new Reichswehr. The army retained him in a division for 'military education'. One of his tasks was to investigate and infiltrate dubious, possibly left-wing, political groups. In this way he came to join Drexler's small German Workers' Party, more a pub-debating society than a genuine party. The transformation of Hitler now began. As a political agitator and an orator who could move his audiences to emotion and hysteria with the violence of his language, Hitler discovered a new vocation. He did not of course see himself as the leader of Germany at this stage, but rather as the propagandist who would help to power the extreme nationalists – men like Ludendorff who would rescue Germany from 'Bolshevism' and the Jews and who would break the shackles of Versailles.

Hitler fulminated against the world Jewish conspiracy, Wall Street and 'Bolshevism', and against the injustices of Versailles, until out of Drexler's debating club a real party emerged with 55,000 supporters by 1923. From 1921 Hitler led that party, renamed the National Socialist German Workers' Party (or by its German initials NSDAP). Hitler the rabid rabble-rousing politician had arrived, a fact made possible only by the totally chaotic political condition of Bavaria where a disparate right had bloodily defeated an equally disparate left (page 123). In November 1923 Hitler misjudged the situation and sought to seize power for the forces of the right in much the same way as Lenin had seized control of Petrograd with a few devoted revolutionaries. His attempted Munich *Putsch* ended ignominiously, Hitler fleeing when the police opened fire. Ludendorff alone, with more courage than good sense, marched through the cordon of police. Hitler had expected that he would seize power without bloodshed and that the police and army would rally to the Ludendorff–Hitler alliance. Later he recognised that failure had saved him. Had he succeeded in gaining control and marched on 'Red Berlin' as he intended, the government would not have capitulated to a fanatic and extremist. Nor, as the Army High Command knew, would the French, who had entered the Ruhr, have tolerated for a moment a coup led by a man who so stridently denounced the Versailles Treaty; the French, moreover, still possessed the strength and determination to prevent such a coup. Hitler might then have been finished for good.

Hitler turned his trial for treason, conducted in Bavaria by judges who sympathised with his cause, into a personal propaganda triumph. Sentenced to the minimum term of five years' imprisonment, he actually only served a few months. While in prison he started writing *Mein Kampf* and after his release he began to rebuild the party which was to carry him to power. The Munich *Putsch* had convinced him that the Nationalist right could not be trusted and was too feeble. He would be the leader, not they. From 1925 to 1928 there were two important developments: a steady but slow growth of membership of the Nazi Party and continuing bitter internal disputes among the leaders, notably Joseph Goebbels, Julius Streicher and the Strasser brothers, Gregor and Otto. Hitler was handicapped by a ban on his making public speeches until May 1928, and he did not dare defy it for fear of being deported from Germany as an Austrian citizen. He nevertheless sought to create a tight, national Nazi organisation, insisting on absolute obedience to himself. Right up to the final triumph of 30 January 1933, when he became chancellor, there was a real threat of defections from the Nazi Party he led.

In 1925 Hitler judged that the established government was too strong to be seized by force. He changed his tactics. He would follow the legal, constitutional road by entering Reichstag elections to gain a majority, and only then establish his dictatorship. He never showed anything but contempt for the Reichstag and, though leader of the party, would never himself take part in its proceedings. He advised his followers 'to hold their nose' when in the Reichstag. During the period from 1925 to 1928 he built up his party as a virulent propaganda machine, insisted that he alone should lead it, without requiring the advice of leading party personalities, for it was an essential element of his plans to cultivate the cult of the Führer or Leader. The party membership reached 97,000 in 1929. Was the economic crisis then not the real cause of this sudden success? The economic crisis which overtook the world is usually dated from the time of the Wall Street crash in 1929. But this is misleading (see Chapter 19). By the winter of 1927–8 distress was already felt in Germany among the small agricultural farmers and workers in northwest Germany and by artisans and small shopkeepers especially. The Nazi party made considerable headway in rural districts in local and state elections in 1929 at the expense of the traditional Conservative and Nationalist Parties.

In that same year with the economic crisis deepening, the conservative Nationalist, Hugenberg, hoped to gain power by forming a broad alliance of the right and using Hitler to win the support of those masses which the conservatives had failed to attract. A vicious campaign was launched against the Young reparations plan of 1929. The reparations and the politicians of Weimar were blamed for Germany's economic ills. The economic and Nationalist assault proved explosive. But the German electorate's reaction in the Reichstag elec-

Who would have considered Hitler the man of destiny as the Nazi Party faithful congregated in Nuremberg for the third Party rally in 1927? Despite the ceremonial pomp, the NSDAP only polled 810,000 votes the following year, winning just twelve seats in the Reichstag.

tion of September 1930 was not what Hugenberg expected: the Nationalists lost heavily and the Nazis made their first breakthrough at the level of national elections, winning 107 seats to become the second-largest party after the Socialists. In a little more than two years their electoral support had increased from 810,000 to 6.5 million.

The period from 1930 to the end of January 1933 was in many ways the most testing for Hitler. Industrialists, however, began to hedge their bets and substantial financial contributions began flowing into Nazi funds. The propaganda campaign against Weimar became ever more vicious. Support among the industrial workers in the big cities could not be won over; the Catholic south remained largely immune too. Although originating in Bavaria, the Nazis gained the greatest following in rural northern Germany. The white-collar workers, the rural voters and elements of what is rather unsatisfactorily labelled the middle class, especially those threatened by Brüning's financial measures with a drop in their standard of living, were the new Nazi voters. The Nazis and Nationalists did all in their power to discredit Weimar democracy. Papen, the new Chancellor in June 1932, hoped to gain Hitler's sympathetic support by lifting the ban

Weimar Germany, 1932, on the brink of collapse. Communist and Nazi flags jostle for space in this Berlin tenement.

on the SA (Sturm Abteilung, or stormtroopers) and, in July, by illegally ousting the socialist government of Prussia.

Papen's Cabinet of 'Barons', as it became known from the titled nonentities of which it was composed, enjoyed no support in the Reichstag. The effect of the two elections which Papen induced Hindenburg to call in July and November 1932 in an unsuccessful attempt to secure some support in the country and parliament were the coffin nails of democracy, for those parties which were determined to destroy the Weimar republic between them won a comfortable majority in the Reichstag. The Nazis in July won 230 seats and 37 per cent of the vote, becoming the largest single party; in the election of November 1932 they held on to 33 per cent of the electorate, saw their seats drop to 196, but remained the largest party; the Nationalists secured almost 9 per cent, and the communists 17 per cent (100 seats) – nor did the three anti-democratic parties have any scruples about acting together. The Socialists slipped from 133 seats to 121. Papen had gambled on making the Nazis more amenable by inflicting an electoral defeat on them. The Nazis did indeed suffer a setback in November 1932. Papen was pleased, but Hitler had lost only a battle, not a war. On 17 November Papen resigned. Hitler thought his moment had come. Summoned to Hindenburg, he was told by the Field Marshal that he would be considered as chancellor only if he could show that a parliamentary majority backed him and that unlike Papen he could govern without special presidential decrees. Such conditions, Hindenburg and Hitler perfectly well knew, could not be met. They amounted to a rejection of Hitler.

Hindenburg wanted his favourite, Papen, back. Papen planned to prorogue the Reichstag and change the constitution. However, General Kurt von Schleicher, who represented the right of the Army High Command and who had played an influential political role behind the scenes, persuaded Hindenburg that Papen's plans would lead to civil war and that the army had lost confidence in Papen's ability to control the situation. With obvious reluctance Hindenburg appointed Schleicher on 2 December 1932 to head the last pre-Hitler government. Schleicher's own solution was to try to split the Nazi Party and to win the support of Gregor Strasser and his more left-wing section of the party. Strasser, who was very influential as the head of the party's political organisation, had become disillusioned with Hitler's tactics of demanding total power and his adamant refusal to share power with coalition partners. Despite evidence of falling Nazi support in the November 1932 election, Hitler won. Strasser made the task easier for him by resigning from the party in early December 1932 after bitterly quarrelling with Hitler, who accused him of treachery. Hindenburg's opposition and internal disputes made many Nazis feel that their chance of gaining power was ebbing away. But Hitler was proved right only a few weeks later. Schleicher announced his government's programme for relieving unemployment and distress; wages and benefits were raised, but even so the divided Reichstag was united on one issue alone – to refuse Schleicher their backing. Papen meanwhile ensured that the only outcome of Schleicher's failure would be a new coalition ostensibly led by Hitler but which Papen expected to control.

Hindenburg was cajoled into concluding that the parliamentary crisis could be ended only by offering the chancellorship to Hitler, the leader of the largest party, even though Hitler had not set foot in the Reichstag as a parliamentary leader. The ins and outs of the final intrigues that overcame Hindenburg's obvious reluctance are still debated by historians. Papen and the conservative and Nationalist right totally misjudged and underestimated Hitler. They believed they could tame him, that he would have to rely on their skills of government. Instead Hitler ended the parliamentary crisis in short order by doing what he said he would do, that is by crushing the Weimar constitution and setting up a totalitarian state. But Papen's intrigues were merely the final blow to the already undermined structure of Weimar's democracy; it cannot be overlooked that Hitler, whose party had openly proclaimed that it stood for the destruction of the Weimar constitution, had won one-third of the votes in November 1932; this meant a higher proportion of electors supported the Nazi Party than had supported any other single party at previous post-1920 Reichstag elections. Given the multiplicity of parties and the system of proportional representation a greater electoral victory than the Nazis achieved is difficult to conceive. It was not backstairs diplomacy alone then that brought Hitler to power, but also the votes of millions of people which made his party the largest in the Reichstag by far. In November 1932 the Nazis had polled 11, 737, 000 votes against 7,248,000 of the second-largest party, the Social Democrats.

There is a strong contrast between the long wait for power and the speed with which Hitler silenced and neutralised all opposition to establish a totalitarian regime. The destruction of Weimar democracy, and the civic rights that were guaranteed by the constitution to all German citizens was accomplished behind a legal façade which stilled the consciences of all those in the state who should have resisted. The reasons for the lack of opposition had their roots in the past. The elites which led the German state – the majority of administrators, civil servants, the army, the Churches too – had followed a long tradition of defaming democracy; Hitler's anti-Semitism and his attacks on minorities were nothing new in their thinking. This weakness is as noteworthy as Hitler's rise. All the more honour to the minority who refused to accept the changes and actively resisted or left the country. Almost half the German electorate was prepared to support Hitler in the hope of better times, to be brought about by a 'national revolution' and an end to Weimar and disunity.

The Nazis occupied only three posts in the coalition Cabinet. Hitler was chancellor; Hermann Göring was placed in charge of Prussia as minister without portfolio and Prussian minister of the interior under Vice-Chancellor Papen; and Wilhelm Frick was minister of the interior. The government posts had been carefully arranged so that the army and the Foreign Ministry, as well as other key ministries, were not under Nazi control. Papen and the Nationalists soon discovered that Hitler was not inhibited from exercising control by the constitutional niceties that had been devised to restrain him. This was no Weimar coalition government!

The easy, almost effortless path to total dictatorial power makes melancholy reading. The setting alight of the Reichstag on 27 February 1933, probably by the unbalanced Dutchman van der Lubbe alone – though there can be no certainty – became the pretext for an emergency decree signed by Hindenburg suspending personal liberties and political rights.

Hitler had insisted on new elections as a condition for accepting office, intending to gain an absolute majority, and he meant to make sure of it. Accordingly, despite Papen's supposed seniority, Göring seized control of Prussia, which comprised two-thirds of Germany, and under cover of the emergency decree terrorised the opponents of the Nazis. After an electoral campaign of unparalleled violence and intimidation, with Joseph Goebbels manipulating press and radio to help secure a Nazi victory, the Nazis just failed to gain the expected overall majority. Their votes, rose to over 17 million; the Socialists held on to over 7 million votes and the Communists, despite the Nazi campaign, polled 4.8 million votes; the Centre Party secured nearly 4.5 million and the Nationalists (DNVP) a disappointing 3.1 million. But, together with the Nationalists, the Nazis could muster a majority against all other parties, sufficient to govern with the support of the Reichstag. This was obviously not Hitler's aim. He sought dictatorial power and a change of the constitution, but this required a two-thirds majority and shrewdly he wished to proceed in a pseudo-legal way to assure himself of the support of the country afterwards.

Not a single communist deputy of the 81 elected could take his seat. All were already in the hands of the Gestapo (Geheime Staats Polizei, or Secret State Police) or being hunted down. More than twenty of the Socialists also were under arrest or prevented from attending. Still Hitler needed the support of the Nationalists and so to reassure them and the army and the President, he staged an opening ceremony of the Reichstag in the shrine of monarchical Junkerdom, the old garrison church of Potsdam where Frederick the Great lay buried. But even with the communists prevented from voting and the Nationalists voting on his side, Hitler still lacked the two-thirds majority he needed. It will always be to the shame of the members of the once great Centre Party that they tempered their principles and threw in their lot with Hitler, and agreed to vote for his dictatorial law. They lost the will to resist, and the leadership later came to an

Reichstag Elections, 5 March 1933

	seats	percentage of votes
National Socialists (NSDAP)	288 seats	43.9%
Nationalists (DNVP)	52 seats	8%
Centre (Zentrum)	74 seats	11.2%
Socialists (SPD)	120 seats	18.3%
Communists (KPD)	81 seats	12.3%
Others	32 seats	6.3%

The Reichstag sits, 23 March 1933. All seems orderly in this Nazi propaganda photo; there is no hint of the violence and intimidation that succeeded in burying democracy with the passing of the Enabling Law that day. Göring presides over proceedings from the chair in the top right.

agreement to secure Catholic interests. It was left to the Socialist Party alone to vote against Hitler's so-called Enabling Law, which acquired its two-thirds majority on 23 March 1933 with the stormtroopers howling vengeance outside the Reichstag on anyone who dared to oppose Hitler's will.

Now Hitler was able to put his aims into practice with far less restraint. Under the sinister application of the term *Gleischaltung* (co-ordination or literally a switch used to bring one current in line with another), a vague all-embracing aim was set out forcibly to subordinate all the activities of German society – government, administration, the free press and trade unions – to Nazi bodies set up specially to supervise them. Thus while in some cases the old institutions remained, they were subject to new Nazi controls. The whole process was haphazard and new Nazi organisations proliferated, frequently in rivalry with each other as well. Hitler in the final resort would decide between conflicting authorities. Until he did so there was the inevitable chaos and infighting. For a time he might decide it best not to interfere too much in a particular administrative branch or, for example, leave the High Command of the army intact. The complete process of *Gleischaltung* would be applied later to the army also. Hitler insisted on his own final say, on maintaining some of the traditional structures as long as he thought this tactically necessary to overcome misgivings among broad sections of the German people or powerful groups such as the army. His revolution would be complete but gradual. The Nazi state was thus no efficient monolith. Within the overall framework of acceptance of the Führer as leader, rivalries flourished and independent policies were still pursued for short periods. During the early years there were even islands of legality and normality to confuse opinion at home and abroad.

Among the first steps that Hitler took was to abolish the independent powers of the federal states in March 1933. In April a decree purged the civil service of Jews and those of Jewish descent, and of anyone whom the Nazis deemed to oppose the regime's aims. In Prussia a quarter of the higher civil service was dismissed, including judges who were supposed to be irremovable. The Supreme Court in Leipzig secretly debated whether they should make a protest at this unconstitutional act and decided on discretion. No wonder the German public was misled by the seeming legality of these new 'laws'. During the course of the summer of

1933, the remaining independent parties were disbanded. The communist leaders were already in the new concentration camps. The Vatican now decided to conclude a treaty – the Concordat – with Hitler in a misguided effort to protect Catholic interests. The independent trade unions were quickly brought to heel and suppressed, and the workers enrolled in the Nazi Labour Front. The press and broadcasting were placed under Goebbels's direction. The universities did not put up any real resistance either. There were famous professors like the philosopher Martin Heidegger who, at least for a short time, gave public support to the Nazi movement. Some became ardent Nazis out of conviction; many, opportunistically, for the sake of their careers.

Thus there were many who tried to please the new rulers. Academics participated in the famous burning of the books by Jewish and anti-Nazi authors. Many of Germany's internationally known scientists, writers and artists joined the 'national revolution' of the Nazis. Nor were theologians immune from the Nazi corruption: Christ became an Aryan even. The dismissed Jews, such as Albert Einstein, began to leave the country. So did a few Christian Germans, including the Nobel Prize-winning writer Thomas Mann. Germany's other literary giant, who had also won the Nobel Prize for literature, Gerhart Hauptmann, remained in Nazi Germany, adorning the new regime.

Hitler was sensitive to German public opinion. The German people, he understood, would need to be 'educated' to accept the harshness and final brutality in stages. So, when Jews were dismissed from the civil service, some were granted their state pensions provided they had completed at least ten years of service. Those Jews who had fought in the First World War or whose sons or fathers had died in the war were temporarily excepted from dismissal at Hindenburg's request. Terror was exercised against specific opponents. Dachau was the first concentration camp, established near Munich in 1933 by Heinrich Himmler, head of the Bavarian political police. It became the model for others, and by the summer of 1933 at least 30,000 Germans were held in concentration camps. Himmler soon advanced to become the Reichsführer of the SS (Schutzstaffel) and head of the police throughout the Reich. The courts and police also continued to function.

Germany was left as a mosaic where the normal process of law and administration continued to function fairly in some instances. In other areas the Nazis or the terror arm of the SS were supreme, and no appeal to the courts was possible. Jewish students were for a time permitted to continue their university studies on a quota system. Until 1938, some Jewish businesses continued to function, though many went bankrupt. 'I always go as far as I dare and never farther,' Hitler told a meeting of party leaders in April 1937. So Hitler, at the same time as he breached the vital principles of basic civic rights, gave the outward appearance of acting mildly and reasonably, and always in conformity with proper 'laws'. And did not the person of President Hindenburg guarantee decency? The German people did not realise how completely the President had lost all power. But knowledge of the concentration camps was a deterrent to any thought of opposition from all except the most courageous.

Hitler was especially careful to appease the army. He assured it of an independent status and of its position as the sole armed force in the state. The army wished to draw on the young stormtroopers whom it would train as a large armed force that could quickly augment the regular army in time of crisis. This meant the subordination of the SA to the needs of the army. The head of the stormtroopers, Ernst Röhm, had entirely different ideas. The stormtroopers were not only a separate army in the state, but he saw them under his command as the untainted force which would carry through the complete Nazi revolution in opposition to Hitler, who appeared willing to compromise with the old elements of power, the army and industrialists. Hitler reacted ruthlessly and, with the help of the Reichswehr during what became known as the Night of the Long Knives on 30 June 1934, had Röhm and many senior officers of the SA murdered. The same opportunity was taken to murder General von Schleicher, Gregor Strasser and two of Papen's close associates, as a warning to Papen's nationalist 'allies'. Hitler, with the connivance of the army, had now openly set himself above the law.

On 2 August 1934, Hindenburg, the one man probably still more popular than Hitler, died. He was buried at a great funeral ceremony and for the last time Hitler took a back seat. With Hindenburg were laid to rest symbolically the last vestiges of the Prussian Junker and military traditions of honour and service. The moment Hindenburg died, Hitler took another important step towards supreme power. A decree announced that the offices of president and chancellor were merged in one person, Hitler, who now became the Führer and Reich Chancellor. The Reichswehr generals, believing that they would still control all military decisions, did not oppose Hitler's demand that the army should swear a personal oath of loyalty to him as head of state. Enormous power was now concentrated in Hitler's hands. But still he moved with caution, step by step, accepting that he would need time to achieve his goals.

The year 1934 also witnessed the belated small beginnings of protest against the implications of Nazi anti-Semitism though only as far as it affected the Church's own administration, and the largely unsuccessful attempts by Hitler to subordinate the Protestant Church. That Hitler did not choose immediately to crush the opposition of the Confessional Protestant Church movement and other protests, however, was due not to moderation, as people mistakenly thought, but to his caution, his wish to dominate only gradually all spheres of German life. He bided his time.

Hitler had a clear view of priorities. At home the most important issue was unemployment. If he could get the out-of-work back into factories and construction, enable the small businesses to become sufficiently profitable again and provide security and promotion opportunities for civil servants and army officers, their support for him would be sure. If he failed on the economic front, he would be likely to fail all along the line. That is why Hitler was prepared to tolerate the continuation of Jewish businesses, to allow Jewish salesmen to remain prominent in the export trade until 1938, and to make use of unorthodox financial management to achieve a rapid reduction of the unemployed; real incomes would cease to fall.

Between March 1933 and March 1934 unemployment fell by over 2 million, in part but not wholly due to the ending of recession. Able men served Hitler, including the brilliant financial expert, Hjalmar Schacht, whom the Führer appointed president of the Reichsbank. Plans worked out in advance by Hitler's economic advisers were now put into action. With guaranteed prices for their produce, farmers recovered during the first three years of the regime; small businesses were helped with state spending; taxes were reduced; grants were made to industry to install new machinery; work was created in slum clearance and housing and *Autobahn* construction. The economy was stimulated out of recession. Though wages did not rise in real terms, security of employment was a greater benefit for the wage-earners. The pursuit of autarky or self-sufficiency helped the construction, chemical, coal and iron and steel industries. The industrialists welcomed the opportunities for expansion and increased profit and applauded the destruction of free trade unions. But industry lost its independence as its barons became dependent on state orders and state allocation of resources. The First and Second Four-Year Plans imposed state controls severely limiting the capitalist economy. Armament expenditure remained relatively low from 1933 to 1935, but from then on was rapidly increased, putting Germany on a war footing and eliminating unemployment. Belts had to be tightened, – 'guns before butter' – but it was too late for any opposition to loosen the Nazi hold on power; there was in any case no opposition that could any longer command a mass following.

By 1934 Hitler's regime had established a sufficient base of power and secured enough willing co-operation of 'experts' in the administration, business and industry as well as the army for his Nazi state to function, though often with much confusion. The Nazi ideologues and fanatics had formed an alliance with the educated and skilled who served them. Without them the Nazis could not have ruled Germany. What German history of this period shows is that parliamentary democracy and the rule of law, once established, will not inevitably continue. If they are not defended, they can be destroyed – not only by violent revolution, but more subtly by determined and ruthless men adopting pseudo-legal tactics.

And what of the outside world – they too not only gave Hitler the concessions he demanded or unilaterally took by breaking treaties but in 1936 handed him the spectacular triumph of holding the Olympic Games, dedicated to freedom and democracy, in Berlin.

CHAPTER 22

The Mounting Conflict in Eastern Asia, 1928–1937

It is often said that the Second World War began in China in 1931. According to this view the global rise of fascism first blossomed into external aggression when Japan attacked China; then the tide of war spread to Europe and Africa, to Abyssinia and Spain, until Hitler unleashed the Second World War by marching into Poland in 1939. Undeniably there was some interdependence of European and Asian events in the 1930s. Britain and the United States were in a sense sandwiched between conflicts on the European continent and eastern Asia, with vast interests bound up in the future of both worlds, West and East. But to view the earlier history of eastern Asia from the point of view of the European war of 1939 is to see that history from a Western focus, and thus to distort it. The problems of eastern Asia were coming to a head irrespective of the rise of fascism and Nazism. The problems of Europe, too, had entirely independent roots. 'Interdependence' between Asia and Europe before the critical months of 1940 and 1941 has thus been exaggerated.

It is important to recognise also that seen through Japanese and Chinese eyes Western policies appeared to change with confusing rapidity in the first three decades of the twentieth century. Conscious of their military and industrial weakness in comparison with the West, the Chinese and Japanese accordingly had to calculate how best to adapt to constantly shifting external conditions. Critical too was the question of what their relationship to each other should be. All these problems arising from 'modernisation' and changing external and internal Asian relationships were to reach explosive intensity during the 1930s. The different strands can be seen more clearly if separated.

In Japan the orderly coherent structure of national government and decision-making began to fall apart in 1930. Extremism and lawlessness and a decentralisation of power occurred. Japan's disintegration was political and internal. In China there was physical disintegration. No 'government' of the 'republic' of China could rule the whole vast country. Foreign control had been established over China's principal ports during the nineteenth and twentieth century and over Manchuria, Outer Mongolia and Tibet. To add to these setbacks Chiang Kai-shek and his Kuomintang Party became involved in civil war after breaking with the communists. Then there were constant conflicts between the greater and lesser warlords who ruled much of China as military–feudal commanders in the 1930s. Chiang Kai-shek fought some of these warlords but was never strong enough really to control them or their armies. Most made their peace with him, however, by assenting to nominal allegiance to Chiang Kai-shek and his government of the Republic of China, while continuing to rule independently over their fiefs large and small.

From 1928 to 1937, while Chiang Kai-shek established his capital and government in Nanking, no unified Chinese republic really existed; his reforms had made an impact on urban life but did not reach millions of peasants. His vision of a unified China which as yet bore no relationship to reality. To the Western world he nevertheless embodied China; his ambassadors were accredited to other countries and represented China at the League of Nations in Geneva. Here it was that Chiang Kai-shek sought to mobilise the help of the Western powers when in 1931 the Japanese began transforming their special rights in Manchuria into outright occupation and control of the whole province. The issue appeared to be a simple one for the Western powers of supporting the League and China against Japanese aggression. The contrast between the real condition of China and her international legal position, together with her image in the eyes of the public in the Western world, was one critical factor in the eastern Asia crisis of the 1930s.

The struggle between a central power claiming to speak for and to rule China and regional and provincial rulers was nothing new in modern Chinese history; or, to put it more briefly, the contest between integration and disintegration had been going on for decades and continued until 1949. China's chronic weakness had allowed the European powers to establish colonies and special rights in Shanghai and other treaty ports. Since the beginning of the century the Japanese leaders had been conscious of a great divide in their options for a China policy. Japan could identify with China as a fellow Asian nation and help her to achieve independence from the 'white' imperialists; or she could copy the Western imperialists and join them in acquiring colonial possessions and 'spheres of influence' in China. To combine with China after dominating her meant certain conflict with the more powerful Western powers. Japan's best interests seemed to be served by emulating the Western powers and joining in the scramble for China. This meant participating fully in Western great-power diplomacy, which Japan did when concluding an alliance with Britain in 1902. Britain for her part welcomed the Japanese alliance to check Russia and to preserve her own position in China. After the Russo-Japanese war three years later Japan acquired her own considerable empire by annexing Korea and by replacing Russia and carving out a sphere of interest in southern Manchuria. During the next fifteen years the Japanese sought to extend their influence in northern China in agreement with the Russians and at China's expense. The First World War gave Japan her biggest opportunity and for the first time her ambition now encompassed controlling the government of China itself. But hostile Chinese and international reactions forced the Japanese to withdraw from these extreme pretensions. This was a blow. Worse was the army's profitless Siberian intervention from 1918 to 1922. It had brought neither glory nor gain.

The Japanese in the 1920s then appeared ready to limit their empire to what they already held with the acknowledgement of the Western powers, and beyond this to work with the Western powers within an agreed framework of international treaties, military and territorial. At the Washington Conference of 1921–2 this framework was set up. Japan, as has been noted (page 149), accepted an inferior ratio of battleships to Britain and the United States (3:5:5), but this inferiority was counterbalanced by the agreement of Britain and the United States not to build any naval bases in the Western Pacific. Then the Japanese also signed the Nine-Power Treaty (1922) whereby the powers undertook 'to respect the sovereignty, the independence, and the territorial and the administrative integrity of China', and not to take 'advantage of conditions in China' to seek special rights or create 'spheres of influence'. But what of existing rights? The Western powers were not about to relinquish their rights in Shanghai. Japan also interpreted the treaty as not affecting her existing rights and 'special interests' which, the United States had acknowledged in the past, she should exercise wherever her own territories were close to China's.

Since the opening of the twentieth century the United States had tried to secure the consent of the other powers with interests in China to two propositions. First, they should allow equal economic opportunity to all foreign nations wishing to trade in China (the Open Door). The behaviour of the foreign nations, however, showed that this 'equal opportunity' was not extended to the Chinese themselves, who did not exercise sovereign power over all Chinese territory. Secondly, the United States urged that China should not be further partitioned (respect for sovereignty and territorial integrity), but in practice the United States had acknowledged Japan's special rights and spheres of influence. The second proposition was more a moral hope than real politics. These principles nevertheless were not abandoned. They were reasserted in the 1920s and 1930s.

For Japan, the Washington treaties of 1921–2

stabilised international conduct towards disintegrating China and lessened the chance of conflict with the Western powers. Japan would now maintain her existing rights against a new possible threat, Bolshevik Russia, without fear of conflict with Britain and the United States. A third reason for Japan's peaceful adaptation to the entirely new post-war world was her inability to compete in a naval race with the United States. Japanese finances were exhausted. Japan was dependent on the West to a degree matched by few modern nations. Her capacity to modernise was at the mercy of the Western powers, especially the United States. A Japanese journalist in 1929 summed up Japan's position, reflecting views widely held at the time: 'Japan is a country whose territory is small and whose resources are scarce. It has to depend upon other countries for securing such materials. Furthermore, to sustain the livelihood of its excessive population, Japan finds it imperative to place a high priority upon exporting its products abroad.'

Yet surprisingly the worldwide depression hit Japan less seriously than the West. Japan had an industrious and well-organised people to further economic progress. With the help of a large devaluation of her currency, she had pulled out of the slump by 1932. But now the need for capital, especially from the United States, and for raw materials (cotton, coal, iron ore and oil) from abroad became increasingly essential. The Japanese believed that their own continued economic existence, the ability of the nation to progress, depended on developing the resources of Manchuria (where the Japanese could secure some of the raw materials they needed) and on continued access to the American market. The heavy rearmament programme launched in 1936 and the needs of the military in China, moreover, could not be sustained without American imports of scrap metal and oil. Thus the poverty of resources was Japan's heel of Achilles.

Recognition of this weakness united the Japanese leadership in the military, business, diplomacy, bureaucracy and politics in one aim: that Japan had to maintain her economic empire in China. Four-fifths of all her overseas investment at the close of 1929 were in China. On the importance of China there was no difference between the 'pacific' 1920s and the militaristic 1930s. The rift occurred between the leaders who argued that Japan could achieve this while staying within the legal framework of treaties and concessions held in common with the West, and those who wished to extend the Japanese economic empire not only at China's expense but regardless too of Western economic interests in China. The whole of eastern Asia and south-eastern Asia would become a Japanese-dominated empire serving Japan's interests under the high-sounding guise of a co-operative Japanese commonwealth of Asian nations called the Greater Asia Co-prosperity Sphere. Foreign Minister Matsuoka of the later 1930s, looking at Western behaviour with its earlier emphasis on imperialism and its later support for the League of Nations, simply derided it as a cynical way of changing the rules of international law to suit the West's own selfish interests. 'The Western Powers had taught the Japanese the game of poker,' he once remarked, but then, 'after acquiring most of the chips they pronounced the game immoral and took up contract bridge.'

One significant strand in Japanese thinking about the world was the belief that only by her own endeavours would Japan be accepted as an equal of the 'white' world powers, which did not treat her as an equal. She was still in the process of catching up militarily and industrially with the leading Western nations; to survive among the world powers she must grow in strength or go under. Since the days of Meiji, Japan, for all her later talk of Asian co-operation against the West, did not seek a new role as the leading anti-imperialist nation; she wanted to join the imperialist powers and foresaw a partition of the whole world among them. In that partition Japan and her empire would dominate Asia. Now inevitably this set her on a collision course with Western possessions and economic interests in Asia. Against the European imperialist nations, Japan, though weaker than their combined strength, had a chance of success. Just as the weaker United States in the eighteenth century had made herself dominant in the Western hemisphere – a parallel not lost on Japan – by taking advantage of Europe's distress, of Europe's great internecine wars, so Japan in the twentieth century would profit from the conflicts of Europe. But unlike in the eighteenth century, there was one great power not so affected by these conflicts and standing aside from them and that was the United States. The fulfilment of Japanese ambitions came to depend on the United States.

American policy in Asia in the twentieth century

has been beset by some confusion and contradictions. Paradoxically, one basic tenet of American policy – to uphold the unity and national independence of China in the face of Japanese and European ambitions of piecemeal territorial partition – triumphed in 1949 with the communist victory. For the first time in the century the Chinese mainland was then fused into a genuine national unity. What the Americans had always maintained, that China rightly belonged to the Chinese, had come about. China was set on the road to joining the world's great nations. Only a vestigial presence today remains of the former Western imperial era – Portuguese Macao and British Hong Kong – and both outposts are due to return to full Chinese control by the end of the century. The Chinese became masters of their own internal economic development, their trading relations and their policy towards the outside world. The fulfilment of the Americans' objectives was followed by more than two decades of bitter dispute between the United States and China, including war in Korea. One reason for past ambiguities in US policy was that it was rooted in the genuine desire for eventual Chinese unity on the one hand and equal commercial opportunities for all Western powers on the other. During the 1920s and 1930s the United States was determined to participate in a share of China's market, whose potential was believed to be of critical importance for future Western prosperity.

In 1930 American investment in China, concentrated in Shanghai, was less than American investment in Japan. The Japanese had also acquired rights and privileges, especially in southern Manchuria, based on the Japanese control of the south Manchurian railway and the concessions that went with it. But these rights in Manchuria could not compare with the outright colonial possessions of the European powers acquired by force from a weak China in the nineteenth century, or the semi-colonial 'extra-territorial rights' which the Europeans and Japanese enjoyed in the treaty ports. In southern Manchuria, Japanese control was not absolute but had to be attained by manipulating China's difficulties and working through the local Manchurian warlord. Thus, what came to be regarded as the 'nation's lifeline' was threatened by chaotic conditions and the internal conflicts of China. The Japanese in the 1920s considered China's claims to Manchuria to be purely nominal, arguing that without Japan's defeat of Russia Manchuria would have been annexed by Russia in 1905 and that Japan's presence in Manchuria for a quarter of a century had ensured peace there. That was not the view of the United States, which upheld China's sovereignty over Manchuria; it should be preserved for a future time when China had overcome her internal problems.

But successive American presidents from Theodore to Franklin Roosevelt never contemplated the possibility that America's commercial or strategic interests were sufficiently large in China to justify the United States' defending them by force of arms and so risking war with Japan. It was not in defence of *American* interests in China that the Pacific War of 1941 to 1945 was fought. For Franklin Roosevelt much wider and more fundamental issues were at stake. These were based on American ideological assumptions which were neither shared nor understood in Japan. The fascinating account of American – Japanese relations from 1939 to 1941 needs to be told later where it belongs chronologically (pages 271–9).

With the onset of the depression after 1927, Japan was beset by additional problems. Though industry recovered more quickly than elsewhere in the world, the farmers suffered severely. The domestic silk industry provided an important additional income for the peasantry and the price of silk plunged in the United States. The countryside became the breeding ground for militarism. A strident nationalism, a sort of super Japanese patriotism with a return to emperor-worship, marks the 1930s. It unified most of the Japanese people. Harsh repression in any case ensured broad conformity, and the educational system was geared to uphold military national values. The more 'liberal' tendencies of the 1920s, which saw a strengthening of the Diet, of political parties, of the influence of big business (the *zaibatsu*) on politics, of the civilian politicians as against the military, was engulfed by the new militaristic nationalism.

All these changes occurred without any formal changes in the Meiji constitution. It had never been a part of that constitution to guarantee personal liberties and thereby to limit the powers of the state. Whenever necessary, censorship and control were instituted. The Japanese were taught to obey the state, and patriotism centred on the veneration of the emperor. But it was characteristic of formal

Japanese institutions and laws that they allowed for enormous flexibility and change in practice. The fount of all power, however, remained the emperor. This meant that whichever group succeeded in speaking in his name could wrap itself in his unchallengeable authority. The Meiji Emperor had taken a real role in the decisions of crucial national policies on the advice of his elder statesmen, the *genro*. The position of his successors was weaker. Emperor Hirohito was elevated to an object of worship and, as a god, was thereby moved away from practical influence on national affairs. Temperamentally gentle and scholarly, the emperor followed rather than controlled the tide of events.

But, despite the introduction of universal male suffrage, Japan was not about to turn into a parliamentary constitutional state in the 1920s. She was ruled from above. Her uniqueness as a society, blending emperor-worship and authority with elected institutions, would not be essentially changed by any democratic demands. A Peace Preservation Law imposed severe prison penalties on anyone who even advocated such a change. So the description of the 1920s as the years of Taisho Democracy is a misnomer. The people were not prepared or encouraged to think that they should decide the policies of the state through their elected parties in the parliament. Thus the political parties had no real roots and were the easy victims of military reaction in the 1930s.

There was of course a real difference between the policies pursued by the Japanese in the 1920s and those followed in the 1930s. That difference was due to the change of balance among the groups that exercised power in the state. The army and navy were not subject to the control of the government but, through the right of separate access to the emperor, constituted a separate position of power. The informal *genro* had co-ordinated civilian and military aspects of national affairs. With the passing of the original *genro* through the deaths of its members, no other body advising the emperor was ever again able to exercise such undisputed overall control. The civilian politicians, leaning for support on parliament and backed by some moderates in the army and navy, in the 1920s seemed to have gained the upper hand over the more extreme officers in the navy and army. This split in the military between extremists and moderates indeed made possible their predominance. It found expression in Shidehara's foreign policy and especially in the naval disarmament treaties of the Washington Conference. But both in the Kwantung army stationed in Manchuria and in the navy a violent reaction to civilian control was forming.

From 1928 until 1936 the leadership groups were caught in cross-currents of violent conflict. They were no longer able to provide a unified Japanese policy. So there is the contrast between the outwardly unified nation embodied in the emperor's supremacy and the breakdown of government culminating in the assassination of those politicians who had fallen foul of nationalist extremists. The army was no longer under unified control. The army command in Tokyo was rent by conspiracies to encourage the Kwantung army to act on its own in Manchuria regardless of the policy of the government. In 1928 the Kwantung army attempted to seize military control over Manchuria and so to anticipate Chiang Kai-shek's attempts to extend his rule by conquest or diplomacy. Chiang Kai-shek might decide to strike a deal with the Manchurian warlord at the expense of Japan's ambitions. The Japanese Kwantung Army Command organised the warlord's murder by blowing up the train on which he was travelling. Although at the time there was an aggressive Japanese government in power in Tokyo which was certainly ready to use military force in China to prevent northern China from falling under Chiang Kai-shek's control, the Kwantung army had overreached itself and its attempt to take over Manchuria was disavowed. The murdered warlord's son took over control of the Chinese Manchurian administration and army. A much more moderate Japanese government came to power in 1929 and the pacific Shidehara returned to the Foreign Ministry. The army smarted under its humiliation. But the Kwantung army was not punished – the colonel in command was merely retired – and two years later, in September 1931, it struck again more effectively.

Meanwhile the new Cabinet of Prime Minister Hamaguchi was soon involved in a confrontation with the navy. The government had consented to a new treaty of naval limitation at the London Conference of 1930, this time applying to cruisers. The Japanese navy had not secured the ratio of cruisers which the Chief of the Naval General Staff, Admiral Kato Kanji, and those naval officers who supported him considered indispensable. The Navy Minister, another admiral, supported the Prime Minister, who won after months of bitter debate.

The split into factions even within the armed services themselves is illustrated by this whole episode. It ended tragically when a nationalist fanatic shot Hamaguchi, who lingered several months before succumbing to his wounds.

In September 1931 the insubordination of the Kwantung garrison army in Manchuria attracted the attention of the world. Its plot to seize Manchuria by force from theoretical Chinese suzerainty and the warlord's actual control was an ill-kept secret. The government in Tokyo was powerless. Shidehara received worthless assurances from the War Minister that the plot would be quashed. In fact there was sympathy within the Army General Staff for the plotters. During the night of 18 and 19 September the Japanese themselves blew up the tracks of the South Manchurian Railway just outside Mukden in Manchuria. On this flimsy pretext the Kwantung army attacked the Chinese and occupied Mukden. The Japanese army in Korea now concerted with the Kwantung army and units crossed into Manchuria. Soon the whole of Manchuria was under military administration.

If this action had been the work of only the middle-ranking subordinate officers of the Kwantung army, as was thought for a long time to be the case, then the government in Tokyo might have re-established its authority. We now know that this authority had already been severely undermined by the lack of confidence of the military in the general course of policy adopted. The conspiracy at Mukden extended to the army leadership in Tokyo. Government was disintegrating. Shidehara tried to hide this fact from the outside world and to make the diplomatic best of it. The difficulty which Shidehara and the politicians, supported by big business, faced was also in part self-made. While they strongly disapproved of the armies' insubordination and interference in politics, as well as their resort to force, they held in common with the army the belief in Japan's China destiny. The army was pursuing essentially the same goals as they. Only their means differed.

Internally the army was out of control and followed its own policy of solving Japan's China policy by force. In February 1932 it set up a puppet state which it called Manchukuo and so declared that Manchuria was severed from Chinese sovereignty. Then it placed the last boy emperor of the ousted Manchu dynasty, with the unlikely name of Henry Pu-yi, on the puppet throne. Possibly the motive for this bizarre move was to have a useful symbol under their control who might be put forward as a Japanese-backed emperor of China. What is certain is that during the next few years the army's ambitions were not limited to securing Japan's rights in southern Manchuria. The Kwantung army was soon extending Japanese influence beyond Manchuria, which was completely conquered by 1933. The Great Wall, the ancient traditional defensive boundary which the Chinese had built to keep out the northern barbarians, proved no barrier to the Japanese. The Japanese army crossed the Great Wall along the railway line running from Mukden in Manchuria to Peking.

Chiang Kai-shek's Nationalist government was far too weak to oppose the Kwantung army by force. In many provinces warlords persisted in exercising power and the communists, from the bases they had established, disputed the Kuomintang's right to speak for and unite China. Resistance against Japan would be hopeless unless China could first be effectively united, and this became Chiang Kai-shek's first priority. He was therefore glad of a truce, which the Japanese were ready to conclude with the Nationalist government in May 1933. Chiang Kai-shek concentrated his forces against the communist stronghold in the south, to crush peasant uprisings and the Red Army. He almost succeeded in the autumn of 1934. But the Red Army broke through the encircling Nationalist armies and set out on the epic Long March, a military manoeuvre without parallel in the annals of history. The Red Army and the communist political and administrative cadres, about 80,000 people in all, sought safety from the pursuing Nationalist forces by walking a long circuitous route to the last-surviving communist base in the north-west of China. They had to fight all the way. The distance which this army covered, through mountains and swamps, in heat and freezing cold, was almost 6000 miles. The Long March took just over a year to accomplish and of the 80,000 who had set out possibly only 9000 reached Yan'an in Shaanxi in October 1935, though others joined on the way. In this province Mao Zedong then rebuilt the communist movement from an initial nucleus of 20,000 to the eventual millions that drove Chiang Kai-shek's armies from the mainland in 1949.

The Kwantung army meanwhile was not idle. It was rapidly expanded from 10,000 officers and men in 1931 to 164,000 in 1935 and by 1941 it had

Chinese Communist leader Mao Zedong on the arduous Long March of nearly 6000 miles, 16 October 1934–20 October 1935. Of the 80,000 who set out, only some 9000 reached the sanctuary of Yan'an.

reached an astonishing strength of 700,000. These figures alone provide a graphic illustration of the escalation of Japan's military effort in China. Chiang Kai-shek did not declare war on the Japanese; nor did the Tangku truce in May 1933 between the Nationalist Chinese and the Japanese stop the Kwantung army. By the end of 1935 large regions of northern China and Inner Mongolia were occupied. This brought the Japanese army into contact with the Soviet Union along hundreds of miles of new frontier. The Kwantung army regarded Soviet Russia as the real menace to Japan's aspirations in eastern Asia: Russia alone could put a modern army of millions into the field of battle on land. The Chinese the Japanese disregarded as a serious military force. But just because there were no real obstacles to expansion in China, it was difficult for the Army General Staff to decide where to stop. They argued that the war in China should be limited so that the army could concentrate on the Soviet Union. Other officers wanted first to expand in China. It was the latter who won out in July 1937 when a clash of local Chinese and Japanese troops on the Marco Polo Bridge outside Peking became the Japanese excuse for launching a full-scale war on China.

Chiang Kai-shek had used the years from 1933 to 1937 to consolidate the power of the Kuomintang in the rest of China with some success. But the Western image of republican Chinese democracy was removed from reality. Chiang's regime was totalitarian, with its own gangs and terror police and an army held together by fear and harsh discipline. Supported by intellectuals as the only rallying point for anti-Japanese resistance, and by big business and the landlords as the bulwark against communism, Chiang ruled the country through harshness and corruption. The peasantry were the principal and most numerous victims. Chiang prided himself on having copied techniques of government from Mussolini and Hitler. German military advisers were attached to his army. He also cultivated American friendship by his attitude to business and his welcome to American educators and missionaries. The achievements of the Kuomintang in modernising China during a decade of reforms from 1928 to 1937 also should not be overlooked. Industry grew, communications improved, new agricultural techniques raised produce, education was extended. The cities benefited the most. Tens of millions of peasants, however, remained sunk in abject poverty. Further progress in modernising and unifying China was terminated by the all-out war launched by Japan in 1937.

The educated elite in particular displayed a sense of national pride in the face of internal conflicts and foreign aggression. Trade boycotts were organised against the Japanese and students demonstrated. Groups argued that the Kuomintang and the communists should form a new united front to fight the Japanese. Chiang Kai-shek's priority, however, was to follow Mao to the base he had recently set up in Yenan and smash the 'bandits', before turning to meet the Japanese aggression. He sent Zhang Xueliang, called the Young Marshal, to Xi'an in the province of Shensi with the intention that he should march his troops to Yenan and liquidate the communist stronghold. What happened then is one of the most astonishing episodes in the Chinese war. The Young Marshal installed in Xi'an with his army had ideas of his own. Mao skilfully undermined his loyalty to Chiang Kai-shek appealing to him to make common front against the Japanese. The Young Marshal then looked for allies and sought the support of the powerful warlord in the neighbouring Shansi province; he found him guarded but not unsympathetic. When in October 1936 Chiang Kai-shek left

Nanking and flew to Xi'an to rally the generals against the communist 'traitors' the response was lukewarm. So in early December 1936 Chiang Kai-shek returned to Xi'an hoping for better success.

The Young Marshal now brought matters to a head. He probably saw himself as replacing Chiang Kai-shek in a united national movement against the Japanese who were starting a full-scale military drive in the north. On 12 December the Young Marshal's troops stormed Chiang's headquarters just outside Xian, killed many of his bodyguards and took Chiang Kai-shek himself captive. Two weeks later he was released and allowed to fly back to Nanking. He owed his release, and possibly his life, to the intervention of Mao Zedong. It was an extraordinary turn of events. Mao had received a telegram from Moscow conveying Stalin's advice that Mao should form a united front with Chiang Kai-shek against the Japanese. Mao sent Zhou Enlai to Xi'an to negotiate, to propose that the communists unite in the fight against the Japanese with Chiang Kai-shek and to offer to subordinate their forces. Zhou Enlai also persuaded the Young Marshal that Chiang Kai-shek was the only possible leader of a 'united' China. A formal communist offer in February 1937 was not officially accepted by Chiang Kai-shek, but the military effort of the Kuomintang did switch to resisting the Japanese.

As for the Young Marshal, he was arrested and imprisoned. But the 'Xi'an incident' did mark the beginning of cooperation at least in theory between the Kuomintang and Mao's communist forces. After the Japanese had resumed a full-scale war in the summer of 1937, the two sides reached agreement that the 30,000 soldiers of the Chinese Red Army should become the Eighth Route Army under nominal Kuomintang control. It was not a union of spirit, but a tactical move on both fronts and Mao retained control of the communist base areas.

Of all the Western powers, Britain had most at stake in China. Her total trade and commercial investment in China were very large in 1930, just exceeding Japan's. Together, Britain and Japan dominated all foreign investment in China, accounting for 72 per cent of the total. The United States' investment was far behind at 6 per cent, about the same as France's. No other power had any significant investment. The most sensitive point of Western interests and influence was the great city of Shanghai. The Western powers and the Japanese held 'concessions' there which virtually removed the heart of the city and its port from Chinese control. In January 1932 the Japanese bombed the Chinese district, army reinforcements attacked the Chinese parts of Shanghai, meeting fierce resistance from a Chinese army.

The conflict in China was now brought home to the ordinary people in the West. For the first time the cinema newsreels showed the effects of modern warfare. People were horrified by the sufferings inflicted on civilian populations and by the terror bombing from Japanese planes on the hapless Chinese. This new image of war, which was to become even more familiar after the outbreak of the Spanish Civil War in 1936, had a tremendous impact on public opinion. It produced contradictory currents. It provoked a revulsion against war, thus underpinning later attempts at conciliating Hitler in Europe. The public also identified with the sufferers and therefore cast attackers in the role of aggressors to be stopped. China was seen as the innocent victim. The Japanese did incalculable harm to their cause by adopting such a ruthless style of warfare within the range of Western cameramen.

When the League of Nations met to consider China's appeal immediately after the Japanese launched their operation in Manchuria, public opinion in the West sided with China. There was an element of wishful thinking that the League of Nations would be able to punish the aggressor by using the machinery of sanctions set up to provide for collective security. Governments were urged to support the League. But the League of Nations could not fulfil such unrealistic expectations. To oppose Japan by military force on the Chinese mainland would have required an enormous military effort. Who would be ready in the midst of deep depression to raise and supply the large armies? Alternatively, by a great effort and with large funds the Chinese armies might be better equipped and led. Germany was doing all she could in providing military advice to Chiang Kai-shek's forces. The political divisions of China, however, made it difficult in 1932 and 1933 to conceive of any effective check on Japan.

The British Foreign Office and the American State Department had a more realistic appreciation of the situation. With so much at stake, the British attitude to Japan was ambiguous. Chinese nationalism threatened Britain's imperialist interests as much as Japan's. In the United States it was clear from the start that American material interests were not sufficient to justify the possibility of conflict with Japan or even a trade embargo, which would have deeply injured Japan. That remained the view of official America throughout the 1930s. Yet there was a genuine sense of outrage that Japan had offended against the ethical code that should dictate how she was to conduct her relations with neighbours. She had broken solemn treaties, and this was to be condemned. Secretary of State Henry Stimson issued a famous statement on 7 January 1932 that became known as the Stimson Doctrine – much to President Hoover's chagrin since, he claimed, he had first thought of it. The United States, it declared, would not recognise any treaties or situations brought about in violation of earlier treaties. The United States thus refused to accept all Japanese attempts to regularise her control of Manchuria. The League endorsed this view a little later.

The League of Nations meanwhile had sent Lord Lytton as British chairman of a commission to investigate on the spot Chinese claims and Japanese counter-claims. His report in October 1932 largely condemned the Japanese military action and suggested a compromise solution which would have given Manchuria autonomy while preserving Japanese rights. In February 1933 these recommendations were accepted by the League Assembly; the Japanese delegation thereupon left the League Assembly and never returned. The League of Nations had pinned its hopes on conciliation and when this failed had nothing more to offer in the absence of will on the part of Britain and the United States to back further action. The League suffered greatly in prestige. This in itself did not bring a general war between the other powers nearer; indeed it might have served a useful purpose if the peoples in the democratic countries had thereby gained a greater sense of realism. Too often the call to 'support the League' was believed to be all that was required; it could be comfortably combined with pacifism and a refusal to 'fight for king and country'. Many preferred to believe that they did not need to shoulder the responsibilities of peacekeeping or make the sacrifices required to check aggression – that was the job of the League. An ardent desire for peace and further wishful thinking thus led to blame being transferred to the League of Nations.

In Japan itself the success of the Kwantung army and the failure of the League had important effects too. A wave of patriotism and ultra-nationalism swept the population. Japanese governments now seemed to those Japanese patriots much too cautious. Patriotic secret societies, with sometimes only a few hundred members, sought to influence policy decisively. One method was to assassinate ministers who, in the societies' view, did not follow patriotic policies. Frustrated army officers joined such societies and there were repeated attempts to stage military coups. Several prominent ministers were murdered. This reign of terror did succeed in intimidating many opponents of extremism. The army meanwhile did not try to put its own house in order – at least not until several hundred officers and rebellious troops in February 1936 had seized the whole government quarter of Tokyo and assassinated a number of Cabinet ministers. All this was done in the name of the Emperor. The Japanese navy now played a leading part in putting down the insurrection. But it proved no victory for moderation. From then on, civilian ministers came to be even more dominated by the military. Japan was set on an expansionist course. Although Britain and the United States did not wish to fight Japan, in the last resort the issue of peace with the West would depend on whether Japan's aims in China were limited or whether ambition would drive her on to seek to destroy all Western influence in eastern and southern Asia. That day came perceptibly closer when, in July 1937, the Japanese resumed full-scale warfare with China.

CHAPTER 23

The Crumbling Peace, 1933–1936

In chess what matters is the result, the endgame. The opening moves and the middle play are all directed to achieving such a superiority of position that the endgame is preordained, the annihilation of the opponent. The analogy holds for Hitler's foreign policy. Much confusion of interpretation is avoided if one essential point is grasped: Hitler never lost sight of his goal – wars of conquest that would smash Soviet Russia, and subordinate France and the smaller states of the continent of Europe to the domination of a new Germany. This new order would be based on the concept of race. 'Races' like the Jews were so poisonous that there was literally no place for them in this new Europe. Other inferior races would be handled ruthlessly: the Slavs would not be permitted any national existence and could only hope for a servile status under their Aryan masters. Logically this biological foreign policy could not be confined to Europe alone. From the mastery of the European continent, the global conflict would ensue. Hitler was vague about details; this would be a task for his successors and future generations. But he took some interest in German relations with Japan in the 1930s because he recognised that Japan's war in Asia and threat to British interests could be exploited. He preferred to concentrate on the 'limited' task of gaining mastery of the European continent.

It is interesting to compare Hitler's aims with those of his Weimar and Wilhelmine predecessors. The desire for predominance on the continent of Europe was shared by both Wilhelmine Germany in 1914 and Hitler's Germany of the 1930s. The foreign policy of Weimar's Germany, like Hitler's, included secret rearmament and the objective of restoring German military power by abolishing the restrictions imposed by the Treaty of Versailles. Furthermore, Weimar's foreign policy was ultimately directed towards recovering the territories lost to Poland. (It is difficult to see how this could actually have been achieved without a war on Poland; but as Weimar Germany was not prepared to risk war with Poland's ally, France, it seems unlikely that Weimar's policies could have forced Poland to relinquish territory and her special rights in Danzig.)

Differences between Hitler's policy and earlier policies are also very evident. Wilhelmine Germany was brought to the point of launching war only after years of trying to avoid such a war; she rejected even the notion of 'preventive' war when the opportunity was most favourable, in 1904–5 (page 22). The final decision for war was reached only when the ostensible leader, the Kaiser, desperately and unsuccessfully backtracked, seeking to reverse earlier policies of forcing the tensions of August 1914 to a crisis point in the hope that Russia and France would yield. In 1914, furthermore, an alternative to war was always considered both possible and desirable. War would become unnecessary if the alliance between France and Russia 'encircling' Germany could have been broken by the threat of force alone. Even when Wilhelmine Germany made peace plans in the autumn of 1914 in the flush of early victories, the German leaders did not contemplate the enslavement of peoples or mass murder. Wilhelmine Germany's vision was a utopian one of a prosperous Europe led by a powerful Germany. Her occupation policies, moreover, show that she did not regard non-German people as inferior or as her perpetual enemies. Of course what appeared as utopia to the German leaders, a Pax Germanica, was intolerable to her neighbours.

When we next contrast Hitler's aims with those of Stresemann the differences are equally great. Weimar Germany was not bent on either racialist barbarism or continental domination. The reconciliation with France was genuine, as was Stresemann's assumption that another European war with France and Britain would spell Germany's ruin. A realistic objective, he believed, was for Germany to recover the position she had held as a great power before 1914. To strive for more was to make the mistake that had led other powers to combine against imperial Germany and so had brought about the catastrophic defeat of Germany and the harsh peace. The essence then of Stresemann's diplomacy was to win as much for Germany as possible without provoking the slightest chance of war. It followed that his 'weapon' was to make repeated pleas for trust and reconciliation. He never threatened war. His policy was at times devious but also essentially sincere in that avoidance of war was his real aim. He conducted Weimar's diplomacy with extraordinary skill and considerable success, overcoming many difficulties. Tragically it was Hitler who became the heir of Germany's much improved international position; furthermore he derided Weimar's achievements as the work of the 'November criminals'.

Many historians have commented on Hitler's political skills and on his extraordinary personality, which won the support and allegiance of the majority of German people. This achievement cannot be minimised. But his skill in building up German power and in conducting German foreign policy can very easily be exaggerated. It is a commonplace since the publication of A. J. P. Taylor's *The Origins of the Second World War* to discredit the findings of the Nuremberg War Crimes Tribunal that Hitler and his associates carefully and precisely planned their aggressions culminating in the attack on Poland in September 1939. It is true that Hitler was following no such *precise* and *detailed* plan of aggression. He clearly reacted to events and, as the documents show, was ready at times to be flexible when it came to timing and detail. After all he could not totally disregard contemporary circumstances or the policies of the other powers, nor could he foretell what opportunities would arise for Germany to exploit.

But all this does not lead to the opposite conclusion that he had no plan. That is totally to misunderstand Hitler. No one can read *Mein Kampf*, or his other writings and the few existing documents expressing his views, without being struck by their general consistency. His actions, moreover, conformed to the broad plans he laid down. This was no mere coincidence. Unlike his predecessors, Hitler was working towards one clear goal: a war, or several wars, which would enable Germany to conquer the continent of Europe. Once a dictator has acquired sufficient power internally there is nothing difficult about launching a war. The difficulty lies in winning it, and in getting right the timing of aggression. The task of preserving peace, of solving conflicts, of deciding when war cannot be avoided because of the ambitions and aggressions of other nations – that requires skill and good judgement. Hitler was not prepared to compromise his ultimate goal. Only to a very limited degree, as will be seen, was he prepared to modify the steps by which he intended to attain this goal. Hitler showed a greater degree of skill as a propagandist by hiding his true objectives for a time when in power. His repeated assurances that he was making his 'last territorial demands' fooled some people abroad, as well as the majority of Germans, who certainly did not imagine they would be led again into another war against Britain, France, Russia and the United States.

With hindsight, it is easy to ask and to answer the question why Hitler and resurgent Germany were not stopped before German power had become so formidable that it was too late, except at the cost of a devastating war. Equally, there can be little doubt that British and French policy between the wars and, more especially, in the 1930s was disastrous. But the real interest of these years lies in the contrast between a single-minded Hitler bent on a war of conquest from the start and the reaction of his neighbours who were uncertain of his ultimate intentions, who had to grapple with the problem of how best to meet ill-defined dangers abroad, while facing economic and social difficulties at home. The leaders of the Western democracies, moreover, were incessantly concerned with the problems of domestic political rivalries and divisions within their own parties. In France political divisions had escalated into violence and greatly weakened the capacity of unstable governments to respond decisively to the German danger. In the circumstances it is perhaps all the more remarkable that a real attempt on the level of diplomacy was made by the French to check Hitler. In Britain, despite the overwhelming parliamentary strength won by the nationalist government in 1931, continuing widespread distress and unemployment gave the Conservatives much cause for concern from an electoral point of view. Foreign policy also played a considerable role in the November election of 1935. Baldwin reflected the public mood by simultaneously expressing Conservative support for the League of Nations while reassuring the electorate that there would be no great rearmament. After another electoral victory in 1935, almost as massive as the 1931 landslide, the Conservatives had most to fear from their own supporters, and from one in particular, Winston Churchill, who from the backbenches constantly attacked the government's weak response to German rearmament.

When, on coming to power, Hitler accelerated German rearmament in defiance of the Versailles Treaty, he was in fact taking no real risk. The lack of effective Allied reaction during the period from 1933 to 1935 was not due to the finesse of Hitler or of his diplomats, nor even to Hitler's deceptive speeches proclaiming his peaceful intentions. The brutal nature of the Nazi regime in Germany revealed itself quite clearly to the world with the information leaking out of beatings and concentration camps, and these impressions were reinforced by the exodus of distinguished, mainly Jewish, refugees. Britain tolerated Hitler's illegal actions just as rearmament in the Weimar years had been accepted. France, though much more alarmed than Britain by the development of German military strength, would not take action without the certainty of British support in case such actions should lead to war with Germany. But until 1939 British governments refused to back France unless France herself were attacked by Germany. The French army would have been much stronger than Germany's in 1933 and 1934 at the outset of any war, but France's military and industrial potential for war was much weaker.

It is not quite accurate either to ascribe the failure of the French response to a totally defensive military strategy symbolised by the great Maginot fortress line. It was rather that the French had reached a conclusion diametrically opposite to the Germans. The French did not believe that a lightning strike by her own armies before Germany had a chance to mobilise her greater manpower and industry for war could bring rapid victory. In short, the French abandoned the notion of a limited punitive military action such as they had undertaken in the Ruhr ten years earlier (page 144). Any military response, so the French High Command advised the governments of the day, could lead to general war; therefore, it could not be undertaken without extensive prior mobilisation placing France on a war footing. This left the French governments with no alternative but diplomacy, aimed at aligning allies against Germany in order to exert pressure in time of peace. But no British government was prepared to face another war unless Britain's national interests were clearly imperilled to the point where her very survival as a great power was at stake.

This nexus between the rejection of any limited military response and Britain's and France's perfectly understandable desire to avoid outright war unless there was an attack on their territories, or a clear threat of one, made possible Hitler's rake's progress of treaty violations and aggressions until the serious crisis over Czechoslovakia in September 1938. All Hitler required was the nerve to seize where there would be no resistance. He had only to push against open doors, and occasionally to display temporary hesitations and tactical withdrawals from his original intentions. Even these were probably unnecessary.

A disarmament conference under the auspices of the League was proceeding in Geneva when Hitler came to power. It served as a useful smokescreen for the Nazis. The Germans argued a seemingly reasonable case. It was up to the other powers to disarm to Germany's level, or Germany should be allowed to rearm to theirs. The French could never willingly give their blessing to this proposition, so they were placed in the position of appearing to be the unreasonable power, blocking the progress of negotiations which the British wished to succeed for they had no stomach for increasing armaments expenditure in the depth of the depression. The British argued that some agreement, allowing but limiting German rearmament, was better than none.

The French, however, refused to consent to German rearmament. In fact it made no difference whether the British or the French policy was pursued. In April 1933 the German delegate to the disarmament negotiations confidentially briefed German journalists, telling them that, while Germany hoped to secure the consent of the other powers to a standing army of 600,000, she was building the army up to this size anyway. Hitler was giving rearmament first priority, regardless of the attitude of other nations, though any cover which Anglo-French disagreements gave for his own treaty violations was naturally welcome to him. In June 1933 he happily signed a four-power treaty proposed by Mussolini which bound Britain, France, Germany and Italy, in no more than platitudes of goodwill, to consult with each other within the framework of the League.

In Germany, meanwhile, a National Defence Council had been secretly set up in April 1933 to co-ordinate military planning. It would take time to build up the necessary infrastructure – to set up and equip factories to manufacture large quantities of tanks, planes and the weapons of mechanised warfare. The lack of swift early progress was an inherent problem of complex modern rearmament, as Britain was to discover to her cost later on. So it is erroneous to cite the slow start of German rearmament as good evidence that Hitler was not preparing for war from the beginning. Financial responsibility for providing the regime with all the credit it needed belonged to Hjalmar Schacht, who was appointed head of the Reichsbank by Hitler when the incumbent showed reluctance to abandon orthodox financial practice. Hitler in February 1933 secretly explained to the army generals and to the Nazi elite that the solution to Germany's problems could be found only in the conquest of territory in the east. It is clear that Hitler did not expect France simply to stand by and allow Germany to aggrandise her power in the east. 'I will grind France to powder,' he told the visiting Prime Minister of Hungary in June 1933. But until a superior German military strength could be built up, Hitler explained to his associates, he would have to talk the language of peace. In fact he coupled peaceful gestures, such as offers of friendship to France in the autumn of 1933, with decidedly bellicose action.

Deeds were more convincing than words. In October 1933, in a deliberately aimed blow at the League of Nations, Germany withdrew from the disarmament conference at Geneva and from the League of Nations as well. Hitler then sought approval by a plebiscite and claimed in November that 95 per cent of the German people had expressed their approval in the ballot box. The world is today quite familiar with this device of totalitarian regimes whereby astounding statistical unanimity is expressed. In 1933, it is probable that the majority of Germans believed Hitler's claim. They were undoubtedly elated by Hitler's handling of this aspect of the Versailles diktat – Germany would no longer be pushed around. What followed? An outburst of anger by the other powers? Talk of sanctions? The British government decided Germany should be conciliated and coaxed back to Geneva, and put pressure on the French to make concessions.

Hitler's priorities in 1933 and 1934 were clear: first rearmament and conscription, then a Nazi takeover in Austria and the return of the Saar, and at home the consolidation of power. Although Hitler's next diplomatic move startled Europe it was obvious *Realpolitik*. He wished to weaken the two-front threat posed by the alliance between Poland and France. And so in January 1934 he concluded a non-aggression pact with Poland, thereby renouncing German claims to Danzig and to the Polish corridor, the strip of territory separating East Prussia from the rest of Germany. It was no more than a temporary expedient. It shows how little faith the Poles placed in the French alliance. In April 1934 the French broke off further disarmament discussions with Germany. French political weakness at home after the Stavisky scandal (page 166) turned this apparently new tough stand into an empty gesture. French policy had no teeth. French ministers were under no illusions about Hitler's intentions, but a preventive war before German rearmament had reached an unassailable point was again rejected. So all that was left was diplomacy; but the mood was profoundly pessimistic, and although France would seek closer ties with Britain, little headway was made until 1936.

The Foreign Minister, Louis Barthou, made a determined effort for some months in 1934 to revive France's Eastern and Danubian alliances and alignments of the 1920s and to couple this pressure on Germany with the offer to bind Germany to an 'Eastern Locarno', whereby the Soviet Union, Germany, Poland, Czechoslovakia, the Baltic states and Finland would all guarantee each other's territories and promise to assist one another. This pact was to be linked to the League of Nations. No one can deny that Barthou was a man of real energy, but the idea of an 'Eastern Locarno' was pure moonshine. Hitler had rather cleverly pre-empted Poland's possible involvement. Poland preferred to maintain her own non-aggression treaty with Russia and with Germany and to retain a free hand. Hitler would not agree either. Although he did not feel bound by treaties, he preferred, for the sake of public feeling at home and in order not to antagonise Germany's neighbours prematurely, to sign no unnecessary treaties which he would have to break later on.

More promising was France's rapprochements in 1934 with Russia and with Italy, which were to bear fruit in 1935. Barthou also sought to draw closer to Yugoslavia. His diplomacy was tragically cut short in October 1934 when he met King Alexander in Marseilles. A Croat terrorist assassinated both Alexander and Barthou, an event dramatically captured by the newsreel cameras. His successor, Pierre Laval, who was to play an infamous role in the wartime Vichy government, in 1935 pursued Barthou's policy skilfully. Barthou had wooed Mussolini for Italy's friendship and even an alliance for France. In 1934 and 1935 this was a realistic aim – though Mussolini was notoriously fickle and impulsive – but, militarily speaking, the Italian alliance was of decidedly limited value.

Although Mussolini had hoped that Germany would follow the fascist path of Italy, he was not so sure about Hitler personally. Hitler for his part admired the Duce, who, so he thought, was trying to make something of the Italian people. The Duce was seen by Hitler as a ruthless man of action who like himself believed in superior force. His framed photograph stood on Hitler's desk in Munich in 1931. (Frederick the Great and Bismarck were the two other leaders whom Hitler acknowledged as worthy predecessors.) Mussolini's admiration for Hitler was not uncritical. He patronised him and sent him advice; there were times when Mussolini suspected Hitler might be mad. Many Italian fascists naturally resented Germany's emphasis on Nordic racialism and the supposed superiority of light-skinned blonds over swarthy Latins. In Italy there was no tradition of anti-Semitism. Indeed few Jews lived there. Mussolini's objection to anti-Semitism was not moral; he simply did not believe in the value of Hitler's racial theories and thought that his diatribes against the Jews were impolitic. In June 1934 Mussolini and Hitler met in Venice. Mussolini stage-managed the whole visit to impress Hitler with his superiority. Hitler looked decidedly drab in his raincoat. He was seen to be the junior partner.

They discussed the questions over which German-Italian conflict might arise, the agitation of the German-speaking inhabitants in the South Tyrol and the future of the Austrian Republic. Hitler said he was ready to abandon the Germans of the South Tyrol in the interests of Italian friendship, but Mussolini remained suspicious as the irredentist movement was encouraged by Nazi Party officials. More immediately serious was Hitler's pressure on Chancellor Engelbert Dollfuss to resign and allow an internal takeover by the Austrian Nazi movement. Dollfuss reacted robustly. The Austrian Nazis were now conspiring to seize power.

Austria, with a population of 6.5 million, was one of Europe's smallest nations. Some 3.5 million former German Austrians were now subjects of the Italians and the Czechs. Austria had not exactly been created by the Allies at Paris; she consisted of what was left of the Habsburg Empire after the territories of all the successor states had been decided upon. The Austrian state made very little economic sense with her large capital in Vienna and impoverished provinces incapable of feeding the whole population. Economically the Republic had been kept afloat only by loans arranged through the League of Nations, whose representatives supervised the government's finances. The depression had hit Austria particularly hard and unemployment soared. Not surprisingly it was in Vienna in 1931 that the general European banking collapse began. This impoverished state was also deeply divided politically and socially. Austrian labour was united behind the Social Democratic Party, which supported the parliamentary constitution and rejected the solutions both of revolutionary communism and of fascism. On the right, supported by the Catholic Church, stood the Christian Social Party and groups of right-wing nationalist extremists. For a short while from 1918 to 1920 the Social Democrats had held power. After 1920, although the Social Democrats maintained their strength they no longer commanded an absolute majority. Except for a year from 1929 to 1930, the *Bürgerblock*, a coalition of Christian Socials and Nationalist and Pan-German parties, was in power until the extinction of the multi-party system in 1934. The only issue that united this coalition was a common hatred of labour and socialism.

So deep were the political and social divisions that the danger of civil war was always close. The (Catholic) Christian Socials favoured authoritarian solutions, and their fascist and Nazi allies set up paramilitary organisations such as the SA, the SS and the Heimwehr. The Social Democrats also sought to defend themselves by enrolling armed workers in a Republican Defence Corps. Meanwhile many Austrians regarded their state as a wholly artificial creation; loyalties were provincial rather than national. There were many Austrians who looked towards a union with Germany. Austria's internal problems were exacerbated by her more powerful neighbours. Germany posed a threat to her independence. But Mussolini would defend Austrian independence only if Austria modelled herself on the fascist state. He specifically insisted that the Social Democrats should be excluded from participation in politics. Dollfuss, who became chancellor in May 1932, leant increasingly on the Duce's support against the Nazis. In the spring and summer he banned the Communist Party, the Republican Defence Corps and the Nazis, and a few months later, early in 1934, banned the Social Democrat Party as well. The Social Democrats determined to oppose this attack on their existence. They offered armed resistance when their strongholds were attacked. They were then brutally beaten into submission during a brief civil war in February 1934. Democratic Europe was particularly shocked by the bombardment of the municipal blocks of flats of the workers in Vienna. In fact, Dollfuss had destroyed the one political force able to resist the Nazis, who were the real threat to Austria's independence.

The Austrian Nazi conspiracy to take over power came to fruition in July 1934. The Nazis seized the government buildings in Vienna and forced their way into Dollfuss's office and there murdered him. Although Dollfuss had lost much of the support of the ordinary people, no one rallied to the Nazis. The coup failed. Kurt Schuschnigg was appointed chancellor and promised to continue the policies of Dollfuss. Whether Hitler had connived at this Nazi

Below: *the murdered Austrian Chancellor, Dollfuss, lies in state, July 1934.* Above: *battle-scarred workers' housing in Vienna, during a lull in the civil disturbances of 1934.*

conspiracy and, if so, how far remains uncertain. But, coming as it did just a month after his visit to Venice, Mussolini was outraged and rushed troops to the Brenner frontier, warning Hitler not to interfere in Austria. For a few years longer Austria lived on under Mussolini's protection.

In Britain, the growing turbulence in Europe and in Asia alarmed even a government as committed to pacific solutions as that led by Ramsay MacDonald. Even before Hitler had come to power, the famous 'ten-year rule' was scrapped. It had been adopted in 1919 to save on armaments expenditure and postulated that such expenditure should be based on the assumption that there would be no war for ten years. But there was no real move to rearm for several years after 1932. Throughout the 1920s and in the 1930s, too, every British government, Labour and Conservative, believed that to spend money on arms would worsen Britain's economic plight, making her weaker and less able to resist aggression. It was a perverse and paradoxical conclusion. In February 1933, the Cabinet was informed of the gross military deficiency on land, sea and air caused by a decade of inadequate finance, but the Chancellor of the Exchequer and future Prime Minister, Neville Chamberlain, replied, 'today financial and economic risks are far the most serious and urgent that the country has to face . . . other risks have to be run until the country has had time and opportunity to recuperate and our financial situation to improve.' The depression was Hitler's best ally. When Churchill in Parliament attacked the government's neglect of Britain's security, especially in the air, Anthony Eden, Under Secretary of State at the Foreign Office, replied that the solution was to persuade the French to disarm so that Germany would limit her rearmament. Otherwise 'they could not secure for Europe that period of appeasement which is needed'. And, speaking in Birmingham, Chamberlain added, 'it is our duty by every effort we can make, by every influence we can exert, to compose differences, and to act as mediators to try and devise methods by which other countries may be delivered from this great menace of war'. These speeches from the government side in 1933 encapsulate the main tenets of British policy over the next few years.

Something, but too little, was done for defence. The great fear was that the new form of aerial warfare would lead to devastation and huge civilian casualties. German superiority in the air could thus become a potent form of blackmail. Increased defence spending was accordingly concentrated on the air force. Curiously, though, it was spent not on defensive fighter planes but on bombers. The thinking behind this was that the 'bombers would always get through' anyway. The only credible form of defence was to build up a deterrent bomber force that could carry the war to the enemy. Deterrence was preferable to war. In the Far East, the construction of the Singapore naval base was resumed, even though neglect of the British fleet meant that there would be no warships to send east if trouble simultaneously occurred in Europe. Worst affected by the parsimony of defence expenditure was the British army. In the event of war, only a token force could be despatched to France. This limited military commitment to the defence of the European continent was adhered to by governments and critics until 1939. On the French would rest the main burden of containing Germany on land, even though political conditions in France raised grave doubts about the capacity of the French army to deal with the Germans.

Provided one overlooks many mistaken assumptions, British foreign policy followed its own logic. Both France and Germany needed to be restrained. Britain would mediate between them. Even though Hitler secretly and openly defied treaties, Britain would go far to conciliate Germany and assure her that 'reasonable' rearmament would be acceptable to the other powers. When Eden visited Berlin in February 1934 he attempted to persuade Hitler to return to the League, and thought him sincere in wishing to conclude a disarmament convention. Eden's policy was to gain Hitler's signature to a treaty which would permit German rearmament but also, by its very provisions, place a limit on it. When the British government in July 1934 announced rearmament in the air, the search for an Anglo-German agreement did not slacken. Hitler was outwardly cautious during the six months from the summer of 1934, which opened with the failure of the Nazis in Austria and ended in January 1935 with the holding of the plebiscite in the Saar which would decide that region's future.

The Saar was 'brought home' to the Reich by votes through the ballot box and not by force, under the supervision of the League of Nations. Dr Goebbels had, however, mounted a great propaganda campaign and so ensured a Nazi 'yes' vote of 90 per cent. Hitler's prestige was further enhanced.

In the spring of 1935 Hitler was simply waiting for a good opportunity to announce the reintroduction of conscription and Germany's open repudiation of the military restrictions of the Versailles Treaty. Everyone, of course, already knew that they had been 'secretly' broken for years. Indeed a British defence White Paper, published in March 1935, which justified modest British rearmament by referring to Germany's 'illegal' rearmament, provided the kind of pretext Hitler sought. It was followed by the approval of the French Chamber on 15 March 1935 to extend military service from one to two years. On the very next day Hitler sprang a 'Saturday surprise', repudiated the Locarno Treaties, proclaimed conscription in Germany and 'revealed' the existence of the Luftwaffe. Britain's reaction was characteristically weak. Sir John Simon, the Foreign Secretary, and Anthony Eden, Minister for League Affairs, hastened to Berlin to exchange views with Hitler. The Führer was now ready to receive them. With conscription in the bag, Hitler could afford to be affable. Britain's conciliatory gesture vitiated the meeting of the other Locarno powers at Stresa a short while later in April 1935. Hitler's unilateral breach of Versailles and Locarno was condemned and the need to uphold treaties spelt out in the final communiqué. Significantly Mussolini had lined up with Britain and France and not with Germany. The League then joined in the condemnation.

If Hitler was impressed by this united front – and there is no reason to believe he was much – any apprehensions he might have felt were soon dispelled by the British government. Without consulting her French ally, Britain signified that Germany could also breach the Versailles limitations on her naval development by concluding the Anglo-German Naval Agreement in June 1935. This now permitted Germany to develop her formidable 'pocket' battleships and submarines; all Germany undertook was not to construct a fleet whose total tonnage would exceed 35 per cent of the combined fleets of the British Commonwealth. Even so this treaty also held out the eventual prospect of equality with Britain in submarines. Hitler did not have to push open doors, they were flung open for him. Already Hitler was considering his next step, the remilitarisation of the Rhineland in violation of that part of the Versailles Treaty which France held dear as a guarantee of her own security. Had he moved in the summer of 1935 he would almost certainly have got away with that too – but the cautious streak in his make-up gained the upper hand. There would be a much better opportunity in 1936 when Mussolini was looking for German support instead of opposing her.

The Stresa meeting in April 1935 was not only concerned with Germany. Mussolini was himself planning a breach of the League Covenant, at Abyssinia's expense. The French were willing to connive at Mussolini's aggression. They were searching for a diplomatic bargain to gain Mussolini's support against Hitler. Foreign Minister Laval had paved the way when he visited Rome in January 1935. Mussolini and Laval then agreed that France and Italy would check Hitler's militaristic ambitions. On the question of Abyssinia, Laval appears to have reassured the Duce that France would not impede Italy. But at Stresa Mussolini was left in no doubt about the strength of British public feeling if Italy should attack Abyssinia. The final Stresa communiqué, which upheld the sanctity of treaties and condemned Germany's breach of them, carefully avoided reference to any but *European* conflicts. What was left undone was more important. The powers realised that Hitler's next step would be to remilitarise the Rhineland. But the three Stresa powers, Italy, Britain and France, took no decisions on how this threat might be met in time. The British government remained more anxious to conciliate than to warn.

In the autumn of 1935 Europe's attention was fixed not on Hitler but on Mussolini's war of aggression waged against Abyssinia, the practically defenceless kingdom of Emperor Haile Selassie. Mussolini felt he had adequately prepared the ground diplomatically with France and Britain and that in view of the German danger, which he exploited, the two democracies would acquiesce. The British government, he believed, would defy pro-League outbursts of public opinion. But Mussolini had miscalculated the British government's resolve in an election year. Throughout 1935 he built up a huge army, eventually reaching 650,000 men, with modern weapons and poison gas, to overcome the Abyssinian tribesmen. On 3 October 1935 he launched his war on Abyssinia. The Italian army after some initial success became bogged down. The democratic world admired the plucky resistance of the underdog. At Geneva the League condemned Italy as an aggresor and voted

The World Re-Arms. Armies begin to march again during the 1930s, as the League of Nations and 'collective security' fail to sustain peaceful equilibrium. In Asia, the Japanese invade Manchuria (1931–3) and the Chinese prove no match for them (top). *Then in 1937 they move further into the Chinese heartlands* (left). *Meanwhile, in Africa, Mussolini conquers Abyssinia. The picture* (right) *shows Italian troops entering Gondar, capital of the Amhar province, in 1935.*

for sanctions. But sanctions were not rigidly imposed nor did they include oil, necessary to fuel Italy's war machine. In any case Italy had stockpiled oil in Africa in expectation of sanctions. Sanctions proved an irritant, the main result of which was to create a patriotic reaction in Italy herself.

In Britain in June 1935, Ramsay MacDonald finally retired and Stanley Baldwin became prime minister. Sir Samuel Hoare, who replaced Sir John Simon at the Foreign Office, conferred with Laval in December 1935 on partition plans of Abyssinia which, it was hoped, would bring the war to an end through secret mediation between Mussolini and the Abyssinians. The so-called Hoare-Laval Pact was a 'compromise' plan which would have given Mussolini a large part of Abyssinia. He might well have accepted such a solution but when the French leaked the agreement in Britain there was a great public protest that the League was being betrayed and the aggressor rewarded. The British Cabinet, finding itself in an embarrassing position after fighting an election on the issue of support for the League, placed the blame on Hoare and refused to endorse the proposals he and Laval had agreed upon. Hoare resigned on 19 December 1935. That is how Anthony Eden, who had himself favoured compromise, now inherited the Foreign Office.

Mussolini resumed his military campaign, and his troops occupied Addis Ababa in May 1936. The war was being conducted in the most barbarous fashion. The Abyssinians had no means of defence against air attack or poison gas. The brutality of the Italian occupation and the suppression of tribesmen still resisting in 1937 was a precursor of Nazi terror in occupied Europe during the Second World War. Thousands of defenceless Abyssinians were massacred, while Haile Selassie made his dignified protests in Geneva. The war had brought Mussolini cheap glory, but it also isolated him and drove him to seek closer relations with Germany.

The disunity of the 'Stresa front' made Hitler's next move, the remilitarisation of the Rhineland, even less risky than it appeared to be. Hitler later was to call his boldness in March 1936 the great turning point when he had 'bluffed' the French. It was not a real turning point, but just another step along the road he had already successfully followed. Hitler was looking for a new pretext. The Franco-Soviet pact, concluded in 1934, provided it (page 190). When the French Chamber ratified the treaty, Hitler on 7 March 1936 declared it to be contrary to the Locarno Treaties and ordered the Wehrmacht to move into the demilitarised zone of the Rhineland. In its final timing Hitler's move came as a surprise, but the occupation of the Rhineland had been anticipated and discussed. French ministers were clear they could not react with anything but immediate protests and later on possible recourse to the machinery of League sanctions. The Chief of the Army General Staff, General Maurice Gamelin, insisted that no military moves were possible without prior full-scale mobilisation, placing more than 1 million Frenchmen under arms. He pointed out to the French ministers that there was no immediate striking force available. The British, meanwhile, were not prepared to consider mere German troop movements into the Rhineland zone as sufficient reason for a military counterstroke.

Thus France, rent by internal conflict, could not and Britain would not consider stopping Hitler. Hitler, for his part, was careful to enter the Rhineland with only a small force of lightly armed Wehrmacht troops. Rather like rearmament, the open remilitarisation of the Rhineland had been preceded by 'secret' remilitarisation as the so-called 'police' already stationed in the demilitarised zone were in fact trained infantry. The total force of 'police' and Wehrmacht amounted to less than 40,000 men and could not possibly threaten France.

German troops re-enter the Rhineland in 1936 – with horses still more in evidence than tanks. Here, in Heidelberg, they are greeted with flowers by proud Germans.

But Hitler was not bluffing. He had no intention of accepting defeat had the French marched. It is a myth that all that was required to humiliate Hitler in March 1936 was a French show of strength. In the hastily drawn-up final war plans, the German troops were to withdraw as far as the Ruhr and there to stay and fight. But in view of earlier French political and military decisions it was obvious that the only French counter-moves would be diplomatic.

These counter-moves were handled with skill by the French Foreign Minister, Pierre Flandin. He proposed to the British that economic and military sanctions be applied to force Hitler to withdraw. But Eden was looking for mediation. The British Cabinet had ruled out force. Flandin's sanction plan raised the spectre of war with Germany. But tortuous negotiations in London and Geneva did not this time end entirely without result. The expected League condemnation was the usual empty gesture. But Flandin extracted from the British government an avowal that Britain still stood by her Locarno commitment to France and Belgium. The British Cabinet had been pushed by the French further than it wished to go in the direction of a strictly *defensive* Anglo-French alliance backed up by staff talks in place of the more flexible Locarno agreements (page 137). Arguably, therefore, Hitler had lost more than he gained by his Rhineland coup. There was now a much closer Anglo-French alignment and Britain began to rearm, though still at far too slow a pace. On the debit side, Belgium reverted to absolute neutrality.

Nineteen-thirty-six was to be the year of international goodwill. Berlin was host to the Olympic Games that year. Defiance of treaties and the Nuremberg laws proved no obstacle to the holding of the Games in Berlin. Hitler wanted the world to come to Berlin and admire the National Socialist state. No effort was spared to make the Games a spectacular success. For the duration of the Games

The Berlin Olympic Games, 1936. Fraülein Fleischer has just thrown the javelin further than any other woman. She receives her gold medal and a handshake from the Führer.

anti-Jewish propaganda was toned down in Berlin. Hitler, moreover, assured the Olympic Committee that there would be no discrimination between 'Aryans' and 'non-Aryans'. Even Jewish sporting organisations were allowed to function. It was of course discomfiting that the outstanding athlete of the games was the black Jesse Owens. Nazi commentators explained this success, embarrassing to racial doctrines of superiority, by stressing that blacks were racially lower in the scale of development and hence naturally faster. Nevertheless, for Hitler the holding of the Games in Berlin served as an international recognition of his regime.

CHAPTER 24

The Spanish Civil War and Europe, 1936–1939

The Spanish Civil War, to many contemporaries outside Spain, represented a great struggle between the totalitarian forces of the fascist right against the resistance of the Republic, whose legitimate government was composed of the Popular Front parties defending democracy. The war as it dragged on indeed came to resemble such an ideological contest. This was because, unlike earlier internal Spanish conflicts, the Civil War occurred at a time of deep European division, when fascism, democracy and communism were seen to be moving towards some sort of showdown, which it was thought would decide the fate of Europe. Fascism had spread from Italy to Germany and Eastern Europe. Fascism, so its fervent opponents believed, should be finally stopped in Spain. The battle in Spain was seen as marking the turning point of victory or defeat for the fascists. This was a popular illusion. Governments, communist, democratic or fascist, understood better that events in Spain were a secondary problem. The real question mark hanging over the future of the rest of Europe was how Hitler's Germany and Mussolini's Italy would act in Europe and in Africa. Would they be satisfied with a negotiated revision of the Versailles settlement, or was Europe facing a new contest for supremacy as in 1914–18?

For the major governments of Europe, Spain was a sideshow and policy towards Spain was subordinated to other more important policy objectives. In France and Britain in particular (even in the Soviet Union), there consequently developed a schism between passionate popular feeling, especially among intellectual adherents of the broad left, and governments which appeared incapable of acting against the fascist menace. In Spain, the simple line of ideological division, as seen from abroad, was exploited by both sides since foreign volunteers, and even more so foreign supplies, played a critical part in military success. The warring factions in Spain became known simply as the insurgent Nationalists (the right) and the Loyalists defending the Republic (the left). The battle lines between the parties were not so simple, and the defenders of the Republic, particularly, were deeply divided. On the right the analogy with fascism was not a simple one either. That is not to deny fascist elements in their policies.

The rise of contemporary fascism and communism in the 1920s influenced the political struggle in Spain herself. Mussolini's movement had served as a model to some Spaniards, although the dictator of the 1920s, Primo de Rivera, owed only a slight ideological debt to Mussolini. Socialism and Marxism and anarchism, rather than communism of the Stalinist variety, won adherents in Spain also. But Spanish traditions were strong too. Although political contest assumed some of the forms of the great European ideological schisms of the twentieth century, its roots lay also in the conditions of Spain and in the evolution of past social and political tensions. In searching for the origins of the Civil War the purely Spanish causes always lie just under the surface and explain why in 1936 Spain was split into two warring sides which inflicted savage cruelties on each other during the course of the conflict.

In the north the Republicans held most of Asturias and the Basque region; Catalonia, with the large city of Barcelona, became a Republican stronghold; Valencia and the whole Mediterranean coast and central Spain, the eastern regions of Andalucia and New Castile with the capital of Madrid were also Republican regions. The other bigger cities, except for Seville and Saragossa, were republican too. Western Spain, western Aragon, Old Castile, León and the south – mainly the arid and agricultural regions of Spain – fell into the hands of the Nationalists. Within each of the regions of Spain controlled by Nationalists and Republicans, there were minorities who adhered to the opposite side and so were subject to murderous reprisals. The Church, an object of Republican hatred, suffered grievously in the Republican areas. Landless peasants recruited in the south by the socialists and anarchists were exposed to Nationalist terror.

If we look back no further than to the nineteenth century, the contest over how Spain was to be governed was already splitting the country and leading to civil wars. The more extreme monarchists, supported by the Church, fought the constitutionalists and liberal monarchists who then enjoyed the support of much of the army. Superimposed on this constitutional conflict was the desire of the northern regions for autonomy: they opposed attempts to centralise and unify these regions which enjoyed extensive local rights and traditions. Spain's internal turbulence did not come to an end during the last quarter of the nineteenth century with the establishment of the constitutional monarchy and the granting of universal male suffrage. The votes of the peasants in the countryside were managed by the wealthy and by local men of influence. Despite the liberal constitution, the parliamentary system did not embody the hopes of all the reformers: rather the whole parliamentary democracy appeared something of a sham. Popular discontent was further increased by Spain's poor showing abroad. The loss of colonies, the war with the United States at the turn of the century and the failures of her imperial policies in Morocco, where the Spanish army also suffered defeats, weakened the authority of government.

Besides the constitutional conflict, the problem of the regions and the failures of foreign and imperial policies, Spanish industrialisation, though slow, was concentrated in the north and so added to regional particularism as well as leading to bitter economic conflict between worker and employer. Spain was a very poor country, and suffered perennially from the agricultural problem of her landless and impoverished peasantry. In the early twentieth century, socialism made headway in Spain. As in France, the movement was divided and the anarcho-syndicalists who believed in direct action had won many adherents among the workers of the north and some of the peasants in the south. The strength of their main trade union organisation, the CNT, lay in Catalonia and especially in Barcelona. (Before 1936, however, the Communist Party was small.)

On more than one occasion in the early twentieth century Spain seemed to be poised on the brink of civil war; Barcelona, the capital of Catalonia, was a focal point of bloodshed and civil conflict. The civil guard, hated by the workers, kept unrest just in check by ruthless force and imprisonment. Spain was disintegrating amid warring factions, while the politicians of the Cortes, the Spanish parliament, proved unable to provide effective and stable governments. In September 1923, repeating a pattern familiar in the nineteenth century, an army general seized power to bring peace to Spain and save her from monarchist politicians. Compared with other dictators, this general, Primo de Rivera, was an attractive figure. The King, Alfonso XIII, acquiesced in the overthrow of the constitution. Primo de Rivera followed a policy of repression of politicians, the Socialist Party, anarchists and supporters of Catalan regionalism. But the socialist trade union, the UGT, became a mainstay of the regime. He also inaugurated public works which, in the 1920s, seemed to promise some economic progress. Yet by 1930 he had exhausted his credit and lost support in the army, and the King dismissed him. The King himself did not long survive. The cities had turned against him and he left for exile in 1931.

The second Republic was then established without violence or bloodshed. Its history was brief and filled with mounting political and social conflict. The left had drawn together, temporarily as it turned out, to take charge of the country. But it was characteristic of the politics of the left and the right that, once the electoral victory was won by electoral pacts, rivalry between the parties would thereafter prevent any coalition from providing stable government.

First, until the end of 1933, the Republic was governed by a coalition of the left and moderate Republicans under the leadership of Manuel Azaña. He sought to solve the regional question by granting autonomy to the Catalans; he promoted educational reform, and plunged into a programme of agricultural reform which achieved little. In the summer of 1932, there was an abortive generals' rising against the government of the Republic. It was a fiasco.

What caused the greatest bitterness was the anticlerical legislation of the government, which regarded the Church as the bulwark of reaction. It drove moderate supporters who were faithful Catholics into opposition. The anarchists stirred up the workers in violent strikes which the government suppressed with bloodshed, thus alienating supporters on the left. As in the last days of the Weimar Republic the moderate politicians, of whom Azaña was an example, were assailed by extremists on the left and right, and even the more moderate Socialists looked fearfully over their shoulders lest supporting the government should lose them the allegiance of their followers to those political groups further to the left, especially the anarchists. During the election of November 1933, the left no longer fought by means of electoral agreements. It was the turn of the right to strike such bargains, forming a common opposition to the government's anticlerical legislation. Gil Robles founded CEDA, a confederation of right-wing Catholic groups. A new electoral pact, with the radicals changing sides and now supporting CEDA, gave the centre–right a resounding victory. From 1934 to 1936 the republic struggled on amid mounting tensions towards civil war.

The coalition government of the centre supported by CEDA reversed the 'progressive' aspects of the legislation of Azaña's government. With the roles reversed, the miners in Asturias, under the united leadership of socialists, communists and anarchists began a general strike in October 1934 and seized Oviedo, the provincial capital. Simultaneously there occurred an abortive separatist rising in Catalonia. The government retaliated by using the Foreign Legion and Moorish troops from Morocco bloodily to suppress the Asturian rising. The shootings and tortures inflicted on the miners increased the extreme bitterness of the workers, while there was strong Catholic feeling against the godless Marxist conspiracy. Both the left and right were strengthening their following. Among groups of the right, José Antonio, son of Primo de Rivera, attracted increasing support to the Falange Party, which he had founded in 1933 and which came closest to a fascist party in Spain. But in the election of February 1936 the parties of the left, which were out of power, organised an effective electoral pact and presented themselves as the Popular Front. Its cry was that the Republic was in danger and that the parties of the right were fascist. The parties of the right called on the electorate to vote for Spain and against revolution. Spanish politics had become so polarised that neither the parties of the right nor those of the left were ready to accept the 'democratic' verdict of the people. The Popular Front combination gave the left the parliamentary victory, but the country was almost equally split between left and right in the votes cast. What was now lacking was a strong grouping of the centre, a majority who believed in a genuine democratic peace and parliamentary institutions.

The familiar spectacle of the united left achieving electoral victory, and then falling into division when they got to power, was repeated in the spring and summer of 1936. The left-wing socialists, led by Largo Caballero, rejected all co-operation with left 'bourgeois' governments; Caballero continued the Popular Front but would not serve in the government. He was supported by the communists; but despite all his revolutionary language, he had no plans for revolution. On the right, however, plans were drawn up to forestall the supposed revolution of the left. The generals justified their July 1936 rising on precisely these grounds. Attacked by those who should have supported the Republic, the government was too weak to suppress the generals' rising as easily as in 1932. But the right, on its own, was unable to wrest power from the government, either electorally or by force. It called on the army to restore conservative order and to uphold the values and position of the Church. And the army assumed this task in an action that had more in common with nineteenth-century Spanish tradition and the military seizure of power by Primo de Rivera in 1923, than with Nazi or fascist takeovers which were backed by their own paramilitary supporters, the army standing aside.

The government of the left in 1931–2 had offended army feeling by attempting its reform, replacing many officers with those whose loyalty to the Republic seemed certain. A large number of such promotions after the victory of the Popular Front in 1936 offended the traditionalist officers, and General Francisco Franco, 'banished' to the military governorship of the remote Canary Islands, protested that such unfair practices offended the dignity of the army. The leader of the officers' conspiracy was not Franco, however, but General José Sanjurjo, and General Emilio Mola was its chief organiser. The army itself was divided between those ready to overthrow the Republic and those still prepared to serve it. Franco himself hesitated almost to the last moment. The increasing disorder in Spain – the lawlessness and violence of demonstrations of the left, which the government seemed unable to control – finally decided the army conspirators in July 1936 to carry out a military coup, 'planned' since the previous April, to take over Spain.

Franco had finally thrown in his lot with the conspirators and secretly, on 18 July, left the Canary Islands to take charge of the army in Africa. On 13 July, the murder of a well-known anti-Republican politician by members of the Republican Guard provided a further pretext for the military rising, which had actually already been set in motion. A day early, on 17 July, the army rose in Morocco. General Mola had ordered the risings to begin in Morocco on 18 July and the garrisons in mainland Spain to take power a day later. But the risings on the mainland also began earlier, on the 18th, and the following day spread to Spain's two largest cities, Madrid and Barcelona. Here the risings were successfully suppressed. Thus the army failed to take over the whole of Spain in one swift action. Within a short time the Nationalist and Republican zones were becoming clear. Their respective military resources were fairly equally balanced in metropolitan Spain with about half the army and most of the air force and much of the fleet siding with the government of the Republic.

What decisively tipped the balance was the help Hitler and Mussolini gave to Franco, providing transport planes to ferry the African army to the peninsula. Franco decided not to risk crossing by sea. The Republican fleet's doubtful capacity was thus not tested. The disorganisation on the Republican side extended to the air force, which made no efforts to intercept the German and Italian transport planes. The Nationalists speedily dominated the west and much of the south. By the end of July, Burgos in the north had become the capital of Nationalist Spain. Mola had set up there a junta of generals. However, it was Franco who was accepted by all the generals as their commander-in-chief; by the end of September he was also declared head of the Spanish state as well as of the government. This marked the beginning of a long, undisputed hold on absolute power which was to last until his death thirty-nine years later in 1975.

As the Nationalists captured Republican-held territory, prominent Republican leaders, civil and military, were murdered in their tens of thousands. Terror was a weapon used to cow working-class populations. On the Republican side attacks were indiscriminately directed against the Church. The Church's political identification with the right (except in the Basque provinces) was beyond doubt, but the Church had not participated in the uprising. Twelve bishops and thousands of priests and monks were murdered. Many thousands suspected of sympathy with the Nationalists were summarily executed. The government of the Republic could not control its followers in this bloody lawlessness. The bitter hatreds of the fratricidal war have, not surprisingly, lived on as long as survivors of both sides remain to recall the atrocities of three years of war. These murders on both sides have been estimated by Professor Hugh Thomas to total a ghastly 130,000 (75,000 committed by the Nationalists and 55,000 by the Republicans). To these losses must be added deaths in battle – 90,000 Nationalists and 110,000 Republicans – and death from all other causes, about 500,000, out of a total population of 25 million.

The Republicans had the difficult task of welding together an effective central government in Madrid from all the disparate forces of the left, and a cohesive army from the many military formations that had gathered spontaneously. The communists, declaring that the 'revolution' had to be postponed, joined the moderate Socialists and Republicans. Largo Caballero headed a Popular Front government in the autumn of 1936 which even the anarchists, dominant in Catalonia and Barcelona, joined. But the left could not maintain unity through the war. Their 'fraternal' strife, with the communists fighting the anarchists and the anti-Stalinist Marxists (known by their initials as POUM), was the main cause of the ultimate defeat of the Republic. On the other side, despite the heterogeneous

The Spanish Civil War. Above left: *General Franco receives the fascist salute from the nursing staff of a Nationalist hospital.* Above right: *Republican militiamen celebrate their defence of Madrid.* Left: *Republican soldiers like this one at the Aragon front fought on, despite inferior resources, to the bitter end.* Right: *POUM, a Trotskyist party, calls on the peasants to rise up to claim their land.*

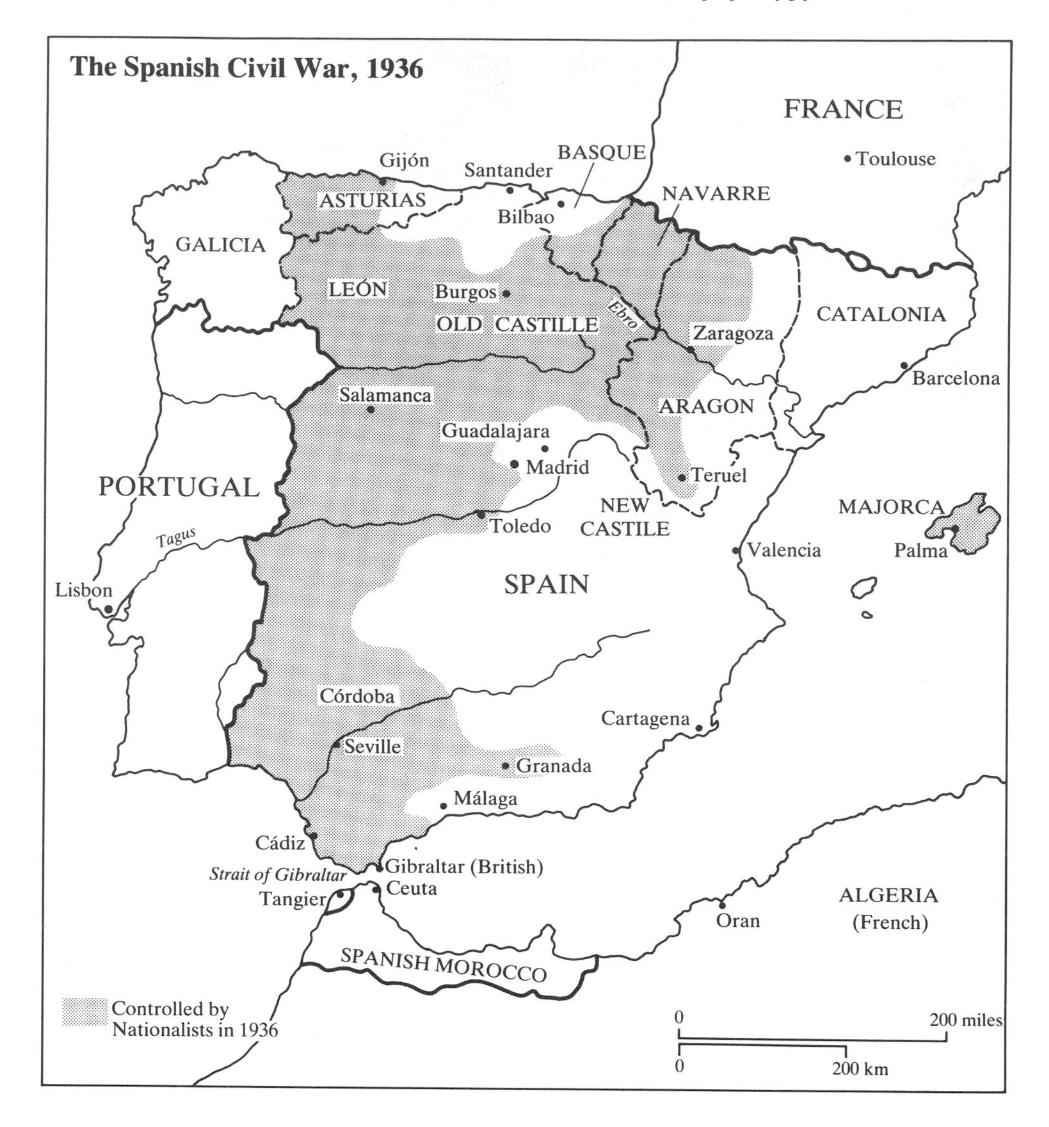

political complexion of the Nationalists, Franco and the army dominated and created an effective unity and an impressive fighting force.

German and Italian help had been critical in the early stages of the war and favoured Franco's advance to the gates of Madrid. But massive Soviet military assistance including planes and tanks saved Madrid in November 1936. Britain and France, ostensibly with German, Soviet and Italian agreement, set up a Non-Intervention Committee whose undertaking not to send weapons to either side was honoured only by the two Western democracies. The Germans sent tanks and experts and the notorious Condor Legion, which, with a hundred planes, played an important role and horrified the democracies by bombing defenceless towns. The wanton destruction of Guernica (26 April 1937) symbolised the terror of war on civilians. The lesson was not lost on the British who week after week saw on their cinema screens the horrible effects of those air raids. Not surprisingly it strengthened the desire of the British people to keep out of a general war and to support those politicians who were trying to do so, though the committed did go to fight in Spain. Mussolini sent over 70,000 volunteer troops. The Russians, from headquarters in Paris, organised the volunteer International Brigades and sent tanks and planes. All this foreign aid succeeded in staving off defeat for either side, but it was not sufficient to ensure a victory.

After the Nationalist advances in August to October 1936, the Republic still held half of Spain – the whole east and south-east, as well as a strip in the north. Madrid remained in government hands, having repulsed the Nationalist advance. In 1937 the Nationalists finally overcame Basque resistance in the north. In Madrid the government was reorganised to take a stronger line against dissidents. The communists, whose strength rapidly grew, took a lead in fighting against the POUM and the anarchists. Caballero was replaced as premier by a socialist professor, Dr Juan Negrín. By now the Republicans had organised a well-disciplined army. In the winter of 1937 the Republican army launched an offensive against the Nationalists. Franco's counter-offensive, however, recovered all the lost territory and went on to split the Republic in half, separating Barcelona and Catalonia from central and southern Spain. The defeat of the Republic appeared imminent. Unexpectedly the Republicans won a short-lived victory in the summer of 1938, but then in the autumn suffered a catastrophic defeat when Franco counterattacked. Internationally the Republic simultaneously sustained devastating blows. France, which intermittently had allowed arms to pass the Pyrenees frontier, closed it, and Stalin gave up sending aid to the Republic. Franco's victories and the desertion of the Soviet Union and France doomed the Republic. In January 1939 Barcelona fell. Still Negrín inspired the final resistance. The Republic came to an end in confusion, with part of her own armed forces in rebellion. At the end of March 1939, Madrid finally capitulated to Franco's army.

The Spanish Civil War was over. It had dragged on with enormous loss of life. Refugees now flooded across the Pyrenees into France. But Europe's attention was only momentarily fixed on the final agony. War between the European powers had been only narrowly averted in the autumn of 1938, and now in March 1939 Hitler again held the centre of the stage. The world would soon turn upside down. The communists, seen by the left-wing idealists as the real opponents of the fascists and Nazis in Spain, would that same year, in September 1939, praise Hitler and condemn the imperialist–capitalist Western democracies for going to war to check Nazi expansion in Europe.

CHAPTER 25

The Outbreak of War in Europe, 1937–1939

Responsibility is a portmanteau word covering many different meanings. All the nations in a complex international society are to some degree involved with each other and in that sense share 'responsibility' for the most important international events such as war. In that sense, too, it is both true and misleading to conclude that Hitler's Germany was not alone responsible for the outbreak of war in 1939 – misleading when responsibility is equated with blame, and blame, like responsibility, is considered something to be shared out between all the nations involved. Such an analysis of responsibility for the outbreak of the second great war in Europe, however, confuses more than it illuminates. This point is vividly brought out when we compare the attitudes of Hitler and Chamberlain as revealed in accounts not at the time intended for the general public.

Hitler, in September 1939, posed before the German people as the injured party, as acting in *defence* of Germans persecuted by Poles, and in response to actual Polish attacks across the frontier (in fact secretly organised by the Gestapo). Hitler knew this pose was a blatant lie. Since coming to power he had built up the armed forces of the Reich, not simply to gain his ends by the bluff of overawing Germany's weaker neighbours: the Wehrmacht and Luftwaffe were fighting instruments prepared for real use. Although not precisely certain of the right timing, Hitler intended all along to pass from a policy of piecemeal territorial acquisition by blackmail to actual wars of conquest. In September 1938, he was frustrated when he could not make war on Czechoslovakia. A year later he was not again deterred. On 23 November 1939, a few weeks after war began, he summoned the chiefs of the armed services and explained that he had not been sure whether to attack first in the East or in the West (it should be noted that it was not a question of either/or); but Polish resistance to his demands had decided the issue:

> One will blame me [for engaging in] war and more war. I regard such struggle as the fate of all being. No one can avoid the fight if he does not wish to be the inferior. The growth of population requires a larger living space. My aim was to bring about a sensible relationship between population size and living space. This is where the military struggle has to begin. No people can evade the solution of this task unless it renounces and gradually succumbs. That is the lesson of history. . . .[1]

There can be no reasonable doubt now, with hindsight and the evidence available, that while Hitler remained in power he intended passing from the phase of preparation for war to actual wars of conquest, and that the purpose of these conquests was the aggrandisement of Germany herself, and the reduction of the conquered nations who would

[1] Max Domarius, *Hitler Reden und Proklamationen*, Vol. 2, pp. 1421–6.

retain a separate existence only as satellites. The dominated people would all have to conform to Hitler's racialist plan for the New Order of Europe. This racialist basis of Nazi policy meant not that Hitler aimed at a Wilhelmine German domination of Europe, but that he planned a European revolution entailing mass population movements in the East, murder and the enslavement of 'inferior' races. For Hitler, then, the question of war and peace was a question of timing, of choosing the moment which promised the greatest chance of success.

As has been seen, the French, whose assessment of Hitler's aims tended to be more realistic than that of the British, would not in any case risk war with Germany without a cast-iron guarantee of Britain's backing. Even then doubts about France's survival as a great power if she were further weakened by heavy losses of men and reserves made Frenchmen look at the prospect with horror. What was true of France was also true of Germany's smaller neighbours. As for the Soviet Union she shared no frontier with Germany and hoped to contain her by deterrence in association with the Western powers; but that policy was bluff since the Soviet alternative to the failure of deterrence was not war but a truce, an accommodation with Germany. The United States was fervently pro-democratic (and Roosevelt gave eloquent expression to these beliefs) but equally fervently neutral if it should come to war in Europe. That gave Britain the key role.

Until the spring of 1939, Neville Chamberlain dominated the Cabinet as few prime ministers had before him. He was Hitler's most formidable protagonist. Chamberlain too, though subject to public opinion and the pressure of his colleagues, would have to decide when to accept that general European war was inevitable, unless Britain were simply to stand by while Hitler secured the domination of the European continent. The conquest of Poland would have been followed by other conquests, though no one can be sure in what direction Hitler would have struck *first* and so what precise sequence he would have followed. Nor did he intend to spare a hostile and independent Britain. When Hitler passed from 'cold' war to 'hot' war, Chamberlain reluctantly accepted that a great European war would become inevitable if civilisation in Europe and Britain's independence and security were to survive.

Chamberlain's attitude stands in stark contrast to Hitler's. Chamberlain abhorred war. He belonged to the generation of the Great War. Humanitarian feelings were the positive motivations of his life. He wished to better the lot of his fellow men, to cure the ills, in particular unemployment, which still beset Britain's industrial life. War, to him, was the ultimate waste and negation of human values. He believed in the sanctity of individual human life and rejected the crude notions of a people's destiny, purification through violence and struggle, and the attainment of ends by brute force. He had faith in the triumph of reason and, believing himself to be fighting the good fight for peace, he was prepared to be patient, tenacious and stubborn, drawing on inner resources to maintain a personal optimism even when conditions all around pointed the other way. To the very end he hoped for some miracle that would ensure a peaceful outcome. Only a week away from war at the end of August 1939 he expressed his feelings in a private letter to his sister Hilda, 'I feel like a man driving a clumsy coach over a narrow cracked road along the face of a precipice . . . I sat with Annie [Mrs Chamberlain] in the drawing room, unable to read, unable to talk, just sitting with folded hands and a gnawing pain in the stomach.'[1] When Chamberlain spoke to the nation over the BBC at the outbreak of war, he, unlike Hitler, could say with sincerity:

> You can imagine what a bitter blow it is to me that all my long struggle to win peace has failed. Yet I cannot believe that there is anything more or anything different that I could have done and that would have been more successful. His [Hitler's] action shows convincingly that there is no choice of expecting that this man will ever give up his practice of using force to gain his will. He can only be stopped by force.

There is no meaningful way in which Chamberlain's responsibility for war can be discussed or compared on the same basis as Hitler's, any more than a man who violently attacks his neighbour is less responsible for his action because of the weakness of the police force.

This is not to suggest of course that the origins of the war in Europe can be reduced to a contrast between two men, Hitler and Chamberlain. Hitler

[1] Chamberlain to Hilda, 27 August 1939, Chamberlain Papers, University of Birmingham, England.

could not safely wage war without the assurance that rearmament had progressed sufficiently – an assurance which required the co-operation of industry and the management of finance. Nor could he totally ignore technical military considerations. He needed the co-operation of the army. The overlapping party and state machinery of government, and the gearing of the economy to war preparations under Hermann Göring's overall direction, created many problems. The 'court' of leading Nazis around the Führer – Himmler, Goebbels, Hess, Bormann, Göring, and lesser sub-leaders such as Rosenberg, Ribbentrop, Ley – were engaged in bitter infighting, jockeying for Hitler's favour and a more influential place in the hierarchy. German policymaking was not monolithic; various highly placed people and organisations influenced policy. Hitler certainly had the last word on all major issues, but took care to try and carry the leaders of the army, industry and the mass of the people with him. His speeches were a torrent of untruths, carefully calculated; he was well aware that war with Britain and France was widely regarded with apprehension.

The many dimensions of British policy and all influences shaping it are just as complex, though different. Party political considerations play an important role in the making of policy in a parliamentary democracy. Governments were more directly affected by public feeling, which could be freely expressed, unlike in Germany. Decisions in Britain were taken by committees, the supreme government committee being the Cabinet, which met at the prime minister's residence. Chamberlain's control was never dictatorial as Hitler's was. Chamberlain's ascendancy over his ministerial colleagues was at its height in 1938, but he could not act without carrying them with him – resignations had to be contained to the single minister in disagreement. In 1939, Chamberlain's influence lessened as the assumption behind his policies was seen to be more and more at variance with unfolding events in Europe. Belated rearmament was a particular handicap, narrowing Britain's policy options.

There was one further, striking difference between German and British policy. Hitler paid relatively little attention to his two 'allies', Italy and Japan, and fashioned policy without allowing their reactions to affect his own decisions. Not so the British government, which, while taking the lead in the framing of the policy in the West, could not ignore France's reactions and later Poland's. Britain stood at the centre of the Commonwealth, and the views of Canada, South Africa, Australia and New Zealand also made themselves felt.

The greatest difference between Britain's and Germany's position derived from Britain's role not only as a European but as a world power with imperial interests in every continent. These interests were each supported by different politicians and pressure groups which conflicted with each other when the priorities of policies came to be resolved. Britain's commitments to defend Australia, New Zealand and India from the Japanese threat were as absolute as considerations of security at home which required Britain to stand by France if she were attacked by Germany. The Defence Requirements Committee, specifically assigned the task of analysing Britain's military needs, came to a clear decision when it reported to the Cabinet in February 1934 that Germany was 'the ultimate potential enemy against whom all our "long range" defence policy must be directed'.

For many years none of Britain's armed forces would be strong enough to meet all potential enemies. At first there were only two of these: Germany in Europe, rapidly arming, and Japan in Asia. With the outbreak of the Italian-Abyssinian war and Britain's support for League sanctions there was now a third potential enemy with naval forces in the Mediterranean – Italy. The need to defend every British possession was equally absolute. How then was the lack of resources to be matched to these requirements? That was the task of diplomacy. The real question was not whether or not to 'appease', but which nation to stand up to and which to conciliate. In the Far East much would depend on the attitude of the United States. Britain's situation *via-à-vis* the United States in Asia was similar to that of France *vis-à-vis* Britain in Europe. France could not risk war with Germany without British support; Britain could not afford to contemplate war with Japan without the guarantee of American support unless driven into war in defence of the territory of the empire and Commonwealth. In Europe also, Britain could only act defensively. Her air force, intended as a deterrent, lagged behind the strength of the German air force and so its deterrent value never materialised. It did not even figure in Hitler's calculations: Germany made great efforts towards self-sufficiency (autarky) under Göring's Four-Year Plan after 1936, though Hitler recognised that, without conquests, self-sufficiency could not be completely attained. Nevertheless, dependence on foreign supplies was reduced and to that extent the damage which a British blockade by sea could inflict much lessened. How then did Britain conceive a war with Germany might be conducted so that it would end in Germany's defeat?

The one consistent military assumption that the politicians in the British Cabinet made until February 1939 was the extraordinary one that Britain needed no large army to fight Germany on the continent. Chamberlain, as chancellor of the Exchequer, argued that there was not enough money to expand all three services and everyone, except the Chiefs of Staff, agreed that the British public would never accept that Britain should, as in 1914–18, send an army of millions to France and Belgium. The French realised that they could not opt out of providing the land army to repel Germany. All the heavy casualties would thus fall on them. No wonder that in the circumstances they sought to protect their depleted manhood by reliance on the Maginot Line and felt some bitterness towards their British ally.

While the British and French service chiefs were agreed that the most dangerous enemy would be a rearmed Germany, their policy towards Italy was never co-ordinated. When France wanted to conciliate Mussolini in 1935, Britain gave no backing and in January 1939 the reverse occurred. British attention, moreover, and French too, was not exclusively fixed on Germany. From 1931 to 1933 Japanese aggression in Manchuria and the question of support for the League of Nations occupied the attention of the public and of governments. Alarm at Germany's growing armament was next diverted by the Italian–Abyssinian war in 1935. Hitler was singularly lucky at having these 'diversions' during his years of military preparations. In just the same way the remilitarisation of the Rhineland, Germany's own 'backyard', soon came to be overshadowed by the outbreak of the Spanish Civil War. While Hitler incessantly worked in his foreign policy to extend and strengthen Germany, he was simultaneously transforming the country from inside with increasing emphasis on Nazi ideology and the militarisation of the whole of society. German women were admonished to 'give' the Führer many babies, the soldiers of the future. The Führer cultivated the image of the lone leader on whom rested all the burdens of his people. He was occasionally shown more humanly in the company of children and dogs. But the existence of his blonde mistress, Eva Braun, was one of the best-kept secrets of the Third Reich.

The middle 1930s were years of feverish preparation for the great moment when Nazi Germany would consummate Hitler's revolution and establish the new racial order in Europe. The preparations were still taking place within the frontiers of Germany, though party propaganda was reaching out and spawning local parties not only in Austria but as far afield as Latin America. Within Germany, incessant propaganda was directed against one arch-opponent in Nazi demonology, the Jews. Despite widespread anti-Semitism Hitler felt he had to move with caution so as not to arouse sympathy for the Jews: many good 'Aryans' knew at least 'one good' Jew and did not grasp the literal meaning of the SA bands' obscene shout, *Judah verrecke*, 'perish the Jew'. The Jews were bewildered. Many saw themselves as patriotic Germans, tied to German culture, and thought the Hitler phenomenon was mere summer's madness. The tide of emigration was slow. They could transfer only a fraction of their possessions out of the country. Opportunities of earning a living abroad were restricted, and the language and customs were strange. Most German Jews hung on. Despite all the discrimination against them they continued to enjoy the protection of the law from common violence. By and large they were not physically molested before November 1938. Nevertheless the screw was being turned more tightly year by year.

The notorious anti-Semitic Nuremberg laws, first proclaimed at the Nazi Party rally in 1935, and in subsequent years constantly extended, were but a logical step in the direction of the new Nazi world which Hitler and his followers were creating. The persecution of the Jews was not an accidental blemish of Hitler's government, which, it has been mistakenly argued, should be seen as just another aggressive nationalist German regime. Without hatred of Jews and the relentless persecution waged against them, the core of Nazi ideology collapses. In 1935 all Jews remaining in the civil service were dismissed. The definitions of 'full' Jew, 'half' Jew or *Mischlinge* – 'mixtures' of various degrees – were determined not by a man's baptism or personal belief but by descent. Three Jewish grandparents made the second-generation descendants all Jews.

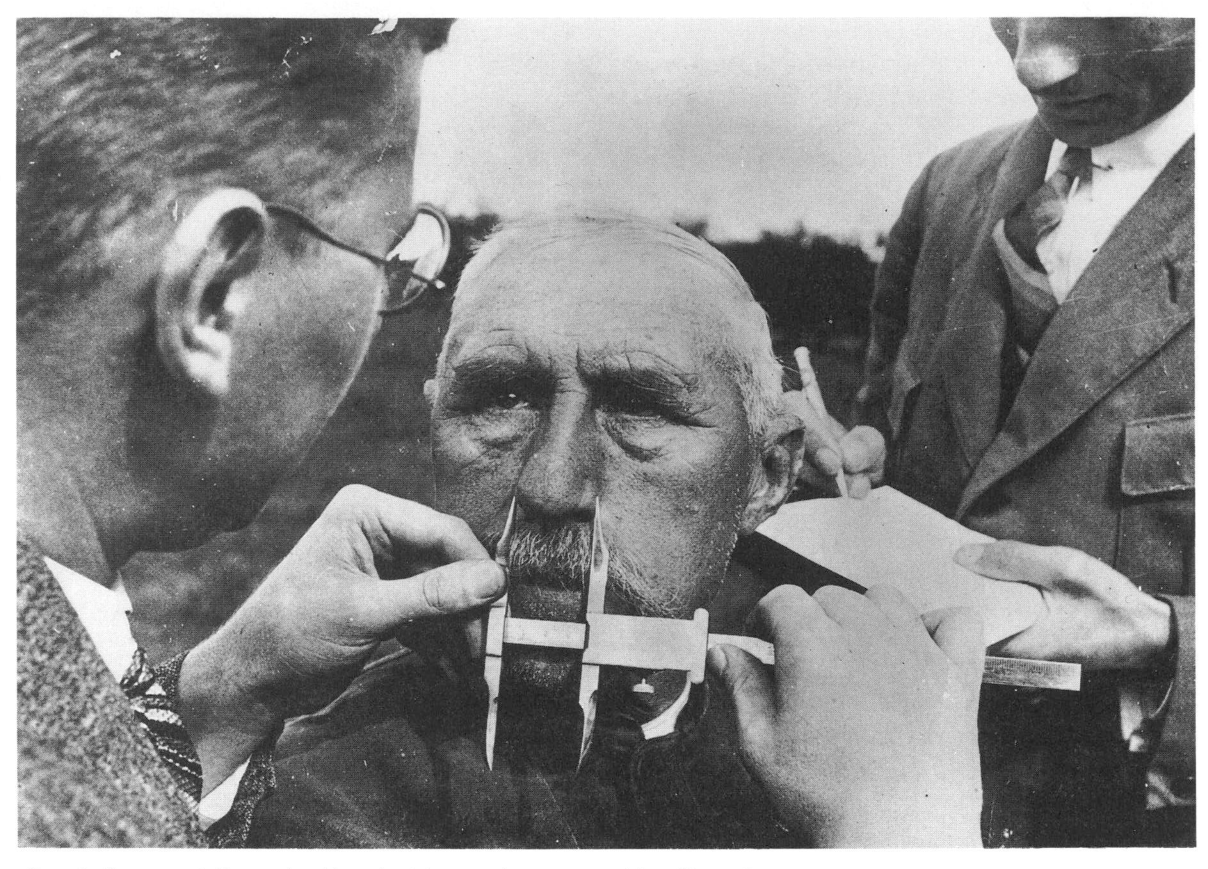

Eugenics Rampant. A German has his credentials as an Aryan measured by calliper rule.

The definition thus was racial, based on pseudo-science, not religious. The 'full' Jews, or 'Non-Aryans' as they were called, felt the total weight of persecution from the very start. The only *temporary* exception was made in cases where Jews were married to Aryans and there were 'mixed' children from the marriage. Pressure was placed on the Christian partner to divorce the Jewish spouse. Some did so. Other German wives and husbands protected their partner and children with the utmost courage and loyalty throughout the years of persecution and so saved their lives, for the war ended before Hitler could take measures against them. These brave people came from every walk of life and included officers in the armed forces and at least one admiral. Their behaviour alone should serve as a caution against crude generalisations about the 'German character', even though they formed, like the active resistance, only a tiny minority of the population. The Nuremberg laws made the German Jews second-class citizens officially and forbade further marriages between Jews and non-Jews and any sexual relations between Aryans and Jews. This latter crime was called *Rassenschande* and death sentences were passed where Jewish men were accused. Over a period of time Jews were removed from all professional contact with non-Jews. Only in business activities were Jews permitted to carry on until 1938, since it was feared that their sudden removal would harm the German economy. This concession was not due to Hitler's moderation – rather it is an indication that he was prepared to countenance a tactical delay while never deviating one inch from his ultimate ideological goals.

This pressure on the helpless small German Jewish population in 1933 – there were about 500,000 racially defined as Jews – drove them into increasing isolation and hardship. Even so they did not emigrate to Palestine or elsewhere fast enough. The majority of German Jews wanted to stay in their homes and in their country, whose cultural heritage, the works of Lessing, Goethe and Beethoven, they cherished. German culture was their culture. Not in moments of blackest nightmare could they imagine that in the twentieth century in Western Europe women and children would be murdered in factories of death. They were not, after all, stuck in the Middle Ages. Many Jews were still living in reasonable comfort, and for the most part relationships with their fellow Germans were correct and occasionally even friendly. But official discrimination steadily increased; Jews were expelled by the autumn of 1938 from all professions, they could no longer study in universities, and their shops were compulsorily purchased and Aryanised. It was by then clear that there was no future for young Jews, but the older generation expected to live out the rest of their days in Germany on their pensions and savings. During the summer of 1938, however, the Nazi leadership had decided to take far harsher measures against the Jews. First it was the turn of Jews from Poland who had not acquired German citizenship to be expelled brutally overnight. Then concentration camps were readied inside Germany. The German people would be given a practical demonstration of how to treat their Jewish neighbours as their enemies. Only a pretext was needed.

It was provided on 7 November 1938 by the fatal shooting of the third secretary of the German Embassy in Paris. The perpetrator was a half-crazed young Jew whose parents (of Polish origin) had just been deported; perhaps there were other reasons too. Paradoxically, the diplomat, Ernst von Rath, was no Nazi. After news of Rath's death reached Germany on the afternoon of 9 November, a pogrom all over Germany was launched. Synagogues were set on fire, Jewish shop-windows smashed. With typical black humour, Berliners dubbed the 9 November 'Kristallnacht', the night of crystals. Gangs of ruffians roamed the streets and entered Jewish apartments – it was a night of terror. Jewish men were arrested in their homes on the following day and incarcerated in concentration camps. A recently discovered entry in Goebbels's diary fully implicates Hitler, thus adding more evidence, if any were needed, that no major action could be undertaken in the Reich without the Führer's explicit approval. It so happened that 9 November was the annual occasion when all the Nazi leaders met to commemorate the abortive *Putsch* of 1923. In Munich, Goebbels wrote in his diary:

> I report the situation to the Führer. He decides: let the demonstrations continue. Pull back the police. The Jews should be made to feel the wrath of the people. . . . As I head for the hotel, I see the sky is blood-red. The synagogue is burning. . . . the Führer has ordered 20,000–30,000 Jews to be arrested immediately.

The purpose of the great November pogrom of 1938 was to force the remaining Jews into emigration. A visa to a foreign country gained release from concentration camps. The question is often asked: why did Hitler try to force the Jews out of Germany even after the war began? Does this mean he would have preferred this solution to murdering them later? We do not know exactly what was in Hitler's mind but it is safe to conclude that humanitarian considerations did not come into his calculations on so central a question as his hatred of the Jews. He certainly was sensitive to German public feeling and presumably concluded that the German people were not ready to back his rule with increasing enthusiasm if he simply massacred all Jews, men, women and children *within Germany*.

During the war, vain efforts were made to preserve the secrecy of the death camps. Hitler wished to remove physically all Jews from the territory ruled by him. Emigration would 'export' anti-Semitism. And when he had won his wars the Jews would be done for in any case, as Nazi policies in all occupied Europe were to show during the war. After November 1938 the Jews in panic belatedly attempted to leave: the civilised world debated but could not agree to absorb the remaining 300,000. But tens of thousands of people were saved, with the 'children's transports' to Britain forming a poignant part of these emigrants. Many children said goodbye to the one parent who was permitted to come to the railway station in Germany. Most of these children never saw their parents again. The exodus was made possible by the response of thousands of concerned individuals who collected money and pressurised their reluctant governments to let the refugees in.

The Jewish persecution by bureaucratic machine involved and implicated more and more Germans in the criminal activities of the Nazi regime under pseudo-legislative cover. Opposition became more risky as the grip of the totalitarian state tightened. There were still a few who spoke out openly, like the Protestant pastor Martin Niemöller, and were placed in concentration camps. Amid the general enthusiasm for the Nazis, it must be remembered that there were many too who were terrorised into silence.

The Jews were the most obvious and open targets of persecution. But there were hundreds of thousands of others who suffered. In ruthless pursuit of the supposedly racially healthy German *Volk*, laws were passed in 1933 which permitted mass sterilisation of those deemed able to pass on genetic defects, such as medical handicaps, epilepsy and deafness, mental defects or even social defects, one of which was identified as drunkenness and another as habitual criminality. Not only were pregnancies aborted and sterilisation ordered for the individual affected, but the whole family, including young adolescents, were sterilised. Convicted homosexuals were incarcerated in concentration camps. In the interests of 'racial hygiene' it was then but a step to proceed to murder the handicapped during the war under the pretence that they were being released from their suffering – this was the 'euthanasia' programme. But, as with the murder of the Jews, Hitler decided that the extermination of 'lives not worthy of life' would have to wait for the cover of war. Racial discrimination after 1935 was also suffered by the 22,000 gypsies living in Germany. They too, men, women, children and babies, together with the tens of thousands of Polish and European gypsies, were designated for extermination.

Hitler was still telling the German people that he wanted peace and desired no more than to bring home to the Reich those German people living beyond the German frontier: not just the people of course but also the lands in which they were living. At a meeting of his military commanders and in the presence also of the Foreign and War Ministers in his Chancellery on 5 November 1937 Hitler spoke his mind. Colonel Hossbach recorded the meeting. The aims Hitler expressed contained nothing new; they were all familiar from his previous statements and writings. He referred to the need to realise these aims within six to eight years at the latest. The German *race* needed space in the east to expand and multiply or it would be doomed to decline. More land and resources were an economic necessity. The solution to Germany's problems could be found only by using force. Beyond the years 1943–5 the rearmament of Germany's enemies would exceed the ageing equipment of the German military. Germany had to assume the enmity of Britain and France. Hitler speculated on international complications like a civil war in France or a war between the Mediterranean powers which would divide Germany's enemies to her advantage. As a first step, a strategic necessity was an 'attack' on Austria and Czechoslovakia. It was therefore obvious that rearmament expenditure could not be reduced. The immediate objective of winning Austria and Czechoslovakia, however, would be attained by a little war conducted with lightning speed; and Hitler assured the generals that this would not lead to general war.

What is noteworthy about Hitler's policy from 1937 to 1939 is the acceleration of pace – his reluctance simply to await events and to exploit suitable opportunities. He became more confident and reckless; he wanted to carry through his grand design without waiting much longer. He became obsessed with his health, nerves and stomach disorders. He was ageing and would do so rapidly during the war. Such independence as the army had retained, as a professional body whose independent judgement was expressed on the military feasibility of Hitler's plans, was an obstacle to their realisation. The Commander-in-Chief of the Wehrmacht as well as the War Minister were forced to resign early in 1938. Hitler assumed personal supreme control with his own military staff by replacing the War Ministry with the Oberkommando der Wehrmacht (OKW, or High Command of the Armed Forces). The General Staff of the Army was subordinated to the OKW. The army was purged of generals unenthusiastic about Nazi plans, though opposition to them from within the officer corps was not silenced. The Foreign Minister Konstantin von Neurath was also replaced – by an ardent Nazi, Joachim von Ribbentrop – and the diplomatic service was purged. Before embarking on action, Hitler had thus powerfully strengthened his authority.

Hitler had no immediate plans for the annexation of independent Austria. Yet within a few weeks it was a fact. The events as they unfolded made possible a quick finish to Austria's independence and convinced Hitler in the spring of 1938 that the tide was running more swiftly and favourably towards Germany's destiny than he had thought. He had wished to cow Austria into satellite status without, for the time being, openly destroying her independence. From 1936 to February 1938 he succeeded well with the Austrian Chancellor Schuschnigg, who was finally summoned to his mountain retreat

Scapegoating the Jews. Above: *the incineration of Jewish, 'degenerate' and 'un-German' books, May 1933.* Top right: *Viennese Jews scrub the paving stones in the public humiliation that swiftly followed the* Anschluss, *March 1938.* Top left: *The shell of Königsberg's synagogue, burnt out during* Kristallnacht, *9/10 November 1938.*

The Expansion of Germany,
January 1935–October 1939
Memel
LITHUANIA
Vilna
Gdynia
Königsberg
Danzig
EAST
PRUSSIA
Hamburg
Bremen
Rhine
Berlin
Poznan
Warsaw
Brest
Litovsk
GERMANY
Cologne
SUDETENLAND
Lublin
POLAND
Frankfurt
Prague
Lvov
Teschen
Pilsen
CZECHO-SLOVAKIA
SAAR 1935
German
Protectorate
Danube
Munich
ALSACE
Bratislava
Vienna
Budapest
RUTHENIA
AUSTRIA
SWITZERLAND
HUNGARY
ROMANIA
Milan
Zagreb
Venice
Turin
Belgrade
ITALY
YUGOSLAVIA
Sofia
Rome
Durazzo
Tirana
ALBANIA
to Italy 1939
GREECE
Germany January 1935, Saar, plebiscite in Germany's favour
March 1936, Rhineland (German sovereign territory remilitarized)
March 1938, Austria annexed
October 1938, Czechoslovak frontier regions (Sudetenland) annexed
March 1939, Memeland from Lithuania
March 1939, annexation of Bohemia and Moravia
September 1939, German occupation of Poland
Hungary
November 1938, Czechoslovak frontier region
March 1939,
Ruthenia
Poland October 1938, Teschen from Czechoslovakia
Soviet Union
September 1939, Occupation of eastern Poland
Lithuania
October 1939, Vilna region from Poland

at Berchtesgaden a month before the *Anschluss* to be bullied into agreeing to make far-reaching further concessions to the Nazis in Austria entailing the certain erosion of what independence had remained. Deserted by Mussolini, he had little choice but to agree to German demands.

Mussolini preferred a German alignment ever since his conflict with Britain over Italian aggressions in Abyssinia and involvement in Spain. He was jealous of German success, but in 1936 bombastically claimed that European affairs now revolved around the Axis of Berlin and Rome. He visited Hitler in September 1937 and was very impressed by the spectacle of Germany's might and flattered by the Führer's attentions. He had already secretly removed his objection to German dominance over Austria and had been assured that her independence would not be too blatantly destroyed.

That is one reason why Hitler as late as 28 February 1938 sought an 'evolutionary' Austrian course. But Schuschnigg in the end would not play the game; the rabbit bolted. When he returned to Austria he announced he would hold a plebiscite on 13 March, intending to ask the people whether they desired independence or union with Germany. Despite the suppression of the socialists and trade unions, who had no love for Schuschnigg, their vote would certainly have been cast against Hitler's Germany. Hitler demanded a 'postponement' of the plebiscite. Schuschnigg conceded and resigned. But now the President would not appoint the National Socialist nominee in his place, a new demand. Göring, given responsibility for the Austrian Nazi takeover, had completed the military preparations. On 12 March 1938 the Wehrmacht crossed the frontier; Hitler followed close behind. There was no military opposition. Hitler was received in Linz with cheers and flowers by part of the population. He decided on an instantaneous acceleration of his plans. Instead of a gradual fusion of the two countries, complete union, or the *Anschluss*, was announced on 13 March and later approved by a charade of a plebiscite.

It all happened so quickly that international reaction in the first place consisted merely of some ineffectual protests. But this ruthless expansion of Germany's frontiers forced the British and French governments into a fresh stock-taking.

In February 1938 Eden resigned and Halifax replaced him at the Foreign Office. Eden had resigned over the immediate difference of opinion with Prime Minister Chamberlain on whether Mussolini should be appeased before he had given concrete proof of abiding by international undertakings and withdrawing troops from Spain. Eden was testing the specific, the good faith of the dictators, while Chamberlain was following a grand design of foreign policy and was ready to subordinate 'secondary' questions to its fulfilment. Chamberlain's grand design for peace and stability involved working separately on Hitler and Mussolini. His ideas had already been clearly formulated the previous November 1937 when he sent Halifax, then Lord President of the Council and not Foreign Secretary, on a mission to Hitler. Halifax, according to the official British record, told Hitler that England accepted 'possible alterations in the European order which might be destined to come about with the passage of time. Amongst these questions were Danzig, Austria, Czechoslovakia. England was interested to see that any alterations should come through the course of peaceful evolution . . .' The German record is more pointed and has Halifax expressing the view that he 'did not believe that the *status quo* had to be maintained under all circumstances'. As further baits to persuade Germany into the paths of peace, Chamberlain was prepared to make economic concessions and even envisaged some eventual African colonial appeasement.

Privately Chamberlain explained to his sister Ida that he regarded the visit as a great success because it had created an atmosphere which would make possible discussions with Germany on 'the practical questions involved in a European settlement':

> What I wanted to do was to convince Hitler of our sincerity and to ascertain what objectives he had in mind . . . Both Hitler and Göring said separately and emphatically that they had no desire or intention of making war and I think we may take this as correct at any rate for the present. Of course they want to dominate Eastern Europe; they want as close a union with Austria as they can get without incorporating her in the Reich and they want much the same thing for the Sudeten Deutsch as we did for the Uitlanders in the Transvaal. . . . But I don't see why we shouldn't say to Germany give us satisfactory assurances that you won't use force to deal with the Austrians and Czecho-Slovakians and we will give you similar assurances that we won't use

> force to prevent the changes you want, if you can get them by peaceful means. . . .[1]

The flaws in Chamberlain's reasoning were several and serious. First, it was wrong that Hitler was pursuing a nationalist foreign policy which could be satisfied by limited territorial adjustments. Down to the outbreak of war in 1939 Chamberlain failed to comprehend the central racialist kernel of Hitler's policy and therefore the significance of the persecution of the Jews. There is one interesting piece of evidence about this in an unpublished private letter. His sister Hilda had passed the absurd information to him that it was possible for Jews to be admitted to the Hitler Youth, and Chamberlain replied in July 1939:

> I had no idea that Jews were still allowed to work or join such organisations as the Hitler Youth in Germany. It shows, doesn't it, how much sincerity there is in the talk of racial purity. I believe the persecution arose out of two motives: a desire to rob the Jews of their money and a jealousy of their superior cleverness.[2]

Chamberlain, unlike Churchill, did not have warm feelings for Jews in general. He wrote that he did not regard them as a 'lovable people' but condemned their persecution: 'I don't care about them myself' but that was not sufficient reason to explain pogroms. Chamberlain failed to grasp early on the limitless nature of Hitler's demands. He worked for a 'reasonable' settlement so that a great war would be seen as a needless and criminal sacrifice of life.

The second flaw, which led to the taint of moral guilt, was that Chamberlain believed in the justification of the greater good, or more precisely the avoidance of the greater evil, which for him was a general war. This played into Hitler's hands. Hitler intended to secure the maximum advantages at minimum cost. He would thus without risk of general war provide Germany with a strong base before launching his ultimate wars of conquest. The sacrifices Chamberlain called for, moreover, were not of British territory. It would be the Austrians, Czechs and other 'foreigners' who would actually suffer the consequences. So too the colonial concessions in Africa would be offered largely at the expense of Portugal and Belgium and, far more importantly, would have placed racist Nazis in control of black peoples whom they looked on as subhumans. It is doubtful whether Chamberlain really grasped this fact.

The third flaw was the weakening of Britain's allies, actual and potential, on the continent. But Chamberlain was essentially right when he assessed the United States as an unlikely ally at the outset of any war in Europe. Whatever Roosevelt might say, he was the prisoner of an overwhelmingly isolationist Congress. Also Chamberlain was right that no reliance could be placed on the Soviet Union, which was not ready for war and would not fight Germany in alliance with Britain and France as long as she could divert the German attack from her own territory.

By the spring of 1938 the Anglo-French alliance had reached a pretty low point. The British Cabinet was forging ahead with the grand design of Chamberlain's peace policy, intermittently consulting French ministers. A consistent British policy was followed throughout 1938. It was obvious that the German-speaking inhabitants of Czechoslovakia would be the next target. Germany was informed that the November 1937 assurances to Hitler still held (page 241). Britain was willing to come to an agreement over the Sudeten question on Germany's terms provided this could be accomplished peacefully. The new French government of Prime Minister Édouard Daladier and Foreign Minister Georges Bonnet was promised the support of the British alliance if Germany launched an unprovoked attack on France. The sting in this seemingly satisfactory guarantee was that it was not extended to the case where France declared war on Germany in fulfilment of her commitment to the Franco-Czechoslovakian alliance. In this way the British alliance became a potent weapon which Chamberlain and Halifax used to force the French into line behind a policy of concessions to Germany at Czechoslovakia's expense. Not that the French had much spirit of resistance given the pessimism of General Gamelin and the British attitude. French policy too was to reach agreement with Germany. The French consistently sought to influence British policy, without ever taking a position in advance of Britain's which risked war. France, the ministers

[1] Chamberlain to Ida Chamberlain, 26 November 1937, Chamberlain Papers.

[2] Chamberlain to Hilda Chamberlain, 30 July 1939, Chamberlain Papers.

had decided in March 1938, 'could only react to events, she could not take the initiative'.

In dealing with Germany, Britain offered the carrot and the stick. The colonial, territorial and economic carrots dangled before the Germans have already been noted. The 'stick' consisted of refusing to bind Britain to neutrality if Hitler did resort to force. Chamberlain declared in the House of Commons after the *Anschluss*,

> His Majesty's Government would not however pretend that, where peace and war are concerned, legal obligations are alone involved and that if war broke out it would be likely to be confined to those who have assumed obligations. It would be quite impossible to say where it might end and what Governments might become involved.

It was a clear warning to Hitler not to attack Czechoslovakia, though secretly the Cabinet had already concluded that there was no way in which Czechoslovakia could be helped militarily.

British policy from March 1938 until September 1938 thus put pressure on all who might precipitate a conflict – the French, the Germans and, not least, the Czechs if they resisted German demands. Chamberlain got his way because the military were only too aware of Britain's woeful weakness, especially in the air; the Dominions counselled peace; and British public opinion, however indignant about Hitler, was overwhelmingly for peace as well. These pressures corresponded to Chamberlain's innermost convictions that his mission was to save the peace of Europe.

Plans for attacking Czechoslovakia were discussed by Hitler and the generals in April 1938. To ensure that Czechoslovakia would receive no support, a crisis was to be worked up. At the end of May Hitler declared to his generals his 'unshakeable will that Czechoslovakia shall be wiped off the map'. He signed a military directive which set a final date, 1 October 1938. He had been infuriated by indications that Czechoslovakia would not tamely submit as Austria had done. Rumours of German military moves had in May led to a partial Czech mobilisation and warnings from Britain and France. Hitler had actually been anticipated, and he raged at the public loss of face. He was not yet ready to smash Czechoslovakia but soon would be – that mixed 'racial' state was for him a monstrosity that challenged his ideology of racial purity.

Among all the Eastern European states, only Czechoslovakia had retained her Western democratic constitution – an added reason to make it unfit for German partnership. Another sin was the prominent support Czech statesmen gave to the ideals of the League of Nations. Czechoslovakia, largely because of her national composition, faced grave difficulties as a new successor state. In 1930 the country was inhabited by 7.1 million Czechs, 3.3 million Germans, 2.6 million Slovaks, 720,000 Hungarians, 569,000 Ruthenes, 100,000 Poles and a smaller number of Romanians and Yugoslavs. The cohesion of the state depended on the co-operation of Slovaks and Czechs as symbolised by the founding fathers, Thomas Masaryk and Eduard Beneš. The peasantry of Slovakia was administered mainly by the more educated Czechs, which caused discontent and the creation of a Slovak People's party, led by Father Hlinka, demanding autonomy. But the most serious difficulty was caused by relations with the German-speaking ex-Habsburg population living in Bohemia and Moravia and along the frontiers with Germany and the new Austria. Most of the Germans, once the masters, now resented their subordination to the 'Slav' state. Czech suspicions of German loyalties and attempts to favour Czech education and discriminate against Germans aroused anger and resentment.

The depression of the 1930s and the consequent economic crisis sharpened nationality conflicts as both Slovaks and Sudeten Germans blamed the Czechs. It coincided with the rise of Hitler, whose movement inspired imitations. In Bohemia and Moravia Konrad Henlein led the German National Front, which claimed rights for the Germans within the state, but secretly in 1938 worked for its disruption and union with Germany. Meanwhile Hitler publicly proclaimed that he would 'protect' the Sudeten Germans, who were unable to protect themselves. But not all Germans were enamoured of the Nazis. A significant minority of Social Democrats opted for Czechoslovakia out of hatred for Hitler, as the Austrian Social Democrats had also done. In 1938 the Czechs made far-reaching attempts to satisfy the German minority in negotiations with Henlein. But as Henlein had been told at a meeting with Hitler always to ask for more than the Czechs would accede to, these negotiations were doomed. Despite the genuine catalogue of internal difficulties, the 'multinational' army was patriotic and loyal and Czechoslovakia was in no danger of internal disruption. It was Hitler's aggression and Anglo-French diplomacy that destroyed Czechoslovakia in two stages, in September 1938 and in March 1939.

The agony of Czechoslovakia had its counterpart in Chamberlain's triumphant reception after saving the peace in September 1938. For the first time the Western democracies had been brought to the brink of war. The German Army High Command was alarmed as well by Hitler's tactics and warned Hitler that the Wehrmacht was not ready for war against France and Czechoslovakia. In August 1938 Colonel Ludwig Beck, the Chief of the Army General Staff, courageously resigned in protest at Hitler's insistence that Czechoslovakia must be attacked regardless of the risks of war with France. His successor was General Halder. In August both Halder and Beck plotted against Hitler and planned to arrest him before he could plunge Germany into war. The attitude of the majority of the army, including General von Brauchitsch, the Commander-in-Chief, makes it extremely doubtful whether the plot would have succeeded had it ever materialised. It depended in part on the appeal sent to London secretly urging Chamberlain to stand firm. Not unreasonably, Chamberlain was not prepared to risk the issue of war and peace on the success of a few conspirators in Germany who were trying to remove a powerful and popular dictator.

Chamberlain was pursuing his own peaceful policy. He induced the Czech government to 'invite' Lord Runciman early in August to assist as 'mediator' in the negotiations between the Czech government and Henlein. In view of Hitler's instructions to Henlein not to reach a settlement the mission was futile from the start. On 7 September Henlein broke off the negotiations. Hitler now deliberately worked for his pretext to attack Czechoslovakia, having carefully made all the necessary military preparations. The last stage of the German propaganda campaign began with Hitler's attack on the Czech President Beneš in a speech to the faithful at Nuremberg. But Chamberlain now began to interfere with Hitler's well-laid plans. Chamberlain's personal diplomacy, his flight to visit Hitler at Berchtesgaden on 15 September, caught the public imagination not only in Britain but also in Germany. He had come to find out what Hitler wanted. The crisis would be solved by diplomacy not force. The Czechs were diplomatically bludgeoned into agreeing on the cession of the Sudeten region to Germany and the French were persuaded to desert their Czech ally. But when Chamberlain met Hitler with these fruits of his diplomacy on a second occasion in Godesberg, the Führer refused to give up the use of force and Chamberlain broke off the negotiations. The Czechs mobilised. It looked as if war might still result.

What made Hitler draw back on the brink at the end of September and forgo his *Blitzkrieg* or 'lightning war'? We can only surmise. He delivered another almost unbelievably insulting speech abusing Beneš on 26 September. But the likelihood of war with France and Britain made Hitler hesitate. A probable major influence on his decision not to force a war was the 'unsatisfactory' state of German public opinion. Watching the dramatic newsreels, the German cinema audiences applauded the old gentleman with his umbrella so determined to struggle for peace. The Germans feared the consequences of another war with Britain and France. And so Hitler allowed Mussolini the glory of arranging for a peaceful outcome. A conference was called at Munich and Hitler, Mussolini, Daladier and Chamberlain assembled on 29 September. By the early hours of 30 September the formalities of arranging for a German occupation of the Sudeten areas between 1 and 10 October were agreed and a few other details such as a declaration that what was left of Czechoslovakia would be guaranteed once the Poles and Hungarians too were satisfied. Chamberlain even got Hitler to sign the piece of paper he waved at the airport on his return to Britain promising to settle all future Anglo-German differences by diplomacy. The Czechs were not allowed to participate. Nor the Russians, who in 1938 were still the sworn Bolshevik enemies of Nazi Germany.

The new rump Czech-Slovak state did not last long, although she tried to avoid all offence in Germany. The Slovak autonomy movement proved disruptive and in March 1939 Hitler browbeat the Czech President Hacha in Berlin to sign away what was left of the independence of his country. Göring threatened that he would otherwise obliterate Prague with bombs. The Czech will to resist had already been broken at Munich. On 15 March 1939 the Wehrmacht moved in and Hitler hastened to Prague to savour his new triumph. But his cynical breach of the Munich settlement caused an immense revulsion in the West and the crowds which had so recently applauded Chamberlain on

Mussolini's last appearance as Hitler's equal took place at the Munich Conference in September 1938.

But will Hitler honour his signature? On his return from Munich, British Prime Minister Neville Chamberlain waves the 'Anglo-German' agreement promising peace.

his triumphant return from Munich demanded that something should now be done to stop Hitler. Thirty-five well-equipped Czechoslovak divisions were lost to the French ally. Could the French without a 'second front' in the east still check Germany on land? Fears were voiced in the British Cabinet that France might even abandon the British alliance and make the best terms she could with Germany. These worries drove both the Cabinet and the military advisers of the government to accept the need for a continental commitment. At the end of March 1939 plans were approved which would double the strength of the British Territorial Army from thirteen to twenty-six divisions.

Britain's foreign policy now had to be aligned to the recently perceived shift in the balance of power on the European continent. After initial hesitations Chamberlain responded in a speech he delivered in Birmingham on 17 March 1939. He accused Hitler of breaking his word and taking the law into his own hands, and asked rhetorically, 'Is this the end of an old adventure or is it the beginning of a new? Is this the last attack upon a small state or is it to be followed by others? Is this, in effect, a step in the direction of an attempt to dominate the world by force?' In London, the Cabinet insisted on steps to create a deterrent alliance to save the peace if it could still be saved. They believed that only the threat of force might stop Hitler. Rumours of an impending German ultimatum to Romania, false as it turned out, served as the initial impetus which led to a unilateral Anglo-French guarantee, announced on 31 March 1939, to defend Romania and Poland against German aggression. Although Chamberlain continued to place faith in conciliating Hitler, he too was converted to the need for a deterrent alliance. Halifax and the Cabinet also urged that the alliance of the Soviet Union, too, should be sought. A sceptical Chamberlain had to give way. The long and weary Anglo-French–Soviet negotiations which followed lasted until 23 August 1939 when Stalin decided that Soviet interests were best served by concluding a non-aggression treaty with Nazi Germany instead (page 248).

If Britain's negotiations with Russia and her guarantee (and later alliance) with Poland prove anything, it is that the British never sought to

March 1939: German troops march into the Hradcany Castle in Prague, seat of Czechoslovakia's president.

embroil the Germans in a war with Russia while they themselves stood aside. Hitler could have invaded Russia on a broad front only by way of Poland or Romania, and Britain's policy had put up a barrier which could not be breached without involving Britain and France in war as well. It was ironic that the Western democracies should now be aligned with authoritarian Poland, having sacrificed democratic Czechoslovakia.

It has been argued that Britain and France were unnecessarily dragged into war by the March 1939 guarantees to Poland. Hitler, so this reasoning runs, would have followed the attack on Poland with an invasion of the Soviet Union. Would this not have been in Britain's and France's interest? The speculation about benefit is highly dubious. The evidence, moreover, is by no means so conclusive. At various times after Munich Hitler spoke of having to strike at France first before turning eastwards, on other occasions of finishing Poland first. He hoped by coercion and cajolery to keep Britain neutral. Logically the strategy of the lightning war suggested a quick campaign against Poland, then France, before resuming the war in the East again. In any case this was the path Hitler eventually followed. Our uncertainty concerns only his timing and strategic priorities.

Hitler's well-tried step-by-step policy of aggrandisement entered a new phase in 1939. He recognised that further bloodless successes were unlikely; he welcomed the opportunity of war, preferably against a small, weaker neighbour. Britain and France fought in September 1939 not because Hitler had *then* forced war on *them*. They fought because there could no longer be any doubt about the pattern of Hitler's violent diplomacy nor about his ultimate goals. It would have been madness to allow him to pick off his victims one by one and to choose his time for overpowering them while reassuring those whose turn had not yet come. Belatedly, by September 1939, Hitler was no longer able to call the tune. For Chamberlain, Hitler's choice of how to settle his Polish demands was the ultimate test.

The intricate diplomacy of the powers from March to September 1939 can only be briefly summarised here. The British and French governments were still seeking a settlement with Hitler and were even prepared to make far-reaching concessions to him after March 1939. They had accepted his seizure of Memel on the Baltic only a week after his entry into Prague. Poland, moreover, had not been guaranteed unconditionally. Her frontiers were not regarded as inviolate. As in the case of Czechoslovakia, if Hitler made 'reasonable' demands the Western powers hoped that the Poles would be 'reasonable' too. What the two Western powers ruled out, however, was that Hitler should simply seize what he wanted by launching with impunity a war against Poland.

In October 1938 Poland was first approached by the Nazi Foreign Minister Ribbentrop with demands that she return Danzig to Germany, create an extra-territorial corridor to East Prussia and join with Italy and Japan in the anti-communist alignment known as the Anti-Comintern Pact. Then in January 1939 the Polish Foreign Minister Colonel Beck visited Hitler and was offered a junior partnership as Germany's ally, with promises of Czech territory and the Soviet Ukraine. During the earlier Czech crisis Hitler had already been helpful in permitting the Poles to acquire the Czech territory of Teschen. It seems that because of Poland's strong anti-communist past, and the 'racial' mixture of Balt and Slav in her population, Hitler was ready to see the 'best' Polish elements as a suitable ally. Fervent anti-Semitism and the Polish government's desire to force Poland's own Jewish population into emigration was another link between them. But the Poles proved stubborn. They overestimated the worth of their own army and with a population of more than 34 million regarded themselves as almost a great European power. The cession of territory was anathema to them; in Polish history cession of territory had been the prelude to partition.

Hitler had offered the Poles what amounted to an alliance in the East. Later during the war against the Soviet Union other Slav nations, the Slovaks and Croats, were to become allies. Does this mean that Hitler was flexible about his definition of 'subhumans' other than the Jews? Might Poland have been spared the carnage that followed? For 3 million Poles who were Jews the outcome would have been no different; for the rest of the Poles, of whom another 3 million were murdered, the great majority would probably have survived the war as the Czechs did. But in the longer term Hitler was inflexible. The new greater German Reich after victory would have annexed large tracts of land in the East for 'living space'. These territories would have been 'racially cleansed' and resettled by Germans. Some Slav *Untermenschen* might have been retained as slave labour; Poles, Ukrainians and Russians capable of being Germanised would have been absorbed; of the millions driven out, few would have survived sickness and starvation. But the rejection by the Poles of Hitler's offers as late as 1938 sealed their immediate fate.

Beck's rejection and the Anglo-French guarantee determined Hitler to smash the Poles at the first opportunity. In May 1939 Germany and Italy ostentatiously signed the bombastically named Pact of Steel, which by its terms committed Italy to go to war whenever Hitler chose that Germany would fight, despite the Duce's explanations that Italy would not be ready for war for another three years. The conquest of Abyssinia and the more recent occupation of little Albania by Italian troops (in April 1939) were one thing, war with France and Britain quite a different prospect. The alliance nevertheless served the purpose of dashing any

As Molotov signs the Nazi-Soviet Non-Aggression Pact on 23 August 1939, Ribbentrop and Stalin look on.

hopes Chamberlain might have had left of detaching Italy from Germany after his own abortive attempt to achieve this on a visit to Rome the previous January. It was intended to pressurise Britain into neutrality. Far more important was the conclusion on 23 August of a Nazi–Soviet Pact, which Hitler hoped would convince Britain and France that it was useless to fight for Poland.

August 1939 turned out to be the last full month of peace. The crisis started when Poland insisted on her treaty rights in Danzig and Hitler chose to regard this as a provocation. However, Danzig was not the real issue; nor even was the future of the territory lying between East Prussia and the rest of Germany – the Polish corridor. Rather, it was that Hitler could not tolerate an independent Poland which blocked his road to *Lebensraum* in the East. The Poles were not impressed either by efforts at intimidating them by the Nazis on the one hand and pressure to be 'reasonable' exerted by Britain and France on the other. They had no intention of suffering the fate of Czechoslovakia. But the Chamberlain Cabinet in London and Daladier's government vainly hoped that the dispute was about no more than Danzig and the corridor and that war could be avoided if Poland gave way.

However, from Hitler's point of view, war with France and Britain would only be postponed, not avoided, that is postponed until he decided that the balance of power was most advantageously in Germany's favour. To the extent that one can fathom Hitler's mind, war with Poland was by now a certainty. He told his commanders-in-chief on 22 August that the destruction of Poland was necessary even if it meant conflict with Britain and France. He added that he did not believe it likely that Britain and France would go to war. What was desirable, politically and militarily, was not a settling of all accounts, but concentration on single tasks. Hitler had no intention of allowing the British or French any role as mediators.

According to Hitler's original plans, the attack on Poland was to begin on 26 August. On 25 August at 3 p.m. the order to attack was given and then, much to the annoyance of the Wehrmacht, countermanded at 7 p.m. when the final troop movements were already under way. The attack was postponed by Hitler for a few days. How significant was the postponement? Was there a real chance of peace somehow missed by lack of communication or misunderstanding? Chamberlain was aware of the parallel with July 1914. In a personal letter to Hitler on 22 August he made it clear that Britain would stand by her Polish commitments regardless of the German–Soviet Pact. Hitler received the letter on 23 August. The flurry of negotiations principally between London and Berlin during the last days of peace were undertaken by Britain to induce Germany and Poland to negotiate the differences over Danzig and the corridor. In that respect there was a parallel between the Czech crisis of 1938 and the Polish crisis. Britain and France would have acquiesced in any territorial gains Germany succeeded in obtaining from Poland without use of force. Mere German blackmail had become almost an acceptable fact of life as far as diplomacy was concerned. But if Germany attacked Poland to gain her ends by force then there was no doubt that Britain would support Poland by declaring war on Germany. The British Cabinet knew no other policy was possible and that the country would not accept another Munich, especially with the Poles, unlike the Czechs, fighting for their country. In France, Daladier firmly controlled his government and Bonnet, the Foreign Minister, counted for little now; there was no doubt here too that an actual German invasion of Poland meant war.

That is not to say that Britain and France wanted to fight Germany. Quite the contrary; the two governments were ready to talk and negotiate as long as Hitler did not actually attack. There was no certainty in their minds that he would actually go to war – so talk they did from 25 August until the outbreak of war with Poland, and even for two days beyond that. Only Hitler was sure that he was going to attack Poland and that his military timetable allowed only a few days' leeway. He used these days not to make any genuine attempt to draw back from the war with Poland, but to try to persuade Britain and France to abandon her. He wanted to postpone war with them until after Poland had been defeated and so avoid, if he could, a war on two fronts. Hitler concentrated on Britain. The 25 August was the most dramatic day of the crisis in Berlin. At 1.30 p.m. Hitler talked to the British Ambassador, Nevile Henderson, and he put on a very good act; he declared that he wanted to live on good terms with Britain, that he would personally guarantee her world empire, that Germany's colonial demands were limited and that his offer of a general settlement would follow the solution of the Polish–German disputes, which in any case he was determined to settle. This, he emphasised, was his last offer. He overdid it a little, stretching credulity too far by confiding to Henderson that once the Polish question was out of the way he would conclude his life as an artist and not as a war-maker.

About half an hour after Henderson had left the Chancellery in Berlin to fly with this offer to London, Hitler ordered the attack on Poland to commence the following day. The war machine was set in motion at 3 p.m. At 5.30 p.m. Hitler received the French Ambassador to tell him Germany wanted to live at peace with France and that the issue of peace and war was up to the French. But Hitler was unsettled that afternoon by the news of the imminent conclusion of the Anglo-Polish alliance, and by Mussolini's message revealing his unwillingness to join Germany in war. In London, meanwhile, the news that the Soviet Union and Germany had signed a treaty, and that the Anglo-French alliance negotiations with Russia had thus ended in failure, meant that nothing now stood in the way of the formal conclusion of the Anglo-Polish alliance, which was signed on 25 August. It promised Poland that Britain would go to war with Germany if Germany attacked Poland. In Berlin it was dawning on Hitler that Britain might not simply desert Poland the very moment Germany attacked her. Then in the late afternoon of 25 August Mussolini informed Hitler that Italy did not have the resources to go to war.

Not surprisingly Hitler now thought it prudent to give his 'offer' to Britain a chance of being accepted and not to jeopardise his overture by simultaneously attacking Poland. Hitler did not rely on Henderson alone. Göring had initiated the use of an unofficial emissary, Birger Dahlerus, a Swedish businessman, who shuttled between London and Berlin from 25 to 30 August. After his first return from London he saw both Göring and Hitler; unwittingly he became a tool of Hitler's diplomacy to detach Britain from Poland. If that succeeded, then France also could be counted on to remain out of the war. The British reply on 28 August to Hitler's 'last' offer was to welcome the opportunity of an Anglo-German settlement, but not at Poland's expense. Instead, the British Cabinet urged direct Polish–German negotiations, offered to act as mediators and informed Hitler that the Poles were willing to enter such negotiations. Germany was warned against the use of force. Henderson saw Hitler on the 28th and again on the evening of 29 August when Hitler angrily conceded direct negotiations – solely, so he claimed, to prove his desire for lasting friendship with Britain. Such proof, he hoped, would dissuade the British from supporting an unreasonable Poland. As Goebbels recorded in his diary, Hitler's aim was 'to decouple Warsaw from London and still find an excuse to attack'.

Hitler demanded that a special envoy must reach Berlin the very day following, on 30 August. Henderson was upset by the peremptory German reply. He gave as good as he got, shouting back at Hitler and warning him that Britain was just as determined as Germany and would fight. The British Cabinet refused to 'mediate' what amounted to an ultimatum. The German demands were unknown yet Hitler was insisting that the Poles should come immediately to Berlin to settle all that Germany required within a time limit of only a few hours. The time limit was ignored in London and discussions about starting direct negotiations were still proceeding on 31 August. Hitler's time limit for a Polish plenipotentiary to present himself in Berlin expired at midnight on 30 August. The Poles were not prepared to rush cap in hand to Hitler.

Polish policy has been characterised as crazy and suicidal. How could the Poles hope to maintain their independence sandwiched, as they were, between Germany and the Soviet Union? But such an argument denies small nations a policy of independence, which in practice they have retained. How can they be expected to give in without at least attempting to resist? Nevertheless it is perfectly true that Poland's military situation in September 1939 was hopeless. The Poles overrated their capacity to resist in the short term. So did the French Commander-in-Chief, General Gamelin, who expected the Poles to be able to hold out until the following spring. The Poles also counted on effective help from France and Britain. There was logic and reason in Poland's refusal to contemplate significant concessions to Germany in 1939. The recent example of Czechoslovakia showed only too clearly that independence could not be bought for long by making concessions to Hitler. Once started on that road, the Poles believed with good reason, the end at best would be that they might be permitted to remain Germany's satellite. So they reasoned that if the Germans intended the destruction of Polish independence, it would be better to fight them at the outset with Britain and France as allies than to accept piecemeal subordination to Germany and to risk the loss of the French and British alliance. Furthermore, there was just the possibility that Hitler's objectives were limited to Danzig and access through the Polish corridor. For such aims alone, Hitler, so they thought, might not risk a great European war. But if his aims were not limited, then Poland's only choice was to submit or fight. Accordingly the Polish government came to the conclusion that Poland's national interests were best served by resisting Hitler's territorial demands, by holding tight and so testing his real intentions. Hitler's determination, the Poles vainly hoped, might crack if his policy was based on bluff.

Did this Polish attitude then dash hopes of a peaceful settlement? That would have been so only to the extent that, if the Polish government had submitted to *whatever* Hitler demanded in August 1939, then France and Britain would have had no cause for war in September 1939. But while the British Cabinet and the French government were anxious for the Poles to explore all possibilities of a peaceful settlement with Germany by opening direct negotiations with Hitler, they did not expect the Poles simply to submit to time limits and the threat of force. Hitler, too, would have to demonstrate Germany's desire for peace by putting forward reasonable terms for a settlement, and by negotiating in a reasonable way without ultimatums.

At first sight he appeared to be putting forward what in London and Paris might be considered 'reasonable' terms. The German demands were embodied in sixteen points; they struck the British Ambassador in Berlin as moderate, when he *eventually* heard what they were! They included the immediate takeover by Germany of Danzig and a plebiscite later in the corridor to decide whether it was to remain Polish or become German, with the loser being granted extra-territorial rights across the strip of territory. But the method of negotiation belied the apparent moderation of the sixteen points. They were drawn up in strict secrecy and not communicated until *after* the time set for the appearance in Berlin of a Polish plenipotentiary with full powers to negotiate. In fact they first reached the ears of the British Ambassador just after midnight – in the early hours of 31 August. Henderson had called on the German Foreign Minister, Ribbentrop, who after a stormy discussion pulled a piece of paper out of his pocket and then read the sixteen demands aloud in German, according to Henderson, at 'top speed'. Ribbentrop added that since no Pole had arrived they were superseded anyway. He refused the Ambassador's request for a copy. Henderson was astonished at this breach of diplomatic practice and had to rely on his memory for the gist of the proposals.

Henderson in Berlin, and Halifax in London, nevertheless tried to persuade the Poles to act quickly to open discussions in Berlin. Not until noon on 31 August did Dahlerus, the innocent intermediary, who was being used by Göring and Hitler in an attempt to keep Britain out of the war, communicate the full terms to the British and Polish ambassadors in Berlin. All the efforts of the professional and amateur diplomats were in vain. The sixteen points and Hitler's diplomatic manoeuvres in August were designed to provide an alibi to put the Poles in the wrong and so justify war to the German people. Furthermore, Hitler almost to the last seemed to have had some hopes that, if the Poles could be shown to be unreasonable, then France and Britain would refuse to live up to their alliance commitments. He intended to drive a wedge between Poland and her Western allies. But in the last resort he was prepared to risk war with France and Britain rather than abandon the war he was preparing to launch against Poland. The first order to the Wehrmacht to attack Poland at 4.35 a.m. on 1 September reached the Army High Command at 6.30 a.m. on 31 August, that is several hours *before* the full text of the 'moderate' proposals was communicated to the British and Polish ambassadors in Berlin. It was finally confirmed by Hitler at 4 p.m., little more than three hours after the full text of the sixteen points was first revealed.

Would Hitler have accepted a settlement based on these demands if the Poles had rushed cap in hand to Berlin and agreed to everything? This would have avoided a war with Britain and France, which at this stage Hitler did not want. On the other hand Hitler was driven by his conviction that the Wehrmacht, navy and Luftwaffe needed a *Feuertaufe*, a baptism of fire, to maintain their fighting fibre. The German people too had to be taught to accept a real war, not be softened into believing that every victory would be bloodless. Hitler did not hesitate for long. If war with Poland risked a great European war, that risk had to be taken. As Henderson later wrote in his memoirs, the conclusion that Hitler did not want to negotiate at all on the basis of these proposals is inescapable.

The invasion of Poland began at 4.45 a.m. on 1

September. Now it is true that in both Paris and London, while Poland fought back, the ministers were still clutching at hopes of restoring peace even less substantial than straws. Mussolini offered again, as at the time of Munich, his mediation and held out hopes that another conference of the powers might be called. But the British Cabinet made it a firm precondition that Germany should first withdraw her troops from Poland. As Hitler would never have accepted this, Mussolini told the British and French that there was no point in his attempting further mediation. Meanwhile, between Paris and London, there was an extraordinary lack of co-ordination on the very eve of the war. On 1 September, Germany was warned about the consequences of war on Poland only by Britain. On 2 September, Chamberlain faced a hostile and suspicious House of Commons. Was another Munich in the making? But there was no chance that Britain and France this time could avoid war. On 3 September, separate British and French ultimatums led to the declaration of war on Germany, the French actually going to war a few hours after the British, though they did not start attacking Germany for a while longer, and then only ineffectually.

There could be no other outcome but a European war once Hitler had decided to attack Poland. Not a single country in Europe wished to attack Germany, but in September 1939 the British and French governments were forced to the conclusion that they must fight in their own defence and not allow Hitler to pick off one European state after another. There can be little doubt that this is precisely what Hitler would have done had he been allowed his war against the Poles. Hitler's aggression against Poland, despite the clear warnings he received of its consequences on the one hand and the perception of the British and French governments of his real intentions after the unprecedented concessions to his demands in the previous year on the other, thus led to the outbreak of the second great European war within twenty-five years of the first.

PART V

The Second World War

CHAPTER 26

Germany's Wars of Conquest in Europe, 1939–1941

During the first two years of war, Germany won a series of victories on the continent of Europe that staggered the world and made the Wehrmacht appear invincible. Apprehensive at the outset, the German people were intoxicated by military success; all that Hitler had done appeared justified by this unanticipated and brilliant outcome. The nightmare that the experiences of the First World War would be repeated seemed for the Germans no more than a bad dream in 1940. Europe learned the reality of the *Blitzkrieg*. The Wehrmacht used the tactics of speedy penetration by tanks, followed by mechanised infantry and then more slowly by infantry on foot, supported closely by the Luftwaffe; towns were subjected to indiscriminate air raids, and the terrorised populations jammed the roads to escape the advancing Germans. The *Blitzkrieg* required careful planning, a well-co-ordinated command structure and highly disciplined, well-equipped troops. The armed forces, from the most senior officers to the newest conscript, served Hitler's cause, which they identified with Germany's, with efficiency and the utmost devotion. The home front supplied the means. It was their war, too, though Hitler's lightning wars did not require the entire mobilisation of the home front as in Britain. Women were not conscripted and luxury items continued to be produced to keep the Germans happy. Military victory alone made possible the horrors that Hitler's regime inflicted on the millions of people who, as a result, fell into Germany's grasp.

In September 1939 Poland was conquered; in April 1940, Denmark and Norway; during May the Netherlands and Belgium; and then in June 1940 the greatest victory of all, France was defeated. With France prostrate, Britain withdrew from the continent of Europe. Did not the 'good' which Hitler had achieved outweigh the 'bad'? – so many Germans now reasoned. Hitler even publicly offered peace to Britain. In July 1940 the war, so it seemed, was virtually over, an astonishingly short war rather than the expected long and bloody struggle, leaving Germany victorious. Why were these German dreams shattered so soon?

Hitler was not satisfied with what he had achieved so far. He had not won sufficient *Lebensraum* in the East or the undisputed hegemony of Europe. Any 'peace' for him now would have been tactical and short-lived. Everything he said to his associates, either secretly at the time or in conversations and writings before, points to the fact that he regarded the victory in the West as only a prelude to greater conquests. Plans for a great fleet had been carried forward not with a view to winning the continental European war but with an eye to the wars after that, including the world war with the British Empire and the United States. The struggle would continue as long as Hitler lived and until Europe was racially transformed and world power was won; but naturally Hitler preferred to proceed according to his own timetable. The Germans were not allowed for long to enjoy the fruits of victory, the victory parades accompanied by champagne and other luxuries

Warsaw capitulates to the Germans on 27 September 1939. Polite formalities are on display here, but millions of Poles were to die at German hands during the occupation.

looted from France. After the war was finally over in 1945, Hitler's megalomania was rightly seen as Germany's undoing. Her defeat then was so complete that it is easy to overlook the fact that four years earlier it had been a much more close-run thing.

Germany's defeat of Poland was rapid. Surrounded Warsaw resisted until 27 September 1939. Badly led, the Poles bravely fought the Wehrmacht, which enjoyed overwhelming strength. In the earliest days of the war, the Luftwaffe destroyed the Polish air force, mostly on the ground. Any chance the Poles had of holding out a little longer was lost when the Russians on 17 September invaded from the east in accordance with their secret agreement with Germany of the previous August (page 248). Still it was no walkover. The Poles inflicted heavy casualties and the Wehrmacht was in no fit state to switch immediately to the west and to attack France in November 1939 as Hitler desired.

Hitler's public 'peace' proposals to Britain and France early in October 1939, after the victorious Polish campaign, were almost certainly meant for German public opinion. He would not, of course, have rejected the idea that Britain should accept and withdraw from involvement on the continent. Then France could not have continued the war on her own and would have been in his power even without a battle. Did Britain contemplate any sort of peace? Had Chamberlain altogether abandoned his previous policies? Much recent manuscript material, including Chamberlain's private papers, add to our knowledge of the so-called 'phoney war' period in the West. There remain gaps in our knowledge. But, whatever differences of opinion may have existed, peace terms involving the eventual abandonment of France were unthinkable in 1939.

Militarily, on land and in the air, the war scarcely got started in terms of real fighting on the western front. The French were not ready to take *quick* offensive action against the weak screen of German troops facing them behind the incomplete fortifications of the Siegfried line. By the time the army was fully mobilised and in a state of readiness for offensive action – had the Commander-in-Chief,

Maurice Gamelin, desired it – the Polish campaign was drawing to its close and the German High Command was rushing reinforcements westwards from Poland. The military inaction on land corresponded to the doctrine, Poland notwithstanding, that the army which attacked would be forced to suffer huge casualties. All the advantage was believed to lie with the defence behind such powerfully constructed fortifications as the Maginot line. In preparing the defence of France one section of the front – the Franco-Belgian frontier to the Channel – had been left 'open', designed to act as a limited region for offensive manoeuvre. But when the Belgians returned to a position of complete neutrality in 1936 this strategy was more difficult to execute. The Anglo-French campaign plan of 1939–40 was nevertheless designed to meet the expected German advance through Belgium, by a forward movement of their own into Belgium the moment the Germans attacked that country; no earlier move was possible as the Belgians fearfully clung to absolute neutrality.

These military assumptions about how best to conduct the war were paralleled by political assumptions held by Chamberlain about the war and its likely outcome. It would be ended, if possible, without great sacrifice of life by imposing a strict blockade on Germany. The British and French governments even considered blowing up the sources of Germany's oil supplies in Romania and the Soviet Caucasus. With neutral Scandinavia, the Balkan states and the Soviet Union delivering oil and other essential raw materials, the British blockade by sea was far less effective than during the First World War. It did not seriously impede Hitler's intended lightning strikes against the West. For fear of massive reprisals, the French and British dropped nothing more lethal than pamphlets on the industrial Ruhr. But then Chamberlain did not believe that the war would be won by military force. In December 1939 he wrote to the Archbishop of Canterbury, 'I feel before another Christmas comes the war will be over, and then the troubles will really begin!' What was in his mind when he wrote that? Was it that he expected reasonable negotiations and a peace treaty? He certainly thought that the war would end in a stalemate and that, once the Germans were convinced that they could not win, they would negotiate for peace. The war would be won on the home front. Chamberlain was certainly anxious whether the British people would stand for a long stalemated kind of war. He feared there was in Britain a 'peace at any price' party whose influence might become powerful. He thought it probable nevertheless that the German home front would crack first, forcing Hitler into the wrong policy of attack!

Whether all aspects of 'appeasement' completely ended after the outbreak of war in September 1939 poses questions which can as yet be answered only tentatively. The future situations which Chamberlain envisaged were hypothetical and no one can say for certain how he, his Cabinet colleagues, Parliament or the country would have reacted to events which never happened. From existing evidence we can reasonably conclude that Chamberlain would never have consented to peace on Hitler's terms; also that Chamberlain thought Britain and France would not be able to impose a Carthaginian peace on Germany. Indeed he would have been likely to insist on Hitler's removal from any real exercise of power in Germany. He appears to have thought that some reshuffle of power setting Hitler aside might offer a solution. 'Until he disappears and his system collapses there can be no peace,' he wrote a week after the outbreak of the war. Chamberlain's assumptions were mistaken. Events turned out very differently, when what was to him unthinkable occurred and the French armies collapsed. Only then did the pre-war illusions on which policies had been based for so long finally collapse.

While at sea Britain had the better of the war, serious fighting on land began not on the frontiers of France but in Norway. Winston Churchill had rejoined the Cabinet as First Lord of the Admiralty at the beginning of the war and was anxious that some visible blow be struck at Germany's war effort. The attack by the Soviet Union on Finland on 30 November 1939 seemed to provide a good pretext and opportunity. British experts calculated that Swedish iron ore was vital to the German war machine. During the winter months it was shipped through the Norwegian port of Narvik. For weeks under Chamberlain's chairmanship the cabinet discussed the possibility of an operation which would disrupt its flow. The favourite idea was to help the Finns against the Russians by sending volunteers who would, on the way so to speak, control the railway line from northern Sweden to the coast. This scheme made use of the public indignation in the West about Russia's attack to

Well-equipped Finnish troops successfully resist Russian attacks during the winter of 1939.

damage both Germany and the Soviet Union, which was seen as Germany's partner in the European war of aggression. The Finns successfully resisted the ill-prepared Soviet troops for weeks, inflicting heavy casualties on them in what became known as the Winter War.

The French too were keen to fight, but not in France. They agreed in February 1940 to a joint Anglo-French expedition of 'volunteers' to aid the Finns and occupy the strategic northern railway. British scruples about infringing neutral rights, and Norway's terrified adherence to neutrality – the Norwegians did not wish to give Germany an excuse for invasion – led to delays, until finally the British decided to mine the waters off Narvik through which the ore ships sailed (though only until spring had opened the other route by way of the Baltic, blocked by ice in the winter). Before an expedition could be sent to the Finns, however, they were defeated, making peace on 12 March 1940. French politicians were so outraged at the inability of the government to help that Daladier's ministry fell; the more militant Paul Reynaud became prime minister. Chamberlain's own fall was delayed by another month and historically was far more important.

The public was tiring of the phoney war and the easy successes of the dictators, Hitler and Stalin. Poland and now Finland had fallen. Fortunately the British Cabinet (unlike the French) never contemplated any steps that might lead to outright war with the Soviet Union as well, even though, or perhaps because, the Soviet Union represented a far greater threat to Britain's imperial interests than to France. Chamberlain was singularly unlucky in some of his public utterances. After Munich he had rashly repeated the phrase about 'peace in our time'. Early in April 1940 he coined one phrase too many when he told the nation that Hitler 'has missed the bus'. It was Britain that missed the bus. After relatively small forces had secretly begun the operation at sea on 3 April 1940, the main force following during the night of 7 and 8 April, the Germans in a daring move occupied all Norway's major ports, including the capital, Oslo, on 9 April. The Norwegians resisted and inflicted casualties, especially on the German warships making for Oslo's harbour. But Germany's attack was almost entirely successful, even though it was not a complete surprise to Britain and France. The British navy missed the German. Executing the policy decided on by the Cabinet, the Royal Navy on 8 April was proceeding to lay mines in Norwegian territorial waters accompanied by a small force of troops which was ready to land in Norway should the Germans retaliate by invading. In fact they had already anticipated the British move. The instructions to the British force were unclear and reveal Britain's moral dilemma about landing in Norway if the Norwegians chose to resist. In many ways the Norway fiasco was an 'honourable' defeat.

The question arose whether Britain and France could defeat Hitler with such a sense of 'honour'. Only in the extreme north, in Narvik, were Anglo-French forces able to inflict a temporary setback to the small German forces far from their base. The British navy sank the German destroyers in the port and a month later Narvik was reoccupied. After Dunkirk, these forces had to be withdrawn and the whole of Norway fell under German occupation. Nevertheless German naval losses had been so severe that in July 1940 there was no surface fleet in active service; only a few lighter warships were undamaged.

The most important political consequence of so evidently acting too late once again in Norway was the fall of the Chamberlain Cabinet, and the outcome – surprising at the time of the crisis – was that Winston Churchill became prime minister on 10 May 1940 of a national government joined by Labour and the Liberals. With the passage of time the adulation of Churchill as war leader has rightly given place to a more critical and detailed assessment of his role in policy making at home, in foreign relations and in military strategy, which together make up what is called the conduct of the war. Churchill's shortcomings do now stand revealed. But this does not totally alter the older picture of him. By filling in the shadows, showing his mistakes as well as his successes, Churchill becomes more real and believable. The shadows only bring into sharper relief the predominance of that galvanising spirit, the enormous energy and undaunted faith in final victory which became an asset of inestimable value to Britain and to the war effort of the whole alliance. And, despite wartime restrictions, Churchill still led a democracy rooted in Parliament, and was dependent upon the support of the people. The nation thrilled to the rhetoric of his radio speeches and sensed that Britain now had a war leader who was at last a match for Hitler. Churchill, more than any single man, sustained national morale and hope in the future.

Winston Churchill, 1941.

It is therefore all the more remarkable that the secrets now emerging from private papers and official records reveal how insecure Churchill's position really was during the first four months of his administration. Chamberlain was no broken reed. His government had actually won what amounted to a vote of confidence, though many Conservatives had abstained or voted with the Opposition. It was Chamberlain who was deeply injured by so many of his former supporters turning against him. It was he who decided that for the 'duration' what was required was a truly national government. But he would remain leader of the Conservative Party and quite possibly thought that he might return to power when sanity returned and that the time might come when his unrivalled experience would be used to bring back peace. As yet he had no inkling of the cancer that, within a few weeks, turned him into an invalid and caused his death early in November 1940. Churchill was prime minister, but Chamberlain and Halifax remained the most powerful Conservatives in the Cabinet. When Churchill first presented himself to the House of Commons, it was Chamberlain whom the Conservatives loudly cheered. Chamberlain was soon to earn those cheers for far more than his readiness to accept second place under Churchill.

*

Norway was a serious defeat for the Allied war effort. The Norwegian fjords could now serve as ideal bases for the German submarines threatening to sever the lifeline of war supplies crossing the Atlantic from the United States. The most shattering blow of all was the defeat of France, on whose armies the containment of Germany overwhelmingly rested. It seemed unthinkable that a great power like France would succumb as quickly and as totally to the onslaught of the *Blitzkrieg* as smaller nations like Poland and Norway had done. Yet that is what occurred.

The military débâcle of the Allied campaign in France can only be briefly summarised. The total strength of the German army on the one hand and the French, British, Belgian and Dutch forces on the other were roughly comparable, as were the numbers of tanks on each side. Arguably the French had the edge in the quality of their tanks and artillery. Germany achieved superiority in the air but this in itself was not decisive and, contrary to popular belief, the Maginot line, to which so much blame came to be attached, was of advantage to the Allies: it deterred the Germans from attacking more than half the frontier and it could be held by a relatively small force. This meant that the Allies did not have to concentrate on the Franco-German border but could predict that the main battles would occur in the regions not covered by the Maginot line. They could not, or rather should not, have been taken by surprise. The Allies then had apparently good reason for quiet confidence before the Germans opened the offensive.

The Allies realised that the obvious route of invasion lay through the north, the Netherlands and Belgium, and made all their plans accordingly. The Germans, when they attacked, should not be allowed to turn industrial northern France immediately into a battle zone as they had done in the First World War. The French and British forces would, and did, have time to meet the German thrust in Belgium before it reached France. The Maginot line ran alongside the whole frontier with Germany, alongside that of Luxembourg and alongside the southern tip of the Belgian frontier. Just beyond was the heavily wooded Ardennes region, believed by the Allies to be impassable to any major German offensive with tanks, and this section of the front was lightly held. Beyond the Maginot line to the sea, one careful calculation – others did not differ appreciably – indicated that forty French divisions and nine British were facing two German armies totalling seventy-four divisions. But alongside the Allies another twenty-two Belgian divisions were expected to fight, even discounting ten Dutch divisions which were quickly overwhelmed. The purely Anglo-French/German disparity would have disappeared if thirty-five French and one British division had not been allotted to the Maginot line and upper Rhine. The total German and combined French and British forces were roughly comparable. Germany's success was based not on superiority of numbers or equipment but on taking and choosing the offensives and in so distributing the German divisions that (as in chess) they would appear in overwhelming strength at the weak point of the Allied front. The massed, co-ordinated use of armour would ensure that the initial breakthrough could be exploited with great speed.

As has been noted, the Allies anticipated no major thrust through the Ardennes and the Germans achieved complete surprise there. The second unexpected development was the direction of the thrust. Even now the French High Command thought in terms of 1914. They thought the Germans would continue straight from Sedan in a south-westerly direction for Paris. Instead, in a great arc the massed Panzers co-ordinated with aircraft followed by infantry, turned west towards the Channel coast at Abbeville, and north-west to Boulogne, Calais and in the direction of Dunkirk. The BEF (the British Expeditionary Force) and northern French armies were now caught in a nutcracker, with one German army pressing them through Belgium and the other swinging behind their rear. It was like a mirror image of the Schlieffen Plan and had the advantage that the wheel to the coast was a finite and limited distance, whereas Schlieffen's arc had been huge, and of virtually indefinite length. Had the Wehrmacht attacked in November 1939, the plan would then have corresponded to Anglo-French expectations of an offensive predominantly through Belgium, the old Schlieffen formula.

In short, German victory was due to the brilliance of the amended war-plan carried out in May 1940, its successful execution by the German High Command and the fighting qualities of the well-trained troops, particularly the Panzer divisions. Obversely, Allied failure was primarily a failure of strategy. French armies were thrown into total confusion, their generals lost control over communications and over the movements of whole armies. No soldier can successfully fight in such a situation, except in local actions. Later, the generals and politicians were quick to blame all sorts of factors – the communists, sabotage, poor equipment, low morale – as having greatly contributed to defeat. The blame must lie overwhelmingly with Gamelin and the Allied generals themselves.

The devastating timetable of defeat can be tersely set out. On 10 May 1940 the Germans launched the western offensive, simultaneously attacking the Netherlands, Belgium and Luxembourg. The terror-bombing and destruction of Rotterdam added a new term to the war vocabulary. The French and British troops moved forward according to a plan which, as it turned out, placed them more securely in the noose. On 13 May the Germans broke through on the Meuse. The French Prime Minister Reynaud telephoned Churchill the following day telling him that the situation was grave, and on the 15th that the battle was lost, the way to Paris open.

The first rift now appeared between the British and French conduct of the war. The French wanted the outcome of the whole war to depend on the battle for France. Churchill already foresaw that if indeed the battle for France was lost the war would go on. There would then be the battle for Britain before Hitler could win. So 15 May 1940 is an important date. Reynaud appealed to Britain to throw the whole of her air force into the battle as the only chance left to stop the Germans. Churchill and the Cabinet were ready to send further squadrons of fighters to France. But twenty-five squadrons would be retained as indispensable for the defence of Britain, as the Commander-in-Chief of Fighter Command, Air Marshal Sir Hugh Dowding, insisted that this represented the minimum necessary protection. On 15 May, to Reynaud's desperate plea, Churchill responded: 'we would do everything we could, but we could not denude England of her essential defences'.

On 16 May Churchill crossed the Channel to see the situation for himself and to infuse some of his fighting spirit into Reynaud's government. As the full disaster became evident, there was near panic in Paris in the ministries and government. Gamelin was dismissed and replaced by General Weygand on 19 May. But Hitler slowed the advance to the Channel. He did not wish to risk his tanks in unsuitable terrain; to Göring and his *Luftwaffe* was to be left a share in annihilating the trapped British. The tanks were temporarily halted. General de Gaulle, of later fame, managed a small-scale counterattack on 17 May but it could not affect the outcome of the battle. In the north the BEF and French divisions were retreating in good order – much too slowly. On 20 May Reynaud had brought Marshal Pétain into his new government. Defeat was in the air. On 24 May the German Panzers reached the coast at Abbeville on the mouth of the Somme. The Allied northern armies were now cut off.

The story of the French capitulation is well known. Increasingly the French began to blame the British for not throwing their last reserves into the battle. They could not conceive how Britain would continue the war without France. Churchill was back in Paris on 23 May to discover how the northern Allied armies including the BEF might be saved. It was trapped, he reported back to the War Cabinet in London the next day. On 25 May, General Lord Gort, the commander of the BEF, in spite of instructions on the 19th from Churchill and the Chiefs of Staff to link with the French, independently began the manoeuvre, subsequently approved, that eventually made it possible to save the British divisions, and many French troops too, from the beaches of Dunkirk. Weygand's planned counter-offensive against the German flanks never had a chance; there were no French forces left who could seriously threaten the Germans. Meanwhile in Paris on the night of 25 May Pétain and other members of the government were already searching for a way to conclude a separate peace with Germany. Prime Minister Reynaud was despatched to London to sound out British reactions to peace initiatives. That same day contingency arrangements to evacuate the BEF were acted on.

The last week of May 1940 was one of the most critical and dramatic periods of the Second World War. The full story of British Cabinet deliberations on possible peace negotiations with Hitlerite Germany, some of which were so secret that their record was kept in a separate and special file, are extraordinarily interesting in the light of later history.[1] Churchill's 'finest hour' was to come: Britain withstood the German Blitz, later that summer and autumn. Government and people were

[1] The file of the relevant Cabinet Records is kept at the Public Record Office, London, 65/13.

determined to repel invasion from their shores. In Churchill's speeches the spirit of resolution and the will to fight were accurately encapsulated. Yet the 'finest hour' might never have struck.

The picture of Churchill as the indomitable war leader towering over colleagues is so deeply etched in the history of the Second World War that it comes as a surprise that his position as prime minister during the first weeks of office was far weaker than that enjoyed by any of his predecessors since the fall of Lloyd George. Chamberlain probably at first saw Churchill as the best war leader for the duration of the conflict and he was also the one Conservative whom Labour and Liberals could agree to serve under. Churchill presided over a small War Cabinet of five. Neville Chamberlain and Halifax, the two most powerful Conservatives, were now joined by two Labour Party ministers, Clement Attlee and Arthur Greenwood. But Churchill was regarded with much suspicion by many Conservatives, who continued to look to Chamberlain for guidance. Within the War Cabinet, Chamberlain's role was still decisive. If he sided with Halifax against Churchill, given the continued party loyalty Chamberlain still enjoyed and the overwhelming strength of the Conservatives in the House of Commons, Churchill would not be able to make his views prevail even with the support of Labour and its two representatives in the War Cabinet. The government might then break up – as the French did – with disastrous results at a moment of crisis. This political reality has to be borne in mind when assessing what Churchill, Chamberlain, Halifax, Attlee and Greenwood said during the long hours of Cabinet discussion in May 1940. What was at stake was more than the fate of a government. Whether Britain would remain in the war, the future of Western Europe and the course of world history would be affected by the outcome.

Halifax, the Foreign Secretary, made a determined bid to persuade the War Cabinet to sanction peace feelers. The Cabinet had authorised him on 24 May to try to discover what terms might keep Mussolini out of the war. But Halifax went beyond his brief when he spoke to the Italian Ambassador on 25 May.[1] He reported back to the Cabinet on the morning of Sunday, 26 May, that the Italian Ambassador had sounded him out on whether the British government would agree to a conference; according to the Ambassador, Mussolini's principal wish was to secure peace in Europe, and he wanted Italian and British issues to be looked at as 'part of a general European settlement'. Halifax agreed emphatically and replied that peace and security in Europe were equally Britain's main object and that 'we should naturally be prepared to consider any proposal which might lead to this provided our liberty and independence were assured'.[2] In this way efforts to keep Italy out of the war – efforts which the Cabinet had already sanctioned involved seeking Roosevelt's good offices – were being widened to draw in Germany and France in an attempt to reach a general peace. Halifax now wanted to secure the authorisation of the Cabinet to seek the Duce's mediation for this purpose. Churchill opposed Halifax; the Prime Minister's instincts were sound. Even if 'decent' terms were offered in May 1940 they would have been no safeguard against fresh demands later, once Britain was at Hitler's mercy. Churchill also knew that if he consented to the commencement of any negotiations it might then prove impossible to fight on. He was therefore determined by any and all means to block Halifax's manoeuvres.

After the Cabinet meeting on Sunday morning of 26 May Churchill lunched with the French Prime Minister Paul Reynaud, who had flown over from France. Churchill urged him to keep France in the war. Reynaud, according to Churchill, 'dwelt not obscurely upon the possible French withdrawal from the war'. Reynaud's immediate request was that negotiations should be started to keep Italy out of the war by bribing Mussolini with offers including the neutralisation of Gibraltar and Suez as well as the demilitarisation of Malta. But Churchill wanted no approach to Italy. He knew how easily this could slide into peace negotiations with Germany. He told Reynaud that Britain would not give up on any account but would rather go down fighting than be enslaved to Germany.

After further discussions with the French Prime Minister, the British Cabinet reassembled in the afternoon. Halifax urged that the mediation of Mussolini be sought; Hitler, he observed, might not present such unreasonable terms. Churchill repeatedly opposed such a move. In the diary Cham-

1 Record of conversation Halifax and Bastiani, 25 May 1940, Cabinet 65/13, PRO.

2 Record of conversation Halifax and Bastiani, 25 May 1940, Cabinet 65/13, PRO.

berlain kept of these vital hours he records Churchill as saying, 'It was incredible that Hitler would consent to any terms that we could accept though if we could get out of this jam by giving up Malta and some African colonies he would jump at it. But the only safe way was to convince Hitler that he could not beat us. We might do better without the French than with them if they tied us to a conference into which we should enter with our case lost beforehand.' What are we to make of Churchill's remark that 'he would jump' at the chance of getting out of the war? If this one remark is considered alone it might appear that not much separated Churchill from Halifax. But Churchill's actions throughout these critical days, and all the arguments he marshalled, make it absurd to suppose that he had any other intention but that of defeating Halifax and of winning over the remaining Cabinet ministers in order to fight on. An approach to Mussolini, Churchill warned, would not only be futile but would involve Britain in 'deadly danger'; 'let us therefore avoid being dragged down the slippery slope with France'.

Nevertheless in making an effort to appear reasonable, by apparent concessions to Halifax's arguments, Churchill was manoeuvred into a dangerous corner at the Cabinet meeting on the following day, 27 May. He reiterated his view that no attempt should be made to start any negotiations by way of Mussolini. Halifax, who was a formidable opponent, now accused Churchill of inconsistency, saying that when on the previous day he had asked him whether he were satisfied that if matters vital to Britain's independence were unaffected he would be prepared to discuss terms, Churchill had then replied that 'he would be thankful to get out of our present difficulties on such terms, provided we retained the essentials and the elements of our vital strength, even at the cost of some cession of territory'. Yet now, Halifax pointed out, Churchill spoke only of fighting to a finish. Churchill was flustered; he attempted to reconcile what could not be reconciled by saying, 'If Herr Hitler were prepared to make peace on the terms of the restoration of the German colonies and the overlordship of Central Europe, that was one thing. But it was quite unlikely that he would make any such offer.' Halifax immediately followed up his advantage, pressing Churchill by asking him whether he would be willing to discuss Hitler's terms. Churchill rather feebly responded that 'He would not join France in asking for terms; but if he were told what the terms offered were, he would be prepared to consider them.' The Cabinet ended. Churchill had gained just one important point: Britain would not initiate direct negotiations with Hitler.‡

The Cabinet met again on 28 May. Halifax once more, on the pretext of starting negotiations to keep Italy out of the war, was trying to find a way of discussing peace with Hitler's Germany. The War Cabinet well understood this. The real difference between Halifax and Churchill was simple. Halifax believed the war already lost; to fight on would entail useless sacrifice. What he actually said was that Britain might get better terms before France left the war and before Britain's aircraft factories were bombed by the Luftwaffe. The Italian Embassy now wanted to know, Halifax said, whether 'we should like mediation by Italy'. Churchill retorted that Britain could not negotiate from weakness; 'the position would be entirely different when Germany had made an unsuccessful attempt to invade the country', he added, and he argued that even if defeated later Britain would get no worse terms than now. A nation that went down fighting would rise again whereas those that tamely surrendered were finished. Any negotiations, furthermore, would undermine the nation's morale. Churchill was supported by both Attlee and Greenwood. The cold, calculating Foreign Secretary thought that Churchill was indulging in rhetorical heroics. But the decisive voice was Chamberlain's.

Chamberlain had been deeply shocked by the débâcle in France. The basis on which he had previously conducted the war had been shattered. In his diary a little over a week before these crucial Cabinet discussions he had noted that he expected a German ultimatum, and that it might be necessary to fight on but that 'We should be fighting only for better terms not for victory.' Chamberlain thought with Halifax that realism could only lead to the conclusion that the war was lost. But he jibbed at bribing Mussolini while Britain and Germany remained at war. On the issue of whether Mussolini's help should be invoked to bring Germany, France and Britain to the conference table his views fluctuated. Halifax worked hard on him to get him to force Churchill's hand. Chamberlain, however, attempted to reconcile Halifax and Churchill. In addressing the Cabinet, Chamberlain said on 28

‡ Cabinet Record, 27 May 1940, 65/13, PRO.

May, 'He felt bound to say that he was in agreement with the Foreign Secretary in taking the view that if we thought it was possible that we now get terms, which, although grievous, would not threaten our independence, we should be right to consider such terms.' But, he added, he did not think the French idea of an approach to Mussolini would produce 'decent terms', especially with France in Hitler's grasp. Chamberlain therefore said he had come to the conclusion that an 'approach to Italy was useless at the present time, it might be that we should take a different view in a short time, possibly even a week hence'. Churchill had won, at least for the time being.

One cannot say with certainty what would have happened if Chamberlain, not Churchill, had been prime minister. Halifax might then have carried the day. The impression the documents leave is that Chamberlain had acted less from conviction than out of loyalty to the Prime Minister. The Cabinet adjourned at 6.15 p.m. Churchill had called a meeting of the ministers not in the War Cabinet to his room in the House of Commons that evening. He told them that 'of course whatever happens at Dunkirk, we shall fight on'. He reported back to the reassembled War Cabinet at 7 p.m. that his message had been greeted with enthusiasm. Churchill then agreed to a long and tactful message to be sent to Reynaud explaining that Halifax's 'formula' prepared on the occasion of Reynaud's visit two days previously, which had contemplated asking Mussolini to act as mediator, was now dead; 'we are convinced that at this moment when Hitler is flushed with victory . . . it would be impossible for Signor Mussolini to put forward proposals for a conference with any success'.*

Churchill's victory would not be final as long as Halifax remained in the Cabinet and could influence Chamberlain. Indeed the following day the Foreign Secretary challenged Churchill's fighting despatch to Lord Gort. Halifax wanted a despatch sent that left to Gort's judgement the decision whether to surrender the BEF. 'It would not be dishonourable to relinquish the struggle in order to save a handful of men from massacre.' Churchill was not strong enough to offer outright opposition to such defeatism but evaded the issue by asking for time to consider the position. The evacuation from Dunkirk soon made any reconsideration unnecessary. Churchill was successfully playing for time.

In mid-June 1940, with the imminent withdrawal of France from the war, there were more anxious moments for Churchill. In July Hitler in a speech finally called on Britain to be reasonable and to make peace. At the same time he mocked Churchill, whose position was still far from assured. On 2 August, the King of Sweden secretly offered his mediation but the Cabinet on 7 August approved Halifax's reply which made Germany's withdrawal from all her conquests a precondition.† The full story of continuing attempts by those under Churchill to seek peace remains to be told but there is no reason to doubt Chamberlain's continued loyalty to the Prime Minister. It enabled Churchill to survive and at least to neutralise his opponents.

Chamberlain was incapacitated in the summer of 1940. Inoperable cancer was diagnosed. It was Chamberlain's terminal illness and resignation from the government in October 1940 that transformed Churchill's position. He now became leader of the party and in November 1940, when Chamberlain died, he paid tribute to Chamberlain's sincerity. During those critical first weeks of his administration he had owed much to him. Britain had survived. The Chiefs of Staff in a grave report in May 1940 had not rated Britain's chances very highly, concluding that 'Germany has most of the cards; but the real test is whether the morale of our fighting personnel and civil populations will counterbalance the numerical and material advantages which Germany enjoys. We believe it will.' That Britain had fought back was due to a unified people, to the Royal Air Force, the Royal Navy and the army, whose morale remained intact. This unity would have been severely tested if Churchill's leadership had been repudiated at the heart of government. But the doubts and divisions within the War Cabinet remained a well-kept secret until long after the war was over. In December 1940, Churchill reconstructed the War Cabinet and sent Halifax to Washington as ambassador, bringing Eden into the Cabinet as foreign secretary. But we must now retrace our steps to the course the war took during the last days of May and the summer of 1940.

*

* Cabinet Record, 28 May 1940, 65/13, PRO.

† Cabinet Record, 7 August 1940, 65/14, PRO.

Dunkirk. The Germans blundered, the British improvised and the French fought stubbornly to defend the beachhead. That is why 338,226 British, French and other Allied soldiers were able to escape the French coast when the Cabinet in London had already given most of them up for lost; waiting to embark was tense for all (above)*; the relief at reaching English shores unbounded* (right)*. The evacuation began on 24 May and ended on 4 June. Eva Braun, Hitler's mistress, no doubt gloated over the 40,000 who did fall into German hands. This photo* (left) *of British prisoners was found in her private collection after her death.*

On 28 May Leopold, King of the Belgians, capitulated, ignoring the contrary advice of his ministers. The evacuation of the BEF had begun the previous day. Every possible boat, including paddle pleasure steamers, was pressed into service. The Royal Navy conducted the evacuation, and some air cover could be provided by the air force. Göring's Luftwaffe strafed the boats and the men waiting on the beaches. But the calm seas favoured the Allies. The evacuation went on day after day until 3 June. A total of 338,226 Allied troops were snatched from certain capture, including 139,097 Frenchmen, but all the equipment was lost. To the south the war went on in France, and Britain even sent reinforcements to encourage the French. But Weygand viewed the situation as nearly hopeless. The French were given a few days' grace while the German divisions redeployed.

On 10 June 1940 Mussolini – having contemptuously rejected Roosevelt's earlier offer of good offices (page 262) – declared war on an already beaten France. Even so the French forces along the Italian frontier repulsed the Italian attacks. But the Germans could not be held. On 14 June they entered Paris. The government had fled to Bordeaux and was seeking release from the British alliance so that it could negotiate separately with Germany. Churchill at first replied that Britain would be willing to grant this wish provided the powerful French fleet were sent to British ports. Hard on the heels of this response, General de Gaulle, who had come to Britain to call on the French to continue the fight from a base still free from the enemy, telephoned from London an extraordinary proposal. Britain, as evidence of solidarity, was now offering to all Frenchmen an 'indissoluble union' of the United Kingdom and the 'French Republic'. Churchill had been sceptical from the first about whether this dramatic gesture would have much effect in Bordeaux and so keep France in the war. In Bordeaux Reynaud favoured acceptance but the French Cabinet never considered the idea seriously. During these critical days there remained much doubt about Britain's actual conditions for releasing France from her alliance. The final agonies ended with Pétain replacing Reynaud as prime minister. He immediately began armistice negotiations. On 22 June the French accepted the German terms and later signed them in the same railway carriage in which Marshal Foch had accepted the German capitulation at the end of the First World War.

A photo that none would have thought possible ten months previously. It depicts Hitler arriving on a surprise early morning visit one June day in 1940 to satisfy his curiosity about Parisian architecture. He found much to criticize.

France was divided into occupied and unoccupied areas. The whole Atlantic coast came under German control. South and south-eastern France was governed by Pétain from a new capital established in Vichy. The colonial empire remained under the control of Vichy. The French sought to ensure that their fleet would not be used by Germany against Britain. The armistice provided that it would be disarmed under German supervision. Not unreasonably the British Cabinet remained unsure whether or not the Germans would in the end seize the fleet. For Britain the war had become a fight for national survival. In one of the most controversial military actions of the war, British forces attacked units of the French fleet at

Mers-el-Kebir on 3 July, after the French Admiral refused a British ultimatum requiring him to follow one of four courses, each of which would have denied the Germans use of these warships. The British action cost the lives of 1297 French sailors so recently their allies. It was an indication that Churchill would pursue the war with all the ruthlessness necessary to defeat a ruthless enemy. Vichy decided not to declare war but to break off diplomatic relations with Britain.

In London, General de Gaulle rallied the small Free French Forces. But the great majority of Frenchmen and most of the colonial empire accepted the legitimacy of Vichy and Pétain. Vichy France remained an important strategic factor in Britain's calculations, so de Gaulle was not granted the status of the leader of a French government in exile, even though such Polish, Dutch and Belgian governments had been recognised. He deeply resented this as an insult to the honour of France as now embodied in his movement.

The course of the war from the fall of France to December 1941 needs to be followed in three separate strands. First there was the actual conflict between Britain and Germany and Italy on land, sea and air. The most critical of the struggles was the battle in the air. Hitler believed that unless he won command of the air he could not, in the face of the strong British fleet, successfully mount Operation Sea Lion, codename for his invasion of the British Isles. On 10 July the preliminary of the Battle of Britain started over the Straits of Dover, then in mid-August the main attack switched to British airfields. The Luftwaffe could use some 2500 bombers and fighters in the battle. Britain's first-line fighter strength was some 1200 fighters. The radar stations on the coast which gave warning of the approach of the German planes and the cracking of the German operational code, as well as the superior Hurricanes and Spitfires, of which 660 could be used, were to Britain's advantage. But had the Germans persisted in their attacks on airfields they might nevertheless have succeeded in their aim of destroying Britain's air strength. Instead the German attack switched to cities. London was heavily raided on 7 September in reprisal for an RAF raid on Berlin. On 15 September it was clear that the German air force had failed to establish command of the air and two days later Hitler abandoned plans for the invasion of England. But now the night raids against cities were causing tremendous damage to London and other British towns. On 14 November 1940 Coventry was blitzed. The night raids continued, but for all their damage, for all the loss of life they caused, they were not a decisive factor in the outcome of the war. The people emerged from the air-raid shelters to work in the war factories.

More critical was the war at sea. Although Britain controlled the surface of the oceans, submarine warfare once again brought her into desperate danger by disrupting essential supplies from America. The submarine threat reached its most serious peak between March and July 1941. The losses of British tonnage were heavy, but the United States increasingly assumed a belligerent attitude in guarding the convoys on her side of the Atlantic. The Germans never won what Churchill called the battle of the Atlantic.

On land Britain at first won spectacular victories in Africa during General Wavell's campaigns against the Italians in the spring of 1941. With the help of Dominion troops from South Africa, Australia and New Zealand as well as Indian troops, a much larger Italian army was defeated and chased out of Libya and Cyrenaica. In East Africa Abyssinia was freed and Haile Selassie restored to his throne. Hitler responded by sending General Erwin Rommel and an Afrika Korps to assist the Italians in the western desert. Wavell was forced back to the Egyptian frontier.

Britain had weakened her forces in the Middle East by sending an expedition to Greece. Mussolini had attacked Greece in October 1940 to show Hitler that he too could act independently. Unfortunately he could win no battles and soon the Greeks were chasing the Italians into Albania. In April 1941, Hitler came to Mussolini's rescue once more. By the end of the month the Greeks were defeated and the British expeditionary force withdrew. Britain's last forces were defeated in Crete which was spectacularly captured at the end of May 1941 by German paratroopers, who, however, suffered heavy casualties in the operation.

The second strand of the period from June 1940 to the end of 1941 is formed by the growing informal alliance between Britain and the United States. During Britain's 'finest hour', she did not stand alone. Besides the forces of her European Allies who had formed new fighting units in Britain she enjoyed from the beginning of the war the full support of the Dominions, all of whom had chosen to stand by Britain. Only Eire (Ireland) declared her neutrality. The support of the Dominions and empire was an important addition to Britain's ability to wage war. But without the United States Britain's survival would have been problematical. Until the fall of France, President Roosevelt was convinced that to make available the capacities of American industry to provide war supplies to Britain and France would be sufficient to ensure an Allied victory. In the mid-1930s Congress had attempted to prevent the United States from playing a role similar to that of the First World War by passing the Neutrality Laws in 1935, 1936 and 1937 so that the United States would not be 'dragged' into war. This legislation denied belligerents the right to purchase arms and munitions or secure American credit for such purposes. In November 1939, Roosevelt secured the repeal of some of its provisions. Belligerents could now obtain arms and munitions provided they paid for them and transported them home in their own ships ('cash and carry'). Britain and France took immediate advantage of the opportunity. Germany, lacking the means to transport purchases to Europe, could not do so.

The collapse of American neutrality was rapid. Roosevelt was determined to help Britain in every way possible to continue the war against Germany once he became convinced in July 1940 that Britain was not about to be knocked out of the war. Congress, concerned to keep the United States out of the war, was the major impediment. Bypassing Congress, Roosevelt agreed in September 1940 to Churchill's repeated pleas for fifty First World War destroyers in return for leases on naval bases in the British West Indies. He also obtained a formal promise from the British government never to surrender the British fleet to the Germans. But he felt it politically essential during the presidential election of the autumn of 1940 to promise the American people simply, 'Your boys are not going to be sent into any foreign wars.' When the votes were counted in November, Roosevelt's victory was decisive.

Following the election, Churchill appealed to Roosevelt for all-out aid. He wanted arms and ships and planes if Britain were to match Germany's strength. Roosevelt did his best to marshal American public opinion, declaring in a speech on 30 December 1940 that the United States would become the 'arsenal of democracy'. The Lend-Lease Act (March 1941) made all these goods available to Britain without payment. By May 1941 Roosevelt had concluded that the United States would have to enter the war, but given the attitude of Congress and of the majority of the American people he wanted Germany to fire the first shot. Hitler did not oblige. He cleverly avoided treating the United States as a hostile state even though the US Navy was now convoying merchant vessels – British, American and neutral – halfway across the Atlantic, and was occupying Iceland. In August 1941 Roosevelt met Churchill off Newfoundland and they jointly enunciated the principles on which a post-war settlement (known as the Atlantic Charter) would be based after the final destruction of the Nazi tyranny. Roosevelt and Congress supported all such unneutral behaviour partly out of hatred of Nazi rule but above all because the safety of the United States depended on Britain's successful resistance. Roosevelt and Congress had virtually placed the United States in a state of undeclared war against Germany, but did not cross the rubicon of declared all-out war until after the attack by Japan in December 1941 – and then it was Germany which first declared war on the United States.

The third decisive strand of these years was the transformation of the Nazi–Soviet partnership into hostility, marked by the beginning of the great war which Germany launched against Russia on 22 June 1941. Since 23 August 1939, when the Nazi–Soviet Non-Aggression Pact had been concluded, Stalin had avoided being drawn into war against Germany. Military unpreparedness in 1939 would have made war even more catastrophic for Russia then than in 1941: the West would have remained behind their defensive line leaving Russia to face the full force of the Wehrmacht. If the Wehrmacht had succeeded in defeating the Soviet Union, admittedly a hypothetical question, the military picture of the Second World War would have been totally different. Stalin in 1939 had no wish, of course, to save the Western democracies. He wanted to protect Russia and never lost his belief in the ultimate hostility of the Western capitalist powers. From the Soviet point of view the pact with the Germans had other advantages in enabling her to take on Japan without fear of a German attack in Europe. The Japanese were stunned by Hitler's U-turn of policy. Left isolated, they hastened their own undeclared war with the Soviet Union on the borders of Manchuria and Mongolia and were defeated. The

Non-Aggression Pact also brought other gains for Russia. In a secret additional protocol the Russians secured German acknowledgement of the Russian sphere of interest in Eastern Europe. The Baltic states, Finland, Estonia, Latvia and Lithuania, fell into Russia's sphere. Russia also expressed her 'interest' in Bessarabia, then part of Romania. Poland was partitioned 'in the event of a territorial and political rearrangement' taking place, a fine circumlocution for the imminent German attack on Poland.

Germany's unexpectedly rapid defeat of the Poles nevertheless surprised and alarmed the Russians, who extensively mobilised and entered Poland on 17 September 1939. But Hitler did not plan to attack the Soviet Union next. France was to be defeated first. Stalin in any case was confident that he could 'appease' Hitler. A new Soviet–German treaty of friendship was concluded on 28 September, adjusting the Polish partition in favour of the Germans. The Russians also denounced France and Britain as responsible for continuing the war. From the end of September 1939 to June 1941, the Soviet Union supplied Germany with grain, oil and war materials.

In this way the Soviet Union, though officially neutral, became aligned with Germany. The faithfulness with which Stalin carried out his part of the bargain indicates his fear of being exposed to Germany's demonstrated armed might and he expected no real help from the West. Fears of Allied hostility, especially now that the Soviet Union was collaborating with Germany economically, were well founded. Until May 1940, when the German victories in the West revealed the desperate weakness of their own position, the British and French were considering not only sending volunteers to Finland, but also stopping the flow of oil from the Baku oilfields by bombing them or by some other means. Fortunately, the kind of action which could have led to war with the Soviet Union was never taken by France and Britain.

Soviet aggression in 1939 and 1940 was in part pure aggrandisement to recover what had once belonged to the Russian Empire and more, but also to improve Russia's capacity for defence. The Baltic states were occupied without a war. But the Finns refused to accept Soviet proposals for naval bases and a shift of the frontier on the Karelian isthmus, which was only twenty miles from Leningrad. In return Finland was offered Soviet territory. The three months Soviet–Finnish War from 30 November 1939 to 12 March 1940 that followed did nothing to enhance Russia's military prestige. Hitler must have well noted her military incompetence, but her turn had not yet come, and Germany did nothing to help the 'Nordic' Finnish defenders against the Russian Slavs. Stalin was undoubtedly severely shaken by Hitler's victory in France, but he did not show it. On the contrary, he was in June 1940 unexpectedly tough, demanding that Romania return Bessarabia to Russia and, for good measure, the province of Bukovina. He wished to anticipate German dominance in a strategic region bordering on the Soviet Union. Hitler put pressure on Romania to comply. But secretly he had already made his first plans for the invasion of Russia.

Fears in the Kremlin of German dominance in the Balkans led to a sharp deterioration of good relations. This became evident when Molotov, the Soviet Foreign Minister, visited Berlin in November 1940. Molotov's demands infuriated Hitler and reinforced his determination to 'smash' Russia. Yet at the same time Stalin was anxious not to give Germany any pretext for attack and loyally fulfilled to the bitter end all Russia's economic undertakings to deliver war materials. When the Germans struck on 22 June 1941, the Soviet forces were totally unprepared. Despite all the information on the impending German onslaught reaching Stalin from spies and from the Allies, he either disbelieved it as an Allied plot to involve the Soviet Union in war or was afraid to take precautionary military counter-measures for fear of provoking the Germans. His failure in June 1941 was perhaps one of the most extraordinary displays of weakness by this hard and ruthless dictator.

Hitler's decision to launch his war on Russia marks a great turning point in the Second World War and made his ultimate defeat certain when he failed to destroy Russia militarily in this new *Blitzkrieg* during the first few months. Previous German military successes had made him overconfident. The war with the Soviet Union in fact repeated the 'war of attrition' which alone had brought the First World War to an end. Of course the Russian war from 1941 to 1945 was a war of dramatic movement, unlike the trench warfare on the western front – but its effect in destroying millions of soldiers and huge quantities of material in the end bled the Third Reich to death. Why did

Hitler attack the Soviet Union?

After the fall of France, Hitler hoped Britain would sue for peace. After the failure of the Luftwaffe in the battle of Britain, Hitler for the time being abandoned the alternative of subjugating the British Isles militarily. He also failed in October 1940 to win Franco's and Pétain's support for a joint Mediterranean strategy of destroying Britain's Mediterranean power. Hitler now reasoned that the war against Russia, which he had all along intended to wage as the centrepiece of his ideological faith and territorial ambition, should be launched before Britain's defeat. It was to serve the additional, though not primary, purpose of convincing Britain that it was useless to continue the war any longer. Hitler gave the order to prepare Operation Barbarossa on 18 December 1940.

A series of brief Balkan campaigns in the spring of 1941 ensured that the invasion of Russia would be undertaken on a broad front without any possibility of a hostile flank. Fear of Germany, together with hostility to Russia, had turned Romania, Hungary and Slovakia into more or less enthusiastic junior German partners who all declared war on Russia, as did Italy and Finland. They felt safe under Germany's military umbrella. Bulgaria, though practically occupied by German troops, remained neutral. Greece was also involved since Mussolini had decided on his own little war of conquest. In the end German troops had to rescue the Italian army and so Greece was occupied. Hitler thought Yugoslavia too was in the bag when the Regent, Prince Paul, signed a treaty with Germany in March 1941. But there was a revolt against the Regent and the new government repudiated the German alignment. Yugoslavia's resistance did not last long. The Germans attacked on 6 April and the Hungarians faithlessly joined in three days later. In less than two weeks Yugoslav resistance was overpowered. Until recently it was believed that these two wars against Yugoslavia and Greece, though minor for Germany, had momentous consequences by delaying the attack on the Soviet Union – a delay that meant the Wehrmacht ground to a halt in front of Moscow in the bitter winter of 1941/2. In fact the Greek and Yugoslav military diversion was too slight to affect significantly the time it took to assemble the huge build-up of men, equipment and supplies for the Russian invasion. In the early hours of 22 June 1941 the Germans launched the attack in the air with approximately 190 German and satellite divisions. The Soviet Union was thereby given no choice but to enter into an alliance with Britain and, later, into alignment with the United States as well. The consequences of this new war unleashed by Hitler proved momentous for the course of world history.

CHAPTER 27

The China War and the Origins of the Pacific War, 1937–1941

The Pacific War grew out of Japan's China War renewed in 1937. Though there are doubts about how far the Japanese pre-planned a large-scale conflict, a small incident became for the Japanese the starting point for an all-out war against China. It was essentially the future of China that four years later led Japan to war with the United States. The decision for war was taken in Tokyo in September 1941 because the United States was seen as the enemy unalterably opposed to Japan's concept of her right to a dominant role in China and eastern Asia. The only chance for peace was a change in the course of American policy as perceived by the Japanese, and this did not happen. The Japanese leaders believed that the choice before them was to fulfil the task of conquest or to acquiesce in Japan's national decline. Why, the Japanese wondered, should the United States of all nations deny Japan the right to an Asian Monroe Doctrine?

But the course of events that led to war was not so straightforward when looked at in depth, and raises fascinating questions. Was the Japanese perception of US policy correct? Britain and the United States, moreover, were not the only two strong Western powers with interests in eastern Asia. From the beginning of Japan's expansion in China, the only country capable of challenging Japan's army on land with an army of millions other than Nationalist China was Russia. At the time, in the mid-1930s, the Japanese military asked themselves whether Japan's empire could ever be completely safe without first removing the potential Russian threat. Should therefore a war against her northern neighbour precede the efforts to control China? Indeed, might an alliance with China against the Soviet Union be possible? And if the Soviet Union was to be fought, or checked from interfering in Japan's China policy, then might not Europe help – calling in the old world to balance the new?

Such a view corresponded with the traditions of Japanese foreign policy. From 1902, until its dissolution at the Washington Conference two decades later, Japan had enjoyed the support of the Anglo-Japanese alliance. In the new conditions of the 1930s, Hitler's Germany was the obvious counterweight to Bolshevik Russia. The history of German–Japanese relations from 1936, when Japan first joined the Anti-Comintern Pact, to the close of the Second World War is another important theme for study: how the Germans and Japanese viewed this relationship, and whether the British and more importantly American perceptions of that relationship were accurate. The origins of the war in Asia are less well understood than the origins of the war in Europe.

The roots of the conflict lie in the militaristic–spiritual values that Japanese education inculcated. During the 1930s these values were translated into politics by the small group of military, naval and political leaders who exercised power. They now controlled a highly centralised bureaucratic state, having reversed the earlier broadening of political participation which had taken place during the so-called era of Taisho 'democracy' of the 1920s (page 89). Men like Prince Konoe, prime minister in 1937–9 and 1940–1, believed that Japan had a right to achieve equality with other great powers. Unlike the United States and the British Empire, Japan lacked the necessary resources within her own tightly packed islands to fulfil the role of a great power. She was a have-not nation, so some Japanese argued, claiming only the opportunity for prosperity and strength to which her advanced culture, civilisation and capacity for modern technical development entitled her. For Konoe's foreign minister, Matsuoko, Japan's international conduct was also a question of national pride. No Japanese must accept the insulting, inferior role the Western imperialists assigned to him. Only by showing forceful courage would the West ever be convinced of the equality of Japan. The view of many American politicians was precisely the counterpart of this; the Japanese would give way if shown a firm hand.

Confrontation was unavoidable given the Japanese leaders' concept of their national honour's requirements. They saw themselves as guiding a unique people with a divine emperor. While Western *Realpolitik* was certainly practised by Japanese policymakers, the ultimate factor deciding national policy was not rational policy but chauvinism masquerading as spiritual values. The Chief of the Japanese Naval General Staff, for instance, urged in 1941 that Japan should wage war to remain true to the spirit of national defence, saying, 'even if we might not win the war, this noble spirit of defending the fatherland will be perpetuated and our posterity will rise again and again'. The 'spirit' of war itself was glorified; a nation which denied this spirit and did not rise against injustice would deserve to decay. The 'injustice' referred to was America's denial that Japan had the sole right to shape China's destiny. All this chauvinistic spirituality was not the inevitable heritage of Japanese beliefs. There were opposing views, socialist, pacific views based on different Japanese traditions. The moods of governments of the 1930s and 1940s mark a distinctive period in Japanese history, as the post-1945 changes in attitude further confirm.

Britain and the United States formally protested at Japanese aggression in China, but there was no thought in the 1930s of resisting it by force so long as only China was involved. Japan, moreover, stressed the anti-communist aspect of her policy when concluding the Anti-Comintern Pact with Germany in November 1936. The following summer of 1937 was decisive in the policies pursued by the Kwantung and Manchurian armies. In June Russia's capability to hinder Japanese objectives in China was tested. There was more sporadic fighting on the borders with Russia in 1938. The fighting capacity of the Soviet Union had recovered sufficiently from Stalin's purges of the armed forces to inflict a severe defeat on the Japanese army at Nomonhan in August 1939. More than 18,000 Japanese were killed (page 190). This evidence of Soviet strength, coming close on the heels of the German–Soviet Non-Aggression Pact, led the Japanese to revise their estimate that Russia was too weak to interfere in China. The Soviet Union became an important factor in Japan's calculations. Meanwhile the die in China had long been cast, but the Japanese army, despite its victorious advances, could not bring the China War to an end.

The Japanese army had continued to interfere and expand its influence in northern China from 1933 to 1937, but in the whole of northern China the Japanese garrison was only 6000 men. Then, near Peking, on an ancient bridge, Chinese and Japanese soldiers clashed in July 1937. The Marco Polo Bridge incident was in itself minor; exactly how a small number of Japanese and Chinese troops came to clash is still obscure. There is no evidence (unlike in Manchuria in 1931) that the Japanese army had planned war against China and provoked the conflict. There were divided counsels in Tokyo. The hawks won. At first, sharp local actions were undertaken in the expectation that Nationalist China would be overawed. Full-scale war ensued when Chiang Kai-shek chose to resist instead. The war quickly spread from northern China. The Japanese attacked Shanghai and by December 1937 the Nationalist capital of Nanking had fallen. Japanese reinforcements had been rushed to China. In the Shanghai–Nanking operation the Japanese suffered 70,000 casualties and the Chinese at least 370,000. By then 700,000 Japanese troops were engaged in China. After 1938 close to 1 million Japanese troops were fighting some 3 million Chinese troops. The Japanese troops behaved with the utmost brutality, massacring, raping and looting. The fall of Nanking was not the end of the war, as the Japanese hoped, but its beginning. Although one of the world's most devastating wars, the China War is little known in the West. It became a three-

Japan's War in Asia, 1937–1945
SOVIET UNION
KAMCHATKA
MONGOLIA
MANCHUKUO
1931–45
Peking
KOREA
CHINA
1938
Tokyo
JAPANESE EMPIRE
Nanking
Shanghai
Chungking
BURMA
1944
FORMOSA
Hong Kong
Dec. 1941
MARIANAS
ISLANDS
PACIFIC
OCEAN
THAILAND
PHILIPPINES
1942
FRENCH
INDO-CHINA
1940
Guam
1942
MALAYA
SUMATRA
BORNEO
CELEBES
1942
SOLOMON
ISLANDS
NETHERLANDS EAST INDIES
NEW
GUINEA
1942
JAVA
Japanese Empire and occupied land to 1938
Japanese conquests until 1942
0
1000 miles
0
1000 km
AUSTRALIA

sided struggle between the Chinese communists, the Chinese Nationalists and the Japanese. The communists' main priority was to gain control over as much of the territories evacuated by the Nationalists as they could. The Nationalist Chinese armies bore the brunt of the regular fighting.

The sinking of the US naval vessel, *Panay*, and damage to the British *Ladybird* in December 1937 directly involved the two Western powers in the conflict. Since the autumn of 1937 Roosevelt had been searching for some effective counterblast to German, Italian and now Japanese aggression. He gave expression to his desire for 'positive endeavours to preserve peace' in his well-known 'Quarantine' speech in Chicago on 5 October 1937. He called on the peace-loving nations to make a 'concerted effort' in opposition to the lawless aggressors; that lawlessness, he declared, was spreading and the aggressors, like sick patients, should be placed in 'quarantine'. It was rousing stuff but meant little in concrete terms. The depression preoccupied the United States and Britain at home. Neither Congress in America nor Parliament in Britain would contemplate war with Japan. After the *Panay* incident, and before full Japanese apologies were received, Roosevelt for a short while had considered economic sanctions. What destabilized relations further was a renewed naval race between Japan and the United States.

Meanwhile, the powers with interests in China had met in Brussels but the conference assembled there could achieve nothing. Britain would not act without US backing, or in advance of American policy. The needs of the Dominions, Australia and New Zealand, for adequate protection or peace in the Pacific were obvious. But Britain could not match the worldwide defence requirements of her Commonwealth with her available military resources, which had been neglected for years. As the crisis mounted in Europe the British navy was needed in home waters and the Mediterranean and could not be spared for Singapore. Although recognising clearly the threat Japan posed to British interests in China and Asia, a cautious policy had to be followed: conciliation and firmness without risking war at a time of European dangers. In 1939 the Japanese blockaded the British concession in Tientsin, demanding that Britain in effect abandon Nationalist China. It was a serious crisis but the simultaneous threat of war in Europe decided the British Cabinet in June 1939 to reach a compromise with Japan.

The first tentative shift of American policy, nevertheless, did occur just after Britain's climb-down in the summer of 1939. Of fundamental importance for the history of eastern Asia was that for a decade the United States felt somewhat uncritically anti-Japanese, while Chiang Kai-shek became almost an American folk hero.

The Prime Minister, Prince Fumimaro Konoe, would have liked to bring the war in China to an end but his 'solution' implied Chinese acceptance of Japan as the senior member of the Asian 'family'. That is how the Japanese deluded themselves that their aggression was really for the good of all the Asian people. The vastness of Chinese territory denied the Japanese army the possibility of conquering the whole of China, even after eight years of warfare. Within the huge areas they did occupy, despite the utmost barbarity of the occupation, which would have been unthinkable in the Meiji era, much of the countryside remained under communist or Nationalist control. The Japanese for the most part could make their occupation effective only in the towns and along the vital railway lines.

Encouraged by moral and some material American support, Chiang Kai-shek refused all peace terms which would have subjugated China in the manner of Japan's Twenty-One Demands. In November 1938 Konoe sought to make it clear to Chiang Kai-shek, and the world, that Japan would never leave China. Japan would establish a New Order in Asia through the economic, political and cultural union of Japan, Manchukuo and China. The New Order served notice to the Western powers that there would be no room for Western interests of the kind that had existed in China before. Early in 1939 Konoe resigned. It is certainly mistaken to see him as a peaceful moderate, though he endeavoured to avoid war with the United States without abandoning Japan's anti-Western policy in east Asia. German victories in Europe from September 1939 to July 1940 greatly strengthened the impatient military. With the abolition of political parties Japan became more authoritarian.

In July 1940 Konoe headed a second government. Japan drew closer to Germany, concluding, as a result of Foreign Minister Matsuoka's urging, the Three-Power Pact (Italy was also a signatory) on 27 September 1940. It purported to be an agreement on the division of the world. Japan recognised Germany's and Italy's leadership in the establishment of a 'new order in Europe'; Germany and

Italy recognised the 'leadership of Japan in the establishment of a new order in Greater Asia'. With the reservation of Japanese neutrality towards the Soviet Union, the three powers promised to help each other by all means, including military, if attacked by a 'Power at present not involved in the European War or in the Sino-Japanese Conflict'. That article (three) pointed to the United States. What was the purpose of the alliance? Both the Japanese and the Germans at the time hoped it would act as a deterrent against the United States involving herself in a war over Asian issues. Hitler, furthermore, hoped Japan would attack Singapore, thus increasing the pressure on Britain to make peace with Germany or to face even worse military complications in defence of her empire. In Tokyo, in all probability without Berlin having any knowledge of it, the German Ambassador in an additional exchange of notes with Matsuoka conceded to the Japanese a good deal of flexibility in the honouring of their obligations to help Germany militarily if in fact the United States went to war with Germany alone and not with Japan.

The existence of the treaty made a deep impression on Roosevelt, who saw it as confirmation that all the aggressors in Europe and Asia were linked in one world conspiracy of aggression. That this was *not* so in fact Roosevelt discovered when the Japanese–American confrontation had reached the point in September 1941 at which war was seen by the Japanese as the only way out. But the prime cause of US–Japanese tension was not the German–Japanese alliance. That lacked all substance on the Japanese side. Konoe instructed the Japanese Embassy in Washington in September 1941 to tell the United States that, if she went to war with Germany in Europe, Japan would not feel herself bound to declare war on her in the Pacific but that the 'execution of the Tripartite Pact shall be independently decided'.

The story of how the United States and Japan came to be engaged in the Pacific War is a twisted and tangled one. Roosevelt did not want a war in the Pacific, believing that the defeat of Nazi Germany should take priority. Hitler urged the Japanese to strike at the British Empire in Asia, thereby weakening Britain's capacity to oppose him in Europe and the Mediterranean. If the Japanese decided they had to attack the United States simultaneously, they were assured of Germany's alliance. What the Japanese wanted was to finish the war in China and not have to take on America as well.

In Britain both Chamberlain before May 1940 and Churchill afterwards wished to avoid the extension of war in the Pacific. In 1940 and 1941 Britain was engaged in fighting in the Mediterranean and the Middle East to preserve her power there. The Dominions of New Zealand and Australia, moreover, clamoured for adequate defence in eastern Asia; that defence would best be served by peace and deterrence. But Churchill believed that for deterrence to have credibility the United States and Britain would need to form a counterpart to the Triple Alliance of Japan, Germany and Italy, so that Japan would realise that her expansion beyond the limits which Britain and the United States were prepared to accept in south-east Asia would result in war. Thus both Churchill's and Roosevelt's thinking was based on the theory of deterrence. Except that Roosevelt, dependent upon support in Congress, could not go so far as to threaten war or to ally with Britain.

The mutual policies of deterrence – of the Japanese on the one hand, and of the United States and Britain on the other – totally failed in their purpose. The United States was not deterred by Japan's alliance with Germany and Italy from continuing to play a role as an eastern Asian power. Indeed she stepped up her support for Chiang Kai-shek. Without Nationalist Chinese resistance, the ever-growing pretensions of Japan's co-prosperity sphere would become a reality, placing Western interests completely at Japan's mercy. For Britain, the vital regions were those bordering on the British Empire in Malaya, Burma and India. In this way the French colonies of Indo-China, the Netherlands East Indies, independent Thailand and the American Philippines came to be seen as the key areas to be defended against Japan. But the 'firm' policy towards Japan eventually adopted by the United States to impede Japanese expansion triggered off among Japan's leaders an almost fatalistic response that war with the United States and Britain was preferable to the kind of peace, a return to the Washington peace structure of the 1920s, which the two Western powers sought. The crux was China. Britain and the United States were not prepared to accept Japanese domination over China. Roosevelt held to the simple truth that China was for the Chinese. Furthermore, if the Japanese were allowed to achieve their aims in China no Western interests in eastern Asia would be safe.

The course of US policy from 1940 to 1941 was nevertheless not clear or consistent. It is sometimes difficult to fathom precisely what was in Roosevelt's mind. He was sensitive to American public opinion, which increasingly demanded tough measures, short of war, to restrain Japan from ousting US commerce from China. Yet, with war raging across the Atlantic, Roosevelt genuinely wished to preserve peace in the Pacific for as long as possible, though not on Japan's terms. The United States possessed powerful retaliatory economic weapons: the American market for Japanese goods, American raw materials essential to Japan, including oil, and capital for Japanese industry. Secretary of State Cordell Hull advised caution in applying any economic sanctions; but some of Roosevelt's other advisers, including the powerful Secretary of the Treasury, Henry Morgenthau, believed that Japan would have to accept American conditions for a just settlement in China once the United States made use of her economic muscle, for oil and raw materials were essential to sustain a Japanese war against the West. Roosevelt followed an uncertain middle course. In July 1939, the Japanese were informed that the treaty of commerce with the United States would be terminated in January 1940. This was the first tentative application of economic pressure and shocked the Japanese leaders. After its termination it would be possible to impose sanctions other than 'moral embargoes'.

With the defeat of the Netherlands and France by Germany in the summer of 1940, the chances of peace in the Pacific grew less. French and Dutch possessions in south-east Asia now became tempting targets for Japan, which cast covetous eyes particularly on the Netherlands East Indies with their valuable raw materials of tin, rubber and oil. But the American administration made clear that it would regard any change in the *status quo* of these European possessions as endangering American interests and peace in the Pacific. In 1940 Japan increased the pressure on France and Britain to block aid to China. Vichy France had to accept the stationing of Japanese troops in northern Indo-China and for a time Britain agreed to close the Burma Road along which supplies had been sent to Nationalist China. If the United States were not prepared to use her economic weapons, then, the British argued, there was nothing left for them to do but to attempt to appease Japan.

In July 1940, Roosevelt took a second step to apply economic pressure on Japan. He ordered that the export of petrol suitable for aviation fuel be restricted, in addition to lubricants and high-grade scrap metal. Although this was intended as a limited embargo, there were those in Washington who, as it turned out, rightly foretold that turning the screw would not make for peace but would lead the Japanese in desperation to attack the Netherlands East Indies. Roosevelt was well aware of the danger and characteristically wanted to apply some pressure but not push Japan too hard. The Tripartite Pact which Japan, Germany and Italy concluded in September 1940 hardened Roosevelt's attitude (page 275). In a speech soon after the conclusion of the pact, Roosevelt declared, 'No combination of dictator countries of Europe and Asia will stop the help we are giving to . . . those who resist aggression, and who now hold the aggressors far from our shores.' All the same, from the summer of 1940 to the summer of 1941 Roosevelt attempted to dampen down the crisis in the Pacific. He gave some additional help to China, but also urged restraint on Japan. He also made it clear that he was still willing and anxious to negotiate a settlement. Meanwhile he rejected Churchill's urging that the United States and Britain should jointly take steps so that the Japanese should be left in no doubt that further aggression in Asia meant war.

Negotiations got under way in Washington between the Japanese Ambassador Nomura and Secretary of State Cordell Hull in the spring of 1941. Meanwhile, the Japanese signed a neutrality pact with the Soviet Union and were extending their military bases to southern Indo-China in the obvious direction of the Netherlands East Indies. A crucial decision was taken in Tokyo that affected the whole course of world history. The plan to strike north from China and join Germany in the war against the Soviet Union was rejected. Japan would advance to the south to secure the raw materials vital to her own needs. An imperial conference on 2 July 1941 gave its seal of approval to that decision. The goal was the Dutch East Indies. Japan did not wish to go to war with the United States and the British Empire. Her diplomats would try to convince London and Washington that for her this was a question of survival. If Britain and the United States, however, opposed the southern drive, the Japanese Empire would not shrink from war either.

Roosevelt proposed that, if Japan withdrew from southern French Indo-China, the raw materials she needed could be guaranteed by the powers and the region would be neutralised. What impressed the Japanese more was the order freezing Japanese funds in the United States and an American trade embargo which, despite Roosevelt's initial intentions, included oil. But Roosevelt's object was still to avoid war in the Pacific, while somehow getting the United States in on the side of Britain in Europe. After the German invasion of Russia during the summer of 1941, he also ordered that ways be found to provide all-out aid to the Soviet Union.

So when in mid-August 1941 Nomura suggested the continuation of informal negotiations to settle American–Japanese differences, Roosevelt gladly agreed. Nomura suggested a meeting between Prime Minister Konoe and the American President. Roosevelt was excited by the idea, but followed the advice of the State Department and insisted that first the Japanese government should accept a number of basic propositions: they should desist from a southern drive of conquest (that is, in the direction of the Netherlands East Indies), they should agree to withdraw troops from China and to give up any economic discrimination, and they should detach themselves from the Tripartite Pact. All but one of these preconditions were entirely unacceptable to the Japanese. They might have been willing to halt their southern expansion on their own terms, but not to make any but token withdrawals from China.

What the Americans were really demanding was the Japanese abandonment of the basic tenets of their co-prosperity sphere. The negotiations dragged on through October and November. The gulf between the Japanese and American concepts of the future peace of eastern Asia was as wide as ever, despite the search by the diplomats for some middle ground. As late as mid-November 1941, Roosevelt was searching without success for a compromise which would lead to a postponement of war for at least six months. This shows that for Roosevelt, in any case, Germany still came first, but his judgements proved very changeable.

In Tokyo the basic countdown to war was decided upon at the Imperial Conference which took place on 6 September 1941. Prime Minister Konoe opened the meeting saying that Japan must complete her war preparations, but that diplomacy should be given a last chance to resolve peacefully the problems facing her. If diplomacy failed, and only a limited time could be allowed for its success, then Japan must fight a war of self-defence. The United States' conditions for a settlement, involving not only a barrier to the southern drive of Japan but also American insistence that Japan withdraw her troops from China and abandon her demands for exclusive economic control, were, Konoe claimed, tantamount to denying Japan's right to exist as an equal and Asian power. Without oil and a certain source of essential raw materials Japan was at the mercy of foreign powers. That was her interpretation of the American proposals for a peaceful settlement. The Chief of Naval Staff, Admiral Osami Nagano, moreover, was confident that the Japanese navy's early victories would place Japan in an 'invincible position' even in a long war. The Japanese Army Chief of Staff urged the opening of hostilities as soon as possible while Japan still enjoyed a relative military advantage. The tone of the conference was therefore that war with the United States and Britain would become inevitable unless American policy rapidly altered course. In October, Konoe resigned and made way for a new government headed by General Hideki Tojo, a clear indication that the moment for war was drawing close.

The outcome of these Tokyo conferences became known in Washington from the intercepted instructions cabled from Tokyo to Ambassador Nomura, who was still negotiating with Cordell Hull in Washington. The Japanese code had been broken by the Americans, who were now privy to the Japanese secrets. The Americans thus learnt that the Japanese had a time limit in mind for the success of these negotiations. Furthermore, that there could be no question of any genuine Japanese withdrawal from China and that when the time limit expired the Japanese army and navy would extend the war by continuing their drive southward against the Dutch and British possessions. What was not clear to the Americans was whether the Japanese intended to attack the United States simultaneously in the Pacific. The Americans, therefore, were aware while negotiating that unless they were prepared to abandon China war would become inevitable. The Japanese might be brought to compromise on their 'southern' drive in return for American neutrality but not on the issue of the war in China. The Hull–Nomura negotiations were thus unreal, maintained on the American side

Pearl Harbor, 7 December 1941.

mainly in the hope of delaying the outbreak of war.

It is in this light that Roosevelt's remarks at a policy conference which took place on 25 November must be judged. Roosevelt by this time regarded war as virtually inevitable, observing, 'The question now was how we should manoeuvre them into the position of firing the first shot without allowing too much danger to ourselves.' But the well-known Hull Note of the following day, sent in reply to an earlier Japanese note, was couched in the form of a 'tentative outline' to serve as a 'basis for agreement'. It set out America's ideas for a settlement point by point. The Japanese could look forward to a normalisation of trade and access to raw materials in return for peace in eastern Asia; the Japanese must promise to respect the territorial integrity of all her neighbours; the 'impossible' American condition from the Japanese point of view was that both Japan and the United States should give up their special rights in China and that Japan should withdraw all her military forces from China and Indo-China.

At the Imperial Conference in Tokyo on 1 December 1941, this note was placed before the assembled Japanese leaders as if it were an ultimatum. It was a deliberate misrepresentation by the Japanese themselves, intended to unite the ministers. Differences were now indeed reconciled. The decision was reached to attack Britain, the Netherlands and the United States simultaneously.

The Japanese sent a formal declaration of war to Washington, intending it to be delivered fifty minutes before the carrier planes of Admiral Yamamoto's task force, which was at that moment secretly making for Pearl Harbor, attacked America's principal naval base in the Pacific. Unfortunately, the

Japanese Embassy was slow in decyphering the message and so the Japanese envoys appeared at the State Department almost an hour after the start of the Pearl Harbor attack on the United States fleet. That made 7 December 1941 an unintentional, greater 'day of infamy'. It was Admiral Isoruku Yamamoto, commander-in-chief of the Japanese navy, who had planned the daring pre-emptive strike on Pearl Harbor. The actual task force was commanded by Vice-Admiral Chuichi Nagumo. The Japanese warships reached a position 275 miles north of Pearl Harbor, escaping detection; Nagumo ordered the carrier planes, two waves of bombers and fighters, into action and they hit Pearl Harbor on a Sunday morning. The naval base was unprepared. Six battleships were sunk and the remaining two damaged; many planes were destroyed on the ground; 2,403 servicemen and civilians were killed. The unexpected position of the Japanese task force, and lack of proper service cooperation in Washington, were responsible for the disaster. That Roosevelt and Churchill wanted it to happen belongs to the legend of discredited conspiracy theories, once popular. The US Pacific fleet, however, was only temporarily crippled; of the eight battleships six were repaired and saw action again.

Japan had decided to start the war having clearly set a time limit for negotiations in September. It was self-deception to believe that the United States was about to make war on Japan after Hull's note on 26 September, even if Roosevelt thought war virtually inevitable. There is no evidence that Congress would have allowed the President to declare war for the sake of China or of any non-American possessions in Asia attacked by the Japanese. The traumatic loss of lives and ships, the fact and manner of the Japanese attack, now ensured a united American response for war. For Churchill a great cloud had lifted. With the United States in the war, he knew for certain that Hitler would now be defeated. Furthermore the United States found herself simultaneously at war with Germany, not by resolution of Congress, which might still have been difficult to secure, but by Hitler's own decision to declare war on America. In this way it came about that in December 1941 all the great powers of the world were at war.

CHAPTER 28

The Ordeal of the Second World War

The Second World War was the last world war to be fought with conventional weapons and the first to end with the use of the nuclear bomb, which raised the threat that any third world war could end in the destruction of the majority of the human population. The Second World War also became a new kind of total warfare with the deliberate killing of many millions of civilian non-combatants.

The major technical advance was aerial warfare. That cities could be reduced to rubble from the air the Germans first demonstrated in Spain in 1937 with the destruction of Guernica. In 1939 it was the turn of Warsaw, and in 1940 Coventry suffered a similar fate. Britain and the United States from 1942 to 1945 retaliated with mass bombing of the majority of Germany's cities. The results of such raids were to cause heavy casualties to civilian populations and widespread destruction. The Allied bombing of Dresden, crammed with refugees from the East, just before the war ended has been singled out for particular condemnation. By February 1945 the devastation of German cities no longer affected the outcome of the war. The impact on the capacity of a country to wage war despite such bombing was throughout the war less than anticipated. The Germans fought on in desparation. There was no alternative. Fear, especially of Russian revenge, maintained the resistance. Nor did the devastation prevent the rapid expansion of war production in Germany. Was the great loss of human life – post-war official Germany calculated that 593,000 civilians were killed – justified by the military results?

Vengeance on the Allied side was a subsidiary motive for the bombing offensive. For mere vengeance the lives of more than 50,000 aircrew and an enormous industrial war effort would not have been expended. Photographic reconnaissance of the destruction of the industrial Ruhr region and other cities seemed at the time to justify these raids as crippling blows against Germany's capacity to wage war. There can be no doubt that German resources were destroyed and wasted in reconstruction and that this weakened Germany's war effort. But one cannot quantify what contribution the air war made to bringing the war to an end, or how much longer it would have lasted if mass 'carpet' bombing had not been adopted. It did not reach its most devastating dimensions until 1944, and by then the German armies had already been defeated and could only delay the inevitable end. But there can be little doubt that more specific strategic bombing of, for instance, synthetic fuel plants and communications did impede the German war effort from 1944 to 1945 and that the brilliant German Armaments Minister, Albert Speer, could no longer make good the losses within the frontier of a shrinking Reich. Important, too, was the fact that before the invasion of France in 1944 the land war waged by the Allies was minor relative to the struggle on the eastern front. The bombing offensive was the only major weapon available to wage a war whose impact would be felt by the Germans until the Allied military build-up was sufficient to defeat the German armies in the West.

During the Second World War the distinction between combatants and non-combatants was not so much blurred as deliberately ignored. The factory worker was seen as a combatant. In most contemporary eyes, as the war progressed, this justified his destruction and the destruction of his home from the air. Children, women, the old and the sick were killed and maimed in this new type of warfare. The Germans, Japanese and Italians went beyond even what in the Second World War came to be considered legitimate warfare against all those involved in the war effort. What would have been in store for Europe, Asia and Africa if Germany and Japan had won the war can be seen from their ruthlessly brutal behaviour as occupying powers. The contrast with the First World War in this respect could not be greater. Murder and terror became deliberate acts of policy.

The destruction of towns and villages during the German military campaigns and the machine-gunning of fleeing columns of refugees was just a beginning. Hitler's Reich was no respecter of the human values of those regarded as belonging to lesser races, or of the lives of the Germans themselves. The 'euthanasia' programme, for example, was designed to murder 'useless' incurably ill or mentally handicapped German men, women and children. Many thousands of gypsies, classified as 'non-Aryans', were murdered in Auschwitz. Jehovah's Witnesses, whose faith would not allow them to be subservient to Hitler's commands, were persecuted and killed, as were countless other civilians of every nationality who were defined as opponents of the ideals of the regime. Hostages were picked off the streets in the occupied countries and shot in arbitrary multiples for the resistance's killing of German soldiers. Offences against the occupying powers were punishable by death at the discretion of the local military authorities. To hide partisans or Jews meant the death penalty if discovered or denounced. For the Jews in Europe, who were not so much opponents as defenceless victims, a unique fate awaited: physical destruction, as foretold in Hitler's Reichstag speech of 30 January 1939.

Yet, side by side with these horrors, the German armies fighting the Allied armies in the West behaved conventionally too and took prisoners who were, with some notable exceptions, treated reasonably. In Russia, however, the German army became increasingly involved with the specially formed units attached to the army commands which committed atrocities on a huge scale. Here there was to be no 'honourably' conducted warfare.

More than 3 million Russian prisoners of war in German hands died through exposure and famine. Himmler, who as head of the SS organisation wielded ever-increasing power, later in the war recognised the waste of manpower involved, and Russian prisoners of war and civilians were used as forced labour in German war industries. Many died from exhaustion. On the Allied side, some 300,000 German prisoners of war in Russian hands never returned to Germany. There was also the Soviet murder of Polish officers at Katyn, their bodies discovered by the Germans in mass graves in April 1943. The full horror of this slaughter was only revealed by Russia's new leaders in September 1992. The orders to shoot Polish officers and civilians in prison for suspected enmity to the Soviet Union were signed in March 1940 by Stalin himself and by three Politburo comrades, Voroshilov, Molotov and Mikoyan, at the suggestion of Beria, chief of the secret police. In the forest of Katyn, near Smolensk, 4421 Polish officers were shot. They were only a small proportion of the total victims. Another 17,436 soldiers and civilians were murdered as well. All the Soviet leaders, Khrushchev, Brezhnev and Gorbachev, were told of the dark secret in the files, which were kept in a special safe. Brezhnev minuted, 'Never to be opened'; Gorbachev passed on some information to the Polish government. The Yeltsin government revealed the full account of the murders.

Japanese troops also became brutalised. To be taken prisoner was regarded as a disgrace. Allied prisoners of war were treated inhumanely by the Japanese military authorities, and thousands of them died. Many were employed together with forced Asian labour on such projects as the construction of the Burma–Siam railway. By the time that death line was completed in October 1943, 100,000 Asians and 16,000 Europeans had lost their lives.

The horrors and ordeals, the depravity and brutality behind the battlefronts, the mass murder of millions are an inseparable part of the history of the Second World War. But the historian, confronted with such enormities, must not allow the atrocities simply to become merged into one impenetrable blackness. The separate strands have to be analysed if some understanding is to be reached of why civilisation collapsed on so vast a scale. Nor can the atrocities be set aside by the misguided argument that those on one side cancel out those on the other.

In Poland, and then in Russia, the German conquerors displayed a degree of barbarism which has no parallels with Germany's conduct during the First World War. In the 1930s, for tactical reasons, Hitler had been prepared to work with the Poles, and his view of them was quite favourable. The authoritarian Polish state, the Polish brand of anti-Semitism and official Poland's anti-Bolshevism made them, in Hitler's eyes, suitable junior partners. But Poland's courageous resistance in 1939 changed all that. With the exception of the Jews, who were all seen as destroyers of the Aryan race, Hitler's views of what to do with other 'races' such as Slavs was opportunistic. He cared nothing for their lives. In destroying the Polish intelligentsia he was not so much following a racial policy as taking what he regarded as the most efficacious practical steps to root out the strong sense of Polish nationalism. The same 'racial' inconsistency is noticeable in the treatment of the Ukrainian population. Vengeance for the slightest resistance to his will was a dominant element of Hitler's character. With the exception of the parts of the Soviet Union which the Germans occupied, no state, once independent, was treated worse than the Polish. Hitler planned that the Poles should lose their national existence altogether. Intellectual leaders and members of the professions were murdered wholesale. Polish culture and national consciousness were to be wiped out. Parts of western Poland were annexed by Germany and settled with 'German' farmers, mainly the so-called *Volksdeutsche*, ethnic Germans who for generations had lived in Eastern Europe.

The greater part of the rest of Poland was organised as a colony called the General Government of the Occupied Polish Territories headed by Hans Frank, a fanatical, brutal Nazi since the earliest days of the party. In this colony the Poles were to rise to positions no higher than workers. Frank described his fief in November 1940 as 'a gigantic labour camp in which everything that signifies power and independence rests in the hands of the Germans'. Frank, typically for the strife-torn Nazi German administration, himself engaged in much infighting with the SS, who obeyed no one except the leader, Heinrich Himmler. The Ukraine, with Frank's General Government, was selected by the SS for the majority of the sites of the extermination camps, such as Treblinka. Frank approved of the murder of the Jews, objecting to their settlement in the General Government. In December 1941 he declared, 'Gentlemen, I must ask you to arm yourselves against all feelings of pity. We must destroy the Jews wherever we meet them wherever possible.'

The majority of the Polish people were expected to survive so long as they served their German masters and lost all national consciousness. What the Nazis had in store for the Jews was so incredible that, even when the facts leaked out, most of the Jews still surviving in German-occupied Europe could not believe it, nor was the horror fully grasped abroad. Indeed the hell the Nazis created in the death camps of the East, like hell itself, is so far removed from human experience as to be scarcely real and credible. The Holocaust forms one of the most difficult aspects of modern history to explain and understand.

Hitler's ultimate intention about the fate of the Jews before 1941 remains a subject of intense historical debate. From all the available evidence, however, some definite conclusions are possible. In conditions of peace, that is before the outbreak of war in 1939, he could not order the mass murder of German, Austrian and Czech Jews within Germany. If the German sphere was to be made *Judenrein*, free of Jews, their forced emigration was the only option. For Hitler, the Jews had another possible value; they could be used to blackmail the West. He believed National Socialist propaganda that behind the scenes the Jews were influential in pulling the strings of policy in Washington, London and Paris. His aim was to conquer continental Europe piecemeal. The next target was Poland. In January 1939 he therefore threatened in his well-known Reichstag speech that the Jews would perish if Britain, France and the United States resisted his aggression on the continent by unleashing a general war.

Until Germany attacked the Soviet Union in June 1941, there seemed to be a small chance of a Western peace. Jews in Germany and conquered Europe were still allowed to live. Hitler liked to keep options open: alternative solutions to isolate the Jews and drive them out of Europe altogether were considered, such as the plan to banish them to Madagascar. That from the start he had no moral inhibition against mass murder, if that should prove the best course, cannot be doubted. During the summer and autumn of 1941, millions of 'Bolshevik Jews', the mortal enemy in his eyes, were added to the millions of European Jews already under German control, and mass emigration or expulsion overseas was no longer a possibility. Nor, with so much non-Jewish slave labour falling into German hands, Hitler calculated, would Jewish slave labour be needed. The option of mass murder as the final solution now became the most desired and practical course.

As Hitler's own pep talks to the generals during the spring of 1941 show, on the eve of the attack on Russia, the 'racial' war was now being openly launched. That spelt doom for the Jews, the race which Hitler hated and saw as a pestilence in human society. He could now repeat his Reichstag speech of January 1939, this time as a justification to the German people for the destruction of Jewry. In the light of this analysis Nazi policies can be seen to have followed a path that had inevitably to end in genocide.

By every means available the Nazis attempted before 1939 to 'clear' Germany of Jews by forcing them to emigrate. The Germans were not alone in following such policies. The Poles, too, before the war hoped to 'solve' their Jewish problem by promoting forced emigration of the Polish Jews. Anti-Semitism was virulent all over Europe and in the United States. But discrimination was not a part of government policy in any Western country, offending as it does against basic civil rights and freedoms. Entry of Jews to settle outside Germany was restricted. Unemployment was everywhere high so any increase of labour was not welcomed, especially if caused by immigrants deprived of their money and possessions. Nevertheless, can guilt be turned away from Nazi Germany by blaming her neighbours for not enabling more Jews to leave Germany before their later destruction? It is true that Western governments were preoccupied with their own problems during the depression years. And it always has to be remembered that before 1942 no government in the West could conceive what 'Final Solution' lay in store for the Jews on the German-dominated continent.

Britain, holding the League Mandate for Palestine and having promised the Jews a National Home there (page 130), had a special responsibility to aid the Jews. Until German persecution became more severe, the majority of German Jews, however, did not wish to emigrate to Palestine. When they desperately sought to leave Germany after November 1938 and would have gladly escaped to Palestine, the British government was more concerned to safeguard its vital strategic interests in the Middle East. Palestine had become a cauldron of conflict between Arab and Jew and the British occupiers. In Arab eyes both the Jews and the British authorities were European colonisers of Arab lands. The Arabs, moreover, could see that the increased Jewish immigration had its roots in European anti-Semitism, which strengthened Zionism. British governments tried to extricate themselves from these conflicting interests without satisfying either the Zionists or the Arabs. Finally, in May 1939 the British government took the decision that the Arabs would have to be appeased by promising to limit Jewish immigration to 75,000 over the next five years and, after that, the government promised the Arabs that further immigration would be subject to the consent of the Arab majority.

Public opinion and voluntary organisations before 1939 gave the efforts to rescue the Jews a dynamism which governments lacked. Germany's European neighbours, and the United States and Latin America, accepted German and Austrian Jews in tens of thousands. Although the Nazis were ready at first to expedite their exit even after the war broke out, the exodus was slowed down to a trickle by the war. In all, more than half the German Jews, some 280,000, succeeded in finding refuge between 1933 and 1939, many, however, only temporarily as Hitler overran the continent. The Jews so saved came from Germany and from the countries – Austria and Czechoslovakia – occupied by Hitler before the outbreak of war in 1939. They represented only a very small proportion of Europe's total Jewish population.

In Poland in 1940 many Polish Jews were killed wantonly, and the whole Jewish population was herded into ghettos, as in the Middle Ages, by fencing off or building a wall around a part of a city and leaving the Jews to fend for themselves. The two largest were in Warsaw and Lodz. In the ghettos the Germans could secure what was practically slave labour to supply the German armies. Undernourished and overcrowded, the ghetto population was decimated by disease and exhaustion. The planned massacre designed to kill every last Jew was begun on the day, 22 June 1941, when the German armies invaded the Soviet Union. These terrible killings of men, women and children in Russia, machine-gunned next to the open graves they had been forced to dig, had been deliberately worked out beforehand. It is not conceivable that they were undertaken without Hitler's knowledge. Hitler's full brutality is revealed by the record of a Führer Conference held at his headquarters on 16 July 1941 in which he spoke of his aims and referred to Russian orders to start partisan warfare behind the German front. Hitler saw in this order 'some advantages for us; it enables us to exterminate everyone who opposes us'. The actual task for the open-air killings was assigned to special SS detachments, the *Einsatzgruppen*. The German army, too, became heavily implicated in the mass murder. Nazi ideology had come to be widely accepted by ordinary people. Hitler and a small leadership group could not have committed such crimes without thousands of active helpers and an uncaring attitude to the victims by many more even where it was not actually hostile. The Final Solution in the Soviet Union avoided all need for transport and special camps or ghettos.

In Poland, the Jews were not perishing fast enough. Then the destruction had to be planned of the Jews remaining in German-occupied Europe, and of the Jews living in the countries of Germany's allies. After discussions among the Nazi leaders an order to Heydrich, a subordinate of Himmler, was issued by Göring on 31 July 1941 to draw up plans for the destruction – the so-called Final Solution – of non-Russian Jewry on a systematic basis. In accordance with these instructions Heydrich called the notorious conference on 20 January 1942 of senior administrators from the various Reich ministries who would be involved and which took its name from Wannsee, a favourite picnic area just outside Berlin where they met. It was assumed that the Jews in the rest of Europe could not be massacred as in Russia. Though there were several concentration camps in Germany herself, these could kill only tens of thousands, not millions! The greatest concentration of Jews was already in Poland, so to Poland and the East the Jews were to be transported: 'Europe will be combed from west to east.' What 'resettlement' really meant was clear from the record of the conference: 'the Jews capable of work will be led into these areas in large labour columns to build roads, whereby doubtless a large part will fall away through natural reduction . . . The inevitable remainder will have to be dealt with appropriately, since it represents a natural selection which upon liberation is to be regarded as a germ cell of a new Jewish development.'

No one present could doubt that what was being planned was indeed mass murder. Adolf Eichmann of the SS, who was present and was one of the principal organisers of the Holocaust, later testified that the atmosphere was one of general agreement; no one raised difficulties or moral objections. The eastern ghettos now became transit stations as the plans were implemented. The construction of the Auschwitz extermination camp had already begun before the Wannsee Conference. Others followed, among them Chelmo, Belzec, Sobibor, Treblinka. These camps of mass murder were specifically equipped to kill thousands *every day*, generally in large gas chambers. The 'selection' of those to be murdered as unfit to work was done on arrival from the rail transports arriving straight at the camps; the remainder, a smaller number and never the old, the sick or children, were allowed to survive some weeks longer. There were only very few long-term survivors.

Mass murder was so huge in extent that historians cannot tell for certain even to the *nearest million* how many people perished. Despite the virtual hopelessness of their situation in some ghettos and camps, a few Jews did resist, and with such weapons as could be smuggled in fought against German troops, thus at least selling their lives dearly. The whole world learnt of the Jewish rising of the Warsaw ghetto in April and May 1943 and its destruction. Less well known were risings in a number of extermination camps, in Treblinka in August 1943 and Sobibor in October of the same year, for instance. A few thousand more Jews were able to escape into the forests in Poland and the Ukraine, and operated as partisan units. They were not always welcome, and they were sometimes killed by their compatriots as well as by the Germans. Before the war was over, between 5 and 6 million Jews had been murdered. Nazi ideology was so widespread that it is unrealistic to limit responsibility for these crimes to Hitler and his henchmen. While Germans, soldiers, the SS and officials were overwhelmingly responsible, they were aided in their work of destruction by some sections of the conquered peoples of Europe in every country.

In Germany knowledge was widespread, brought home by soldiers and SS on leave from the East.

Survivors of the Warsaw Ghetto Rising of April 1943 are chaperoned by the Wehrmacht out of the city to be killed soon after.

How much the Germans were actually told can be seen from an article written by Goebbels and published in the 'respectable' weekly journal *Das Reich* on 16 November 1941. That world Jewry started the war, he wrote, was proven beyond dispute:

> The Jews wanted their war, and now they have it. What is now coming true is the Führer's prophecy of 30 January 1939, in his speech to the Reichstag, when he said that if international Finance Jewry once more succeeded in driving the peoples into a world war, the result would not be the bolshevising of the world and thereby the victory of the Jews, but the destruction of the Jewish race in Europe. We are now witnessing the fulfilment of that prophecy, and a destiny is being realised which is harsh but more than deserved. Feelings of sympathy or pity are entirely inappropriate ... [Jewry] according to its law, 'an eye for an eye, a tooth for a tooth', is now perishing.

The demand of the German authorities that all Jews be handed over for the terrible Final Solution being prepared for them was one of the deepest moral challenges faced by occupied Europe and Germany's allies during the Second World War. There was not one response that was uniquely French, Polish, Dutch or Hungarian. The response was multi-faceted. There was the 'official' collaboration of governments – and even this was not uniform – and then there was the response of institutions, the Churches above all, and of ordinary people. In every corner of Europe there were some individuals who risked their lives to shelter Jews. Otherwise, the Jews who survived in Germany were mainly those in mixed Jewish–Christian marriages. They too were on the list for murder but they came last in the plan for the Final Solution and the war was over before they could be exterminated as well. Several hundred Jews were hidden from humanitarian motives or managed with forged papers to pass themselves off as Aryan. The Christians who protected Jews in Germany were heroic, their number pitifully small – far fewer than in Poland or other occupied countries. In Germany the opportunities for the non-privileged Jews (those not married to Christian spouses with offspring) to survive were so slight as to be negligible in practice.

Poles and Jews had lived for centuries together, but in separate communities. Even in 1931, most of the 3 million Jews in Poland were largely unassimilated, although those who were assimilated were well represented in the professions and the middle class. Under the Nazi occupation anti-Semitism was reinforced by propaganda, but there were Poles who, though they did not like Jews, helped them because they hated the Germans more. There were also Poles who actively assisted the Germans to round up Jews. Several thousand Poles, however, out of feelings of pity, hid Jews at great risk to themselves, for the penalty was death. It has been estimated that between 50,000 and 100,000 Polish Jews survived, some fighting as partisans or with the Red Army. In Warsaw 15,000 found hiding places, many more than in Berlin. Had more Germans made efforts to protect the Jews, Hitler would have found it far more difficult to carry out the Holocaust.

In the Netherlands, Belgium, France and, above all, Italy the Jews stood a better chance of survival. Many Jews were hidden in homes, in monasteries and in villages. Official Vichy France, however, gave some aid to the Germans in rounding up the Jews, including French citizens of Jewish faith, for transportation to the death camps in the East. Uniquely, all but 500 of about 7000 Jews living in Denmark were rescued by the Danish resistance by being ferried across to Sweden. The Danish resistance had been alerted to their imminent deportation by Dr Duckwitz, a courageous German official in Copenhagen who had learnt of their intended fate from a leak passed on by someone in the Gestapo. The fate of the Danish Jews who did not escape was extraordinary. The Nazi rulers in Berlin maintained the fiction that Denmark had remained a sovereign country and the Danes were therefore permitted to continue to protect all Danish citizens, including Danish Jews. The 500 Danish Jews were deported to the privileged ghetto of Theresienstadt, where they were housed separately in much better conditions than the other Jews. They remained in contact with the Danish authorities, who insisted on providing for them to the end of the war. None was transported to the extermination camps further east and almost all of them survived and returned to Denmark after the liberation. They were the fortunate exception. Dr Duckwitz also survived and is honoured as 'one of the righteous' at Yad Vashem, the Holocaust Memorial in Jerusalem.

Germany's ally, Italy, on the other hand, in practice protected Jews despite Mussolini's anti-Jewish legislation. Until Italy's capitulation and the consequent German occupation, the Italian military authorities in their Croatian zone and in the Italian zone of France prevented both German troops and police from arresting Jews for transportation east or murder by the Croatian Ustachi on the spot. The Italian army would have nothing to do with the brutal mass murder of the Jews being instigated by the Germans and their 'allies' and either sabotaged orders or simply refused to carry them out. Feelings of humanity and decency were not extinct.

In occupied Europe local police could be found to do the dirty work of the Germans for them. In some cases they would have been shot had they disobeyed. In others the work was done with enthusiasm. The public silence of the Pope and the Vatican and of the *German* Protestant Churches signifies a massive moral failure. In contrast, in Holland Catholic churches and many Protestant churches read protests from the pulpit after the first Dutch transport of Jews. Priests and pastors, wherever Germany held power, suffered martyrdom for their personal protest. Bishop Galen of Münster publicly condemned the murder of some 60,000 to 80,000 feeble-minded and incurably ill Germans in the so-called 'euthanasia' programme: Hitler feared that the people's war effort might be undermined by an open onslaught on religious beliefs. A strong public movement by the *German* Churches and military might also, therefore, have saved countless Jewish lives. Hitler and his regime were sensitive to, and watched, the reactions of the German people. There was no such public movement as, for instance, in the Netherlands.

The importance and nature of resistance to the Nazis within Germany herself and in Nazi-dominated Europe varied enormously. Conspiratorial by necessity, it came into the open in acts of violent sabotage and several attempts on Hitler's life, the most spectacular – the 20 July 1944 plot – almost succeeding when an explosive charge went off a few feet from Hitler at his headquarters in East Prussia. The composition of the resistance ranged from members of the pre-Nazi Weimar political parties to individuals moved by moral considerations. Thus in Munich a small group of students and teachers who called themselves the White Rose distributed, until they were caught and executed, thousands of leaflets condemning the barbarities of the Nazis. But the only resistance that had the power actually to remove Hitler came from within the army and culminated in the bomb plot of 20 July 1944. The officers involved saw clearly that the war was lost and hoped by removing Hitler to be able to make peace with the Western allies while keeping the Russians out of Germany. Others were less materialistically motivated. Had Hitler been killed, the plot might have succeeded, though Britain and America would certainly have refused to make peace on any terms other than unconditional surrender.

Successful armed resistance, tying down considerable numbers of German troops, was carried out by Tito's partisans in Yugoslavia. And in France, while Pétain and the Vichy regime enjoyed overwhelming support, a sizeable minority joined the French resistance, undertaking sabotage and supplying a 'secret army' which returned aircrew shot down in France and Belgium on an escape route back to England by way of neutral Spain. In the East, Russian partisans acted as auxiliaries of the Red Army and interrupted the supply routes of the Wehrmacht. But in occupied Europe there was not one simple struggle against Nazi Germany. Among the resistance fighters themselves there was conflict after the communists joined the resistance after Hitler's invasion of the Soviet Union in June 1941.

The struggle in Yugoslavia between the royalist Colonel Mihailović and the communist leader, Tito, led to civil war between them as well as war against the Germans. In Poland, the Home Army was as bitterly opposed to the Polish communist partisans as to the common German enemy. Here Stalin had the last word. The Polish government in exile in London and the Home Army, which took its orders from London, attempted to frustrate or at least impede Stalin's plans to bring Poland under communist control. In August 1944, as the Red Army reached the River Vistula, the Home Army began to rise in Warsaw against the Germans. Their intention was to prove to the world that Poles, not the Russians, had liberated the Polish capital. The Poles seized half the city and fought bitterly for two months until their capitulation to the Germans on 2 October. Warsaw was entirely destroyed. Soviet help was cynically withheld by Stalin. Only during the last stages were Russian supplies dropped; they could only prolong the doomed struggle, resulting in the deaths of still more Polish Home Army fighters holding out in the sewers of the city. The Soviet command had even prevented Polish units fighting with the Red Army from battling their way to the city. Soviet airfields were closed to relief flights from the West. Surrender terms were finally agreed by the Home Army with the Germans on 2 October 1944 and three days later General Bor-Komorowski, with the exhausted remnants of the fighters, gave up the struggle. Surprisingly the Home Army were well treated as prisoners of war probably in order to increase hatred between the Poles and the Russians.

During the early stages of the rising auxiliary SS units committed terrible atrocities against the civilian population, until regulars were brought in

Holocaust Victims and Survivors

	Victims	Survivors (*after 1939*)
Germany	165,000	20,000
(Austria)	65,000	6,000
France	76,000	230,000
Belgium	28,500	36,000
Netherlands	102,000	38,000
Denmark	116	7,380
Norway	760	1,000
Italy	6,500	29,500
Greece	59,000	12,700
Poland pre 1939 frontier	2,700,000	
post 1939 frontier	1,600,000	50,000
Soviet Union pre 1939 frontier	1,000,000	
post 1939 frontier	2,100,000	
Czechoslovakia 1937 frontier	260,000	40,000
(Slovakia)	65,000	20,000
Romania	211,200	381,200
Bulgaria	11,000	50,000
Yugoslavia	65,000	14,500
Hungary	550,000	290,000

These approximate statistics of the Holocaust have been calculated primarily on the basis of *Dimension des Völkermords*, editor W. Benz (Munich 1991).

to crush resistance. The total (mainly civilian) casualties in Warsaw reached about 200,000. The Germans lost some 2000 killed and 9000 wounded. Polish military casualties were far higher: 17,000 killed or missing and 9000 wounded. Politically and militarily the anti-communist Polish underground had been destroyed, leaving a vacuum which Stalin was able to fill with communists ready to follow Soviet orders. The Warsaw rising marked one more milestone in the tragedy of Poland and signalled to the rest of the world the ruthlessness of which Stalin was capable in furtherance of the Soviet Union's post-war plans.

In the West this conflict between the communist and anti-communist resistance did not flare into civil war but a similar pattern emerges. As the defeat of Nazi Germany drew close, the resistance was as concerned with questions of post-war political power as with fighting the Germans. The Nazi answer to all resistance from whatever quarter was terror.

Houses were burnt to the ground in reprisals and people not involved in the resistance were killed wholesale. The destruction of the village of Oradour-sur-Glane in France and of Lidice in Czechoslovakia, and the massacres which took place there, are among the best known of such barbarities. But these were just two of the thousands of atrocities that became a common occurrence in German-occupied Europe. The terrible reprisals taken by the German occupiers raise the question whether the Allies should have actively encouraged resistance and parachuted agents into the occupied countries, many of whom lost their lives. Was the sabotage to the German war effort sufficiently great to justify this policy? It is impossible to balance such an equation, or to estimate the importance of maintaining morale on the continent, of sustaining belief that Hitler's Germany would be beaten. All over Europe, from northern Italy to Norway, large German forces were tied down. The Nazi New Order could not be imposed anywhere unchallenged, and the German forces could not relax their vigilance amid populations of which significant sections were hostile. Even though the active resistance was a minority, it made an impact out of proportion to its numbers.

The Japanese had been at war since 1937. They sought to justify their wars of expansion at home and abroad both as self-defence and as fulfilling a mission of liberating Asia from Western imperialism. In its place Japan would build a Greater East Asia Co-Prosperity Sphere. The Japanese, to emphasise the solidarity of eastern Asia against the West, chose to call the war they had launched the Greater East Asian War. The real intentions of the Japanese leaders can be deduced from the decisions taken at secret conferences in Tokyo rather than from the rhetoric of their propaganda. First consideration in all the conquered regions was to be given to military needs. Local economies were to be strictly controlled and independence movements discouraged. No industry was to be developed in the southern region, which was to become the empire's source of raw materials and a market for her goods. The Japanese saw themselves as the superior people who possessed the right to subordinate and exploit the conquered peoples. Everywhere propaganda and indoctrination sought to reinforce the superiority of everything Japanese. For the indigenous peoples, foreign Western rule was replaced by more brutal foreign Japanese rule. Japanese colonialism had taken the place of Western imperialism. The 'natives' were regarded as inferiors.

Even before the war had been launched a secret conference in Tokyo on 20 November 1941 settled the general principle of Japanese occupations. Local administrations were to be utilised as far as possible, but each territory was placed under military government and subordinated to Japan's needs. The Japanese government never worked out any really coherent plan for the future of eastern Asia. Some territories of particular strategic importance such as Malaya would remain under direct Japanese control; others, the Philippines and Burma, were promised eventual 'independence' but only if they became co-operative satellite states. Japanese attempts to win over the mass of Asian peoples to support the war against their former colonial masters was almost totally a failure. The great majority of the ordinary people did not see the conflict as *their* war. Equally, there was little active support for the departed Westerners against the Japanese, except in the Philippines. In Burma, and especially in the Philippines, sections of the population became vehemently anti-Japanese. But on the whole the peoples saw themselves as suffering from a war between two foreign masters struggling for ultimate control over them. In India, as has been seen, the political leaders sought to make use of the situation to promote genuine independence.

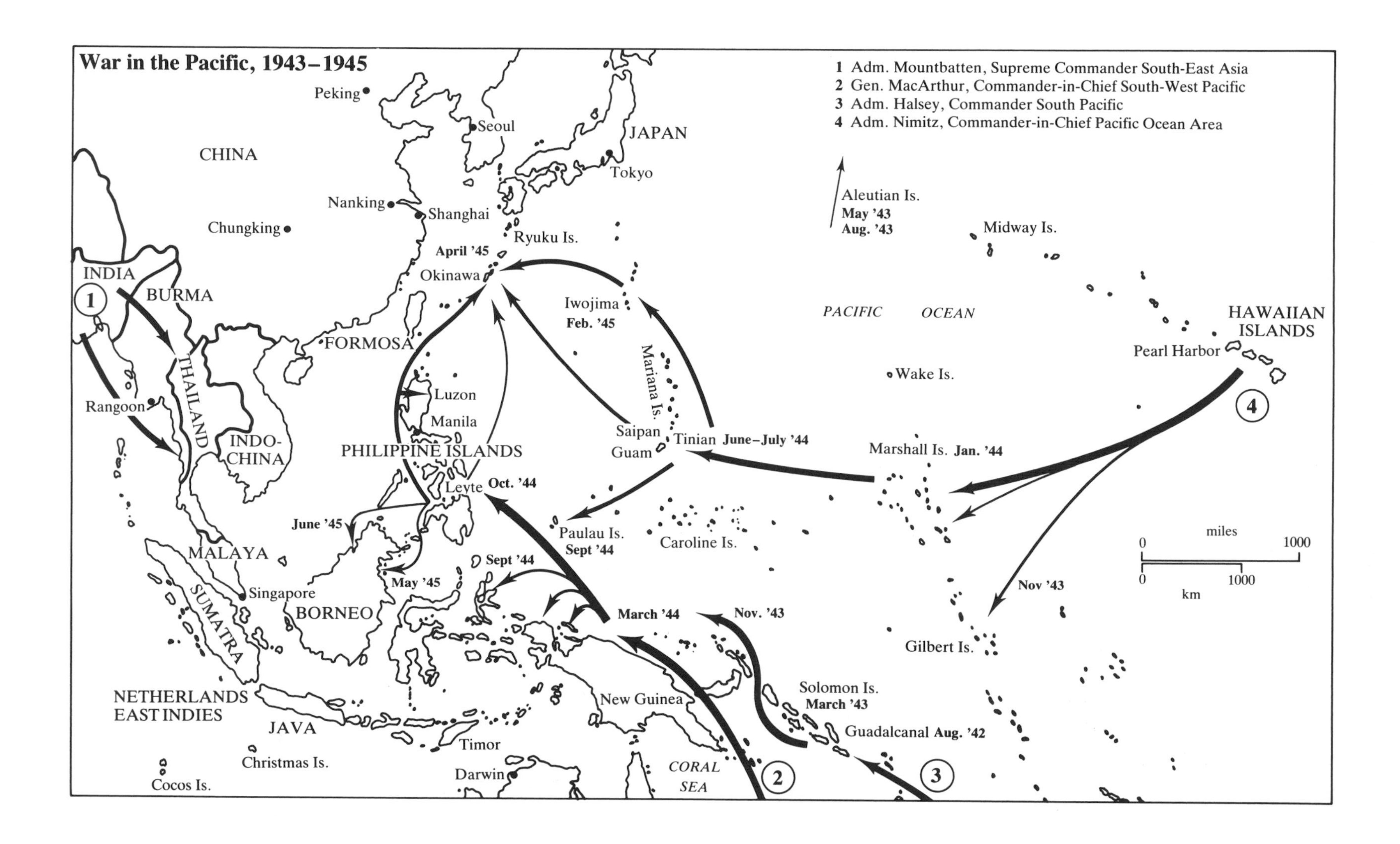
War in the Pacific, 1943–1945
1 Adm. Mountbatten, Supreme Commander South-East Asia
2 Gen. MacArthur, Commander-in-Chief South-West Pacific
3 Adm. Halsey, Commander South Pacific
4 Adm. Nimitz, Commander-in-Chief Pacific Ocean Area
Peking
CHINA
Chungking
Nanking
Shanghai
Seoul
JAPAN
Tokyo
Ryuku Is.
April '45
Okinawa
INDIA
BURMA
THAILAND
Rangoon
INDO-CHINA
FORMOSA
Luzon
Manila
PHILIPPINE ISLANDS
Leyte
Oct. '44
June '45
May '45
MALAYA
Singapore
SUMATRA
BORNEO
NETHERLANDS EAST INDIES
JAVA
Christmas Is.
Cocos Is.
Timor
Darwin
CORAL SEA
New Guinea
Sept '44
March '44
Nov. '43
Solomon Is.
March '43
Guadalcanal Aug. '42
Iwojima
Feb. '45
Mariana Is.
Saipan
Guam
Tinian June–July '44
Paulau Is.
Sept '44
Caroline Is.
Aleutian Is.
May '43
Aug. '43
Midway Is.
PACIFIC OCEAN
Wake Is.
Marshall Is. Jan. '44
HAWAIIAN ISLANDS
Pearl Harbor
Nov '43
Gilbert Is.
miles
0
1000
km
0
1000

Of all the peoples under Japanese rule, the Chinese suffered the most – both in China and wherever Chinese communities had settled in south-eastern Asia. In Singapore after her fall, there was a terrible bloodbath of Chinese and at least 5000 were massacred. Japanese barbarities against the Chinese population, which constituted about a third of the total population of Malaya, drove them into armed resistance. Japanese terror tactics thus proved counter-productive. But though undeniably harsh, and though atrocities were committed, the Japanese did not emulate their German allies in resorting to an irrational and carefully planned and executed policy of extermination of whole peoples. With the Japanese as masters instead of the Europeans, local administrations continued to function smoothly, with the indigenous junior administrators carrying out the orders of their new masters. With the need to fight the war, the Japanese left the social order intact and tried to preserve the *status quo*. To win over the population and channel nationalist feelings, they set up Japanese-controlled mass movements. The constant emphasis on Japanese superiority, however, alienated the local populations.

Some nationalist leaders because of their great popularity, like Sukarno in Indonesia, were able to gain a degree of genuine independence in return for promising to rally the people to co-operate with the Japanese war effort. More concessions were promised to the Burmese and Filipinos in 1943 as the war began to go badly for the Japanese. In August 1943 Burma was proclaimed independent, but in alliance with Japan and at war with the Allies. In October the Japanese sponsored an independent Philippine republic and in the same month Bose proclaimed a provisional Indian government in exile. In mainland China puppet governments had been set up from the first; Manchuria had been transformed into Manchukuo in 1932 with its own emperor Pu-yi; another Japanese-controlled government of China was set up in Nanking in 1938. But plunder, rape and massacre were routinely perpetrated by the Japanese troops in China. Despite a veneer of local autonomy in some regions under Japanese occupation, the reality of the co-prosperity sphere was not liberation but Japanese domination and imperial exploitation.

In 1942 the Japanese had won large territories in Asia at small cost. The Americans prepared their counter-offensive across the Pacific, straight at the Japanese heartland. This is how Japan was defeated while her armies still occupied the greater part of what had been conquered at the outset of the war. The fall of the Japanese-held island of Saipan, in July 1944, placed American bombers within range of Tokyo. The Americans hoped to bomb the Japanese into submission. The massive indiscriminate raids brought huge destruction on the flimsily constructed Japanese houses. On 10 March 1945 one of the most devastating air raids of the whole war was launched against Tokyo. The fire storm created destroyed close on half the city and caused 125,000 casualties. In May and June 1945 the bomber offensive spread to sixty other major towns throughout Japan.

On 6 August 1945, for the first time, a new weapon was used, the atom bomb that devastated Hiroshima. The destruction and suffering were appalling. Most of the city was destroyed and more than 70,000 people were killed immediately. About the same number were to succumb to a new man-made illness, radiation sickness. For decades the atom bomb claimed victims from among the survivors. The casualties from the spring raid on Tokyo by fleets of Super-Flying Fortresses were greater, but what filled the whole world with awe and horror was that a single plane dropping just one bomb from out of the blue sky could produce such suffering and destruction. A second bomb was dropped on Nagasaki three days later, again causing great loss of life. In the face of such a war the Japanese surrendered.

The Second World War was waged simultaneously in Asia, Europe and North Africa by huge armed forces on all sides, backed by tanks and aircraft in numbers hitherto unknown and, in its closing stages, with a new weapon releasing the devastating power of nuclear fission. The destruction and maiming on a global scale consequently exceeded anything known before. The war caused not only many millions of dead and wounded, but also inflicted on millions more forcible population migrations and wholesale destruction of towns and villages – a sum total of virtually unimaginable human misery.

As the tide of the war turned, the German people increasingly suffered the ravages of war. The losses on the eastern front alone matched the bloodbath of the First World War on all fronts. The great majority of the German war dead died fighting

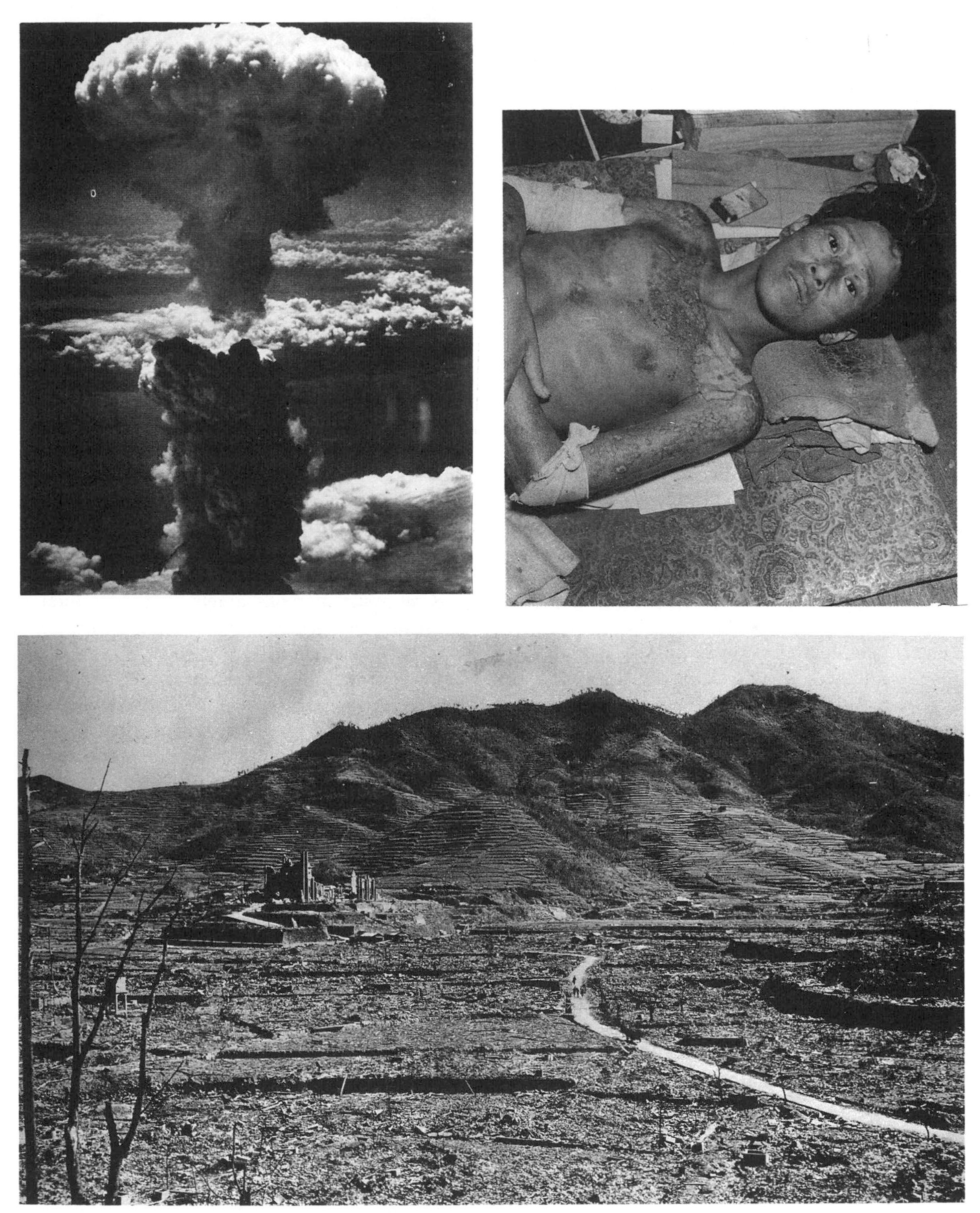

On 9 August 1945, the mushroom cloud rose 60,000 feet into the sky (left). *Below lay Nagasaki. Once the cloud cleared, little was left intact in the city save the Catholic Cathedral* (below). *The lucky people were those who were killed outright. Makeshift shelters housed the survivors* (right), *but medics were flummoxed by new injuries and new diseases like 'radiation sickness', which claimed many more lives in the years to come, and afflicted the unborn.*

in Russia. The Bomber Commands of the Allies inflicted terrible devastation as city after city was laid waste during the last months of the war. Above all else, the German people feared the Russians, bent on revenge for the German invaders' actions in Russia. Ethnic Germans and German colonisers fled from the advancing Russian armies, retreating into Germany. The Sudeten Germans, who had lived in Czechoslovakia before 1938, were driven out. Most of the Germans living in Polish-occupied eastern German regions from East Prussia to Silesia – assigned to the Poles for administration in compensation for territorial losses to the Soviet Union – were driven out or fled in terror from the Poles and Russians. 'Orderly and humane' population transfers were sanctioned by the Allied Potsdam Conference in the summer of 1945. But the mass exodus of 15 million people immediately after the war was certainly not orderly and was frequently inhumane. Pent-up hatreds against the Germans burst out and were vented not only on the guilty supporters of Hitler's regime but also, indiscriminately, on tens of thousands of innocent people, on children and the sick. The exodus from Eastern and central Europe began during the last months of the war and continued after the war was over. Although relatively few were deliberately murdered, in all as many as 2 million Germans are estimated to have died as a result of the privations they suffered.

Mere statistics cannot convey the tragedies which befell almost every family in Europe. The Soviet Union suffered the most: at least 28 million military and civilian people died – a staggering figure. Germany's dead numbered between 4.5 and 5 million. Proportionately to their population, the Jews suffered the most; only a minority of those in Europe at the outbreak of the war survived to its end. For Britain, France and Italy, however, the Second World War casualties did not repeat the bloodbath of the First World War. British military and civilian deaths totalled 450,000, to which must be added those of the empire: 120,000. The French figures are approximately 450,000 dead; the Italians lost 410,000 dead. Yugoslav, Hungarian, Polish and Romanian losses were heavy. In central Europe, the Poles suffered far more even than their neighbours. American deaths on the European and Pacific fronts were 290,000. No one knows how many million Chinese died in the war; the figure may well be in excess of 10 million; about 2 million Japanese are estimated to have lost their lives in the war. The physical destruction has largely been made good in the years since the war. But the loss of lives will continue to be mourned as long as the generations that experienced the war are still alive. The ordeal of the Second World War also serves a lasting warning to future generations of what national aggression and the intolerance of peoples can lead to.

CHAPTER 29

The Victory of the Allies, 1941–1945

The war that began in September 1939 has been called the European War, in contrast to the World War that ensued when the Soviet Union, the United States and Japan became involved in 1941. Militarily there is an obvious reason for seeing 1941 as a dividing line. In Asia, the China War being waged since 1937 was a separate conflict until it was widened into the Pacific War by Japan's attack on Pearl Harbor. In Europe Hitler's invasion of the Soviet Union marks a turning point in the course of the war. But in a deeper sense the global implications of Hitler's attack on Poland in 1939 were there from the beginning. Long before Germany declared war on the United States, the USA was throwing her support behind Britain and actually engaging in warfare in the battle of the Atlantic. Then Nazi–Soviet 'friendship', affirmed in August 1939, was clearly nothing but a temporary expedient. Hitler did not abandon his goal of winning living-space in the East and conquering 'Jewish-Bolshevism'. The outcome of the war between Germany and Russia would decide whether the Soviet Union or Germany would emerge as a superpower in the second half of the twentieth century.

In 1940 and 1941 Britain on her own was incapable of inflicting serious damage on Germany. Was her survival as a belligerent therefore of much importance? Without the war in the East, it is difficult to imagine how Britain could have launched even a destructive bomber offensive against Germany. Not only was much of the German air force fighting the Russians, but had the war against Russia not continued, and so frustrated his plans, Hitler would have diminished the size of his victorious continental army and transferred the main German war effort to building up an air force which in sheer size alone would probably have overwhelmed the Royal Air Force. Hitler was never able to realise this plan as Germany's war resources continued to be fully stretched in holding the eastern front. Britain was the only Western European democracy left in 1940. Her refusal to accept the apparent logic of the military situation saved post-war Western Europe from suffering the fate either of continued German overlordship or of a future under Stalin's Red Army if, as seems more probable, the Soviet Union had won the war. Instead democratic Britain provided the link, and later the base, for an Anglo-American counter-offensive in Western Europe that created the conditions for recovery free from the totalitarian control of the left or the right. Without Britain still fighting from 1940 to 1941, the likelihood of an American involvement in the European theatre of the war was remote.

The powers victorious in the Second World War recognised that they would be faced with world problems and worldwide confrontations after the war was over. The future of the millions who were largely tacit observers of the war, the subjects of the colonial European empires, or under Japanese rule, would be dependent on its outcome. A new world was in the making and its history would have been different had Germany and Japan instead of the Soviet Union and the United States emerged as the post-war superpowers.

The size and destructive capability of the armies which fought on each side during the Second World War exceeded even those of the Great War of 1914–18. Behind the fighting fronts, the industrial war was waged, pouring out guns, tanks, aircraft and ships. One of the most intriguing aspects of the war was that of spies and of science. Secrecy about the espionage war has only partially been lifted. Much may never be known. Generalisations are therefore particularly hazardous. It does appear, however, that despite spectacular coups, the achievement of the spies in affecting the course of the war was less than might have been expected. The decision-makers could never be certain whether in the world of deceit and intrigue in which the various espionage networks operated the information obtained was real or planted. The success of espionage and counter-espionage meant that they tended to cancel each other out. One of the best-known illustrations of this was the failure of Richard Sorge, the master spy working for the Russians in Tokyo, to convince Moscow that his information from the German Embassy of Hitler's intentions and the timing of the invasion of the Soviet Union was true. On the Allied side a more demonstrable espionage success, was the breaking of the German code machine Enigma, used by Germany's armed forces. The Poles had built a replica and just before the start of the war passed its secret to the British, who continued the decyphering work at Bletchley Park. The intelligence data, code named 'Ultra', thus secured, helped Britain and her allies in the air war, in the Mediterranean and in the North African campaigns, but most crucially in the battle of the Atlantic.

There can be no uncertainty about the advantage the Allies derived from their successful application of science to warfare. Radar was in use early in the war in both Germany and Britain; Germany was probably ahead in its development at the outset of the war. But during 1940–1 small airborne radar sets were produced in Britain which allowed night fighters to defend cities during the Blitz. Airborne radar also became an indispensable adjunct to the Allied bomber offensive, enabling the bombers to pinpoint their targets at night. At sea, advanced types of radar gave the Allies a decisive advantage against German submarines in the spring of 1943 and helped to turn the tide of battle in their favour. But the scientific breakthrough that did most to shape the future was the atomic bomb; the decision at the end of the war to use this weapon brought about the rapid Japanese surrender.

Allied scientists from many nations, British, American, French, Danish, Italian and German too (for German refugees played a crucial role), made the construction of a nuclear bomb possible. It was eventually in the United States that science was matched by the technical know-how and the immense production facilities necessary for its manufacture were provided. First tested in the empty spaces of the New Mexican desert, the bomb was dropped just three weeks later in August 1945 over Hiroshima.

An early indication of Allied suspicions about the likely post-war attitude of the Soviet Union can be seen in the decision not to share the secrets of nuclear development with the USSR. Indeed, despite an agreement with Britain, the United States sought to retain a monopoly on the manufacture of these awesome weapons. The Soviets were well aware they would need to develop their own atomic bomb and in 1942, despite the immediate German threat, pressed ahead vigorously with their own research. The Danish atomic scientist Niels Bohr advised Roosevelt that the Russians would succeed in building their own bomb some time after the Americans did so. Would it not be better to share secrets with them and to work for international control? The Russians made their own bomb in 1949. The atom spy Klaus Fuchs had provided some help but the Russians could eventually have built their own bomb in any case. It seems unlikely that the course of Stalin's policy would have differed much even if the Americans had passed on the atomic secrets. German atomic research – despite the eminence of some of the scientists ready to work for the Nazis – lagged behind. Hitler, according to Armaments Minister Albert Speer, was not prepared to earmark the vast resources necessary to make the bomb, regarding nuclear physics as 'Jewish physics'. Instead the Germans did devote great resources to the development of new rockets, which by themselves could have no decisive effect on the war. The outcome was the pilotless plane, the V-1, and the advanced supersonic rocket, the V-2, against which there was no defence when it came into use in 1944. But the later combination of Allied and German science, the new delivery system and new explosive force – in other words, rocket technology and nuclear weapons – led to our present-day nuclear-missile age.

In the summer of 1940 it was difficult to see how Germany's victorious armies would ever be defeated. But by attacking the Soviet Union in June 1941 and then declaring war that December on the United States the balance *potentially* swung against Germany. Allied superiority was only potential in the sense that it depended on Britain and Russia not being defeated. The United States would make her military weight felt in Europe only in 1943 and 1944.

For Britain the danger of invasion finally passed in 1941. With Germany fully engaged in the East, there remained no possibility of her mounting an invasion of the British Isles as well. But this did not mean that there was no longer any danger that Britain might be forced to submit. She remained beleaguered, dependent for longer-term survival on supplies reaching her from overseas, above all from the United States. Her own resources, great though they were when fully mobilised, were not sufficient both to sustain the war effort and to feed all the people. For Britain's success in mobilising her material and human resources much credit must go to Ernest Bevin, a leading trade unionist who had entered Churchill's national government as minister of labour in 1940. The British people accepted an unprecedented degree of direction of labour and of rationing. Even so, supplies from overseas became increasingly essential. Lend–Lease made possible the purchase of war supplies in the United States without payment of cash. But they still had to reach Britain.

The conflict at sea, the battle of the Atlantic, was therefore as vital to Britain as the land battles had been to France in 1940. The sinkings by German U-boats in 1941 and 1942 could only be made good by the output of ships from US yards. Before Pearl Harbor on 7 December 1941, Hitler had given orders that American vessels supplying Britain and their escorting US warships were not to be attacked. His hands had been tied. After Pearl Harbor he welcomed the outbreak of war between Japan and the US, and declared war on the Americans himself, removing the restrictions on the U-boat war in the Atlantic. Now, he thought, Britain would be forced to her knees. In November 1942 U-boats sank 729,000 tons, and for the year as a whole almost 8 million tons or 1664 ships. These losses were inflicted by about 200 submarines and could no longer be made good. The tide was turned in the spring of 1943. Airpower, improved radar and 'Ultra' by the end of May practically drove the U-boats from the Atlantic. The submarine had been the greatest threat. Germany's surface fleet was not sufficiently strong to challenge Britain's supremacy. Hitler's battleships were eliminated after some spectacular engagements. The *Graf Spee* sank in 1939, the *Bismarck* in 1941 and the crippled *Tirpitz* by air attack in 1944. Supplies were carried across the Atlantic by convoys. By far the most hazardous route for these merchant vessels was from Scotland and Iceland to Murmansk to aid Russia. But by the end of 1943 not only had the Germans lost the battle of the seas, but they had also sustained defeats on land from which there would be no recovery. The darkest years of the Second World War were over for Britain. Winston Churchill's contribution to maintaining British morale would be difficult to overestimate.

Britain's warfare with Italy and Germany on land in 1941 and 1942, judged by the numbers of men engaged, was secondary when compared with the millions of German and Russian troops locked in battle in the Soviet Union. Yet strategically the region of the eastern Mediterranean, known loosely as the Middle East and lying between neutral Turkey and the Italian colony of Libya, was a vital one. During the inter-war years it was dominated by Britain and France not as outright colonial powers but as the powers holding League Mandates. Both Britain and France had problems with their Mandates. From 1936 onwards, Arab militancy forced Britain to station 30,000 troops in Palestine. But after the British government's decision in 1939 to restrict the immigration of the Jews there was relative calm until 1944.

Hitler's Arab policy was ambiguous. While welcoming Arab hostility to Britain, the Nazis were not prepared to give unequivocal promises of future independence to the Arab states. But Arab attitudes were determined by Arab hostility to Britain and France as the occupying powers. Thus Egypt, nominally independent, and though being 'defended' by Britain, was pro-German during the war and was actually occupied by Britain. Iraq, Britain's Mandate, achieved independence in 1930 under British sponsorship but was closely linked to Britain economically and militarily. What was important to Britain was that Iraq and her eastern neighbour, Persia, were the major suppliers of oil in the region.

Britain's Middle Eastern dominance was seriously threatened in 1941 by Germany. Germany's victory over France stimulated Arab nationalism. The Vichy French authorities in the Lebanon and Syria, moreover, were not pro-British in their sympathies; while in Iraq, a group which favoured Germany staged a military coup and drove out the regime in power which had been friendly to Britain. Turkey, fearful of German power, decided on neutrality and so did not, as expected, join Britain. If Hitler had followed his Balkan campaigns in the spring of 1941 by advancing into the Middle East, there would have been no sufficiently strong British forces to oppose the Germans. Instead, Hitler attacked the Soviet Union in June 1941. Germany might nevertheless have reached Persia and the Persian Gulf by way of southern Russia. But Russia's defence of the Caucasus blocked that path. Britain, meanwhile, despite her militarily weak position, decided on offensive action. Together with Free French troops, a relatively small British force invaded Syria and the Lebanon and overcame Vichy French resistance. Britain intervened in Iraq and restored the pro-British regime. Persia was also invaded in conjunction with the Russians. In Persia and the Arab world, including Egypt, Britain had secured her strategic interests by force against local political nationalist groups. From her point of view, Arab national feelings could not be permitted to jeopardise the war effort.

In North Africa on the western frontiers of Egypt, Britain and Dominion troops fought the Axis. The fortunes of this desert war varied dramatically until October 1942 when the battle of Alamein finally broke the offensive power of General Erwin Rommel and the Afrika Korps. General Bernard Montgomery had built up an army of 195,000 men with a thousand tanks, almost double the size of the German–Italian army. At Alamein he outgunned and outwitted Rommel, who had to withdraw hastily.

Britain's Alamein victory ended the disastrous sequence of British defeats. A trap was sprung. Rommel's line of retreat was being simultaneously cut off by Anglo-American landings at his rear. There had been much inter-Allied dispute on where an Anglo-American force could best strike against Hitler's Europe in 1942. Roosevelt and the American generals favoured an assault on France. Their reasoning was political as well as military. Stalin was pressing for a 'second front' to relieve

The Battle of El Alamein of 23 October 1942 was the first decisive land battle the British won in the Second World War.

Black Military Service. An aspect of the story of the twentieth century still not fully told is the contribution made by black servicemen to all of the wars in which the United States has taken part. During the First World War, 370,000 were enlisted, but they were rigidly segregated (though separate regiments of the 92nd Division served with French troops). In the Second World War, one million black American men served in the armed forces alongside several thousand black women. Again segregated, they were mainly assigned service roles. Above: *the most senior black officer, Brigadier-General Benjamin O. Davis, inspects combat troops in England in October 1942. The all-black 93rd Division served in the Pacific. The gun crew of Battery "B" 598th Field Artillery 92nd Division* (below) *on the banks of the Arno, Italy, 1 September 1944. In 1948, President Truman ended segregation by executive order. During the Korean War, all races were integrated in the armed forces.*

pressure in the East by forcing the Germans to transfer forty divisions to the West. But the Americans were quite unrealistic about the time needed for so difficult an undertaking. An unsuccessful commando raid on Dieppe in August 1942 showed how hard it would be to establish a bridgehead. Shortage of landing craft meant that no more than ten Allied divisions could have been sent across the Channel in 1942. Churchill and the British Chiefs of Staff were in any case opposed to a premature invasion of France. Agreement was eventually reached that an Anglo-American force should land in Vichy French North Africa in November 1942. General Dwight Eisenhower commanded this whole operation, codenamed Torch. At first the Vichy French forces resisted the landings but then agreed to an armistice. The Allies were thus able to occupy French Morocco and Algeria virtually unopposed.

Hitler responded to the Allied invasion of North Africa by sending his troops into the hitherto unoccupied regions of Vichy France. Britain had always feared that this would happen and that the French fleet would then fall into German hands. In fact the French fleet in Toulon eluded a German takeover by scuttling itself. Hitler also sent in troops from Sicily to occupy French Tunisia in North Africa. Rommel, meanwhile, fought and retreated westwards from Libya. The real fighting between the Allies and the Italian and German forces then occurred in Tunisia and lasted until May 1943, when a total of 150,000 troops (both Italian and German) finally capitulated. It was a major victory for the Anglo-American forces. Even so, the scale of the fighting in North Africa cannot be compared with that of the Russian front. Here the main war on land was being waged.

On 22 June 1941 a massive military force invaded the Soviet Union with almost 3.6 million German and Axis soldiers, 3,600 tanks and 2,700 planes. This great show of force included fourteen Romanian divisions. With the Panzers racing ahead in best *Blitzkrieg* tradition, the Soviet armies in the west were to be smashed by a three-pronged attack by the three army groups – North, Centre and South. The army of the North drove through the former Baltic states with Leningrad as their goal. The German army of the Centre made its thrust in the direction of Smolensk and Moscow, and the army group South invaded the Ukraine. The purpose of these deep thrusts was to encircle and to destroy the Red Army in western Russia, and to prevent a Russian retreat into the vastness of Soviet territory. The victorious German armies expected to control European Russia from the Volga to Archangel. A 'military frontier' could then be established against Asiatic Russia, where the Japanese ally later might be encouraged to colonise parts of Siberia. Territorially Germany almost achieved her objective of conquering the whole of European Russia in 1941 and 1942. Yet the Soviet Union was not defeated and the *Blitzkrieg* turned into a war of attrition, during which the greater Soviet reserves of manpower and the increasing output of her armament industry turned the tide of the war against Hitler's Germany.

After the initial and spectacular victories of the battles of the frontiers during the first weeks of the war, when the Germans took hundreds of thousands of Russian prisoners and whole Russian armies disintegrated, the German generals and Hitler disagreed which of the three offensives was to be the main effort. Thus already in August of 1941 the basic weakness of Germany's latest *Blitzkrieg* became evident. Speaking to Goebbels on 18 August, Hitler bitterly complained about the failures of military intelligence before the war. Instead of the expected 5000 tanks, the Soviets disposed of 20,000. Goebbels reflected that had the true strength of the Soviet Union been known, 'Perhaps we would have drawn back from tackling the questions of the East and Bolshevism which had fallen due.' What a momentous 'perhaps', on which the whole course of the war was to depend! During the first six weeks the Germans lost 60,000 dead; newspaper columns in Germany were filled with small black iron crosses announcing a son or husband fallen for Führer and Fatherland. As the Germans penetrated the Soviet Union the already vast front from the Black Sea to the Baltic of more than 500 miles lengthened even further. The same tactics that had worked in the 'confined' space of France failed in the vastness of the Soviet Union. Though Stalin was completely stunned by the German attack, not expecting it, despite all warnings, to be launched before 1942, huge Russian reserves of manpower and the setting up of industrial complexes beyond the Urals meant that the Soviet military capacity to resist was not destroyed.

But Stalin's fear of provoking Germany by taking adequate preparatory measures had left the Soviet

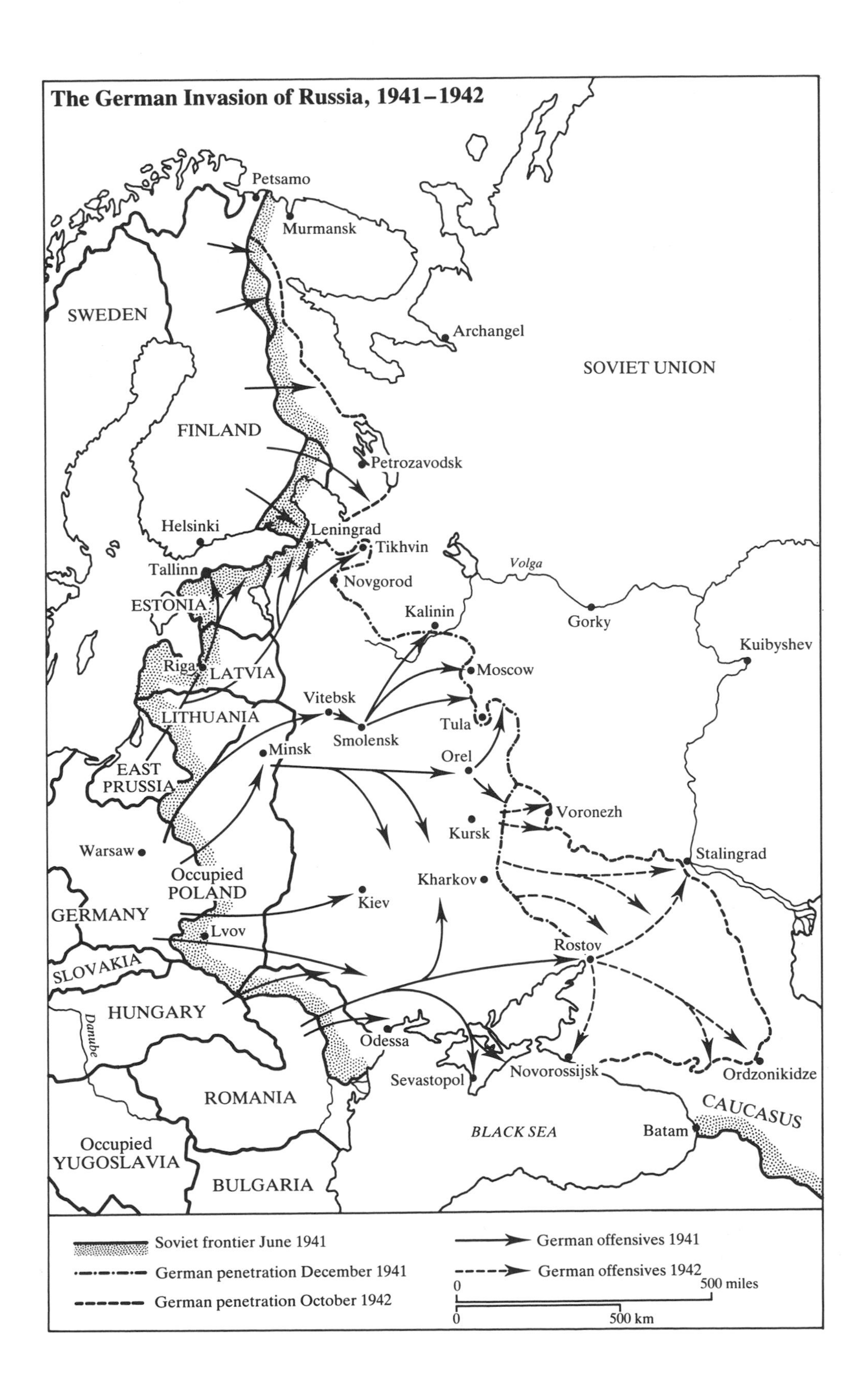
The German Invasion of Russia, 1941–1942
Petsamo
Murmansk
SWEDEN
Archangel
SOVIET UNION
FINLAND
Petrozavodsk
Helsinki
Leningrad
Tikhvin
Tallinn
Novgorod
Volga
ESTONIA
Kalinin
Gorky
Kuibyshev
Riga
LATVIA
Moscow
Vitebsk
LITHUANIA
Tula
Smolensk
Minsk
Orel
EAST PRUSSIA
Voronezh
Kursk
Warsaw
Stalingrad
Occupied POLAND
Kharkov
Kiev
GERMANY
Lvov
Rostov
SLOVAKIA
HUNGARY
Danube
Odessa
Sevastopol
Novorossijsk
Ordzonikidze
ROMANIA
CAUCASUS
BLACK SEA
Batam
Occupied YUGOSLAVIA
BULGARIA
Soviet frontier June 1941
German penetration December 1941
German penetration October 1942
German offensives 1941
German offensives 1942
0
500 miles
0
500 km

armies unprepared and exposed to German encirclements at the outset. The Germans captured more than 3 million prisoners between June and December 1941. But if the Soviet Union could avoid actual defeat in 1941 and 1942 it would then become impossible for the German armies to defeat the more numerous Soviet armies, whose weapons matched, and in the case of the T-34 tank even outclassed, those of the Germans. First the autumn rains and the mud and then the winter weather caught the German armies unprepared. Not only did the troops freeze during the particularly severe winter of 1941/2, but much of the mechanised equipment became unusable in the Arctic frosts. Russia's two greatest cities, Leningrad and Moscow, were the goals of the central and northern German armies. Leningrad was almost surrounded by the Germans and the Finns.

The siege of Leningrad is one of the epics of the Second World War. It lasted from September 1941 to January 1944. During the siege 641,803 people died from hunger and disease alone. The Soviet spirit of resistance was not broken. Almost three-quarters of a million German troops were bogged down around the city for 900 days. The Germans were also denied the capture of Moscow, although they reached the southern suburbs. Germany's defeats were not due to 'General Winter' alone, but owed much to the skill and heroism of the Soviet forces facing the invaders. The German High Command was forced to admit that for the first time a *Blitzkrieg* had failed. The war was not over in the East; the war of attrition which had defeated Germany in 1914–18 and which Hitler had done everything to escape was just beginning.

There are occasions when secret intelligence plays a crucial role in war. The Soviets had a spy in Tokyo, Richard Sorge, a German press correspondent who had predicted the date of the German attack almost to the day. The warning appears to have fallen on deaf ears. But when he passed on the information that the Japanese would strike south and not attack the Soviet Union just before his arrest as a spy, and Japanese military inactivity confirmed his tip off, Stalin, though still suspicious, gradually withdrew those troops facing the Japanese after the Siberian campaigning season was over (Sorge was imprisoned and executed in 1944). With the help of these troops and other reinforcements, Marshal Zhukov, the most outstanding general on the Soviet side during the war, organised the defence of Russia's capital. In December 1941 fresh Soviet divisions counterattacked and the Germans were forced to give up territory, but their own retreat was orderly. They were not routed or captured in huge numbers as the Russians had been. Although the Russians probably did not yet enjoy superiority in men or materials on the Moscow front, the Germans were severely disadvantaged by the length of and lack of adequate rail and road supply lines to their own troops.

Stalin's own mistakes in carrying on the Russian offensives in the spring of 1942, believing the German armies virtually beaten, led to major military disasters on the Kharkov front in the south in May and June 1942 and in the Crimea. Hundreds of thousands more Soviet troops were lost. Stalin, expecting the Germans to renew their main drive on Moscow, concentrated Russian reserves on the central front. Instead the main German blow was delivered in the south. The Crimea, including Sevastopol, was taken. The Germans drove forward to the city of Stalingrad on the Volga, intending to cut off the whole of Russia south of that city including the oil-rich Caucasus, which formed the gateway to Persia.

In the ruins of Stalingrad the Russians, fighting from house to house, made their stand. The battle lasted from mid-August to mid-November 1942. Stalin and Hitler were locked in a titanic proxy struggle for supremacy. Hitler decided that Stalingrad would be taken come what may and that Germany would not withdraw. Stalin sent Zhukov to mastermind the defence of the city regardless of casualties. Most of the city was taken by the Germans in October, and the Russian defenders' reinforcements were limited as fresh divisions were being husbanded in preparation for a great counter-offensive. On 19 November 1942 the Russians launched their attack and encircled the 200,000 men of Germany's Sixth Army fighting in Stalingrad. Hitler ordered the Sixth Army to stand fast. Losing the opportunity to link up with the German armies to the rear it was doomed. Fierce fighting continued until the 91,000 survivors including Field Marshal von Paulus surrendered on 31 January 1943. The Wehrmacht had been decisively defeated, and, more than that, the myth of Hitler's infallible military genius had been exploded. The world felt Stalingrad marked a turning point in the war. Soviet strength would increase as Germany's diminished. By the summer of 1943 the Russians

The Battle for Stalingrad, August 1942–January 1943. Every house, every factory a fortress. The German Army was never to recover from its defeat and Hitler's reputation as the 'greatest military leader of all times' was finally shattered.

had also won superiority in the air, with thousands of planes engaged on each side.

Had there been wholesale defections from the forced union of Soviet Socialist Republics the whole prospect of the war might have changed. The almost unbelievable number of prisoners that the Germans took in 1941 suggests not only military defeat but also large-scale desertions. But Hitler resisted those of his advisers who wished to utilise this anti-communist and anti-Russian sentiment. The peasants hungered for land and for release from the collective farms. A captured Russian general, Andrei Vlasov, even offered to raise an army from prisoners of war to fight Stalin's Russia. But Hitler's racist fanaticism stood in the way of winning the war by these means. European Russia was designated as colonial territory, eventually to be depopulated as necessary to provide room for the New German settlers. The Slavs were 'subhumans'; nearly 3 million were sent to Germany to work as virtual slave labour. With the Germans ransacking the Russian territories they occupied, the early welcome which they received turned to hatred. Partisan resistance increased behind German lines and was met by ruthless terror. Only too late in 1943 and 1944 did Himmler try to change a German policy bound to alienate the local population and to recruit for the German army from among the minorities. Meanwhile Stalin skilfully appealed to Russian patriotism and encouraged all the peoples of the Soviet republics to turn out the invaders.

Hitler tenaciously clung to one hope even when surrounded in his bunker in burning Berlin in April 1945, that the 'unholy' and unnatural alliance between Britain, the United States and the Soviet Union would fall apart and that the Western powers would recognise that he was fighting the common Bolshevik enemy. There is not the slightest evidence that Roosevelt or Churchill would for one moment have contemplated any kind of pact with Hitler. Though Churchill, more so than Roosevelt, foresaw that there would be post-war conflict with the Soviet Union, his conviction of the need to destroy the evils of Nazism was unshakeable. The holding together of the grand alliance was a precondition of victory.

Was this also Stalin's perception of British policy? Did Stalin, pathologically suspicious of the motives of all possible enemies, have any faith in Britain's determination to fight Hitler's Germany to the finish? Despite Churchill's immediate and unqualified promise of support the moment the Germans invaded Russia, suspicion of any antagonist past, present or future was second nature to Stalin. The continuing delays in the opening of a second front in France through 1942, then 1943, must have confirmed his fears that the reason for delay was mainly political not military. He bitterly complained to Churchill, charging him with breaches of faith. The Soviet archives are only just being opened and the workings of Stalin's mind remain a matter of conjecture. But he may well have concluded that the West was deliberately prolonging the war to weaken the Soviet Union in the bloodbath of the eastern front in order to dictate the future from a position of strength. The longer European Russia remained in German hands, the more difficult it would be to re-establish communist autocracy over the non-Russian peoples. Hence it became for Stalin almost a test of Britain's good faith that Russia's right to her *1941* frontiers should be accepted by Britain and the United States and not become a matter of negotiation after the war was won. The 1941 frontiers included the additional territory the Soviet Union had acquired as a result of the deal struck with Nazi Germany: eastern Poland, the Baltic states, Bessarabia and northern Bukovina, and also the territories taken from Finland after the Soviet–Finnish War.

The British position at first was to reject any frontier changes until after the war was over and peace negotiations took place. Roosevelt, mindful of his own Polish minority in America and of the condemnation of the 'secret deals' of the First World War, at first resisted even more firmly European frontier discussions. But Churchill and Eden were anxious to appease Stalin at a time when the Red Army was bearing the brunt of the war on land. An Anglo-Russian agreement for jointly waging war against Germany had been signed in Moscow on 12 July 1941; on 26 May 1942 it was replaced by a formal twenty-year alliance. Churchill also responded courteously to Stalin's angry and wounding messages about the lack of a second front. But there was much apprehension in London that Stalin might lose confidence in his Western allies and strike a deal with Hitler. Everything was avoided that might add to his suspicions. This had one important consequence. Discussions with emissaries from the German resistance, or with representatives sent by Himmler's SS to bargain over the lives of the Hungarian Jews, were avoided for fear that they would compromise Britain and lead Stalin to the wrong conclusion that a separate peace was being considered.

Among Hitler's entourage were advisers and allies who urged him to seek a separate peace with the Soviet Union. But the struggle against the Bolsheviks and Jews lay at the core of his ideology. He rejected peace with his arch-enemies though he admired Stalin's ruthlessness. His barbarity in Russia and the carrying through of the Final Solution while the war was being lost militarily show that ideology ultimately dominated Hitler's actions when *Realpolitik* would have served the interests of the Third Reich. As for Stalin it is possible that he welcomed the West's belief that he had an alternative to war with Germany for it would make Britain and the United States more willing to accede to Russia's military and political demands.

The question of the future of Poland was the most difficult for Britain and the United States to solve. The Polish government in exile demanded that the independence of its state be restored within the frontiers of 1939, that is of pre-war Poland. But Stalin had already annexed and incorporated in the Soviet Union the portions of Poland occupied in September 1939 and insisted on a post-war Poland 'friendly' to the Soviet Union. With the Red Army inevitably overrunning Poland there was little in effect the United States and Britain could do to force Stalin to renounce territory which he claimed as Soviet already. The Polish government in exile in London was in a hopeless situation. General Sikorski, who headed the Polish government in exile in London, had at first tried to work with the Russians. He had signed an agreement for Russo-Polish co-operation with Stalin in 1941, but from the first two issues clouded Polish–Soviet relations: the question of Poland's eastern frontier and the thousands of missing Polish officers who should have re-emerged from Russian prisoner-of-war camps after the 1941 agreement had been concluded. The corpses of Polish officers found by the Germans near Smolensk in the Katyn forest provided a grisly explanation for their disappearance and ruptured relations between the Polish government and the Kremlin in April 1943. The Russians formed their own Polish military units and an embryonic rival Polish government, the Union of Polish Patriots.

The fate of Poland was virtually decided at the first summit conference when Roosevelt, Churchill and Stalin met in Teheran in Persia from 28 November to 1 December 1943. There was no formal agreement, but Churchill agreed on behalf of Britain, and Roosevelt personally acquiesced too, to the Soviet Union's retaining eastern Poland as far as the Curzon line (the armistice line between Poland and Russia proposed by the British Foreign Secretary Lord Curzon in 1920) and that Poland should be compensated with German territory east of the rivers Oder and Neisse. At the Yalta Conference more than a year later (4–11 February 1945), with Poland by then overrun by the Red Army, despite some ambiguities in the official declarations Stalin secured his territorial ambitions at Poland's expense. For his part Stalin promised that he would allow all the liberated peoples in Eastern and central Europe to choose their own governments freely and democratically. Power had passed to a Polish provisional government which was based in the Soviet Union and which some 'London' Poles were permitted to join. At Teheran and Yalta, military needs and realities, as well as hopes for post-war co-operation, decided Churchill and Roosevelt to accept Stalin's demands that Soviet conditions concerning the future frontiers of Russia be met in all but formal treaty form before the conclusion of the war.

Until 1945 there was little link between the war waged in Europe and Africa and the war waged by Japan, Britain, China and the United States in eastern and south-eastern Asia. The Soviet Union was not a party to the Pacific war until shortly before its end. Japan and the Soviet Union signed a neutrality treaty in April 1941 and the two countries remained at peace until Russia declared war on Japan just one week before Japan's surrender.

Roosevelt and Churchill never wavered from their early determination after Japan's attack on Pearl Harbor in December 1941 that despite the military disasters in eastern Asia the defeat of Germany must come first. Japan's victories came as a tremendous shock to British and Dominion public opinion. The Western empires of the Dutch, French and British and the American hold on the Philippines collapsed in just a few weeks and the whole region fell for the first time under the control of one power, Japan.

In Malaya, Britain had constructed the Singapore naval base and Churchill had insisted on sending to it two battleships, the *Prince of Wales* and the *Repulse*, intending thereby to deter the Japanese from going to war. The British commanded in Malaya 89,000 troops, including 37,000 Indian, 19,000 British and 15,000 Australians. In the Netherlands East Indies 35,000 Dutch regular troops were stationed. The Americans had posted 31,000 regulars to the Philippines. But the British, Dutch and American troops were poorly equipped. Air defence in particular was inadequate, which gave the Japanese a decisive advantage. The Japanese almost immediately after the outbreak of the war sank the *Prince of Wales* and the *Repulse* from the air. There were now no battleships left to oppose them. The attack on Pearl Harbor had knocked out the capacity of the United States fleet to challenge Japan's offensive. The capture of Guam and Wake islands denied the United States naval bases beyond Hawaii. In Malaya the well-equipped and skilfully led Japanese army began the invasion on 8 December and, though only 60,800 in strength, overwhelmed the British defence forces, which finally capitulated in Singapore on 15 February 1942. Some 80,000 troops under British command surrendered, a stunning military defeat when added to the shock provoked by the sinking of the *Repulse* and *Prince of Wales*. The fall of Singapore was also a great psychological blow which undermined the faith of Asian peoples in 'white' superiority.

General Douglas MacArthur defended the Philippines. The Japanese gained air control and their invading army defeated the Americans, who withdrew to the Bataan peninsula in January 1942; the Americans finally had to surrender their last fortress defence on 9 April with 70,000 troops, a disaster comparable to Singapore, except that the defence had been long drawn out and skilfully conducted. Simultaneously with the invasion of Malaya, another Japanese army crossed from Thailand into Burma and by the end of April had driven the weak British forces into India. The Netherlands East Indies were captured between January and March 1942. Throughout these five months of victorious campaigns the Japanese had suffered only some 15,000 killed and wounded and had taken more than ten times as many Allied troops prisoner. The whole of south-east Asia had fallen under Japanese domination.

British rule seemed to be threatened now at the very heart of the empire, British India. The position was regarded as sufficiently desperate for the British Cabinet to send out Sir Stafford Cripps with a promise to the leaders of the Indian Congress Party that India would be granted independence after the war. A constituent assembly would be called to decide whether she would remain within or outside the Commonwealth. Meanwhile, during the war, the Congress Party would be granted some participation in but not control of government. Congress rejected the proposals, partly because Cripps also offered to the Muslim League the possibility of secession for the predominantly Muslim parts of India (later Pakistan). Gandhi, India's greatest voice of non-violent opposition, now called on Britain simply to 'quit India'. He expected non-violence to defeat Britain and Japan and to win India for the 385 million Indians. The Viceroy of India reacted with repression and arrested the Congress leaders and Gandhi. India did not rise against the British, and the Indian army fought under British command against the Japanese. The Japanese also created an Indian 'liberation' army from prisoners of war mainly taken at Singapore and founded the Indian Independence League. In 1943 an Indian nationalist, Subhas Chandra Bose, ex-president of the Indian Congress, took over the Indian 'government' operating with the Japanese. Though Bose had a good deal of success among Indians beyond British control, his impact within India was limited and never threatened British rule. The problem of Indian independence was now shelved until the war was won.

Militarily the Japanese expansion in the Pacific and south-east Asia was checked by the summer of 1942. In the naval battle of the Coral Sea in May 1942 Japan's thrust towards Australia was blunted when the Japanese attack on Port Moresby in New Guinea was called off as a result of the naval engagement. Far more serious for the Japanese was the failure of their attack in June on the American-held Midway Island. Admiral Yamamoto was in overall command of the most powerful fleet of battleships, aircraft carriers, cruisers, destroyers and submarines the Japanese had ever assembled. Its task was not only to cover the Japanese landing force, but to destroy the remaining US Pacific fleet. Yamamoto had separated his fleet. It was a naval battle dominated by the aircraft carriers on both sides. The Japanese lost four of their eight carriers, the Americans only one before Yamamoto's main fleet could join the engagement. Yamamoto decided to break off the battle and from then on had lost the initiative in the Pacific. It was now certain that the American war effort, which was once fully developed, would overwhelm Japan eventually. Just as in Europe, where Hitler's *Blitzkrieg* had failed finally in 1942, so did Japan's oriental *Blitzkrieg* now fail in its purpose of forcing the country's principal enemies to accept her claim to predominance in eastern and southern Asia.

The American counter-offensive in the Pacific began in August 1942 with the attack on the tiny Japanese-held island of Guadalcanal, one of the Solomon group of islands. The fighting between the American marines and the defending Japanese was ferocious and casualties on both sides were heavy, until the Americans overwhelmed the fanatical defenders. This was to become the pattern of the remorseless Pacific war until the Japanese surrendered to the Americans.

The Japanese war with Britain, the Dominions and the United States brought relief to the Chinese, who had been at war with the Japanese alone since 1937. Chiang Kai-shek now avoided active battles with the Japanese as far as possible. His eyes were firmly set on the future when, with the Anglo-American defeat of the Japanese, he would gain mastery over all China, including the communists, his theoretical allies against Japan. Despite the growing corruption of the Kuomintang and the inefficiency of Chiang Kai-shek's armies, the United States based her hopes for the future peace and progress of eastern Asia on the emergence of a strong and democratic Chinese republic linked in friendship to the United States. Roosevelt did not wish to see the restoration of the pre-war special rights of Europe in China or the re-establishment of the European empires in eastern Asia. In January 1945 he expressed his hopes to his Secretary of State that United States policy 'was based on the belief that despite the temporary weakness of China and the possibility of revolutions and civil war, 450 million Chinese would someday become united and modernised and would be the most important factor in the whole Far East'.

The problem during the last two years of the land war in Asia was to get Chiang Kai-shek's armies to put up any resistance at all to the Japanese, who renewed their offensives and occupied large new areas of eastern China in 1944. The Japanese overran the American-built airfields from which they had been bombed. Chiang Kai-shek meanwhile positioned half a million of his best troops in the north to contain the communists and was preserving his armies for a future war of supremacy in China after the Western powers had defeated Japan. Throughout 1944 the tension between Roosevelt and Chiang Kai-shek grew. Roosevelt had little faith in the Chinese leader. He wished to force on him the appointment of an American general to command all the Chinese armies and to bring about effective co-operation between the communists and the Kuomintang against the Japanese. A China policy that would reconcile China and serve America's global interests continued to elude the United States.

During the course of 1943 the tide of war turned decisively against Japan, Italy and Germany. The enormous industrial resources of the United States alone, when fully mobilised for war, exceeded all that Germany, Japan and their allies could produce together. The Soviet Union was by now more than a match for the military strength Germany had built up in the east. It was only the tenacity and skill of Germany's armies, despite Hitler's disastrous interferences as at Stalingrad, that enabled

Germany to stave off defeat for so long. Germany did not collapse even when the ordinary man in the street knew the war was lost and had no confidence left in Hitler's promised 'wonder' weapons. She fought to the bitter end, until Hitler had shot himself and the crushing superiority of the Allied armies closing in from all sides made further resistance a physical impossibility. Until close to the end of the war, Hitler's regime could still successfully terrorise and kill anyone who openly refused orders to fight to the last. Equally important was German fear of Russian conquest and occupation. Nazi propaganda had successfully indoctrinated the German people into believing that the Russian subhumans from the east would destroy, loot and kill and that it was better to die resisting than to fall into Russian hands. Early experiences of the Russian armies when they first invaded East Prussia appeared to confirm this belief.

But a separate peace with the West, the principal hope of those who during the later stages of the war had plotted against Hitler, was not a possibility. In practice the Western Allies could follow no other policy than to demand that Germany must surrender unconditionally on *all* fronts simultaneously. The actual phrase 'unconditional surrender' emerged during discussions between Roosevelt and Churchill when they met at Casablanca in January 1943 to co-ordinate and agree on Anglo-American strategy. Roosevelt gave it official public backing in speaking to the press. It meant that Britain and the United States would not entertain any bargaining over peace terms with Germany, Italy and Japan and would fight until complete military victory had been achieved.

It has been argued that the call for unconditional surrender made the enemies of the Allies fight more fanatically to the bitter end and that the war might have been shortened by a more flexible Allied attitude. The evidence of Germany's and Italy's behaviour in 1944 and 1945 does not support this view. The Italians were able to overthrow Mussolini and in fact negotiate their surrender, whereas Hitler's grasp over Germany remained so complete, and his own attitude so utterly uncompromising, that no negotiated peace was possible short of Germany's total collapse, even if any of the Allies had desired to negotiate for peace. The advantages of having proclaimed as a war aim 'unconditional surrender' on the other hand were solid. Allied differences on how to treat a conquered Germany could be kept secret since the Allied public had been satisfied by the demand of 'unconditional surrender'. Moreover, Roosevelt and Churchill hoped that the call for unconditional surrender would reassure Stalin in the absence of an early second front. In January 1943 Britain's and America's military effort on land did not compare with that of Russia, where the final phase of the Stalingrad battle was raging.

Within the Grand Alliance, or United Nations as all the countries fighting Germany came to be called, there was an inner Anglo-American alliance. A joint strategic body, the Combined Chiefs of Staff, was set up soon after Pearl Harbor to provide a forum for debate on strategy and eventual decision-making. Joint Anglo-American commands were created as necessary. There are no parallels in modern history of such close co-ordination of policy as was achieved by the United States and Britain during the last three and a half war years. It was based on the trust and working relationships at the top between Roosevelt and Churchill. Stalin would never have agreed to a joint command, and the Soviet Union remained an outsider fighting her own war with Germany, which engaged in 1942 and 1943 two-thirds of the total number of German divisions.

Joint Anglo-American planning bodies did not mean, however, that there was perfect harmony. The American military argued for a concentration of all effort on the earliest possible cross-Channel attack on France and so a blow at Germany's vitals. Churchill and his British military advisers warned against any premature landings, which might fail. Roosevelt, fearful in 1942 of the possibility that the Soviet forces might collapse unless some of the German forces were diverted, was inclined to listen to Stalin's appeals more sympathetically. Churchill mollified Stalin, convincing him that the projected landings in Vichy North Africa were a genuine second front. The successful completion of these operations in May 1943 was too late to allow for a switching of resources necessary to mount a cross-Channel attack in 1943. Churchill argued in favour of a Mediterranean strategy and attacking Italy, the 'soft underbelly' of the Axis. Churchill's reasons were based on his appraisal of military alternatives. The Germans were weakest in the Mediterranean and if the Allies carried the war into the Balkans then the German armies would be trapped between them and the Russians. The Allies, moreover, would

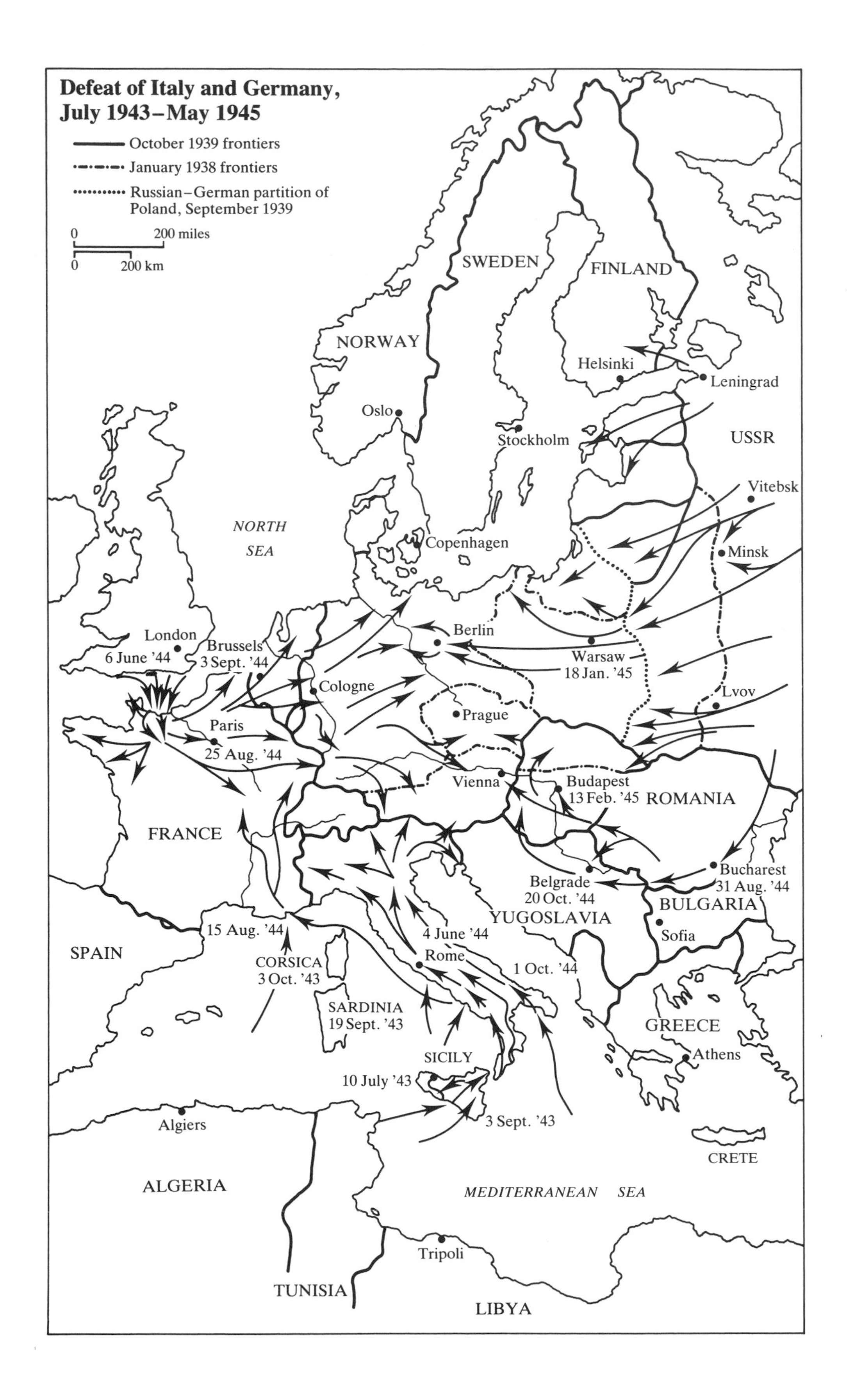

Defeat of Italy and Germany, July 1943–May 1945
October 1939 frontiers
January 1938 frontiers
Russian–German partition of Poland, September 1939
0
200 miles
0
200 km
NORWAY
SWEDEN
FINLAND
Helsinki
Leningrad
Oslo
Stockholm
USSR
Vitebsk
Minsk
NORTH SEA
Copenhagen
Berlin
Warsaw
18 Jan. '45
London
6 June '44
Brussels
3 Sept. '44
Cologne
Prague
Lvov
Paris
25 Aug. '44
Vienna
Budapest
13 Feb. '45
ROMANIA
FRANCE
Bucharest
31 Aug. '44
Belgrade
20 Oct. '44
BULGARIA
YUGOSLAVIA
Sofia
SPAIN
15 Aug. '44
4 June '44
Rome
1 Oct. '44
CORSICA
3 Oct. '43
SARDINIA
19 Sept. '43
GREECE
Athens
SICILY
10 July '43
3 Sept. '43
Algiers
CRETE
ALGERIA
MEDITERRANEAN SEA
Tripoli
TUNISIA
LIBYA

be able to link with Tito's Yugoslav partisans. The Americans wanted to concentrate all forces on an attack on France, but agreed that the North African forces could be used to invade Sicily next.

The rapid fall of Sicily to the Anglo-American forces in July 1943 marked the end of Mussolini's hold on power. The fascist leaders and King Victor Emmanuel could see the writing on the wall. The way out for Italy was to jettison the German alliance and to change sides if possible. Military defeat and the imminent invasion of Italy had weakened Mussolini's position sufficiently to make it possible to overthrow him. The Duce was dismissed from his office not by a popular revolution but by the King and his fascist collaborators on 24 and 25 July 1943. He was then imprisoned until rescued by the Germans. The King appointed Marshal Pietro Badoglio as Mussolini's successor. But Badoglio and the fascist leaders failed to save Italy from becoming a battleground. Despite the promise to continue the war, German suspicions were aroused and reinforcements were sent to Italy. The new regime held secret negotiations with the Allies, but did not persuade them to land in northern Italy to enable the Italians to avoid a German occupation. The Anglo-American plan envisaged occupying only southern Italy. This made it possible for the Germans to seize the remainder of Italy when Italy's surrender was made public on 8 September 1943. Naples was reached by the Allies on 1 October. The Germans by then had established a strong defensive line across the Italian peninsula. The King and the Italian government fled south behind the Allied lines and then declared war on Germany, while Hitler restored Mussolini to act as a puppet dictator over the republic he had proclaimed. Until the close of the war in May 1945, the Allied armies had to fight their way gradually north, piercing heavily fortified lines which the Germans created in their path. Meanwhile a guerrilla war was fought in the north by the partisans, whose aim was not only to drive out the Germans but also to bring about radical social change in Italy.

Mussolini did not survive the military defeat of his ally. Captured by Italian partisans, he, together with his mistress, was executed by them. The Italian campaign did not prove to be a rapid success and entailed some of the heaviest fighting of the war. But Hitler's decision to defend Italy and so keep the Allies as far as possible away from south Germany diverted many divisions to her defence and to the defence of the Balkans, which had become vulnerable.

While in July 1943 the British and American armies invaded Sicily, the largest tank battle of the war was being waged at Kursk on the Russian front. The German attack on the Russian salient was beaten back by Marshal Zhukov. It was the last occasion on which the Germans were able to mount a major offensive in Russia. Both sides suffered huge casualties, but the Russian armour had proved superior and the Russians, unlike the Germans, could make good such losses. Successive Russian offensives drove the German armies back in heavy fighting into Poland, but they halted the Russians on the River Vistula. The Warsaw rising (1 August –2 October 1944) did not induce the Red Army at all costs to reach the Polish capital. In mid-September Russian attempts to advance were repelled by the Germans, who remained in control of Warsaw until the end of the year. Further south, Russian armies advanced from the Ukraine into Romania, Bulgaria, Yugoslavia and Hungary. As in Italy, new governments attempted to change from the German to the Russian side. But the Germans were still strong enough to remove the Hungarian Regent Admiral Horthy from power and to make a stand against the Russian armies. Budapest did not surrender to the Russians until February 1945. But Hitler could no longer in 1944 place the bulk of his armies to defend the eastern front.

On 6 June 1944 under General Dwight Eisenhower's supreme command the successful cross-Channel invasion of France began. The tremendous obstacles to this enterprise had been overcome by meticulous planning and brilliant execution. Beaches and bases were won and by the end of July 1944 1.5 million men had been landed in France. After the battle of Normandy, Paris was taken on 25 August and the German troops were pursued as they retreated from France. A landing in southern France against the depleted German forces there enabled the Allies rapidly to liberate most of France. The Allies reached the southern Netherlands and the northern Franco-German frontier between Aachen and Trier in September.

Meanwhile Hitler had launched his promised wonder weapons, the pilotless aircraft-bomb, the V-1, and the missile bomb, V-2, against London. The attacks by these new weapons on London and

An immense armada brought the Allied invasion forces to the Normandy beaches, 6 June 1944.

Antwerp in the summer and autumn of 1944 did much damage but could not alter the course of the war. The last of these ingenious bombs hit Antwerp in March 1945.

One problem that could not await any longer for solution was who was to be recognised as representing the free government of France. There could be no question that Pétain's Vichy regime had forfeited all its claims by collaborating with the Germans. Of all the countries that had been overrun by the Germans, France was the most important, the only indubitable pre-war great power. Yet ironically it was the one ally not represented by a government in exile in London. The Free French, who had rallied to General de Gaulle in 1940 and formed their own administration in London, were recognised only as the French Committee of National Liberation. De Gaulle felt his inferior status deeply. But it cannot be denied that his status corresponded to reality in that the majority of Frenchmen in France and in the French Empire accepted Pétain's authority. Not that this would have stopped the British and Americans in wartime from according recognition to de Gaulle. Expediency, however, persuaded them not to challenge Vichy France openly. A powerful French fleet after all was still in Vichy hands in 1942. When the Allies made their North African landings in November 1942, Operation Torch, it was with the Vichy authorities there that secret negotiations were conducted to avoid the hostility of the French army units stationed there. Admiral Darlan, who happened to be in Algiers, decided to support the Americans. Soon after that he was assassinated. De Gaulle was regarded as something of an embarrassment; but despite Allied intrigues he succeeded in reasserting his leadership over all the Free French.

Roosevelt was particularly averse to committing himself to de Gaulle, who reacted by asserting all the more strongly his rights and those of France. The disparity between the reality of the French position and de Gaulle's behaviour struck Churchill and Roosevelt at the time as incongruous. But Churchill, with more imagination, insight and sympathy

Liberation. Left: *in Belfort, France, in November 1944, an American GI receives a warm welcome.* Right: *In Paris, the penalty for taking a German lover during the Occupation was public humiliation.*

than Roosevelt, urged after the Allied invasion of France in June 1944 that de Gaulle's administration should be recognised as the provisional government of France. Such recognition nevertheless was delayed until October 1944. The manner in which de Gaulle had been treated by the 'Anglo-Saxon' powers made the deepest impression on him and still rankled years later. The restoration of France to great-power status, and her independence from Anglo-American dominance, became almost an obsession with de Gaulle in the post-war years.

The war was clearly drawing to a close in the autumn of 1944. But stiff German resistance frustrated a quick victory. In the East, the Germans continued to fight fiercely. In the West, they were even able to inflict temporary reverses on the Allies. Montgomery made a bold attempt in September 1944 to cross the lower Rhine at Arnhem with the help of parachute divisions dropped in advance, but just short of Arnhem the Germans were able to halt his thrust. The Allied armies, however, were slowly pushing on to the Rhine along a broad front and had reached practically the whole length of the German frontier by mid-December. The Germans had still one surprise left. Powerful German divisions, led by tanks, together with what was left of the Luftwaffe in the West, opened an offensive through the Ardennes on 16 December 1944. The Germans advanced sixty miles before they were halted. It was their last offensive of the war.

With the imminent collapse of Hitler's Germany, agreement with the Russians on the military division of the territories the Allies would occupy, and on the post-war delimitation of frontiers and spheres of influence, took on a new urgency. In October 1944, Churchill flew to Moscow. Russian armies were by then already in Romania and Bulgaria and a British force was about to enter Greece. Churchill in Moscow proposed to Stalin a division of influence in the Balkan states. Stalin readily consented. But the resulting agreement was little more than a piece of paper. The Red Army would dominate Romania, Bulgaria and Hungary as it advanced towards Greater Germany. But Stalin allowed Britain freedom of action in Greece, provided a broadly based government including communists was formed in that country. British troops who landed in Greece soon found themselves fighting the communist-organised partisans. The uneasy peace established by the British force was to be shattered two years later in 1947 by civil war. Despite Stalin's promises to respect the sovereignty and the rights of self-determination of the nations of central Europe and the Balkans, in his mind there was always one overriding qualification: the free choice of the people would be forcefully set aside if it led, as was likely, to anti-Soviet governments. Greece, Yugoslavia and Albania were able after 1945 to assert their independence from Soviet control. The realities of Soviet 'freedom' were already apparent before the war with Germany was even won. A division of Europe was emerging between the Soviet-controlled territory of Eastern, central and south-eastern Europe and the West.

Roosevelt's hope of achieving some solid understanding between the three world powers, Britain, the Soviet Union and the United States, was severely tested by Soviet behaviour in 1944 and 1945. He pinned his hopes on creating a new international organisation – the United Nations – under the tutelage and based on the agreement of Britain, the Soviet Union and the United States. But Stalin was making unreasonable demands. All sixteen Soviet Republics were to be among the founder members of the United Nations. He also insisted that the six permanent members of the proposed council of the United Nations should be able to exercise an all-inclusive veto, that is to say, have the right to a veto when disputes were being dealt with in which they themselves were involved. The Dumbarton Oaks Conference which had met to organise the United Nations thus ended in September 1944 without agreement on these vital issues. What was seen as Stalin's intransigence brought the United States and Britain more closely together.

In Quebec, Churchill and Roosevelt met that same month, September 1944, to devise their joint military and political strategy. Plans were made to move troops from Italy into Istria and Austria ahead of Russian troops. To help Britain economically, Roosevelt also agreed to continue Lend–Lease during the time that would elapse between the defeat of Germany and the defeat of Japan. Britain's likely post-war economic weakness was thus foreshadowed: Britain would not remain an equal superpower with the United States and the Soviet Union. Britain and the United States next agreed to co-operate in the military and civilian development of atomic energy and, significantly, to exclude the Soviet Union from sharing this information.

The future of Germany was another subject of primary importance discussed at Quebec. Roosevelt's advisers had prepared both a 'soft' plan for peace terms and the famous plan associated with the name of the Secretary of the Treasury, Henry Morgenthau, which intended to deprive Germany of her major industries, reduce the German standard of living and turn her into an agricultural country. At first Churchill was violently opposed to this 'hard' option. It would too clearly be repeating the error of the First World War. A prosperous Europe could not develop without German economic recovery. But in return for concessions for the continuation of American economic aid to Britain he finally assented to 'converting Germany into a country primarily agricultural and pastoral in its character'. What were Roosevelt's motives in advocating a course that would have been so disastrous for European recovery? He spoke of punishing the German people for their wars of aggression; more important to him was to win Stalin's co-operation by reassuring the Soviet leader that the Western Allies would not try to rebuild Germany as a bulwark against Russia. In the autumn of 1944 Roosevelt's hand was greatly strengthened by his re-election as president. He would not have to enter peace negotiations without the certainty of public support as Wilson had done in 1919.

At Yalta in February 1945 Stalin, Roosevelt and Churchill finally met together again for the first time since Teheran. Roosevelt and Churchill arrived with some 700 officials. The photograph of the three leaders in front of the tsarist Livadia Palace implied an equality that did not exist. Roosevelt as a head of state was seated in the centre flanked on his left by Stalin and on his right by Churchill. Roosevelt's exhaustion and illness were plain to see, a shocking transformation from the confident President pictured only fifteen months earlier at Teheran. He was in a hurry and wanted the conference to be quickly over. He telegraphed to Churchill that it ought not to last more than five or six days. Churchill replied, 'Even the Almighty took seven.' In the event it lasted eight days from 4 to 11 February 1945.

Roosevelt was determined to come to terms with the Soviet leader and saw in Churchill almost as great an obstacle to establishing a good post-war partnership between them as Stalin himself. He had even been reluctant to meet Churchill in Malta before flying on to the Crimea for fear that Uncle Joe would interpret this as the Anglo-Saxons ganging up on him. The peaceful future of the world rested, as Roosevelt saw it, on a good Soviet–American understanding founded on trust. He regarded Churchill's 'Victorian' imperialism and his lifelong anti-communism as outdated in the post-war world.

As for Churchill, he felt keenly on the eve of Germany's defeat that Europe was in danger from the overbearing, immensely powerful Russian bear. He was looking to a less rosy future than Roosevelt was, in a world in which a United Nations organisation could no more be relied upon to preserve peace with justice than the League of Nations had been. He wanted to dilute the bilateral relationship between the United States and Russia that Roosevelt was trying to establish. Like Talleyrand at Vienna in 1814, conscious of Britain's comparative weakness Churchill tried to bring in another European ally, France. He failed. De Gaulle was not invited and would henceforth refer to the Yalta carve-up with bitterness and blame the 'Anglo-Saxons' for it.

The only concession Churchill did win, finally gaining Roosevelt's support for it, was to secure for France participation on the Allied Control Commission for Germany, which was to co-ordinate Allied rule over the defeated Reich. France would thus have her own occupation zone and her own sector in Berlin. On reparations there was an acceptance that the Soviet Union had a special claim but the final amount was left to a commission to propose. Perhaps the most significant thing about Yalta was what was *not* discussed and agreed. The question of Germany's future was really shelved. Churchill and Roosevelt had moved away from turning Germany into a 'pastoral' country. The dismemberment of Germany was *not* now determined. The destitute plight of the Germans, so Stalin may well have calculated, would strengthen communism throughout Germany. To gain material ends, he was ready to make promises which would appear as major concessions. He agreed to modify the Soviet stand on the organisation of the United Nation, whose success was closest to Roosevelt's heart. But Roosevelt had incautiously told him that American troops would be withdrawn from Europe within two years. Stalin therefore knew that he had only to wait until 1947; no military threat would then be able to stop him from doing whatever he then deemed to be in the Soviet interest.

The debate about Poland occupied much of the conference and was the most vexed. History did not have the same meaning for Churchill, Roosevelt and Stalin. Stalin looked at the frontiers of post-Versailles Europe through different eyes. For the West, 1937 was the last year that was 'normal', when the political geography of Europe reflected the peace settlements reached after the First World War. After 1937, Hitler first blackmailed the West and then redrew the map of Europe by force. For Russia, international injustice predated Hitler and had occurred after she had lost the war in 1917. The settlement then of the post-1918 Versailles era represented the humiliating acceptance of the superior force of the capitalist West at a time of Soviet weakness.

From her own perspective, the Soviet Union had simply not in her infancy had the necessary strength to regain Russia's 'just' frontiers. And so she had to acquiesce in the detaching of the Baltic provinces, which became independent states – Latvia, Lithuania and Estonia. Large territories were also carved out of what was formerly imperial Russia to create the Polish state, which included many Ukrainians and White Russians. Bessarabia was detached and added to Romania. As Stalin saw it, the frontiers of 1918–20 were those imposed on Russia; they were neither 'just' nor settled. He took advantage of the war between Germany, Poland, Britain and France in 1939–40 to put right what he believed were past wrongs by first making deals with Hitler. By 1941, with the absorption of eastern Poland, the three Baltic states and Bessarabia, Russia had regained most of her 'historic' frontiers. Stalin claimed that the Russian frontiers of 1941 should be regarded as the settled ones and not those of 1921 or 1937; he was prepared to consider only minor concessions. With remarkable consistency, he took his stand on this issue in discussions and negotiations with his Western allies from the earliest to the last months of the war.

The Czechs in 1943 had arranged their own settlement over the frontiers and future government of their country. Beneš, head of the exiled government in London, after the Munich experience of 1938 was not prepared to rely on Western support again. He did not allow a confrontation to develop between the communist-led Moscow Czechs and the London Western-oriented Czechs and accepted certain Soviet conditions and some loss of territory. But the Poles in London had not made their peace with Moscow. On the contrary, relations between the Polish government in exile and Moscow were little short of outright hostility, and had been aggravated by the establishment in Lublin of a communist-dominated provisional government.

Beyond Russia's frontiers the smaller nations in an arc from the Baltic to the Balkans had recently acted, in Stalin's view, as the springboard of aggression from the West against the Soviet Union. He insisted to Roosevelt and Churchill that they must not be allowed again to serve as hostile bridges to the heart of Russia. Soviet security, he emphasised, would depend on guarantees that they would be 'friendly' to the Soviet Union and would act in co-operation with her. What, however, did 'friendly' mean? To Stalin it meant that they could not remain capitalist, with anti-Russian governments based on the kind of society that had existed before the war; only societies transformed by a social revolution would be 'friendly' in the long term. The Western leaders rejected this link between the social and economic composition of the Soviet Union's neighbours and her own security. They in turn insisted on free elections, meaning that the people of the nations in question should be allowed to choose the kind of government and society they desired.

The prospect of reconciling these opposite views was slight. From Stalin's point of view the West had no business to dictate the social and political reconstruction of Poland, Czechoslovakia, Romania, Bulgaria or Hungary, any more than he himself wished to dictate the shape which the societies and politics of France, Italy, Belgium and the Netherlands should take. In these countries, Moscow had instructed the communist parties to work constructively in coalitions dominated by non-communists. He expected a *quid pro quo*. The West saw the issue in simple terms of democracy and self-determination.

For the Polish government in London the relationship with the Soviet Union was one of understandable enmity. The Russians had invaded Poland in September 1939 and now were annexing a large part of eastern Poland. The mass graves of 4421 Polish officers, shot in the back of the head by the Russians, had been discovered in 1943 in the forests of Katyn by German occupying forces and exploited by Joseph Goebbels for Nazi propaganda purposes (page 281). This unforgettable atrocity tormented Polish-Soviet relations. During the Second World War, Poland had been the conquered nation which, with Russia, had endured the most. Should she also become the nation that would now be made to suffer the consequences of victory? Britain and the United States agreed at Yalta to accept the Curzon line, with some deviations, as Poland's eastern frontier, thus giving a third of her pre-war territory to the Soviet Union. This, the London Polish government felt, was a betrayal. Churchill and Roosevelt had been driven to the reluctant conclusion that they had no realistic alternative. The Red Army occupied Poland and could not be forced to withdraw unless the Anglo-American armies were prepared to fight. Stalin for his part was well aware of the bitterness of the Polish government in London, which constituted an obvious danger to the Polish settlement he had in mind. The Poles were traditionally anti-Russian. They would not be allowed to assert their freedom at Russia's expense.

The major tussle was over the western boundary of Poland. Stalin had promised the communist Lublin government that the frontier would be marked by the Western Neisse. It was agreed that Poland would receive Pomerania and the larger half of East Prussia. Churchill and Roosevelt held out for the Eastern Neisse, which would not have assigned the whole of Silesia to Poland in addition. This question was left open to be settled later. These territories were only to be 'administered' by Poland until the conclusion of a final peace treaty with Germany.

Despite these calculations Stalin signed the Declaration on Liberated Europe at Yalta. According to its provisions the Allies would act as trustees, reaffirming the principle of the Atlantic Charter – the right of all peoples to choose the form of government under which they would live – and ensuring the restoration of sovereign rights and self-government to those peoples who had been forcibly deprived of them by the aggressor nations. Interim governments representing all democratic elements were to be set up, followed later by governments established 'through free elections'. This apparently unambiguous undertaking was ambiguous after all because it permitted only 'democratic and anti-Nazi parties' to put up candidates.

The Soviet Union twisted this to suit her own purpose of securing communist-dominated governments.

Churchill and Roosevelt wanted more specific arrangements for Poland to ensure that the Lublin provisional government, subservient to Moscow, would be replaced by a broad coalition, including exiled Polish leaders from the London-based government. The British and American ambassadors in Moscow, together with the Soviet Foreign Minister Vyacheslav Molotov, were to facilitate negotiations between the rival Polish governments in Lublin and London. Once a unified provisional government had been established, free elections were to be held. The suspicious Stalin had agreed to this for the sake of Allied unity before the final defeat of Germany. As the Red Army was in occupation of Poland he held all the cards and believed that there were enough loopholes in the Yalta agreement to ensure Soviet control in reality. For the Soviet Union an independent Poland in the post-war world was likely to be a hostile Poland, so her future was for Stalin a critical issue. Yalta had only papered over the cracks between West and East.

One reason why Roosevelt had been conciliatory in dealing with Stalin, frequently isolating Churchill, was his anxiety to secure Soviet help against the large Japanese armies deployed in China and in the Japanese home islands. The future of the atom bomb was still in doubt. Roosevelt told Stalin nothing about the progress that had been made. Actually, through agents, Stalin was already well informed. But it still appeared likely in February 1945 that the defeat of Japan would require bitter fighting, culminating in the invasion of mainland Japan, fanatically defended by the Japanese. Stalin at Yalta agreed to the Soviet Union's entry into the Pacific war two or three months after the defeat of Germany, but he named his price. With American lives at stake, Roosevelt did not allow anti-imperialist sentiments to stand in the way. Stalin demanded that Japan should relinquish southern Sakhalin and the Kurile Islands and that China should concede the warm-water port of Dairen and use of the Manchurian railway. The former imperial rights that tsarist Russia had enjoyed in China before 1904 were to be restored to the Soviet Union. The Chinese were not consulted, though in one part of their secret agreement it was stated that Chiang Kai-shek's consent was to be secured; but elsewhere, inconsistently, another paragraph was included: 'The Heads of the three Great Powers have agreed that these claims of the Soviet Union shall be unquestionably fulfilled after Japan has been defeated.' Stalin also promised to support efforts to bring about the co-operation of the Chinese Nationalists and the communists. For him this had the advantage of preventing the far more numerous Nationalists from simply attempting to wipe out the communists once the war with Japan was over.

Although Roosevelt had conceded Soviet predominance in Manchuria, he believed he had done his best to strengthen the post-war position of a weak China and that he had reduced the risk of civil war. The actual consequences of his diplomacy turned out differently and Harry S. Truman, his successor, did not welcome the last-minute Soviet declaration of war on Japan. Roosevelt in public spoke of Yalta as a triumph and a new beginning which would see the replacing of alliances and spheres of influence by the new international organisation of the United Nations. In private he was far more doubtful whether Stalin would fulfil what he had promised. But the war against Japan was still to be won and in the new year of 1945 he would contemplate no confrontation with the Soviet Union in Eastern or central Europe. Co-operation with her was possible, he believed, but he was at one with Churchill in concluding that firmness in dealing with Stalin was equally necessary. Roosevelt was not duped by Stalin but he could see no peaceful future unless coexistence could somehow be made to work. It was best to express confidence rather than misgivings.

Churchill's conscience was troubled by the Yalta agreement, which had once again partitioned Britain's brave wartime ally Poland. The shadow of appeasement, of Munich and Czechoslovakia lay not far behind and there was discontent in the House of Commons where a hard core of votes were cast against what had been concluded at Yalta. Poland was potentially damaging politically, a sensitive spot for Churchill at home. Internationally that spring of 1945, with the defeat of Germany in sight, his apprehensions also grew, as he contemplated a prostrate Western Europe and Britain being left to face the Soviets alone. The Americans, he feared, would withdraw to concentrate on the war in the Pacific. At Yalta, he had not been able to influence the outcome as the third and equal partner, because Roosevelt and Stalin had negotiated directly with

each other. The Soviets had secretly agreed to help defeat Japan so it was tempting, especially for the Americans, to appease the Soviet Union in Europe. In the war theatre, General Eisenhower also appeared too trusting of the Russians, ready to concert military strategy with his Soviet counterparts, rather than to occupy as much of northern Germany as could be captured and then to drive on to Berlin, as Churchill urged in March 1945.

Stalin meanwhile was accusing the West of secretly arranging for the German armies to stop fighting on the western front while they continued to resist the Russians ferociously all along the eastern battle zones. This was indeed partially true. The German forces were disintegrating in the West, with many soldiers deserting. Cities and towns surrendered to Anglo-American forces, disobeying Hitler's senseless orders to fight to the last, and the German High Command would have liked to reach a separate military surrender in the West. This was rejected. This did not mean that Churchill was complacent about the threat he discerned from the Soviet advance deep into Western Europe.

Churchill kept up a barrage of warnings in telegrams to Roosevelt. He urged that Stalin be treated firmly and made to adhere to the Yalta engagements. At Yalta, he cabled to Roosevelt, they had sided with Russia on the question of her western border. 'Poland has lost her frontier. Is she now to lose her freedom?' Churchill asked rhetorically. For Roosevelt too the Poles were a sensitive domestic political issue: there were 6 million Americans of Polish descent in the United States. But at the time he was anxious to secure Soviet co-operation to found the United Nations. He was therefore inclined to more conciliatory tactics to avoid alienating Stalin and so jeopardising his vision of a new world order. He also wanted to make sure of the promised Soviet help against Japan. Nevertheless he joined Churchill in firm appeals to Stalin.

On 12 April 1945 Roosevelt suffered a stroke so severe that he died shortly afterwards. He had responded with a growing sense of urgency to the threat posed by the totalitarian states. He recognised that freedom and democracy were being endangered throughout the world. His 'Quarantine' speech in 1937 had marked an important stage in his realisation that domestic problems at home would have to take second place to world problems. Working within the context of an overwhelming isolationist sentiment, Roosevelt had provided the indispensable, if at times devious, leadership which placed on the American people the burden of accepting the role of the United States as a superpower. In his post-war plans he worked for Soviet–American understanding, and for the creation of a viable United Nations organisation. He placed the United States on the side of independence for the peoples of Asia, including the dismantling of the European empires. He pinned his hopes on China achieving unity and stability. In Western Europe he was ready to provide American support to bring about a recovery that would enable these liberated nations, together with Britain, to safeguard their own freedoms. But he was under no illusions that all this had already actually been achieved. The behaviour of Stalin's Russia filled him with anxiety, yet it was an anxiety not without hope for the future. For all his limitations, Roosevelt's contribution to the reorientation of America's vision of her responsibilities in the world was all important. The news of his death came as a shock to the world. A half-crazed Hitler buried in his Berlin bunker saw it as the miracle that might save his Reich from defeat. By then the final offensives in the East and West were striking into the heart of Germany.

In March 1945 the American and British armies crossed the Rhine. During April they passed well beyond the military demarcation zones agreed at Yalta. Suspicion of Russian intentions was high and Churchill urged that the Anglo-American forces should withdraw only when the Russians had fulfilled their undertakings. It had been agreed that Berlin, although deep within the Russian zone of Germany, should be occupied by the United States, Britain and the Soviet Union, as well as France. But would the Soviets, once they had taken Berlin, honour their obligations?

The final Soviet offensives began in January 1945. Hitler ordered fanatical resistance on all fronts and the adoption of a 'scorched earth' policy. If Germany were not victorious, he concluded, the German people had not proved themselves worthy of the ideals of the Aryan race. He thus condemned Germany to senseless destruction. With Goebbels and Bormann at his side, he issued streams of orders from his underground headquarters in Berlin. But his orders were no longer unquestioningly obeyed. Armaments Minister Albert Speer attempted to prevent Germany's industry from being totally destroyed. He was looking beyond Hitler and defeat to Germany's recovery. Himmler tried to save his skin by seeking to negotiate an end to the war. Göring, who was in southern Germany, fancied himself as Hitler's successor, but an angry Hitler ordered the Field Marshal's arrest. The Reich ended in intrigue, ruins, bloodshed and shabby farce. Hitler concluded his life marrying his mistress, and on 30 April they both committed suicide. Goebbels and his wife then killed themselves with all their children. On 2 May Berlin surrendered to Soviet troops. Despite Germany's rapid disintegration, Admiral Karl Dönitz, nominated by Hitler as new leader of the Reich, took over as head of state observing legal niceties. He even formed a new 'government'. It lasted but a few days. On 7 May Germany unconditionally surrendered on all fronts. Britain and the United States now confronted the Soviet Union amid the ruins of continental Europe. Thus began a new era of international realities and conflict.

The sudden death of Roosevelt was a great blow for Churchill. While the Prime Minister's influence over the peace settlements had diminished, his special relationship with Roosevelt, an old friendship and appeals to past loyalties still counted for something. But would the new inexperienced President listen to the advice of the elder statesman, as Churchill now directed his warnings about Russia to Truman? He sent a cable to Truman expressing his foreboding that an 'iron curtain is being drawn down on their front', his first use of this phrase, which was to become famous later when he uttered it in public at Fulton in March 1946. He wanted Truman to come to London to co-ordinate a show-down with Stalin at a new conference. Truman rejected the idea as signalling to Stalin that the Anglo-Americans were ganging up against him.

Churchill further urged Truman to delay implementing the agreements reached on the respective occupation zones of Germany and not to withdraw the Allied forces which held territory deep in the zone assigned to the Soviet Union. It would be a bargaining counter and at least force the Russians to relinquish control over the whole of Berlin. But Truman was his own man. He was not enamoured of the Russians, to put it mildly, yet he was determined to honour previous agreements, so that he could hold Stalin, so he thought, to what the Russians had undertaken. If Churchill had prevailed, the Cold War would have begun earlier, more of Germany would have been kept out of the Soviet sphere, and the West would not have become entangled in Berlin; alternatively, Stalin would have had to give way in central Europe. But a major difficulty of standing up to the Russians at this early date was public opinion in the West, where an unbounded admiration was felt for the Red Army, which had played the major role on land in the defeat of the Wehrmacht.

Far from co-ordinating policy with Churchill, Truman sought a direct Soviet–American understanding on all the issues not settled at Yalta, to which end he sent Harry Hopkins to Moscow in May 1945. Churchill was upset by this move, which left Britain out in the cold. He was anxious to secure settlements with the Soviet Union concerning frontiers and spheres of influence before the British and American armies on the continent had been demobilised, for he feared that if such settlements were delayed the Russians would be able to do what they wanted. Truman and his advisers were more anxious to establish the United Nations as an institution that would ensure peace and solve all future world problems. It was a case of realism versus idealism.

The conference to negotiate the United Nations Charter convened in San Francisco on 25 April 1945. The Americans feared that the UN would be stillborn unless Russian co-operation could be won. The problem of how the veto would operate on the Security Council had not finally been settled at Yalta, and Molotov's widening of its application was creating difficulties. It was common ground that the five permanent members – the United States, the Soviet Union, Britain, France and China – could veto any *action*; the dispute was about whether the veto also applied to a discussion, an examination or a recommendation concerning an issue brought before the Security Council. If it did, any one of the permanent members could stop a dispute from even being considered. The Russian attitude, however, was understandable given that the West looked like enjoying a permanent majority in the General Assembly. In addition the question of whether any government could represent Poland raised the unsolved Polish question once more.

It was to straighten out these and other differences that Truman sent Hopkins to Moscow in May. At their meetings, Stalin cleverly tried to drive a wedge between the United States and Britain, while Hopkins listened sympathetically. Stalin certainly got the better of the bargain. His concession that the Polish government would be widened by the admission of some of the London Polish leaders still left the communists in a dominant position. Hopkins meanwhile accepted as sincere Stalin's promise not to interfere in Polish affairs, especially during the holding of 'free elections', and to show respect for individual rights and liberties. Yet when Stalin refused to release Poles he had arrested for what he described as 'diversionist' activities, the reality behind the words became only too clear. Hopkins was also anxious to gain confirmation of the secret agreement concerning the Far East reached at Yalta. Stalin promised to attack the Japanese on 8 August 1945 and to respect Chinese sovereignty in Manchuria. On the veto issue which was blocking progress on the UN Charter, Stalin made genuine concessions and the final agreements reached in San Francisco represented a complicated compromise of the American and Soviet view (page 373). It made possible the completion of negotiations for the Charter on 25 June 1945.

Hopkins returned from his mission in early June, with the way now clear for the summit meeting in Potsdam. Truman's idea that he should meet Stalin alone before being joined by the British Prime Minister was angrily rejected by Churchill, who was adamant that he was not 'prepared to attend a meeting which was a continuation of a conference between yourself and Marshal Stalin'. He insisted on a simultaneous meeting on equal terms.

The Potsdam Conference was the final confer-

The 'Big Three' at the Potsdam Conference, 17 July–2 August 1945. Soon hereafter only Stalin among the wartime leaders remained at the helm of his country.

ence, and the longest, of the Grand Alliance. It lasted from 17 July to 2 August 1945, forming a bridge between the world at war and the coming peace. Churchill had hoped Britain would recapture part of her lost influence, that the inexperienced new President would listen to the elder statesman. De Gaulle was again snubbed; although France was to become a member of the Control Commission for Germany, French representatives were not invited to join in discussions over Germany. Agreement was reached on many post-war issues, especially the Allied treatment of Germany, but suspicion between the Allies had grown. The military necessity of holding together was gone. The relationship between East and West lacked trust and, in the personal contact between the big three, Churchill, later Clement Attlee, Truman and Stalin, the old sense of comradeship was lacking. Despite the rounds of dinners and receptions, there was a palpable absence of warmth. Averell Harriman, US Ambassador in Moscow, tried to make a friendly remark to Stalin at Potsdam: 'Marshal, you must be very proud now to be in Berlin.' He received the rather disconcerting reply, 'Tsar Alexander got to Paris' – a reference to Alexander I, who with the allies entered Paris on the defeat of Napoleon in 1814. Distrust was to widen as the agreements reached at Potsdam were broken. The West accused the Soviet Union of bad faith; this made little impression on Stalin, who faced the enormous task of rebuilding the Soviet Union and tightening the dictatorial reins once more so that his regime would survive the capitalist external threat which he perceived.

Stalin did not trust the West and the West did not trust him. That was very clearly shown by the fact that Britain and the United States had been building the atomic bomb in great secrecy, without sharing their knowledge with their Soviet ally during the war. The Russians too had been secretly engaged on making a bomb, but the Americans got there first. After hearing that an experimental bomb had been successfully tested in New Mexico on 16 July, Truman obliquely referred to this success in talking to Stalin, without specifically mentioning that an atomic bomb would soon be dropped on Hiroshima. Stalin did not betray his anxiety that the United States had tilted the balance of power in her favour. Churchill was elated. The atomic bomb would redress the balance: despite the strength of the Red Army, Stalin no longer had all the cards in his hands. After Stalin had returned to the Kremlin, he ordered Soviet scientists to redouble their efforts to make a Soviet atomic bomb. Now that the world knew it could be done, the basic obstacles were more industrial than scientific, the difficulty of extracting the fissionable materials. Klaus Fuchs helped the Soviet scientists to reach their goal in 1949, but they would no doubt have solved the problems, without him, albeit perhaps a little later.

On the whole Stalin could be well satisfied with the outcome of the conference at Potsdam. Churchill did not stay to the end. He returned to be in London when the outcome of the general election was announced. He was replaced on 28 July in Potsdam by Clement Attlee and the redoubtable Ernest Bevin, the new foreign secretary, who in the last days of the conference conducted most of the negotiations for Britain. Truman also left most of the critical bargaining to his Secretary of State James Byrnes. The Polish issue once more proved highly contentious. There was much argument about Poland's western frontier. To the end Stalin insisted on the Western Neisse, facing the West with a *fait accompli*. Bevin and Byrnes had to accept this but did so with the proviso that these German territories were only to be 'administered' by Poland and a final settlement of the western frontier would have to await the signature of the peace treaty with Germany. In fact the provisional was to prove permanent.

The Polish agreement was part of a deal whereby the Soviet Union reluctantly accepted the American proposal on reparations. From a reparations point of view, Stalin had wanted to have Germany treated as a whole so that he could participate in spoils from the West and the industrial Ruhr as well as take away all that could be moved from the Soviet zone – in other words, so that he could get the best of both worlds. But he had to be satisfied with a formula that left each of the occupying powers to take reparations from her own zone. The reparation claims of Poland too would have to be met from the Soviet share. In addition, the Soviet Union would receive 10 per cent of industrial capital equipment taken as reparations by the West and a further 15 per cent in exchange for food and raw materials from the East. The agreement soon led to bitter recriminations.

Stalin did better on the question of the reconstituted Polish government. The London Poles were pressurised into accepting a settlement which incorporated some London ministers in the communist-dominated government in Warsaw. Poland would not emerge again from communist rule and Soviet domination for two generations.

The redrawing of Poland's frontiers only ratified what had already happened on the human level. Millions of Poles moved west to the Polish side of the Curzon line. Millions of Germans too had fled westward from the Red Army and the Polish forces, as well as from the German territories now under Polish rule and from the Sudeten areas of Czechoslovakia. Young and old were driven out with only the possessions they could carry. The Russians, Poles and Czechs, after the way they had been treated under Nazi occupation, were now indifferent to the suffering of the Germans. Retribution fell on guilty and innocent alike and many Germans perished from the ardours of migration. When at Potsdam the Allies recorded their agreement that the 'transfer' of Germans from Poland, Czechoslovakia and Hungary should be carried out 'in an orderly and humane manner', the West was therefore doing no more than expressing a pious hope largely after the event.

A central issue at Potsdam was the need to reach agreement on the treatment of Germany. The idea of dividing Germany into a number of separate states was finally abandoned. But the principles on which control of Germany were based were contradictory from the start: the Allies sought to treat Germany as one while at the same time partitioning her into zones of occupation. The Allied Control Council was supposed to oversee Germany as a whole, but each of the commanders-in-chief in his own zone had complete authority as well. The plan to establish 'central German administrative departments, headed by State Secretaries . . . in the fields of finance, transport, communications, foreign trade and industry', but under the direction of the Control Council, proved impossible to carry through as long as each occupation zone fell under the separate control of one of the four Allies. There was to be 'for the time being' no central German government, but local self-government and democratic parties were encouraged. On the one hand, the Allies agreed that during the occupation 'the German economy shall be treated as a single economic unit'; on the other, reparations were a matter for each occupying power to settle in her own zone.

The immediate consequence of all these decisions in practice was to move towards the division of Germany into four separate zones. Four years later, the three Western zones would combine and create a democratic Western central government, and a communist regime would be imposed on the Soviet Eastern zone. There were some areas of agreement, however; the trial of war criminals, the destruction of Nazi ideology, the complete disarmament of Germany, and control of such German industry as could be used for war led to no real differences at Potsdam. But already the West and the Russians were compromising these principles. German scientists were too valuable a 'war booty' to be punished as Nazi war criminals. Rocket scientists who had perfected the V-1 and V-2 in Peenemünde were, despite their past, seized by the Americans and bribed to contribute their know-how to Western military technology. Many who should have been convicted of war crimes prospered instead in the West and worked for the United States in the space race. Other German rocket scientists were captured by the Russians and assisted in Soviet missile development. In the Cold War, ex-Nazis with expertise in military intelligence were recruited by both sides. Former Wehrmacht officers served both NATO and the Warsaw Pact armies. Only recently has the veil been lifted from some of the darker aspects of what happened in the aftermath of the victory over Germany.

Austria was separated once more from Germany and was fortunate to escape reparations. Austrian guards in concentration camps had not behaved with any less bestiality in the SS than their German counterparts, nor can a distinction be drawn between Austrian and German members of the Wehrmacht. Austria was allowed to establish a central government but was occupied like Germany and divided into four zones, American, British, French and Soviet, with Vienna under joint control.

The Potsdam Conference established a Council of Foreign Ministers, which it was expected would normally meet in London. Its main task was the preparation of peace treaties with Italy, Romania, Bulgaria, Hungary and Finland. A peace settlement with Germany was also mentioned, but it seemed a distant prospect in 1945 since it required the prior establishment of a German government with the consent of the Allies. Only those countries which were signatories to the terms of surrender of each state would be allowed to participate, with the exception of France, which was admitted to discuss peace terms with Italy. During the eighteen months of its existence and after much acrimony, peace treaties with all these states except Germany were agreed. The Council, which still represented the wartime alliance, came to grief over the German question, and the Cold War began (pages 378–9).

Potsdam marked the beginning of the end of any hope that the wartime alliance would outlast the defeat of Germany, Italy, Japan and the minor Axis allies and, as Roosevelt had hoped, continue to safeguard the peace. It had achieved victory over the most powerful and barbaric threat ever faced by Russia and the Western democracies in modern times. Nineteen-forty-five marks a division in world history. This side of it the West once more perceived the Soviet Union as its most dangerous enemy. But this division should not obscure what lies on the other side, what the civilised world owes to the sacrifices made by the Soviet Union, by China, by Britain and by the United States, the great powers of their day which saw the struggle through together.

No one expected that the Japanese would be forced to surrender within three months of the Allied victory in Europe. In fighting as savage as any in the Second World War, the United States Navy, the marines and the army, under the command of Admiral Nimitz, had pushed the Japanese back from one tropical island base to the next. By the summer of 1943 the Japanese had been forced on to the defensive. A year later the Americans were closing in on Japan, capturing Saipan, Tinian and Guam. Meanwhile a Japanese offensive from Burma into India was halted by British and Dominion troops. In October 1944 General MacArthur began the attack on the Philippines. There ensued the last great naval battle of the Second World War – the battle of Leyte Gulf. The Japanese navy had planned a counterblow to destroy MacArthur's supply line and then his army. With the defeat of the Japanese navy in Leyte Gulf the United States had won command of the sea in Japan's home waters.

In the central Pacific, Nimitz advanced from Saipan to the island of Iwojima and then in the fiercest fighting of the war, lasting from April to June 1945, attacked and captured Okinawa, an island in the Ryukyu group just 500 miles from Japan. Japan's cities were being systematically reduced to rubble by the fires caused by constant air attacks. In south-east Asia, Admiral Lord Louis Mountbatten commanded the Allied forces which between December 1944 and May 1945 recaptured Burma from the retreating Japanese. But skilfully as this campaign was conducted, it was secondary in its impact on the war. The Americans in the Pacific were thrusting at the heart of the Japanese Empire.

In 1944 the Japanese military and naval leaders knew the war could not be won. Yet even as late

Okinawa, 1945. The Americans begin the process of revitalizing Japan – leading her through the minefield of authoritarianism to the haven of democracy, much as this military policeman here steers a child clear of an unexploded shell.

as May 1945 they hoped that the evidence of Japan's fanatical defence at Okinawa and elsewhere would deter the Allies from invading Japan herself, where the Allies, for the first time, would have to come to grips with large Japanese armies. Rather than lose tens of thousands of men, might not the Allies be prepared to offer reasonable terms?

Those advisers of the Emperor who were in favour of an immediate peace were not strong enough to assert themselves openly against the military and naval leaderships. But war supplies, especially oil, were rapidly running out and Japan's situation was deteriorating fast. By July 1945 even the military accepted that it was worth taking the initiative to explore what kind of peace terms the Allies might put forward. Approaches were made to the Soviet Union to act as mediators. The Soviets refused brusquely to help Japan to a negotiated peace. With the prize of Manchuria promised at Yalta, Stalin had his own reasons for wishing to prolong the war long enough to enable the Red Army to advance into Manchuria. Nevertheless, Stalin did inform Churchill of Japanese overtures when they assembled with Truman at the Potsdam Conference in July 1945, urging that the Allies should insist on 'unconditional' surrender.

But Churchill pressed moderation on Truman to save American and British lives. The upshot was that Truman and Churchill on 26 July issued an 'ultimatum' to Japan setting out basic conditions of peace. They called for the 'unconditional surrender' of the Japanese military forces. The influence of the military and all those who had wished Japan into the path of aggression would be removed. War criminals would be punished and reparations required. Japan would have to give up all her imperial conquests. Finally, Japan would be occupied. But, beyond this, the declaration went out of its way to promise Japan a future: 'We do not intend that the Japanese shall be enslaved as a race nor destroyed as a nation . . .' Japan's industries would be preserved, her soldiers allowed to return home, and democracy and justice would be established under the guidance of the occupation. Once this was securely rooted in Japan, and a freely elected Japanese government could safely be given responsibility, the occupation forces would withdraw. In short, imperial Japan with her divine emperor would be transformed into a Western-type democratic state. What was not clear, and it was a critical point for the Japanese, was whether the Emperor would be permitted to remain on the throne.

Japan's eighty-year-old prime minister, Admiral Suzuki, responded to the ultimatum with a non-committal statement. He was temporising in the face of the powerful military opposition; mistranslation unfortunately made his reply sound contemptuous. But was it really necessary to drop the atomic bomb or would a few more days have given the upper hand to the peace party in any case? The evidence suggests that only after Hiroshima – realising what terrible havoc would result from more such bombs – did the Emperor Hirohito conclude that he could no longer merely accept the decision of his leading ministers and the military, but that he would have to assert himself and overrule the military who still were inclined to continue the war. Ironically it was the last act of the Emperor's divine authority, soon to be destroyed, that saved countless American and Japanese lives. President Truman was probably therefore right in believing that only the atomic bombs could shock Japan into *immediate* surrender.

On 6 August an American plane dropped just one small bomb on a Japanese city still untouched by war. 'Hiroshima' henceforth has become a byword for a nuclear holocaust, for a threatened new world. There was instant recognition that the

Europe after 1945
FINLAND
SWEDEN
NORWAY
Helsinki
Oslo
Stockholm
NORTH
SEA
DENMARK
SOVIET UNION
ATLANTIC
Copenhagen
NETHER-
LANDS
Dublin
POLAND
OCEAN
London
Berlin
DDR
Warsaw
Elbe
FEDERAL
GERMAN
REPUBLIC
BELGIUM
CZECHOSLO-
VAKIA
Curzon line
1919–20
Lvov
Seine
Paris
LUX.
Vienna
AUSTRIA
HUNGARY
ROMANIA
FRANCE
SWITZ
Bucharest
Rhône
ITALY
YUGOSLAVIA
Belgrade
Free Territory of
Trieste 1947–54
BULGARIA
PORTUGAL
ANDORRA
Sofia
Rome
CORSICA
Madrid
ALBANIA
TURKEY
SPAIN
SARDINIA
GREECE
Athens
MEDITERRANEAN SEA
Tangier
GIBRALTAR
Algiers
SICILY
CRETE
Tripoli
Former German territory
Post-1945 frontiers
0
1000 miles
0
1000 km

nature of war had been transformed. Scientists had harnessed the innermost forces of nature to a weapon of destruction that had hitherto been unimaginable. In one blinding flash the humans who were instantly vaporised were perhaps the more fortunate; 66,000 men, women and children were killed immediately or succumbed soon after the atom bomb had struck. Another 69,000 were horribly injured – they were found to suffer from a new illness, radiation sickness, and many died later in agony. Even future unborn generations were affected, deformed by the mutation of genes in the sick. The suffering has continued for decades. Four square miles of the city were totally destroyed on that terrible day. Three days later Nagasaki was the second and mercifully last city to suffer the effects of an atomic attack. It was not the end, however, of the development of even more destructive nuclear weapons of annihilation. The single Hiroshima bomb possessed the explosive power of 20,000 tons of TNT. Later hydrogen bombs were tested in the 1950s with a power 250 times greater than the bomb dropped on Hiroshima. There was and is no effective system of defence in existence that can stop the missile delivery of a destructive power that can wipe out civilised life on whole continents. The Japanese were the first victims and the last, if the world is to survive.

Ever since the horror of Hiroshima the debate has raged whether a weapon so indiscriminate in its mass destruction of human life should have been used. It has been argued that the main reason why it was dropped was to warn the Soviet Union of the new invincible power of the United States. No doubt the possession of the atomic bomb made it possible for the United States to feel that she was safe to demobilise even in the face of the superior weight of the Soviet armed forces. But the bomb would have been dropped even had the Soviet Union not existed. The investment in the construction of the two nuclear bombs available for use in 1945 had been huge. It was thought that using them would prove decisive in ending the war without more fighting and the expected further losses of hundreds of thousands of Allied lives from storming the Japanese home islands against fierce resistance. Okinawa and Iwojima would come to seem a picnic by comparison. The killing of enemy civilians in order to shorten the war was seen as entirely justified after so much death and destruction. No one thought in terms of drawing up a balance sheet of losses of enemy men, women and children as against the lives of Allied soldiers. That is shown by the devastating raids on German and Japanese cities with conventional weapons. Loss of civilian lives was greater in Tokyo and Dresden than in Hiroshima and Nagasaki, and no moral issue appeared involved whether this was the result of one bomb or 5000. So Truman had no hesitation.

The Soviet Union's declaration of war on Japan on 8 August and her invasion of China were fresh disasters but not decisive factors in forcing Tokyo's leader to make a decision. Messages sent by the Allies and received in Tokyo on 13 August 1945 indicating that the Emperor would not be removed from the throne were more important in the final deliberations. On 14 August the Emperor broadcast Japan's surrender. Over the radio he spoke for the first time to the Japanese people, saying that the unendurable had to be endured. The Second World War was over.

The outcome had been decisively influenced by the separation of the Second World War in reality into two separate wars, one in Asia, the other in Europe, despite the alliances spanning the hemispheres. This sealed Germany's fate. What if Germany and Japan had coordinated their onslaught on the Soviet Union in 1941? Who can be sure that the outcome would not have been different? There never, however, was a chance of such coordination. The Japanese followed their own war aims in China and Asia. Surprisingly, this was welcomed by Hitler. He believed it would weaken Britain and the United States while in Europe Germany's defeat of Russia without Japanese help would demonstrate once and for all time who was the racially superior, the 'aryan' or the subhuman Bolshevik-Jew. Too late, and only when facing disaster at Stalingrad, did Hitler in January 1943 urge the Japanese to come to his aid by attacking the Soviet Union. By then any chance that might have existed earlier of defeating Russia was gone. The war was lost, though it dragged on for another two years, with the loss of the lives of millions more until in 1945 both Japan and Germany finally succumbed.

PART VI

Post-war Europe, 1945–1947

CHAPTER 30

Zero Hour: The Allies and the Germans

In May 1945 a world seemed to have come to an end in Germany. So cataclysmic was the change that the Germans coined the phrase 'zero hour'. Their country was occupied and at the mercy of foreigners, who now took over the government. The victors' ideologies and values were imposed on the new Germany for good or ill; but nothing could be worse than what had gone before.

In the Western zones of Germany, constituting two-thirds of the former Reich, the social basis did not radically alter. Factory owners, managers of industry, and the professional classes, despite their involvement with Hitler's Germany, adjusted themselves to the new circumstances. Only the best-known collaborators like Alfried Krupp were arrested and tried. Expertise and efficiency does not have to coincide with morality. Defeated Germany thus did not lose the skills of her managers, engineers and workers, who thus made possible the later economic miracle of the 1950s. During the early years of the occupation from 1945 to 1949 their first task was to try to resist or circumvent and soften the draconian economic directives of occupiers bent on deindustrialising Germany.

In 1945, the Allies were amazed to discover how much of Germany's industrial strength had survived the war. The lost production of the steel industry did not exceed 10 per cent, and no key industry had suffered more than 20 per cent losses. Industrially, then, 1945 was not the zero hour, despite the huge problems of restoring some sort of normality.

The physical appearance of the German cities belied their underlying strength. Corpses still lay under huge mounds of rubble, and many were to remain permanently entombed there. The new Germany would have to be built on top of streets turned into cemeteries. Parts of Berlin, Cologne and Hamburg were totally flattened. In Hamburg, one district had even been walled in. No one had been permitted to enter it for fear that disease would spread from the corpses left there. Only the most rudimentary shelter could be made available for those civilians who had not already fled to the countryside.

The last weeks of the war, although it was lost for certain, had added to the needless destruction of life. The Germans had fought on, obeying orders. Some even believed that the Führer had a wonder-weapon which would rescue them or that the Americans and British would join them to fight the Russians 'to save civilisation'. There was also a good reason for holding on as long as possible in the east. The surviving German navy made it a last mission to evacuate the refugees stranded on the coast of East Prussia and now cut off from the rest of Germany by the Soviet advance. Tens of thousands were ferried to Hamburg and other ports in west Germany. German losses during the war had been horrendous. As best as can be established more than 3 million German soldiers had been killed or were missing, millions more were wounded and disabled; the Western Allied camps were filled with prisoners of war. Those in Soviet captivity who survived would not return home for ten years. More

In a devastated Dresden (above) *the war is over and life must go on. Elsewhere in rural Germany* (below), *it was possible to think that there had been no war at all.*

than half a million civilians killed were victims of the Allied bombing offensive.

Allied soldiers commandeered the more habitable buildings; military headquarters were set up; local administrative offices were supervised by Russian, British, French or American army officers. The war had displaced millions. German soldiers and civilians were trying to find their way home. Poles and Russians brought to Germany as slave labour were now stranded; there were also tens of thousands of Russians who had changed sides and had sought to escape death by helping the Germans. Some Ukrainians and Latvians, Lithuanians and Estonians had participated with the SS in terrible atrocities. Victims and murderers were now all intermingled. The concentration-camp survivors were released. Millions of 'foreigners' were on German soil; many were sick and unable to work – what was to happen to them? What was to be done with the pitiful remnants of the European Jews? A new and prosaic term was found for this flotsam of humanity, 'displaced persons'. They were put in camps again, in simple huts, and were fed by relief workers. It was to take years to sort them all out and settle them – not always in the country of their choice.

More than 20 million were on the move in Europe in the early summer of 1945, escaping something, going from somewhere to somewhere else. The roads were crammed with people on foot, on bicycles and with bundles of possessions. Some arrived crowded into or clinging to the outside of the few trains that were still running. The sheer scale of the forced migration during the war and in 1945, continuing for another two and three years, almost defies the imagination. From mid-1944 Germans and their allies were fleeing from the advancing Red Army in the east, where the Wehrmacht tried to hold a front line even during the last days of the war to enable millions more to reach the West. The loss of life probably exceeded 2 million, as the fighting at times overran the fleeing civilian columns. Nazi Germans who had lorded it over the Poles might have deserved their fate but not the children. Tragedy overtook both the guilty and the innocent.

When the war was over, under the terms of the Potsdam Agreement the Poles drove out most of the Germans who had settled in Poland during the war, as well as the ethnic Germans who had lived in Poland long before it became a sovereign state again; millions more were driven from the newly occupied German territories east of the Oder–

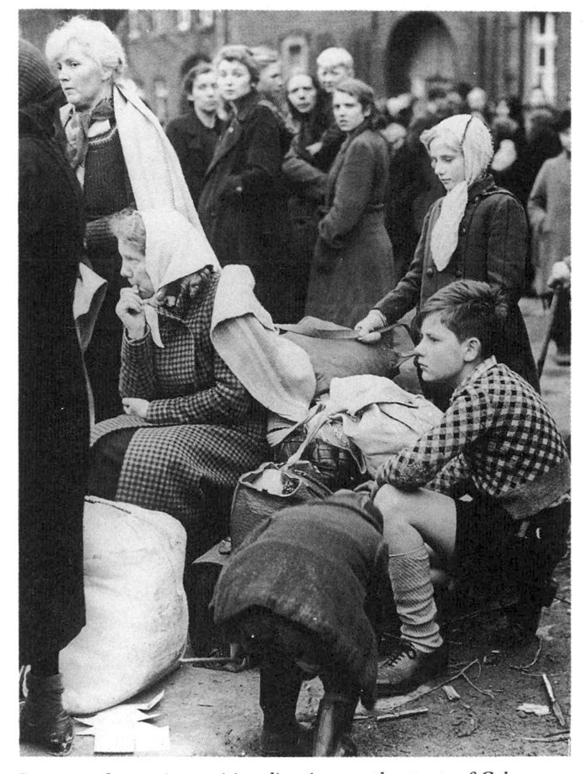

German refugees sit, awaiting direction, on the streets of Cologne.

The last major German naval operation of the Second World War: rural Germans fleeing from the Russian armies sweeping through East Prussia are evacuated by ship.

Neisse, which to all intents and purposes became part of the Polish state. From Czechoslovakia, the Sudeten ethnic Germans were likewise expelled. It was supposed to be done humanely, but pent-up hatreds often got the better of humanity. Atrocities were committed by both Poles and Czechs. In all, as many as 10 million Germans and ethnic Germans reached the Western zones of Germany without much more than the clothes they stood up in. At least they were 'home' with their own people, though not always welcomed by the local residents. They were not displaced persons (DPs for short) in the same sense as the 1.5 million Russians, the million Frenchmen, the 600,000 Poles and the hundreds of thousands from every country the Germans had conquered, whose people had been forced to work in German factories. Some of these DPs, like the Western nationals, had a home to go to; others, including many Russians, did not want to return – they knew what fate awaited them for collaborating with the Germans. The British, in accordance with agreements made with the Russians and Yugoslavs, forced thousands back at the point of the bayonet. Among the most pathetic DPs, who sought their home but were prevented from going there, were the Jews, the survivors of the death camps, who longed to enter British-controlled Palestine.

Rations for the Germans were very short, sufficient only to maintain life. Coal was lacking for heating and for industry. Hardly a tree that could provide fuel for a fire was left standing in the towns. The lovely Berlin park, the Tiergarten, was soon denuded of its trees. The destruction of the transport system made it even harder to provide basic needs for an estimated 25 million homeless and rootless people, as well as for the rest of the population. Many families had lost their breadwinner at the front, 'fallen for Führer and country'; many more men, women and children were crippled by war wounds. The immediate challenge in 1945 was mere survival. Curfews and the lack of postal and telephone systems cut off one community from another during the early weeks of peace; in Kassel the population did not know what was happening in Frankfurt. Only German farmers, in the countryside, were still relatively well off. They had their houses, their land, and flour, milk, vegetables and meat which they could exchange for a Persian carpet or jewellery brought to them by hungry city-dwellers. There was little fellow feeling in misfortune. Allied soldiers too swapped necessities and cigarettes for expensive cameras and watches. Cigarettes became a currency.

That mass starvation and epidemics did not sweep through Germany and central Europe in 1945 and 1946 is a remarkable tribute to the victors and to the relief workers. It was also due to the efficiency of new pesticides: there was no repeat of the influenza epidemic that claimed millions of victims after the First World War; lice, the main carriers of disease, were killed by DDT. Much of the management of these huge tasks was entrusted to young inexperienced Allied officers. But the Germans who acted under their direction and succeeded in bringing some semblance of order out of chaos also deserve credit.

Contemporary observers remarked on the apathy and listlessness of the German population. In the towns only the bare rations to keep people alive could be distributed, and the first winter of peace, one of the coldest on record, claimed many victims among the elderly and the sick in Berlin, Hamburg, Munich and other cities, where makeshift shelters had to serve as homes. Germany was completely defeated and at the mercy of the occupying armies. But would Allied disunity rescue the Germans from their plight, as the Russians, the Americans and the British vied to enlist German help?

The Allies distrusted the Germans: that was the one point, amid all the disputes, on which in 1945 they were agreed. But they still expected Germany to remain unified under their supervision. Soviet and Western leaders shared what turned out to be an accurate perception of the capacity of the German people for recovery; but they also feared that the Germans, unless controlled, would be capable of rebuilding not only their shattered industry and their cities, but also their destructive military potential. In their hearts, the Allies thought the German people had not changed and were only temporarily submissive in the face of overwhelming defeat. They saw the great majority of Germans as incorrigibly militaristic and as a threat to a peaceful Europe. The German people, so history appeared to prove, were ready to subordinate individual ethical values to the good of the state, whose leaders then ruthlessly exploited Germany's strength at the expense of her neighbours. A new and terrible dimension of barbarism had been added by Hitler's German nation in arms. German victories from 1939 to 1942 were accompanied by destruction throughout continental Europe and by suffering and the killing

On liberation by the Allies, the concentration camps in Germany were overflowing with survivors of the death marches that had brought Jews and other prisoners from the eastern extermination camps as the Russians continued to advance through Nazi territory (above and left). *Thousands died of the diseases that swept the camps before they were liberated – among them a young Jewish girl called Anne Frank. Despite intensive medical efforts thousands more could not be saved even after being restored to freedom* (top right). *One such camp, with the idyllic name Buchenwald (Birchforest)* (right), *was situated close to Germany's cultural shrine, Weimar.*

of millions of men, women and children. By the end of the war, virtually every German was suspected of having been in league with the evil-doers. These Allied attitudes cannot be understood today without seeing again the newsreels of the liberated concentration camps shown in all the cinemas, especially (by Allied command) German ones, immediately after the end of the war, with their piles of naked corpses, the skeletal appearance of the survivors. For the first time, ordinary people in the West came face to face with the full evil of National Socialist Germany. In Russia and Poland newsreels were not necessary. The inhabitants had actually experienced on their own bodies the cruel and ruthless occupation.

Allied planning was based on the belief that, since Europe and the world had to go on living with some 70 million Germans, they represented a threat for the future unless they could be led to change fundamentally. The Russians, as well as the British, French and Americans, meant to impose these changes from above – though they had very different conceptions of what needed to be done. They were agreed, however, on the wholesale removal of the Nazi political leadership as a prerequisite.

The expediency of demanding the unconditional surrender of the German state has been much debated by historians, but to no purpose. Britain, Russia and the United States, together with France and the other Allied nations, had fought Germany in an all-out war for survival. How could they be expected to negotiate with the military successors of Hitler, on the basis of any terms that left Germany intact and her armies short of defeat? Germany had to be taught a lesson in defeat that would allow no false sense of military honour to survive. Germany's neighbours would not be able to live in peace unless control over Germany was taken away from the Germans – as had conspicuously not been done in 1919. That meant occupation and Allied rule over a completely powerless Germany (some spoke of this lasting twenty-five, even forty, years). On this interpretation of 'unconditional surrender' at least, Stalin, Churchill and Roosevelt were agreed in 1944 and 1945.

The first solutions suggested during the war to this problem of containing Germany proposed to render her harmless by standing down her armed forces and eliminating the general staffs, supposedly imbued with Prussian military traditions. In its original form, the Morgenthau Plan of 1944 allowed Germany no heavy industry to manufacture cars and no machine tools; instead light industries could make furniture and tin-openers. Germany would thus become a 'pastoral' country; the industrial region of the Ruhr would be no more. The standard of living of the Germans would be at subsistence levels, no higher than that of the poorest of the countries in the east which Germany had occupied. There was, of course, a strong punitive element in these plans, felt to be justified by Germany's barbaric behaviour during the war. The large labour force, which would not be able to find employment in Germany, would provide reparations as forced labour working for the Allies to make good some of the damage done. But the plan was too unreal to survive. Seventy million Germans could not live without export industries. Europe could not manage without Ruhr coal and steel. Short-term reparations would not make up for the cost the Allies would have to bear to keep the Germans alive. The plan's shortcomings were realised immediately, but its opponents could not eliminate it altogether; they could do no more than introduce some changes.

After the war was won, US occupation aims were embodied in the order of the Joint Chiefs of Staff (US) JCS 1067, dated 26 April 1945, Germany; British policies did not differ from it significantly, though they embodied a more constructive view of the future rehabilitation of Germany. Sweeping deindustrialisation and the dismantling for reparations of German factories were mandatory. The German people would be allowed only the lowest standard of living that avoided death and disease. Yet they could not be condemned to mass starvation: $700 million annually were needed to pay for food imports to keep the Germans in the British and American zones alive. For Britain especially, with her desperate dollar shortage, this was an unacceptable drain. The Germans should be made to pay for what they needed themselves, but could do so only if they were allowed to manufacture goods again for export. This stimulated a revision of thinking about limitations placed on industrial production from the early draconian four-power decision of March 1946, to reduce it to 50 per cent of that in 1938. The economic occupation policies from 1945 to 1949 were a mass of contradictions: continuing to dismantle factories as reparations, desiring to break Germany's industrial potential for war, and removing possibly successful commercial rivals from world markets, such as the pharmaceutical industry. Patents became war booty. At the same time there was growing acceptance that Western Germany had to be rebuilt, that her prosperity was an essential support of West German and European democracy, threatened by the Cold War. Not until 1952 were all attempts to limit Germany's basic heavy industry, steel, abandoned.

Through the hardships of the early years, the Germans had survived better than anyone would have thought possible in 1945. They accepted certain limitations – for example, not to manufacture nuclear weapons or poison gas. For the rest, Allied efforts to restructure German industry, break up the powerful cartels and loosen the hold of the banks were soon reversed.

At the start of the occupation there was a haphazard mass internment of those deemed to have served the Third Reich in an important capacity. German prisoners of war in Allied hands and labouring abroad, on British farms for instance, were not sent home at the end of the war. The Western Allies only agreed to return them by the end of 1948. But most of the millions taken prisoner in Germany itself during the last stages of the war were released after a short time. From Soviet captivity hundreds of thousands never returned. German women had to undertake the heaviest manual labour, clearing the rubble. Where were strong men? Three and a quarter million were missing or dead, millions were crippled, and millions had been taken prisoner. Shortly before his death Roosevelt wrote, 'The German people are not going to be enslaved. . . . But it will be necessary for them to earn their way back into the fellowship of peace-loving and law-abiding nations.' They would never be entrusted again to bear arms. The captains of industry and the National Socialist leaders would be tried and treated as criminals. What was left of industry would be supervised and ceilings of production imposed.

The Germans were told they had been liberated, but Allied soldiers were strictly ordered not to 'fraternise' with them – to avoid all social contact. Shunned and struggling to survive hunger and cold,

Guilty of perpetrating crimes against humanity: from left to right, Göring, Hess, Ribbentrop and Keitel in the front row of the defendants' box at the Nuremberg trials.

Scenes from Occupied Germany. Many Russian soldiers had even fewer possessions than the defeated enemy (top right). *Money became worthless and cigarettes, originally from the fabled US Army stores, were the currency in most frequent use* (top left)*; while young Germans were being 're-educated'* (left), *the Fraüleins looked to simpler pleasures* (right). *To the GIs they did not look much like the enemy: the order against fraternization was readily disobeyed.*

the German people were obliged to submit to 're-education', the attempt to change their hearts and minds. Punishment and 'denazification' was one side of the coin, the inculcation of virtue and democracy the other. Control of the media and the re-establishment in schools of sound teaching of the right values were priorities. Gradually, decentralised political life was encouraged. The adoption of punitive measures, it was quickly realised, ran counter to the attempt to reform the German people. If they were to be treated as pariahs, how could they be convinced at the same time of the blessings of liberty?

Within occupied Germany, despite many absurdities and contradictions, denazification and re-education made a positive contribution. The Nuremberg trials of the leaders of Hitler's state, which began in November 1945, culminated in the death sentence on twelve of the accused eleven months later, and revealed the barbaric nature of the occupation in the east. This evidence confronted the ordinary German people with unpleasant truths which many of them had known about but could not face, and only the totally incorrigible still insisted that the gas ovens of Auschwitz were propaganda. No respect was felt for Hitler's lieutenants, who had led Germany into destruction and suffering, though some satisfaction was felt that Göring had outwitted his jailers by committing suicide before he could be hanged. The SS was condemned wholesale by the Allies as a criminal organisation.

Rough justice was meted out to the lesser supporters. All Germans were required to fill out a questionnaire, the famous *Fragebogen*, which served as a basis for denazification. Many millions of Germans had been National Socialists out of conviction, many opportunistically in hope of gain, some only under pressure; most had joined the party or one of its organisations. But only a minority, some 209,000 out of a population of 44.5 million, were actually prosecuted in the special courts set up in the British, American and French zones (more were tried in the American than in the British zone). In the Soviet sector, with a population of 17 million, the figure given for those tried is also small, just over 17,000. This did not imply that the Russians were more forgiving; they simply did not trouble with court procedures. Tens of thousands were put in former Nazi concentration camps and thousands lost their lives, not only Nazi criminals but also opponents of communism. When categorised, of those charged with being Nazis only 1667 were regarded as chief perpetrators of crimes, 23,060 as partially guilty (*belastet*), 150,425 as less guilty and just over 1 million as 'fellow travellers'. Over 5 million suspects were not prosecuted in any way. Even the Allies came to realise how unsatisfactory the process was. Minor offenders were not infrequently treated more harshly than men with far more on their conscience, including the Gauleiter of Hamburg, who after imprisonment and a quiet period, prospered again in post-war West Germany. Justice proved too subjective, too haphazard, and punishment too arbitrary; there was no clean sweep of all those involved in the crimes of the Third Reich. The judges, with few exceptions, continued to sit in judgement, as they had in the Nazi years; the majority of civil servants now served their new masters and the files they kept frequently show no break around May 1945! There were simply too many National Socialists; the task of punishment had to be abandoned for all but the worst criminals.

Nevertheless, the great majority of Germans did change after the war. Allied re-education contributed to this but it was not the only or even the main reason for it. Correct as Allied assumptions were about Germany's capacity to recover from defeat, so they were wrong in believing that, given half a chance, the German people would once again turn to another Hitler with a policy of expansion and conquest. Henry Morgenthau even wrote a book about it in 1945 entitled *Germany Is Our Problem*, describing how some still unknown corporal was very likely plotting secretly that very moment how to rebuild Germany in order to prepare for a war of revenge. After more than four decades of peace, Morgenthau has been proven to have been wrong. The total military collapse and its immediate consequences did in fact convince the German people (except for a small extremist fringe) that in Hitler they had followed a false prophet. To the surprise of the Allies the expected Nazi underground movements, such as the Werewolves, came to nothing. The German people soon showed themselves anxious to learn from their victors, who had after all proved themselves stronger and more successful. Defeat of all things German had proved a radical cure for the mentality of *Deutschland über Alles*. British representative institutions now became the model, and the American way of life an aspiration – at least that part portrayed in Hollywood films and by the comparative illusion of wealth now sustained by the occupying GIs in their smart uniforms. From the Russians the benefits were less obvious and no one in Germany, except hardened communists, wished to emulate their style of life and lower standards of living. There is no doubt that the year 1945, unlike 1918, thus marks a decisive breach in German history. The lure of conquest and physical expansion, of lording it as the supposed *Herrenvolk*, had ended in evident ruin.

That is not to say that there was an immediate moral renaissance in Germany. Many Germans had fanatically believed in Hitler and in Germany's survival to the end; those who felt genuine shame and regret for the crimes of the regime were probably a minority. Most were sorry they had lost the war; fortunately some did recognise that they had been 'liberated' by the Allies – they would form a small nucleus for creating a better society.

Living conditions proved desperate during the first two years of occupation, and its rule by Russian, American, British and French soldiers and administrators brought home to every German the totality of the defeat. They were now faced with the practical task of material survival amid the ruins of their cities. Feelings of guilt did not in the circumstances spring first to mind; there were more immediate needs to attend to. Many of the older generation of Germans did not repudiate the Nazi past, but Hitler was dead and new masters had to be served, new political realities to be faced. It was different for the young. They increasingly questioned the values of their parents and could find no pride in German history or indeed in being Germans at all. They saw a way ahead in showing themselves to be good Europeans. And so the two Germanies became the first modern nations whose citizens consciously turned their backs on the past, some concentrating on rebuilding a new life and giving little thought to moral questions, others genuinely feeling shame for the past. The Western Allies were not confronted with a task they had thought would take at least a generation to complete. Instead, within two years of the German surrender, the East–West confrontation of the Cold War hastened Soviet and Anglo-American readiness publicly to accept at face value the 'new' reformed Germany, though in private there were still strong reservations about the trustworthiness of Germans. This residual suspicion of the dangers of too strong a Germany remained alive after almost half a century when German unity once more became a reality.

Stalin was just as anxious to 're-educate' the German people in the Soviet zone his way. His own life's experiences in the USSR may well have made him more optimistic about the prospects than the West was. The German people had shown an enviable readiness to follow strong leadership. For some it was only a question of exchanging a brown for a red shirt. It was particularly easy to form new red youth brigades. The Russians and their German nominees would now provide that leadership. As the victors they would carry away from Germany all the reparations they could, but Stalin saw no reason why he should wait before undertaking political re-education and the transformation of German society. Confident that sufficient power at the top could ensure the loyalty of those below, he was ready to use as instruments not only the Moscow-trained communists, but even leaders of the Wehrmacht, taken prisoners of war, who as early as 1943 had been formed into the Free Germany Committee. Former supporters of Hitler, provided they were useful enough, could now rehabilitate themselves by promising unswerving loyalty to Moscow. Others were simply set to work, like the scientists and rocket specialists. The Western Allies in this respect acted no differently. For Stalin the struggle in Germany would be between 'capitalism' and 'socialism', and the only safe Germany would be a country whose previous political and social patterns had been transformed. Given Stalin's ideological assumptions he was bound to be extremely apprehensive about developments in the Western zones of occupation, where the majority of Germans lived. In such fears the blossoming of the Cold War can be traced.

In their relations with the Allies the Germans were not entirely supine. A nucleus of post-war German political leaders, unsullied by the Nazi years, resurfaced, hardened and toughened. They had a vision of a new Germany and a better future. It was difficult for the communist leaders Wilhelm Pieck and Walter Ulbricht, returning from Moscow in 1945, to be anything but cynical after Stalin's terror years, which had claimed so many of their German comrades as victims, and after Stalin's sacrifice of the German Communist Party to the Nazis. But there were also idealistic communists, survivors of the concentration camps and returning exiles, who preserved their illusions of Stalin's Russia and now were ready to work for an 'anti-fascist' Germany.

It was the Soviet authorities in their zone of occupation in June 1945 who first announced the revival of the democratic political process by permitting the setting up of political parties – the Communist Party of Germany (KPD), of course, but also the German Social Democratic Party (SPD), the new conservative Christian Democratic Union (CDU) and the Liberal Democratic Party, better known in the West as the Free Democratic Party (FDP). One-party rule, the cornerstone of the Soviet political system founded by Lenin, was refined into Stalin's totalitarian state, in which no dissenting group was permitted any voice or even the right to exist. In Germany, then, Stalin was ready, according to his own lights, to make enormous concessions and to provide communist predominance with a more acceptable face for the local population and for the Western Allies.

When the Austrian communists in genuinely free elections in November 1945 secured only 5 per cent of the vote, Stalin knew that more would be required in Germany than just to let the parties compete freely. The Soviet authorities cajoled and pressurised the Social Democratic Party, led by Otto Grotewohl in their zone, to fuse with the Communist Party and so form the Socialist Unity Party (SED). In provincial elections in the autumn of 1946, the SED, despite Soviet help, failed to win outright majorities over the competing CDU and Liberals, so the SED had to resort to anti-fascist popular-front tactics to gain control in the *Länder* assemblies. Berlin, although it fell within the Soviet zone, had been placed under the joint authority of all the four powers, so its political parties could not be manipulated by Moscow like those in the Soviet zone. For that reason, moves to fuse the Socialist and Communist Parties in Berlin were comprehensively defeated.

This result marked a decisive split in Germany. Given the freedom to choose, the country's emerging political leaders rejected totalitarianism. Instead, the two most outstanding political figures of the immediate post-war German years, Kurt Schumacher (SPD) and Konrad Adenauer (CDU), laid the foundations of a party political system on which could be based the stable parliamentary democracy of the two-thirds of Germany that formed the Western zones, which together with West Berlin later became the Federal Republic of Germany. It is to the lasting credit of Schumacher as well as of Adenauer that German democracy was not stifled at birth. In the Soviet zone, on the other hand, the German people were not to be given a free choice until forty-five years later. It should also be conceded that the Germans in the Western zones did not have a completely free choice: after all, the Western Allies would not have permitted their zones to be turned into a totalitarian communist state. The more important point, however, is that the Allies' aim to create a democratic society reflected the wishes of the majority of Germans.

The contrast between the two West German leaders, Kurt Schumacher and Konrad Adenauer, was striking. Schumacher's health but not his spirit had been broken after long years of incarceration in a concentration camp, an experience which had inspired him with a hatred of all forms of totalitarianism. He now looked to the British Labour Party as an example of a democratic socialist party supporting a parliamentary form of government. Schumacher was uncompromising on any issue he believed involved principle: it was a lack of firm principles that had driven the Germans into the abyss. He intended to lead a strong independent party committed to democracy, socialism and the recovery of dignity, and eventually sovereignty for a reunited Germany. The victorious Allies would once again be compelled to respect such a re-emerging German nation.

Adenauer was in an altogether different position. No political party except the SPD had emerged with credit during the Hitler years. They had either played Hitler's game before January 1933 or had compromised immediately after to hand him dictatorial powers. (The rank-and-file communists had no choice: they had to change allegiance or face persecution.) So Adenauer had to create an entirely new party, the CDU and its Bavarian ally, the CSU. This called for flexibility, adroitness and a high degree of political skill. Party political aims would need to be limited to essentials. A staunch Catholic and a Rhinelander, Adenauer enjoyed the better things in life, and, although he had courageously defied the Nazis as mayor of Cologne in 1933, thereafter he had played no active role in Germany's opposition. He had lived a comfortable retired life, storing up his energies for a better future. It was only during the last six months of the war that he was arrested and imprisoned by the Gestapo in the wake of the Hitler bomb plot of 20 July 1944, in which likewise he had played no part.

Unexpectedly, it was Adenauer in his seventies,

and not Schumacher, who dominated post-war German politics. Adenauer's re-entry into politics was not at first auspicious. Reinstated by the Americans as mayor of Cologne, his gritty personality and the scheming of political opponents led to his dismissal after the British took over control of the city. He re-emerged to challenge the support for Schumacher and the SPD. A third party, smaller than the other two, was the Liberal Free Democratic Party (FDP), which at times exercised a disproportionate influence because it held the balance between the two major parties.

In the summer of 1946 regional states (*Länder*) were created in the British, French and US zones, and local and regional elected assemblies reintroduced two-thirds of the German people to the democratic parliamentary process. Political party organisations were revived. The Social Democratic Party, led by Schumacher, competed with the Christian Democratic Union, which was opposed to socialism and to centralised state power at the expense of individual rights, and emphasised Christian ethical values as the foundation of the state.

Each of the *Länder* was headed by a minister-president answerable to a parliamentary assembly democratically elected. It was in the *Länder* that Germany's leading post-war political leaders first came to prominence – men like Reinhold Maier, Minister-President of Württemberg-Baden, Theodor Heuss, Heinrich Lübke and Professor Ludwig Erhard. The Western Allies, who had vetted and approved them (though not all had been active opponents of the Nazi regime) had chosen this leadership group wisely; in this they made a crucial contribution to Germany's post-war democratic development. Political life recovered. Its progress, however, depended on Allied willingness to transfer responsibilities to the Germans, to obtain their co-operation rather than their mere acquiescence. The process was accelerated by Western suspicions of the Soviet Union and the onset of the Cold War.

Political leadership is one thing, but how would the majority of Germans behave when asked to participate again in a democratic process after twelve years of dictatorship? How many politically active Germans were there who had been compromised? The majority of those whose hands were clean belonged to the left. They felt that their sufferings in concentration camps, their exclusion from the German state or their years in exile now gave them a moral right to lead the new Germany. Business, big and small, had formed a part of the National Socialist state. German businessmen and farmers had accepted the help of 'slaves' from the east, had frequently exploited their forced labour and had only rarely treated them with humanity and consideration. The majority of Germans were saddled with the guilt of not having cared sufficiently for foreigners and for their own German Jewish neighbours. There were thus millions of Germans who wished to lie low. Survival might depend on not drawing attention to one's self unnecessarily by prominence in politics.

The more educated, the professional leaders of the state, civil servants, judges and lawyers, the better off and propertied, the doctors, many of whom had been implicated with Nazi measures, all those who had lived well and comfortably through the Hitler years and had provided expertise and leadership, were most heavily compromised and could least afford to play an active role in post-war politics. The workers, the poor, the conscripts in the army could more easily claim that they had been misled and were themselves the exploited, even though such a simple social division of those who supported and those who opposed National Socialism does not correspond to the facts. In the immediate months after the collapse, even the Western occupying forces looked with more favour on the communist resistance than on Germans with an uncertain political past. Gradually, the Western Allies sifted out a small elite group of political leaders in the *Länder*. It seemed likely at first that the left would dominate post-war German politics; adherents to the centre and the right of the political spectrum were willing to share power with the left for two or three years, ostensibly for the sake of national reconstruction, but in truth because they were too obviously compromised to assert their residual electoral strength more forcibly.

In the ill-fated Weimar Republic, there had been a disastrous political backlash from the extremists once Germany had regained most of her independence. That did not happen after 1945. The political leaders who convinced the Western Allies that democracy was safe in their hands and who complied with their terms were subsequently endorsed and won power through free elections. Most Germans had been cured of aggressive nationalism by their total defeat and the disastrous consequences. A new Germany was born of prosperity.

CHAPTER 31

The Soviet Union: The Price of Victory and the Expanding Empire

Victory over Nazi Germany and her allies came as an immense relief to the Soviet Union. No victorious power had suffered more. The war had devastated European Russia, 25 million were homeless, factories were destroyed, railways disrupted, mechanised farm machinery virtually non-existent. Of the population of 194 million before the war, twenty-eight million had lost their lives; more than one in four Russians had been killed or wounded. Stalin did not expect much help from the capitalist United States once the defeat of the common enemies was accomplished. Supplies had been shipped to Russia under the wartime Lend–Lease programme, but this was severely curtailed after the victory over Germany, and was ended altogether in August 1945 after Japan's defeat for all countries. But crucial Western food supplies still reached the Soviet Union in 1946 under the United Nations Relief and Rehabilitation Administration (UNRRA), mainly financed by the United States. This programme saved devastated regions from famine.

The Soviet Union tried to obtain immediate assistance by taking away from the former enemy countries everything that was movable: rails, factory machines and all kinds of equipment. It was an inefficient operation and probably only a small proportion could be used again when it reached the Soviet Union. The rest rusted away in railway sidings. Joint Soviet and Eastern European companies were formed on terms dictated by the Russians; special trade agreements were reached with former allies, generally favouring the Soviet Union. Another important source of help came from reparations exacted, not only from the Soviet zones of Germany and Austria, but for a short time, with Anglo-American co-operation, from the Western occupation zones as agreed at Potsdam. Destruction in the Soviet Union was on a scale almost unimaginable, and during the war the Germans had treated the Russians worse than animals. This helps to explain the Soviet insistence on huge reparations from the production of west German industry. But Soviet demands soon ran counter to Western occupation policies. The Western Allies realised that it was they who would in the end have to make good these losses or continue to support the Germans in the Western zones with their own subsidies for years to come (page 330). The inter-Allied conflict on the reparations issue became one of the causes of the Cold War.

There were desultory negotiations for a US loan after the war which never came to anything. In the last resort, Stalin had to rely on the sweat of the Russian people. There was work for the millions demobilised from the Red Army. During the war there had been some ideological relaxation. Now there was a return to orthodoxy. Stalin had not mellowed in old age: coercion resumed and an army of forced labour was herded into the Gulag Archipelago, the vast network of labour camps east of Moscow. Hundreds of thousands labelled as traitors were transported from the Baltic states, which had been annexed in 1940; many more from all over the Russian empire were also deported to virtual slavery. The Communist Party was allowed to re-emerge as Stalin's instrument of control over Soviet society. There was rigid ideological censorship of science and all forms of culture, even of composers. The party exploited to the maximum the labour of the peasants and the workers. Military heroes were relegated to the status of ordinary citizens.

The last decade of Stalin's rule was stifling. Terror returned. Stalin's Soviet Union was a country of immense hardship. Nascent internal nationalism was savagely crushed but could never be entirely suppressed. Jewish national feelings, especially after the foundation of Israel, drew world attention to another aspect of Soviet persecution. Rights, taken for granted in the West, did not exist in Stalin's Russia.

A new five-year plan was inaugurated in 1946. Enormous difficulties had to be overcome. Soviet statistics need to be treated with caution, but expert Western evaluation confirms that there was a remarkable recovery of Soviet heavy industry, coal, iron and steel, cement, oil, electricity and transport. As in the 1930s, Stalin's economic plans gave precedence to heavy industry at the expense of consumer goods, so the standard of living recovered only to a rudimentary level. Draconian labour laws deprived workers of all freedom and exposed them to punishment for lateness or drunkenness. Heavy burdens were laid particularly on the peasantry: the collectives were more tightly regulated and controlled; the productive private plots of the peasantry were taken away; in 1947 collectivisation was extended to the former Baltic states of Estonia, Latvia and Lithuania. But agricultural production, unlike industrial activity, hardly recovered from the wartime lows. Food was forcibly taken from the peasantry for ridiculously low prices. There was widespread famine in the Ukraine in 1946–7. By 1952 the grain and potato harvests had still not reached the 1940 pre-war level. The failure of 'socialist' agriculture has remained a permanent feature of the Soviet economy.

Stalin's emphasis on heavy industry was conditioned by his fear of Western industrial superiority. He took for granted the implacable hostility of the capitalist West to the Soviet Union. His grip over Eastern Europe and the maintenance of a large peacetime Red Army were to compensate for Russia's economic inferiority. Every effort was also made to catch up in the field of nuclear weapons. But Stalin clearly wished to avoid a war with the West. In 1946 he cautiously withdrew demands made earlier on Turkey, and later pulled the Red Army out of northern Iran and Manchuria. Yet the Soviet position in the post-war world would depend in the first instance on the Red Army. Globally the Soviet Union stood on her own, exhausted and deeply wounded by war.

Stalin feared that the Red Army, as it advanced westwards, would become aware of the much higher standard of living enjoyed by the 'fascists' and capitalists. The success of Soviet propaganda depended on keeping the Russian peoples from Western contact. Fraternisation with local populations was therefore severely limited where it was allowed to occur at all. Within the Soviet Union, rigid censorship about the world outside continued and a distorted picture of Western hostility and hate was propagated. 'Bourgeois culture' was condemned as decadent and everything Soviet praised as superior. The party and Stalin's leadership were glorified for winning the war.

Stalin's post-war revenge was indiscriminate. The victims of Yalta, those Russians who were forcibly repatriated by the British and Americans after the war from the zones of occupation, were lucky if they ended up in the Gulag Archipelago. Others were simply shot. But these thousands of men, women and children were just the tip of the iceberg. Whole national groups, such as the Muslim Tatars and Kalmycks, were deported with great brutality from the Caucasus when it was reoccupied by Soviet armies in 1943 and 1944. Possibly more than 1 million people were collectively punished and deported. Stalin's ferocity exposed his fanatical determination to wipe out any danger to 'Russian' communist power and Soviet unity from within. The years from 1945 to Stalin's death in 1953 were as repressive as the terrible 1930s had been. Stalin ruled by coercion and terror; he was omnipresent yet totally remote, never meeting the Russian people face to face. His character was, in Khrushchev's words, capricious and despotic, brutal tendencies that only increased as his faculties weakened in old age. But he never lacked henchmen and supporters for his policies, policies that no one man could have carried through alone. Coercion and terror formed one essential element; the other was compliance. To this end, Stalin's immediate helpers received material benefits; for the rest of the population, socialist idealism was perverted by propaganda. A slave army of millions of Russians, arrested for one reason or another, arbitrarily or not, and housed in the Gulag Archipelago, provided the forced labour to assist Soviet recovery.

The Western Allies had little inkling of Stalin's paranoid fear for his continued unchallenged rule at home and little understanding of his determination that no national group within the Soviet Union should be able to challenge Russian dominance. Stalin, a Georgian by birth, was convinced by their conduct in the war of the superiority of the Russian people. This did not inhibit him from condemning nationalism at home or abroad according to Marxist–Leninist doctrine as a phase belonging to bourgeois societies. To the Soviet Union nationalism posed a threat in two ways: 'bourgeois' and 'nationalist'. Wherever nationalist consciousness manifested itself, especially in communist states, such as Yugoslavia, its advocates were fiercely denounced.

In the communist states the leadership exercised its will through the one (communist) party that was allowed to function. The party's control was usually in the hands of one man, sometimes a small group, whose wills then became ultimate law. The party apparatus was essential as a means of government, providing the link between policy decisions and their execution. Only one party could be tolerated in the classic communist state as it existed until 1989, or the whole execution of policy would fall into confusion. After 1948, the nations which the Soviet Union dominated had to conform in leadership and party organisation to the Soviet model, even down to the details of the 'personality cult' and the theatrical plaudits for the leader. Their alliance with the Soviet Union was not a question of free choice: loyalty to this alliance was the price exacted for freedom from direct Soviet military control.

Between 1940 and 1945 Stalin expanded Soviet rule over new territories, though he was well aware of the difficulties such absorption of hostile ethnic groups could create for the Soviet empire. Where possible, he reasserted the historic rights of pre-1917 tsarist Russia. Poland was a special and most difficult case if only because there were so many Poles – some 30 million in 1939, but reduced to 24 million in 1945. In re-establishing the 1941 Soviet frontier, a mixed population of Belorussians and Ukrainians in the countryside and Poles in the towns was brought within the Soviet Union, and this was only mitigated by population exchanges of Poles, Ukrainians and White Russians. The frontier between Poland and the USSR had some historical justification, since it basically followed the demarcation proposed at the Paris Peace Conference by Lord Curzon in 1919. Finland too lost territory but retained more of her independence. Stalin shrank from incorporating the fiercely independent and nationalist Finns. Instead, he made sure that they understood that as Russia's neighbour, and located as they were far from possible Western help, they would have to follow a policy friendly to the USSR as the price of their comparative freedom.

In 1945 Stalin shamelessly retained, without Allied approval, the territories of the once independent Baltic states of Lithuania, Latvia and Estonia, which it had been agreed in the Stalin–Hitler pact of August 1939 should fall within the Soviet sphere. The Red Army occupied them in 1940 and set up puppet assemblies, which promptly abandoned their countries' independence and acceded to the USSR. Also in 1945, but this time in agreement with the Allies, the northern third of pre-war East Prussia was 'administered' by the Soviet Union – in practice incorporated into it. In the Balkans, Stalin wanted Bessarabia (Moldavia). It had been Russian until 1918. After the First World War ethnic Romanians of Moldavia had declared for union with Romania. In 1940, with the acquiescence of Hitler, Russia forced Romania to cede the territory back to her. Finally, to gain a direct link and common frontier with Hungary, Stalin pressured the Czechs to cede a part of their territory, Ruthenia, to the USSR. In this way he accomplished large acquisitions of land all around the periphery of the Soviet Union from the Baltic through central Europe to the Balkans in the south. But, even beyond these annexations, the Soviet Union desired further influence and control, to destroy the pre-war block of hostile states, the cordon sanitaire, with which the West had tried before 1939 to surround and contain communist Russia.

During the years from 1945 to 1948 Stalin brought Eastern and central European politics and societies under Soviet control. He was obsessed by the fear that eventually the capitalist powers would take advantage of their superiority to attack the Soviet Union, which therefore had only a few years in which to prepare. In Asia, he was reticent and pacific. He had little time for that continent. The real danger, he believed, would develop in Europe. To avoid the danger of too vehement a Western reaction, central and Eastern Europe was only gradually integrated into the Soviet system. One-party communist states tied to the Soviet party remained the goal. To reach it, Stalin had to overcome the obstacle not only of Western opposition but more seriously of the intense nationalism of the ethnic groups living in this region of Europe. It proved impossible to extinguish the loyalties to their own countries of Yugoslavs, Hungarians, Poles and Romanians. Their acceptance of the communist embrace, despite some genuine gratitude for their liberation, fell far short of seeing in the Soviet Union a desirable overlord. Polish history had consisted of the struggle for freedom from Russia; the powerful Catholic Churches in both Poland and Hungary identified themselves with their countries' national feelings. Added to such opposition was the resistance to the social and economic revolution demanded by the communists. The relationship between the Soviet Union and her allies in the socialist camp thus moved uneasily between attempts at rigid party and Soviet control and relaxation of that control to the extent of limited independence.

The central and East European states through which in 1944 and 1945 the Red Army marched on its way to Vienna and Berlin can be divided into two groups: the Allied nations, Poland, Yugoslavia, Czechoslovakia and technically Albania too; and the former enemies, Bulgaria, Romania and Hungary. The ability of Britain and the United States to intercede effectively for allies was paradoxically smaller than the ability to secure some say in the future of the enemies. In the case of allies, the only option was to withhold recognition of the government installed by the Russians in 1945. This was done, only for recognition to be granted two years later.

Over the future Czechoslovakia Allied influence was especially weak. President Beneš had decided long before 1945 that Czechoslovakia's post-war future left no choice but to accept Soviet 'friendship', which meant acquiescing in whatever limits Stalin chose to place on her independence. Beneš was rewarded by being the only Allied head of state to return to his own country by way of Moscow. As for Yugoslavia, the royal government in exile could not conceivably be re-established without the support of a large Allied army, for Tito and his communist partisans had assumed control of the country, moreover without direct Soviet help.

The position of the enemies, of Hungary, Romania and Bulgaria, was different, although each was under Red Army occupation. Their governments and frontiers could not be regularised without peace treaties involving the consent of Britain and the United States. The Allies kept up a constant stream of protest at the undemocratic conduct of these regimes set up by the Soviet Union and withheld their recognition and their signature to the peace treaties until 1947.

In Poland, which he recognised as the most vulnerable country under Soviet control, Stalin kept the tightest grip, making few concessions. Poland remained under the thinly veiled direct military occupation of the Red Army. The Polish army which had accompanied the Red Army was largely officered by reliable Soviet officers. In the new communist-dominated government, the only politician with a considerable following was Stanislav Mikolajczyk, a non-communist and leader of the Peasant Party who had joined the Lublin government from London and now served as a deputy prime minister. The communist secretary of the Polish Workers' Party, Wladyslaw Gomulka, was the real power in Poland. The communists adopted their usual tactics of attempting to secure the agreement of the Peasant Party and the non-communist coalition partners to elections on a 'single list'; this meant the voters would be presented not with a choice of parties, but with one agreed list of candidates, of which the Peasant Party and others would be allowed only a minority. Stalin had promised the Western Allies early free elections. But, because the communists could not guarantee the results in 1945 despite holding key internal ministries and controlling the police, the army and much of the administration, they simply postponed the elections for two years. During these years there was open violence and armed struggle.

The Home Army, operating in Poland but loyal to the London government in exile, was dissolved in July 1945. Embittered by their experiences, some desperate units went underground again and with a few thousand members of the Ukrainian Independence Army began terrorist attacks on administrative officials of the Communist Workers' Party.

In parts of the countryside fighting escalated into civil war. Civilian administrators and police were attacked and killed. Jewish survivors once more became the murder victims. Not until 1948 could this violence be broken. Until then, the terrorist attacks served the interests of the communists, for they made the postponement of elections plausible.

By fair means and foul the communists did all they could to undermine support for their political opponents, who happened also to be their coalition partners in government. Nevertheless, the road to socialism was to be Polish and not Soviet. The economic plans were publicly declared to be based on the coexistence of a private, a co-operative and a public state sector. All the same, there was not much left but the state sector of industry by 1947. All industrial undertakings employing more than fifty workers per shift were nationalised, which effectively brought 91 per cent of industry and banking under state control. The land question was the most immediately important. In 'old' Poland all the large farms and estates were broken up and distributed to the peasantry. In the 'new lands', vacated by the Germans, peasant settlers were encouraged to join collective farms. This largesse politically neutralised the peasantry. Few lamented that the pre-war gentry and wealthy industrialists would not be allowed back their possessions. Intimidation of political opponents did the rest. Despite the appalling conditions, huge efforts were made to rebuild the devastated economy and the towns and villages of Poland, especially Warsaw.

In the election, finally held in January 1947, the communists won and almost eliminated their principal rivals the Peasant Party, many of whose candidates had been intimidated or imprisoned. The Catholic Church remained intact, however, sustaining its links with the majority of the Polish people. Gomulka tried to reconcile the Poles to communist rule, but his efforts were to be negated by the need to abandon the Polish road to socialism. During the barren harshness of Stalin's last years the Communist Party was disrupted by purges and Gomulka was disgraced in January 1949.

Soviet policies in Romania exemplified a different, gradualist approach determined by internal events and by the military situation. At first, Stalin may well have planned a ruthless and simple takeover, with communist-trained Romanians such as Anna Pauker setting up an administration in the wake of the Red Army's conquest. But the unexpected happened. In August 1944, King Michael led a coup which overthrew the fascist government and then changed sides, from Hitler's Germany to that of the Allies. This threw the country open to the Red Army, which with Romanian troops chased the Wehrmacht into Hungary. Romania again lost Bessarabia to the Soviet Union, but was rewarded by the return of Transylvania, which in 1940 had been transferred to Hungary by Hitler. Meanwhile a Romanian government, including pre-war Romanian communists, was established, though these 'native' communists were not trusted by Stalin. At Moscow's behest, the popular-front-type governments, which included non-communist parties, were reshuffled in December 1944 and March 1945 to provide the communists with greater though still incomplete power.

Soviet army intervention in local administration eroded popular support for the non-communist parties. Joint Soviet–Romanian companies were founded, landed estates were broken up, communists and fellow travellers were labelled 'democratic' and other parties showing any signs of independence were stigmatised as 'fascist'. So-called 'free elections' were held in November 1946. There was intimidation, and the results may well have been doctored, but the communists had won for themselves a sufficient power base to make their overwhelming electoral victory acceptable to the Romanian people. In any case the people had little choice beyond acceptance since Western protests would be limited to words. Britain and the United States had already recognised the communist-controlled government *before* the elections. Despite the unsatisfactory elections and the Anglo-American detestation of communist regimes, Romania had been written off as inevitably forming part of the Soviet camp, and a peace treaty was signed in February 1947 which recognised this. King Michael was forced into exile and Romania became a 'people's democracy', the beginning of four terrible decades.

Although Bulgaria was not at war with the Soviet Union, Churchill had made it clear to Stalin in 1944 that she would be allowed to fall within the Soviet sphere. War having been hastily declared on her, Soviet troops entered and overran the country in September 1944, without real Anglo-American opposition. Unlike its Romanian equivalent, the Bulgarian Communist Party had had a substantial popular following before the war and in Georgi Dimitrov a leader of international reputation following his acquittal in Nazi Germany for complicity in the Reichstag Fire. Although he became an influential figure in Moscow as general secretary of the Comintern in the 1930s, Dimitrov was not at first allowed to return to Bulgaria in the wake of the Soviet invasion. Instead Bulgarian communists were installed in 1944 in another popular-front government, the Fatherland Front, and to begin with the opposition was not ruthlessly suppressed. But the respite was only temporary. With the Red Army stationed in the country and Stalin determined to consolidate Soviet power, and with no effective Western counter-measures forthcoming, the fate of the Social Democratic and Agrarian Peasant opposition and its party leader Petkov was sealed. Dimitrov was now allowed to return to Bulgaria to strengthen the communists.

Despite the muzzling of the press, the elections held in October 1946 saw a striking success for the non-communist opposition. For a few months 101 deputies elected by over a million votes were able to act as a parliamentary opposition to the communist regime. But in August 1947 Petkov was arrested, tried and sentenced to death on trumped-up charges of working for 'Anglo-American Imperialism'. He was shot the following month. Britain and the United States had made public protests before his execution, but Dimitrov only reinforced the impression of judicial murder by declaring that Petkov might have been spared but for the Anglo-American protests. Of course, the execution could not have taken place without Stalin's acquiescence. To Britain and the United States events in Eastern Europe showed the extent to which Stalin was prepared ruthlessly to ignore his international obligations. Like their Romanian counterparts, the Bulgarian communists turned their country into a particularly brutal and repressive 'people's democracy'.

The Hungarians had been ruled from 1919 until 1944 by anti-communist regimes under the Regent Admiral Horthy. It was his fatal error to throw in his lot with the German invaders of the Soviet Union in 1941. When events revealed his error, he tried to disengage and achieve a peace with the Soviet Union, but it was too late. It was the Germans instead who first occupied his country. In pre-war Hungary army support for the authoritarian structure had been decisive, and the need for social reform had gone unsatisfied. The dominant aspiration of successive Hungarian governments was the recovery of territory lost principally to Romania (Transylvania) by the Peace Treaty of Trianon in 1920. It was this aspiration which drove Hungary into the arms of Germany and even to declare war on Russia in 1941. By then Hungary had already been rewarded, in 1940, by the transfer of northern Transylvania from Romania, as well as of portions of Czechoslovakia. Defeat in 1945 entailed the loss once more of all these gains as Stalin redistributed the territories, Britain and the United States again raising no objections.

Stalin's opportunism is well illustrated by the first anti-German Hungarian government set up by the Red Army in the part of Hungary they had liberated. Soviet military requirements at this time made it expedient to include many former supporters of Horthy, as well as communists and members of other parties. As circumstances changed, so would the composition of the government. The leading Hungarian communist was Mátyás Rákosi, who had lived in Moscow since 1940; he now returned to participate in coalition governments. He began with patriotic appeals in 1944 promising democracy and peaceful progress, yet within four years Hungary was transformed into one of the most ruthless of the Stalinist 'people's democracies'. Rákosi's approach corresponded to Stalin's own: cautious opportunism ruthlessly pursued. Hungarians, not Russians, would be allowed to transform politics and society and would guarantee national loyalty to the Soviet Union. Three parties besides the communists were allowed to organise and participate in national politics.

The Catholic Church too played an important role, acting as a bulwark against atheistic communism. Stalin proceeded in Hungary with caution, permitting free elections in November 1945. The communists lost badly. Stalin was not going to repeat such an error.

Still, Rákosi, with Soviet backing, retained the key to power through his control of the Interior Ministry and the secret police. He skilfully exploited differences between the government coalition parties, cynically commenting later that he had sliced them away like salami until only the communists were left. First the Smallholders' Party was eliminated, then the Social Democrats. In the 1947 elections, communist victory was no longer left to the whim of the voters. Within a few months, Rákosi and his lieutenants had taken over the country, and a new 'constitution' in 1949 turned Hungary into a Moscow-style 'people's democracy'.

There were few indications in 1945 that Yugoslavia would differ in any significant way from the other states in Eastern Europe liberated from the Nazis with the help of the Soviet Union. If anything. Yugoslavia was more obviously communist, controlled from the start by Marshal Broz Tito as undisputed leader organising a one-party state, ideologically bound to Marxism–Leninism. The military victory of the partisans who had been fighting the Germans left little alternative but to accept Tito's terms for the post-war reconstruction of Yugoslavia. Only a military occupation, Soviet or Allied, could have altered that. Interestingly, in 1944 Stalin had encouraged the idea of an Allied landing in Yugoslavia, evidently already seeing in Tito's Yugoslav communism a dangerous national deviation. A closer study of Yugoslavia shows both similarities with and important differences from the general pattern of the communist takeover of the central and East European states. None of the communist resistance forces was strong enough to defeat the Wehrmacht without the victories of the Red Army. This was no less true of Yugoslavia, although there the partisans actually liberated the country from German occupation.

Tito was well aware that the partisan victory would be dependent upon the victory of the Soviet Union. He also followed Lenin's precept of a tightly disciplined party as indispensable for maintaining communist power. During the war the German and Italian occupation had destroyed the pre-war social and political order. Yugoslav communists and the royalists fought each other for predominance at the same time as they fought the Germans. This triangular struggle was complex, the two Yugoslav sides accusing each other of helping the Germans to eliminate the internal enemy. Initially Tito drew his support overwhelmingly from Serb peasants attracted by promises of greater social justice and by appeals to their patriotism. The Serbs were the largest national group and Tito succeeded in winning over far more to his side than the royalist Chetniks did. But from the first he was also aware that Yugoslav unity required the support of all the major national groups – Croats, Macedonians, Montenegrins and Slovenes. He created people's committees in villages, towns and provinces, promising full national rights to the major nationalities in a post-war federal Yugoslavia.

Milovan Djilas, Tito's friend and supporter until 1954, has described Tito vividly as a man born a rebel, who combined a distinctive zeal for communism with a personal zest for power; like some Eastern potentate Tito, once the hardened partisan leader, built villas and palaces after the war for his exclusive pleasure, even though he could spent little time in any one of them. The dictatorship of the proletariat became in practice personal power wielded by an autocratic leader. Tito created a new party hierarchy, himself at the pinnacle and the secret police as the instrument for securing compliance by dealing ruthlessly with his opponents. In 1946 a constitution on the Soviet model was established, which guaranteed the cultural and administrative rights of all the nationalities in a federal Yugoslav state; this went some way towards solving the nationality conflicts of pre-1945 Yugoslavia, at least for a time. Tito's second achievement was his resolute defence of Yugoslavia's own road to socialism in 1948 in the face of Stalin's onslaught, and the assertion of Yugoslavia's independence from Moscow's control. The monolithic Soviet empire was cracked for all the world to see.

The road to total communist power was different again in Czechoslovakia. Edvard Beneš, the President of the Czech government in exile in London, had signed a formal alliance and friendship treaty with the Soviet Union in December 1943 by which the Russians undertook not to interfere in Czechoslovakia's internal affairs. But Stalin had already established a communist émigré group in Moscow, led by Klement Gottwald. The experience of Munich in 1938, when Britain and France had forced the Czechs to give in to Hitler's territorial demands, had convinced Beneš that he should stay on good terms with the Russians, because Western protection could not be relied upon. He hoped that by demonstrating the Czechs' genuine friendship he would be allowed to maintain democracy and Western values. He saw Czechoslovakia's role as forming a bridge between East and West. As if to emphasise Czech reliance on the Soviet Union, Beneš returned to Czechoslovakia via Moscow in the spring of 1945. Ominously he now had to agree to new terms which further limited his freedom of action. The government in exile would be replaced by a new National Front government for liberated Czechoslovakia in which only the parties of the left would participate, and key ministries for the internal control of the country would be in communist hands. In return Beneš received Stalin's empty promise that the Soviet leader would deal with any communists who gave him trouble. Beneš had also to agree to a social and economic transformation (designed to pave the way to communism) and to the expulsion of the Sudeten Germans. Real democracy through representative government was not re-established in 1945, only its appearance. Czechoslovakia was bound to follow the Soviet Union in any policy Stalin regarded as important, even before the communist takeover in 1948; the Czech recantation of participation in the Marshall Aid programme in 1947, on Moscow's insistence, was a good illustration of this.

The Czech communist leader, Klement Gottwald, was told by Moscow to content himself with a gradual path to absolute power. During the war the communists had organised a resistance movement against the Germans; after it they not only held the key ministries and dominated the trade unions, but established their national committees in villages, towns and provinces. Economic transformation began with the nationalisation of large industries and businesses even before the provisional parliament met in October 1945. But later that month the American forces and the Red Army, who had jointly liberated the country, agreed to withdraw, giving hope to the democrats, although the country was split between the communists and the democratic parties of the left. Elections were held in May 1946, but they were not absolutely free since only the parties comprising the National Front were allowed to participate. Furthermore, many Czechs feared that, if the communists failed to win, the Red Army would return. Given all their preparatory work and control, it is hardly surprising that the communists polled 37 per cent of the votes. But, even with their fellow travellers among the Social Democratic Party, this did not give them absolute control. Nonetheless the democratic opposition, stronger in Slovakia than Bohemia and Moravia, was weakened by being split among three parties.

In the new government, formed after the elections, Klement Gottwald became prime minister; the two Czechoslovaks best known abroad retained their former positions, Beneš as president and Jan Masaryk as foreign minister. But soon the communists inside and outside the government started to behave high-handedly, and mass arrests of their opponents were ordered. Clashes in parliament and between government ministers became increasingly heated and the supporters of the democratic parties were considering whether they would not have to resist violations of justice if democracy was to survive. But to the outside world the presence of Beneš and Masaryk appeared to guarantee the preservation of civil rights; that illusion was shattered early in 1948 (pages 386–7).

A survey of Eastern and central Europe shows a considerable variation of national experience and of the role played by the communists. Not everything that happened could be controlled by Moscow. Indeed one of the major headaches for the Eastern European communist leaders was the difficulty of discovering what Stalin really wanted. At lower levels, Russian advice and influence were at times confusing or contradictory. Gottwald, a loyal communist, believed in 1947, for example, that Stalin would not object if Czechoslovakia participated in the Marshall Aid programme; as we have seen, he was rapidly obliged to recant. But whenever Stalin made his views known the communists made speed to fall into line.

A façade of representative institutions would placate the West; meanwhile the United States was pulling most of her armed forces out of Europe. Firm communist bases in Czechoslovakia, Romania, Hungary, Bulgaria, Poland and the Soviet zone of Germany were established. Everywhere communists were strongly entrenched and dominant in coalition National Front governments. The political activities of other parties were controlled, and those labelled 'fascist' were banned. The influence of the landowners was removed by dividing up their estates, and for the time being the peasantry benefited from the redistribution of land: for this, the communists gained the credit. Large industries were nationalised, and progressively the smaller ones as well. The economic base of the dominant wealthy pre-war social groups was destroyed; in Poland it had already been destroyed by the Germans, who had also killed many members of the professional classes. Everywhere, in local committees established in every community down to the smallest village, the communists entrenched their influence to prepare for ultimate control. Communism could move only one way – into a position of dominance – and would do so as soon as the Kremlin judged the time right.

In each country there were differences too. The Catholic Church was powerful enough in Poland and Hungary to form an opposing force. Social and economic conditions also differed, Poland having suffered more grievously during the Second World War than any other Eastern European state apart from the Soviet Union. The strength of the anti-communist opposition varied from country to country too, as did the tactics adopted by the communist leaders. In Czechoslovakia, the communists were sufficiently strong to seek control by semi-legal means; in Yugoslavia, the communists took control from the start. But all the countries in the Soviet orbit had this in common: the dynamics of the social and political changes introduced after 1944–5 were bound to end in a communist victory.

Communist domination after 1948 did not mean the end of political strife. This was now transferred to struggles within the party, between the groups which had the ear of Moscow and those which were denounced as the enemies of the Soviet Union. The Moscow-trained communist leaders turned on the 'native' communists in great purges during the closing years of Stalin's rule. The revolution began to eat its own children. Moscow's was a savage dominance over a turbulent region.

CHAPTER 32

Britain and the World: A Legacy Too Heavy to Bear

Victorious British armies had shared with the Americans the reconquest of Italy, France and Germany in arduous campaigns from the beachheads of Salerno and Normandy to the Elbe. What the British now feared was that the Americans would depart from Europe and simply return to pre-war isolationism and so leave Britain facing the Soviet Union alone.

The British people rejoiced on VE (Victory in Europe) Day and saw it as proving the powers of endurance and the superiority of the British; Churchill's government knew better and recognised the serious problems that lay ahead. The war in Asia against Japan had still to be won. Hidden from general public recognition were other facts: the bleak position of Britain's financial resources, her foreign assets decimated by the purchase of war supplies; the extent to which the United States had provided essential foods, raw materials and weapons under the wartime 'lend–lease' arrangement which meant postponing payment, not avoiding it altogether. Without US help, the British economy – geared until mid-1945 to the war effort – was not able to provide the British people even with the standard of living possible during the war. And now in addition came the cost of maintaining the minimum living standards of the former enemy in the British zone of occupation. The food imported into Germany had to be paid for by Britain from her small dollar reserves.

If continental Western Europe was to be prevented from sliding into chaos and protected from Soviet expansion or subversion, the active support of the United States was essential. Yet there were considerable and persisting Anglo-American differences. In the United States there was still a widespread belief that Britain remained an unrepentant imperialist power and a potentially formidable trading rival. British policies in Palestine restricting Jewish immigration caused bitterness on both sides of the Atlantic (pages 455–6). Finally, despite his robust language, President Harry S. Truman thought that the United States and the Soviet Union could reach an accommodation and that it was Britain, bent on defending her worldwide colonial interests, which might provoke the Soviet Union into conflict.

Until the United States was ready to recognise her new responsibilities in regions of the world which she had hitherto not regarded as falling within spheres essential to her own security, Britain had to fill the vacuum. Meanwhile, there was uncertainty about America's long-term commitment to Western Europe, and about her readiness to defend Western interests in Asia, the Middle East and the Mediterranean. So, until March 1947, it was Britain which financially as well as militarily took up the burden of supporting the anti-communist government in Greece.

With resources so overstretched, there was an urgent need to limit Britain's more costly responsibilities. India had been promised her independence, and after the end of the war it could no longer be delayed. The Labour government grasped this nettle: Lord Mountbatten arrived in Delhi as the last viceroy to India on 22 March 1947. On 14 and 15 August India and Pakistan gained their independence. Partition had proved unavoidable, and the tragedy of communal violence and murders marred Britain's wise decision to give up willingly the 'jewel' of her empire (see Chapter 40).

In the summer of 1945 there were among government ministers no illusions about Britain's own economic weakness and the need for American help. Even so, there seemed no reason to doubt that, after a transition period of five or six years, Britain would recover.

The first important post-war decision to be taken was a political one – who was to govern Britain? The election in July 1945 took place while the war was still continuing in the Pacific. British troops were fighting in Burma and the Japanese were fanatically resisting the advance of the Americans on the island approaches to their homeland. The war was expected to last many more months, until the atomic bomb revealed its awesome power and unexpectedly ended the fighting. But in the weeks following Germany's surrender all this was momentarily put aside. Churchill had contributed to a carefree post-war mood by ensuring the celebration of VE Day. There were parties in every street. Burma was far away except for those with relatives still fighting there or whose next of kin were starving in Japanese prisoner-of-war camps. The great majority of people in Britain were now hopefully anticipating the rewards of peace. Churchill wanted the coalition with Labour to continue until the defeat of Japan; when the Labour ministers in his government rejected this proposal, he fought the election in July on the appeal that he should be given the mandate to 'finish the job'. But he had unwittingly undermined his own election chances by helping to create the feeling that the war was already over.

Outside Britain it seemed incredible that the British people, who owed so much to Churchill, should now with apparent ingratitude turn him out of office. Even in his own constituency the Labour candidate attracted substantial support. But the election was not about the conduct of the war. Indeed, Churchill's electoral tour was a personal triumph, with ordinary people everywhere mobbing him to express their gratitude and genuine affection. The Labour leader Clement Attlee appeared a colourless little man by comparison. Yet it was Attlee not Churchill who entered 10 Downing Street after the biggest landslide since the election of 1906, which had given the Liberals victory. However much the British 'first past the post' electoral system might exaggerate the disparity of the parties' fortunes, it was a striking turnaround from the last election, held in 1935, when the Conservatives and their supporters had returned 432 members and the opposition parties could muster only 180.

Parliamentary Election, 1945

	Seats	Votes
Labour	393	11,995,152
Conservative	213	9,988,306
Liberal	12	2,248,226
Communist	2	102,780

Why was the swing of votes to Labour so large, especially among the servicemen? Churchill himself, as the electoral asset on which the Tory Party managers were banking, proved insufficient to turn the tide. Conservative promises of a new deal based on the Beveridge Report of 1942 were not so very different from those of the Labour Party, but the electorate doubted whether the Conservative heart was really in reform. It is also true that Churchill mishandled the electoral campaign by overdoing his condemnation of 'socialism' as embodied in the Labour Party's programme. He denounced Labour as setting out on a path to totalitarian rule which would lead to a British Gestapo. Did Churchill really persuade himself of this nonsense? His judgement proved equally fallible when he derided Attlee as a 'sheep in wolf's clothing'. It was impossible to persuade a sophisticated British electorate that Attlee, Bevin and Morrison were now not to be trusted despite their outstanding accomplishments as ministers in Churchill's all-party War Cabinet. The Gestapo jibe badly misfired.

But probably none of this explained the magnitude of the Conservative defeat. There was one factor more powerful than any other: the memories of the bitter hardship of unemployment during the 1930s, of slums, of ill-health and of a society that had failed to provide fair opportunities to the majority of the British people. In July 1945 millions of troops faced imminent demobilisation. Were the Conservatives likely to have their interests at heart? Would the government ensure that worthwhile work was found for everyone or would the employers be allowed to pick and choose, to depress wages in free-market style, careless of the poverty of the masses? It was this deep distrust of the Conservative Party, regarded by Labour supporters as the party of the well-to-do, that induced a larger proportion of working people and soldiers than ever before, together with traditional Labour supporters, to put their faith in a socialist government and in a prime minister, Clement Attlee, who had previously been overshadowed by Churchill. Ernest Bevin and Herbert Morrison had had a far greater impact during the pre-war and war years. Yet Attlee proved a most effective and even wily leader; with his pipe, his baggy trousers and his mousey moustache, his mild-mannered image was in sharp contrast to the larger-than-life Churchill.

The transfer from military service to peacetime employment was managed by the Labour government with considerable skill, an effective example of good planning. But the women who had manned the factory benches now frequently had to give up their jobs to the men. This time soldiers, unlike after the First World War, were demobilised in an orderly and fair fashion and only as fast as they could be reabsorbed in civilian work. This meant Britain still had more than 900,000 men in the forces in 1948. The free 'utility' civilian clothes supplied to everyone on leaving the army were just the first sign that the future had been thought out. Retraining facilities and vacancies in industry became available as wartime production was switched to that of peacetime. There was great demand for goods and a need for new housing and public works.

A most important feature of the celebrated Beveridge Report of 1942 agreed by all three parties at the time, Conservative, Labour and Liberal, was a commitment that the government's running of the nation's economy would ensure full employment. Never again should the hungry 1930s, with the hated means test, be allowed to return. Labour and Conservative governments were able to fulfil that pledge for a generation, unemployment rarely rising above 2 per cent or half a million. The other promises of the Beveridge plan, more wholeheartedly supported by Labour and the Liberals than by Conservatives, were to provide insurance for the whole of the population for the basic needs of life, and on death a grant for their burial. The state would take care of its citizens from the 'cradle to the grave'. A health service would provide medical treatment for the whole family regardless of who was working and who was not. Together, these measures laid the intellectual foundations of the post-war welfare state. They represented a tremendous advance in working people's standards of living, an indirect 'social wage' provided by the Exchequer from the differential contributions and taxes of the whole population. The Conservatives were committed to similar provisions of state aid but would have proceeded differently and possibly at a slower pace. They doubted from the start whether the state could afford to make such far-reaching promises entailing vast expenditure. There were reforming Tories in the wartime coalition too, but by 1945 they had passed only one important measure through parliament, R. A. Butler's Education Act of 1944, which when implemented raised the school-leaving age to fifteen and reorganised the educational system so that better opportunities would be opened to all. The Labour government translated theoretical welfarism into practical measures. The Insurance Act of 1946 and – after a struggle between Aneurin Bevan, the fiery Welsh Minister of Health, and the doctors which ended in a compromise over the continuation of private medicine – the National Health Service Act of the same year were the two most important measures of the new government, which carried out and extended the Beveridge plan.

The commitment to socialism, however, remained largely a matter of theory. In practice the Attlee administration's approach was pragmatic, aiming at the gradual transformation of the British economy. This reflected the electorate's mood accurately enough. The majority of the people were interested, not in theories of socialism, but rather in gaining a better standard of living, a fairer share of the nation's production, more equal opportunity – in short, 'social justice'. The continued rationing of food was one way of sharing out what was essentially in short supply. Basic foods were subsidised, so even the poorest people could afford to buy their rations. State ownership was extended only where it seemed most obviously necessary. The Bank of England was nationalised, but not the commercial banks or the insurance companies. The coal mines, civil aviation, the railways, and gas and electricity production were also brought under state control by the close of 1947, with the employers and shareholders receiving compensation. But although now 'owned by the people', the workers did not play a new and significant role in running state industries. The government appointed a management team, who were frequently none other than the former managers, and the workers at best exchanged one set of employers for another. Consequently nationalisation had little impact on good industrial relations.

More important in this respect was the Trade Disputes and Trade Union Act 1946, which repealed the restrictions placed on trade union power after the General Strike of 1926. A generation later new efforts would be made by both Labour and Conservative governments to restrict trade unions once again in the actions they could take without incurring legal penalties. By then, the majority of the electorate had come to feel that the balance of power had swung too far in favour of the trade unions and against the national interest.

The ability to feed Britain during the immediate post-war years, to pay for raw material and to revive industry was dependent not only on following sound policies, which Labour did, nor on the mobilisation of Britain's depleted capital resources, but also on American help. By themselves, the British could not earn enough dollars to pay for the imports necessary for Britain and the German zone of occupation. There were no illusions about the country's plight in this respect. Yet, as we have noted, it was expected that, given help during the early post-war years, a reconstructed British industry would thereafter be able to cope. The problem thus appeared to be a transitional one.

The Roosevelt administration had made it clear that it was prepared to help in post-war reconstruction and that it would not return to isolationism. It was obvious that the United States would emerge from the war as the world's economic superpower, unscarred and unscathed by the ravages of fighting at home. In this task of reconstruction, Britain was America's principal partner, and Anglo-American economic plans for the post-war world had been prepared in continuous rounds of discussion since 1942. They took concrete form at a conference held under the aegis of the United Nations in a Washington suburb at Bretton Woods.

*

In their planning of the world economic future the British and American administrations knew they were dealing with crucial problems that went far beyond technical details. If the mistakes after the First World War, which led to international economic warfare, mass unemployment and the great depression, were not simply to be repeated, a sensible method of achieving economic co-operation and mutual support would need to be worked out. The United States would, for a time at least, have to provide massive assistance. On this the Americans and the British were agreed. It corresponded to American custom that the form of this co-operation should be institutionalised. At Bretton Woods the foundations were soundly laid, even though solutions were not found for every international economic problem likely to arise in the post-war world.

The details of the Bretton Woods agreements are complex, but the essential points can be simplified and understood without expertise in high finance. The key was US concern about discrimination in worldwide trade. Individual countries in the 1930s had rigidly attempted to control their foreign imports. One important mechanism which national governments could most effectively use to this end was exchange control: the imposition of restrictions on the exchange of their own currency for those of other countries. Sterling was a currency used in world transactions; if its exchange into dollars were restricted, then Britain, the Commonwealth (except Canada) and many other countries trading in sterling would not be able to buy from the United States, and worldwide there would be a barrier to trade. An important part of the Bretton Woods agreements was an undertaking to make all currencies freely convertible after a transitional period of five years; exchange rates between currencies, including the dollar, would be fixed and regulated by a new international institution, the International Monetary Fund (IMF). It was intended that exchange rates should be stable and that they should be changed only with the consent of the IMF. The resources of the Fund were to be made up of contributions from each member country in gold and currencies in proportion to the strength of her economy. The United States supplied by far the biggest single contribution. Each country could draw on the Fund to make up a shortfall in foreign currency if its trade was not in balance; but if it drew on the Fund beyond a certain limit the IMF could prescribe conditions for its loan and demand that measures it thought necessary should be adopted to correct the trade imbalances. The decision-making apparatus of the IMF was a crucial feature. Members did not each have an equal vote with decisions by majority on important issues. It was intended that rates of exchange, for instance, could be changed only by a four-fifths majority of the Fund's board of directors. Each member country appointed one director, but his vote was weighted in accordance with his country's share in the IMF. This gave the United States a preponderant influence, and the IMF is appropriately located in Washington. In return for the large US contribution to the resources of the IMF, conditions were agreed which were aimed at preventing discrimination in world trade, and thus discrimination against the United States for lack of dollars. A twin to the IMF is the World Bank, which provides development loans, but it has played a much less important role than the IMF in post-war international trade and the world economy. But the hopes placed in these institutions for facilitating the free flow of world trade and the free convertibility of currencies were only partially realised after 1945.

It is curious that, in the pursuit of freer trade, import duties or tariffs did not play a more important role in American thinking. The United States retained her own high tariffs against imports and thought only in terms of their gradual international reduction by international agreement. The bargaining for reductions of tariffs began in April 1947 when twenty-three countries met in Geneva; in October that year they concluded the General Agreement on Tariffs and Trade (GATT). What the United States particularly wanted to achieve was the elimination of large trading blocks which traded among themselves preferentially, erecting higher tariffs against outsiders. The British Commonwealth had set up such a system in 1932 by the Ottawa Agreement, which established imperial preference. The American negotiators offered large reductions in US tariffs, but Britain – faced with myriad financial difficulties – clung to imperial preferences until obliged to eliminate most of them when joining the European Economic Community in 1973. Further rounds of trade bargaining continued under the auspices of GATT without resulting in the freeing of all trade barriers as originally envisaged. Nonetheless GATT has made a valuable contribution over the years to the increase in the volume of world trade.

The arrangements worked out at Bretton Woods did not, however, solve Britain's or Western Europe's immediate problems. With the United States alone able to supply what Britain and the Western European nations needed for their reconstruction, and with inadequate recovery in Europe producing insufficient exports to the United States, not enough dollar funds were available to make the necessary purchases in America. This was called the 'dollar gap'.

In fighting Nazi Germany, Britain had subordinated all her economic policies to just one aim, to maximise the war effort. As a result her export trade had dwindled to a third of the pre-war level; not enough was produced at home to match wages, so inflation resulted; Britain's dollar and gold reserves and her large overseas assets had been used to finance the war; Britain had also accumulated large sterling debts as a result of wartime expenditure; the national debt had tripled and Britain's industry, adapted to produce armaments, now had to be transferred to peacetime manufacture for the domestic and export markets. The dislocation was enormous, in Britain as elsewhere. Millions were still in the services and could only gradually be demobilised. The dilemma for Britain was that she had to import food and raw materials to supply her people and industry, and to pay for them she needed to export manufactured goods as well as to earn returns from the City of London's financial and insurance services (invisible earnings). It was impossible to achieve such a turnaround from wartime production instantly. During the war itself, Britain's essential needs had been met by American Lend–Lease. Then came the crunch. In August 1945, with the President's economic advisers judging that the special circumstances of war were now over, and with Congress unlikely to agree to fund the arrangement in peacetime, Truman abruptly ended Lend–Lease.

Something had to be done about the yawning dollar gap that was immediately in prospect. Britain's most distinguished economist, John Maynard Keynes, was despatched to Washington to negotiate a loan to tide Britain over. The Lend–Lease debts now had to be settled. This seemed especially unjust in British eyes since the money had been spent fighting the common enemy:

furthermore Lend–Lease had been made available only in 1942 when Britain had been at war for three years. By then Britain had already spent most of her foreign reserves and assets. The Lend–Lease debts were settled with a loan, not cancelled. A loan of $3750 million at 2 per cent interest was granted to Britain to overcome her dollar shortage. Repayments were to begin in 1951 in fifty equal annual instalments. The loan was not as much as Britain had hoped for but the Canadians helped with an additional $1287 million. The total was sufficient to cover Britain's own immediate needs, including those of the British zone in Germany, though not those of the whole sterling area. The problems that arose related to some of the conditions the Americans had attached to the loan.

There was also the serious problem of the 'sterling balances'. (If all the sterling-area countries sought to convert their holdings of sterling at the same time, Britain could not have paid and would therefore have defaulted.) At Bretton Woods, Britain had reserved to herself the way she would settle the large sterling balances with her creditors during the transitional period, rather than accepting American help and making a joint Anglo-American approach to her creditors. Britain, with some justice, was suspicious of US anti-imperialist attitudes and did not wish the Americans to be able to meddle in Britain's Commonwealth and colonial relationships. Nevertheless these sterling balances were a Damocles sword overhanging the British economy because they were so large at $3,355 million. The United States in loan negotiations concluded in December 1945 made it a condition that within one year of drawing on the loan (that is, early in 1947) all *current* transactions by all the sterling-area countries should be freely convertible. As for the huge credits, the parties could do no more than reach an agreement in principle, without figures attached: some small part of these balances were to be immediately convertible to dollars; another tranche would become convertible in 1951; and as regards the rest Britain would seek agreement to write them off. Without figures this was a pretty meaningless arrangement, except that, in some magical way which no one could really envisage, the sterling balances would be made to disappear. There was much opposition to these American conditions in Britain, but there was little choice. They were accepted.

In February 1947 Britain honoured the loan agreement and made sterling convertible. The result was a disaster. The British Treasury could not control all the countries which now converted sterling into badly needed dollars. Not only current transactions as provided for in the loan agreement but some sterling balances held by other countries were converted as well. In August 1947, with the dollar reserves near exhaustion, Britain was forced to suspend convertibility. Her recovery was not far enough advanced to stand the strain. Exchange control was reintroduced and thus one important plank of Bretton Woods was abandoned. The Americans had misjudged the situation and had forced the issue of free convertibility too soon. By the 1950s sterling became partially convertible and in December 1958, almost thirteen years from the time of the first dollar loan, it became fully convertible. By then West European exports had recovered, the European dollar gap had disappeared and American overseas trade and expenditures were beginning to move into deficit. Other planks of Bretton Woods, however, continued to function for three decades. Fixed exchange rates were adjusted from time to time until they were abandoned in the early 1970s, to be reintroduced in the European Community in 1979 and in Britain in 1990 (to be abandoned by her in 1992).

Back in 1947, for Britain and Europe the situation would have become serious, with a new dollar gap in prospect once more, had not Marshall Aid come to the rescue the following year.

The effect of these abstract financial matters on the lives of ordinary people in Britain was very damaging. The manmade financial crisis came on top of an act of God, a terrible winter of heavy snowfall and ice. Coal was running out, unemployment temporarily soared, and now in the summer the government announced an austerity programme to cut imports. Rationing became more severe. Sir Stafford Cripps, gaunt and ascetic, symbolised the new era of austerity when he took charge of the Treasury as Chancellor of the Exchequer in November 1947. Food rations were small, though the population judged as a whole was in better health than before the war. Wages were low, and modest increases kept them low. Working people were asked to produce more without more pay – a theme to become familiar in the post-war era. Britain was probably one of the few countries in the world where a sense of fair play and discipline could make rationing work year after year without a large black market developing. Output in 1948 was already 36 per cent higher than before the war, and this production was being directed to support an export drive. Given the difficult conditions with which the government was faced, it could take credit for its achievements so far. 'Better times' for the people were nevertheless still a long way off. Full employment was taken for granted, so Labour would run into difficulties when people tired of the unending prospect of austerity.

Britain's dire financial plight forced the Cabinet to sort out British priorities in the rest of the world; Hugh Dalton, when at the Treasury (1945–7), constantly urged Ernest Bevin at the Foreign Office to cut back on Britain's overseas responsibilities. The Foreign Office, which rapidly came to admire him, had never known a Foreign Secretary like the tough, blunt and ebullient Bevin, proud of his working-class background and his long experience as leader of the largest trade union, the Transport and General Workers' Union; he had also been an effective Minister of Labour in Churchill's wartime coalition. Deeply committed to the democratic left, he was just as determined as Churchill not to allow communism any power base in Britain or in any region abroad where vital British interests were involved. Nor did he lag behind Churchill when it came to safeguarding Britain's empire. Thus he supported Churchill's policy of suppressing the communist-dominated front (EAM) in Greece (pages 380–1), despite vociferous protest from the British left, because, as he put it, 'the British Empire cannot abandon the position in the Mediterranean'. In Europe, Bevin in 1945 still regarded resurgent Germany as a greater danger than the Soviet Union. He shared Roosevelt's vision rather than Churchill's realism, however, in his belief that war could be avoided by a strong world organisation, the United Nations, with the United States, Britain and the Soviet Union guaranteeing the peace each in her own global region. Bevin was at first more ready than the Americans to accept the place of the Soviet Union in this scheme as having special interests and security concerns in Eastern and central Europe; he believed business could be done with Stalin. In the conduct of that business, Bevin's lifelong experience as a negotiator helped him to appreciate when to be tactically aggressive and when to be emollient. He did not wish to see the wartime Allies split into Eastern and Western blocs, and he was in any case suspicious of US policies. In speaking to Stalin in December 1945, he made it clear that Britain's intentions were peaceful, but that 'there was a limit beyond which we could not tolerate continued Soviet infiltration and undermining of our position'.

The hostility of Soviet propaganda until the summer of 1946 was directed mainly against Britain, with threats to Turkey and Iran and complaints about Allied policies in Germany souring British relations with the Soviet Union. In March 1946, at Fulton, Missouri, Churchill delivered his famous 'Iron Curtain' speech. He saw Britain in the front line of halting communist expansion and subversion beyond the Soviet Union's own acceptable sphere of power in Eastern Europe. He was now trying to get the Americans to take these threats seriously. Bevin also saw the Soviet threat but he had not yet given up trying to persuade Stalin to work out problems co-operatively while remaining firm towards him. A Western alliance directed against the Soviet Union would only provoke her, and Bevin regarded public condemnations such as Churchill had delivered as counter-productive. Patient firmness was Bevin's policy until 1948; meanwhile his suspicions of the Germans continued to play a considerable part in his European outlook.

Bevin's main worry was that the United States would carry out her stated intention of completely withdrawing her military forces from Europe. He therefore encouraged the French to play a role in Germany as Britain's ally, but the Anglo-French relationship was not an easy one. After much difficulty, particularly over the French desire to detach the Ruhr from Germany, something Britain opposed, the Dunkirk Treaty of alliance was concluded with the French on 4 March 1947. Its terms were designed to meet the danger of renewed German aggression, but it was also intended to serve as the nucleus of a Western European grouping of nations without causing offence to the Soviet Union and so ruining any chance of future agreement and co-operation. The grouping would strengthen social democracy internally in Western Europe – after all, the communist parties were strong in both France and Italy. In following this policy Britain provided the important lead that two years later became the sheet anchor of Western security, the North Atlantic Treaty Organisation.

In 1947, Bevin was faced with two difficult problem areas on opposite shores of the Mediterranean – Palestine and Greece. The intractable problem of Palestine did more than anything else to cast a shadow over his reputation and indeed over the morality of the whole of Britain's attitude to the persecuted Jews since before the war, when the British government had restricted the entry to Palestine of the Jews wishing to escape from Hitler's Germany to no more than 75,000 over a period of five years. As a result fanatical Zionists accused Britain of acting as an accomplice to the Holocaust, though other countries, especially the United States, were even more reluctant to accept Jewish refugees. During the war British warships had patrolled the Palestine coast and prevented escaping Jews from landing (the Jews were not inhumanely sent back, however, but were interned in Mauritius). This set the secret Jewish militia, the Haganah, against the British. More extreme groups, such as the Irgun Zwai Leumi (National Military Organisation) and a small terrorist group, the Fighters for the Freedom of Israel (known as the Stern Gang in Britain after their leader), began attacking British policemen and installations in 1943. In November 1944 the Stern Gang assassinated Lord Moyne, the British Resident Minister in Cairo. Nonetheless, the majority of Jews in Palestine and those who lived in Allied countries fought with Britain against the common enemy.

While the great majority of Zionists condemned terrorism, British sympathies for the Jews after the horrors they had suffered during the Second World War were tempered by the effect which terrorism against British soldiers had on British opinion. One of the worst incidents was the blowing up on 22 July 1946 of the King David Hotel in Jerusalem, which housed the British Army Headquarters. Ninety-one people were killed – forty-one Arabs, twenty-eight British, seventeen Jews and five of other nationalities. Another outrage which caused the deepest revulsion was the hanging of two British sergeants in 'reprisal' for the execution of two Irgun terrorists. In all, some 300 people lost their lives as a result of terrorism between August 1945 and September 1947, almost half of them British.

After the war, the British government was pilloried for continuing to prevent large-scale immigration of Jewish survivors interned in Europe. Truman pressed for 100,000 entry permits, a plea which Bevin condemned as cynical political pandering to American-Jewish voters. The newsreels meanwhile were showing film of the Royal Navy intercepting ramshackle boats overloaded with refugees and forcibly detaining the ragged passengers. The most famous of these interceptions concerned the *Exodus*. There was an outcry when the Jews were returned to Germany, of all places (page 453).

Britain's policy was far from heroic but she should not be saddled with all the blame for what happened. The search for a peaceful settlement between Arabs and Zionists had been going on since before the war. It always ran into the same blind alley. The Jews were not willing to live in an Arab state; they wished to create their own state in Palestine and to allow unrestricted access to all Jews who wanted to come. This meant some form of partition, which the Zionists would accept. But the Arabs rejected the partition of Palestine, so if partition was the only solution, it would have to be imposed on the Arabs by military force. Yet Britain was not willing to use her troops to fight the Arabs, given her widespread interests in the Arab Middle East. In any case, why should Britain alone be made responsible for the creation of a Jewish state in Palestine? It was an international obligation. Even that leaves open the question whether partition corresponded to justice for the Arabs.

There was thus a certain logic when Britain in April 1947 decided to end her thankless responsibilities and to hand them back to the United Nations, the successor of the international organisation which had conferred the Mandate on Britain. Britain gave the UN until 15 May 1948 to find a solution. But Bevin's last hope that the terminal date of British rule in Palestine might, as in India, force the contending parties to the conference table proved a vain one. Meanwhile Palestine gradually descended into civil war. It was not so much Britain that seemed to abandon the Jews to the apparently superior might of the Arabs surrounding them as the nations at the UN, which duly voted for partition but, just as Britain had done, then left the Arabs and Jews to fight out the consequences (pages 455–6). For the time being at least the British had safeguarded their own interests in the Middle East, and the Americans had done the same. That need to safeguard British interests, in the Mediterranean as well as the Middle East, also lay behind the support for the royal Greek Government against the communists.

It was largely due to British intervention that Greece was not taken over by the communists after German forces withdrew in October 1944. The Greeks had fought the invading Italians and Germans courageously in 1940–1, and had gone to defeat despite the spirited intervention of British troops. In December 1944 British troops returned, for Greece, with Turkey, occupied a vital strategic position in the eastern Mediterranean. Stalin had accepted Western predominance in Greece and did not challenge the British directly, but communist Albanian, Bulgarian and Yugoslav partisans provided aid to the communist-led Greek National Liberation Front (EAM), with its military wing, ELAS. EAM had earned the admiration of the Greek people by their resistance to the Germans during the occupation. George II, the Greek king, was in exile with his government in Cairo. The majority of the Greek people did not wish to return to pre-war political and social conditions, with the result that EAM received wide support among non-communists. Opposed to EAM and ELAS was another, much smaller republican resistance group, EDES. Fighting broke out in Athens in December 1944. With the assistance of the British, EAM was prevented from taking over the country. A truce was patched up in January 1945, but it was to provide no more than a pause in the mounting tension (with atrocities committed by both sides) that led to the outbreak of civil war in May 1946. Britain insisted on elections in March 1946, but these were boycotted by the left, so a right-wing government came to power and, with a plebiscite in his favour in September 1946, the King returned to Athens. British troops continued their support, but EAM retained strongholds in the devastated countryside.

By the time of the King's return the civil war had begun. For a country that had already suffered so much from foreign occupation and starvation during the war, this was the crowning tragedy. With the help of communist neighbours Bulgaria, Albania and Yugoslavia, EAM was able to continue the civil war for three years until October 1949. The great majority of the Greek people may have been in favour of change and moderate left policies, but the country was being destroyed by extremists.

The civil war in Greece played a major role in the post-war relations of the Second World War Allies. The communist insurrection, it was assumed,

A plebiscite in Greece in September 1946 decides in favour of the monarchists. Unrest grows on the eve of full-blown civil war.

was being masterminded from Moscow. As with later crises producing great international tensions, the 'domino theory' was brought into play. It was suggested in London and Washington that if Greece fell to communism the whole Near East and part of North Africa as well were certain to pass under Soviet influence. Bevin was in a dilemma. He had no sympathy for the corrupt royal Greek government and sensed that what the Greek people really wanted was social and political change. But his paramount motivation lay in his anti-communism. He was also constantly pressed by his colleagues not to squander Britain's limited financial resources in propping up the Greek regime with taxpayers' money. The Foreign Secretary decided on a bold stroke to help rivet US attention on the Soviet threat in the Mediterranean and at the same time relieve the financial burden on Britain. On 21 February 1947 he sent a message to Washington that British economic aid to Greece would have to be terminated by the end of March. Militarily the British actually continued to support the royalist government until the communists were defeated in 1949. The United States stood in the financial breach. This took the dramatic form of the Truman Doctrine announced on 12 March 1947, which pledged American help to defend the cause of the 'free peoples' (page 382).

The Truman Doctrine was followed in June 1947 by the offer of Marshall Aid. Bevin promptly responded by concerting with the French a positive Western European response. Stalin, on the other hand, ordered the Eastern satellite nations to pull out of the conference in Paris which met from July to September 1947 to discuss the details of Marshall Aid. The division of the East and West was becoming ever clearer, as was America's support for Western Europe. But this support still fell short of a firm military commitment, let alone an alliance. Thus in 1947, despite her weakened state, Britain was still the only major power which could be relied upon to defend Western Europe.

The breakdown in December 1947 of the London Foreign Ministers' Conference on the question of the future of Germany had finally convinced a reluctant Bevin that priority would have to be given to strengthening Western Europe economically and militarily. The communist coup in Czechoslovakia in February 1948 (pages 386–7) was interpreted in the West as signalling a new phase of Soviet aggression. Bevin was not willing to place total reliance on an American readiness to defend Western Europe and Western interests in the Middle East and Asia. It was true that Britain and Western Europe were shielded by the umbrella of the US monopoly of nuclear weapons, but America had only a small stockpile of atomic bombs and not until the Berlin crisis of 1948 were US bombers sent to Britain to act as deterrent to the Soviet Union. So Western Europe had to grasp the nettle of providing for its own defence. Bevin tackled this energetically. The outcome of his diplomatic efforts was the conclusion of the Brussels Treaty in March 1948, an alliance between Britain, Belgium, the Netherlands, Luxembourg and France. Its aims were not only to promote economic collaboration in Western Europe; Article IV provided for military assistance to any member of the alliance who became 'the object of an armed attack in Europe'. Although the preamble of the treaty referred only to Germany as a potential enemy, the defensive alliance applied to any aggressor in Europe – and the aggressor warned off in March 1948 was the Soviet Union. Britain had now joined a Western bloc and Bevin was its principal architect.

The Labour government's vision of acting as a peacemaker and mediator without exclusive alliances with any one group of nations, a vision which corresponded to a long tradition in British foreign policy, had been abandoned by Bevin and the Attlee Cabinet as the post-war dangers inherent in the Cold War became ever more apparent in 1948. But it was only a partial abandonment. Neither the Conservatives nor Labour intended to join a united Western Europe, a supra-national Europe. Britain's alliances with her continental neighbours were not exclusive: she valued her worldwide Commonwealth ties too highly. Bevin also believed that Western Europe was not strong enough to defend itself. For him, the Brussels Treaty was a stepping stone to a wider transatlantic alliance to be constructed when the United States was ready for it. In the event, that was not to be until 1949, when NATO was created. Thus in a significant sense the British Foreign Secretary was a principal architect of the most important Western alliance from 1949 to 1990. Bevin's desire that Western Europe should strengthen itself to avoid becoming a mere appendage of the United States was also sound. For many years, however, the power of the United States was dominant within the Western alliance.

CHAPTER 33

France: A Veil Over the Past

The Nazi victories in Europe cast a long shadow over all the countries the Germans occupied. For none is this more true than France. Hitler had allowed a French government to continue to function, and this Vichy regime under Marshal Henri Philippe Pétain enjoyed the support of the great majority of Frenchmen in 1940: for them the war was over. Vichy represented adjustment to the new realities and reconstructions, for the 'old France' had demonstrated her rottenness in defeat. There appeared to be no real alternative to 'honest collaboration', carrying out the terms the Germans had imposed. But where did honour end? Vichy militia and police helped the Germans to arrest other Frenchmen to be handed over to Gestapo torturers. Then the Jews were rounded up to be sent to their deaths in the east, not only the foreign refugees admitted before the outbreak of war, but French men, women and children. The war produced great heroes in France: men and women risking their lives for the persecuted, and for the Allied cause. But there were tens of thousands of Frenchmen who served Vichy France, some in important roles, others in minor capacities, from Pierre Laval, the Prime Minister to the lowliest policeman or civil servant. They made their living serving the state, and the great majority were able to continue their careers after the war, with no apparent stain on their character.

In France the situation changed only gradually in de Gaulle's favour, gaining added impetus after the German invasion of the Soviet Union in June 1941. The strong French Communist Party now reversed its policy of collaboration, and the resistance, until then scattered and weak, now with the adhesion of the communists developed into a strong movement. As the chances of German victory receded with defeats in Russia and North Africa, and as the Nazis more and more ruthlessly exploited the human resources of French labour, forcing many Frenchmen to work in German factories, so support for Vichy dwindled. In 1943 the various resistance groups agreed to combine, and, looking to de Gaulle in London for leadership, formed a National Council of Resistance with the help of a Gaullist emissary parachuted to France from England. Of course, this did not mean that all rival political ambitions had ended. While the communists fixed their eyes not only on liberation, but on a post-war communist transformation of France, de Gaulle skilfully laid his plans for frustrating them and for placing himself at the head of a national government. This meant controlling the resistance movement and subordinating it to his own administration. With liberation in 1944, the unity based on fighting the Germans came to an end, and France's political future stood shrouded in uncertainty. Would the communists take power? Would de Gaulle be able to do so? Or would there be a civil war and an Anglo-American occupation?

In the event, millions of ordinary people were now only too happy to identify with a French hero and to rally around a new saviour to replace the discredited eighty-year-old Marshal Pétain. With the help of the BBC, de Gaulle had projected the myth of an unconquerable France, and he himself fitted the desired image. It was an extraordinary feat, as he imbued the people with an inflexible faith in France and in the recovery of her rightful place as a world power, thereby relegating 1940 to no more than one defeat in battle that could not alter France's destiny. A gift for oratory enabled de Gaulle to do for France what Churchill had accomplished during the darkest hours of the war for Britain. Politicians in France, of all shades of belief, accepted de Gaulle as indispensable in the months immediately following the expulsion of the Germans. On 26 August 1944, in scenes preserved by the newsreel cameras, de Gaulle strode through liberated Paris, with snipers still firing from the rooftops. Even so, largely because of American reluctance, the Allies waited until October before granting full recognition to de Gaulle's provisional government.

In the resistance movement, the communists were the largest and most disciplined element. The socialists, as in Italy later, were divided on the issue of whether or not to collaborate with the Marxist communists in a broad-left front. The president of the Resistance Council was Georges Bidault, an anti-Marxist who identified with progressive Catholic aims; he headed a new party, the Mouvement Républicain Populaire (MRP), which after the communists and socialists formed the third and smallest group in the Resistance. But de Gaulle deliberately stood aloof from party politics in 1944 and 1945, refusing to lead any party of his own; he claimed to speak for France above parties. Yet, by stating as the aims of his policy the restoration of national greatness and the political, social and economic renovation of France, he appealed to popular feelings on the left: liberation from the Germans would go hand in hand with reform. Big business, which had collaborated with the Germans, and the conservative supporters of Vichy, as well as all those who had done well under German occupation, had to lie low politically. Until the eve of liberation, supporters of de Gaulle represented only a minority of Frenchmen; after liberation they were able to lay claim to the government without opposition.

How did this come about? The communists were on the spot, well armed and well organised. They had worked with the non-communist resistance under de Gaulle's aegis, but would they now capitalise on their strong position in the country to seize power? Again, as in Italy, the communists made no such bid to challenge de Gaulle directly. Their leader, Maurice Thorez, returned from Moscow in November 1944 and gave his public approval to communist co-operation with the other parties and their participation in a provisional government headed by de Gaulle. The French communists, like the Italian, had probably received their instructions from Moscow. The Germans were not yet defeated and it was in Russia's interest to maintain Allied unity. An open attempt by communists to take power in a Western country might alienate Britain and the United States. Stalin even thought that such an event could open the way to a change of alliances, the Western Allies siding with Germany against Russia – his ultimate fear. De Gaulle succeeded therefore more easily than anyone expected. The provisional government was able to establish its authority over the whole country, with the communists securing only the less important ministerial posts. The independent local committees and militia were dissolved without resistance. For two years, from 1944 to 1946, the communists participated in governments with the socialists and the MRP. Despite their strength, the communists could not dominate French politics in succeeding years and were excluded from government. De Gaulle's first period of office was short and ended in 1946, but he had already made a permanent impact on French politics.

During the first year de Gaulle had acted cautiously at home. The obligatory trials of prominent Vichy collaborators had taken place. The Vichy Prime Minister Pierre Laval was sentenced to death and executed, though Pétain's death sentence was commuted to life imprisonment. Newsreels showed pictures of girls with heads shaven for consorting with Germans. Wild summary 'justice' was meted out by the forces of Liberation; this gave opportunities, too, for the simple settling of old scores. The best estimate is that nearly 10,000 Frenchmen were killed. Regularly constituted law courts passed 7037 sentences of death, but most received the presidential pardon and only 767 executions were actually carried out. Of the just over 167,000 tried, almost half were acquitted and 27,000 received jail sentences. So the prisons were filled with collaborators. Even so, not all the French citizens who saw in Vichy a legitimate government which they actively supported could be tried. After 1950, less than

5000 remained in prison. The trials ceased. They had been intended to cleanse France from the Vichy taint. In fact the only practical policy was to draw a veil over the Vichy years, to conciliate and to unite the nation. It was left to a few ardent individuals to continue to the present day to uncover those responsible for Vichy crimes, much to the embarrassment of some of the older generation of Frenchmen. Somehow sleeping dogs will not lie; the whole war generation will have to pass away first.

The provisional government after Liberation was faced with daunting problems of restoring the dislocated and shattered French economy. There were grave shortages of food and fuel. The infrastructure of transport, bridges and railways had to be rebuilt. State intervention and the takeover of ailing industries were seen as necessary to enable the nation to recover rather than as policies in conformity with socialist ideology. The provisional government in 1945 responded to the demands of the resistance and nationalised the big banks, insurance, gas, electricity and coal as well as companies that, like Renault, had collaborated with the Germans. This created the large state sector of industry which has been characteristic of post-war France. Joint committees were set up in firms employing more than fifty workers to give employees a role and a stake in the success of the company. But hopes for 'industrial democracy' were unfulfilled, because employers continued to take the critical financial decisions. Employees did, however, gain from the increase of family benefits and the introduction of compulsory insurance. But this did little to relieve the grim economic situation. Workers' standards of living were under constant pressure from inflation. During the Vichy years (1940–4) retail prices had risen more than three times but hourly wages had only doubled. At the end of the war, with too much paper money chasing too few goods, prices shot up. There was much industrial unrest, made politically more dangerous because the largest union, the Confédération Générale du Travail (CGT), was controlled by the Communist Party. De Gaulle rejected the restrictive monetary policy necessary to reduce the flood of paper money held by the population and so defeat inflation and restore the value of the currency. Instead, to maintain his popularity, he decreed salary increases and simply postponed tackling France's economic problems.

Nevertheless, de Gaulle's greatest achievement must be recognised. He stopped France from sliding into a civil war between the active supporters of Vichy, including the police and militia, on the one side and the resistance on the other. Amid the chaos he used his enormous prestige as the embodiment of France to impose a centralised, unified state on the warring factions.

De Gaulle knew that, once the emergency was past and the war was over, the provisional government would need to be transformed into a democratically elected one, and the provisional state into a stable republic. Following a national referendum held in October 1945, the French people voted overwhelmingly for a new constitution to be framed and for a constituent assembly to be elected and given the task of drafting the constitution. In the unique post-war circumstances the left gained more seats in the Assembly than its usual electoral strength warranted, given that half the electorate tended to be conservative: the communists benefited most with 160 seats, and the socialists won 142. The new progressive Catholic Party, the MRP, also did surprisingly well, gaining 152 seats. The socialists and communists thus achieved an absolute majority in the Assembly of 586 deputies.

A deep rift soon opened up between de Gaulle and the majority in the Assembly on the question of the future constitution. De Gaulle was clear about the essentials: France must not relapse into the political instability of the Third Republic. He therefore insisted on a strong executive headed by the president, and on an assembly that would have a share in government but should not be able to exercise sovereign power. Meanwhile, in the Constituent Assembly the communists attempted to gain the agreement of the socialists to a common programme that would exclude the MRP, but the socialists, who held the key and had no wish to be swallowed up by the communists, insisted on a three-party (communist, socialist, MRP) alignment. The communists chose to bide their time, all parties agreeing to offer de Gaulle the presidency. In the complicated political manoeuvrings that followed, de Gaulle refused to give the communists any of the key ministries they claimed – War. Interior or Foreign Affairs – and threatened to resign. The socialists and MRP supported him, and the communists, faced with a choice of exclusion or participation, gave in. So the first round, with the critical help of the socialists and MRP, went to de Gaulle. The political crisis of November 1945 provoked by the communist demands was thus resolved and a government, headed by de Gaulle and comprising ministers drawn from all the major parties, was formed.

But the fundamental issue remained to be settled: despite deep divisions between the socialists and communists in the Assembly, it became clear that these two parties would reject de Gaulle's concept of a strong, independent presidency and executive in favour of leaving controlling powers with a parliamentary assembly. In many ways the Assembly was already asserting the right to make judgements on the policies that de Gaulle wished to adopt. On the constitutional question de Gaulle could count only on the support of the MRP, and he reacted with bitterness to the prospect of defeat in the Assembly. He believed that he could rely on the support of the mass of the French people. The politicians in the Assembly, he was convinced, were combining against him to safeguard their own selfish interests rather than those of France. Feeling nothing but contempt for the parliamentarians, he decided to force their hand. He confided to one of his ministers at this time,

> I don't feel that I am made for this kind of fight. I don't want to be attacked, criticised, challenged every day by men who have no other distinction than the fact that they got themselves elected in some little place in France.... I can't resign myself to enduring criticisms of parties and irresponsible men, to seeing my decisions challenged, my ministers criticised, myself attacked, my prestige diminished. Since I cannot govern as I wish, that is to say fully, rather than see my power dismembered, I'm going!

That conversation took place shortly before de Gaulle dropped his bombshell on 20 January 1946 and resigned.

His frustration and anger were genuine. All his policies abroad, in Germany, Indo-China and the Middle East, had experienced setbacks as well. But there was calculation too. He did not believe the nation would be able to manage without him. It was a tactical retreat and he expected to be recalled on conditions he himself would set. Several years later he acknowledged his miscalculation: 'I have made at least one political mistake in my life: my departure in January 1946. I thought the French would recall me quickly. Because they didn't do so, France wasted several years.'

After de Gaulle's resignation, the French people – influenced by his opposition – rejected the draft constitution in a referendum held in May 1946. Then a second constituent assembly was elected to draft an amended constitution. This gave women the vote, adopted proportional representation and created a second chamber but left the real political power in the lower chamber, the National Assembly, which also elected the president. The constitution resembled in most important respects that of the Third Republic and was to create the same governmental instability. But despite de Gaulle's strong opposition the new constitution was narrowly approved in a referendum in October 1946, nearly 8 million dissenting and just over 9 million in favour, with almost a third of the electorate not bothering to vote at all. It was an inauspicious start for the Fourth Republic.

Nineteen-forty-seven was a particularly bad year for France. Food became still scarcer in the cities, and coal production fell. Prices doubled. Workers whose real wages were rapidly diminishing came out on strike, needing little encouragement from the communist-controlled CGT. The Communist Party found itself in the spring of 1947 faced with a choice between remaining in the three-party government (with the MRP and the socialists), which opposed the strikes, and supporting the workers in their strike demands. Moreover, France's harsh policy of re-establishing her authority over the colonies, and the developing Cold War, made it increasingly difficult for the communists to collaborate with their coalition partners. The socialist Prime Minister solved the problem for them by dismissing the communist ministers. Despite their hold over the trade unions and their support among the electors, the communists could henceforth play only an oppositional role in French politics and society. They were not to regain a share of power in government for thirty-four years.

The stability of the Republic was also threatened from the right. Admirers of de Gaulle were secretly plotting to found a party as a vehicle for the General's early return. De Gaulle himself was thinking along the same lines and began recruiting supporters in the autumn of 1946 to set up a national movement drawing support from all Frenchmen to 'save France'. In April 1947, boosted by the wave of strikes, he went public in a speech in Strasbourg. He denounced the communists and proclaimed his new movement, a kind of anti-party party, calling for the 'Rally of the French People' under the banner of his leadership, the Rassemblement du Peuple Français (or RPF).

The question remained: if it was not a party, how would de Gaulle regain power under the constitution? The answer was far from clear, except that de Gaulle had no dictatorial intentions and would accept the presidency only if offered it constitutionally. But the movement still looked dangerously authoritarian, certainly unparliamentary, given de Gaulle's contempt for 'rigid parties' and his call for an 'orderly, concentrated state'. He promised that the movement would act within the framework of the law, but 'over and above differences of opinion', so that 'the great effort of common salvation and the profound reform of the state may be successfully undertaken'. It looked for a time as if de Gaulle would succeed, as millions of Frenchmen were ready to support him during that difficult year. In the local elections in October 40 per cent of the electorate gave their vote to candidates of the Rassemblement. But just four years later, in the elections for the new National Assembly in 1951, de Gaulle's support had nearly halved. The 'Gaullists' had become just another, albeit strong, parliamentary group. The game was up for the time being and two years later de Gaulle withdrew to the village of Colombey-les-Deux-Églises.

The economy of the Fourth Republic was recovering. A landmark in that recovery was the adoption in January 1947 by the National Assembly of what became known as the Monnet Plan. De Gaulle had appointed Jean Monnet after the Liberation to head a committee to prepare a plan for the reconstruction and modernisation of the French economy. Monnet's roots were deeply embedded in traditional France: he was born in 1888 in Cognac into a family of brandy distillers. But he learnt to combine his understanding of conservative France with the international experience he gained as a salesman for the cognac concern. In particular he was able to observe at first hand the drive, flexibility and efficiency of twentieth-century America. His international perceptions and idealistic belief in the betterment of society through co-operation were heightened by service for the League of Nations and the French government before the outbreak of war in 1939. Monnet joined the Free French and came to Britain after the débâcle of 1940; it was he who suggested to Churchill the idea of an Anglo-French union. In 1943 he became a member of the French Committee of National Liberation, for which he organised a group of experts. The work of his committee bore fruit in the plan he proposed in 1947. Monnet was to exert a lasting influence, not only on French economic planning, but on the co-ordination of the West European economies and the establishment of the Common Market. Drawing on his practical experience he passionately believed that collective action, nationally and internationally, was necessary to solve the problems confronting France and Europe.

The plans produced by his Commission, the Commissariat Général du Plan, were not directives, but targets and guides showing how the different elements of the economy could best be co-ordinated in order to achieve the proposed increases in production. Monnet had no intention of controlling industry as was done in communist countries. Much depended on his personal influence. The nationalised industries provided a good starting point because they were more amenable to government planning, and Monnet's Plan dealt primarily with improving supplies of fuel and energy, as well as with oil refineries, transport, steel, cement and tractors to increase agricultural productivity. The aim of the Plan was to raise industrial and agricultural output by 25 per cent over 1929 within three years. This would make possible a substantial rise in the standard of living. It was presented as an emergency plan of action. Instead it was to become a much more permanent institution with a series of five-year plans. The remarkable success of continuous economic planning based on long-term objectives contrasted with what appeared to be the hopelessly inefficient political scenario so characteristic of France. This political instability led many to underrate her fundamental strength.

In world affairs, France had not won an equal place with Britain in 1945. France's German policy of attempting to detach the Rhineland and the Ruhr achieved no success. The United States and Britain were co-ordinating and centralising western Germany, isolating France in her German occupation zone. De Gaulle's cherished hope of establishing France as a third force and as a bridge between the Anglo-Saxons and the Russians, which had led him to Moscow and to the conclusion of a new treaty between France and the Soviet Union in 1944, was an idle dream. Stalin had no intention of using de Gaulle as an intermediary, and the realities of the Cold War destroyed any notions of French bridge-building. In reasserting French colonial rights by the use of force in Madagascar, the Middle East, Algeria and Indo-China, France enmeshed herself in Third World struggles for independence which for more than two decades caused many deaths, bled her of resources and weakened her at home and abroad, only to end in failure. Finally, 1947 was a year of economic crisis and industrial unrest. Yet in retrospect, it was those very failures and difficulties which turned French thoughts in new directions.

French economic recovery was not possible without German economic recovery and Franco-German co-operation. De Gaulle was the first French statesman to offer the German people reconciliation but it was on condition that they became junior partners and accepted a weakened German state deprived not only of the Saar but also of the Rhineland and Ruhr, which would be internationalised and formed into a separate 'European' state. But such aims were as much opposed by the United States and Britain as they were by Germany. As conflicts with the Soviet Union deepened, so earlier anxieties receded. Germany was likely to remain divided between the West and the Soviet Union; control over armaments and the Ruhr would continue in any case. But west German support would have to be won: this meant concessions and no further amputations of German territory.

For the governments of the French Fourth Republic it was, therefore, not so much a perceived *direct* Russian threat, the fear that Soviet tanks would cross the Elbe and head for France, that provided the impetus for a change of policy; it was rather the realisation that French aims in continental Europe – dominance over Germany, bridge-building to the East and maintenance of French independence in the face of the Atlantic Anglo-Saxon powers – were doomed to failure as an indirect consequence of the Cold War. France herself was now threatened with isolation as Britain and the United States chose to start building up west Germany. France might, nevertheless, have taken her time to change course had it not been for her dire economic condition, which obliged the government to rely on American aid.

Internally and externally in 1947 pressures were thus mounting for a reorientation of French policies. There was soon tangible evidence that a new course was being followed. An Anglo-French treaty of alliance was concluded in March 1947 (the Treaty of Dunkirk) to reassure France as Germany revived, and as a first step towards closer economic and political collaboration in Western Europe. In June 1947, General George Marshall, the American Secretary of State, delivered his famous address at Harvard (page 382) promising American aid on condition that the European nations co-ordinated their planning. His proposal was welcomed in France, and Anglo-French agreement on how to proceed followed speedily. On the initiative of the French and British foreign ministers, Bidault and Bevin, the European nations were invited to a conference in Paris with the purpose of formulating their responses to Marshall's offer. West Germany was included in Marshall's plan for European economic co-operation (theoretically the German Eastern zone, all the nations under Soviet control and the Soviet Union were likewise included, but they were expected to reject the conditions of aid). Acceptance of Marshall Aid was as essential for France as it was for the other Western nations if recovery was to be accelerated. The Plan also held out the hope that Western Europe might one day be better able to maintain its independence from United States influence. De Gaulle realised this as quickly as anyone and the Gaullists called for a European union based on a federation of states. Although their motivation and aims of policy were by no means identical, the United States, Britain and France found their policies converging in 1947. Britain still saw herself as separate from continental Europe but also favoured a strengthening of the Western continental states through collaboration.

Thus, despite earlier differences, perhaps the most significant outcome of the early post-war years was not only the recovery of France, but the drawing together of Western Europe under Anglo-French leadership with firm United States support. The shape of the future Western Europe and the broad Atlantic economic partnership had begun to emerge in 1947. The shocks of the crisis years 1947 and 1948, the coup in Czechoslovakia and the Berlin blockade, created a sense of common danger which reinforced these ties, but Britain, having first provided a strong impetus, was to draw back from closer economic co-operation with the beginnings of West European integration in the 1950s.

CHAPTER 34

Italy: The Enemy Forgiven

Nazi Germany's principal ally during the Second World War was Benito Mussolini's fascist Italy. There had been much destruction, particularly of housing, as the Allied armies pushed up the Italian peninsula after their landings in the south, but the country's industrial north-east region, where the Germans surrendered without severe fighting taking place, would allow Italian industry to recover quickly. Agriculture too could be brought back to normal within one or, at most, two seasons. The immediate dislocation caused by the war was, nevertheless, enormous. Even though most Italian cities, unlike Germany's, had not been turned into rubble heaps, the standard of living of most Italians had dropped to subsistence level and below. Communications and infrastructure had to be rebuilt. Relief from abroad was essential if the poorest Italian families were not to starve, and it came principally from the United States. In 1945 Italy was producing less than half of what had been her Gross National Product in 1938, yet three years after the end of the war the Italian economy had already caught up with pre-war levels.

In many respects the Italians were in a more fortunate position than the Germans at the end of the war. Italy was not divided; it was occupied and in reality under the control of the Western Allies alone. The Allied perception of Italians, reinforced by the way the war came to an end in Italy, was far more favourable than their perception of the Germans. At about the same time in the autumn of 1944 as the Morgenthau Plan of pastoralisation and minimal living standards was being regarded as appropriate treatment for the Germans, Britain and the United States promised to help Italy recover from the wounds of war. Why the great difference? Mussolini had presided over a vicious puppet regime in northern Italy while the Allies in 1944 were slowly battling up the Italian peninsula. But the fighting had not been left to the Allies alone. A powerful anti-fascist partisan movement had attacked and harried the German troops and the Italian fascist militia. In this way the Italians had actively assisted in the liberation of their country. The Germans had fought for Hitler's Germany to the end.

The Allies had looked upon the fascists with contempt rather than hatred during the war. The Italian fascists, moreover, had not committed atrocities on the terrible scale of the Germans. Although Mussolini's regime was increasingly ready to accept German dictation, the Italian Army High Command during the Second World War had not become as depraved as much of the Wehrmacht leadership became; Italian generals had even shown resistance to criminal orders. The Italian people had tired of the war and genuinely welcomed the British and American troops as liberators. The cause of Italy was also assisted by the presence in the United States of a large Italian-American community whose members had not lost their love for their homeland: Roosevelt wanted to secure their support in the presidential election of 1944. Most importantly, the Italians themselves had overthrown Mussolini when the Fascist Grand Council and the King had dismissed him. The Allies were prepared to deal with his successor, Marshal Pietro Badoglio, even though he was the brutal conqueror of Abyssinia; what mattered most to them was that he was prepared to take Italy out of the war. The Italians were thus allowed by the Western Allies to change sides and become 'co-belligerents' – not exactly allies, but not enemies either.

Italy had achieved something remarkable. Without a revolution the old fascist establishment and the monarchy had transformed their fascist rule to one acceptable to the Allies. To all intents and purposes they had escaped the consequences of the Allied demand for 'unconditional surrender'. As far as Italy was concerned, the needs of war overrode other considerations in Allied counsels. For Churchill and the British, Badoglio and the monarchy represented the best bulwark against communism; the liberal politicians of the pre-fascist era had failed once and were not to be trusted again.

The southern half of Italy had always been predominantly conservative and royalist. With the Allied armies in the south and the Germans in the north, Italy was, in 1944, more physically split than ever. In central and northern Italy a coalition of anti-fascist parties was formed in September 1944 embracing all anti-fascists from the Liberals to Catholic Christian Democrats and from the socialists to the communists. Calling themselves the Committee of National Liberation, they demanded war against the German occupiers. By contrast, the King and his government, who had earned the contempt of many Italians by fleeing south to safety behind the Allied lines, seemed paralysed and hesitant. The Committee of National Liberation filled the vacuum and acted decisively, despite the German occupation of central and northern Italy. For this reason it became the effective political authority in Italy in 1945.

With 250,000 armed partisans, a fierce war was fought in the north against the well-armed German divisions. The partisans suffered heavy casualties in 1944 and 1945 but succeeded in liberating Milan and Italy's other northern cities even before Allied troops advancing from the south could reach them. Mussolini's puppet regime in the north collapsed and he tried to flee. He was captured by partisans and executed together with his mistress. Their bodies were then exposed to the savagery of public vengeance. The newsreels which showed these horrible scenes, though they shocked many in the West, provided a glimpse of the passions the war had aroused.

Why then did the communists not seek to exploit their organisational strength among the partisans of the centre and north and their military success in sweeping through the Po Valley during the spring of 1945, 'the wind from the north', to try to hold on to effective power? Palmiro Togliatti, the communist leader, a cool and calculating politician, had left Moscow and reached southern Italy a year earlier, in March 1944. He had immediately declared that the communists would collaborate with the royal government and anti-fascist parties and he did not waver from this course at the moment of victory in 1945. It is probable that the strategy had been co-ordinated in Moscow. The similarity with the attitude of the French communists is striking. Stalin was anxious to maintain Allied unity until the war was won, and indeed after; he had pressed for spheres of influence in the Europe overrun by the Allied armies and he now tried to demonstrate to the Western Allies that the communists in the sphere he accepted as Western would not be allowed to cause any trouble. Realism, so Stalin believed, dictated that the Western Allies, whose armies would conquer the whole of Italy, would also decide future politics in Italy. The Soviet recognition of Badoglio's royal government in the south in March 1944 sent this signal clearly. Stalin, of course, was also anxious as an obvious *quid pro quo* to have the Western Allies accept Soviet dominance in Eastern and central Europe. Moscow, therefore, urged the communist parties of the West to follow popular-front tactics, to bide their time and to gain strength by working constitutionally within the system.

Togliatti too was committed to a policy of caution. An insurrection now would only have been crushed by the Allies; the path of legality, on the other hand, guaranteed the survival of the Communist Party, particularly when it was combined with the call that all Italians should unite to defeat fascism and the Germans. Togliatti's aims were long-term, to rally the Italian masses to an Italian Marxist line *after* the war, to establish what he enigmatically called 'progressive democracy'. The inevitable drawback of his policies was that by supporting the royal government he also strengthened the anti-communist forces, which, as it turned out, have dominated Italian politics ever since 1945.

The party in greatest difficulty after the war was the 'other party' of the left, the socialists. Should it be ready now to unite the left, to gain a majority in the country and to collaborate with the communists? It was led by Pietro Nenni, a warm and popular 'man of the people' who believed that it was the disunity of the working class which had allowed Mussolini and the fascists to gain and retain power. Hence his decision after 1945 to urge close collaboration with the Communist Party. This policy eventually split the party in 1947, a majority following Nenni; a minority under Giuseppe Saragat distrusted Moscow and the communists, left the party on this issue and formed their own party, the Social Democrats.

The Christian Democrats were to play the decisive role in post-war Italian politics. The principal aim of the party was to re-establish the constitutional parliamentary state of the pre-fascist era. Fervour for reform varied among party members, those on the left being the keenest. But the Christian Democrats enjoyed one large electoral advantage: the full backing of the Vatican. The leader of the party, who dominated Italian politics in the immediate post-war years was Alcide De Gasperi, a practising Catholic. Although not solely a Catholic party, the Christian Democrats depended on the support of the Church for their electoral success. Yet De Gasperi was no mere captive of the Church. Despite Vatican disapproval he was ready to work with the communists in the National Liberation Council during the war and he encouraged communist participation in the post-war coalition governments until 1947. It served the interests of the governments he led after December 1945 not to drive the communists immediately into opposition.

In post-war Italy the Church resumed its enormous influence over the lives of believers, the Vatican and priests backing from their pulpits the Christian Democrats against the godless communists. The Christian Democrats succeeded in attracting by far the largest support of any one party. However, the alliance of Togliatti's communists and of Nenni's Socialist Party, both strongly based in industrial northern and in central Italy, obtained as much support as the Christian Democrats, but, with the Allies occupying Italy until the peace treaty was signed in 1947, they had to content themselves with the position of coalition partners in governments led by the Christian Democrat De Gasperi. The communists and their socialist allies were in any case anxious to prove their good behaviour as a non-revolutionary political grouping. Dominating the reborn trade unions, the communists urged restraint on the workers in the north, and at the end of the war ensured that the partisans gave up their arms, so ending any possibility of revolution. Were these tactics a betrayal of the working class and the revolution, as extreme-left theoreticians later claimed? Revolution in the circumstances prevailing in Italy was unlikely to have succeeded. Stalin would have given no support. The overwhelming strength of the Anglo-American armies, the fact that the partisans were not all communists and their need for Allied supplies against the Germans made the notion of a seizure of power in 1944 and 1945 quite unrealistic.

Despite the support the Church gave to the monarchy Italy became a republic in 1946, in response to a national referendum. The majority for the republic had been slender, reflecting the small preponderance of the left. A constituent assembly was elected at the same time, with three parties gaining most of the votes: the Christian Democrats secured 35 per cent, the socialists nearly 21 and the communists just under 19. The revived extreme right, quasi-fascists, managed to obtain 5.3 per cent. On crucial issues, communists and socialists behaved moderately, so that a constitution setting up a parliamentary form of government was agreed on in 1947. It left many issues ambiguous and would allow the shift to the right to continue.

All three government parties collaborated on the urgent task of post-war reconstruction; unemployment, rampant inflation and shortages of food created enormous difficulties for the government and people of Italy. Flour was brought in by the United Nations Relief and Rehabilitation Administration (UNRRA), largely financed by the United States. American emergency loans further emphasised Italy's dependence on the United States. Reconstruction, it was held, must precede socialisation. The fascist economic controls over industry were dismantled and private enterprise was favoured over state-run industry by the orthodox economists who dominated the Treasury. They had little faith in Keynesian interference in the economy, after years of a corporate fascist state. The trade unions won some relief for the workers against rising prices, but distress remained widespread, even though production picked up and the yield of the 1946 harvest was better than that of 1945. As elsewhere in Western Europe, the hard winter of 1946/7 caused a grave crisis in Italy. The first two years after the war were a period of great hardship for the Italian people, with 1 million unemployed in industry alone. It was followed by an extraordinary upswing of production, which cannot simply be attributed to Marshall Aid. It was dubbed an economic miracle, but its foundations had been laid in the hard years after the war. Confidence in the currency was restored. The danger of a communist political and economic takeover receded. De Gasperi underlined the waning need for communist and socialist support when he excluded those parties from his new government in the spring of 1947. With their departure the last vestiges of the wartime Committee of National Liberation vanished. The politics of war, of possible revolutionary change, were over and Italy was returning to a kind of normality. Thus in little more than two years a certain political stability had been attained, and vital issues such as the future control of industry, the monarch and the role of the Catholic Church had all been defined.

No former enemy was quite so rapidly forgiven nor so speedily embraced as a new ally as was Italy. In February 1947, unlike Germany, Italy secured a peace treaty. The loss of her colonies appeared a heavy blow at the time, but later it was to spare Italy the trauma of decolonisation suffered by the victors. The Western Allies demanded no reparations, and those paid to the injured victims in the Balkans and the USSR were kept to a modest level, funded by grants and loans supplied by the United States. Yet the Italians did not escape entirely unscathed. Besides losing their colonial territories, Italy also had to give up Albania and her wartime Balkan gains. The most bitterly disputed territory was the province of Venezia Giulia, until 1918 part of the Austro-Hungarian Empire, its port of Trieste populated predominantly by Italians. Italy had had little to show for her heavy losses in the First World War, and her 1918 gains had enormous emotional significance. But the Yugoslavs, who had suffered so much from German and Italian occupation, were in 1954 granted most of the territory by the wartime Allies, the Italians regaining control only of the city of Trieste itself, which was made a free territory.

Of great economic, as well as national and emotional, importance was another former Habsburg territory, the South Tyrol, its predominantly German-speaking population antagonised by Italian rule. The Italians had gained this territory with the blood of more than 1 million war dead in the Great War. They would not now lightly give up the Brenner Pass frontier or the hydroelectric power they had developed in this region. Hitler had recognised Italian sensitivities and had assured Mussolini that he harboured no designs on the Tyrol. The Allies in 1946 rejected Austrian claims, not to mention the wishes of the majority of the population. The Austrians, who had helped the Germans, were after all easier to deny than the Yugoslavs, who had fought with the Allies. Even so, the Italians were far from satisfied with the peace terms. They claimed that, having changed sides in 1943, they should have been better treated. No war or peace since the Risorgimento had ever fulfilled all Italian aspirations. But today Italy has overcome the evils of nationalism and only an occasional bomb in the South Tyrol serves as a reminder of past injustices in the new era of West European co-operation.

The Russians consented to the peace treaty, which might appear surprising in the Cold War climate of 1947. But the treaty also marked the logical outcome of the Yalta Agreements. The occupying powers' decisions were not to be challenged in the spheres of influence recognised by the Soviets. In return for agreeing to the Italian terms, the satellite regimes in Soviet-controlled Bulgaria, Romania and Hungary received recognition and peace treaties at the same time, as also did Finland. Their gains and territorial adjustments as allies of Germany were reversed, but the Soviet Union retained Bessarabia (Moldavia) and northern Bukovina, which they had first occupied in 1940. Finland had to confirm the cession of territory made to the USSR in 1940, and the Soviet Union in addition secured a fifty-year lease of the Porkkala naval base. Unlike the Balkan states, Finland never became a satellite and was allowed complete independence while following a policy friendly to the USSR. Relations proved so satisfactory that the Soviets returned the naval base in 1955.

From the start Italy was not treated as Germany was. Even under American occupation from 1945 to 1947, the military supervisory government dropped the word 'Control' from its title of Allied Commission. Fascism was suppressed, but political life never came to a standstill. After the peace treaty, Italy participated on the same terms as France and Britain in the Marshall Plan (though receiving much less) and could take her place in the United Nations. Italy had been treated generously, and harboured no grudges against the nations that had defeated her. Italians escaped too the heavy burden of guilt that would continue to haunt the German people for more than a generation.

SUGGESTIONS FOR FURTHER READING

CONTENTS

This bibliography represents only a fraction of the immense, rich and varied literature concerned with the history of the twentieth-century world. On the whole I have concentrated on books available in English – either written in that language or in translation. (English has become something of a universal language but that does not mean of course that *all* the most important works of scholarship are available in English.) It is fortunate that many books have appeared in paperback and these are marked with an asterisk. Hardcover editions of those paperbacks which are out of print are frequently available in libraries. In the first instance I have chosen books which provide an overview of large subjects, as these are likely to be particularly useful to the student and general reader. The main difficulty is to know how many books of detailed scholarship additionally to cite. In compiling not too long a reading list, I have made some pretty arbitrary judgements. The suggestions made here should not, therefore, be regarded as including all the more important books. My aim has been a different one: to provide a list of further reading which will introduce the reader to some of the complexities and controversies of interpretation which syntheses tend to iron out. I should have liked to mention all the books from which I have profited, but unfortunately that is not practicable. This is not so much a bibliography, then, as a useful starting point for further study. (Quotations from the papers of Neville Chamberlain are cited by permission of the University of Birmingham, and quotations from the unpublished Goebbels diaries are from the microfilm at Stanford University.)

1. GENERAL HISTORIES

Two stimulating world histories are P. Johnson, *Modern Times: History of the World from 1920s to 1990s**, a revised edition of a book first published in 1983 (Weidenfeld & Nicolson, 1992), and T. E. Vadney, *World since 1945: A Complete History of Global Change from 1945 to the Present**, revised edn (Penguin, 1992). Older but still useful, D. C. Watt, F. Spencer and N. Brown, *A History of the World in the Twentieth Century*, really three books in one, is a more detailed treatment (Hodder & Stoughton, 1967). G. Barraclough examines some underlying forces in *An Introduction to Contemporary History* (Penguin, 1969). *The New Cambridge Modern History* had two shots at covering the twentieth century, a volume edited by D. Thomson, *The Era of Violence 1898–1945* (Cambridge, 1960), which was incomplete for events after 1933, and C. L. Mowat's *The Shifting Balance of World Forces, 1898–1945* (Cambridge, 1968). Both volumes contain good individual narrative chapters. Two French interpretations are M. Crouzet, *L'Epoque contemporaine: á la recherche d'une civilisation nouvelle* (5th edn, Presses Universitaires, 1969); and a factual overview, J. Bouillon, P. Sorlin and J. Rudel, *Le Monde contemporaine* (13th edn, Bordas, 1968). For a good introduction to the forces shaping culture and society, see M. Biddiss, *The Age of the Masses** (Penguin, 1977).

EUROPE. J. Joll, *Europe since 1870** (Penguin, 1990) is outstanding; also excellent is H. S. Hughes, *Contemporary Europe: A History* (4th edn, Prentice-Hall, 1976). Three volumes of the Rise of Modern Europe series cover the first half-century: O. J. Hale, *The Great Illusion, 1900–1914**, R. J. Sontag, *A Broken World 1919–1939**; and G. Wright, *The Ordeal of Total War, 1939–1945** (Harper & Row, 1971 and 1968), all well worth reading.

EASTERN ASIA. J. K. Fairbank, E. O. Reischauer and A. M. Craig, *China: Transition and Transformation** (2nd edn, Unwin & Hyman, 1989); H. Tinker, *South Asia: A Short History** (Praeger, 1966); D. G. E. Hall, *A History of South-east Asia* (3rd edn, Macmillan, 1968); E. O. Reischauer and A. M. Craig, *Japan: Tradition and Transformation** (2nd edn, Unwin & Hyman, 1989).

AFRICA. The best one-volume history from origins to independence is J. D. Fage, *A History of Africa** (2nd edn, Unwin Hyman, 1993).

LATIN AMERICA. B. Keen, *A History of Latin America* (vol. 2, 4th edn, Houghton Mifflin, 1992) provides an excellent survey of the nineteenth and twentieth centuries.

THE MIDDLE EAST. Two good general surveys are P. Mansfield, *The Middle East** (Penguin, 1992) and W. R. Polk, *The Arab World Today** (4th edn, Harvard, 1991). A. H. Hourani, *A History of the Arab Peoples** (Faber & Faber, 1991) and M. E. Yapp, *The Near East since the First World War** (Longman, 1990) are also useful.

THE WORLD ECONOMY. For a one-volume survey, see H. van der Wee, *Prosperity and Upheaval: The World Economy 1945–1980** (Penguin, 1991). In the same series the first half of the century is covered in more detail by D. H. Aldcroft, *The European Economy, 1914–1990** (Routledge, 1989). See also A. S. Milward, *War, Economy and Society, 1939–1945** (Methuen, 1987). An interesting theory of modernisation and economic development is propounded by W. W. Rostow, *The World Economy: History and Prospect* (Macmillan, 1978). W. Ashworth, *A Short History of the International Economy since 1850** (4th edn, Longman, 1987); W. M. Scammell, *The International Economy since 1945** (2nd edn, Macmillan, 1983); and F. B. Tipton and R. Aldrich, *An Economic and Social History of Europe, 1890 to the Present** (2 vols, Macmillan, 1983) are of value.

WORLD INTERNATIONAL RELATIONS. Two good textbooks are available in paperback: the well-tried P. Calvocoressi, *World Politics since 1945** (7th edn, Addison Wesley Longman, 1996) and W. R. Keylor, *The Twentieth Century World: An International History** (3rd edn, Oxford, 1997). These can be supplemented by J. A. S. Grenville, *The Major International Treaties, 1914–1945: A History and Guide with Texts*, and J. A. S. Grenville and B. Wasserstein, *The Major International Treaties since 1945: A History and Guide with Texts* (Methuen, 1987). Contemporary problems and their origins are set out in G. Segal, *The World Affairs Companion** (new edn, Simon & Schuster, 1991).

2. SOME GENERAL NATIONAL HISTORIES

FRANCE. From among the rich choice, A. Cobban, *A History of France, 1871–1961** (vol. 3, Penguin, 1961) remains one of the best introductions. It may be supplemented by Georges Dupeux, *French Society, 1789–1970** (Methuen, 1976), a very useful survey with statistics. See also W. L. Shirer, *The Collapse of the Third Republic** (Pan, 1969); T. Zeldin, *France, 1849–1945** (2 vols, Oxford, 1979); and J. Néré, *La Troisième République* (Oxford, 1967). A lucid one-volume survey with a good bibliography is J. F.

McMillan, *Twentieth Century France** (Arnold, 1992). For a good social and economic analysis, see C. Flockton and E. Kofman, *France** (Paul Chapman, 1989). For France since the First World War, a sound general treatment is H. Tint, *France since 1918** (2nd edn, Batsford, 1980). M. Larkin, *France since the Popular Front: Government and People 1936–1986** (Oxford, 1988) covers the later years.

GERMANY. There are a number of excellent one-volume histories, including W. Carr, *A History of Germany, 1815–1990** (4th edn, Arnold 1991) and Hajo Holborn, *A History of Modern Germany* (Knopf, 1969). G. Mann, *The History of Germany since 1789** (Penguin, 1974) offers a personal and stimulating view. A well-written survey paying attention to the 'moods' of different periods is Gordon A. Craig, *Germany, 1866–1945* (Oxford, 1978). A critical analytical study is V. R. Berghahn, *Modern Germany: Society, Economy and Politics in the Twentieth Century** (2nd edn, Cambridge, 1988).

ITALY. D. Mack Smith, *Italy: A Modern History* (revised edn, Michigan, 1969); C. J. Lowe and F. Marzari, *Italian Foreign Policy, 1870–1940* (Routledge, 1975); S. B. Clough, *Economic History of Modern Italy* (Columbia, 1968); A. C. Jemolo, *Church and State in Italy, 1850–1950* (Blackwell, 1960); R. A. Webster, *Christian Democracy in Italy, 1860–1960* (Hollis & Carter, 1961); C. Seton-Watson, *Italy from Liberalism to Fascism, 1870–1925* (Methuen, 1967). In addition there are a number of excellent one-volume histories to choose from: P. Ginsborg, *A History of Contemporary Italy: Society and Politics, 1943–1988** (Penguin, 1990); N. Kogan, *A Political History of Postwar Italy** (Praeger, 1983); M. Clark, *Modern Italy, 1871–1995** (Addison Wesley Longman, 1996); and H. Hearder, *Italy: A Short History** (Cambridge, 1990).

BRITAIN. There are some very good general histories; among the older, C. L. Mowat, *Britain between the Wars** (Methuen, 1968) has stood the test of time well. For a comprehensive account, among the most reliable and perceptive is W. N. Medlicott, *Contemporary England, 1914–74** (Longman, 1976). A. J. P. Taylor, *English History, 1914–45** (Oxford, 1965) is stimulating. A good recent account is T. O. Lloyd, *Empire to Welfare State: English History, 1906–92** (4th edn, Oxford, 1992); see also W. N. Medlicott, *British Foreign Policy since Versailles, 1919–63** (2nd edn, Methuen, 1968). For brief and perceptive accounts, see D. Thomson, *England in the Twentieth Century** (Penguin, 1965) and H. Pelling, *Modern Britain, 1885–1955* (Nelson, 1960). A fresh approach is offered in A. Marwick, *Britain in the Century of Total War** (Penguin, 1971). The best survey of Britain and her Commonwealth is W. D. McIntyre, *The Commonwealth of Nations: Origins and Impact, 1869–1971* (Minnesota, 1977). R. R. James, *The British Revolution: British Politics, 1880–1939** (Methuen, 1978) is very good. For the period before 1915 there is an outstandingly good paperback, R. Shannon, *The Crisis of Imperialism, 1865–1915** (Paladin, 1976). For post-1945 Britain there are two excellent one-volume histories, K. O. Morgan, *The People's Peace: British History, 1945–1990** (Oxford, 1991) and A. Sked and C. Cook, *Post-War Britain: A Political History, 1945–1992** (4th edn, Penguin, 1993).

TSARIST RUSSIA AND THE SOVIET UNION. A good recent survey is J. N. Westwood, *Endurance and Endeavour: Russian History, 1812–1992** (Oxford, 1993). For the last decades of Tsarist Russia, see L. Kochan, *Russia in Revolution** (Paladin, 1970). An invaluable analysis of Tsarist society is R. Pipes, *Russia under the Old Regime** (Penguin, 1977). M. T. Florinsky, *The End of the Russian Empire** (Collier-Macmillan, 1961); B. Dmytryshyn, *USSR: A Concise History** (3rd edn, Scribner, 1978); and M. McAuley, *Soviet Politics, 1917–1991** (Oxford, 1992) are also useful. A good survey that takes the collapse of the USSR into account is G. Hosking, *A History of the Soviet Union, 1917–1991** (HarperCollins, 1992). The history of the freed Baltic nations can be studied in J. Hiden, *The Baltic Nations and Europe: Estonia, Latvia and Lithuania in the Twentieth Century** (Longman, 1991).

HABSBURG EMPIRE AND AUSTRIA. C. A. Macartney, *The Habsburg Empire, 1790–1918* (Weidenfeld & Nicolson, 1969) is probably the best general survey in any language. For a good study in German, see E. Zöllner, *Geschichte Österreichs* (4th edn, Munich, 1970). See also A. J. P. Taylor, *The Habsburg Monarchy, 1815–1918** (Penguin, 1964); A. J. May, *The Habsburg Monarchy, 1867–1914* (Cambridge, Mass., 1951); R. Kann, *The Multinational Empire* (2 vols, Columbia, 1964). For the history of the Austrian republic, Karl R. Stadler, *Austria* (Benn, 1971) is sympathetic and outstanding.

UNITED STATES. There are many excellent general histories of the United States and many others besides those here mentioned could equally well be commended. In paperback there is William Miller, *A New History of the United States** (Paladin, 1970). For a well-written and beautifully produced one-volume history, see M. B. Norton, D. Katzman, P. Escott, T. Patterson, H. Chardacoff and W. Tuttle, *A People and a Nation: A History of the United States* (2nd edn, Houghton Mifflin, 1986); two good surveys are D. Grantham, *Recent America: The United States since 1945** (Harlan Davidson, 1987) and W. La Feber,

The American Century: A History of the United States since the 1890s (4th edn, McGraw-Hill, 1991). A concise economic history is H. N. Scheiber, H. G. Vatter and H. V. Faulkner, *American Economic History* (9th edn, Harper & Row, 1976). See also J. A. Garraty, *The American Nation** (7th edn, Harper & Row, 1990). For a broad view, see R. H. Wiebe, *The Search for Order, 1877–1920* (Greenwood, 1980). Foreign policy is carefully surveyed in S. F. Bemis, *A Short History of American Foreign Policy and Diplomacy* (Holt, 1959).

CHINA. J. Chesneaux, F. Le Barbier and M.-C. Bergère, *China from the Opium Wars to the 1911 Revolution** (Harvester, 1976) and *China From the 1911 Revolution to Liberation** (Harvester, 1977) provide a sound factual survey, though somewhat disjointed. For a stimulating analysis and good narrative, see J. E. Sheridan, *China in Disintegration, 1912–49** (Collier-Macmillan, 1977). Brief but informative is M. Gasster, *China's Struggle to Modernize** (Knopf, 1972). See also J. Ch'en, *China and the West** (Hutchinson, 1979); I. C. Y. Hsü, *The Rise of Modern China* (4th edn, Oxford, 1992); A. Feuerwerker, *The Chinese Economy, 1870–1911* (Michigan, 1969); and *The Chinese Economy, 1912–49* (Michigan, 1977). Information on many aspects is to be found in C. Mackerras and A. Yorke, *The Cambridge Handbook of Contemporary China** (2nd edn, Cambridge, 1991) and B. Hook and D. Twitchett, *The Cambridge Encyclopaedia of China* (Cambridge, 1991). The doyen of America's historians of China, J. K. Fairbank, has produced *China: A New History** (Harvard, 1992). The authoritative multi-volume history of China is *The Cambridge History of China*, vol. 10 (*1800–1911*, pt 1), ed. J. K. Fairbank; vol. 11 (*1800–1911*, pt 2), ed. J. K. Fairbank and Kwang-Ching Liu; vol. 12 (*1912–1949*, pt 1), ed. J. K. Fairbank; vol. 13 (*1912–1949*, pt 2), ed. J. K. Fairbank and A. Feuerwerker; vol. 14 (*1949–1965*), ed. R. MacFarquar and J. K. Fairbank; vol. 15 (*1966–1982*), ed. R. MacFarquar and J. K. Fairbank (Cambridge, 1978–92). See also S. Karnow, *Mao and China: Inside China's Cultural Revolution** (Penguin, 1985); M. Yahuda, *Towards the End of Isolationism: China's Foreign Policy after Mao* (Macmillan, 1985); J. Gittings, *China Changes Face: The Road from Revolution, 1949–1989** (Oxford, 1990); C. Riskin, *China's Political Economy: The Quest for Development since 1949* (Oxford, 1987). An account by Chinese scholars of the development of the economy can be found in *China's Socialist Economy: An Outline History (1949–1984),** ed. Liu Suinian and Wu Qungan (Beijing Review, 1986).

JAPAN. Among the best one-volume histories is R. Storry, *A History of Modern Japan** (Penguin, 1976). Another good survey is W. G. Beasley, *The Rise of Modern Japan** (Weidenfeld & Nicolson, 1990). Full of stimulating insights is E. O. Reischauer, *The Japanese* (Harvard, 1977). On Japan's relations with the West, see R. Storry, *Japan and the Decline of the West in Asia, 1894–1943** (Macmillan, 1979). See also K. B. Pyle, *The New Generation in Meiji Japan* (Stanford, 1969); I. Nish, *Japanese Foreign Policy, 1869–1942* (Routledge, 1977); M. Schaller, *The American Occupation of Japan: The Origins of the Cold War in Asia* (Oxford, 1986). A lively and critical account is J. Woronoff, *Politics the Japanese Way** (St Martin's, 1990). For the book of a first-rate BBC Television series, see W. Horsley and R. Buckley, *Nippon New Superpower: Japan since 1945* (BBC Publications, 1990). See also M. Morischima, *Why Has Japan 'Succeeded'?: Western Technology and the Japanese Ethos* (Cambridge, 1982).

SOME OTHER COUNTRIES. R. Carr, *Spain, 1808–1939* (Oxford, 1966); H. V. Livermore, *A New History of Portugal** (2nd edn, Cambridge, 1976); J. Rothschild, *East Central Europe between the Two World Wars** (Washington, 1975); H. Roos, *History of Modern Poland* (Eyre & Spottiswoode, 1966); A. Polonsky, *Politics in Independent Poland, 1921–39* (Oxford, 1972). H. G. Skilling (ed.), *Czechoslovakia, 1918–88: Seventy Years from Independence* (Macmillan, 1991); H. G. Skilling, *Czechoslovakia's Interrupted Revolution* (Princeton, 1976); B. Lewis, *The Emergence of Modern Turkey* (2nd edn, Oxford, 1968); A. G. Mazour, *Finland between East and West* (Greenwood, 1975); V. S. Vardys and R. J. Misinnas (eds), *The Baltic States in Peace and War, 1917–45* (Pennsylvania, 1978); C. P. Woodhouse, *Modern Greece: A Short History** (4th edn, Faber & Faber, 1986); R. Clogg, *A Short History of Modern Greece** (2nd edn, Cambridge, 1986); T. B. Millar, *Australia in Peace and War* (Hurst, 1978); P. Mansfield, *The Ottoman Empire and Its Successors** (Macmillan, 1973); B. N. Pandey, *The Rise of Modern India* (Macmillan, 1967).

3. ORIGINS AND COURSE OF FIRST WORLD WAR

ORIGINS. The classic account is the immensely detailed L. Albertini, *The Origins of the War of 1914* (3 vols, Oxford, 1952–7). A 'revisionist' debate over German war-guilt began with F. Fischer, *Griff nach der Weltmacht* (Droste, 1961), translated as *Germany's Aims in the First World War* (Chatto & Windus, 1967). These ideas were supported and supplemented in V. R. Berghahn's excellent study, *Germany* *and the Approach of War in 1914** (Macmillan, 1973). By far the best book on British policy is Z. Steiner, *Britain and the Origins of the First World War** (Macmillan, 1977). For the foreign policy of Austria-Hungary there is the well-researched and sympathetic study by F. R. Bridge, *From Sadowa to Sarajevo* (Routledge, 1972). A good brief introduction is L. C. F. Turner, *Origins of the First World War** (Arnold, 1970); see also J. Röhl, *Delusion or Design* (Elek, 1973). For Serbian policies, see V. Dedijer, *The Road to Sarajevo* (MacGibbon & Kee, 1967). For a French view, see P. Renouvin, *La Crise européenne et la Première Guerre Mondiale* (4th edn, Presses Universitaires, 1962). The outstanding account of British relations with Germany is P. Kennedy, *The rise of the Anglo-German Antagonism, 1860–1914* (Allen & Unwin, 1980). The best general synthesis is J. Joll, *The Origins of the First World War** (Longman, 1992). See also John C. G. Röhl, *The Kaiser and His Court* (Cambridge, 1996).

MILITARY. P. M. Kennedy (ed.), *The War Plans of the Great Powers, 1880–1914* (Allen & Unwin, 1979); C. Falls, *The Great War** (Putnam, 1961). An older study still useful for the western front is Basil Liddel Hart, *History of the First World War**, first published in 1930, also in paperback (Pan, 1972). For links between strategy and politics, see L. L. Farrar, *The Short War Illusion** (Clio, 1973) and M. Kitchen, *The Silent Dictatorship* (Croom Helm, 1976). For the conflict between Russia, Germany and Austria-Hungary, see N. Stone's stimulating assessment in *The Eastern Front* (Hodder & Stoughton, 1975). See also J. M. Bourne, *Britain and the Great War, 1914–1918** (Arnold, 1989).

GENERAL AND DIPLOMATIC. M. Ferro, *The Great War 1914–18** (Routledge, 1973); Z. A. B. Zeman, *A Diplomatic History of the First World War* (Macmillan, 1971); E. R. May, *The World War and American Isolation, 1914–17** (Times Books, 1966); E. Kedourie, *England and the Middle East: The Destruction of the Ottoman Empire, 1914–21* (Harvester, 1977); V. H. Rothwell, *British War Aims and Peace Diplomacy* (Oxford, 1971); D. Stevenson, *First World War and International Politics* (Oxford, 1987); B. Hunt and A. Preston (eds), *War Aims and Strategic Policy in the Great War, 1914–18* (Croom Helm, 1977); R. A. Kann, B. K. Kiraly and P. S. Fichtner (eds), *The Habsburg Empire in World War I* (Columbia, 1977); A. Marwick, *The Deluge: British Society and the First World War** (Macmillan, 1973).

4. THE RUSSIAN REVOLUTION 1917

W. H. Chamberlin, *The Russian Revolution, 1917–22** (2 vols, Grosset, 1965) was written close to the events it describes, a vivid portrait first published in 1935. See also A. B. Ulam, *Lenin and the Bolsheviks** (Fontana, 1969); E. H. Carr, *The Bolshevik Revolution 1917–23** (3 vols, Penguin, 1950–3); S. P. Melgunov, *Bolshevik Seizure of Power** (Clio, 1972); I. Deutscher, *The Prophet Armed: Trotsky, 1879–1921** (Oxford, 1954) and *The Prophet Unarmed: Trotsky, 1921–9** (Oxford, 1970). E. H. Carr's classic fourteen-volume *History of Soviet Russia* is likely to be studied only by the specialist; the first three volumes have already been cited under their sub-heading, *The Bolshevik Revolution*; E. H. Carr distilled the multi-volume work into one very readable volume to serve as a general introduction, entitled *The Russian Revolution: From Lenin to Stalin, 1917–29** (Macmillan, 1980). See also under national histories. More recent works include E. Acton, *Rethinking the Russian Revolution* (Arnold, 1990); E. Mawdsley, *The Russian Civil War** (Allen & Unwin, 1987); and, from the doyen of American historians, R. Pipes, *The Russian Revolution, 1899–1919** (Collins Harvill, 1990).

5. PEACEMAKING AND DIPLOMACY IN THE 1920s

For a good synthesis, see A. Sharp, *The Versailles Settlement: Peacemaking in Paris, 1919** (Macmillan, 1991). For British policy, see E. Goldstein, *Winning the Peace: British Diplomatic Strategy, Peace Planning and the Paris Peace Conference* (Cambridge, 1991). See also S. P. Tillman, *Anglo-American Relations at the Paris Peace Conference of 1919* (Princeton, 1961); H. Nicolson, *Peacemaking, 1919* (Constable, 1934); J. M. Keynes, *The Economic Consequences of the Peace* (reprint, Macmillan, 1976); E. Mantoux, *The Carthaginian Peace* (reprint, Arno, 1978); J. M. Blum, *Woodrow Wilson and the Politics of Morality* (Little, Brown, 1956); A. S. Link, *Wilson the Diplomatist** (Johns Hopkins, 1957). For a brief general survey, see G. Schulz, *Revolutions and Peace Treaties, 1917–20** (Methuen, 1972). Also of value are H. I. Nelson, *Land and Power: British and Allied Policy on Germany's Frontiers, 1916–19** (David & Charles, 1971); and A. Mayer, *Politics and Diplomacy of Peacemaking: Containment and Counter-revolution at Versailles*

1918–1919 (Weidenfeld & Nicolson, 1968). A good general survey is S. Marks, *The Illusion of Peace: International Relations in Europe, 1918–33** (Macmillan, 1976). J. Jacobson, *Locarno Diplomacy* (Princeton, 1972) is based on new research. Also important is P. Wandycz, *France and Her Eastern Allies, 1919–25* (Minneapolis, 1962), and *Soviet-Polish Relations, 1917–21* (Harvard, 1969). See also R. Ullman, *Anglo-Soviet Relations, 1917–21* (3 vols, Princeton, 1961–7); F. P. Walters, *A History of the League of Nations* (2 vols, Oxford, 1952); H. A. Turner, *Stresemann and the Politics of the Weimar Republic* (Greenwood, 1979). Interesting contributions are to be found in H. A. Turner (ed.), *European Diplomacy between Two Wars, 1919–1939** (Quadrangle, 1972). Also useful are G. A. Craig and F. Gilbert, (eds), *The Diplomats, 1919–39** (2 vols, Athenaeum, 1963); and A. Orde, *Great Britain and International Security, 1920–36* (Royal Historical Society, 1978).

6. CHINA AND JAPAN AND THE WEST BEFORE THE SECOND WORLD WAR

CHINA. V. Purcell, *The Boxer Uprising* (Cambridge, 1963); Y. C. Wang, *Chinese Intellectuals and the West, 1872–1949* (Carolina, 1966); M. C. Wright, *China in Revolution: The First Phase, 1900–13** (Yale, 1971); J. E. Rue, *Mao Tse-tung in Opposition, 1927–35* (Stanford, 1966); Lucien Bianco, *Origins of the Chinese Revolution** (Stanford, 1971); C. Tse-tung, *The May Fourth Movement: Intellectual Revolution in Modern China* (Harvard, 1960); R. C. Thornton, *China: The Struggle for Power, 1917–72** (Indiana, 1973); J. Gittings, *The World and China, 1922–72* (Eyre Methuen, 1974); J. Ch'en, *Mao and the Chinese Revolution** (Oxford, 1968). See also under national histories.

JAPAN. J. Livingston, J. Moore and F. Oldfather, *The Japan Reader: Imperial Japan, 1800–1945** (Penguin, 1976); A. Iriye, *After Imperialism** (Athenaeum, 1973); R. Storry, *Japan and the Decline of the West in Asia, 1894–1943** (Macmillan, 1979); A. D. Coox and H. Conroy (eds), *China and Japan: Search for Balance since World War I* (Clio, 1978); J. B. Crowley, *Japan's Quest for Autonomy: National Security and Foreign Policy, 1930–8* (Princeton, 1966); R. D. Burns and E. M. Bennett (eds), *Diplomats in Crisis** (Clio, 1975); *The Cambridge History of Japan: The Twentieth Century*, ed. P. Duus (Cambridge, 1989); W. E. Beasley, *Japanese Imperialism, 1894–1945* (Oxford, 1987).

7. THE DEPRESSION YEARS: THE UNITED STATES, BRITAIN AND FRANCE

GENERAL. P. Fearon, *The Origins and Nature of the Great Slump, 1929–32** (Macmillan, 1979) surveys the literature and sums up. J. K. Galbraith, *The Great Crash 1929** (new edn, Deutsch, 1980) is a stimulating account. More technical are D. H. Aldcroft, *From Versailles to Wall Street: The International Economy, 1919–29* (Allen Lane, 1971); and C. P. Kindleberger, *The World in Depression, 1929–39* (Allen Lane, 1973). See also D. E. Moggridge, *Keynes** (Fontana, 1976).

UNITED STATES, DEPRESSION AND NEW DEAL. There is a rich choice of stimulating general treatments. See especially R. Hofstadter, *The Age of Reform: From Bryan to F.D.R.** (Vintage, 1973). For a good survey of the period with bibliographical discussion, see R. S. Kirkendall, *The United States, 1929–45: Years of Crisis and Change** (McGraw-Hill, 1974). See also W. E. Leuchtenburg, *The Perils of Prosperity, 1914–32** (Chicago, 1958); A. M. Schlesinger's three volumes, *The Age of Roosevelt: The Crisis of the Old Order, 1919–33*, *The Coming of the New Deal* and *The Politics of Upheaval* (Houghton Mifflin, 1957, 1959, 1960); and H. Stein, *The Fiscal Revolution in America** (Chicago, 1971). An outstanding treatment is W. E. Leuchtenburg, *Franklin Roosevelt and the New Deal** (Harper & Row, 1963). A valuable series of studies of the New Deal can be found in J. Braeman, R. H. Bremner and D. Brody, *The New Deal* (2 vols, Ohio, 1975). See also E. A. Rosen, *Hoover, Roosevelt and the Brains Trust* (Columbia, 1977). A fine biography of Roosevelt is F. Freidel, *F. D. Roosevelt* (4 vols, Little, Brown, 1952–73). Stimulating analysis in one volume is J. MacGregor Burns, *Roosevelt: The Lion and the Fox* (Harcourt, 1956). A good biography from outstanding New Dealer is S. F. Charles, *Minister of Relief: Harry Hopkins and the Depression* (Syracuse, 1963).

BRITAIN. In addition to books already cited under national histories for the traumatic industrial breakdown of the mid-1920s, see M. Morris, *The General Strike** (Penguin, 1976); S. Pollard, *The Development of the British Economy, 1914–67** (Arnold, 1969); M. Cowling, *The Impact of Labour* (Cambridge, 1971); T. Wilson, *The Downfall of the Liberal Party, 1914–35** (Macmillan, 1975); and P. Rowland, *Lloyd George* (Barrie & Jenkins, 1975). A recent study of the critical 1929–34 period is D. Marquand, *Ramsay MacDonald* (Cape,

1977). Other biographies of especial value are K. Middlemas and John Barnes, *Baldwin: A Biography* (Weidenfeld & Nicolson, 1969); R. Skidelsky, *Politicians and the Slump** (Macmillan, 1967); R. Skidelsky, *Oswald Mosley* (Macmillan, 1975); C. Cross, *The Fascists in Britain* (London, 1961); K. Feiling, *The Life of Neville Chamberlain* (Macmillan, 1946); M. Gilbert, vol. 5, *Winston S. Churchill, 1922–1939* (Heinemann, 1976). For a fascinating social history, see N. Branson and M. Heinemann, *Britain in the Nineteen Thirties** (Panther, 1973). See also D. Winch, *Economics and Policy** (Hodder & Stoughton, 1969); R. Blake, *The Conservative Party from Peel to Thatcher** (Fontana, 1985); T. F. Lindsay and M. Harrington, *The Conservative Party, 1918–70** (Macmillan, 1979); H. Pelling, *A Short History of the Labour Party** (Macmillan, 1978). Providing a controversial but stimulating link between politics and foreign policy is M. Cowling, *The Impact of Hitler** (new edn, Chicago, 1977). A provocative and stimulating account is A. J. P. Taylor's *English History, 1914–45** (Penguin, 1970).

FRANCE. For an overview, see D. Thomson, *Democracy in France since 1870** (5th edn, Oxford, 1969). See also J. P. T. Bury, *France: The Insecure Peace** (Macdonald, 1972); J. Lacouture, *Léon Blum* (Seuil, 1977); R. Rémond and J. Bourdin (eds), *Édouard Daladier, Chef de Gouvernement* (Fondation Nationale des Sciences Politiques, 1977); A. Sauvy, *Histoire économique de la France entre les deux guerres, 1918–39* (2 vols, Fayard, 1965–7); J. Plumyène and R. Lasierra, *Les Fascismes français, 1923–63* (Paris, 1963); R. Rémond, *The Right Wing in France from 1815 to de Gaulle* (2nd edn, Pennsylvania, 1966). See also under national histories.

8. ITALY AND THE RISE OF FASCISM

Covering not only Italy but fascism in general, is the very useful W. Laqueur (ed.), *Fascism: A Reader's Guide** (Penguin, 1976). See also R. De Felice, *Interpretations of Fascism* (Harvard, 1977); A. J. Gregor, *Fascism: The Contemporary Interpretations** (General Learning Press, 1974) and the same author's *Italian Fascism and Developmental Dictatorship* (Princeton, 1979); A. Lyttelton (ed.), *Fascism in Italy, 1919–29** (Princeton, 1988). A classic study is the same author's *The Seizure of Power, 1919–29* (Scribner's, 1973). A useful overview is G. Carocci, *Italian Fascism** (Penguin, 1975). See also E. Nolte, *Three Faces of Fascism** (Mentor, 1970); F. Carsten, *The Rise of Fascism** (Methuen, 1970); E. Wiskemann, *Fascism in Italy** (Macmillan, 1972); S. J. Woolf (ed.), *European Fascism* (Weidenfeld & Nicolson, 1968); and A. Cassels, *Fascist Italy** (Routledge, 1969). P. F. Sugar, *Native Fascism in the Successor States, 1918–45** (Clio, 1971) is a stimulating collection of essays on the spread of fascism in central and south-east Europe.

For biographies of Mussolini, see L. Fermi, *Mussolini** (Chicago, 1966); M. Gallo, *Mussolini's Italy* (Macmillan, 1973) is a treatment of the man and his times, and I. Kirkpatrick, *Mussolini* (reprint, Greenwood, 1976). A stimulating book is D. Mack Smith, *Mussolini's Roman Empire* (Longman, 1976). A marvellous study of the last years is F. W. Deakin, *The Brutal Friendship: Mussolini, Hitler and the Fall of the Italian Fascism** (Penguin, 1966). See also A. J. Gregor, *Young Mussolini and the Intellectual Origins of Fascism* (California, 1980).

9. THE SOVIET UNION: GENERAL, AND THE STALIN ERA

(Books additional to those cited under national histories.) There are a number of outstanding biographies, not least I. Deutscher, *Stalin: A Political Biography** (Penguin, 1970); the leading work for the early period is R. C. Tucker, *Stalin as a Revolutionary, 1879–1929* (Norton, 1973); by the same author is *Stalin in Power: The Revolution from Above, 1928–1941* (Norton, 1990). See also I. Deutscher, *The Prophet Unarmed: Trotsky, 1921–9** (Oxford, 1970) (two further volumes deal with the remainder of Trotsky's life); for a useful and more brief discussion, see I. Howe, *Trotsky** (Fontana, 1978); in the same Modern Masters series, see R. Conquest, *Lenin** (Fontana, 1972). Also valuable is A. B. Ulam, *Lenin and the Bolsheviks** (Fontana, 1969). The best single overview of the economy is A. Nove, *An Economic History of Russia** (revised edn, Penguin, 1996). On party and politics, see M. Fainsod, *How Russia is Ruled* (revised edn, Harvard, 1965); L. B. Schapiro, *The Communist Party of the Soviet Union* (2nd edn, Eyre & Spottiswoode, 1970); A. Nove, *Stalinism and After** (Allen & Unwin, 1975); and M. Fainsod, *Smolensk under Soviet Rule* (Harvard, 1958). An outstanding study of the problems of the peasantry and Soviet policies is M. Lewin, *Russian Peasants and Soviet Power** (Allen & Unwin, 1968). R. W. Davies, provides the authoritative account of collectivisation in two volumes, *The Socialist Offensive, 1929–30* and *The Soviet Collective Farm, 1929–30*

(Macmillan, 1980). A condemnation of Stalinism can be found in R. A. Medvedev, *Let History Judge** (Spokesman, 1976). On the military, see J. Erickson, *The Soviet High Command: A Military-Political History, 1918–41* (St Martin, 1962). An outstanding history of Soviet foreign relations in A. Ulam, *Expansion and Co-existence: A History of Soviet Foreign Policy* (2nd edn, Praeger, 1974). A brief and stimulating survey is G. F. Kennan, *Russia and the West** (Mentor, 1967). J. Haslam, *Soviet Foreign Policy, 1930–41* (5 vols, Macmillan, 1983–91) is a re-examination of Soviet foreign policy in a multi-volume study.

10. SPAIN AND THE CIVIL WAR

A good general history is R. Carr, *Spain, 1808–1939* (Oxford, 1966); see also S. G. Payne, *A History of Spain and Portugal* (vol. 2, Wisconsin, 1976), and the same author's *Politics and the Military in Modern Spain* (Stanford, 1967). Stimulating is R. Herr, *Modern Spain** (California, 1971). Other outstanding books dealing more generally with the 1930s, include G. Brenan, *The Spanish Labyrinth** (2nd edn, Cambridge, 1950); G. Jackson, *The Spanish Republic and the Civil War, 1931–9** (Princeton, 1965); S. G. Payne, *The Spanish Revolution** (Norton, 1969); R. A. H. Robinson, *The Origins of Franco's Spain* (Pittsburgh, 1971); S. G. Payne, *Falange History of Spanish Fascism** (Stanford, 1961); H. Thomas, *The Spanish Civil War** (3rd edn, Penguin, 1977). The impact on Britain is discussed in K. W. Watkins, *Britain Divided* (reprint, Greenwood, 1976).

For Portugal, see A. H. De Oliveira Marques, *History of Portugal* (vol. 2, Columbia, 1972).

11. GERMANY: THE WEIMAR REPUBLIC AND THE THIRD REICH

An interesting general account is M. Kolinsky, *Continuity and Change in European Society since 1870** (Croom Helm, 1974). On Weimar, the classic account is E. Eyck, *The Weimar Republic* (2 vols, Harvard, 1962–4); see also S. W. Halperin, *Germany Tried Democracy: A Political History of the Reich from 1918 to 1933* (New York, 1946), and E. J. Feuchtwanger, *From Weimar to Hitler: Germany, 1918–1933** (2nd edn, Macmillan, 1995). For the foundation year, see F. L. Carsten, *Revolution in Central Europe, 1917–19* (Temple Smith, 1972); and a crucial aspect of the history of the Republic, *The Reichswehr and Politics 1918 to 1933* (Oxford, 1966). Indispensable for a view of the origins and impact of National Socialism is K. D. Bracher, *The German Dictatorship** (Penguin, 1978); see also M. Broszat, *German National Socialism** (Clio, 1966). Lively but somewhat dated is W. Shirer, *The Rise and Fall of the Third Reich** (Pan, 1960). A brief account of Weimar's collapse is A. J. Nicholls, *Weimar and the Rise of Hitler** (2nd edn, Macmillan, 1979).

Thousands of books have now been written on all aspects of Hitler and the Third Reich. The following are likely to be found especially useful. I. Kershaw, *The Nazi Dictatorship** (2nd edn, Arnold, 1989) is a valuable discussion of problems of interpretation. Also useful for elucidating different approaches is J. Hiden and J. Farquarson, *Explaining Hitler's Germany: Historians and the Third Reich** (2nd edn, Batsford, 1989). Both these books refer to the extensive literature on the subject. The classic biography is A. Bullock, *Hitler: A Study in Tyranny** (Penguin, 1962); see also, by the same author, *Hitler and Stalin: Parallel Lives** (Fontana Press, 1993). A stimulating discussion can be found in W. Carr, *Hitler: A Study in Personality and Politics* (Arnold, 1978). J. P. Stern, *Hitler: The Führer and the People** (Fontana Press, 1975) is outstanding. On more specialised topics, see A. Tyrell, *Vom 'Trommler' zum 'Führer'* (Fink, 1975); J. Gordon, *Hitler and the Beer Hall Putsch* (Princeton, 1972); J. Noakes, *The Nazi Party in Lower Saxony, 1921–33* (Oxford, 1971); and G. Pridham, *Hitler's Rise to Power: The Nazi Movement in Bavaria, 1923–33* (Hart-Davis, 1973). A series of studies of Nazi leaders appears in J. C. Fest, *The Face of the Third Reich** (Penguin, 1970). An excellent survey of the Third Reich is R. Grunberger, *A Social History of the Third Reich** (Penguin, 1974). See also I. Kershaw, *The 'Hitler Myth': Image and Reality in the Third Reich** (Oxford, 1989).

For foreign policy a good synthesis is W. Carr, *Arms, Autarky and Aggression** (Arnold, 1972). The early years are authoritatively analysed by G. L. Weinberg, *The Foreign Policy of Hitler's Germany: Diplomatic Revolution in Europe, 1933–6* and *Starting World War II* (Chicago, 1970 and 1980).

On the SS, see H. Krausnick and M. Broszat, *Anatomy of the SS State** (Paladin, 1973). On the churches in the Third Reich, see J. Conway, *The Nazi Persecution of the Churches* (Weidenfeld & Nicolson, 1968). On relations with the army, see R. O'Neill, *The German Army and the Nazi Party* (Heinemann, 1976). A good survey of the resistance is P. Hoffmann, *The History of the German Resistance, 1933–45* (Macdonald & Jane's, 1977). See also D. J. K. Peukert, *Inside Nazi Germany** (Penguin, 1996); M. Burleigh and W. Wippermann, *The Racial State: Germany, 1933–1945** (Cambridge, 1994).

12. THE ORIGINS OF WAR IN ASIA AND EUROPE

The books on foreign policy mentioned in the previous sections are relevant.

ASIA AND THE PACIFIC. J. W. Morley (ed.), *Japan's Foreign Policy, 1868–1941: A Research Guide* (Columbia, 1974) contains essays and bibliographies. See also I. Nish, *Japanese Foreign Policy, 1869–1942* (Routledge, 1977); S. N. Ogata, *Defiance in Manchuria: The Making of Japanese Foreign Policy, 1869–1942* (London, 1977); and S. E. Pelz, *Race to Pearl Harbor: The Future of the Second London Naval Conference and the Onset of World War II* (Harvard, 1974). J. W. Morley (ed.), *Japan's Road to the Pacific War: Deterrent Diplomacy, 1935–40* (Columbia, 1976) and S. Ienaga, *Japan's Last War* (Blackwell, 1979) offer two very different Japanese views. Also useful is C. Thorne, *The Limits of Foreign Policy: The West, the League and the Far Eastern Crisis of 1931–3* (Hamish Hamilton, 1972). A. Iriye (ed.), *Mutual Images: Essays in American Japanese Relations* (Harvard, 1975) provides a stimulating broader series of excellent essays. By the same author is *The Origins of the Second World War in Asia and the Pacific** (Longman, 1987). A detailed analysis of aspects of the origins of the war in the Pacific can be found in D. Borg and S. Okamoto, *Pearl Harbor: A History. Japanese–American Relations, 1931–41* (Columbia, 1973). For British policy, see P. Lowe, *Great Britain and the Origins of the Pacific War: A Study of British Far Eastern Policy* (Oxford, 1977). A good analysis appears in R. Dallek, *Franklin D. Roosevelt and American Foreign Policy, 1932–45* (Oxford, 1979) which deals not only with eastern Asia, but with the whole range of United States policy. An older classic work on United States foreign policy in Europe and Asia and American entry into the Second World War is W. L. Langer and S. E. Gleason, *Challenge to Isolation, 1937–40* and *The Undeclared War, 1940–1* (Harper & Row, 1952–3). Also valuable is D. Reynolds, *The Creation of the Anglo-American Alliance, 1937–41* (North Carolina, 1981).

EUROPE. A collection of essays on the controversy aroused by A. J. P. Taylor, *Origins of the Second World War** (Penguin, 1963) is in E. M. Robertson (ed.), *The Origins of the Second World War** (Macmillan, 1971). A good brief synthesis is P. M. H. Bell, *The Origins of the Second World War in Europe** (Longman, 1986). The most authoritative treatment of the immediate crisis years is D. C. Watt, *How War Came: The Immediate Origins of the Second World War, 1938–39** (Mandarin, 1990). A stimulating German survey is K. Hildebrand, *The Foreign Policy of the Third Reich** (Batsford, 1973). A. Adamthwaite provides a valuable study of *France and the Coming of the Second World War, 1936–9* (Cass, 1977). A French view of the coming of the war can be found in M. Baumont, *The Origins of the Second World War* (Yale, 1978). See also J. Néré, *The Foreign Policy of France, 1914–45* (Routledge, 1974). British foreign policy is well surveyed in F. S. Northedge, *The Troubled Giant* (Bell, 1966). Detailed analysis of British policy on the eve of the war from 1937 to 1939 appear in K. Middlemas, *The Diplomacy of Illusion* (Weidenfeld & Nicolson, 1972) and S. Aster, *The Making of the Second World War* (Deutsch, 1973). Provocative older books are M. Gilbert and R. Gott, *The Appeasers** (Weidenfeld & Nicolson, 1967) and N. Thompson, *The Anti-appeasers* (Oxford, 1971). See also D. C. Watt, *Personalities and Policies* (Longman, 1965). Of general importance is M. Howard, *The Continental Commitment** (Penguin, 1974). Polish policy is set out in A. M. Cienciala, *Poland and the Western Powers, 1938–9* (Routledge, 1968) and in P. Prazmowska, *Britain, Poland and the Eastern Front, 1939* (Cambridge, 1987). Italian policy is discussed in M. Toscano, *The Origins of the Pact of Steel* (Johns Hopkins, 1967); E. Wiskemann, *The Rome–Berlin Axis** (2nd edn, Fontana, 1966); G. Salvemini, *Prelude to World War II* (Gollancz, 1953); C. J. Lowe and F. Marzari, *Italian Foreign Policy, 1870–1940* (Routledge, 1975); and D. Mack Smith, *Mussolini's Roman Empire* (Longman, 1976). For a Soviet view, see I. Maisky, *Who Helped Hitler?* (Hutchinson, 1964). A good survey of the last two years is C. Thorne, *The Approach of War, 1938–9** (Macmillan, 1967). Specialist studies include J. T. Emmerson, *The Rhineland Crisis* (Temple Smith, 1977); J. Gehl, *Austria, Germany and the Anschluss* (new edn, Greenwood, 1970); K. Robbins, *Munich, 1938* (Cassell, 1968); the same subject is covered in great detail and at length by T. Taylor, *Munich: The Price of Peace* (Hodder & Stoughton, 1979).

13. THE SECOND WORLD WAR

Among the best one-volume histories are P. Calvocoressi, G. Wint and J. Pritchard, *Total War** (Penguin, 1995); R. A. C. Parker, *Struggle for Survival: The History of the Second World War** (Oxford, 1990), an outstanding synthesis; M. Gilbert, *Second World War* (Collins, 1990); G. L. Weinberg, *A World at Arms* (Cambridge, 1994). W. S. Churchill, *The Second World War* (6 vols, Cassell, 1948–54) is indispensable for a feel of the war as seen through Churchill's eyes. For a Soviet view, see P. N. Pospelov and others, *The Great Patriotic War of the Soviet Union, 1941–5* (Progress, 1974). The classic Western account is J. Erickson, *Stalin's War with Germany* (2 vols, Weidenfeld & Nicolson, 1975–83).

Britain at war is also interestingly discussed by P. M. H. Bell, *A Certain Eventuality* (London, 1974) and in H. Pelling, *Britain and the Second World War** (Fontana, 1970). A. Calder presents a vivid portrait in *The People's War: Britain, 1939–45** (Panther, 1971). Also good is P. Addison, *The Road to 1945** (Quartet, 1977).

R. Paxton, *Vichy France* (Barrie & Jenkins, 1972); A. S. Milward, *The New Order and the French Economy* (Oxford, 1970); H. R. Kedward, *Resistance in Vichy France, 1940–42* (Oxford, 1978) all reveal important facets of events in France. See also R. Griffiths, *Marshal Pétain* (Constable, 1970); J. Isorni, *Philippe Pétain* (2 vols, Table Ronde, 1972–3); G. Hirschfeld and P. Marsh (eds), *Collaboration in France: Politics and Culture during the Nazi Occupation, 1940–1944* (Berg, 1989).

Important for a study of Germany are A. S. Milward, *The German Economy at War* (Athlone, 1965); M. G. Steinert, *Hitler's War and the Germans* (Ohio, 1977); E. K. Bramsted, *Goebbels and National Socialist Propaganda* (East Lansing, 1965); Z. A. B. Zeman, *Nazi Propaganda** (2nd edn, Oxford, 1973); M. Balfour, *Propaganda in War, 1939–45* (Routledge, 1979).

A perceptive short book on the murder of the Jews considered in its widest setting is Y. Bauer, *The Holocaust in Historical Perspective* (Sheldon, 1979). See also F. H. Littell and H. G. Locke (eds), *The German Church, Struggle and the Holocaust* (Wayne, 1974) and, outstanding, R. Gutteridge, *Open Thy Mouth for the Dumb* (Blackwell, 1976). A magisterial study is R. Hillberg, *The Destruction of the European Jews* (new edn, 3 vols, Holmes & Meier, 1985). Interesting contributions have been made by G. Fleming, *Hitler and the Final Solution* (California, 1984); W. Laqueur, *The Terrible Secret** (Penguin, 1982); C. Browning, *The Path to Genocide: Essays on Launching the Final Solution** (Cambridge, 1992); M. Gilbert, *Auschwitz and the Allies** (Mandarin, 1991). J. Steinberg, *All or Nothing: The Axis and the Holocaust, 1941–43* (Routledge, 1990) compares the humanity of the Italian army on the Adriatic with the barbarity of the German. M. Gilbert, *The Holocaust: The Jewish Tragedy** (Collins, 1987) is an unbearably detailed account of atrocities all over occupied Europe. The Israeli scholar D. Bankier, in *The Germans and the Final Solution: Public Opinion under Nazism* (Blackwell, 1992), addresses the important question of what Germans knew and thought. The best one-volume account is L. Dawidowicz, *The War Against the Jews, 1933–1945** (Penguin, 1990). See also D. Cesarani (ed), *The Final Solution* (Routledge, 1994); D. J. Goldhagen, *Hitler's Willing Executioners* (Knopf, 1996).

For Allied diplomacy during the Second World War, see H. Feis, *Churchill, Roosevelt, Stalin** and *Between War and Peace** (Princeton, 1967 and 1960); L. Giovannitti and F. Freed, *The Decision to Drop the Bomb* (Methuen, 1967); G. Kolko, *The Politics of War: The World and United States Foreign Policy, 1943–5** (Pantheon, 1990); W. R. Louis, *Imperialism at Bay, 1941–5: The United States and the Decolonization of the British Empire* (Oxford, 1978). A critical assessment of Allied policy towards Poland can be found in E. J. Rozek, *Wartime Diplomacy: A Pattern in Poland* (Wiley, 1958). Also useful is R. Edmonds, *The Big Three: Churchill, Roosevelt and Stalin** (Penguin, 1992). For a study of Japan's impact and her occupation policies during the war, an outstanding book is J. Pluvier, *South East Asia from Colonialism to Independence* (Oxford, 1975). See also C. B. Dear and M. R. D. Foot (eds), *The Oxford Companion to the Second World War* (Oxford, 1995).

14. WESTERN EUROPE: POST-WAR RECOVERY AND GROWTH

W. Laqueur, *Europe in Our Time, 1945–1992** (Penguin, 1993) provides an overview, as does D. Urwin, *Western Europe since 1945: A Political History* (Longman, 1989). M. J. Hogan, *The Marshall Plan: America, Britain, and the Reconstruction of Europe** (Cambridge, 1989) examines American motivation in seeking to integrate a free-market Western Europe; A. S. Milward's classic study, *The Reconstruction of Western Europe, 1945–51** (Routledge, 1987), shows recovery under way before the Marshall Plan could make an impact.

BRITAIN. K. O. Morgan, *The People's Peace: British History, 1945–1990** (Oxford, 1992); the same author has made a special study of the post war Labour record in *Labour in Power, 1945–51** (Oxford, 1985) and *Labour People** (Oxford, 1990). Of the biographies, interesting reading is B. Pimlott's *Hugh Dalton** (Macmillan, 1986) and the same author's *Harold Wilson* (HarperCollins, 1992). See also K. Harris, *Attlee** (Weidenfeld & Nicolson, 1984); A. Horne, *Harold Macmillan** (2 vols, Macmillan, 1988–9); R. Blake, *The Conservative Party from Peel to Thatcher* (Fontana Press, 1985). A good synthesis is A. Sked and C. Cook, *Post-War Britain: A Political History, 1945–1992** (Penguin, 1993). For a stimulating interpretation see P. Calvocoressi, *The British Experience, 1945–75** (Penguin, 1978). See also V. Bogdanor and R. Skidelsky (eds), *The Age of Affluence, 1951–1964** (Macmillan, 1970); D. Marquand, *The Unprincipled Society: New Demands and Old Politics* (Cape, 1988). Violence, not only that caused by the IRA is discussed in R.

Clutterbuck, *Britain in Agony: The Growth of Political Violence** (Penguin, 1978); for a readable and subtle analysis of the British way of life, see A. Marwick, *British Society since 1945** (2nd edn, Penguin, 1990). Two good studies of the Thatcher decade are D. Kavanagh, *Thatcherism and British Politics: The End of Consensus?** (Penguin, 1988) and P. Riddell, *The Thatcher Era and Its Legacy** (Blackwell, 1991). For an antidote to patriotic fervour, see Lieutenant D. Tinker's moving letters, *A Message from the Falklands**, posthumously compiled by H. Tinker (Junction Books, 1982). On the impact and reception of immigrants to Britain, see J. Walvin, *Passage to Britain** (Penguin, 1984). A good overview of Britain's external relations is provided by D. Reynolds, *Britannia Overruled: British Policy and World Power in the 20th Century** (Longman, 1991), with an extensive bibliography

REPUBLIC OF IRELAND AND NORTHERN IRELAND. F. S. L. Lyons, *Ireland since the Famine* (2nd edn, Fontana Press, 1985); R. F. Foster, *Modern Ireland, 1600–1972** (Penguin, 1989); J. J. Lee, *Ireland, 1912–1985* (Cambridge, 1989). P. Arthur and K. Jeffery, *Northern Ireland since 1968** (Blackwell, 1988) chronicles and analyses the conflict.

FRANCE. One of the best general overviews is J.-P. Rioux, *The Fourth Republic, 1914–1958* (Cambridge, 1987); perhaps the most interesting way to tackle post-war France is through the English version of J. Lacouture's brilliant biography, *De Gaulle: The Ruler, 1945–1970* (Harvill, 1991); see by the same author, *Pierre Mendès-France* (Holmes & Meier, 1984). See also J. R. Frears, *France in the Giscard Presidency* (Allen & Unwin, 1981); D. S. Bell and B. Criddle, *The French Socialist Party: The Emergence of a Party of Government** (2nd edn, Oxford, 1988). Two very readable contributions illuminating French politics and way of life are J. Ardagh, *The New France: A Society in Transition, 1945–1977** (2nd edn, Penguin, 1973) and the same author's *France in the 1980s** (Penguin, 1982). On France's war in Indo-China, see J. Dalloz, *War in Indo-China, 1945–1954* (Gill & Macmillan, 1990). The conflict in Algeria is graphically covered in A. Horne, *A Savage War of Peace: Algeria, 1954–1962** (Penguin, 1979); for French policy in the West, see F. R. Willis, *France, Germany and the New Europe, 1945–1963* (Stanford, 1965); economic and social developments since 1945 are analysed in C. Flockton and E. Kofman, *France** (Chapman, 1989).

GERMANY. A. Grosser, *Germany in Our Time: A Political History of the Post-war Years** (Penguin, 1974) is an interpretive study by the German-born author, who emigrated to France. With a demise of the German Democratic Republic, H. A. Turner had to revise his *The Two Germanies since 1945* published in 1987, and he contrasts and recounts the history of the two Germanies from a new perspective in *Germany from Partition to Reunification* (Yale, 1992). See also T. Prittie, *The Velvet Chancellors: A History of Postwar Germany* (Muller, 1979) and M. Balfour, *West Germany: A Contemporary History* (Croom Helm, 1982). For the American occupation, see J. Gimbel, *The American Occupation of Germany: Politics and the Military* (Stanford, 1968). *The Konrad Adenauer Memoirs, 1945–53*, trans. B. Ruhm von Orpen (Weidenfeld & Nicolson, 1966) make for pretty dry reading and can be supplemented by T. Prittie, *Konrad Adenauer* (Stacey, 1972), by the same author, *Willy Brandt: Portrait of a Statesman* (Schocken, 1974) and by G. Pridham, *Christian Democracy in Western Germany* (Croom Helm, 1977). W. Griffith, *The Ostpolitik of the Federal Republic of Germany* (MIT, 1978) traces the changing relationship with the other Germans; see also P. Merkl, *German Foreign Policies East and West* (Clio, 1974), and P. Pulzer, *German Politics, 1945–1995** (Oxford, 1995). The history of the German Democratic Republic until her dissolution will need to be rewritten; meantime D. Childs, *The GDR: Moscow's German Ally* (2nd edn, Allen & Unwin, 1988) and M. McCauley, *The German Democratic Republic since 1945* (Macmillan, 1983) are useful outlines. A sound German account is T. Vogelsang, *Das geteilte Deutschland** (dtv., 1980) and P. Bender, *Neue Ostpolitik vom Mauerbau bis zum Moskauer Vertrag** (dtv., 1986). See also M. Fulbrook, *Anatomy of Dictatorship: Inside the G.D.R., 1949–1989* (Oxford, 1995).

ITALY. There are several good general histories of post-war Italy, including P. Ginsborg, *A History of Contemporary Italy: Society and Politics, 1943–1988** (Penguin, 1990), with an extensive bibliography, and N. Kogan, *A Political History of Postwar Italy* (Praeger, 1981). The early years can be studied in S. J. Woolf (ed.), *The Rebirth of Italy, 1943–1950* (Longman, 1972); corruption and the political way of life are discussed in J. Chubb, *Patronage, Power and Poverty in Southern Italy: A Tale of Two Cities* (Cambridge, 1982) and J. Walston, *The Mafia and Clientilism: Roads to Rome in Postwar Calabria* (Routledge, 1988).

SPAIN AND PORTUGAL. An overview can be found in R. Carr, *Modern Spain, 1875–1980* (Oxford, 1980); for post-civil-war Spain, see R. Carr and J. P. Fusi, *Spain: Dictatorship to Democracy** (2nd edn, Allen & Unwin, 1981). A biography of Franco in English translation is E. de Blaye, *Franco and the Politics of Spain** (Penguin, 1976). See also P. Preston, *The Triumph of Democracy in Spain* (Methuen, 1986); R. Robinson, *Contemporary Portugal: A*

History (Allen & Unwin, 1979). See also K. Maxwell, *The Making of Portuguese Democracy* (Cambridge, 1995).

THE EUROPEAN COMMUNITY. Three good overviews, are J. Lodge (ed.), *The European Community and the Challenge of the Future** (Pinter, 1989); J. Pinder, *European Community: The Building of a Union* (Oxford, 1991); and D. Swann, *The Economics of a Common Market** (6th edn, Penguin, 1988). C. Tugendhat, *Making Sense of Europe** (Penguin, 1986), by a former vice-president of the EC Commission from 1981 to 1985, is a realistic but upbeat appraisal of its achievements and future needs. See also S. de la Mahotière, *Towards One Europe** (Penguin, 1970).

INDEX

bold numbers indicate a reference to an illustration